EIGHTH EDITION

Criminology

John E. Conklin

Tufts University

PEARSON

Boston   New York   San Francisco
Mexico City   Montreal   Toronto   London   Madrid   Munich   Paris
Hong Kong   Singapore   Tokyo   Cape Town   Sydney

Series Editor: Jennifer Jacobson
Editorial Assistant: Amy Holborow
Senior Marketing Manager: Krista Groshong
Manufacturing Buyer: JoAnne Sweeney
Photo Researcher: Katharine S. Cook
Composition and Prepress Buyer: Linda Cox
Cover Administrator: Linda Knowles
Editorial-Production Service: Omegatype Typography, Inc.
Interior Designer: Denise Hoffman
Electronic Composition: Omegatype Typography, Inc.

For related titles and support materials, visit our online catalog at www.ablongman.com.

Between the time website information is gathered and then published, it is not unusual for some sites to have closed. Also, the transcription of URLs can result in typographical errors. The publisher would appreciate notification where these errors occur so that they may be corrected in subsequent editions.

Library of Congress Cataloging-in-Publication Data

Conklin, John E.
    Criminology / John E. Conklin.—8th ed.
        p.   cm.
    Includes bibliographical references and index.
    ISBN 0-205-38177-4 (alk. paper)
    1. Criminology.   I. Title.
HV6025.C59 2004
364—dc21

                              2003041904

Printed in the United States of America

10 9 8 7 6 5 4 3 2 1   CIN   08 07 06 05 04 03

CONTENTS

Feature Boxes   x

Preface   xi

Author Biography   xii

1 The Study of Crime   1

The Nature of Crime and Delinquency   2

The Characteristics of Crime   4

Juvenile Delinquency   5

Social Origins of the Criminal Law   6

Theoretical Perspectives on Crime
and the Criminal Law   6

The Social Construction of Crime   9

Strategies of Criminological Research   10

Comparative and Historical Research   11

Biographies   12

Patterns of Crime   13

The Cohort Study   15

Surveys   16

Other Strategies of Criminological
Research   18

Summary   20

IMPORTANT TERMS   20

REVIEW QUESTIONS   21

FOR FURTHER STUDY   21

2 Measuring Crime   22

The Emergence of Modern Criminology   22

Classical Criminology   22

Cartography   23

Positivism   24

Official Crime Statistics   25

History of Crime Statistics
in the United States   26

FBI Crime Statistics   26

Crime Rates   28

Gathering Crime Statistics   31

Using FBI Data for Criminological
Research   36

Measuring Criminal Victimization   36

History of Victimization Surveys   36

Comparing NCVS and FBI Data   37

The Dark Figure   37

Methodological Problems with
Victimization Surveys   39

Measuring Crime by Self-Reports   40

History of Self-Report Studies   40

The Dark Figure   41

Methodological Problems with
Self-Report Studies   42

Summary   44

IMPORTANT TERMS   45

REVIEW QUESTIONS   45

FOR FURTHER STUDY   45

3 Crime and Its Costs   46

Conventional Crimes   48

Crimes of Violence   48

Property Crimes   58

White-Collar Crime   64

Is White-Collar Crime Different?   65

The Costs of White-Collar Crime   67

Organized Crime   68

The Costs of Organized Crime   69

Victimless Crimes   69

Drug Use   70

Gambling   70

Prostitution   71

Summary   71

IMPORTANT TERMS   72

REVIEW QUESTIONS   72

FOR FURTHER STUDY   73

4 Dimensions of Crime   74

Cross-National Variations in Crime Rates   74

Regional Variations in Crime Rates within the United States   76

Variations in Crime Rates by Community   77

Crime within Metropolitan Areas   78

Migration and Crime   80

Temporal Variations in Crime Rates   81

Seasonal Variations in Crime Rates   81

Annual Trends in Crime Rates   82

Variations in Crime Rates by Sex   83

Sex and Juvenile Delinquency   85

Sex and Crime   86

Sex and Victimization   87

Variations in Crime Rates by Age   88

Age-Specific Arrest Rates   88

Age Distribution and Crime Rates   89

Age and Victimization   91

Variations in Crime Rates by Race   91

Race, Arrest Statistics, and Self-Report Studies   93

Race, Crime, and Background Variables   94

Race and Victimization   95

Variations in Crime Rates by Social Class   97

Social Class and Adult Crime   97

Social Class and Juvenile Delinquency   97

Methodological Problems   98

Social Class and Victimization   99

Summary   99

IMPORTANT TERMS   100

REVIEW QUESTIONS   101

FOR FURTHER STUDY   101

5 Biological and Psychological Explanations of Crime   102

Biological Explanations of Crime   102

History of the Biological Perspective on Crime   103

Modern Biological Research on Crime   104

Biology and Modern Criminology   111

Psychological Explanations of Crime   113

Intelligence and Crime   113

Personality Characteristics   116

Schizophrenia and Mood Disorders   124

Psychology and Variations
in Crime Rates   125

Psychology and the Criminal Law   126

Summary   129

IMPORTANT TERMS   130

REVIEW QUESTIONS   130

FOR FURTHER STUDY   131

6 Social, Cultural, and Economic Sources of Crime   132

**Social, Cultural, and Economic Sources
of White-Collar Crime   133**

Free Enterprise: Profits and Competition   133

Market Structure and Crime   135

Trust and Credit   136

Corporations and Crime   136

Development of New Technology   137

**Social, Cultural, and Economic Sources
of Organized Crime   139**

Prohibition and Organized Crime   140

Organized Crime after Prohibition   140

Organized Crime and the
Economic System   142

**Social, Cultural, and Economic Sources
of Conventional Crime   142**

Modernization and Crime   143

Opportunity and the Economy   144

Unemployment and Crime   144

Relative Deprivation and Crime   147

Anomie, Strain, and Crime   148

Differential Opportunity
and Delinquency   152

Social Class, Values, and Delinquency   154

The Subculture of Violence   156

Gender, Crime, and Feminist Criminology   159

The Generalizability Problem   160

The Gender Ratio Problem   160

Gender Socialization   162

Doing Gender   162

Power-Control Theory   164

Women as Victims, Women as Resisters   165

**Social, Cultural, and Economic Factors
and Variations in Crime Rates   165**

Summary   167

IMPORTANT TERMS   168

REVIEW QUESTIONS   168

FOR FURTHER STUDY   168

7 Social Control and Commitment to the Law   170

Neutralizing the Law   170

Drift   170

Delinquent, Dominant, and Subterranean
Values   171

Techniques of Neutralization   172

Evidence on Techniques
of Neutralization   177

Critique of Neutralization Theory   180

Social Control Theory   181

The Family   181

The School   182

The Peer Group   182

Conventional Lines of Action
and Adult Activities   182

Evidence on Social Control Theory   183

Critique of Social Control Theory   197

Techniques of Neutralization, Social Control
Theory, and Variations in Crime Rates   199

Summary   200

IMPORTANT TERMS   201

REVIEW QUESTIONS   201

FOR FURTHER STUDY   201

8   Learning to Commit Crime   202

Sources of Learning to Commit Crime   202

The Community   202

The Peer Group   203

The General Culture   203

The Media   205

Sports   208

Pornography   210

Correctional Institutions   211

Differential Association Theory   212

Critique of Differential Association Theory   214

Evidence on Differential
Association Theory   216

The Labeling Perspective   221

Labeling and Self-Concepts   222

Labeling and Opportunities   224

Labeling and Subcultures   225

Critique of the Labeling Perspective   226

Rewards and Risks of Crime   226

Reward-Risk Models of Criminal Behavior   227

The Rewards and Risks of Crime   230

Critique of Reward-Risk Models   234

**Learning Theories and Variations
in Crime Rates   234**

Summary   235

IMPORTANT TERMS   237

REVIEW QUESTIONS   237

FOR FURTHER STUDY   237

9   Opportunities and Facilitating Factors   238

Routine Activities Theory   238

A Critique of Routine Activities Theory   240

Targets of Crime   241

Property Crimes   242

Vulnerability of Victims   243

Victim Precipitation   247

**Facilitating Factors: Alcohol, Drugs,
and Firearms   249**

Alcohol and Crime   250

Drugs and Crime   252

Firearms and Crime   254

Summary   260

IMPORTANT TERMS   261

REVIEW QUESTIONS   261

FOR FURTHER STUDY   261

10   Criminal Careers   263

**Theoretical Perspectives
on Criminal Careers   264**

Analyzing Criminal Careers   265

Career Contingencies   265

The Labeling Perspective   266

The "Zigzag Path": Criminal Careers and
Legitimate Pursuits   267

Recruitment into a Criminal Career   268

Typologies of Criminal Careers   269

Delinquent Careers   269

Chronic Offenders   270

Patterns of Delinquent Careers   271

Juvenile Delinquency and
Adult Criminal Careers   272

Criminal Careers of Robbers   274

Career Patterns   275

Planning Crimes   275

Use of the Stolen Money   276

Intensive and Intermittent
Career Criminals   276

**Criminal Careers of White-Collar
Offenders   277**

Leaving a Life of Crime   278

A Model of the Exiting Process   278

Reasons for Leaving a Career
as a Professional Thief   280

Reasons for Leaving a Career
in Violent Crime   280

Reasons for Leaving a Career as a
Drug Dealer or Smuggler   281

Exiting and Theories
of Crime Causation   281

Exiting and the Correctional System   283

Summary   284

IMPORTANT TERMS   285

REVIEW QUESTIONS   285

FOR FURTHER STUDY   286

11 The Organization of Criminal Behavior   287

The Meaning of Organization   288

Juvenile Gangs   290

The Unorganized Gang   291

The Organized Gang   292

Conventional Crime   295

Professional Theft   295

Drug Smuggling and Dealing   299

Violent Crime   301

Organized Crime   301

The Mafia in the United States   303

New Forms of Organized Crime   307

White-Collar Crime   309

Summary   310

IMPORTANT TERMS   311

REVIEW QUESTIONS   311

FOR FURTHER STUDY   312

12 Community Reactions to Crime   313

Fear of Crime   314

Consequences of the Fear of Crime   316

Informal Control of Crime   319

Community and Informal
Social Control   319

Defensible Space and Informal
Social Control   322

Individual Response to Crime   324

Bystander Responses to Crime   324

Collective Response to Crime   328

A Historical and Comparative
Perspective   329

Urban Patrol Groups   330

Neighborhood Watches   332

Community Crime-Prevention Strategies   333

Summary   334

IMPORTANT TERMS   335

REVIEW QUESTIONS   335

FOR FURTHER STUDY   336

13 The Criminal Justice System   337

The Police   338

History of the Police   338

Police Abuses of Authority   340

The Clearance Rate   346

Criminal Courts   347

The Bail System   348

Preventive Detention   348

Prosecutors   349

Defense Attorneys   349

Judges   350

Juries   350

Plea Bargaining   350

Probation   351

Sentence Disparity   352

The Prisons   358

History of Prisons   359

The Prison Population   359

Parole   361

**The Victim in the Criminal
Justice System   362**

Compensation   362

Restitution   363

The Changing Role of the Victim   364

Summary   365

IMPORTANT TERMS   366

REVIEW QUESTIONS   366

FOR FURTHER STUDY   367

14 Deterrence, Incapacitation, Retribution, and Rehabilitation   368

Deterrence   368

Assumptions about Behavior   369

Deterrence and Other Effects
of Penalties   370

Deterrence and the Criminal Act   371

Deterrence and the Sanctioning Process   372

Deterrence and the Criminal
Justice System   374

Incapacitation   382

Selective Incapacitation   382

Career Criminal Programs   383

"Three Strikes and You're Out"   384

Retribution   384

A System of Just Deserts   386

Retribution and the Criminal
Justice System   390

Rehabilitation   397

Rehabilitation and the Criminal
Justice System   398

Types of Treatment   400

Does Rehabilitation Work?   402

Reaffirming Rehabilitation   404

Reintegrating the Offender into Society   406

The Future of Rehabilitation   407

Summary   408

IMPORTANT TERMS   409

REVIEW QUESTIONS   409

FOR FURTHER STUDY   410

15 Solving the Crime Problem   411

Ideological Approaches to Solving the Crime Problem   411

The Conservative Approach   411

The Liberal Approach   412

The Radical Approach   412

Attitudes toward the Causes and Prevention of Crime   413

The Politics of Crime   414

The President's Commission on Law Enforcement and Administration of Justice   414

The Law Enforcement Assistance Administration   415

The 1968 and 1972 Presidential Elections   416

The Crime Issue during the Reagan Administration   416

The 1988 Presidential Election and the George H. W. Bush Administration   417

The 1992 and 1996 Elections and the Clinton Administration   417

The 2000 Presidential Election and the George W. Bush Administration   418

Crime and the Criminal Justice System   420

Overreach of the Criminal Law   420

The Police   420

The Courts   421

The Prisons   424

Situational Crime Prevention   425

Target Hardening   426

Self-Protective Measures   426

Informal Social Control   426

Community Crime Prevention   427

Dealing with the Causes of Crime   427

Economic Factors   428

The Process of Social Change   429

Political Factors   429

Community Ties   430

The Family   430

The School   431

Discrimination   431

Conclusion   432

Summary   432

IMPORTANT TERMS   433

REVIEW QUESTIONS   433

FOR FURTHER STUDY   433

Glossary   435

Bibliography   443

Name Index   478

Subject Index   486

FEATURE BOXES

 ## Crime and the Media

The Police and the News Media   35
Reporting Terrorism   57
White-Collar Crime in the News   66
Race and the Student-Murderer   92
*Internet Crimes against Young People   138
The How-to-Commit-Crime Manual   213
Crime Stoppers   325

Crime on Campus

Measuring the Problem   43
*Fraud and Student Loans   61
Computer Crime and Differential Association Theory   220
Routine Activities and Criminal Victimization   241
The Role of Alcohol and Drugs   250
Just Deserts for Student Offenders?   385

 ## Cross-Cultural Perspectives

*Hate Crimes against French Jews   55
*Violent Crime in South Africa   75
Japanese Corporations and the *Yakuza*   143
Machismo and Murder in Brazil   204
*Terrorism and the al Qaeda Network   288
Rape in Bosnia   302
Lynchings in Brazil   330
*Rape and Adultery in Pakistan   363
*Capital Punishment in China   381

Using Criminology

Can Curfews Stop Juvenile Crime?   90
Neurological and Psychological Problems of Juveniles
   Condemned to Death   110
Gender and the Student-Murderer   163
Holding Parents Responsible for Their Children's Behavior   188
RICO and Organized Crime   306
Profiling the Serial Killer   422

*New to this edition

PREFACE

This book remains organized around a conceptual scheme, unlike the core of most textbooks, which use a "crime-of-the-week club" approach (for example, a chapter on violent crime, a chapter on organized crime, a chapter on white-collar crime, and so on). There is as much material on those crimes here as in other books, but that material appears in chapters that treat conceptual issues, such as learning to commit crime and the organization of criminal behavior.

In revising this book, I have, as usual, paid close attention to professional journals and books in criminology, sociology, and other disciplines. This literature develops and tests hypotheses and theories; it is conceptual in nature, rather than focused on telling the reader everything he or she might like to know about a particular type of crime. I believe that such a conceptual approach is the best way to introduce students to the tools and ideas with which to analyze and understand criminal behavior.

Boxes new to this edition examine Internet crimes against young people, fraud and student loans, hate crimes against French Jews, violent crime in South Africa, terrorism and the al Qaeda network, rape and adultery in Pakistan, and capital punishment in China. New sections deal with violence against intimate partners, terrorism, Internet fraud, rampage killers, the biological basis of antisocial personality disorder, the Enron–Arthur Andersen scandal, the subculture of violence among the homeless, delinquency in Japan, right-to-bear-arms laws, the criminal careers of white-collar offenders, racial profiling, cross-national differences in criminal justice expenditures, the impact of the police and prisons on crime rates, changing attitudes toward the death penalty, the broken windows theory, and the 2000 presidential election. At several points I have integrated material on terrorism and the September 11, 2001, attacks on the World Trade Center and the Pentagon.

Each chapter ends with a detailed summary; review questions that are helpful to students for studying the material and to instructors for preparing essay questions; and a new annotated section of recent books, articles, and websites for further study. Important terms are highlighted in the text, listed at the end of each chapter, and defined in the glossary at the end of the book. References in the text are to an end-of-text bibliography, which is followed by a name index and a subject index.

I would like to thank the following people for their comments and suggestions for this eighth edition: Carol A. Archbold, Marquette University; Martha Karin Dudash, Cameron University; Jerome Rosonke, Northern State University; and Sudipto Roy, Indiana State University. I would also like to thank Jennifer Jacobson, Series Editor at Allyn & Bacon, for her suggestions for improving this book.

J. E. C.

AUTHOR BIOGRAPHY

John E. Conklin, professor of sociology at Tufts University in Medford, Massachusetts, was born in Oswego, New York, in 1943 and raised in Syracuse, New York. He is the father of four children—Christopher, Anne, Lydia, and Gillian—and is married to Sarah Belcher Conklin.

After earning a bachelor's degree from Cornell University in 1965, Professor Conklin attended Harvard University, completing his doctorate there in 1969. He then worked for a year at Harvard Law School's Center for Criminal Justice. He started teaching at Tufts University in 1970 and now offers courses in criminology, sociology of law, and sociology of sexual behavior.

Professor Conklin's first book, *Robbery and the Criminal Justice System* (1972), was based on data he gathered in Boston. He also wrote *The Impact of Crime* (1975), a study of community reactions to crime, and *"Illegal but Not Criminal": Business Crime in America* (1977). Two editions of *Sociology: An Introduction* were published in 1984 and 1987, and the first of eight editions of *Criminology* appeared in 1981. *Art Crime*—Professor Conklin's study of theft, forgery, and fraud in the art world—was published in 1994. His *New Perspectives in Criminology* (Allyn & Bacon, 1996) is an edited collection of papers published by leading criminologists during the 1990s. In 2003, Allyn & Bacon published Professor Conklin's *Why Crime Rates Fell,* a study of the reasons that crime declined so dramatically in the 1990s.

1 The Study of Crime

Watch an hour of local television news tonight, and notice how many stories deal with crime. Murders will probably get the most coverage, but child abuse, domestic violence, fraud, and political corruption may also be represented. Then look through the TV listings for the evening's "entertainment"; crime and violence will be featured. Pick up the newspaper and glance at the advertisements for the latest movies; at least a few will focus on crime. Chances are that several mysteries and suspense novels will be on the best-seller list as well. You can even buy trading cards depicting serial murderers and CD-ROM interactive murder mystery games. All of us are part of a vast audience for crime as entertainment. Crime stories offer escape, stimulation, relaxation, and the drama of a confrontation between good and evil.

The mass media rapidly disperse crime news throughout the nation and inform even the residents of relatively crime-free areas of the extent of crime in the society. The media focus on attention-grabbing events, bringing the most sensational and bizarre crimes to public attention. As a result, people develop a distorted view of crime as inexplicably and unpredictably violent, even though simple theft, burglary, and commercial fraud are much more common than murder and rape.

Because newspapers and television stations in this country are businesses trying to make a profit, the crime news they present is designed to attract as big an audience as possible. The crimes that appeal most to the news media are those that are visible and spectacular, have sexual or political implications, threaten the social order, can be presented in graphic—usually violent—terms, and seem to be the product of individual aberrations rather than social conditions. Newsworthiness is a product of a crime's seriousness, uniqueness, and salience; the characteristics of its victims and offenders; and the background and work environment of reporters and their sources (Ericson, Baranek, and Chan, 1991; Chermak, 1995). Media attention to sensational crimes can produce "echo effects" that influence the way the criminal justice system deals with other high-profile cases (Surette, 1999).

Violent crime, especially murder, occurs on prime-time television programs much more often

1

than in the real world, but more commonly experienced property crimes such as larceny and burglary appear much less often on television. Reality television programs
such as *America's Most Wanted* and *Unsolved Mysteries* emphasize violent crime, especially murder (Cavender and Bond-Maupin, 1993). Television also distorts the
characteristics of offenders. Compared to actual murderers, those appearing on
prime-time shows are older, more likely to be white or Asian, have higher incomes,
are more likely to be professional criminals or businesspersons, and are more apt to
be motivated by greed than by anger. Only in portraying most murderers as males living in urban areas does television present an accurate picture. On television very few
offenders get away with their crimes, but in real life four-fifths of serious crimes produce no arrest (Lichter and Lichter, 1983; Lichter, Lichter, and Rothman, 1994).

The news media sometimes convey incorrect impressions about trends in crime
rates. From 1990 to 1995, the homicide rate in the United States dropped by 13 percent, but coverage of murders on ABC, CBS, and NBC nightly newscasts increased by
1,352 percent if the O. J. Simpson case is included, and by 336 percent if it is excluded
(Center for Media and Public Affairs, 1997).

Media distortion of the reality of crime has important consequences. It generates
anxiety among the public; people who watch a lot of television are more likely than
people who watch less to see the world as violent, dangerous, and crime-ridden
(Gerbner and Gross, 1976). A study of crime news in *Time* magazine from 1953 to
1982 concluded that by focusing on violent rather than property crime, neglecting
the role of unemployment in crime, and emphasizing crime by racial minorities, the
magazine provided ideological support for the capitalist political economy (Barlow,
Barlow, and Chiricos, 1995). Even when corporate crimes resulting in the loss of lives
are reported in the press, they are less apt to be treated as criminal behavior than as
the consequence of lax enforcement of government regulations (Wright, Cullen, and
Blankenship, 1995).

The way that crime is portrayed in the media differs significantly from the actual patterns and causes of crime that criminologists have discovered from their research. Sociologists, psychologists, economists, political scientists, biologists, and
others who study crime gather empirical data to test their ideas and then revise those
ideas to fit the new information.

The Nature of Crime and Delinquency

Most people have an intuitive sense of what crime is, but social scientists try to define in precise terms the phenomena they study. By defining crime in an exact way,
criminologists specify the domain of their study. Definitions of crime serve another,
more subtle function: They influence the causes of criminal behavior that a criminologist will study. Let's look at several definitions of crime, see what they include
and exclude, and consider how they affect the causes on which criminologists will focus their attention.

In their influential book *A General Theory of Crime* (1990: 15), Michael Gottfredson and Travis Hirschi define crimes as "acts of force or fraud undertaken in pursuit
of self-interest." They explicitly avoid defining crime in terms of violating the criminal law, preferring as a definition one that focuses on "the nature of crime," which
they describe in terms of selected research on what they call "ordinary crime." Ordinary or mundane crime is described as providing immediate and easy gratification of
desires, few long-term benefits, little skill or planning, and pain for the victim. They
exclude from their picture such highly organized crimes as Mafia domination of the
garbage industry in the New York metropolitan area (Reuter, 1993) and a conspiracy

in the electrical equipment industry to fix prices in violation of federal law (Geis, 1967). Gottfredson and Hirschi suggest that such highly structured crimes are rare and only seem to be highly organized because scholars or law-enforcement officials have imposed organization on what is really the impulsive behavior of individuals. Their definition of crime also seems to include too much; a student of mine suggested that boxing fit their definition, as would hockey and wrestling. Those sports involve the use of force in the pursuit of self-interest.

A very different definition of crime was developed in an essay by Herman and Julia Schwendinger (1975). They define crime as violations of "the historically determined rights of individuals." They suggest that their broad definition would incorporate most current violations of the criminal law, but it would reconstitute the study of crime by focusing attention on imperialistic war, racism, sexism, and poverty. They would treat as criminals those people who deny basic human rights to others through such practices. A problem with such a definition is that criminologists would disagree over what are basic human rights. For instance, are political leaders who allow poverty to persist by not redistributing income to be regarded as criminal, or might they be seen as criminal if they taxed the rich at such a high rate as to deprive them of their property? The Schwendingers' definition of crime implies that the causes of crime exist in the institutions of society, and more specifically in the institutions of capitalist economies. This definition allows them to develop a radical critique of capitalism and to encourage criminologists to become "guardians of human rights" rather than "defenders of order."

Most criminologists adopt legalistic definitions of crime quite different from those offered by the Schwendingers and by Gottfredson and Hirschi. This book will define **crime** as an act that violates the criminal law and is punishable by the state. Criminal **laws** are formalized or codified **norms**, which are rules that make explicit certain social expectations about what is appropriate behavior for particular people in specific situations. Crimes, which are violations of these codified norms, are treated as offenses against the state rather than as acts against specific individuals. This definition has its origins in medieval Great Britain, where the king replaced formal vengeance by victim against offender with sanctions by the state. Thus, today a robbery is dealt with by the courts as *State* v. *Jones* rather than as *Smith* v. *Jones*. Smith as the victim of the robbery might sue Jones, the alleged robber, in civil court to recover money for damages caused during the holdup, but this rarely happens. Instead, the offense will be dealt with in criminal court, with a prosecutor or district attorney acting on behalf of the state in bringing charges against Jones. A person who is convicted of a crime is subjected to a **sanction**, a measure designed to ensure future conformity to the law and to punish past nonconformity.

In its ideal form, the criminal law is specific in nature, uniform in its application, dispassionate in its enforcement, and reflective of the culture's informal norms (Sutherland and Cressey, 1978). Criminal law is a means to control behavior by allowing or prohibiting certain behaviors for particular individuals in specific situations. Thus, a police officer can use lethal force to stop a felon who poses a threat of serious harm to others, but a private citizen generally is not permitted to do so. The same act is treated differently because each individual occupies a different status. The law is also specific to the situation. A victim who fears for his or her life during a crime may use lethal force in self-protection and have the action treated as justifiable homicide, but people generally are not allowed to use lethal force to prevent a simple theft.

This book treats crime in a legalistic way, beginning with the law's definition of crime and studying behavior that violates the law, rather than regarding the development of the law as the primary topic of study. Some criminologists have criticized this legalistic approach, claiming that it implies acceptance of the values of those who make the law (Platt, 1975). This is not necessarily the case, however, for it is possible to recognize the existence of a body of criminal law and examine the causes of behavior that violates that law, without at the same time giving one's moral support to that body of law or personally condemning behavior that violates it.

The Characteristics of Crime

Crime is behavior that is subject to legally defined punishment. The French sociologist Emile Durkheim (1895/1933) asserted in the late nineteenth century that punishment is the defining characteristic of crime and that other characteristics—such as social harm—are corollaries rather than defining traits. Punishable behavior includes a myriad of actions, from forcible rape to price-fixing, from murder to pollution of the environment. Because crime includes so many diverse acts, it makes little sense to speak of "crime increasing" or "the typical criminal" without referring to specific crimes or specific criminals. However, many crimes have some characteristics in common.

Crime usually involves **criminal intent**, the willed or conscious desire to commit an act that violates a criminal law. Before the twelfth century, the law did not include the idea of a guilty mind or *mens rea* that formed criminal intent; guilt was then based simply on the causing of injury. Over time, the idea of intent was gradually introduced into the law, partly as a result of the influence of Christian teachings about sin and moral blame. However, not all acts now designated as crimes involve criminal intent. Some crimes arise from negligence or recklessness. For example, in 1995 two German executives were charged with murder and attempted murder for distributing blood products contaminated with the HIV virus that causes AIDS. Other crimes are strict liability offenses, meaning that there is no need to prove criminal intent in order to convict the defendant. One strict liability offense is statutory rape, or sexual intercourse with an individual below a legally defined age of consent. In one highly publicized case, a thirty-five-year-old former grade-school teacher from Seattle, who had sex with a thirteen-year-old student and gave birth to his child, served 100 days in jail. She was rearrested and reincarcerated in 1998 after violating the conditions of her release by having further contact with him.

For most crimes, the law requires a causal connection among criminal intent, criminal conduct, and harm. For instance, an act that violates the law and causes harm may not be treated as a crime by the legal system if criminal intent is absent. This practice is based on the idea that punishment makes sense only if the violator of the law is responsible for his or her behavior. For intent to exist, an individual must have criminal capacity or be in control of his or her own behavior. Capacity is lacking in people who are too young to have criminal capacity (usually defined as being under the age of seven) or are not legally adults (often defined as being between the ages of seven and seventeen).

The law allows several excuses and justifications as defenses to criminal charges. **Excuses**, which deny criminal intent, include the insanity defense, which is examined in Chapter 5. The excuse that one committed a crime because of drunkenness or the influence of drugs is less likely to bring exoneration than to reduce the seriousness of the charge for which a defendant is convicted. Ignorance of the law is an excuse that is rarely accepted. Entrapment is the defense that one broke the law only because of illegal inducement by a law-enforcement agent.

A defense that the law allows a person to act in a particular way is called a **justification**. Self-defense against an offender threatening serious bodily injury is permitted if the potential victim uses no more force than necessary to prevent the harm. The defense of duress is the claim that another person coerced one into committing a crime; thus, stealing a bicycle because someone forced you to at knifepoint is not a crime. The justification that one had to violate the law to avoid the threat of some greater harm from a nonhuman force is called the defense of necessity; stealing a car to escape an earthquake is an example.

Juvenile Delinquency

People who violate the law but are not legally adults—defined as those below the age of eighteen in many states—can be tried in juvenile court, an institution that is about a century old, and be "adjudged delinquent" rather than convicted of a crime. These delinquents might have committed an act that would be a crime if done by an adult. The designation **juvenile delinquent** is also applied to those who commit **status offenses**, acts such as underage drinking, running away from home, or truancy, which are violations only because those who engage in them are below the age of majority.

Juvenile courts were originally designed as informal welfare agencies that offered counseling and therapy tailored to the needs of the individual offender. The offender's youth was thought to confer a kind of diminished capacity and to make the offender easier to reform than an adult criminal. A 1988 survey in California found "overwhelming public support for a juvenile justice system, separate from the adult system, with rehabilitation as its primary goal" (Steinhart, 1988: 1; see also Moon et al., 2000a). A national survey of 1,007 adults found significant opposition to the harsher treatment of juvenile offenders proposed in the U.S. Senate's Violent and Repeat Juvenile Offender Act of 1997 (Schiraldi and Soler, 1998).

Since the U.S. Supreme Court's decision *in re Gault* (1967), the juvenile court has become more formalized, more like "a scaled-down criminal court" (Feld, 1993: 197). More punitive measures have come to characterize the treatment of serious juvenile offenders, with every state now specifying conditions under which juveniles can be prosecuted and punished as adults. In 1997, 8,400 delinquency cases were waived to criminal court; juveniles charged with drug offenses were more likely than those charged with violent or property offenses to be tried as adults, and nearly nine-tenths of the juveniles whose cases were waived to criminal court were sixteen or older (Puzzanchera, 2000). In one curious case, a Connecticut judge in 2001 rejected a claim by Michael Skakel, who was thirty-nine years old when charged with a murder he had allegedly committed at the age of fifteen, that he should be tried as a juvenile; the judge ordered that Skakel be tried as an adult in criminal court, where he was eventually convicted.

The "get tough" attitude toward juveniles that developed in the 1980s and persists today resulted from perceptions that juvenile violence and juvenile drug use were increasing and that an increasing proportion of delinquents could not be treated effectively within the juvenile justice system. Highly publicized cases that strengthened these perceptions include the following:

- A twelve-year-old Florida boy was arrested for his fifty-seventh offense in 1993. Over the previous four years, he had been arrested twelve times for car theft, ten times for burglary, and three times for armed robbery.

- Two boys who had killed a five-year-old boy by dropping him from a fourteen-story building when they were only ten and eleven were sentenced to Illinois juvenile penitentiaries in 1996.

- Two boys, aged eleven and thirteen, who killed a teacher and four girls in 1998 with high-powered rifles after luring them from an Arkansas school with a false fire alarm, could be released when they turn eighteen, because state law prevented offenders under fourteen from being punished as adults.

In November 2002, Alex King (front), 13, and his brother Derek King, 14, pleaded guilty in criminal court to killing their sleeping father with a baseball bat a year earlier.

Research suggests that trying youths in criminal court and incarcerating them with adults will not solve the problem of juvenile crime. This approach often imposes severe penalties on minor offenses instead of on the violent ones at which they are aimed, and it therefore may actually increase the chance that juveniles will commit more crimes in the future (Bishop, 2000; Snyder, Sickmund, and Poe-Yamagata, 2000).

Social Origins of the Criminal Law

Criminal law is a social phenomenon; behavior defined as crime in one society can occur in a different society and not be regarded as suitable for punishment there. We can see the social nature of the criminal law by looking at variations in the definition of theft in different societies. Most societies define theft as a crime, but there are significant differences in the way this behavior is treated. In Norway, petty theft from a relative with whom the thief lives is not treated as a crime. Thieves in Colombia are exempted from criminal sanctions if they can show that they or their family had a pressing need for food or clothing, that there was no legal way to meet that need, that no violence was used to perpetrate the theft, and that no more was taken than was necessary. The former Soviet Union distinguished the theft of private property from the theft of socialist property, a distinction based on state ownership of land and the means of production. In industrial societies, taking a neighbor's property for personal use is generally regarded as a crime, but in some tribal societies one is expected to take and use a neighbor's property in time of need. Understanding why one society permits such behavior while another condemns it as crime requires a careful study of the social structure, culture, history, and level of economic development of each society.

Theoretical Perspectives on Crime and the Criminal Law

Criminologists disagree on the origins of the criminal law and, as a result, disagree on the way they see crime. Conflict theorists claim that the law develops to benefit some groups to the detriment of others. Consensus theorists regard the law as a reflection of popular agreement on standards of behavior.

The Conflict Perspective   The **conflict perspective** sees the criminal law as closely intertwined with the distribution of political power and economic resources in a society (Gordon, 1973; Taylor, Walton, and Young, 1973; Chambliss, 1999). Conflict theorists argue that those who control power and wealth determine which kinds of behavior are defined as crime and which kinds are permitted. The criminal law thus reflects the will of the powerful and well-to-do, and behavior that threatens the interests of that elite—such as theft and violence by the poor—will be harshly sanctioned.

Marxist or radical criminology is a form of conflict theory that focuses on social class, defined by the relationship of a group to the means of production. This perspective claims that capitalists, who own and control the means of production, use the law to protect their property from those who threaten it, namely, the lower and working classes. Crime by the wealthy and powerful is attributed to the greed generated by a capitalist economic system, and crime by the powerless is attributed to the need to violate the law in order to survive.

Marxist and radical criminologists assert the relationship between capitalism and crime, but they offer little evidence that capitalism generates crime to a greater degree than alternative economic systems, such as socialism. Some capitalist systems, such as those of Japan and Switzerland, do not have high crime rates, whereas relatively high rates seem to have existed in the Soviet Union before its breakup. Indeed, after more than seventy years of Communist Party rule, Russia had a murder rate significantly higher than that of the United States. Even if some socialist or communist nations do have low crime rates, those rates might not be due to the greater amount of income equality or social justice in those countries, as Marxists suggest. Instead, those low rates might be due to the more oppressive social control that characterizes some of those totalitarian states, or due to the low level of economic development of those countries.

Not all conflict theories are Marxist, but most conflict theories acknowledge that control of the economic system is an important means by which less powerful groups are dominated. Conflict theorists have also examined group differences other than social class, such as disputes over values and between racial, ethnic, and religious groups.

Left realism is a conflict theory that has shifted the emphasis from crime by the ruling class to the impact that crime by the lower and working class has on other members of the same class. Proposing crime-reduction strategies that are more concrete than the Marxist demand for a new social order to replace capitalism, left realists have called for closer attention to the actual circumstances of victims and offenders, the development of programs that increase "human capital" through job training and better wages, more citizen involvement in the fight against crime, a police force that is both more responsive to community needs and a more effective deterrent of crime, greater emphasis on rehabilitation, and less use of imprisonment (Lowman and MacLean, 1992; Matthews and Young, 1992).

Another version of conflict theory is **peacemaking criminology**, a humanistic approach that regards crime as the product of a social structure that puts some groups at a disadvantage, sets people against one another, and generates a desire for revenge. The proposed solution is not to rely on the criminal justice system, which can actually increase crime, but rather to develop empathy with others, resolve social conflicts, and create a more just society (Pepinsky and Quinney, 1991).

Conflict theorists have contributed to the sociology of law by asking why some behavior is defined as crime and other behavior is not. They have shown that behavior that is especially common to powerless groups is more likely to be defined as criminal than behavior that is characteristic of the wealthy and the powerful. Thus, the criminal law does not reflect the values and interests of the whole society, but only those of the groups that are able to use the law to protect their own narrow interests. In tracing the development of criminal laws against vagrancy, drug use, theft, alcohol production and distribution, and antitrust violations, conflict theorists have shown that laws emerge from conflict among various interest groups, with victorious groups imposing their will on the losers through enactment and enforcement of laws. By looking at the process of law formation, conflict theorists have demonstrated that crime is behavior that is socially defined rather than intrinsically wrong. However, the conventional crimes that have been the primary focus of modern criminology are widely supported by all segments of the population: There is little dispute over whether murder, rape, robbery, and even white-collar offenses should be defined as criminal.

By focusing on crime by the wealthy and the powerful, conflict theorists have helped to redirect the attention of criminologists from conventional crime to white-collar crime and political corruption. However, this redirecting of attention to crime by the upper strata is not a unique contribution of conflict theory. Edwin Sutherland made the same point in the 1930s when he introduced the concept of white-collar crime, and most research on white-collar crime has been done by criminologists who do not identify themselves as conflict theorists.

Conflict theorists have focused on the way that laws are enforced as well as the way they are enacted. As Austin Turk (1969: 25) remarks, "Criminality is not a biological, psychological, or even behavioral phenomenon, but a social status defined by the way in which an individual is perceived, evaluated, and treated by legal authorities." Conflict theorists claim that the criminal justice system discriminates against those who are disadvantaged by class, race, ethnicity, and gender. They claim that the lower classes and minorities are more likely to be watched by the police, arrested in suspicious circumstances, held in jail rather than released on bail, tried in court, found guilty, and given harsh sentences (Reiman, 2001). These assertions of bias will be assessed in Chapter 13.

Some conflict theorists have argued that criminology should link the study of crime to the pursuit of social justice and the liberation of oppressed people (Schwendinger and Schwendinger, 1975). They deny the "objective" nature of criminal behavior and instead regard offenders as victims of oppression. Property crime, for instance, is seen as an effort to accumulate property as rapidly as possible, a goal highly valued in capitalist systems. These conflict theorists believe that criminology should be "normatively committed to the abolition of inequalities in wealth and power," rather than search for factors that distinguish offenders from nonoffenders or try to change people who violate the law (Taylor, Walton, and Young, 1975: 44).

The Consensus Perspective   In contrast to the conflict perspective stands the **consensus perspective**, the position that the criminal law reflects broad agreement about which kinds of behavior should be punished by the state. Consensus theorists argue that the law represents shared values and norms held by all members of the society, rather than the norms and values of a particular group. Consensus is derived from discussion and compromise by elected lawmakers, rather than imposed on society by a group that controls political power or economic resources (Durkheim, 1895/1933).

Consensus theorists see crime as behavior that exceeds a society's limits of tolerance. In this view, crime is behavior detrimental to the public interest, rather than behavior detrimental to the narrow interests of organized groups that are able to influence the law. For consensus theorists, the critical question is why some people violate the law, rather than why the law defines their behavior as criminal. These theorists propose that criminals are either inadequately socialized with dominant norms and values or are insufficiently integrated into conventional social institutions.

Using the Conflict and Consensus Perspectives   The best way to view the criminal law is to examine the extent to which consensus and conflict are involved in the passage of laws, as well as the degree to which the public supports existing laws. Some laws reflect a widespread social consensus; for example, murder and rape are almost universally regarded as harmful acts that ought to be punished (Brown, 1952; Clifford, 1978). Other laws reflect the outcome of conflict among groups. For instance, an antitrust law in the United States was the result of a victory by small-business owners, labor, and farmers over large corporations (Quinney, 1970). Sometimes, laws initiated through conflict are perpetuated through consensus; an example is antitrust law.

The Social Construction of Crime

Crime is defined by the criminal law, but the social meaning given to crime varies from group to group and over time. In recent years, criminologists have studied the **social construction of crime**, the way that crime is interpreted by groups with different interests they seek to promote by using their resources to gain ownership of an issue (Jenkins, 1994). Rather than assume that criminal laws are uniformly applied, this perspective proposes that laws are inconsistently applied. Crime is less an objective property of behavior than a definition constructed through social interaction. One form of social constructionism is **cultural criminology**, which focuses on the way that crime and crime control are given meaning by popular culture, especially the media, both as political and social issues and as entertainment (Ferrell and Websdale, 1999).

Law-enforcement officials and political leaders are primarily responsible for establishing the frame of reference within which the crime issue is discussed. Their views are more often cited in newspaper feature stories on crime than are the views of professors and nonacademic researchers, whose opinions are presented as secondary or "nonofficial" interpretations of crime. This marginalization of intellectuals by the press means that their theories of crime causation are slighted in favor of the crime-control model favored by the police and politicians. As a result, public discourse on crime focuses on deterrence and incapacitation rather than on unemployment, poverty, and rehabilitation (Welch, Fenwick, and Roberts, 1997, 1998).

Varying interpretations of the terrorist attacks of September 11, 2001, have raised questions about whether the resulting deaths should be treated as murders. According to the Federal Bureau of Investigation (2002: 302),

> There will be disagreement and debate among academicians, governmental officials, law enforcement, the media, and the general public regarding the perspective from which one should view the events of September 11. Some will argue that they were an act of war; others will say they are a local crime, an international conspiracy, terrorism in its classical meaning, or a myriad of other possibilities.

In its crime report for 2001, the FBI defined the 3,047 deaths as murders, but said that because their inclusion in national crime statistics would have skewed its analysis, it was treating the deaths in a separate section of the report. Including the September 11th deaths in the national murder rate would raise that rate by nearly 20 percent. In its 1995 report the FBI did include the 168 deaths resulting from the terrorist bombing of Oklahoma City's Alfred P. Murrah Federal Building in the national murder rate, but that inclusion raised the murder rate by less than 1 percent. Except for two tables reporting the location of murders, the FBI's 2001 crime report omits the September 11th deaths from national crime statistics, suggesting that the bureau chose to regard the deaths more as an act of war than as local crime.

Gary LaFree (1989) has used the social construction perspective to examine official reactions to reports of sexual assault. Rather than focusing on the causes of sexual assault, he asked how the police and courts decided that a sexual assault constitutes a rape. He discovered that definitions of rape are constructed through social interaction and reflect stereotypes or typifications, which are shared ideas about the kinds of offenders, victims, and situations that characterize something called "rape." For example, he found that men accused of sexual assault are less apt to be convicted of rape if their victims had "bad reputations" and unconventional living arrangements, were chronic alcohol users, and did not report the assault promptly. None of these factors appears in legal definitions of rape, but all influence the way that rape is socially constructed.

The abduction of children by strangers is another crime that has been examined in terms of its social construction. By merging perhaps two to three hundred such abductions each year with millions of runaways and children taken by their noncustodial parents in violation of court orders, "claims makers" such as the news media, politicians, law-enforcement agents, and child-advocacy groups exaggerate the problem of stranger abductions (Best, 1990; Kappeler, Blumberg, and Potter, 1996). Pictures of missing children are widely circulated, sensational cases are given front-page attention, and the sexual exploitation of missing children is highlighted. In this way, a tragic event—the abduction of a child by a stranger—that is only slightly more common than being struck dead by lightning is thrust to the fore of public consciousness and becomes perceived as a major crime problem.

Serial murder is another crime that has commanded great public attention in recent years. As with child abductions, this crime is a serious one, but one that has been exaggerated and distorted by various claims makers (Jenkins, 1994). The FBI's Behavioral Sciences Unit was influential in defining this problem during the 1980s, exaggerating the number of serial murderers active at any given moment and focusing on killers who wandered from state to state, even though most serial killers stay within their own metropolitan region (Hickey, 2002). This picture of serial murder served the FBI's interests by increasing its investigative resources and by redefining some murders as crimes requiring federal attention. Feminists cited serial murder as another example of men's domination of women, often linking serial murder to the influence of pornography. Some feminists even denied the existence of female serial killers, although 10 to 15 percent of serial killers are women. Certain religious groups tried to explain the serial murder problem by linking it to the rituals of satanic cults. Lack of credible evidence and the FBI's resistance to this interpretation led to the failure of this attempted construction of the serial murder problem (Jenkins, 1994).

Crime is behavior that violates the criminal law, but groups with different ideological perspectives emphasize and distort crime stories to make rhetorical points supportive of their own positions. Criminologists need to study criminal behavior, but they also must attend to the ways that crime issues are socially constructed by groups with various interests.

Strategies of Criminological Research

Criminology is a discipline that gathers and analyzes empirical data in order to explain violations of the criminal law and societal reactions to those violations. The personal values of criminologists sometimes influence the kinds of crime they choose to study, yet they can still be relatively detached in their collection and interpretation of data. Stating a hypothesis and gathering data that might support or refute that hypothesis will increase objectivity, even if the selection of the problem for study (for example, robbery or white-collar crime) reflects personal values.

This section looks in detail at five research strategies employed by criminologists, giving an example of each. This will give the flavor of how social scientists go about the task of studying crime. Then several other strategies that researchers have used will be examined more briefly.

Comparative and Historical Research

One way to illuminate the problem of crime causation is to study violations of the law in other societies and at other times. This process offers insight into the relationship between crime and factors such as level of economic development and rate of urbanization. **Comparative research** can be used to evaluate whether a theory of crime developed in one society also explains crime in other societies, that is, whether the theory is universally true or limited in scope. The comparative approach also generates theory, for differences in crime from one society to another must fit a theory of crime.

Comparative research of this sort is uncommon. Crime has been studied in countries other than the United States, but researchers rarely collect data simultaneously in different countries so that they can make direct comparisons. Methodological problems with crime statistics gathered by the police, the courts, or the prisons also make comparisons difficult. Comparative research is hampered, too, by political and linguistic barriers, lack of funding, and the absence of a research tradition in some societies. Moreover, criminologists from one society sometimes approach the study of crime in another nation with an ethnocentric bias or a theoretical preference that distorts their interpretation of the data (Johnson and Barak-Glantz, 1983).

Similar in some ways to comparative research in contemporary societies is **historical research**, which examines the same society at different times and looks at the ways that crime has changed with economic and social development. Historical research often requires reliance on nonstatistical material, although researchers have sometimes used official statistics from the past or quantified material from historical documents. They have also used accounts by observers of the time, records of legislative hearings, narrative material from court files, and other documentary evidence.

Historical studies put contemporary crime into perspective, show how people have reacted to crime in the past, and suggest problems that may be encountered by nations now undergoing change. One historical study that illuminates the nature of crime in today's developing societies is J. J. Tobias's *Crime and Industrial Society in the 19th Century* (1967).

Tobias's Study of Crime in Nineteenth-Century England   J. J. Tobias's study of crime in industrialized England found that the crime statistics of that period were practically worthless for systematic study. As a result, he relied on parliamentary reports and contemporary accounts to piece together a picture of crime.

Tobias discovered that crime rates were high early in the nineteenth century because social institutions had failed to respond to a sizable increase in population. More specifically, the number of young people had increased without a commensurate growth in employment opportunities. Migration from rural areas and small towns to larger towns and cities proved unsettling, and those larger communities provided ample opportunities for crime as well as an anonymity that reduced the risk of arrest.

Crime rates decreased in England during the nineteenth century as social conditions became more settled. This engraving depicts the murder of a traveler by the notorious highwayman Richard Turpin around 1840.

During the nineteenth century, crime decreased as social conditions became more settled. Economic development increased job opportunities and raised incomes, and the government introduced social services for the disadvantaged. The police and the courts also changed over the course of the century, from a system that had a low rate of detection and severe penalties for the few offenders who were convicted to one that had more lenient sentences but a higher rate of detection. Tobias argues that this change enhanced the deterrent effect of the law and reduced crime.

It is difficult to support Tobias's interpretation of the historical changes with precise data, but he provides convincing documentary evidence of the social changes that accompanied the long-term decline in the crime rate. His conclusions are also consistent with evidence about the changing nature of crime in societies now undergoing social and economic development.

Biographies

A fruitful way to study the sources of criminal behavior and the development of criminal careers is to examine the experiences of a single offender. This **biographical method** reveals the needs and motivations of the offender, the way that commitment to the law is reduced, the way that criminal skills are learned, the obstacles encountered in pursuing legitimate careers and illegitimate lifestyles, the pattern of criminal activity over a lifetime, and the consequences of contact with the criminal justice system.

One problem with the biographical method is that the criminal who is studied may not be representative of other offenders. Separating an offender's experiences into those that are idiosyncratic and those that are common to other offenders is a difficult undertaking that requires more information than can be provided by one criminal's biography. The richness of the account of one offender's life sacrifices the representativeness provided by research on a sample of offenders, though the biographical method often yields hypotheses that can be tested on larger samples of offenders.

Another problem with the biographical method is that offenders sometimes distort their experiences. They may do this because of faulty memories, because they view the past in light of their present circumstances, or because they want to glorify and romanticize themselves. This problem of distortion can be minimized by double-checking the accuracy of an account with the offender at different times or by interviewing friends and relatives of the offender.

An early example of the biographical technique is Edwin Sutherland's (1937) study of "Chic Conwell," a professional thief who recounted his life of crime in great detail. William Chambliss (King and Chambliss, 1984) used a similar approach to study Harry King, a "box man" or safecracker. Another valuable biographical study is the story of a heroin addict and thief named Manny (Rettig, Torres, and Garrett, 1977). The biographical method has also been used to good advantage by Carl Klockars in *The Professional Fence* (1974) and by Darrell Steffensmeier in *The Fence* (1986).

Steffensmeier's Study of a Fence   Steffensmeier met his research subject "Sam Goodman" while Sam was serving time in prison for receiving stolen goods. He contacted this fence (an intermediary between thieves who steal property and members of the public who buy stolen goods) through the recommendations of several burglars Steffensmeier had been questioning as part of a different study.

In one chapter of *The Fence,* Sam tells how he became involved in criminal activity. He was self-reliant by the age of fifteen, working full-time and realizing that he was "out for a buck." His attraction to a fast life and hustling was reinforced by an uncle who led a similar life and had been in prison. From occasional petty theft, Sam graduated to burglary at age seventeen, being arrested and serving time for that crime in a juvenile reformatory. After his release, he worked full-time but continued to commit burglaries as part of a gang. Following his release from prison after another burglary conviction, he started to work for a furniture manufacturer. Eventually, he opened a secondhand furniture and antiques shop, though he continued to commit burglaries. Sam used his shop as a front to sell goods he had stolen. Other dealers began to pay him to upholster or doctor stolen goods for resale, and thieves began to bring him stolen merchandise. Sam's fencing operation grew after another prison term, and his burglaries became less frequent. Later he served time for receiving stolen goods, but after his release he seemed to become a legitimate dealer in secondhand goods and antiques, although he did fence on a small scale.

Steffensmeier's study of Sam Goodman offers rich insights into the crime of fencing. He details the network in which the fence is embedded, and the way that the fence interacts with thieves, criminal justice officials, antiques dealers and collectors, truckers, dockworkers, and competing fences. Steffensmeier looks at the rewards of fencing, including money, reputation in the criminal community, excitement, and a sense of mastery over one's life. He also provides insight into the ways that Sam justifies his fencing by claiming that fences are not the same as thieves, do little harm to the victims of theft, are much like legitimate businesspeople, and actually help other people.

Patterns of Crime

Another way to study crime is to look at it as a social phenomenon that has a specific form or structure. This study of **patterns of crime** often involves the use of police statistics to determine where crime is committed, who commits it, who is victimized, and what are the major dimensions of the criminal act. This kind of research examines the spatial distribution of crime in a city, the social background of offenders and victims, relationships between offenders and victims, and the social processes that lead to crime.

The patterns-of-crime approach assumes that police records can provide a comprehensive and valid description of crime and its participants. However, police statistics may not be representative of all the crime that occurs in a community if some offenses are not reported by the public or are not recorded by the police.

Patterns-of-crime studies are useful in describing the criminal act and in providing information on the prior arrest records of offenders and victims. However, they usually do not deal with the issue of crime causation in much depth. They do not tell us much about how offenders reduce their commitment to the law, learn criminal skills, or find opportunities to commit crime. The failure to interview offenders is a major shortcoming of the patterns-of-crime approach. In crimes such as homicide, where a high proportion of offenders are caught and convicted, much could be learned from interviews that cannot be discovered in police reports.

The patterns-of-crime approach has been used extensively at the University of Pennsylvania's Sellin Center for Studies in Criminology and Criminal Law, where Marvin Wolfgang pioneered the approach in his *Patterns in Criminal Homicide* (1958). Robbery and rape have also been studied using the same approach (Normandeau, 1968; Amir, 1971). A national study of four violent crimes in seventeen cities used a similar research strategy (Curtis, 1974).

Wolfgang's Study of Homicide   Wolfgang's pioneering investigation of homicide used police records from 1948 through 1952 in Philadelphia to analyze the race, sex, and age of homicide offenders and victims, the methods and weapons used to commit murder, the temporal and spatial patterns of homicide, the presence of alcohol in the offender and the victim at the time of the crime, the previous criminal records of offenders and victims, and the motives of offenders. He also explored the interpersonal relationships of offenders and victims, homicides committed during other crimes, and the extent to which victims contributed to their own murders. He looked at the solution of homicide cases by the police and at the court's disposition of charges against suspects.

One important finding that emerged from Wolfgang's research was that offenders and victims in homicide cases are often intimately associated with each other. About one-fourth of the homicides involved an offender and a victim who were relatives, and a similar number involved offenders and victims who were close friends. Homicides between strangers were relatively rare, accounting for only one-eighth of the cases. These findings focused criminologists' attention on the interpersonal dynamics of intimate relationships as a factor that can lead to lethal violence.

Another important conclusion was that homicides frequently occur in a context that includes the use of alcohol. Alcohol was absent in the homicide situation in only 36.4 percent of the cases. In 43.5 percent of the murders, both the offender and the victim had been drinking, in 9.2 percent of the cases only the victim had been drinking, and in 10.9 percent of the cases only the offender had been drinking.

Wolfgang's study of homicide provided other important findings. He found that most murders occurred between an offender and a victim of the same race; murders of whites by blacks or of blacks by whites were relatively rare. He also found that murder rates were highest among young black males, a finding he later used to support his theory of a subculture of violence.

The Cohort Study

One problem with some research techniques is the lack of a time dimension; that is, little attention is paid to the way a criminal career develops over time or the way crime rates increase or decrease. One strategy that introduces a time dimension follows a carefully defined group of people who are in a common situation over a period of time. Such a group is called a **cohort.** A cohort of all the individuals born in a given year will experience similar events over their lifetimes, even though they may be affected differently by those events. For instance, all people born in 1915 who lived until 1936 experienced the Great Depression during their adolescence, although some were exposed to abject poverty during that era and others were relatively insulated from its effects.

The ideal way to carry out a cohort study is to begin to collect data at an early age for the members of a cohort and then follow them through adolescence and into adulthood. Such a study could take twenty-five or more years to complete, if we assume that little crime is committed before the age of ten and that most offenders stop their criminal activities by the age of thirty-five. This kind of study would not have to rely solely on official records of delinquency or crime but could use questionnaires to measure violations of the law. Interviews could be conducted periodically to measure changes in an individual's social situation—for example, adjustment to school or family income—that might be associated with violation of the law. Some criminologists believe that such a long-term cohort study would yield information on the causes of criminal behavior and the development of criminal careers that we cannot get from other kinds of studies (Farrington, Ohlin, and Wilson, 1986; National Research Council, 1993).

Cohort studies do have several drawbacks. They are expensive to conduct, because they take so long to complete. A multicommunity cohort study of the biological, psychological, and social roots of violence proposed by the National Research Council would cost as much as $50 million, even though such a project "offers only a reasonable chance of breakthroughs in the understanding and control of violence" (National Research Council, 1993: 344). Pressure on academic researchers to publish scholarly work can inhibit them from undertaking cohort studies that will not yield data for years. In addition, interviewing cohort members on a regular basis could affect their normal process of growing up.

In spite of such difficulties, several cohort studies have been done. An important early one was the Cambridge-Somerville Youth Study (Powers and Witmer, 1951; McCord and McCord, 1959; McCord, 1978, 1981). Another major cohort study was carried out in England (West, 1969, 1982; West and Farrington, 1973, 1977), and a study of the relationship between juvenile delinquency and adult criminal careers was done in Wisconsin (Shannon, 1988). One cohort study that has received much attention is reported in Marvin Wolfgang, Robert Figlio, and Thorsten Sellin's *Delinquency in a Birth Cohort* (1972).

Wolfgang, Figlio, and Sellin's Cohort Study of Delinquency   Wolfgang, Figlio, and Sellin studied a cohort of all males born in 1945 who lived in Philadelphia continuously from ten (the first age at which there was a significant number of arrests) until eighteen (the age at which the juveniles became adults). The researchers studied only boys because of "the greater incidence, frequency, heterogeneity, seriousness, and persistency of male delinquency" (Wolfgang, Figlio, and Sellin, 1972: 30). Records kept by schools, draft boards, juvenile courts, and the police were examined for all 9,945 boys in the cohort. All police contacts that resulted in a written report about a delinquent act were examined. A study of the experiences of some of those boys as adults has also been done (Wolfgang, Thornberry, and Figlio, 1987).

Wolfgang, Figlio, and Sellin looked at the characteristics that distinguished boys who had had contact with the police from boys who had not. Thirty-five percent of the boys had at least one contact with the police as a juvenile, but a mere 6 percent of the boys accounted for 52 percent of all of the police contacts in the cohort. This suggests that a policy that could keep this small group of chronic offenders from engaging in delinquency would have a major impact on the overall rate of juvenile delinquency.

Blacks were more apt than whites to have police contacts, and lower-class boys were more likely than middle-class boys to have police contacts. In fact, the likelihood that a black middle-class boy would have contact with the police was the same as the chance that a white lower-class boy would have contact. The cohort technique permitted such conclusions because nonoffenders as well as offenders were included in the study. Conclusions of this sort would not be possible if the research design had included only people who had had contact with the police.

Because the cohort they studied included only boys whose contact with the police was examined during the relatively tranquil period from 1955 to 1962, Wolfgang and his colleagues later decided to study a second cohort. This cohort of 27,160 included both boys and girls who were born in 1958 and lived in Philadelphia from 1968 to 1975, a time of turmoil that included the Vietnam War, increased drug use, and social protest. In comparing the boys in the two cohorts, Wolfgang and his colleagues found that a similar percentage of each had had contact with the police, that in each cohort blacks were more likely than whites to have had police contacts, and that a relatively small proportion of each cohort accounted for most of the cohort's police contacts. The researchers did find, however, that the boys in the second cohort were much more likely to be involved in serious, costly offenses (Tracy, Wolfgang, and Figlio, 1990). Cohort studies can thus show how patterns of criminal and delinquent activity change over time.

Surveys

A **survey** is a study in which a sample of people representative of some larger population is asked a series of prepared questions. Survey researchers first review the published literature on the topic in which they are interested, then develop hypotheses about relationships among a set of variables, define those variables in precise and measurable terms, write and pretest questionnaires, select samples, administer the questionnaires, gather the data, and analyze and present their findings. Surveys have been used to measure crime by asking people both about their experiences as victims and about their own violations of the law (see Chapter 2).

Researchers have used surveys to measure sexual assaults on college campuses. A study of thirty-two campuses carried out for *Ms.* magazine concluded that 15.3 percent of female college students had been raped at least once and another 11.8 percent had been victims of attempted rape (Warshaw, 1988). This survey found that 6.3 percent of male college students reported that in the previous year they had committed an act that fit the legal definition of rape; another 5.3 percent admitted to attempting such an act. However, 84 percent of the males who admitted to such behavior did not label their behavior rape. According to psychologist Neil Malamuth, "When men are asked if there is any likelihood they would force a woman to have sex against her will if they could get away with it, about half say they would. But if you ask them if they would rape a woman if they knew they could get away with it, only about 15 percent say they would" (cited in Goleman, 1989: C1).

Fisher, Cullen, and Turner's Study of Rape on Campus   The National College Women Sexual Victimization (NCWSV) survey carried out by Bonnie S. Fisher, Francis T. Cullen, and Michael G. Turner (2000: 3) gathered data by telephone from "a randomly selected, national sample of 4,446 women who were attending a 2- or 4-year college or university during fall 1996." The survey was administered between February and May 1997 to students enrolled in schools with at least 1,000 students. The sample was stratified by the total enrollment and location (urban, rural, or suburban) of the schools. The response rate was 86 percent.

An important aspect of surveys attempting to measure rape is the kind of questions used to uncover victimization. Fisher, Cullen, and Turner first asked a series of "behaviorally specific screen questions" to determine if women had been sexually victimized and then used an incident report to gather specific information on each reported victimization. One such screen question was the following: "Since school began in fall 1996, has anyone made you have sexual intercourse by using force or threatening to harm you or someone close to you? Just so there is no mistake, by intercourse I mean putting a penis in your vagina" (Fisher, Cullen, and Turner, 2000: 6). Similar questions were asked about oral sex, anal sex, and the use of foreign objects, as well as about unsuccessful attempts at such sexual assaults. Incident reports recorded the details of the assaults, such as the type of penetration, the means of coercion, the victim's relationship to the offender, where the incident occurred, and whether it was reported to the police.

Fisher, Cullen, and Turner found that 4.9 percent of college women are the victims of rape or a rape attempt during any given calendar year, and that 20 to 25 percent of college women are victimized during the course of their college careers. When rape victims were asked if they considered the incident a rape, 46.5 percent said they did, 48.8 percent said they did not, and 4.7 percent were uncertain. The failure of nearly half of the victims to define their victimization as a rape does not, however, mean that it was not. Factors such as embarrassment, ignorance of the legal definition of rape, unwillingness to consider the offender a rapist, and the belief that they contributed to their own victimization can keep victims from acknowledging assaults that are legally rapes as such.

The NCWSV study was consistent with prior surveys in finding that most victims were acquainted with the men who had committed the rapes. Rape victims described the offender as a classmate, friend, boyfriend, or ex-boyfriend in 93.4 percent of the incidents and as an acquaintance in an additional 2.6 percent of the cases. Nearly 60 percent of the rapes that occurred on campus took place in the victim's

To protect their students against sexual assault, some colleges are buying coasters that test for "date-rape" drugs in drinks. Manufacturers say the coasters are 95 percent accurate, but law-enforcement officials question that assertion and suggest that the coasters might create a false sense of security.

residence, 31 percent occurred in other on-campus living quarters, and 10.3 percent happened in fraternities. Two-thirds of the rapes (66.3 percent) took place off campus, but most of those assaults occurred in bars and nightclubs or in students' apartments near the campus, and so were associated with the victims' lives as students. About 20 percent of the rape victims reported that they had been physically injured by their attackers. The risk of sexual victimization was greater for college women who frequently drank to the point of drunkenness, were unmarried, and had been sexually assaulted prior to the current school year.

Fewer than 5 percent of the rapes were reported to the police, but two-thirds of the victims told someone about the assault, usually a friend rather than a parent. Those who did not report the crime to the police offered the following reasons: The incident had not caused enough harm; it was not clear that a crime had been committed; they did not want others to know of the incident; they could not prove what had happened; they feared reprisals from the assailant; or they were wary of how the police would respond.

By documenting the extent and characteristics of criminal behavior that is often not recorded by the police, surveys provide a basis for developing measures to prevent victimization. For instance, the results of the NCWSV survey suggest that efforts to control the heavy consumption of alcoholic beverages on campuses could reduce sexual assaults.

Other Strategies of Criminological Research

Comparative and historical research, biographies, patterns-of-crime studies, cohort studies, and surveys are but a few of the many strategies that criminologists have used to study crime and the criminal justice system. Other strategies that have provided valuable information include the analysis of official and unofficial records, experiments, observation, and mathematical models and econometric techniques (see Table 1.1).

Official and Unofficial Records   The records of the police, the courts, and the correctional system have been used to study how the police arrest suspects, whether there is racial discrimination in sentencing convicted offenders, and how parole boards decide to release inmates.

Unofficial records of crime have also proved useful. For instance, department store records have been used to study shoplifting, a crime that often is not reported

TABLE 1.1   Some Strategies of
                 Criminological Research

1. Comparative and historical research
2. Biographies
3. Patterns-of-crime approach
4. Cohort study
5. Surveys
6. Analysis of official and unofficial records
7. Experiments
8. Observation
9. Mathematical models and econometric techniques
10. Combining research strategies

to the police by store managers (Cameron, 1964). In recent years, private security forces have patrolled private and public spaces to an increasing degree, and the records of those firms may prove to be an important source of information for criminologists in the future.

Experiments   **Experiments** are controlled studies in which people are treated in different ways to determine the effects of that treatment on their attitudes and behavior. Experiments have been used to evaluate the effectiveness of rehabilitation programs; one such study assessed the impact on inmates of group counseling (Kassebaum, Ward, and Wilner, 1971). A series of experiments conducted by Bibb Latané and John M. Darley (1970) focused on the question of why bystanders often fail to assist the victims of crime. Another experiment tested the impact on ex-convicts' criminal behavior when financial assistance was provided to them after their release from prison (Rossi, Berk, and Lenihan, 1980).

The National Institute of Justice favors experimentation as a research strategy. Some of the experiments it has funded were designed to refine criminal justice policies that had already been found effective in earlier experiments. Experiments sometimes show that the results of one policy do not differ from the results of alternative policies, an important finding that makes it possible to select the least expensive policy (Garner and Visher, 1988).

Observation   Another research method that has been used to study criminal behavior is **observation**, the careful and systematic watching of behavior. One difficulty in using this method is that criminals want to keep their offenses secret and wait to commit their crimes when no witnesses are present. Nevertheless, observation has been used fruitfully by criminologists. Francis Ianni (1972) examined the activities of an organized crime "family" for more than two years. Sociologists have often observed the behavior of juvenile gangs (Horowitz, 1983; Padilla, 1992). In another observational study, Patricia Adler (1993) spent six years investigating upper-level drug dealers and smugglers. Terry Williams (1989, 1992) used this method productively in his studies of teenage cocaine dealers and a crack house. Observational methods have also been used to examine interaction between the police and suspects (Piliavin and Briar, 1964; Reiss, 1971; Skolnick, 1994) and the operation of the courts, including the process of plea bargaining (Rosett and Cressey, 1976).

Mathematical Models and Econometric Techniques   Another way to study crime is to use mathematical models and econometric techniques. These abstract formulations of the relationships among variables have been evaluated with data gathered from the police, the courts, and the prisons (Fox, 1981a, 1981b; Phillips and Votey, 1981). Such methods have been used to study the deterrent effect of punishment, including the death penalty (Ehrlich, 1975; Layson, 1985), and to examine the relationship between crime and unemployment (Grogger, 2000).

Combining Research Strategies   Criminologists sometimes combine several approaches in their study of crime, enabling them to maximize the advantages and minimize the disadvantages of each strategy. Information not found in police records, such as how crime is planned, can be uncovered in interviews with offenders. Material that cannot be gathered by interviewing offenders, such as the overall distribution of crime in a city, can be found in police records. Klockars (1974) relied mainly on the biographical method in his study of a professional fence, but he also examined police arrest records, observed a fence at work, and read historical documents on fencing.

Criminologists thus use a variety of research strategies to study criminal behavior and responses to it by the criminal justice system. Each strategy can provide useful information if properly employed, but none by itself gives a complete picture of crime and the institutions that deal with it. As a result, the following chapters rely on research that has used many different strategies to study crime.

Summary

Criminology is the systematic study of violations of the criminal law, a set of formal norms that define certain behaviors as legally punishable. Criminology also studies societal reactions to those violations of the law.

Crime includes a diversity of behavior, but most offenses are characterized by criminal intent that leads to behavior defined as socially harmful. People who are not thought capable of forming criminal intent, such as the legally insane, are not punished with criminal sanctions.

Crime and the criminal law are social phenomena, for behavior is socially defined as punishable rather than intrinsically criminal. This accounts for differences in the law from one society to another. Conflict theorists point to the criminal law as the social product of the domination of one group by another one that has more economic resources and political power. Consensus theorists see the law as the outcome of compromise and agreement among various groups.

Criminologists use many research strategies. Some employ the comparative method, looking at crime in two or more societies to test or develop theories. Historical work is a kind of comparative research that compares the past with the present, either explicitly or implicitly. Another useful strategy is the biographical approach. This method does not tell us how representative a particular offender is of all criminals, but it provides a richness of detail often missing from research based on official statistics or surveys. Another strategy is the patterns-of-crime approach, which uses police data to investigate the distribution of crime in time and space and to study offenders and victims. A very productive, but expensive and time-consuming, strategy is the cohort study. People who have a common characteristic—usually the same year of birth—are studied over time, allowing for the collection of data on criminal careers. The survey, a method that consists of interviewing representative samples of the population about their experiences as both victims and offenders, has significantly increased our knowledge of crime.

Many other research strategies have contributed to our knowledge of crime, as we will see in the following chapters. Unofficial records of crime, such as those kept on shoplifters by department stores, have been useful. Experiments have evaluated the effects on offenders of prison treatment programs and financial assistance. Social scientists have engaged in systematic observation of criminals and their behavior to uncover information that can be difficult to gather in other ways. Sociologists and economists have used mathematical models and econometric techniques to study crime. Often several of these strategies are used in combination.

IMPORTANT TERMS

biographical method	conflict perspective	criminal intent
cohort	consensus perspective	criminology
comparative research	crime	cultural criminology

excuse
experiment
historical research
justification
juvenile delinquent
law

left realism
Marxist or radical criminology
norm
observation
patterns of crime
peacemaking criminology

sanction
social construction of crime
status offense
survey

REVIEW QUESTIONS

1. What is crime? Why does the kind of behavior defined as crime differ from one society to another?

2. What are the differences between the conflict perspective and the consensus perspective?

3. Make a list of some of the research strategies that have been used to study crime. Then list in one column the advantages or strengths of each strategy. In a second column, list the disadvantages or weaknesses of each strategy.

FOR FURTHER STUDY

Juvenile Delinquency Anthony M. Platt's *The Child Savers: The Invention of Delinquency* (2nd ed., Chicago: University of Chicago Press, 1977) investigates the emergence of the concept of juvenile delinquency and the development of the juvenile justice system.

Social Construction of Crime Jeff Ferrell and Neil Websdale's (eds.) *Making Trouble: Cultural Constructions of Crime, Deviance, and Control* (Hawthorne, NY: Aldine de Gruyter, 1999) is a collection of essays that examine the social construction of the crime problem, policing, terrorism, and the gender–crime relationship.

Criminology A useful website that includes material on criminological theory and research, links to data sets, and other resources is www.crimetheory.com.

Biographical Method Richard P. Rettig, Manual J. Torres, and Gerald R. Garrett's *Manny: A Criminal-Addict's Story* (Boston: Houghton Mifflin, 1977) is a compelling autobiography that examines the criminological significance of a varied criminal career.

Observation Terry Williams's *The Cocaine Kids: The Inside Story of a Teenage Drug Ring* (Reading, MA: Addison-Wesley, 1989) is a richly detailed observational study of a group of young cocaine dealers in New York City.

2 Measuring Crime

The scientific study of criminal behavior originated in Europe in the nineteenth century. Until then, there had been much speculation about crime, but it was abstract and not based on empirical research. Many early ideas about the causes of crime have proved inaccurate or incomplete, but the history of these ideas is important for understanding the emergence of modern criminology.

The Emergence of Modern Criminology

From 1500 until about 1750, philosophers who studied the problem of crime usually proposed that people freely choose how to act. This assumption of free will implies that people are responsible for the consequences of their actions. Another implication is that people can be controlled through fear, especially the fear of pain. Punishment by the state, an institution based on a social contract among its citizens to live together in peace, is the primary means to instill fear and prevent criminal behavior.

Classical Criminology

These ideas were the basis of the **classical school** of criminology. This approach developed during the Enlightenment, an eighteenth-century movement in European thought that emphasized progress, individualism, the use of reason, the questioning of tradition, and the use of empirical data to test abstract ideas.

The major proponent of the classical approach was an Italian, Cesare Beccaria (1738–1794), who sharply criticized the criminal justice system, especially judges who imposed arbitrary and harsh punishments. Along with earlier philosophers, Beccaria believed that punishment was needed to prevent people from violating the law. He thought that people were motivated by pain and pleasure, that they exercised free will, and that rationality and responsibility characterized human action. According to Beccaria, fear of punishment would lead people to conform to the law.

Beccaria claimed that punishment should be based on the harm that the criminal act did to society, rather than on the harm incurred by the victim. Harm was to be judged by the consequences of the act rather than by the intentions of the offender. Marxist critics have argued that this approach contains a basic flaw: In capitalist societies, social harm is inevitably defined in a way that protects the interests of capitalists from interference by other classes (Taylor, Walton, and Young, 1973).

Beccaria hoped that making punishment proportional to social harm would limit the arbitrary punishment meted out by judges. Implicit in his theory is the notion that similar crimes should be punished similarly, an idea violated by the judges of his time as well as those of today. This idea, basic to the theory of retribution or just deserts, suggests that an offender's characteristics and the circumstances of the crime should not be taken into account in meting out punishment.

Beccaria's ideas were the basis of the 1791 criminal code of France, but problems arose in implementing that code. The code ignored differences among offenders and differences in the circumstances of crimes. It treated first offenders and repeat offenders alike when they were convicted of similar offenses, and it gave no special attention to offenders who were minors, insane, or retarded.

The revised French criminal code of 1819 provided for somewhat more judicial discretion, allowing judges to consider the circumstances of the crime but not the offender's intent. The underlying assumption was that the idea of free will was valid, but that individual responsibility could be influenced by pathology, incompetence, or insanity. The notion of premeditation—the consideration of one's behavior prior to acting—developed as a measure of free will. Age, mental capacity, and the circumstances of the crime were accepted as factors that could mitigate punishment, for those factors were thought to reduce personal responsibility. This led to the use of testimony by experts to help the courts decide on the extent to which defendants could be held responsible and punished for their actions.

The idea implicit in the 1819 code was that sentences had different effects on different kinds of offenders. This was the beginning of the rehabilitation rationale for punishment, the idea that the goal of punishment is to change offenders so they will not commit crime again. Individual choice of behavior was the basis of the 1819 code, but choice was increasingly seen as influenced by social and psychological factors (Taylor, Walton, and Young, 1973).

Cartography

Some European nations have been gathering official data on crime since the sixteenth century, but not until the nineteenth century did scholars start to use the statistics to understand crime. Their approach has been called **cartography**, because it involves the use of data to map or chart patterns of crime.

Important studies using this approach were published in 1833 by A.M. Guerry, a French lawyer, and in 1838 by A. Quetelet, a Belgian mathematician. These two cartographers worked independently, but they came to similar conclusions from their studies of national crime data. Both found that the annual total of crime recorded in a country remains fairly constant over time and that each kind of crime remains about the same proportion of the total over time. They concluded that officially recorded crime is "a regular feature of social activity" that is better explained by social conditions than by individual predispositions (Taylor, Walton, and Young, 1973: 37).

The cartographic approach was used to great advantage in a ground-breaking study of suicide by Emile Durkheim (1858–1917), one of the founders of sociology. In his writings on crime, Durkheim (1895/1938) shared with Guerry and Quetelet the idea that crime is a normal feature of social life. He did not mean that crime was good or to be encouraged, but rather that crime exists in all societies and therefore must be studied in its relationship to the social structure. Durkheim did suggest that crime has some positive functions, or consequences, for society: It makes clear what behavior is acceptable to the members of society; it draws official attention to the social conditions that cause crime; and it can create social solidarity in opposition to people who violate important social standards.

Positivism

Modern scientific criminology grew out of the work of three Italian students of crime—Cesare Lombroso, Enrico Ferri, and Raffaele Garofalo. They saw the proper course of criminology as "the systematic elimination of the free will 'metaphysics' of the classical school" (Taylor, Walton, and Young, 1973: 10). Rather than try to reduce crime by relying on the criminal justice system, as did the classical criminologists, they sought to learn the causes of crime and then eliminate the conditions that produce it. Modern criminology has been dominated by this perspective, but the criminal justice system has been dominated by classical thinking.

This perspective, which is called **positivism**, relies on the scientific method, quantifying and measuring behavior and the social conditions associated with behavior. Positivists claim that scientific neutrality is possible in the study of crime and that criminologists should focus on criminal behavior rather than on the criminal law. Positivists see themselves as relatively objective in their work, but critics allege that a positivist approach implicitly supports the existing legal system by adopting the state's definition of crime. However, positivists do have a legitimate claim to objectivity, for compared with the work done by scholars who argue that scientific neutrality is impossible, positivists have generally produced more reliable results—that is, results that different scholars would also get if they applied the same scientific methods to the same data.

Positivists claim that human behavior is subject to causal laws. This assertion that behavior is determined, or at least influenced, by forces outside the control of individuals contradicts the classical position that people are rational beings who exercise free will and determine their own behavior. Positivism sometimes goes too far in denying individual freedom to choose how to behave, but it is a method that lends itself well to the study of social, psychological, economic, political, and biological influences. Research using the positivist method fills the pages of the leading journals in criminology and is cited extensively throughout this book. This research has generated policy recommendations for reducing crime, such as strengthening the family and reducing income inequality, that are examined later in this book.

Cesare Lombroso   Cesare Lombroso (1835–1909) was the first influential proponent of the positivist approach to criminology. He has been called the "father of criminology" because he was able to direct the study of crime away from questions of free will and personal responsibility to a more scientific basis. Although Lombroso's ideas about the biological origins of crime have proved erroneous, and sometimes even ludicrous, his work marked an important turning point in criminology. By stressing measurable characteristics, even if they were the wrong ones, Lombroso made it possible to determine which factors are actually related to criminal behavior. In the early editions of his textbook on the criminal offender, Lombroso attributed crime primarily to biological factors, but in later editions of the book, his research led him to downplay the significance of those factors and give greater emphasis to insanity, poor education, and social background. This change in his views on crime causation is testimony to the positivist method, because by focusing on measurable factors Lombroso was able to test his ideas about the sources of crime and then modify his theory in light of new evidence.

Cesare Lombroso (1835–1909), the "father of criminology," used the positivist approach to study the causes of crime.

Beyond Lombroso   Enrico Ferri (1856–1929) and Raffaele Garofalo (1852–1934) were two positivists who went beyond Lombroso in the study of the causes of crime. Ferri focused on causes such as climate, age, race, sex, psychology, population density, and political and economic conditions. His work has been criticized for failing to specify the relative importance of each factor in the causation of crime. Garofalo shared some of Lombroso's ideas on crime causation, but his work focused on psychological factors such as the lack of compassion among offenders. Positivism is not necessarily associated with any particular theory of crime, but is instead a method that can be used to assess the influence of many different factors on criminal behavior.

By 1900, the seeds of modern criminology had been sown. The emphasis on measurement, scientific neutrality, and the testing of hypotheses with empirical data was a major advance over earlier speculative work on crime. Even if the early positivists' explanations were often inaccurate or incomplete, they did provide criminologists with the methods to determine whether explanations are right or wrong. Recognizing that crime cannot easily be studied by direct observation, positivists try to develop indicators of crime that can be used to test theories and hypotheses. Positivists generate theories to explain their research findings and then test those theories with more research, modifying their explanations to fit new evidence. Before a theory supported by research can be developed, however, it is necessary to collect data on the dimensions of crime that must be explained by a theory. The rest of this chapter looks at several methods for gathering data on crime.

Official Crime Statistics

Criminologists often use measures of crime produced by law-enforcement agencies to study criminal behavior and offenders. Because students of crime frequently use statistics they do not collect, they must have a thorough understanding of how those statistics are produced. Changes in law-enforcement practices over time can alter the way that crime statistics are gathered. When this happens, a change in crime rates may reflect a change in enforcement activity rather than a real increase or decrease in the amount of criminal activity.

History of Crime Statistics in the United States

Support for a police-based system of crime statistics developed in 1926 and 1927 among police organizations (particularly the International Association of Chiefs of Police), philanthropic foundations (primarily the Laura Spelman Rockefeller Memorial Foundation), and social scientists (especially the Social Science Research Council). They saw crime statistics as a way to evaluate police performance, assess newspaper reports of crime waves, develop a scientific criminology, and control crime. In 1929, a manual for reporting crime statistics was distributed to police departments around the country and the collection of data began. The Federal Bureau of Investigation (FBI), which began compiling crime statistics in 1930, now publishes an annual volume, *Crime in the United States: Uniform Crime Reports.*

In 1931, Thorsten Sellin stated that "the value of a crime for index purposes decreases as the distance from the crime itself in terms of procedure increases" (p. 346). This view was widely shared and led the FBI to focus on crimes reported to and recorded by the police, rather than on data on arrested suspects, defendants in court, or prison inmates. The farther we move from the report of the crime, the more likely we are to get a distorted picture of it. For example, some research shows that we cannot accurately measure trends in drug offenses with arrest data. This is because changes in arrests over time are related to changes in the perceived seriousness of drug law violations and changes in patterns of law enforcement (DeFleur, 1975; Stoddart, 1982). However, a recent study suggests that arrests for the use of cocaine and heroin, but not marijuana, measure the prevalence of drug use in urban populations as accurately as other indicators produced by law-enforcement and public health agencies, though the authors do warn researchers to be cautious in using arrest data to measure the extent of drug use (Rosenfeld and Decker, 1999).

Ideally, national crime statistics would include police data on reported crimes and arrested suspects. Suspects would then be followed through the criminal justice system, with information being recorded on the disposition of cases and the sentences meted out to convicted offenders. Maintaining such records would be costly and difficult but would give us a more complete picture of crime than we now have.

FBI Crime Statistics

The FBI has achieved nearly complete coverage of the country in its collection of data from the police. It now gathers statistics from nearly 17,000 law-enforcement agencies, which cover 92 percent of the country's population. Data are gathered either from state-level crime-reporting programs or directly from local police departments.

The FBI presents detailed data on eight crimes, the Part I offenses that together constitute the **crime index.** The FBI presents much less information on twenty-one Part II crime categories. Table 2.1 defines the eight Part I and the twenty-one Part II crimes. The FBI justifies its presentation of more detail on the Part I offenses by claiming that those crimes

- are regarded by the public as very serious
- are relatively frequent in occurrence
- often come to the attention of the police

Criticisms of FBI Statistics   Critics claim that the public may regard Part I offenses as serious because the FBI gives them the most attention. In other words, the FBI's choice of what to include in Part I conveys to the public a particular image of "the crime problem," one that for the most part consists of crimes against persons

TABLE 2.1   Offenses in the FBI's Uniform Crime-Reporting System

PART I (INDEX) OFFENSES

Murder and nonnegligent manslaughter: the willful killing of one human being by another.

Forcible rape: carnal knowledge of a female forcibly and against her will, including attempts.

Robbery: taking or attempting to take anything of value from another person by force or threat of force.

Aggravated assault: unlawful attack by one person upon another for the purpose of inflicting severe or aggravated bodily injury, usually accompanied by the use of a weapon.

Burglary-breaking or entering: unlawful entry of a structure to commit a felony or a theft.

Larceny-theft: unlawful taking, carrying, leading, or riding away of property from the possession of another; excluding motor vehicle theft, embezzlement, con games, and forgery.

Motor vehicle theft: theft or attempted theft of a motor vehicle.

Arson: willful or malicious burning, or attempt to burn, with or without intent to defraud, of a house, public building, motor vehicle or aircraft, or personal property of another.

PART II OFFENSES

Other assaults (simple): assaults and attempted assaults where no weapon is used and that do not result in serious injury to the victim.

Forgery and counterfeiting: making, altering, uttering, or possessing, with intent to defraud, anything false that is made to appear true.

Fraud: fraudulent conversion and obtaining money or property by false pretenses.

Embezzlement: misappropriation or misapplication of money or property entrusted to one's care, custody, or control.

Stolen property: buying, receiving, possessing: buying, receiving, and possessing stolen property, including attempts.

Vandalism: willful or malicious destruction, injury, disfigurement, or defacement of any public or private property, real or personal, without consent of the owner or persons having custody or control.

Weapons: carrying, possessing, etc.: all violations of regulations or statutes controlling the carrying, using, possessing, furnishing, and manufacturing of deadly weapons or silencers.

Prostitution and commercialized vice: sex offenses of a commercialized nature, such as prostitution, keeping a bawdy house, procuring, or transporting women for immoral purposes.

Sex offenses (except forcible rape, prostitution and commercialized vice): statutory rape and offenses against chastity, common decency, morals, and the like.

Drug abuse violations: state and local offenses relating to narcotic drugs, such as unlawful possession, sale, use, growing, and manufacturing of narcotic drugs.

Gambling: promoting, permitting, or engaging in illegal gambling.

Offenses against the family and children: nonsupport, neglect, desertion, or abuse of family and children.

Driving under the influence: driving or operating any vehicle or common carrier while drunk or under the influence of liquor or narcotics.

Liquor laws: state or local liquor law violations, except drunkenness and driving under the influence.

Drunkenness: drunkenness or intoxication, excluding driving under the influence.

Disorderly conduct: breach of the peace.

Vagrancy: vagabondage, begging, loitering, etc.

All other offenses: all violations of state or local laws, except the preceding offenses and traffic offenses.

Suspicion: no specific offense; suspect released without formal charges being placed.

Curfew and loitering laws (persons under age 18): offenses relating to violations of local curfew or loitering ordinances where such laws exist.

Runaways (persons under age 18): limited to juveniles taken into protective custody under provisions of local statutes.

Source: Adapted from Federal Bureau of Investigation, *Crime in the United States, 2001: Uniform Crime Reports.* Washington, DC: U.S. Government Printing Office, 2002, pp. 446–447.

and property by people who have low incomes and who are members of minority groups (Chambliss, 1999; Reiman, 2001).

The FBI's crime report pays little attention to white-collar crime and fails to note that such crime inflicts much greater financial losses on the American public than do all the Part I crimes together (see Chapter 3). Of the eight Part I offenses, only arson is sometimes a white-collar crime. Embezzlement and fraud, which are Part II crimes, are sometimes white-collar offenses. White-collar crimes, such as price fixing and government corruption, fit the FBI's criterion of being relatively frequent, but no mention is made of those offenses in its crime report. Local police departments rarely learn of white-collar crimes, because of their complexity and because the public thinks that the police will not deal with such offenses. As a result, FBI crime reports convey the impression that white-collar crime is of little consequence in American society.

FBI reports are also deficient in failing to indicate the pervasive involvement of organized crime in criminal activities in the United States. Data on arrests for narcotics violations and gambling appear in the FBI's reports, but the statistics do not show gangsters' involvement in those offenses, nor are any data presented on loan sharking (usury), a major source of revenue for organized crime.

Crime Rates

The FBI's Uniform Crime Report (UCR) gives the absolute number of crimes and the crime rates for the index offenses, except for arson for which data are incomplete. The FBI calculates national **crime rates** by dividing the number of reported crimes by the number of people in the country and then expressing the result as a rate of crimes per 100,000 people. For instance, in 2001 there were 15,980 recorded cases of murder and nonnegligent manslaughter in the United States, excluding the deaths resulting from the September 11th terrorist attacks. The estimate of the nation's population in 2001 was 284,796,887. The murder rate per 100,000 is thus calculated as follows:

$$\frac{15,980}{284,796,887} \times 100,000 = 5.6 \text{ per } 100,000$$

Expressing the crime rate in this way makes more sense than simply stating how many homicides occurred in 2001. For example, if the United States experienced 15,980 murders in a year in the past when its population was exactly half as large as its 2001 population, the murder rate in that earlier year would have been twice as high as it was in 2001, or 11.2 per 100,000 people.

Crime rates, rather than the absolute number of crimes, are the appropriate measure for comparing countries, states, or cities. In the following excerpt from an advice column in the *Boston Globe* (May 7, 1980, p. 86), the letter writer asks a question about rates in the correct way, but the newspaper provides an inappropriate response:

Q. I have to make a job choice between New York City and Houston. Can you tell me how the crime rates for these cities compare—V. P., Burlington [Mass.]

A. The latest available annual (1977) FBI major crime statistics for New York City and Houston are as follows: New York—1,553 murders; 3,899 rapes; 74,404 robberies; 42,056 assaults; 178,907 burglaries; 214,838 larcenies; and 94,420 vehicle thefts. Houston—376 murders; 965 rapes; 6,153 robberies; 1,810 assaults; 33,419 burglaries; 60,839 larcenies; and 13,726 motor vehicle thefts.

Here the newspaper gives the total number of crimes in each city, making it impossible for the letter writer to compare the crime rates of the cities without looking up their populations. The letter writer wanted to compare risks of victimization in the two cities, and crime rates are needed to do that. Let us see what happens when we calculate murder rates for New York City and Houston:

	Number of Murders (1977)	**Population (1977)**	**Murder Rate per 100,000 People (1977)**
New York City	1,553	7,298,000	21.3
Houston	376	1,555,000	24.2

New York City had many more murders than Houston in 1977, but it also had a much larger population. When we calculate murder rates per 100,000 people—a measure of the risk that a person such as the letter writer will be killed in a given year—we find that the homicide rate per 100,000 people was actually higher in Houston (24.2) than in New York City (21.3). Based on the faulty answer by the *Boston Globe,* the letter writer might have moved to Houston, even though the risk of being murdered there was greater than it was in New York City.

Sociological criminology often focuses on crime rates. Rather than examining and explaining each and every criminal act, it makes more sense to look at rates of crime and seek explanations for variations in crime rates among different social groups. For instance, if poor people have a higher murder rate than well-to-do people, we might focus on blocked opportunities and frustrated ambitions as causes of murder. We might also suggest that policies increasing available jobs and reducing economic inequality could reduce the rate at which people kill others.

Prevalence and Incidence   The per capita crime rate can be broken down into two components: prevalence and incidence. **Prevalence** refers to the proportion of a population that commits crime in a given time; it is measured by dividing the number of offenders by the size of the population. **Incidence** is the frequency with which offenders commit crime, or the average number of offenses per offender; it is measured by dividing the number of offenses by the number of offenders. As the following formula shows, the crime rate is equal to the product of prevalence and incidence:

$$\text{Crime rate} = \frac{\text{Offenses}}{\text{Population}} = \frac{\text{Offenders}}{\text{Population}} \times \frac{\text{Offenses}}{\text{Offenders}}$$
$$\text{(Prevalence)} \quad \text{(Incidence)}$$

Crimes of Violence   Calculating crime rates in terms of number of offenses per 100,000 people makes sense for murder, robbery, and aggravated assault because in these crimes of violence it is individuals who are at risk. The FBI rates for these and other index offenses are shown in Table 2.2.

According to the FBI's definition, forcible rape can only involve female victims. Because the FBI presents forcible rape statistics only for sexual assaults that involve women as victims, it makes no sense for it to present rates of forcible rape per 100,000 people in the country, because nearly half of the people in the denominator used to calculate the rate are men. For instance, in 2001 the FBI reported that there were 31.8 recorded rapes and attempted rapes per 100,000 people (men and women). The rate of rape would be better expressed by dividing the number of incidents by the number of women in the country, a rate of 62.4 per 100,000 women. This rate provides a

TABLE 2.2   Rates of Crime per 100,000 People, United States, 2001

CRIME	RATE PER 100,000 PEOPLE
Murder and nonnegligent manslaughter	5.6[a]
Forcible rape	31.8
Robbery	148.5
Aggravated assault	318.5
Burglary	740.8
Larceny-theft	2,484.6
Motor vehicle theft	430.6
Arson	[b]
Crime index total	4,160.5

[a]Deaths resulting from the September 11th terrorist attacks are not included in this number.
[b]Sufficient data are not available to estimate crime rate.

Source: Adapted from Federal Bureau of Investigation, *Crime in the United States, 2001: Uniform Crime Reports.* Washington, DC: U.S. Government Printing Office, 2002, p. 65.

better idea of the risk of rape faced by women, although calculating the rate in this way means that it cannot be compared with rates of murder, assault, or robbery, which are calculated per 100,000 people (both men and women).

Property Crimes   Burglary, larceny, motor vehicle theft, and arson are crimes against property, even though it is people who own the stolen or burned property. The FBI calculates crime rates for these offenses by dividing the number of incidents by the number of people in the country and expressing the rates as offenses per 100,000 people. Rates calculated in terms of number of offenses per amount of property available to be stolen or burned would provide more useful information. Rates of property crime per 100,000 people rise dramatically with economic development and increasing affluence, because the amount of property available to be stolen is growing (Clinard and Abbott, 1973; Shelley, 1981a).

The rate of thefts per number of motor vehicles in the country is a more meaningful statistic than the rate of motor vehicle thefts per 100,000 people. From 1963 to 2001, the rate of motor vehicle thefts per 100,000 people increased by 99 percent, while there was only a 9 percent increase in the rate of motor vehicle thefts per 100,000 registrations (a measure of the number of motor vehicles in the country). Using the per capita rate exaggerates the increase in the chance that a given car would be stolen, because over the thirty-eight-year period motor vehicle registrations increased faster than the population.

Comparisons among countries should also take into consideration the number of cars available to be stolen. For example, consider the rates of car thefts per 1,000 people and per 1,000 cars for Italy and Spain for 1987/1988:

	Italy	Spain
Car thefts per 1,000 people	3.6	3.7
Car thefts per 1,000 cars	6.9	12.7

The two countries had about the same rate of car thefts per 1,000 people, but Spain had nearly twice the rate of thefts per 1,000 cars. This was because there were more cars in Italy than in Spain (Clarke and Harris, 1992: 9).

Cars on this street in Barcelona, Spain, are about twice as likely to be stolen as cars in Italy.

The FBI Crime Index   In calculating an overall rate of Part I crimes, the FBI adds the reported number of seven crimes (omitting arson because of incomplete data) and divides by the number of people in the country to get a rate of index crimes per 100,000 people. In 2001 the crime index rate was 4,160.5 per 100,000 people.

The FBI does not attempt to weight the index crimes by their relative seriousness. Obviously a homicide is more serious than the theft of a quarter, but the FBI treats both the same in calculating the crime index rate. The FBI also treats all motor vehicle thefts as index crimes, even though many auto thefts are for joyriding rather than for resale of the car or its parts. A theft in which the car is shipped out of the country for resale would seem to be more serious than a theft in which teenagers abandon a car unharmed after it runs out of gasoline. If the FBI systematically applied a measure of the relative seriousness of various crimes to police crime reports, the informational value of the crime index rate would be improved.

Gathering Crime Statistics

To ensure uniformity in the reporting of crime by local police departments and state reporting programs, the FBI circulates a *Uniform Crime Reporting Handbook* to tell the police how to record crimes. Still, crimes may be counted differently by local police departments. For instance, some departments may record an auto theft the instant a car is reported missing, and other departments may put such a report aside for a few hours to ensure the owner does not call back to say that someone in the family had just borrowed the car. The FBI is aware of the differences among police departments and cautions readers of its reports "against comparing statistical data of individual reporting units," in part because of different "administrative and investigative emphases of law enforcement" (Federal Bureau of Investigation, 2002: v). However, if we cannot compare the crime rates of various communities, then we cannot add the crime rates of those different communities to get a national crime rate, and the FBI does that every year. In January 2000, the FBI formally adopted the Quality Assurance Review, an auditing program designed to ensure uniformity among the states in their crime reporting.

Sometimes multiple offenses are committed during the same crime incident. Thus, if an offender threatens a couple with a knife, forces them into their car, tells them to drive him somewhere, and then steals their money before riding off in their car, he has committed two simple assaults, two kidnappings, one auto theft, and one robbery. In this case, the FBI instructs police departments to count only the most serious offense, or one robbery. Some might consider kidnapping a more serious crime than robbery, but the FBI does not treat kidnapping as an index offense, probably because it occurs relatively infrequently. Information is lost because the FBI ignores some offenses and records only the most serious crime in a series of offenses, but recording each different violation of the law would overstate the extent of crime.

Crime Reporting Because the police can cover only a limited territory and do not have easy access to private places, they must learn of many crimes directly from citizens, usually victims or witnesses. Sometimes people call the police switchboard to report a crime, and other times they report crimes to officers on the street or in patrol cars. Not all citizen complaints to the police are officially recorded as crimes; for example, one study found that only two-thirds of all complaints to the police produced an official crime report (Black, 1970).

In contrast to **reactive police work** in which officers respond to a citizen's report of a crime, some police work is **proactive,** or the result of efforts by the police to discover and deal with crime on their own initiative (Reiss, 1971). Arrests for prostitution and narcotics offenses rarely result from complaints by the public but are typically a consequence of efforts by the police, especially the vice or narcotics squad. In crimes such as these, the number of recorded violations may tell us more about the size of the vice or narcotics squad than it does about the frequency with which such offenses occur. External pressure from political officials or crime commissions can also affect the level of proactive police work. Because the rate of arrests for vice offenses fluctuates wildly with changes in the social climate and changes in law-enforcement practices, the FBI does not include them in Part I of its UCR.

Reasons for Nonreporting People fail to report crimes to the police for many reasons, the most significant of which have to do with the nature of the crime incident itself. Victims are least likely to report offenses that

- are attempted rather than completed
- involve little or no financial loss or physical injury
- do not threaten their sense of personal security
- do not seem serious to them
- do not involve a firearm (Hindelang, 1976; Skogan, 1976b, 1984; Block and Block, 1980)

The effect of loss of property and extent of injury can be seen in the results of a survey that found that only 24 percent of robberies involving no loss and no injury were reported to the police, but that 72 percent of robberies with some loss of property and some injury were reported (Bureau of Justice Statistics, December 1985).

Many victims who do not report crimes to the police say they think there is little or nothing the police can do to catch the offender or retrieve the lost property. This view is supported by police statistics, which show that the police are least likely to arrest suspects in those crimes that the public feels the police can do little about (Skogan, 1976a).

Some victims do not report crimes to the police because they believe the offense is not very important. This may occur, for instance, when an inexpensive item is stolen or when no real harm is done in an assault. The increased ownership of theft insurance—including automobile insurance—leads many victims to report crimes to the police even when they have little hope of recovering their property, because insurance companies often require notification of the police as proof that a theft has occurred before they will pay a claim.

Some crimes are not reported because the victim is afraid of what the police might discover if they investigate the crime. Thus, a drug dealer who is robbed by another dealer may not report the crime. Other victims do not report crimes because they do not want to cause trouble for the offender. A related reason is fear that the offender might take reprisals against the victim for reporting the crime.

Victims are often unwilling to report crimes to the police because they see the offense as a private or personal matter. Rape victims may avoid the police because they feel stigmatized by the sexual attack or anticipate police insensitivity; a telephone survey of 4,008 women found that only one in six rape victims reported the crime to the police (Skorneck, 1992). Victims of assaults sometimes fail to report the crime because the attack was by a spouse or a parent. Police statistics in some developing countries significantly undercount assaults because there is a tradition in local villages of dealing with crime—especially assaults between people who know each other—in an informal way, rather than by bringing in the police (Clinard and Abbott, 1973).

Some victims do not report crime to the police because they think that calling the police is too much trouble, especially if a suspect is later arrested and they have to testify in court. Witnesses, as well as victims, may not report crimes because of inconvenience.

Cross-national surveys have found that crime reporting is not closely associated with attitudes toward the police; in other words, people who are hostile toward the

A police officer in San Francisco takes a report of domestic violence, a crime that many victims do not report because they define it as a private matter.

police seem to be as likely to report crime as people who are friendly toward the police. In addition, demographic variables such as race and income do not seem to be closely related to whether a victim will report a crime. Females are slightly more likely than males to report crimes, and the elderly are more likely than younger people to report crimes (Skogan, 1984). Successful attempts at fraud—the use of deception to take money or property—are most likely to be reported by victims who are highly educated, older, married, strangers to the offenders, suffer larger financial losses, and have more knowledge of and experience with the legal system (Copes et al., 2001). For the most part, however, researchers have found that it is the seriousness and type of the crime incident, rather than social characteristics or attitudes toward the police, that determine whether a victim or witness will report a crime (Gove, Hughes, and Geerken, 1985; Bennett and Wiegand, 1994).

Police Recording Practices   The organization and guiding philosophy of a police department influences the accuracy of its crime statistics. A legalistic department might see the failure to arrest a suspect as a weakness of the officer, but a service-oriented department would stress the solution of problems without formal arrest; the first department would probably record more interpersonal conflicts as crimes and produce more arrests (Wilson, 1968). If a department assigns the collection of crime statistics to precinct captains and rewards them for low crime rates in their precincts, the captains will have an incentive to omit crimes from their official reports. With centralized crime reporting through a switchboard in headquarters, with greater professionalism, and with greater departmental resources, a police department will probably record crime more accurately and more completely, and thereby provide a more valid picture of the crime problem, even though this would mean a higher official crime rate than if some crimes were omitted (Skogan, 1976b; McCleary, Nienstedt, and Erven, 1982).

Sometimes the police record a crime that is reported to them but classify it as a less serious crime than it really is. For instance, forcible rape might be classified as simple assault, and thefts in which force is used might be called larcenies rather than robberies. Recording crimes in this way reduces the rate of serious offenses but inflates the rate of minor ones. Because most public attention is focused on serious offenses, this would make the police look better to outsiders.

Political Use of Crime Statistics   Crime statistics have been used for political purposes at both the local and national levels. The police are selective in the information about crime that they supply to the news media (see the Crime and the Media box). Rising crime rates are sometimes used to justify higher police salaries and increases in police personnel, although police chiefs often acknowledge that police efficiency cannot be evaluated by crime data or arrest statistics. J. Edgar Hoover was a master at using rising crime rates to argue for increased FBI appropriations from Congress. He also argued for more funds when crime rates dropped, claiming that the crime problem was finally being solved and that it was no time to reduce support for the fight against crime.

Politicians sometimes use rising crime rates to attack their opponents as "soft on crime." They claim that reductions in the crime rate during their time in office show that they have successfully battled crime, even if they cannot demonstrate exactly how they did so. An interesting twist on this argument was heard during Richard Nixon's administration, when he asserted that even though he had not actually reduced crime during his first term in office, he had managed to reduce the rate at which crime was increasing. Public opinion polls after both the 1968 and 1972 elections showed that the crime issue was a major reason traditional Democrats had voted for the Republican Nixon.

Clearance and Arrest Statistics   When the police are satisfied that they know who committed a crime, they classify the crime as "cleared" or solved. Most but not all cleared crimes lead to an arrest, and when someone is arrested the police provide information on the suspect to the FBI. In 2001, 19.6 percent of all index offenses were cleared by arrest; 46.2 percent of all violent crimes (murder, forcible rape, robbery, and aggravated assault) were cleared, but only 16.2 percent of all property crimes (burglary, larceny, auto theft, and arson) were cleared.

A study by the Police Foundation (Sherman and Glick, 1984) found that police departments define arrest in different ways, in spite of the FBI's efforts to standardize the definition. As a result, the probability that a citizen will end up with an arrest record depends on the jurisdiction in which the person is apprehended. Because of improper and inconsistent recording practices, the use of arrest data to evaluate police departments or to assess the characteristics of offenders is risky.

The FBI's National Crime Information Center 2000, an expanded version of a program established in 1967, provides law-enforcement agents with rapid access to computerized data on criminal histories, wanted and missing people, fingerprints, mugshots, stolen guns and vehicles, and other information useful for clearing crimes and making arrests. Supporters justify this program in the name of more efficient crime fighting, but critics say that it threatens the privacy of Americans because some of the arrest records are inaccurate, incomplete, or ambiguous (Laudon, 1986).

CRIME AND THE MEDIA

The Police and the News Media

Because newspaper and television reporters get more information about crime from the police than from any other source, the police have the power to provide information selectively and thereby influence public perceptions of crime and the police.

In his study of the news media in a midwestern city, Steven Chermak found that a major source of crime information was the police beat, an office in police headquarters staffed by reporters who monitored police scanners and had ready access to police documents. The police department's spokesperson, who met with reporters daily, decided which crimes were newsworthy and presented information in ways designed to protect the department's public image. The police determined "what information should be revealed and in what form, what details should be highlighted or discarded, and when the story should be released" (p. 19). Sometimes the police cut off media access to police documents or source contacts when they disliked the way the press was portraying the police or reporting a crime story.

Controlling the information supplied to the news media serves several purposes for the police. The release of information can influence the way an offender is punished; for example, the details of a gruesome murder might be provided as the offender is about to be sentenced, pressuring the judge to mete out a severe penalty. The police sometimes talk to reporters about an upcoming crackdown on drunk drivers or drug users in order to deter potential offenders. The police use the press to further their investigations, such as by releasing a photograph of a suspect to elicit information from witnesses and victims. The police also use the press for public relations, hoping to create a positive image by spreading news about awards they have received or crime-fighting measures they have developed.

In exchange for serving the interests of the police, the media gain easy access to information about crime, making it possible to produce news stories efficiently and with little expenditure of resources. The press's dependence on the police for information can mute its criticism of the police. Chermak found that police effectiveness was evaluated in only 4 percent of all crime stories, and those stories tended to focus on a specific incident rather than on problems of the whole department.

Source: Based on Steven M. Chermak, *Victims in the News: Crime and the American News Media.* Boulder, CO: Westview, 1995, pp. 14–22, 30–31.

Using FBI Data for Criminological Research

FBI crime data provide an indicator of the level of police activity in the nation. They have also been used to get a reading on how crime rates have changed over time, although rising crime rates can result from more complete reporting and recording of crime as well as from increases in the actual amount of crime.

In the past, the FBI gathered only summaries of the number of crimes recorded by local police departments and then added the figures from those summary reports to produce the tables in its annual report. This limited the ability of criminologists to do additional analysis of the FBI's data. A 1985 report by a consulting firm suggested changes in FBI practices that would make UCR crime statistics more useful to criminologists. In addition to calling for more thorough auditing of crime statistics to ensure their accuracy and completeness, the report suggested that local police agencies submit short accounts of each crime incident to the national office.

In 1989, the FBI began implementation of its National Incident-Based Reporting System (NIBRS), which collects detailed information on forty-six offenses and their associated arrests. This system distinguishes between completed and attempted crimes, counts rapes of males as well as females, defines three types of assault (aggravated, simple, and intimidation), collects information on the use of weapons in all violent crimes, and records each offense that occurs in an incident. Concern that recording all offenses in an incident, rather than just the most serious one (as does the UCR), would inflate crime statistics was allayed by a study that found little difference between UCR and NIBRS estimates of crime rates. The NIBRS violent crime rate was less than 1 percent higher than the UCR rate, and the NIBRS property crime rate was only slightly more than 2 percent higher than the UCR rate (Rantala, 2000). Nevertheless, administrative and technological impediments have prevented full implementation of the NIBRS program. In 2002, only twenty-two states were certified to report NIBRS data (Federal Bureau of Investigation, 2002).

Measuring Criminal Victimization

Crime rates can be calculated in several ways, and each kind of rate has both merits and drawbacks. Using official crime statistics, we can look at rates of recorded crime per 100,000 people, rates of recorded crime per number of available crime targets, rates of arrests for each kind of crime, and other rates based on crimes or suspects known to the police. Because many crimes are not reported to the police, or are not recorded by the police if they do learn of them, the rate at which people are victimized is likely to be greater than the rate of crime recorded by the police.

History of Victimization Surveys

Apparently the first effort to measure crime by surveying members of households was carried out in 1720 in Denmark. However, the first large-scale, systematic effort to measure victimization by interviewing a cross section of a population was not conducted until 1966 in the United States (Ennis, 1967). This study of 10,000 American households by the National Opinion Research Center sought to determine how often people are victimized by crime. Since 1973, the federal Bureau of Justice Statistics (BJS) has done **victimization surveys** similar to the one carried out in 1966. Beginning with the 1992 survey, it has used a revised questionnaire aimed at jogging subjects' memories about crimes and uncovering more sexual crimes. In 2001, the National Crime Victimization Survey (NCVS) interviewed a sample of 79,950 respondents age twelve and older in 43,680 households to measure both personal and household victimization rates. This survey is perhaps the most costly effort to gather crime data ever undertaken. Victimization surveys have also been used to measure crime in Great Britain, Canada, Australia, Germany, Denmark, the Netherlands, Switzerland, and elsewhere. Surveys have sometimes measured the victimization experiences of subgroups in a population; Table 2.3 shows the results of a 2000 survey of a national sample of American high school seniors.

Comparing NCVS and FBI Data

The NCVS program measures crime in a somewhat different way than does the FBI's UCR data collection program. Consequently, the results of the two efforts to measure crime are not strictly comparable. The NCVS measures the offenses of rape, robbery from the person, aggravated and simple assault, household burglary, motor vehicle theft, and theft. It does not measure murder, kidnapping, or victimless crimes; and for reasons of economy it stopped collecting data on commercial burglary and commercial robbery in 1977. As a result, we cannot compare NCVS data on burglary and robbery with the FBI's UCR data on burglary and robbery, for the latter include burglaries and robberies of commercial establishments as well as of private households and individuals.

In recording crimes against the household, NCVS and FBI methods are the same; for instance, each counts one incident or one victimization for every burglary that is reported. However, NCVS and FBI methods of dealing with crimes against the person differ. If a robbery has two victims, the FBI counts only one robbery incident, but the NCVS records two victimizations. NCVS data are oriented to victimizations and to individuals, whereas FBI data are oriented to crime incidents and to both organizational and individual victims.

The Dark Figure

Victimization surveys have uncovered a substantial **dark figure**, the number of crimes that actually occur but are not recorded by the police. The dark figure exists for many reasons, especially the failure of victims to report crimes and the failure of

TABLE 2.3   High School Seniors' Victimization Experiences in the Previous 12 Months

	PERCENTAGE REPORTING VICTIMIZATION		
TYPE OF VICTIMIZATION	Not at all	Once	Twice or more
Theft of personal property worth less than $50	54.6	25.2	20.3
Theft of personal property worth more than $50	74.3	16.6	9.1
Deliberate damage of personal property	69.7	17.7	12.5
Injury by a weapon	95.5	2.8	1.7
Being threatened with a weapon, without actual injury	83.8	9.6	6.5
Being injured on purpose, without a weapon	85.7	8.2	6.1
Being threatened with injury, without actual injury	71.9	12.8	15.3

Note: Percentages may not add to 100% because of rounding.

Source: Survey data gathered from a national sample of 2,204 seniors, Class of 2000, by the Monitoring the Future Project at the University of Michigan's Institute for Social Research; adapted from Table 3.43 in Kathleen Maguire and Ann L. Pastore, eds., *Sourcebook of Criminal Justice Statistics 2000.* Washington, DC: U.S. Department of Justice, 2001, p. 211.

the police to record all reported crimes. Figure 2.1 shows the percentage of crimes uncovered in the 2001 NCVS survey that were reported and not reported to the police.

Figure 2.2, a hypothetical example that graphically depicts the dark figure, shows an actual total crime rate that is constant over time, as represented by the horizontal line parallel to the time axis. At time 1 (t_1), some of this total amount of crime is recorded (the solid vertical line) and some of it is unrecorded (the dotted vertical line, which is the dark figure). By time 2 (t_2), the amount of recorded crime has increased and the amount of unrecorded crime has decreased, but the actual total crime rate remains the same as at time 1. By time 3 (t_3), the official crime rate and the actual total crime rate are the same; in other words, at time 3, all crime that occurs is reported to and recorded by the police. Figure 2.2 shows how the official crime rate (the slanted line) might increase over time without any increase in the actual total crime rate (the horizontal line). This would happen if people began to report crime that previously had not been reported or if the police began to record more of the crime reported to them. If this happens, official crime rates can rise without any increase in the actual total crime rate.

The dark figure has several important consequences. One is to keep cases, usually the least serious ones, out of the criminal justice system. As we have seen, victims are not as likely to report less serious crimes, and so those offenses that come to

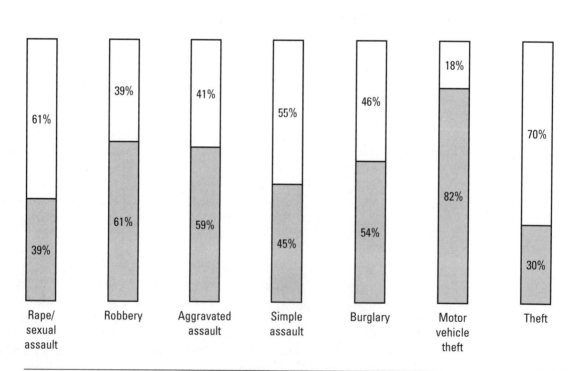

FIGURE 2.1   Percentages of Victimizations Reported and Not Reported to the Police, 2001

Source: Callie Rennison, *Criminal Victimization 2001: Changes 2000–01 with Trends 1993–2001.* Washington, DC: U.S. Department of Justice, September 2002, p. 10.

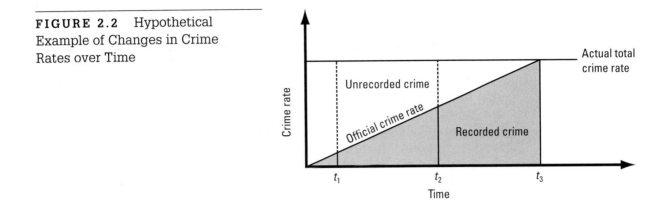

FIGURE 2.2 Hypothetical Example of Changes in Crime Rates over Time

the attention of the police are likely to be completed crimes, to involve larger losses of property and greater personal injury, and to be committed with firearms (Skogan, 1984). Offenders who commit crimes that are not reported to the police cannot be brought to trial, reducing the deterrent effect of punishment. Police and court resources are sometimes allocated on the basis of how much crime is recorded in a community, and thus differences in crime reporting from one area to another could lead to a misallocation of resources. Victim compensation programs and insurance programs may also be affected by the failure to report and record crime, for benefits and premiums may be based on a distorted picture of how much crime occurs. FBI estimates of the financial costs of crime must also be inflated to account for crimes that are not reported or recorded.

Methodological Problems with Victimization Surveys

Victimization surveys are subject to several methodological problems. One problem is the issue of validity, or how well the surveys actually measure the amount of crime in a society. Forgetting can lead to underestimation of the amount of crime that has actually occurred, and it makes it difficult for subjects to tell interviewers exactly when they were victimized. Respondents may also refuse to tell interviewers about crimes for reasons similar to those that keep them from calling the police: the stigma of being victimized, unwillingness to confide in a stranger, and reluctance to take the time to give details of the crime.

Another problem is that victimization surveys can overestimate the amount of crime that occurs. Respondents might incorrectly interpret some experiences—such as the loss of a wallet—and report them as crimes. Overestimation of crime rates can also result if people report crimes that occurred before the period about which they are being questioned. This "telescoping" might result from a faulty memory or from the respondent's wish to have something to talk about with the interviewer. The problem of telescoping can inflate victimization rates by as much as 20 percent, leading to estimates of crime rates that are higher than actual rates. Overreporting can also be encouraged by interviewers who prod respondents to remember crimes, both to keep the interview interesting and to ferret out the "hidden crime" on which the victimization survey is predicated.

Because of these and other methodological problems, the results of victimization surveys should not be regarded as "true" measures of crime. The surveys do measure some of the crime that is not reported to and recorded by the police. However, a comparison of victimization survey results and FBI UCR statistics concluded that "if one defines crime as criminal acts serious enough to be reacted to by both citizens and the police, then [the evidence indicates that] the UCR are at least as valid and probably more valid than the data from victimization surveys" (Gove, Hughes, and Geerken, 1985: 491).

Victimization surveys do not provide a complete and balanced picture of crime. They have not been used to measure white-collar crime, organized crime, or victimless crimes. They offer little or no information on offenders, as do FBI data on arrested suspects. To develop a full picture of crime, victimization surveys must be supplemented with other kinds of data.

Victimization surveys have been used primarily to look at the amount and distribution of crime rather than to test or develop theories of criminal behavior. These surveys have repeatedly shown that much crime is not reported and recorded, but they have added less to our understanding of the social processes that generate crime. As a result, they have contributed relatively little to the development of policies to reduce crime.

Measuring Crime by Self-Reports

Crime can be measured by police statistics or by questioning participants in the incident through a survey. Victimization surveys ask a cross section of the population about its experiences as victims of crime during a specific period. Another way to measure crime is to interview a cross section of the population, or a more limited sample such as high school students, about their involvement in crime and delinquency as offenders. **Self-report studies** reveal that much crime that respondents admit to in confidential interviews or on self-administered questionnaires never makes its way into police statistics.

History of Self-Report Studies

The first use of survey methods to gather self-reported information about involvement in crime and delinquency was Austin Porterfield's (1946) research that used this "self-disclosure" method to compare college students with delinquents who had been through the juvenile court. Porterfield found that both groups had been involved in delinquency in similar ways during their adolescence. In 1947, a self-report survey of adults discovered that 99 percent of a sample of "law-abiding" middle-class people admitted to at least one crime (Wallerstein and Wyle, 1947). These early studies showed that much self-reported crime is never detected by the police.

In 1957, James F. Short, Jr., and F. Ivan Nye (1957) developed a checklist of delinquent activities to be filled out anonymously by respondents. They found that delinquency was more evenly spread across social classes than was indicated by official crime statistics, which showed much more delinquency among the lower classes. Since this pioneering work, many researchers have used self-reports to test and refine theories of crime and delinquency and to provide a more complete picture of violation of the law than is given by official statistics. For example, self-report data collected in the National Youth Survey from 1976 to 1987 have been used productively to test competing theories of delinquency. Table 2.4 shows some of the results of a 2000 survey of self-reported delinquency by a national sample of American high school seniors.

Self-report studies have also been conducted with groups of offenders other than those who engage in conventional crimes and delinquent acts. In 1976 the Internal

TABLE 2.4   High School Seniors' Self-Reported Delinquent Activities
in the Previous 12 Months

TYPE OF DELINQUENT ACTIVITY	PERCENTAGE REPORTING ACTIVITY		
	Not at all	Once	Twice or more
Gotten into a serious fight at school or work	87.7	7.1	5.2
Taken part in a fight where a group of your friends were against another group	80.3	11.0	8.7
Hurt someone badly enough to need bandages or a doctor	88.1	7.3	4.6
Used a weapon to get something from a person	97.2	1.1	1.8
Taken something not belonging to you worth under $50	69.5	12.3	18.2
Taken something not belonging to you worth over $50	87.5	5.6	7.0
Taken something from a store without paying for it	71.3	11.4	17.2
Taken a car that didn't belong to someone in your family without permission of the owner	94.8	2.7	2.5
Gone into some house or building when you weren't supposed to be there	77.3	10.3	12.4
Damaged school property on purpose	86.5	7.3	6.4

Note: Percentages may not add to 100% because of rounding.

Source: Survey data gathered from a national sample of 2,204 seniors, Class of 2000, by the Monitoring
the Future Project at the University of Michigan's Institute for Social Research; adapted from Table 3.49
in Kathleen Maguire and Ann L. Pastore, eds., *Sourcebook of Criminal Justice Statistics 2000.* Washington, DC:
U.S. Department of Justice, 2001, pp. 222–223.

Revenue Service (IRS) mailed questionnaires to 1,200 corporations to ask about their
use of illegal bribes and "slush funds." Of the companies surveyed, 304 corporations
did not respond, but among those that did, the IRS found 481 potentially illegal slush
funds and 71 cases of apparent criminal fraud (Egan, 1978).

The Dark Figure

Self-report studies confirm the conclusion of victimization surveys that the dark figure, or hidden amount of crime, is large. These studies show that nearly everyone in
the general population has broken the law at some time, even though most of the violations are petty. The general population falls on a continuum from highly criminal
to completely noncriminal, rather than being composed of two discrete groups of
criminals and noncriminals. Researchers who compare a sample of convicted offenders with a "noncriminal" sample drawn from the general population usually fail
to consider that many of these "noncriminals" have in fact engaged in crimes. Large
numbers of people commit a few, often trivial, crimes; some commit a larger number; others commit quite a few crimes, including some serious ones; and a small proportion of the population commits many crimes, including large numbers of serious
ones (Elmhorn, 1965). People who violate the law most often are the most likely to
commit relatively serious crimes.

Methodological Problems with Self-Report Studies

Self-report studies have several methodological shortcomings that account for their failure to provide an ideal measure of crime. The questionnaires used in the studies sometimes lack validity; that is, they do not accurately measure the amount of crime that respondents have committed. Subjects might fabricate behavior to impress interviewers, or they might fail to mention some offenses out of fear that the information will be passed on to the police, in spite of guarantees of anonymity. Some studies have found that external control over lying helps to ensure the validity of self-report instruments (Clark and Tifft, 1966; Farrington, 1973).

Self-report studies have been criticized for using school or neighborhood samples that fail to include officially labeled, chronic delinquents. Critics question the assumption of many self-report researchers that "official delinquents are not different from adolescents located at various other points along the delinquency continuum" (Cernkovich, Giordano, and Pugh, 1985: 731). These critics urge researchers to locate and study more official delinquents, because data indicate that the factors explaining relatively minor transgressions are not necessarily the same factors accounting for the actions of chronic delinquent offenders.

Another problem with self-report studies is the way they have been carried out. The use of many different self-report questionnaires by researchers means that their results are often not comparable. Self-report studies would be much more useful if the same questionnaire were administered periodically to national samples. This would allow us to generalize about the amount of crime in the population as a whole and to look at changes in the amount of crime over time. We have accumulated data of this sort on victimization experiences, but we do not yet have such information on self-reported violations of the law. In fact, we know relatively little about self-reported crime by adults, for the vast majority of self-report studies have been carried out on samples of juveniles.

Self-report studies are also flawed in that they ignore certain kinds of behavior. They rarely include questions that add to our knowledge of white-collar crime or organized crime. The way questionnaires are written usually makes it difficult to compare the results of self-report studies with official crime statistics or with victimization survey data. This is partly a result of the use of self-report questionnaires with juvenile samples, for it means that respondents are asked about acts that would be crimes if they were adults as well as about juvenile status offenses such as truancy and underage drinking.

Some self-report studies classify juveniles as delinquents if they admit to one or more delinquent acts. Questionnaires that ask about large numbers of acts are more likely to classify a high proportion of respondents as delinquents, even though many of them might be only minimally involved in trivial acts of delinquency. Self-report studies should emphasize the frequency of delinquency and crime and the seriousness of the acts, rather than whether an individual has ever engaged in any act that violates the law. Increasingly, researchers using self-report methods have focused on "actionable offenses," those relatively serious violations of the law that are likely to lead to arrest and conviction (Junger-Tas and Marshall, 1999: 350).

Because of their methodological shortcomings, self-report studies cannot be employed to assess the efficiency of official crime statistics, even though self-report studies do confirm that there is a large dark figure of crime. They have proved useful, however, in telling us about the characteristics of people who violate different kinds of laws. This information can be compared with official data on arrests, convictions, and sentences to assess the fairness with which the criminal justice system treats different kinds of people.

Because of the methodological problems with each of the three major measures of crime, none is perfect. (See the Crime on Campus box.) When all three measures agree on the extent and distribution of crime, we can have some confidence in the conclusions. When the three measures disagree about the extent and distribution of crime, as they sometimes do, it is difficult to know which one to use. However, each measure can be employed to good advantage by criminologists to answer certain kinds of questions. For instance, victimization data and official crime statistics can be used to examine trends in crime rates. Self-report data have not been used for that purpose, but they can help us to understand the impact on delinquency of child-rearing methods and membership in peer groups, issues not dealt with by either official statistics or

CRIME ON CAMPUS

Measuring the Problem

The Student Right-to-Know and Campus Security Act of 1990 requires all colleges and universities receiving federal funds to publish campus crime statistics, disclose their security policies, and distribute safety reports to employees and prospective and current students. Lawmakers hoped that publication of statistics on campus crime would help students and their families make more informed decisions about campus safety when selecting institutions to attend. They also thought that academic administrators might be underreporting crime because they feared that full disclosure would damage their school's reputation and possibly frighten away potential students, employees, or donors.

The law requires colleges and universities to publish annual crime statistics for murders, sex offenses, robberies, aggravated assaults, burglaries, and motor vehicle thefts that occur on campus and that are reported to campus authorities. Schools are also required to report on-campus arrests for possession of weapons and for alcohol- and drug-related offenses.

Because of inconsistency in how colleges compiled their crime reports, and because of lax enforcement of the 1990 law, a new law was passed in 1998 that required colleges to forward crime statistics to the U.S. Department of Education and to make the data public, or face a $25,000 fine for each unreported incident. In 2000, the department began to post campus crime statistics on a website, www.ope.ed.gov/security.

Criminologists have questioned the validity and reliability of the campus crime statistics produced to comply with these laws. Analyzing the results of their victimization survey of 3,472 students on twelve campuses, John J. Sloan III, Bonnie S. Fisher, and Francis T. Cullen reached the following conclusions:

1. Most of the crimes suffered by students do not have to be reported under the requirements of the act, and as a result the federally mandated statistics overemphasize serious crimes and slight more common forms of victimization. Rapes and sexual assaults, robberies, aggravated assaults, burglaries, and motor vehicle thefts accounted for only 17 percent of all victimizations reported by students in the survey. Crimes that did not have to be reported accounted for the great majority of all reported victimizations: Larcenies were 38 percent of all victimizations; vandalism, threats, and harassments accounted for another 42 percent of all victimizations; and simple assaults were 3 percent of all victimizations.

2. Only 25 percent of all victimizations were reported to any authority, so official campus crime statistics conceal a large dark figure of unreported crime. (When on-campus crimes are reported, they are usually reported to campus authorities rather than to off-campus police forces.)

3. A significant amount of crime victimizes students in off-campus settings, such as their apartments, and this crime is not included in campus crime statistics.

4. Because campus crime statistics are usually presented as raw numbers of reported crimes rather than as rates per number of students in the school, they cannot be used to compare the relative safety of schools or to evaluate the effectiveness of efforts to curb campus crime.

Sources: Based on John J. Sloan III, Bonnie S. Fisher, and Francis T. Cullen, "Assessing the Student Right-to-Know and Campus Security Act of 1990: An Analysis of the Victim Reporting Practices of College and University Students," *Crime and Delinquency* 43 (April 1997), 148–168; Diana Jean Schemo, "Colleges Rushing to Compile Crime Statistics for the Web," *New York Times,* October 19, 2000, p. 22.

victimization surveys. Used appropriately, each measure can contribute to a fuller understanding of criminal behavior.

Summary

The classical school of criminology that developed in the eighteenth century assumed free will and individual responsibility, sought to deter offenders from crime by the threat of punishment, and emphasized punishment in proportion to the social harm caused by the criminal act. During the nineteenth century, cartographers such as Guerry and Quetelet looked for patterns of crime that appeared in official crime statistics. Positivists, reacting to the classical school's emphasis on free will, began late in the nineteenth century to use the scientific method to search for the causes of crime. Cesare Lombroso was the first to use empirical evidence to test hypotheses about why people violated the law, an approach that laid the groundwork for modern criminology.

Today criminologists use several statistical measures to study crime. Sometimes they use official statistics gathered by the police, the courts, or the prisons. The FBI's Uniform Crime Reports provide statistics on crimes known to the police throughout the United States. These reports give detailed information on eight Part I crimes that together constitute the crime index, as well as less detailed information on twenty-one Part II offenses. UCR reports pay little attention to white-collar crime or organized crime and thus present a distorted picture of the crime problem that emphasizes crimes committed by young males who are often poor and members of minority groups.

Official statistics are used to calculate crime rates, usually in terms of number of offenses per 100,000 people. This kind of rate makes sense for crimes in which people are victimized, but it makes less sense when property is the target. Careful thought should be given to the way crime rates are calculated and to the exact meaning of those rates.

Crimes come to the attention of the police when victims and witnesses report offenses and the police react, and when the police uncover crime on their own initiative through proactive work. Crimes are not reported to the police for many reasons: a sense that nothing can be done, a feeling that the offense is unimportant, a belief that the police do not want to be bothered, fear of reprisals, or definition of the crime as a private matter. The police might fail to record crimes, sometimes to keep crime rates down and make themselves look more effective. Official crime statistics have been used for political purposes at both the local and national levels.

A second important measure of crime is the victimization survey. A cross section of a population is questioned in detail about their experiences as victims of crime during a given period. This method was first used on a large-scale basis in the United States in 1966, and today it is employed as part of an ongoing federal effort to measure crime. Because the methods of the NCVS surveys differ from those used by the FBI to collect data, the two kinds of statistics cannot be compared easily. Victimization surveys have found a large dark figure, the amount of crime that occurs but does not make its way into police records. Because victimization surveys have methodological problems, they are not a "true" measure of how much crime there is, but they are important sources of information.

A third measure of crime is the self-report survey, a questionnaire administered anonymously to get respondents to tell about crimes they have committed. Self-report surveys were first used in the United States in 1946, and since then they have been used to measure the extent of crime and delinquency and to test theories of crime and delinquency. Self-report studies find a large dark figure, and sometimes they reach conclusions about who violates the law that differ from research based on official arrest data. Self-report studies have some problems: Most have been done with adolescents; many have asked about involvement in trivial offenses; and the validity of the way they measure crime and delinquency has been questioned. Each of the three measures of crime has strengths and weaknesses, and, when used appropriately, each can contribute to a fuller understanding of criminal behavior.

IMPORTANT TERMS

cartography	dark figure	proactive police work
classical school	incidence	reactive police work
crime index	positivism	self-report study
crime rate	prevalence	victimization survey

REVIEW QUESTIONS

1. What are the differences between positivism and the classical school of criminology? What policies might advocates of each approach recommend for reducing the crime rate?

2. What are the three major kinds of crime statistics used by criminologists? What are the advantages and disadvantages of each measure of crime? What kinds of questions about crime does each measure address most usefully?

3. In 1981, 574,134 robberies were reported to the FBI. The estimated population of the United States in that year was 229,146,000. In 2001, there were 422,921 robberies, and the estimated population was 284,796,887. Calculate the rate of robberies per 100,000 people for each year. What do you conclude from your calculations?

FOR FURTHER STUDY

The Emergence of Modern Criminology   Classical, positivist, and other theories that gave birth to modern criminology are discussed in depth in Thomas J. Bernard, George B. Vold, and Jeffrey B. Snipes's *Theoretical Criminology* (5th ed., New York: Oxford University Press, 2002).

FBI Crime Statistics   Recent FBI UCRs are accessible at www.fbi.gov/ucr/ucr.htm. Other sources of crime data are the link to "Crime Statistics" at the New York Police Department's website (www.nyc.gov/html/nypd/home.html) and the link to "Statistics" at the Chicago Police Department's website (www.ci.chi.il.us/Community Policing).

Victimization Surveys   Reports based on the Bureau of Justice Statistics' NCVS are available at www.ojp.usdoj.gov/bjs/pubalp2.htm.

Self-Report Surveys   Self-report surveys of offending and victimization, as well as data from the NCVS studies and from FBI UCRs, are included in Kathleen Maguire and Ann L. Pastore's (eds.) *Sourcebook of Criminal Justice Statistics 2001* at www.albany.edu/sourcebook.

3

Crime and Its Costs

This chapter looks at the characteristics and costs of four major types of crime: conventional crime, white-collar crime, organized crime, and victimless crime. Conventional crimes are usually divided into two groups: crimes of violence (also called crimes against the person) and property crimes. Crimes of violence include murder, forcible rape, robbery, and assault. Major property crimes are burglary, larceny, motor vehicle theft, fraud, arson, and vandalism. There are a variety of white-collar crimes as well, including crimes by businesses such as deceptive advertising and antitrust violations, and crimes by employees against businesses such as embezzlement and expense account fraud. Organized or syndicated crime has traditionally been equated with the Mafia or La Cosa Nostra in the United States, but it has taken new forms in recent years. Victimless crimes, perhaps more accurately called "crimes without complainants," include drug use, gambling, and prostitution.

After looking at some of the characteristics of these crimes, their financial, physical, and social costs are explored. Estimates of the financial costs of crime, which often appear to be more precise than they really are, can be made only by assuming how much crime actually occurs. Even if we could measure exactly how much crime occurs, it would still be difficult to estimate the cost of each offense. For instance, if a robber beats up a person and steals $25, the victim loses the money but the robber has the use of that money. Placing a monetary figure on the physical and psychological harm to the victim is not easy. If the robber uses the $25 to buy heroin, we might count this expenditure as another cost of crime, even though counting both the initial theft of $25 and the use of that money for heroin might be seen as double counting. If the robber is then arrested, some part of the police budget will be allocated to the crime. The arraignment and trial cost money, and if the offender is convicted and imprisoned, there will be the additional costs of incarceration. The robber's family might have to receive welfare benefits during the period of imprisonment. The absent parent might create a family environment in which the children are more likely to get involved in delinquency. We can see that the initial loss of $25 in the robbery might be quite a small amount when compared with all of the other costs associated with the crime.

There are six distinct kinds of costs of crime (see Table 3.1). One is the **direct loss** of property. For example, arson destroys buildings, and vandalism ruins property. Both offenses reduce the stock of useful things in the world. We can also speak of direct losses from murder, although placing a monetary figure on lost lives is difficult.

A second kind of cost of crime is the **transfer of property.** The theft of a radio in a burglary and the theft of cash in a robbery transfer property from the rightful owner to the thief, and perhaps eventually to a fence and then to a new owner. The victim of the theft regards himself or herself as having lost the property, but from a societal perspective the property has been transferred from one person to another rather than made useless.

A third financial cost of crime arises from crimes of violence in which a victim is physically hurt. These **costs related to criminal violence** include the loss of productivity by incapacitated victims, unemployment compensation paid to victims, fees paid for physical and psychological therapy for victims, and social security payments and funeral expenses associated with homicides.

Yet another type of cost of crime is the expenditure of money on illegal goods and services such as drugs, gambling, and prostitution. **Illegal expenditures** can be considered a cost of crime because they divert money from the legitimate economy and represent a loss of potential revenue for people who produce and supply legal goods and services. However, from another point of view, we might regard illegal expenditures as entertainment expenses, which are often paid for with income earned at a legitimate job. Some of these illegal expenditures do not victimize anyone; no direct and obvious harm to another person necessarily results from spending money on illegal drugs, gambling, or prostitution. Indeed, expenditures on legal goods such as cigarettes and alcohol may produce more obvious harm than do expenditures on some illegal goods and services.

Enforcement costs, a fifth kind of financial cost of crime, include the money spent by various criminal justice agencies. Employees of the agencies regard their salaries as legitimate payments for their work, but from another perspective crime diverts this money from other purposes. If enforcement costs are treated as a financial cost of crime, it follows that redefining some behavior that is now criminal as noncriminal would reduce the cost of crime. The costs of the American criminal justice system are examined in Chapter 13.

A sixth financial cost of crime involves **prevention and protection costs.** This includes the millions of dollars that people spend for alarm systems, spotlights, locks,

TABLE 3.1   Kinds of Financial Costs of Crime

1. Direct loss
2. Transfer of property
3. Costs related to criminal violence
4. Illegal expenditures
5. Enforcement costs
6. Prevention and protection costs

bars, and other "target-hardening" devices, as well as the money they spend on insurance premiums to cover their losses through theft.

Conventional Crimes

Conventional crimes are often divided into violent crimes and property crimes; violent crimes are more feared, but property crimes are more common. The distinction between violent crime and property crime is not always clear-cut. For instance, robbery is the theft of property from a person by force or threat of force, making it both a property crime and a crime of violence. Here we treat it as a crime of violence, because the use of force makes it a more serious crime than simple theft without violence. A second problem with the violent crime/property crime distinction is that one crime event can involve multiple offenses. Thus, after committing a forcible rape the offender may steal the victim's car to get away. Using the FBI's UCR system, law-enforcement officials would record only the more serious offense, forcible rape.

Crimes of Violence

The major types of violent crime are murder, forcible rape, robbery, and assault. Sometimes these offenses take the form of intimate partner violence, hate crimes, or terrorism.

Murder   **Murder and nonnegligent manslaughter** are defined by the FBI as the willful killing of a human being. The taking of another person's life may fall outside this definition if it is excusable, such as an accidental shooting of a playmate by a child, or if it is justifiable, such as a police officer's shooting of a dangerous offender who is about to hurt someone.

In 2001, 15,980 murders were reported to the FBI by local police departments. Because murders are usually reported to the police and because the FBI gathers data from most police departments in the country, the FBI's figure is a good estimate of the number of people actually murdered.

To get some perspective on the meaning of the number of murders that occur each year in the United States, it is instructive to compare the total with deaths that occur in other ways. In 2001, a year that the FBI reported 15,980 murders, there were about 30,000 recorded suicides in the country, though the actual number may have been twice as large. In that same year, 42,116 people died in traffic accidents. Thus, more people committed suicide and more people died in car accidents than were murdered in 2001. The World Health Organization of the United Nations (2002) estimates that worldwide in 2000 there were 520,000 murders and 815,000 suicides—figures greater than the 310,000 war-related deaths in that year.

The financial costs of murder include medical expenses, funeral costs, lost productivity (the total wages the victim would have earned if he or she had lived until the expected age, less the amount he or she would have spent over that time), the cost of welfare or social security payments to the victim's survivors, and such intangible costs as pain and emotional trauma. A study by the Office of Justice Programs (1996) estimates that the tangible costs of an average murder are $1,030,000 and the intangible costs are $1,910,000, for a total cost per murder of $2,940,000. That figure does not include criminal justice expenditures to arrest, prosecute, and punish offenders.

Murder occurs in a variety of circumstances. Of the 12,872 people murdered in Chicago from 1965 to 1981, 69 percent were killed in murders that started as arguments, fights, or brawls; 17 percent were slain in murders that began as robberies; 1 percent were killed in murders that followed rapes; 1 percent were killed in murders that developed from burglaries; fewer than 1 percent were victims of murders that began in some other way, such as a contract killing; and the remainder were murdered in unknown circumstances (Block, 1987).

Murder typically involves an offender and a victim of the same race (see Figure 3.1). This reflects racially based patterns of social interaction in the larger society. Most murders involve a male offender and a male victim. Murders of females by males are the next most common type, although men kill other men more than twice as often as they kill women (see Figure 3.2).

Murder occurs more frequently between an offender and a victim who are known to each other than it does between strangers. In 2001, 13 percent of murders reported to the FBI involved an offender and a victim in the same family; 29 percent

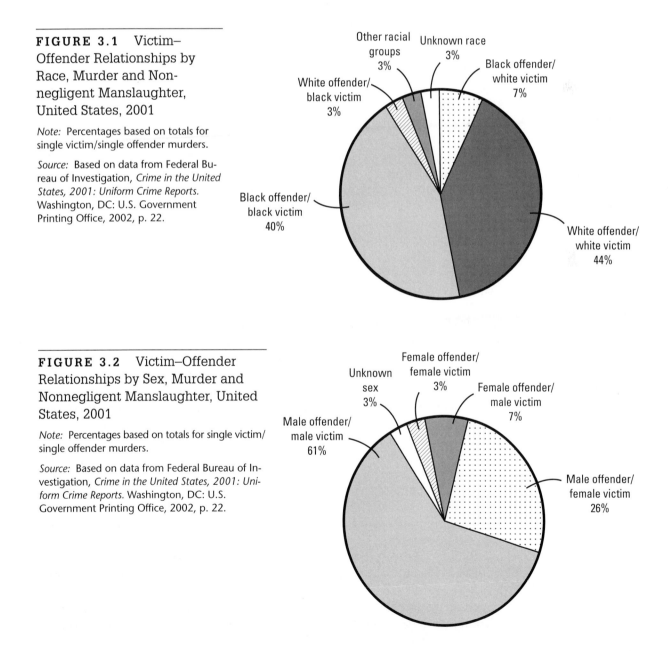

FIGURE 3.1 Victim–Offender Relationships by Race, Murder and Nonnegligent Manslaughter, United States, 2001

Note: Percentages based on totals for single victim/single offender murders.

Source: Based on data from Federal Bureau of Investigation, *Crime in the United States, 2001: Uniform Crime Reports.* Washington, DC: U.S. Government Printing Office, 2002, p. 22.

FIGURE 3.2 Victim–Offender Relationships by Sex, Murder and Nonnegligent Manslaughter, United States, 2001

Note: Percentages based on totals for single victim/single offender murders.

Source: Based on data from Federal Bureau of Investigation, *Crime in the United States, 2001: Uniform Crime Reports.* Washington, DC: U.S. Government Printing Office, 2002, p. 22.

involved boyfriends, girlfriends, friends, acquaintances, neighbors, employers, or employees; 13 percent involved strangers; and in 45 percent of the cases the victim-offender relationship was not known to the police (Federal Bureau of Investigation, 2002: 24). Overall, murders between offenders and victims known to one another outnumbered murders between strangers by more than three to one.

Forcible Rape   According to the FBI, **forcible rape** is "carnal knowledge of a female forcibly and against her will" (Federal Bureau of Investigation, 2002: 29). However, some states now define forcible rape in sex-neutral terms, so that a sexual assault on a male victim, typically by another male, is defined as rape. Some states have also passed laws that distinguish among various degrees of sexual assault, each carrying a different penalty according to the seriousness of the offense, which is a function of the offender's intent, the nature of the sexual act, the amount of injury to the victim, and other circumstances of the crime.

In 2001, there were 90,491 cases of forcible rape and attempted rape reported to local police departments in the United States, but federal victimization surveys have found that many more incidents actually occur. The 2001 NCVS study uncovered 146,000 rapes and attempted rapes, 61 percent more than the number reported by the FBI for that year.

Rape always involves psychological damage to the victim, because by definition it does not involve consent. Rape often involves physical harm as well. NCVS data from 1979 to 1986 show that 39 percent of rape victims were injured, about half of them seriously enough to warrant medical care (Harlow, 1989). A telephone survey of 4,008 women found that of those raped in 1990, 4 percent had suffered serious physical injuries, 24 percent had sustained minor injuries, and 70 percent had not been physically injured; degree of injury was unknown in 2 percent of the cases (Skorneck, 1992). A report by the Office of Justice Programs (1996) estimates that the typical rape or sexual assault has tangible costs of $5,100 and intangible costs (such as pain and emotional trauma suffered by the victim) of $81,400, for a total cost of $86,500 per rape or sexual assault.

Many forcible rapes involve strangers, but a surprisingly large number occur between offenders and victims who have close relationships. Three studies have found that the proportion of all rapes committed by total strangers to the victims ranges from 42 to 53 percent (Amir, 1971; Curtis, 1974; Timrots and Rand, 1987). Two of these studies found that 10 percent and 14 percent of the rapes occurred between an offender and a victim who had previously been intimately related, either as relatives, lovers, or close friends. The third study found that 4 percent of the rapes were committed by relatives. The telephone survey of 4,008 women produced quite different results: only 22 percent of rape victims had been attacked by strangers, 29 percent had been raped by nonrelatives known to the victim, and 46 percent had been assaulted by relatives, ex-husbands, or current or past boyfriends; relationships were unknown in the remaining 3 percent of the cases (Skorneck, 1992).

One relationship between the rapist and the victim that has received considerable attention in recent years is the rape of women by their husbands or ex-husbands. According to one study, one-seventh of women who have ever been married have been the victims of rape or attempted rape by their husbands or ex-husbands (Russell, 1990). All states now permit the prosecution of a husband for the rape of his wife, but in some states the spouses must have been separated at the time of the attack for the case to be prosecuted as a rape. Rape in marriage is an underreported offense, and when it is reported the police often treat it as an assault, if they deal with it as a crime at all.

NCVS data for 1995 reveal the following characteristics of sexual assaults, a category that includes completed and attempted rapes as well as other threatened and completed sexual assaults. Sexual assaults were most common among sixteen to nineteen year olds, people with low incomes, and urban residents; there was no difference by racial group. Two-thirds of the assaults occurred between 6 P.M. and 6 A.M. The majority occurred in the victim's home or in the home of a friend, relative, or neighbor. The majority occurred within one mile of the victim's home. Most victims (84 percent) said that the offender used no weapon; 6 percent reported that the offender used a firearm. Three-fourths of the assaults involved an offender with whom the victim had a prior relationship as a family member, intimate, or acquaintance. About nine-tenths of the assaults were committed by a single offender. Those committed by multiple offenders were much more likely than those by lone offenders to be by strangers. About 7 percent of all sexual assaults involved multiple offenders who were strangers to the victim. Seven of every ten victims reported taking some self-protective measure during the crime, usually struggling to resist or chasing and trying to hold the offender (Greenfeld, 1997).

Robbery   **Robbery** is the theft of property from another person by force or threat of force. More severe penalties are usually meted out to robbers who are armed than to those who do not use weapons. Robberies involve both commercial and financial establishments (banks, stores, gas stations, and taxicabs) and noncommercial targets (people on the street and in residences). (See Table 3.2.)

The FBI reported 422,921 cases of robbery or attempted robbery in 2001. The crimes produced a total loss of $532 million. The NCVS uncovered 631,000 cases of robbery or attempted robbery in its 2001 study (Rennison, 2002). A report by the Office of Justice Programs (1996) estimates that a typical robbery or attempt with injury has tangible costs of $5,200 and intangible costs (such as the victim's pain and emotional trauma) of $13,800, for a total cost of $19,000 per crime. The FBI provides no information on the amount of harm suffered by robbery victims, but an NCVS study using data from 1979 to 1986 found that one-third of robbery victims were injured, half of them seriously enough to require medical care (Harlow, 1989).

Physical injuries during robberies are least common when an offender has a firearm, somewhat more common when a knife is used, and most likely when the

TABLE 3.2   Types of Robbery, as Percentages of All Reported Robberies, with Average Losses, 2001

TYPE OF ROBBERY	PERCENTAGE OF REPORTED ROBBERIES	AVERAGE LOSSES
Street or highway	44.3	$957
Commercial house	14.4	1,881
Residence	12.6	1,364
Convenience store	6.6	618
Gas or service station	2.9	686
Bank	2.4	4,587
Miscellaneous	16.9	1,303
Total (326,277 robberies)	100.1	1,258

Note: Percentages do not add to 100% because of rounding.

Source: Adapted from Federal Bureau of Investigation, *Crime in the United States, 2001: Uniform Crime Reports.* Washington, DC: U.S. Government Printing Office, 2002, p. 218.

About two-fifths of all robberies, such as this one in a convenience store, are committed with firearms.

offender uses no weapon at all (Conklin, 1972; Cook, 1987). Victims confronted by armed robbers are probably least likely to resist and thus least apt to be injured. Victims who believe they can overpower an unarmed robber are more likely to be injured while resisting.

Robberies sometimes lead to murders; these offenses are classified as murders rather than robberies. The FBI estimates that in 2001 there were 1,042 murders that had robbery as the motive. Thus, about one murder in fifteen begins as a robbery. However, only one robbery in every 407 results in a murder.

Many robberies are planned only a few minutes before they occur, with offenders piecing together the elements of the crime by improvisation. One study found that more than 40 percent of juvenile robbers and 25 percent of adult robbers had not intended to commit the crime before it occurred (Feeney and Weir, 1973).

Robbers and their victims do not usually know one another. Because thieves have access to the property of people they know well, they do not need to use force to steal from them. They can simply take the property by stealth in a larceny. They might also explain their need for cash to those with whom they are close, and thus be given or lent the necessary money rather than having to steal it. Concern for people whom they know well can lead robbers to think that if they must use force to steal, they might as well use that force against strangers rather than against relatives or friends. Moreover, strangers are less likely to be able to identify robbers to the police (Curtis, 1974; Hindelang, 1976; Timrots and Rand, 1987). Nevertheless, 20 to 35 percent of robberies involve victims and offenders who are known to one another. Drug dealers are often robbed by other dealers or users, who assume that their victims will be reluctant to call the police (Jacobs, 2000). Acquaintance robbery is also motivated by grievances against the victim, inside information about money or property that can be stolen, and the convenience of stealing from someone close to the offender (Felson, Baumer, and Messner, 2000).

Assault   An **assault** is an unlawful attack by one person on another. The FBI distinguishes between **simple assault**, in which no weapon is used and no serious injury results, and **aggravated assault**, in which the purpose of the attack is to inflict severe bodily injury and a weapon is typically used.

In 2001, there were 907,219 cases of aggravated assault reported to local police departments, according to the FBI. NCVS data revealed 1,222,000 aggravated assaults for that year, 35 percent more than recorded by the FBI (Rennison, 2002). Many victims of this crime are permanently incapacitated. Others suffer injuries from which they eventually recover, but they often lose wages or jobs as a result of being hurt. NCVS data from 1979 to 1986 show that 32 percent of aggravated assault victims were injured, nearly two-thirds of them seriously enough to require medical care (Harlow, 1989). One report (Office of Justice Programs, 1996) estimates that the average assault or attempt has tangible costs of $1,550 and intangible costs of $7,800, for a total loss of $9,350.

A study of 131 patients admitted to a San Francisco hospital with firearm injuries found that their average hospital costs were nearly $7,000 and that 86 percent of those costs were paid for by tax-supported government insurance programs. Extrapolating to the country as a whole, the researchers concluded that firearm injuries cost $429 million per year in hospital expenses and probably more than $1 billion if the costs of ambulance services, physicians' fees, follow-up care, and rehabilitation are added to hospital costs (Martin, Hunt, and Hulley, 1988). A much higher estimate of $63 billion lost due to firearm assault injuries and deaths was derived from estimates of the costs of medical and mental health care, emergency transportation, police services, insurance administration, lost productivity, pain and suffering, and reduced quality of life (Miller and Cohen, 1995).

The exact relationship between victims and offenders in assaults is difficult to determine, because many assaults occur within the family and are not reported to the police and perhaps not even to interviewers who conduct victimization surveys. Fear of retaliation, embarrassment, and the desire to protect even abusive family members contribute to the underreporting of family violence. As a result, assaults between spouses and parental violence against children are more common than is suggested by crime statistics.

In about one-fourth of the aggravated assaults reported to the police, the relationship between the victim and the offender is unknown. About one-seventh of aggravated assaults occur between members of the same family, and nearly one-third more involve lovers, friends, acquaintances, or neighbors. Another one-fifth of aggravated assaults occur between strangers, and one-tenth involve a criminal and a police officer (Curtis, 1974).

Aggravated assaults that are reported to interviewers in surveys of victimization experiences involve strangers 56 percent of the time, a much higher proportion than is the case with aggravated assaults reported to the police. Of the aggravated assaults reported to interviewers, 39 percent are by nonstrangers such as relatives and acquaintances. In 5 percent of the cases, victim–offender relationships could not be determined (Timrots and Rand, 1987).

Intimate Partner Violence   Murder, rape, robbery, and assault by current or former spouses, cohabiting partners, or dates is called **intimate partner violence.** The NCVS estimated that 876,340 females and 157,330 males were victims of such violence in 1998 (Rennison, 2000). Focusing only on rapes and assaults, and using a different research strategy, the National Violence Against Women (NVAW) survey concluded that every year about 1.5 million women and 835,000 men are the victims of intimate partner violence (Tjaden and Thoennes, 2000). Other studies have found that the risk of such victimization is comparable for men and women (Straus, 1995; Schafer, Caetano, and Clark, 1998).

Homicides by intimate partners have declined in recent years in the United States. The number of women killed by intimate partners fell from 1,437 in 1976 to 1,174 in 1997, a reduction of 18 percent. Over that time, the number of men murdered by intimate partners fell from 1,357 to 430, a much larger decline of 68 percent. Expansion of domestic violence programs aimed primarily at women seems to explain these figures: Services encouraging women to take legal action or leave reduce female violence against male partners but increase the rage of men who want to control their female partners (Masters, 1999). In 2001, 1.0 percent of all homicide victims in the United States were husbands killed by their wives, and 4.4 percent of all victims were wives killed by their husbands (Federal Bureau of Investigation, 2002: 24). One study of spouse murder cases found that wives who killed their husbands were less likely to be convicted, and were sentenced less severely if convicted, than were husbands who killed their wives, apparently because the wives had more often been provoked by spouses who had assaulted them (Langan and Dawson, 1995).

The NVAW survey investigated stalking, which it defined as "a course of conduct directed at a specific person involving repeated visual or physical proximity; nonconsensual communication; verbal, written, or implied threats; or a combination thereof that would cause fear in a reasonable person, with 'repeated' meaning on two or more occasions" (Tjaden and Thoennes, 2000: 5). More women (4.8 percent) than men (0.6 percent) reported that they had been stalked at some time by an intimate partner. Stalking was closely associated with actual violence: Four-fifths of women who had been stalked by an intimate partner had been physically assaulted by that person, and one-third of them had been sexually assaulted by that person.

A cohort study in New Zealand found that much intimate partner violence is reciprocal in nature and that much partner abuse by women is not defensive in nature. The risk of being a victim or a perpetrator was associated with both partners' backgrounds and personal characteristics, especially engaging in physically aggressive delinquency before the age of fifteen, being afflicted with mental disorders, and becoming a parent at a young age (Moffitt and Caspi, 1999; Moffit, Robins, and Caspi, 2001). The NVAW survey found that the victims of intimate partner violence were especially likely to have been physically assaulted by adult caretakers as children. That survey found less intimate violence against women in same-sex couples than in heterosexual ones but more intimate violence against men in same-sex couples than in heterosexual ones, showing that the perpetrators of intimate partner violence are especially likely to be males, regardless of the sex of their victims.

Intimate partner violence is costly. The NVAW survey revealed that rapes and physical assaults on female victims were more likely to be repeated and to produce injuries than were attacks on male victims. Women raped by intimate partners were injured in 36 percent of the cases, and those physically assaulted by their partners were injured 42 percent of the time. Males physically assaulted by their intimate partners were injured 20 percent of the time (Tjaden and Thoennes, 2000). Another survey, the National Longitudinal Study of Adolescent Health, showed that young people exposed to intimate partner violence were especially likely to experience depressed feelings and thoughts of suicide, run away from home, drop out of school, or become pregnant (Hagan and Foster, 2001).

Hate Crimes   The FBI defines a **hate crime**, or bias crime, as "a criminal offense committed against a person, property, or society which is motivated, in whole or in part, by the offender's bias against a race, religion, disability, sexual orientation, or ethnicity/national origin" (Federal Bureau of Investigation, 2002: 59). Others add gender to the list of characteristics defining a hate crime. Assaults, vandalism, and intimidation against such victims are especially terrifying because they are aware that they were chosen because of their characteristics. Victims are often seriously injured, but they may be afraid to call the police. By evoking a more general fear in the targeted groups, hate crimes reinforce existing patterns of oppression. (See the Cross-Cultural Perspective box.)

The number of organized hate groups has increased in recent years, partly as a result of the ease with which their messages are spread through websites (Sack, 1998). However, fewer than 5 percent of all hate crimes are committed by organized hate groups. A study in Boston found that the typical offenders are "young white males—teenagers acting in groups of two, three or four, who went out together on a Saturday night looking for someone to bash" (Levin and McDevitt, 1998: A15).

In 1992, the U.S. Supreme Court ruled that the government could not prohibit speech, even hate speech, on the basis of its content, but the following year it held unanimously that it was constitutional to punish crimes motivated by bias more harshly than crimes not motivated by bias. In 1998, thirty-nine states had penalty-enhancement laws that punished hate crimes more severely than similar offenses not motivated by bias. Significant problems remain as to how to prove motivation in a hate crime, assess the precise role of "hate" in the offense, and determine whether provocation and mutual conflict preceded the crime (Morsch, 1991;

CROSS-CULTURAL PERSPECTIVES

Hate Crimes against French Jews

A series of crimes targeting Jewish citizens of France in 2002 included the burning of several synagogues, gunfire at a Toulouse butcher shop, an assault on a young couple in Villeurbanne, and an attack by a gang of masked youths against a soccer team in a Paris suburb. These acts elicited a promise from the prime minister to deploy extra police officers to protect synagogues and schools, but Jewish leaders complained that there was insufficient national outrage at the violence, arson, graffiti, and threatening telephone calls directed against Jews. Some French Muslim leaders decried the attention given to the violence, fearing it would incite further trouble.

These hate crimes were widely attributed to growing anger by France's five million Muslims toward the nation's 600,000 Jews as a result of Israel's military action against Palestinians in Israel's occupied territories. Antisemitic incidents escalated after the Israeli-Palestinian conflict flared up in September 2000; from 1999 to 2000, the number of recorded acts of violence against Jews increased from nine to 116, while other antisemitic acts increased from sixty to 603. According to Jewish leaders, these figures underestimate the extent of the problem, because some victims were afraid to report crimes, while others reported crimes that the police misclassified as youthful misbehavior.

Some French Jewish leaders complained that the government's foreign policy was pro-Palestinian and thereby conducive to antisemitic violence. A public opinion poll did reveal that the French people sympathized more with the Palestinians than the Israelis, by 36 to 19 percent. The government claimed that its foreign policy was even-handed and that it condemned all violence committed by French citizens against fellow citizens. In response, Jewish leaders pointed out that politicians were more vocal in warning citizens not to see all Muslims as terrorists in the wake of the September 11th attacks on the World Trade Center and the Pentagon than they were in condemning hate crimes against Jews. The Jewish leaders suggested that French Muslims had more political clout than French Jews due to their numerical superiority. Some Muslim youths asserted that French Jews were more often given preferential treatment; according to one youth, "The Jews are always the victims, and it is always the Arabs who are always getting pushed around, over there and here" (cited in Daley, p. A3).

Eventually, forty people, fifteen of them under the age of eighteen, were arrested for violence or verbal abuse directed against Jews. A police spokesperson noted that most of the suspects "were people who had been in trouble with the police before. Their actions were not organized and were really just a reaction to whatever was going on around them at the time" (cited in Daley, p. A8).

Sources: Based on Suzanne Daley, "Surge in Anti-Semitic Crime Worries French Jews," *New York Times,* February 26, 2002, p. A3; Donald G. McNeil, Jr., "France Vows Harsh Action after More Synagogues Burn," *New York Times,* April 2, 2002, p. A3; Suzanne Daley, "French Arrest More Suspects in Violent Acts against Jews," *New York Times,* April 9, 2002, p. A8; Adam Clymer, "European Poll Faults U.S. for Its Policy in the Mideast," *New York Times,* April 19, 2002, p. A8.

This rally is protesting hate crimes directed against victims because of their sexual orientation, such as the 1998 murder of openly gay University of Wyoming student Matthew Shepard.

Martin, 1995; Jacobs and Potter, 1998). The police construct hate crimes through their definition of situations and interpretation of the law, a process described as follows:

> They must simultaneously protect the fundamental civil rights of citizens to be free from attacks based on their ethnic or other identity; allow for the constitutionally protected right of persons to express their opinions, including expressions of bigotry; and maintain order and peace in the larger community. (Martin, 1995: 322–323)

Following passage of the Hate Crime Statistics Act of 1990, the U.S. Attorney General assigned the FBI the task of collecting information on bias-motivated offenses. Gathering hate crime data from reports of other UCR offenses, in 2001 the FBI recorded 9,726 hate crime incidents and 11,447 separate offenses, which included the following:

- intimidation (38 percent of all offenses)
- destruction, damage, or vandalism of property (26 percent)
- simple assault (19 percent)
- aggravated assault (11 percent)
- robbery (1 percent)
- burglary (1 percent)
- larceny-theft (1 percent)
- arson (1 percent)
- other offenses (1 percent)

Included in the "other offenses" category were nine murders and four forcible rapes. Race was the motivation in 46 percent of all hate crime offenses (two-thirds of the victims of those crimes were blacks); religious bias was the motivation in 18 percent of the crimes (half of the victims of those crimes were Jewish and one-fourth were Islamic); sexual orientation was the motivation in 14 percent of the cases (two-thirds of the victims of those crimes were male homosexuals); 22 percent of the crimes were motivated by the victim's ethnic or national origin; 0.3 percent of the crimes were motivated by the victim's disability; and 0.2 percent were multiple-bias offenses (Federal Bureau of Investigation, 2002: 60). In addition to the 546 offenses motivated by religious bias against Islam, an unspecified number of the 1,752 offenses motivated by bias against people of non-Hispanic ethnicity or national origin also victimized Muslims. Most of these attacks apparently followed the September 11th terrorist attacks, which were carried out by nineteen Muslims.

Terrorism Terrorism is violence against innocent civilians that is designed to have a psychological impact on a broader audience in order to achieve a political, messianic, or vengeful goal. Some experts argue that terrorists' goals should not be part of the definition, claiming that the essence of terrorism is the means used to evoke fear (*Harvard Magazine,* 2002). (See the Crime and the Media box.)

CRIME AND THE MEDIA

Reporting Terrorism

Terrorists are often "media-motivated," scripting their violent acts to attract publicity that will threaten as large an audience as possible. This makes nations and even cities with prominent media organizations especially vulnerable to terrorism. CNN provided live coverage of the second plane crashing into the World Trade Center, as well as the collapse of both towers, on September 11, 2001. Other news media based in New York City were also well situated to provide up-to-the minute coverage of the terrorist attacks.

Terrorists choreograph their violence to enhance its newsworthiness, choosing a well-known victim, timing an act to coincide with an anniversary or widely watched event, or picking a location where news coverage will be more intensive. One terrorist describes this process as follows:

People in New York's Times Square watch the burning World Trade Center.

We, we give the media what they need: newsworthy events. They cover us, explain our causes and thus, unknowingly, legitimize us. . . . You must understand: the media are very interested in our actions. They look for contacts with us, they try to get information from us and they are eager to report everything we do or say. . . . Take for example the news agencies—within a half an hour after calling them and briefing them, which we did quite often, you are in the headlines all over the world. . . . All you need is one phone call, a threat or a declaration. (p. 61)

The media play an important gatekeeping function in selectively reporting terrorist acts. Weimann and Winn found that the three major American television networks

reported only 15, 17, and 18 percent of a large sample of terrorist acts, and that nine newspapers from around the world reported 22 to 33 percent of the events. For all twelve news media, a terrorist event was most likely to be reported if

- responsibility for the act was known
- there were more injured victims and more fatalities
- the mode of action was a hijacking
- the target was an airline
- the act occurred outside Latin America
- the targets were British or Israeli
- the perpetrators were Irish or Palestinian

Source: Based on Gabriel Weimann and Conrad Winn, *The Theater of Terror: Mass Media and International Terrorism.* New York: Longman, 1994.

Not all crimes that fit this definition are socially constructed as terrorism. The murders, assaults, and bombings by radical anti-abortionist activists that began in 1977 were not treated as terrorism by the government or the media until 1993, even though they fit the definition of terrorism (Jenkins, 1999). After the September 11th attacks, the Bush administration designated some groups, most notably Osama bin Laden's al Qaeda network, as terrorist groups and sought to freeze their assets, but it did not add Hezbollah, Hamas, and other Palestinian groups to that list for another two months, and even then encountered criticism from some of its allies for making those additions.

Calculating the financial cost of the 3,047 deaths on September 11th is difficult. Lawyers argue that monetary awards to surviving dependents should reflect the degree to which the deceased suffered prior to dying, with larger awards going to the dependents of victims who remained alive longer on the higher floors of the World Trade Center than to the dependents of those who died immediately when the planes crashed into the twin towers (Glaberson, 2001a). The financial cost of these crimes vastly exceeds whatever dollar figure is put on the lives taken by the terrorists. Billions of dollars were also lost as a result of the impact of the crimes on the nation's economy, with airlines and other businesses losing money, and employees losing jobs, for months after the attacks.

Property Crimes

Property crimes involve either the theft or the destruction of property. Theft can take the form of burglary, larceny, motor vehicle theft, or fraud. Destruction of property occurs in the crimes of arson and vandalism.

Burglary   **Burglary** is unlawful entry of a building to commit a serious crime, usually the theft of property. A burglary might turn into a robbery if the burglar confronts the occupant of the building and uses force to steal, but most burglary involves no such confrontation. Burglary targets include both private residences and commercial establishments such as stores and offices.

In 2001, the 2,109,767 burglaries reported to the FBI produced estimated losses of nearly $3.3 billion. Residences, which were the targets of two-thirds of the burglaries, suffered an average loss of $1,381; nonresidences suffered an average loss of $1,615 (Federal Bureau of Investigation, 2002: 218). The Office of Justice Programs (1996) estimates that the average burglary or attempt has tangible costs of $1,100 and intangible costs of $300, for a total of $1,400 per burglary.

Burglaries are frequently planned, with burglars examining the architecture of a building for ease of entry and escape. Often they first try to enter through an unlocked door, and only if that fails will they climb in through a window. They might seek a different target if they cannot make a quick entry. They look for alarm systems, occupants of the building, and nearby witnesses. Learning about police and security patrols in the area can also be a part of the planning of a burglary (Letkemann, 1973; Reppetto, 1974; Wright and Decker, 1994).

Although we might expect a prior relationship between burglars and their victims to be rare, because the burglars would have access to the victim's property or would be able to ask for a loan, a 1985 study found that 42 percent of burglaries were committed by a relative, an acquaintance, or someone whom the victim would recognize (cited in Greer, 1986).

Larceny   **Larceny**, or theft, is the "unlawful taking, carrying, leading, or riding away of property from the possession or constructive possession of another" (Federal Bureau of Investigation, 2002: 48). The FBI excludes from this category motor vehicle theft, embezzlement, confidence games, and forgery, although they are forms of theft. Larceny differs from robbery in that it does not involve force or the threat of force, and it differs from burglary in that it does not involve entry of a building.

The FBI recorded 7,076,171 larcenies in 2001. The average loss per larceny was $730, for a total loss of $5.2 billion. Thefts from buildings were the most costly form of larceny, producing an average loss of $1,037 per offense. More than one-third of all recorded larcenies were of car parts, accessories, and contents. Table 3.3 shows the major forms of larceny (Federal Bureau of Investigation, 2002: 51).

Some larcenies are carefully planned in advance, and others are done on the spur of the moment. Shoplifting is carefully planned in advance by "boosters," or professional thieves, and even amateur "snitches" who steal for personal use sometimes plan their thefts before entering a store (Cameron, 1964). Shoplifting often involves the intention to pick up certain merchandise, a plan to get out of the store, and a way to dispose of or use the stolen goods. Other thefts might not be planned. For instance, someone may be tempted to steal an unlocked bicycle or a coat left unattended in a movie theater.

There is little reason to expect that there will be a prior relationship between thieves and their victims. Indeed, one survey found that 90 percent of the victims of personal theft were complete strangers to the perpetrators of the crimes (Hindelang, 1976).

Motor Vehicle Theft   **Motor vehicle theft** is often distinguished from larceny, of which it is actually one form. The reason for this is that motor vehicle theft involves property of much greater value than is commonly stolen in other types of larceny, and often the car thief does not intend to deprive the owner of the property on a permanent basis. Most stolen vehicles are recovered, although the proportion that are

TABLE 3.3   Types of Larceny, as Percentages of All Reported Larcenies, with Average Losses, 2001

TYPE OF LARCENY	PERCENTAGE OF REPORTED LARCENIES	AVERAGE LOSSES
From motor vehicles (except accessories)	25.8	$719
Shoplifting	13.8	182
From buildings	13.3	1,037
Motor vehicle accessories	10.2	451
Bicycles	4.1	318
From coin-operated machines	0.7	286
Pocket picking	0.5	305
Purse snatching	0.5	331
All others	31.0	1,024
Total (5,710,073 larcenies)	99.9	730

Note: Percentages do not add to 100% due to rounding.

Source: Adapted from Federal Bureau of Investigation, *Crime in the United States, 2001: Uniform Crime Reports.* Washington, DC: U.S. Government Printing Office, 2002, p. 218.

Each year there are nearly 50,000 carjackings in the United States. Most are armed robberies, but some result in murders.

never recovered has increased in recent years, apparently as the result of more thefts by professionals who strip vehicles of their parts, repaint and sell them, or even ship them to other countries for sale. The National Insurance Crime Bureau estimates that approximately 20 percent of stolen cars are shipped abroad, most often to Latin America, China, eastern Europe, and the former Soviet Union (Erwin, 2002). Despite this trend, there are still at least twice as many thefts for joyriding and temporary use as there are by professionals (Clarke and Harris, 1992).

In 2001, the 1,226,457 motor vehicle thefts and attempted thefts recorded by the FBI produced an estimated total loss of $8.2 billion. NCVS data showed 1,009,000 motor vehicle thefts and attempts for 2001 (Rennison, 2002). Three-fourths of the stolen vehicles reported to the FBI in 2001 were automobiles, 19 percent were trucks or buses, and the remaining 7 percent were other types (Federal Bureau of Investigation, 2002: 54).

In 1992, newspapers throughout the United States were filled with stories of "carjackings," thefts of automobiles from drivers at traffic lights and stop signs, in parking garages, and in shopping center lots. Carjackers used firearms or caused minor accidents to get drivers to stop. Because the car is a second home for drivers, a private place in which they feel secure, this type of crime was very threatening. FBI officials were quick to point out that carjacking was not a new crime, even if it had increased in frequency, and that the FBI did not classify it as motor vehicle theft. Several carjackings have resulted in the death or kidnapping of the driver, but most carjackings are classified as robberies, because they involve the use or threat of force to steal property. NCVS data indicate that between 1992 and 1996 there were an average of 48,787 carjackings per year in the United States, nearly 10 percent of all robberies. About half of these carjackings involved firearms. Victims were injured in one-sixth of the crimes, and an average of twenty-seven people were killed in such incidents each year (Klaus, 1999).

Fraud   **Fraud** is the crime of obtaining money or property by false pretenses. Facts are misrepresented and deception is employed to mislead victims by promising goods, services, or financial benefits that do not exist or are never intended to be provided. For example, dishonest brokers who fail to deliver on their guarantee to get a college student a scholarship in return for payment of a fee cost consumers an estimated $100 million a year (Bronner, 1998). In addition to being the victims of such schemes, college students sometimes commit fraud: telephone fraud by students costs long-distance companies millions of dollars every year, and some former students have fraudulently avoided repayment of their educational loans (see the Crime on Campus box).

Fraud sometimes involves false or deceptive advertising in which customers lose money by purchasing inferior or misrepresented merchandise. Some fraud is white-collar crime, but fraud is also committed by people who are not white-collar offenders. Concern with welfare fraud led the New York City government to fingerprint recipients, but only forty-three cases of "double dipping" were found among 148,502 recipients. One interpretation was that welfare fraud had never been much of a problem, but another was that the threat of being caught scared off cheats (McLarin, 1995).

Deceiving the government about one's true income and underpaying taxes is a form of fraud. Twenty to 25 percent of Americans cheat on their tax returns. The IRS estimates that in 1998 it was owed $222 billion in unpaid taxes, although the General Accounting Office said that the IRS would probably collect only $26 billion of that amount because of its inability to keep track of unpaid taxes and target those taxpayers most likely to pay. A substantial part of the unpaid taxes is a result of the underpayment of taxes by individuals who fail to report all of their income or exaggerate their deductions, or by corporations that do not comply with tax laws. Tax evasion seems to have increased over time because of a growing perception that there is little risk of being caught by IRS auditors. The agency audited one of every seventy-nine tax returns in 1988, but in 2000 it audited only one in every 232 returns (*New York Times,* January 19, 2002). The IRS audits the returns of the working poor more often than those of wealthy taxpayers, and it pays more attention to wage income than income from self-owned businesses, investments, and trusts (Johnston, 2002).

When people who face a risk insure themselves against financial loss, an opportunity for fraud exists. An estimated 10 to 20 percent of all insurance claims are

CRIME ON CAMPUS

Fraud and Student Loans

Students who borrow money to attend college have their loans forgiven when they die or become totally and permanently disabled. Taking advantage of the U.S. Department of Education's laxness in monitoring the discharge of loans for these reasons, some former students have falsified death certificates or claimed disability to avoid repayment of the money that allowed them to get a college education.

The auditing division of the Department of Education reported in 1999 on its study of loan discharges from July 1, 1994, to December 31, 1996; borrowers whose loans had been forgiven during that time were matched with Social Security Administration records of 1997 earnings. A total of 708 borrowers earned wages in 1997 even though their loans, totaling about $4 million, had been discharged because of death. Those discharges had been based on falsified death certificates or other evidence of death, such as physicians' statements and insurance bills. Another $73 million in loans was mistakenly discharged because former students had fraudulently claimed disability. Nearly one borrower in four who claimed total and permanent disability earned wages after the Department of Education had forgiven his or her loan.

The department announced that it would use garnishment of wages and other means to recover the money lost through fraud, and it promised that in the future it would monitor more carefully the evidence of death and disability it relied on to discharge student loans.

Source: Based on Anjetta McQueen, "$77m in Student Loans Discharged Fraudulently, Audit Finds," *Boston Globe,* June 16, 1999, p. A8.

fraudulent, and 10 percent of the money spent on health care, or $100 billion a year, is lost to fraud and abuse (Rosenthal, 1990; Sparrow, 1998). Some people pad their claims because they assume the insurance company will pay them less than they have lost, but other claims are more blatantly fraudulent. Some people have even faked their deaths to collect life insurance money. One pattern is for an immigrant to return home after buying a life insurance policy while living in the United States, purchase a forged death certificate, and then file a fraudulent claim abroad (Treaster, 1997). Dozens of arrests have been made of people who fraudulently filed claims that they had lost relatives in the September 11th terrorist attacks (D. Barry, 2002).

Arson-for-profit schemes are another source of insurance fraud. Property owners who find their neighborhoods deteriorating and taxes and repair costs rising sometimes burn down their buildings. The building might be overinsured or even insured more than once, and then the insurance claim will exceed the real value of the structure. Insurance companies contribute to the problem of fraud by not inspecting buildings before writing policies, by settling with arsonists if the cost of investigating the fire is too great relative to the size of the claim, and by failing to exercise their option of forcing owners to rebuild rather than collect the money (Brady, 1982).

"True identity fraud" starts with the theft of a social security number, credit cards, and personal checks, often in a purse snatching or robbery. Because social security numbers are widely used for personal identification (for example, on driver's licenses and college I.D.s), offenders can use them to gain computer access to information that permits them to use stolen credit cards, get money from bank machines, forge personal checks, and pass credit checks to open new charge accounts, rent apartments, or secure loans. Complaints about stolen or misused social security numbers nearly quadrupled from 1997 to 1999, an indication that identity theft has increased dramatically in recent years (O'Brien, 2000).

The Internet has brought with it online auction fraud: the failure to deliver items that have been paid for, the dishonest description of goods, the sale of stolen merchandise, and the use of stolen credit cards. Complaints received by the Federal Trade Commission of fraud in online auctions, which started in 1995, grew from 106 in 1997 to 13,901 in 1999 and then dropped to 10,872 in 2000, apparently because of better-educated consumers, self-regulation by auction sites, and policing by outside agencies (Wolverton, 2001). In one highly publicized case, three men tried to sell a painting for $135,805 by "shilling," or conspiring to deceive potential buyers by bidding up the price with no intention of buying the picture. The sale was cancelled by eBay, the largest online auction site, and the men were suspended from further trading; in 2001, they were indicted for wire and mail fraud and charged with entering shill bids in 1,100 auctions that cost art buyers a total of $450,000.

One study of fraud found that it was very common and often quite costly, even though many attempts to commit fraud failed. The only two personal characteristics strongly associated with victimization were age and education: Younger people were victimized more often than older people, and more highly educated people were victimized more often than those with less education. There were no significant differences in victimization by income, race, or gender (Titus, Heinzelmann, and Boyle, 1995).

Arson   Arson is the willful or malicious burning of the building, motor vehicle, aircraft, or personal property of another person. It sometimes involves the intent to defraud an insurance company by filing a claim for the loss of one's own property through a deliberately set fire, though there are other motives for this crime. Revenge is one such motive, with Molotov cocktails or firebombs being used in gang-related attacks and disputes over drugs.

According to one city planner, arson is forty times as common in the United States as in Japan, and the United States has "tallied the worst fire death rate in the industrialized world for decades" (McMillan, 1995: A17). The FBI does not present the total number of crimes of arson because of incomplete reporting, but 42 percent of the cases reported in 2001 involved structures (three-fifths of them residential), 33 percent targeted mobile property such as motor vehicles and trailers, and the remainder involved other kinds of property. Nearly one-fifth of the structures that were the targets of arson were not in use at the time of the fire. The FBI estimates that losses from arson totaled at least $765 million in 2001. Table 3.4 presents the average losses from different types of arson (Federal Bureau of Investigation, 2002: 57).

The National Fire Protection Association (NFPA) provides data on incendiary fires (those for which there is a legal decision or physical evidence indicating they were deliberately set) and suspicious fires (those for which circumstances suggest they may have been deliberately set). The NFPA estimates that in 1999 there were 72,000 structure fires of incendiary or suspicious origin and 370 civilian deaths in those fires, the fewest deaths in the twenty-three years studied by the organization. There were also 45,000 vehicle fires of incendiary or suspicious origin. These 117,000 fires resulted in property damage totalling $1.3 billion (National Fire Protection Association, 2001).

Vandalism   Vandalism is the willful or malicious destruction, injury, disfigurement, or defacement of property without consent of the owner. Breaking the windows in an abandoned building is an act of vandalism that has little social significance, but vandalizing an important painting in a museum can ruin property of great economic and cultural value.

TABLE 3.4   Arson Offenses and Average Property Damage, 2001

TARGET	PERCENTAGE OF REPORTED ARSONS	AVERAGE DAMAGE
Total structure		
Single occupancy residential	17.8	$18,392
Other residential	7.8	18,531
Storage	3.2	20,339
Industrial/manufacturing	0.5	110,925
Other commercial	4.2	33,622
Community/public	4.8	17,343
Other structure	3.9	8,440
Total mobile		
Motor vehicles	30.7	6,813
Other mobile	1.8	9,724
Other	25.4	1,361
Total (68,967 arson offenses)	100.1	11,090

Note: Percentages do not total 100% because of rounding.

Source: Based on Federal Bureau of Investigation. *Crime in the United States, 2001.* Washington, DC: U.S. Government Printing Office, 2002, p. 57.

The Costs of Property Crime   Reliable estimates of the costs of vandalism and fraud are not available, but the FBI estimates that total losses from robbery, burglary, larceny, motor vehicle theft, and arson were about $18 billion in 2001. One study estimated the total cost of crime by adding direct out-of-pocket costs (such as stolen property, lost wages, medical expenses, mental health care costs, and legal fees) to the monetary values of pain, suffering, and fear that have been established by jury awards in personal injury accident cases. This study assigned dollar values to such intangibles as loss of quality of life for crime victims and loss of affection for the members of a murder victim's family. Money spent on police work was included, but correctional costs were not. This broad definition of the cost of crime yielded an estimated annual loss of $450 billion from index crimes, child abuse, and domestic violence. One-fourth of that amount was direct out-of-pocket losses (Cohen, Miller, and Wiersema, 1996).

White-Collar Crime

The concept of white-collar crime was first introduced by sociologist Edwin Sutherland in a speech before the American Sociological Society in 1939 and elaborated on by him in a book ten years later. To modify his definition slightly, **white-collar crime** is any illegal act, punishable by a criminal sanction, that is committed in the course of a legitimate occupation or pursuit by a corporation or by an otherwise respectable individual of high social standing.

One important aspect of this definition is that white-collar crime is punishable under the criminal law, even though it is often not actually punished as a crime but is instead ignored or dealt with by a regulatory agency or civil court. Another important aspect of the definition is that white-collar crime occurs in the course of a legitimate occupation or pursuit; thus, a corporate executive who murders his wife after an argument has not committed a white-collar crime. One problem with our definition of white-collar crime is that it does not make clear what "respectable" actually means. Usually this term is interpreted to mean that the individual offender is held in high social regard, but some have taken it to mean that the white-collar offender has no previous convictions for conventional crimes or does not think of himself or herself as a criminal. Finally, white-collar criminals are of relatively high social standing, although Sutherland and other criminologists have sometimes treated as white-collar offenses certain crimes committed by people of relatively low status, such as fraud by people who repair cars.

Table 3.5 shows some of the many forms that white-collar crime takes. It includes actions by corporations, such as deceptive advertising or collusion to fix prices or divide a market. Embezzlement of the funds with which an employee is entrusted is a white-collar crime against a company rather than by a company. Securities fraud and theft are white-collar crimes. Tax fraud by companies or individuals in the course of their business activities is also white-collar crime. White-collar crime can result in losses to the public, stockholders, and competing companies, or it can involve losses to companies at the hands of their employees. Al Capone once referred to white-collar offenses collectively as "the legitimate rackets."

White-collar crime often involves elaborate planning. A price-fixing conspiracy among electrical equipment manufacturers that resulted in the conviction of companies and executives in 1961 required detailed planning. One conspirator described the techniques used by the offenders as follows: "It was considered discreet to not be too obvious and to minimize telephone calls, to use plain envelopes in mailing material to each other, not to be seen together on traveling, and so forth . . . not to leave

TABLE 3.5   Major Types of White-Collar Crime

CRIMES BY BUSINESSES	CRIMES BY EMPLOYEES AGAINST BUSINESSES
Deceptive advertising	Embezzlement and employee theft
Antitrust violations	Expense account fraud
Insider trading	**CRIMES BY GOVERNMENT EMPLOYEES**
Securities fraud	Police brutality
False valuation of assets	Bribe taking by police officers and political officials
Mail and wire fraud	Embezzlement by political officials
Tax fraud	
Bribery of political officials	**CRIMES BY PROFESSIONALS**
Unsafe workplace conditions	Medical quackery
Production of dangerous products	Health care fraud
Environmental law violations	Fraudulent damage claims by lawyers
Industrial espionage	Embezzlement by lawyers
"Sweetheart contracts" with union officers	
False weights and measures by retailers	
Misrepresentation of credit terms	

wastepaper, of which there was a lot, strewn around a room when leaving" (cited in Geis, 1967: 143). Further evidence that the executives knew they were breaking the law is that they "hid behind a camouflage of fictitious names and conspiratorial codes," called their meeting roster the "Christmas card list," and referred to their gatherings as "choir practice" (Geis, 1967: 143). To ensure their anonymity, they used only public telephones and met at trade association meetings and at remote sites.

Most of the offenses that criminologists study as white-collar crime occur in the business world, but government corruption and police brutality also fit our definition of white-collar crime. The embezzlement of funds by public officials is a white-collar crime. Government officials (including police officers) who take bribes are committing crimes in the course of their legitimate occupations. We can also treat police brutality as a white-collar crime, even though it might be argued that police officers do not wear white collars and are of middle rather than high social status.

Is White-Collar Crime Different?

Sutherland's pioneering work on white-collar crime was important to criminology because it showed that people from other than the lower classes violate the law, even if they are rarely convicted in criminal court. In this way, Sutherland forced criminologists to reject the notion that crime is solely the product of pathological conditions common to poor people and to consider what factors might explain crime by both the poor and the well-to-do. (See the Crime and the Media box.)

Some sociologists have questioned whether white-collar crime really differs from conventional crime. Gottfredson and Hirschi (1990) claim that white-collar crime is indeed crime, because it involves the use of force or fraud for personal benefit, but they assert that it is not the product of any unique causal processes and therefore needs no special theory to explain it. They say that all crime, including white-collar crime, offers the offender immediate benefits with little effort and is the result of acting impulsively rather than considering the long-term consequences of behavior. They cite evidence that criminals are versatile rather than specialized to support their claim that different types of offenders, such as white-collar criminals and conventional criminals, need not be distinguished from one another. According to Gottfredson and Hirschi, the characteristics that employers require of white-collar workers are usually associated with low rates of offending behavior, and therefore white-collar crime is uncommon. They point out that researchers who claim otherwise have usually compared rates of offending over several years by large corporations that have thousands of employees with rates of offending by individuals during a single year. In fact, we have little reliable data to indicate just how common white-collar crime really is.

A study by Weisburd et al. (1991) used presentence reports by probation officers who were advising federal judges on how to sentence offenders convicted of securities fraud, antitrust violations, bribery, bank embezzlement, postal and wire fraud, false claims and statements, credit- and lending-institution fraud, and tax fraud. A significant number of those crimes—especially credit fraud, false claims, and mail fraud—were committed by people without jobs or by employed people of low socioeconomic status, by people who did not have college degrees, and by people who did not own homes. The offenders were also more likely to be nonwhite and to be younger than previous studies of white-collar offenders had led the researchers to expect.

Many of the offenders in the Weisburd et al. study had prior criminal records, usually not for other white-collar offenses, suggesting that they did not meet Sutherland's criterion of respectability. They were less apt to have long or serious records than were conventional offenders, but they had more past involvement in criminal

CRIME AND THE MEDIA

White-Collar Crime in the News

Because businesses support newspapers and television stations with the money they spend on advertisements and commercials, the news media might be expected to avoid white-collar crime stories that would alienate advertisers and sponsors. How do the media report white-collar crime, and what factors influence their reporting?

Steven Chermak's study of a newspaper and a television organization in a midwestern city found that white-collar crime was reported much less frequently than conventional crime, especially murder and other violent offenses. Eleven percent of crime stories in the newspaper, and only 5 percent of television crime stories, dealt with white-collar crime. In contrast, 39 percent of newspaper crime stories and 45 percent of television crime stories dealt with murder and other violent crimes.

Why did the newspaper pay more attention than the television station to white-collar crime? One reason is that the complexity of white-collar crime lends itself better to

coverage in the print media, where articles can go into whatever depth is necessary to explain an offense. Most newspapers have a separate business section, where white-collar crimes can be covered in detail. Television news programs, on the other hand, cover crime news more superficially, rarely spending more than one minute on a story, a time too short to make sense of most white-collar crimes. In addition to their complexity, white-collar crimes have little visual appeal, lacking a specific victim and a definite crime scene, and so they are difficult for television to cover in a way that viewers will find interesting. Television is also unlikely to cover white-collar crimes because "white-collar crime is generally not a threat to the immediate safety of the audience. When a serial rapist strikes, the news report serves as an easily visualized warning. In television it is difficult to warn people about white-collar victimization because too much explanation is needed" (p. 120).

Source: Based on Steven M. Chermak, *Victims in the News: Crime and the American News Media.* Boulder, CO: Westview, 1995, pp. 118–121.

activity than would have been expected from previous work on white-collar crime. Indeed, they were about twice as likely to have a prior arrest record as the population at large.

Weisburd et al. concluded that the typical white-collar offender convicted in federal court bears little resemblance to the wealthy and powerful offenders described in Sutherland's original study, even though the offenders they studied were higher in social class standing than the typical conventional criminal. Most of the white-collar offenders were "average people in a financial jam who [saw] a way out through fraud" (Weisburd et al., 1991: 190). They turned to crime either to move up the ladder of success, especially when they encountered obstacles to further upward mobility, or to keep from falling in social standing. Weisburd et al. (1991: 45–46) were struck by the "banal, mundane quality of the vast majority of white-collar crimes," saying that the offenses involved no particular skills other than the ability to lie and cheat. Nevertheless, these crimes can be distinguished from conventional crimes by their need for access to organizational resources and their financial impact on victims.

The Costs of White-Collar Crime

The 1996 report of the National Criminal Justice Commission estimated that the annual cost of white-collar crime is between $130 billion and $472 billion, seven to twenty-five times greater than the cost of conventional or street crime (Donziger, 1996: 66). However, accurate measurement of losses from white-collar crime is not easy. Not only must direct losses to victims be calculated, but it is also necessary to determine how much prices rise as a result of passing on companies' losses to consumers. The ramifications of a single white-collar crime are often complex and hard to assess. For example, when a bribe is paid by a business executive to accomplish a particular objective, neither the bribe giver nor the recipient will necessarily feel that any loss has been incurred. However, there is a loss to the public from such transactions. For instance, the cost of a bribe paid by a construction firm to a city inspector will be passed on to the individual who has contracted to have the building erected, and that cost might then be passed on to the building's tenants in higher rents.

Perhaps half of the losses from white-collar crime are due to consumer fraud, illegal competition, and deceptive sales practices. Consumer fraud includes the sale of defective merchandise, the misrepresentation of interest terms, and the sale of unneeded or faulty home and car repairs. Illegal competition costs billions of dollars each year, and introducing competition where it has been absent can save consumers much money. For example, an antitrust action against the manufacturer of the drug tetracycline reduced the price of that drug by 75 percent.

The sale of counterfeit merchandise is a deceptive practice that costs companies billions of dollars every year. Fake designer clothing, purses, and cosmetics inflict substantial losses on couturier houses. Products bearing the symbol of the designer firm but made with shoddy materials make customers unwilling to buy the original product. The illegal copying of computer software, compact discs, and audio- and videocassettes also results in billions of dollars in losses for manufacturers each year.

Another business crime that is very expensive is stock fraud and securities theft. Securities are sometimes stolen by brokerage house employees, who may deliver the securities to members of organized crime in return for cancellation of the employees' debts that arose from gambling or borrowing from loan sharks. The gangsters then transport the securities out of the country and use them as collateral for loans from foreign banks.

One costly crime that occurs in the commercial sector is employee theft and embezzlement. Retailers lose in excess of $10 billion a year from "shrinkage," which includes employee theft, shoplifting, shoddy paperwork, misplaced goods, and vendor theft (Traub, 1996). In some urban stores, the percentage of merchandise lost through inventory shrinkage equals or exceeds profits. Theft by employees and fraud by customers cost banks four to five times more each year than bank robberies.

White-collar crimes sometimes cause serious injuries to their victims, more often as a result of negligence than intent. Air pollution and the dumping of toxic waste cause respiratory ailments, cancer, and other diseases. Hazardous and often illegal working conditions result in many deaths and injuries every year. In 1985, three executives were found guilty, fined $10,000, and sentenced to twenty-five years in prison for murder in the cyanide poisoning death of an employee whose job involved the use of that chemical to recover silver from photographic film. In 1990, an appellate court overturned their convictions as "legally inconsistent."

Some of the millions of serious injuries that occur each year as a result of the use of consumer products can be attributed to criminal negligence or deceptive advertising by manufacturers. The Ford Motor Company was charged with reckless homicide for the deaths of three young women in Indiana in 1978. However, a jury acquitted Ford, finding that it had marketed a defective car but had not been reckless in its recall efforts (Cullen, Maakestad, and Cavender, 1987).

White-collar crime has major social costs in addition to the enormous financial losses and physical damage it inflicts on the public. Indirect or secondary effects of white-collar crime include "(a) diminished faith in a free economy and in business leaders, (b) loss of confidence in political institutions, processes, and leaders, and (c) erosion of public morality" (Moore and Mills, 1990: 414). If white-collar crime reduces public willingness to invest in the stock market and engage in commercial transactions, a capitalist economy that relies on public investment can be weakened. Illegal campaign contributions by large corporations can lead to public cynicism toward government. Bribes paid to officials of other nations can weaken foreign relations and diminish national prestige abroad. A company's interest in protecting its foreign investments can even lead to the rigging of elections or the overthrow of a democratically elected regime that is seen as hostile to American business. Business crime might also set an example of disobedience for the general public, with citizens who rarely see white-collar offenders prosecuted and sent to prison becoming cynical about the criminal justice system. A sense of injustice can develop when they or their friends are given long sentences for crimes that cost society much less than offenses committed by wealthy corporate executives or large multinational firms.

Despite these dire predictions, one study found that most of the victims who had lost money when a loan company collapsed due to criminal activity continued to have faith in the economic and political system. Their long-standing faith in the established order was not easily shaken, and they blamed individuals rather than institutions for their losses (Shover, Fox, and Mills, 1994).

Organized Crime

Organized crime is criminal activity by an enduring structure or organization developed and devoted primarily to the pursuit of profits through illegal means. In the United States, organized crime traditionally has been equated with the Italian American Mafia or La Cosa Nostra. In recent years, criminologists and law-enforcement agents have broadened their perspective on organized crime to include criminal enterprises run by Chinese, Japanese, Colombians, Vietnamese, Jamaicans, Russians, Nigerians, Israelis, and other ethnic groups.

Organized crime has the characteristics of a formal organization: a division of labor, coordination of activities through rules and codes, and an allocation of tasks in order to achieve certain goals. The organization tries to preserve itself in the face of external and internal threats.

The opportunities for illegal profits exploited by criminal organizations include the importation and distribution of drugs, the lending of money at usurious rates (loan sharking), gambling, bankruptcy fraud, the disposal of toxic wastes, extortion, labor racketeering, and the smuggling of immigrants. These sources of income are examined in Chapters 6 and 11.

The Costs of Organized Crime

In 1986, in a technical paper written for the President's Commission on Organized Crime, researchers at Wharton Econometric Forecasting Associates in Philadelphia concluded as follows:

> The effects of organized crime on the legitimate economy show up in higher prices for consumers when competition is suppressed, lower wages for workers when labor unions are controlled, and less safety when corners are cut on construction projects or toxic waste is not disposed of properly. (Fishman, Rodenrys, and Schink, 1986: 432)

The researchers stated that the taxes citizens pay

> must be higher by the amount of taxes not paid by these criminals to provide the government with needed revenues. Conversely, if taxes were paid on all income earned by the individuals associated with organized crime, the taxes paid by ordinary citizens could be reduced by this amount. (Fishman, Rodenrys, and Schink, 1986: 486)

From their study, the researchers estimated that organized crime reduces the nation's economic output by $18.2 billion per year, cuts employment by 414,000 jobs, raises consumer prices by 0.3 percent, and reduces per capita income by $77.

The activities of organized crime also have social costs. One essential element of organized crime is the corruption of public officials and police officers who allow gangsters to operate without interference. Reports of corruption undermine faith in government. People might be unwilling to discuss political matters openly for fear that all officials are linked to organized crime. The influence of organized crime with elected officials can lead to public resignation and the belief that young people would be better off pursuing careers other than politics.

Victimless Crimes

A **victimless crime** is an offense that is consensual and lacks a complaining participant (Schur, 1965; Meier and Geis, 1997). It might be more accurate to refer to victimless crimes as crimes without complaints, because some observers question the idea that there is no victim of crimes such as drug use, gambling, and prostitution. What is important is that the offenses usually involve willing participants in activities that violate the law. Because no one complains to the police about being victimized, making arrests and prosecuting suspects are difficult.

What is called victimless crime varies over time as well as among individuals at any given time. When Edwin Schur first used the term "crimes without victims" in 1965, he focused on drug addiction, homosexuality, and abortion. Today, homosexual relations between consenting adults in private are legal in nearly three-fourths of the states. In 1973, abortion was legalized under most conditions by the U.S. Supreme Court in its decision in *Roe* v. *Wade,* although there is still a bitter debate about whether abortion should be legal or illegal.

Estimates of the financial costs of victimless crimes are usually based on a calculation of the amount of money spent on goods and services such as illegal drugs, gambling, or prostitution. The assumption underlying the estimates is that if this money were not spent on illegal goods and services, it would be spent on legitimate goods and services.

Drug Use

The use of illegal drugs can be seen as a victimless crime in the sense that neither the user nor the seller is likely to report the crime to the police. Drugs do have ill effects on users, from physical deterioration to overdose deaths, but some sociologists see those effects more as the consequence of society's laws against drugs than as the result of the pharmacological effects of the drugs themselves. If the drugs were legally available, these sociologists argue, they would be much less expensive and the negative effects on users would be minimized. When drugs are illegal they are expensive, and users need to spend much of their money on drugs. This in turn causes them to neglect food, shelter, and clothing, and such neglect leads to their physical deterioration.

The high cost of illegal drugs also leads users to commit crimes such as robbery, burglary, and larceny to get the money to pay for their drugs; those property crimes do have victims, even if drug use itself is victimless. Moreover, the high cost of illegal drugs leads some users to deal drugs, drawing into drug use some people who otherwise would not have engaged in such behavior. The illegal markets that develop to distribute drugs are dangerous settings. For instance, one-third of all murders in New York City in 1986 were drug-related (Karmen, 2000: 39).

In addition to the money that users pay for illegal drugs, illegal drug use has such costs as revenue lost to the government because required taxes are not paid on those drugs, the expense of enforcing drug laws, losses from the property crimes committed by users to pay for their drugs, murders that occur during drug transactions, losses due to absenteeism by drug-using workers, the artificial inflation of real estate values due to the infusion of money from the drug trade, and the medical costs of treating drug addicts, including intravenous drug users with AIDS and infants born dependent on drugs.

Gambling

One argument for viewing illegal gambling as a victimless crime is that nearly all states now permit some form of legal gambling, such as on-track betting, off-track betting, casino games, and lotteries. If those forms of gambling are not defined as crimes, why then should betting with a bookie on sporting events or playing the numbers be treated as crimes? The variation from state to state in defining what kind of gambling is legal and what kind is illegal makes it clear that there is no national consensus on treating gambling as a crime.

It might be easier to make a case for an economic loss from illegal gambling than to make such a case for illegal drug use or prostitution. Gambling with a bookie produces a loss for the economy in those states that have lotteries or other forms of legalized gambling, if people who can bet legally use their money to bet in illegal ways. Funds are diverted from the state, which would have used that money for education or other social services. This can cause taxes to be higher, or services to be fewer, than would have been the case if the money had been gambled legally.

Another cost of illegal gambling is that money bet with a bookie who has links to organized crime can be used by gangsters to finance the importation of drugs or to engage in loan sharking. However, there is evidence that many, perhaps most, bookies are not members of organized crime and that much money spent on illegal gambling does not make its way into the hands of gangsters (Reuter, 1983).

Pathological or compulsive gambling also has harmful consequences, including alcohol and drug abuse, health and emotional problems, family stress, and absence from work. Moreover, most pathological gamblers eventually engage in crimes such as check forgery, loan fraud, embezzlement and employee theft, confidence games, larceny, burglary, pimping and prostitution, selling drugs, and tax fraud in order to raise money with which to gamble or pay gambling debts (Lesieur, 1987, 1992).

Prostitution

The consensual transactions between prostitutes and their clients typically do not produce complainants, though clients who are robbed by prostitutes or their pimps, and prostitutes who are beaten by their customers, sometimes do turn to the police. Individual prostitutes can be seen as engaging in a crime that has no victim, even though prostitution poses risks to both the prostitute and the client, such as the possibility of contracting sexually transmitted diseases, including AIDS. Prostitutes who work for pimps are often the victims of physical abuse to "keep them in line," but the criminal offense of prostitution itself does not involve participants who define themselves as the victims of a crime.

In estimating the costs of prostitution, as in estimating the costs of illegal drugs, some have assumed that money spent on illegal services is money that otherwise might have been spent on legitimate goods and services and so is lost to the economy. However, from another perspective, it is difficult to see how money spent for sex with a prostitute is any more of a financial loss than money spent to attend a movie or a baseball game.

Summary

Conventional crime, white-collar crime, organized crime, and victimless crime have enormous financial, physical, and social costs. Among the financial costs of crime are the direct loss of property and its transfer from an owner to a thief. Victims of criminal violence suffer lost wages and hospital expenses. Expenditures on illegal goods and services can be treated as a cost of crime because they divert money from the legitimate economy. Also important are the costs of enforcing the law and the money that people spend for prevention and protection.

Conventional crimes of violence include murder, forcible rape, robbery, and assault. Murder often occurs between an offender and a victim who were previously acquainted. Forcible rape frequently occurs between total strangers, but many rapes involve a victim and an offender who are well known to each other. Robbery, the use of force or threat of force to steal property, typically involves strangers. Most assaults are between a victim and an offender who are known to each other. Assaults between people who are intimately associated are probably underreported to the police.

Conventional property crimes include burglary, larceny, motor vehicle theft, fraud, arson, and vandalism. Burglaries involve unlawful entry of a building to commit a serious crime, usually a theft. Larceny or simple theft includes many types of behavior, including shoplifting and pickpocketing. Motor vehicle theft is committed by professionals who sell the stolen car or its parts, or by amateur joyriders who do not intend to deprive the owner of the car on a permanent basis. Other property crimes are fraud, the obtaining of money or property by false pretenses; arson, the deliberate burning of property; and vandalism, the willful destruction of property.

White-collar crime is an illegal act, punishable under the criminal law, that is committed in the course of a legitimate occupation or pursuit by a corporation or by an otherwise respectable individual of high social standing. Financial losses from illegal competition, deceptive advertising, product counterfeiting, stock fraud, price fixing, and other offenses by "respectable" people are greater than total losses from robbery, burglary, larceny, motor vehicle theft, and arson. In addition, white-collar crimes injure their victims through pollution, unsafe working conditions, and defective products.

Organized crime is activity by an enduring organization developed and devoted primarily to the pursuit of profits through illegal means. Because of the great profits to be made, other ethnic groups have taken over some of the criminal enterprises that the predominantly Italian American Mafia controlled in the past.

Victimless crimes, which are consensual offenses that lack complaining participants but which divert money from the legitimate economy, include illegal drug use, gambling, and prostitution. Drug use might be seen as harming users or as hurting the victims of theft by users who steal to buy drugs, but sociologists often argue that it is the law's definition of drugs as illegal, more than the drugs themselves, that produces such negative consequences. Gambling is legal in some form in most states, leading many to question whether illegal gambling can be said to have a victim. Prostitutes can be victimized by pimps and clients, but their transactions with clients are usually offenses that involve no complainant.

IMPORTANT TERMS

aggravated assault	fraud	prevention and protection
arson	hate crime	costs
assault	illegal expenditures	robbery
burglary	intimate partner violence	simple assault
costs related to criminal	larceny	terrorism
violence	motor vehicle theft	transfer of property
direct loss	murder and nonnegligent	vandalism
enforcement costs	manslaughter	victimless crime
forcible rape	organized crime	white-collar crime

REVIEW QUESTIONS

1. What are the four major types of crime? What are the differences among them? What are their similarities?

2. What is intimate partner violence? What are its sources? Are women or men more likely to be the victims of such crime?

3. What is hate crime? What distinguishes it from other crimes? Why did the federal government enact a law to require the collection of official statistics on hate crime?

4. What is terrorism? How would you determine the costs of terrorist crimes?

5. What do sociologists mean by "victimless crimes"? Are people hurt in any way by these so-called victimless crimes? Is it useful to distinguish between victimless crimes and conventional crimes?

6. How would you calculate the financial costs of conventional crime, white-collar crime, organized crime, and victimless crime? Which kind of crime is the most costly in the United States? What physical harm does each type cause? What are the harmful social effects of each type?

Murder   M. Dwayne Smith and Margaret A. Zahn's (eds.) *Homicide: A Sourcebook of Social Research* (Thousand Oaks, CA: Sage, 1999) is a comprehensive collection of papers on theories and research on homicide and proposals for preventing it.

Hate Crimes   Recent FBI hate crime statistics are available at www.fbi.gov/ucr/ucr.htm. Valerie Jenness and Ryken Grattet's *Making Hate a Crime: From Social Movement to Law Enforcement* (New York: Russell Sage Foundation, 2001) looks at the ways that social movements have influenced hate crime laws that cover some vulnerable groups but not others.

Terrorism   Jonathan R. White's *Terrorism: An Introduction* (3rd ed., Belmont, CA: Wadsworth, 2002) is a textbook that examines the origin, organization, and tactics of terrorist groups. Up-to-date material on terrorism can be found at websites sponsored by the Terrorism Research Center (www.terrorism.com), the Federation of American Scientists (www.fas.org/irp/threat/terror.htm), and the Emergency Response and Research Institute (www.emergency.com/cntrterr.htm).

Fraud   The website of the National Fraud Information Center (www.fraud.org) contains current statistics on Internet and telemarketing fraud.

White-Collar Crime   James William Coleman's *The Criminal Elite: Understanding White-Collar Crime* (4th ed., New York: St. Martin's, 1998) is an up-to-date overview of the many forms of white-collar crime, their causes, and possible solutions to the problem. The National White-Collar Crime Center website (www.nw3c.org) provides papers on a variety of topics, including "disaster fraud" that occurred after the September 11th terrorist attacks.

Organized Crime   Howard Abadinsky's *Organized Crime* (6th ed., Belmont, CA: Wadsworth, 2000) is a useful textbook. A website providing access to news articles on organized crime can be found at http://members.tripod.com/~orgcrime/japscenes.htm. The website of the Nathanson Center for the Study of Organized Crime and Corruption at York University in Toronto (www.yorku.ca/nathanson/default.htm) offers a searchable database and links to other websites.

4 Dimensions of Crime

How does the crime rate of the United States compare with those of other nations? Is murder especially common in some regions of the United States? Is the risk of victimization greater in cities than in suburbs? Have crime rates decreased in recent years? How does involvement in crime vary by sex, age, race, and social class? This chapter explores these variations by using data from the FBI Uniform Crime Reports (UCR), the Bureau of Justice Statistics National Crime Victimization Surveys (NCVS), and self-report studies.

Knowledge of how crime rates vary from society to society and from group to group points the way to a theory of crime causation. Statistical variations in crime rates are facts that criminologists' theories must explain, but the variations are not, by themselves, theories of crime. For instance, knowing that men commit more murder than women does not tell us why this difference exists, but it does tell us that a theory of crime should be able to account for this difference.

Cross-National Variations in Crime Rates

In the criminologist's ideal world, all nations would define crime and gather statistics in the same way. Comparison of crime rates in different countries would then facilitate the development of a general theory of crime. Unfortunately, this situation does not exist, nor is it ever likely to. There are significant cross-national variations in laws, the law-enforcement process, and the collection of crime data. In addition, many countries do not have complete and reliable crime statistics that are publicly available. For example, Soviet leader Josef Stalin prohibited the disclosure of crime statistics in 1933, and not until 1989 did the government make that information available, fearing that it would harm the nation's reputation and even contribute to the crime problem. (See the Cross-Cultural Perspective box.)

Crime rates usually rise as a nation develops economically, with property crime rates typically increasing faster than rates of violent crime. However, Japan's experience after World War II shows that social change is not inextricably linked to rising crime rates. In 1948, 1.6 million penal code offenses were recorded in Japan, but by 1973 that figure had dropped to 1.2 million, a decline of 25 percent. In 1986, 1.6 million crimes were recorded, an increase over the 1973 figure but the same as the number reported in 1948, despite significant population growth and urbanization over that time (Hamilton and Sanders, 1992).

Figure 4.1 shows rates per 100,000 people for homicides reported to the United Nations by selected countries; many nations, especially in Africa and Asia, do not report such information. Figure 4.2 presents rates of domestic burglaries per 100,000 households for ten countries, and Figure 4.3 reveals differences among those nations in motor vehicle thefts per 100,000 vehicles. These figures, which are based on crimes recorded by the police, demonstrate that the United States has a high homicide rate relative to other advanced industrial societies but that its rates of property offenses are not especially high. In 2000, England and Wales had more recorded crimes per 100,000 people than the United States for robbery (179.9 to 144.9), burglary (1,579.1 to 728.4),

CROSS-CULTURAL PERSPECTIVES

Violent Crime in South Africa

When South Africa's minister of safety and security imposed a moratorium on the release of crime statistics in August 2000, he claimed that the ban was due to problems with the methods of gathering and analyzing the data. Critics suggested that the moratorium was instead an effort to conceal the country's extraordinarily high rate of violent crime, which was keeping tourists from visiting and international businesses from investing and causing many South Africans to move abroad.

Rates of violent crime in South Africa are among the highest in the world. The country does not report its homicide rate to the United Nations, but in 1999 that rate was 55.3 per 100,000 people, many times higher than the rates shown in Figure 4.1. South Africa's rates of rape and robbery are also among the highest in the world, and the rate of rape has climbed sharply since the mid-1990s. Especially disturbing is the growth in sexual assaults against children; one-fifth of all victims of rapes reported in the first six months of 2001 were under the age of eleven. Many of these sexual assaults are the result of a popular belief that sex with a virgin can cure AIDS, a disease that is rampant in the country. Some of the growth in recorded rapes could be the product of better reporting, because

black South Africans' trust in the police has grown since the end of white political control, but reluctance to prosecute and a low conviction rate seem to have increased the actual number of rapes that are being committed.

South Africa's high rates of violent crime are due to social instability caused by the aftermath of the racist apartheid policy, a high unemployment rate, and extensive poverty. One political leader notes that apartheid "left behind a legacy of a serious breakdown of the moral infrastructure" (cited in Swarns, 2002: A6). Mental health experts agree, suggesting that hungry people do not usually commit rape and proposing that sexual assaults against children are associated with the loss of humanity and moral depravity engendered by years of living in a racially oppressive society. Also contributing to the high rates of violent crime are the difficulty of merging local police forces into a single national agency and the failure to recruit and retain qualified police officers. Thirty percent of the country's police officers are illiterate, and nearly 10 percent of them do not have driver's licenses. In the absence of effective policing, vigilante justice has increased, and many whites have retreated into homes protected by high walls, alarm systems, and private security guards.

Sources: Based on Henri E. Cauvin, "South Africa Veils Crime Data, Faulting System," *New York Times,* August 3, 2000, p. A3; Rachel L. Swarns, "South Africa in an Uphill Fight against Crime," *New York Times,* May 15, 2000, pp. A1, A10; Rachel L. Swarns, "Grappling with South Africa's Alarming Increase in the Rapes of Children," *New York Times,* January 29, 2002, p. A6.

FIGURE 4.1 Homicide Rates per 100,000 People, 1994–1999

Source: Based on data from United Nations, *Demographic Yearbook 1999.* New York: United Nations, 2001, pp. 479–506.

Rate per 100,000

Russian Federation	22.9
Mexico	17.2
Venezuela	15.7
Belarus	11.1
Cuba	6.7
United States	6.6
Argentina	4.6
Poland	2.8
Australia	1.7
Canada	1.4
Italy	1.3
Sweden	1.2
Germany	0.9
France	0.9
United Kingdom	0.7
Japan	0.6

FIGURE 4.2 Domestic Burglaries per 100,000 Households, 1997

Source: Based on data in Frans van Dijk and Jaap de Waard, *Legal Infrastructure of the Netherlands in International Perspective: Crime Control.* The Hague, Netherlands: Ministry of Justice, June 2000, p. 20.

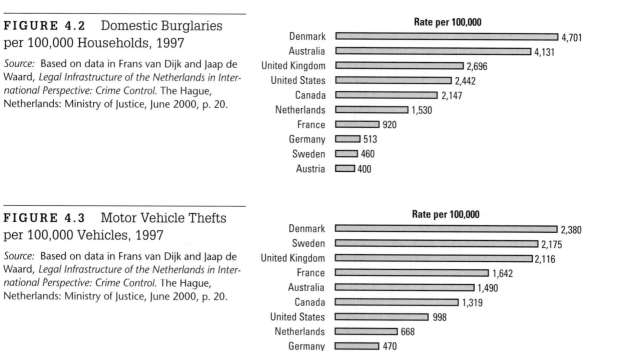

Rate per 100,000

Denmark	4,701
Australia	4,131
United Kingdom	2,696
United States	2,442
Canada	2,147
Netherlands	1,530
France	920
Germany	513
Sweden	460
Austria	400

FIGURE 4.3 Motor Vehicle Thefts per 100,000 Vehicles, 1997

Source: Based on data in Frans van Dijk and Jaap de Waard, *Legal Infrastructure of the Netherlands in International Perspective: Crime Control.* The Hague, Netherlands: Ministry of Justice, June 2000, p. 20.

Rate per 100,000

Denmark	2,380
Sweden	2,175
United Kingdom	2,116
France	1,642
Australia	1,490
Canada	1,319
United States	998
Netherlands	668
Germany	470
Austria	104

and motor vehicle theft (639.9 to 414.2); the murder rate for the United States was much higher (5.5 to 1.6), though the gap between the murder rates has declined substantially in recent years (Federal Bureau of Investigation, 2001; Povey et al., 2001).

Regional Variations in Crime Rates within the United States

The comparatively high murder rate of the United States leads us to ask what causes the differences between this country and other industrial societies. We can begin to zero in on an answer to this question by looking at variations in crime rates within the United States. One such variation is by region of the country.

In 2001, the murder rate for the United States was 5.6 per 100,000. However, there were significant variations in the rates for different regions. The rate for the Northeast was 4.2, the rate for the Midwest was 5.3, the rate for the West was 5.5, and the rate for the South was 6.7 (Federal Bureau of Investigation, 2002: 66–72). The homicide rate for the South had been about twice the rate for the rest of the nation until recently, but murder rates have become more similar for the different regions. Still, the murder rate in the South is now 34 percent higher than the rate for the rest of the country.

Several explanations have been offered for the South's high murder rate. Because both poverty and minority-group status are linked to murder, the South's high murder rate is partly a result of the relatively large amount of poverty and the relatively large proportion of blacks in that region. Regional differences in homicide rates have also been explained by a "subculture of violence," a set of norms that allow violence to be an appropriate response to certain situations (Wolfgang and Ferracuti, 1982). Some claim that those norms are more widespread in the South than elsewhere. Attempts to explain regional variations in murder rates by this subculture-of-violence theory are explored later in the book, but what is important here is the existence of regional differences that a theory of crime causation must explain.

The South and the West had the highest rates of property crime in 2001 (Federal Bureau of Investigation, 2002: 66–73). Larceny and burglary rates were highest for the South. The motor vehicle theft rate was significantly higher in the West than in the other regions. The total rates per 100,000 for the three property crimes were 4,181.0 for the South, 3,834.7 for the West, 3,549.1 for the Midwest, and 2,577.2 for the Northeast. The rate for the country as a whole was 3,656.1.

One possible explanation for the regional variations in property crime rates is that the warmer weather in the South and the West might mean that people there are away from their homes more often and leave their property unguarded, and this could inflate property crime rates by creating more opportunities for theft. We can speculate about the reasons for regional variations in crime rates, but theories of crime causation should make sense of such variations.

Variations in Crime Rates by Community

FBI data show a general tendency for crime rates to increase with the size of the community. For example, in 2001 the violent crime rate per 100,000 people was 332.7 in cities with 10,000 to 24,999 people, 668.3 in cities with 100,000 to 249,999 people, and 1,084.1 in cities with more than 1 million people. Property crime rates were generally higher in more populous communities, but those rates were highest in cities with 500,000 to 999,999 people and lower in cities with more than 1 million people (Federal Bureau of Investigation, 2002: 209).

Victimization survey data for 1993–1998 indicate that rates of rape and sexual assault, robbery, aggravated and simple assault, personal and household theft, household burglary, and motor vehicle theft are higher in urban areas than in suburban ones. All of those rates except household burglary are higher in suburban areas than in rural ones (Duhart, 2000). In general, both official crime statistics and victimization surveys point in the same direction: Conventional crime occurs at higher rates in larger communities, at least within the United States.

Social processes associated with large communities—such as the anonymity of the individual and the disruption of traditional social ties—seem to be associated with more crime, but growth in the size of cities has not always produced higher crime rates. After World War II, Japan became more heavily urbanized, but its crime rate did not increase. Switzerland was also able to keep its crime rate low while urbanizing, with a slow rate of urban growth making it possible to maintain social stability and avoid the disruption of traditional social bonds. Thus, the association between community size and crime rates in the United States should direct our attention to social processes that occur with urban growth, rather than lead us to assume that urbanization inevitably generates crime.

Crime within Metropolitan Areas

The first systematic examination of the distribution of crime within metropolitan areas was carried out in the 1920s in Chicago by Clifford Shaw and Henry McKay (1969). They followed Ernest Burgess in describing the metropolitan area as a series of identifiable concentric rings. In this **concentric-zone model** of the urban community, industry develops near the center of the city in order to be at the crossroads of transportation and communication. This may not be true of cities that developed after the mass ownership of cars and telephones, and in the future, cities may be located at the crossroads of electronic communications rather than at the crossroads of transportation. In Shaw and McKay's model, the central business district is at the center of the metropolis and is immediately surrounded by an area that is changing from a run-down residential area to one occupied by expanding business and industry. Beyond this are residential areas of increasing desirability and respectability.

Shaw and McKay found that rates of arrest for delinquency—as well as rates of adult crime, truancy, tuberculosis, infant mortality, and mental disorder—were highest in the center of the city and declined with increasing distance. Their conclusion that delinquency was a local problem requiring local solutions was the basis for the Chicago Area Project, which was initiated in 1932 to encourage efforts by residents of low-income areas to prevent delinquency. Programs were planned and implemented by members of local churches, unions, business groups, athletic clubs, and other community organizations. One goal was to enhance the well-being of young people through recreation, summer camping, scouting, handicrafts, and field trips and through the creation of job opportunities. Other programs sought to improve housing, sanitation, and the physical appearance of the neighborhood, and to improve schools through the formation of parent-teacher organizations. Systematic evaluation of the Chicago Area Project was impossible because it was implemented in different ways in different communities (Shaw and McKay, 1969).

Others have done work that supports Shaw and McKay's conclusion about the distribution of crime and delinquency in metropolitan areas (see, e.g., Short, 1969: xxv–liv). Rates of crime and delinquency are usually highest in areas characterized by low incomes, dilapidated and overcrowded housing, transiency, unemployment, broken families, and minority groups. These areas are most commonly in the center of large cities. Evidence that the highest rates of crime and delinquency occur in the center of cities also comes from research carried out in Canada, Great Britain, Venezuela, Puerto Rico, Uganda, the Soviet Union, and other countries (Clinard and Abbott, 1973; Ferracuti, Dinitz, and Acosta, 1975; Shelley, 1981b).

Looking at data for Chicago from 1900 to 1966, Shaw and McKay found that the delinquency rate for the members of any given racial or ethnic group was higher for members of the group who lived near the center of the city and lower for members who lived in neighborhoods more distant. For instance, people of German ancestry who lived in the inner city had higher rates of arrest for delinquency than German Americans who lived in the suburbs. This suggests that it is the values and norms that are transmitted from generation to generation in an urban neighborhood, rather than the values and norms of any particular racial or ethnic group, that are conducive to violation of the law.

This conclusion is supported by Shaw and McKay's finding that the same urban neighborhoods generally had the highest rates of delinquency over the years, even when there was considerable change in the racial and ethnic composition of those communities. Areas with high delinquency rates were usually marked by rapid population turnover, socialization into patterns of crime and delinquency, and a lack of good jobs. A more recent study of the distribution of delinquency in Chicago found that Shaw and McKay's conclusion that rates remained the same despite racial and ethnic turnover fit the data for 1940 and 1950. From 1950 to 1970, however, changes in the racial and ethnic composition of a neighborhood were often accompanied by changes in delinquency rates. Rates of delinquency remained about the same when a neighborhood was able to maintain its stability in the face of a changing racial and ethnic composition, but in many neighborhoods racial and ethnic succession destabilized the community and led to an increased rate of delinquency (Bursik and Webb, 1982).

Shaw and McKay claimed that the relationship between local rates of poverty and crime was mediated by neighborhood social organization, defined as the degree to which local institutions allow a community to cope with its problems. Research indicates that a community's control over crime and delinquency also depends on whether its institutions can attract resources from agencies outside the community that deal with health, welfare, education, and criminal justice (Bursik and Grasmick, 1993; Turk, 1993).

Rodney Stark's ecological theory of crime first identifies five characteristics of urban neighborhoods that have high rates of deviance: density, poverty, mixed use, transience, and dilapidation. Stark then develops a set of propositions about the ways that those five characteristics reduce social control and increase moral cynicism, opportunities for crime and deviance, and the motivation to deviate. These responses amplify the amount of crime and deviance in the neighborhood by attracting deviant people and activities, driving out the least deviant people and activities, and further weakening social control. Residence in these "deviant places" is a cause of group differences in crime rates; for example, "high black crime rates are, in large measure, the result of *where* they live" (Stark, 1987: 905).

The Geography of Crime   Geographers have provided a picture of crime in metropolitan areas by mapping the location of crimes, the residences of those who commit crimes, and the residences of victims (Georges Abeyie and Harries, 1980; Brantingham and Brantingham, 1984). Often they use computer graphics to show the distribution of those elements in a metropolitan area.

Crimes of violence are often depicted as a triad of elements: the residences of the offender and of the victim, and the place where the crime occurs. Many crimes of violence occur within the home, where much interaction takes place, so the triad is sometimes a single point, with the residence of the victim and the offender also being the location of the crime.

Crimes against property are usually depicted as a dyad of elements: the residence of the offender and the place where the property is stolen (although larceny from a person may add the third element of the victim's residence). Most property offenses, as well as most crimes of violence, occur fairly close to the offender's home, with the number of crimes decreasing with greater distance from the criminal's place of residence. Offenders are familiar with their own neighborhoods and so can find targets there. They also know what risks they must avoid near home, even though they may run a greater risk of identification near home. Consequently, criminals' "journeys" or "trips" to the places where they commit their crimes are often short (P. Phillips, 1980; Brantingham and Brantingham, 1984). However, the dyads and triads of crime vary with the kind of offense committed and with the age and sex of the criminal.

Geographers have not mapped dyads and triads for white-collar crimes. If they did, they would probably discover that the distance from the home of the offender to the location of the crime, which is usually the place of work, is considerably greater than is the case for most index crimes. Moreover, the residences of the victims of white-collar crimes are probably widely dispersed throughout the metropolitan area, and often throughout the nation or the world.

Chapter 9 explores the way that the routine activities approach explains the geographic distribution of crime in terms of the joint presence of motivated offenders, suitable targets, and a lack of guardianship.

Migration and Crime

There are several reasons that immigrants might have higher crime rates than the native-born residents of a country. Migrants are frequently young males, a group particularly prone to crime in all societies. Moving often disrupts ties to family, friends, and community, thereby weakening traditional controls over deviant behavior. Housing discrimination and lack of resources can force new immigrants to settle in high-crime communities. In addition, there is usually more affluence in the nation to which migrants move than in the country from which they came, and this both provides more opportunities for crime and creates a sense of material deprivation conducive to crime.

During the first few decades of the twentieth century, there was a widespread feeling among native-born Americans that the nation's high crime rate was due to recent immigrants. In *Culture Conflict and Crime,* one of the first studies of the relationship between migration and crime, Thorsten Sellin (1938) showed that immigrants did not have crime rates higher than native-born Americans. In fact, for many crimes and for many nationalities, the immigrants' rates were lower. However, the crime rates of successive generations of the children of immigrants became more like the crime rates of the native-born, suggesting that crime is a learned behavior and that socialization into the dominant American culture is associated with rising crime rates for the offspring of immigrant groups that had lower rates when they came to the country.

In his introduction to a recent collection of essays on immigration and crime, Michael Tonry (1997: 22) states that "the multigeneration immigration and crime model based on American experience is simplistic and is only partly true even for the self-selected immigrants whose experience it describes." He then offers the following generalizations about the relationship between immigration and crime in certain European nations:

1. Self-selected economic migrants from many Asian cultures have lower crime rates than the resident population in the first and in subsequent generations. . . .
2. Cultural differences between structurally similarly situated immigrants can result in sharply different crime patterns. . . .
3. There are grounds for hypothesizing that, all else being equal, some countries' policies for aiding immigrants' assimilation can reduce crime rates, including those of their second- and third-generation descendants. . . .
4. The reasons groups migrate powerfully shape criminality and other indications of successful adaptation. . . .
5. Many categories of immigrants do not fall within any of the preceding generalizations. (Tonry, 1997: 22–24)

Another generalization is that compared to native-born residents, immigrants have high rates of criminal victimization, especially for violent offenses, and frequently by members of their own ethnic group (Marshall, 1997a).

Scholars warn against simplifying the multifaceted relationship between migration and crime. One reason to avoid generalizations is that there is often much diversity among the immigrants in a nation. For instance, Hans-Joerg Albrecht (1997) uncovered four distinct patterns of immigrant crime in the state of Hessen, Germany:

1. For immigrants from India, Afghanistan, Pakistan, and Ceylon, the most common offenses were immigration offenses, fraud, and forgery; the least common were property crimes.
2. For immigrants from Rumania, Poland, Bulgaria, and Russia, property and immigration offenses were common; violent and drug crimes were rare.
3. For immigrants from Turkey, property and violent offenses were relatively common; immigration offenses were rare.
4. Immigrants from Senegal, Gambia, Colombia, Morocco, Spain, Italy, and Turkey were significantly involved in drug offenses.

Not only do patterns of crime vary among immigrant groups, but those patterns often change with successive generations of each group.

In recent years, the globalization of national economies, the easing of immigration restrictions, and the fall of communist governments in eastern Europe have added a new dimension to the relationship between immigration and crime. Drug smugglers, arms dealers, terrorists, and money launderers now move freely across international borders, making the work of law-enforcement agents difficult and producing a new image of the "dangerous foreigner." Increasingly, criminal enterprises based in Russia, China, Japan, and other countries have expanded into nations where there are lucrative opportunities for illicit profits (Marshall, 1997b).

Temporal Variations in Crime Rates

So far we have seen that crime rates vary by country, by region within a country, and by size of the community. In this section, we will see that crime rates also vary over time

Seasonal Variations in Crime Rates

Some studies indicate that homicide is more common in some seasons than in others, but other research finds no such pattern. One comprehensive study concluded that "seasonal fluctuation, if it exists, may be too weak to affect practical policy or administrative decisions" (Block, 1984: 20). An investigation of homicide in Baltimore rejected the idea that there was a season for homicide, finding that it was somewhat more common in July, August, and December, but that month-to-month variations were not large enough to be statistically significant (Cheatwood, 1988).

FBI rates of rape fluctuate over the course of the year, peaking in July, diminishing steadily until February, and then rising again until the following July. In 2001, 9.7 percent of reported rapes occurred in July and only 7.2 percent in February (Federal Bureau of Investigation, 2002: 29). These variations probably reflect differences in the amount of social interaction that occurs in warm and cold weather.

Victimization data show that some crimes fluctuate with the season. The offenses that exhibit the greatest degree of seasonal variation are household larceny, unlawful entry, and rape. Personal larceny with contact, personal larceny of less than $50 without contact, aggravated assault, and attempted forcible entry vary to a moderate degree with the season. Personal larceny of $50 or more without contact, motor vehicle theft, robbery, forcible entry, and simple assault show little variation across seasons. The most common pattern of seasonal variation is for rates to be highest during the summer months and lowest in the winter months, but not all seasonal patterns are of this sort. The clearest exception to the general pattern is for personal larcenies of less than $50 without contact; rates for this offense are highest at the start of the school year from September to January and lowest in the summer months when school is out (Bureau of Justice Statistics, May 1988).

Seasonal variations are relatively small, but they must be explained by theories of crime. The Bureau of Justice Statistics (May 1988: 4) suggests the following approach:

> Individual behavior patterns change with the seasons and with them the opportunity for crime to occur. For example, people spend more time outside in the warmer weather, increasing the number of potential targets for street crime. Doors and windows in homes are more apt to be open or left unlocked at these times and thus provide easier access to intruders. More household articles are likely to be left outside, serving as invitations to theft. Patterns of economic activity may also be related to ebbs and flows of crime, especially the purchase of retail goods and services.

Annual Trends in Crime Rates

Figures 4.4 and 4.5 show fluctuations in rates of the FBI index crimes since 1960. Rates were relatively stable in the early 1960s, but they began to increase significantly around 1963. Since the mid-1970s, rates have declined in some years and increased in other years. Property crimes rates fell from 1991 to 2000, and violent crime rates dropped from 1992 to 2000. Some rates rose slightly from 2000 to 2001. These FBI data must be interpreted cautiously, for changes in crime reporting and recording might account for some of the changes.

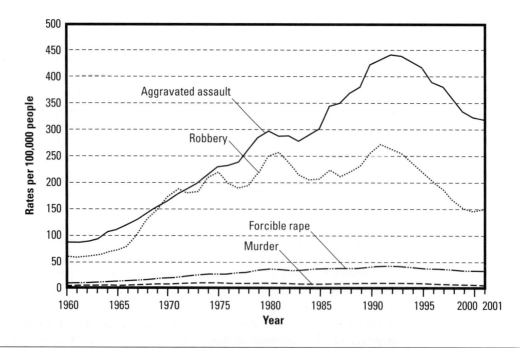

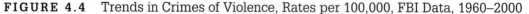

FIGURE 4.4   Trends in Crimes of Violence, Rates per 100,000, FBI Data, 1960–2000

Sources: FBI UCR data from Kathleen Maguire and Ann L. Pastore, eds., *Sourcebook of Criminal Justice Statistics 2000,* Table 3.120, pp. 278–279, retrieved from www.albany.edu/sourcebook; Federal Bureau of Investigation, *Crime in the United States 2001: Uniform Crime Reports,* Washington, DC: U.S. Government Printing Office, 2002, p. 65.

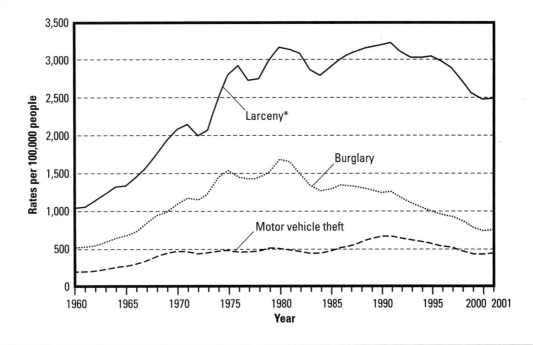

FIGURE 4.5 Trends in Crimes against Property, Rates per 100,000 People, FBI Data, 1960–2000

*Until 1972, the FBI counted only larcenies over $50 as index crimes. From 1973 to the present, it has counted all larcenies as index crimes.

Sources: FBI UCR data from Kathleen Maguire and Ann L. Pastore, eds., *Sourcebook of Criminal Justice Statistics 2000,* Table 3.120, pp. 278–279, retrieved from www.albany.edu/sourcebook; Federal Bureau of Investigation, *Crime in the United States 2001: Uniform Crime Reports,* Washington, DC: U.S. Government Printing Office, 2002, p. 65.

NCVS rates of property crime declined steadily and significantly from 1975 to 2001. Victimization rates for violent crime fell from 1981 to 1986, rose from 1986 to 1993, and then dropped again from 1994 to 2001 (see Figures 4.6 and 4.7). From 1973 to 2001, NCVS victimization rates sometimes decreased while FBI rates increased, but both types of data indicate that crime rates have declined in recent years. The reasons most commonly given for this decline are greater police effectiveness, a growth in the number of offenders who are in prison, the waning of the crack epidemic of the 1980s, more community involvement in crime prevention, a booming economy with plentiful job opportunities, and a drop in the proportion of the population in the crime-prone age groups.

Variations in Crime Rates by Sex

Not everyone is equally likely to commit a crime or to be the victim of one. Offense rates and victimization rates vary with social characteristics such as sex, age, race, and social class.

Perhaps the best predictor of whether an individual will violate the law is sex: Men commit much more crime than women in every society for which we have data. Even though male-female differences in crime rates vary from one society to another, over time, and from one offense to another, sex is a primary factor differentiating criminals from noncriminals. This could be partly a result of hormonal differences that make men more aggressive than women (see Chapter 5), but it is more likely the

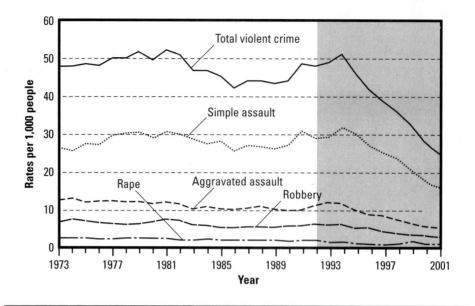

FIGURE 4.6 Violent Crime Victimization Rates per 1,000 People Age 12 or Older, 1973–2001

Note: Data for 1973 to 1991 were collected under the National Crime Survey (NCS) and were made comparable to data collected under the redesigned methods of the NCVS that began in 1992.

Source: Callie Rennison, *Criminal Victimization 2001: Changes 2000–01 with Trends 1993–2001.* Washington, DC: U.S. Department of Justice, September 2002, p. 2.

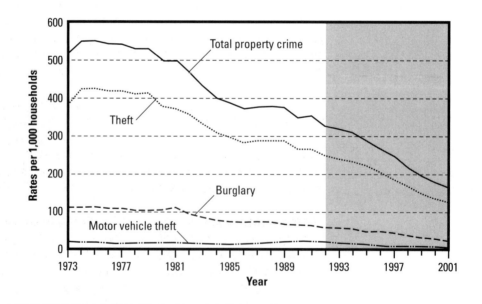

FIGURE 4.7 Property Crime Victimization Rates per 1,000 Households, 1973–2001

Note: Data for 1973 to 1991 were collected under the National Crime Survey (NCS) and were made comparable to data collected under the redesigned methods of the NCVS that began in 1992.

Source: Callie Rennison, *Criminal Victimization 2001: Changes 2000–01 with Trends 1993–2001.* Washington, DC: U.S. Department of Justice, September 2002, p. 2.

result of differences in the socialization of males and females. Boys and girls, and men and women, are taught to behave differently and play different roles. This socialization process, in combination with a social structure that assigns statuses to people on the basis of sex, leads to differences in personality, behavior, and opportunities that are linked to the large difference in crime rates between males and females.

Sex and Juvenile Delinquency

To examine male-female differences most fruitfully, we must look at juvenile delinquency and adult crime separately. Delinquency includes acts that are crimes when committed by adults, but it also includes juvenile status offenses (such as running away from home) that are prohibited only for those below a certain age. Because delinquency is defined so broadly, differences in expected behavior for boys and girls influence the way that each sex is treated by the juvenile justice system.

In 2001, the five offenses for which boys under the age of eighteen were most often arrested were larceny, drug abuse violations, simple assaults, disorderly conduct, and curfew and loitering law violations. For girls under eighteen, the top five offenses were larceny, running away from home, simple assaults, disorderly conduct, and curfew and loitering law violations. The only Part I or Part II offenses for which more girls than boys were arrested were running away and prostitution and commercialized vice. For all Part I and Part II offenses, there were 2.5 times as many boys as girls arrested.

FBI arrest data indicate that the percentage of all arrested suspects under eighteen who were female increased from 15.3 percent in 1963 to 28.4 percent in 2001, evidence that girls became more like boys in their rate of delinquency over that period. This trend also characterized the arrests of young people for major violent crimes (murder and nonnegligent manslaughter, robbery, and aggravated assault, with rape excluded because few females are arrested for that offense). In 1963, 7.9 percent of arrests for these three violent crimes were of females, but by 2001 the figure was up to 19.0 percent.

Self-report studies indicate that when a girl commits an act that would be a crime if committed by an adult, she is less likely than a boy to be reported to the

Girls are more likely than boys to be brought into juvenile court for status offenses, but girls are less likely than boys to be arrested for offenses that would be crimes if committed by adults.

police or to be dealt with in court (Chesney-Lind, 1973, 1997). Boys who engage in conventional crimes are more likely to be arrested by the police and brought before a juvenile court, partly because of the widely held opinions that girls are not as bad as boys and that girls who violate the law are led into crime by bad male companions.

For juvenile status offenses, girls are actually more likely than boys to be arrested by the police and brought into court (Chesney-Lind, 1973, 1997; Canter, 1982; Ericsson, 1998). A girl who runs away from home, drinks alcoholic beverages, violates curfew ordinances, or has sexual relations is more likely to become involved with the legal system than is a boy who does the same things. This difference in treatment by the juvenile justice system is related to norms about appropriate gender-role behavior: Boys are expected to "raise hell" but girls are expected to be "well behaved." These expectations lead to more surveillance and control of adolescent girls than of adolescent boys, and they result in more arrests and court appearances for girls than would be expected on the basis of sex differences in self-reported status offenses.

Sex and Crime

In addition to the male-female differential in juvenile arrests, there is a significant difference between the sexes in adult arrests. In 2001, 3.7 times as many men as women aged eighteen and over were arrested. This is a higher ratio than that for juveniles. In other words, adult crime is even more of a male phenomenon than juvenile delinquency.

For people of all ages, more males than females are arrested for each of the eight index crimes (see Figure 4.8). In 2001, males were four-fifths or more of all suspects arrested for every index crime except larceny; 63.5 percent of the suspects arrested for that crime were males. Despite the predominance of males among suspects arrested for index crimes, there have been important changes over recent decades in the proportion of women arrested for those offenses.

Trends in Arrests of Females   In 1963, females of all ages were 12 percent of all suspects arrested for index crimes, but by 2001 the proportion had risen to 27 per-

---

FIGURE 4.8   Arrests by Sex

Source: Based on data from Federal Bureau of Investigation, *Crime in the United States, 2001: Uniform Crime Reports.* Washington, DC: U.S. Government Printing Office, 2002, p. 251.

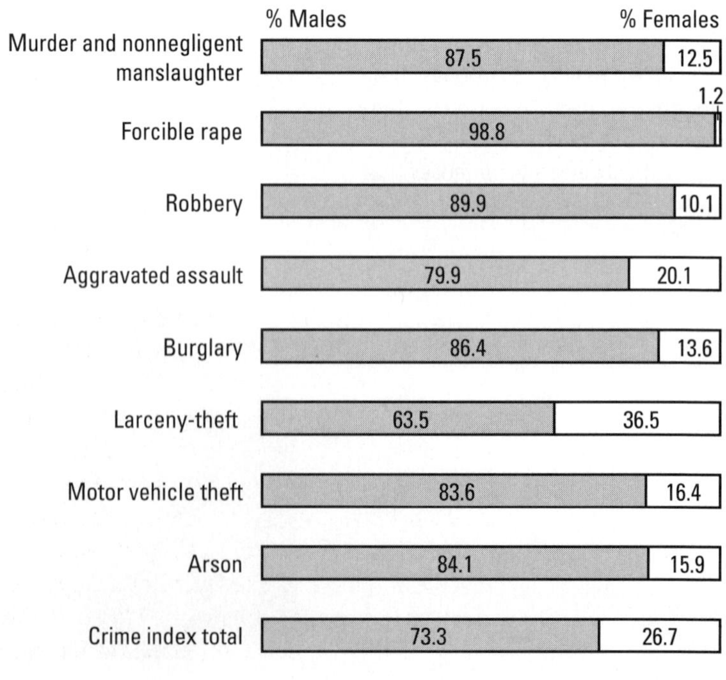

	% Males	% Females
Murder and nonnegligent manslaughter	87.5	12.5
Forcible rape	98.8	1.2
Robbery	89.9	10.1
Aggravated assault	79.9	20.1
Burglary	86.4	13.6
Larceny-theft	63.5	36.5
Motor vehicle theft	83.6	16.4
Arson	84.1	15.9
Crime index total	73.3	26.7

cent. Most of that increase occurred between 1963 and 1976, and most of it was due to the increased proportion of females arrested for larceny, by far the most common index crime for which arrests are made. In 1963, 19 percent of larceny suspects were females, but by 1973 the proportion had climbed to 32 percent, a figure that did not change much thereafter. Without self-report data for females for 1963 and 1973, we cannot determine if the increase in the proportion of larceny suspects who were females reflects an actual increase in theft by females over that time. Perhaps the arrest practices of store detectives and the police changed during that period. One response to the big increase in FBI crime rates over that time may have been a decision to arrest thieves in 1973 who might have been warned and released in 1963.

From 1963 to 2001, there were increases in the proportions of suspects who were females for the crimes of robbery (from 5 to 10 percent), aggravated assault (from 14 to 20 percent), burglary (from 3 to 14 percent), and motor vehicle theft (from 4 to 16 percent). The proportion of females arrested for murder declined from 18 to 13 percent.

Women and White-Collar Crime   In a study of employee theft in a large retail organization, data gathered from personnel records, from files kept by the company's security force, and from interviews conducted with the firm's officials revealed that male employees committed more thefts and took more when they did steal than was true of female employees. Of 447 known dishonest workers, 56 percent were men, even though only 40 percent of the company's work force was male (Franklin, 1979). This study suggests that given similar on-the-job opportunities for theft, men commit crime more often than women, even though we would expect crime by women to increase somewhat as they gain more opportunities to steal on the job (Figueira-McDonough and Selo, 1980).

A study of white-collar offenders convicted in federal courts found that a surprisingly high 17.5 percent of them were female. Nearly as many women as men were convicted of bank embezzlement. The crimes committed by the women in the sample were, on the average, of less organizational complexity and had less impact on victims than was true of the offenses committed by men. However, women in the same positions as men seemed to inflict as much harm as men, suggesting that the reason for the overall lesser degree of harm inflicted by women was that they were less likely to hold positions that provided access to the organizational resources needed to commit serious white-collar crimes (Weisburd et al., 1991). Unlike the study of employee theft, this research suggests that women commit as much and as serious white-collar crime as men when given the opportunity to do so.

Sex and Victimization

FBI UCR data for 2001 show that males are the victims of homicide 3.3 times as often as females. Both male and female victims are usually killed by males. NCVS studies find that males are more likely than females to be the victims of robbery and assault, equally likely to be victims of nonviolent thefts, and much less likely to be the victims of rape and sexual assault (see Figure 4.9).

A national telephone survey of 8,000 women and 8,000 men found that 52 percent of women and 66 percent of men said they had been physically assaulted at some point in their life; 18 percent of women and 3 percent of men had been the victim of a rape or attempted rape. Most violence against women was partner violence, with 76 percent of the women who had been raped or assaulted since the age of eighteen being victimized by a partner. Only 14 percent of women who had been raped or assaulted had been victimized by strangers. In contrast, only 18 percent of male victims of such violence had been victimized by partners; 60 percent had been victimized by strangers (Tjaden and Thoennes, November 1998).

FIGURE 4.9 Victimizations per 1,000 People Age Twelve and Older, by Sex, 2001

Source: Based on Callie Rennison, *Criminal Victimization 2001: Changes 2000–01 with Trends 1993–2001.* Washington, DC: U.S. Department of Justice, September 2002, p. 6.

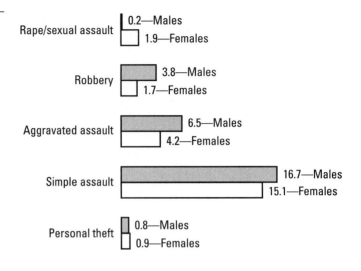

Variations in Crime Rates by Age

Crimes are disproportionately committed by adolescents and young adults. In 2001, when only 14 percent of the U.S. population was between the ages of fifteen and twenty-four, 45 percent of all arrests for index crimes were of people in that age bracket. Overall, 26 percent of suspects arrested for index crimes in 2001 were under eighteen and 54 percent were under twenty-five. Suspects arrested for property crimes tend to be younger than those arrested for violent crimes (Federal Bureau of Investigation, 2002: 244–245).

Age-Specific Arrest Rates

Arrest data do not provide a perfect picture of how involvement in crime varies with age, because young offenders may be more or less likely than older ones to be arrested for any given crime. Arrest data do, however, suggest that there are important age differences in criminal behavior.

Because the rates at which people are arrested vary with age, arrest rates for a whole society can mask important trends for different age groups. For instance, between 1985 and 1993, there was a dramatic increase in the arrest of juveniles for homicide, especially homicides committed with handguns (Blumstein, 1995). Over this time, the homicide arrest rate for people twenty-five and over declined by 20 percent, while the rate for eighteen to twenty-four year olds increased by 65 percent and the rate for fourteen to seventeen year olds rose by 165 percent (Fox, 1995).

Table 4.1 gives the **age-specific arrest rates**—or number of arrests per 100,000 people in each age category—for the crime of robbery for 1970, 1980, 1990, and 2000, four census years. We can see that in each year there is considerable variation in arrest rates among age groups. In each year, the arrest rates rose to a peak at age seventeen or eighteen and then declined with age. Age-specific arrest rates were higher for all age groups in 1980 than in 1970. From 1980 to 1990, robbery arrest rates decreased for all ages up to twenty-three but increased for all age groups between twenty-four and forty-four; this pattern might be the result of the aging of a cohort especially prone to commit robbery. Robbery arrest rates fell markedly for every age group from 1990 to 2000, reflecting the precipitous decline in the nation's crime rates during that decade.

Peak ages and age-specific arrest rates vary considerably from one offense to another. For all index crimes, 26.2 percent of the suspects arrested in 2001 were under

TABLE 4.1   Robbery Arrests per 100,000 People for Age Groups,
1970, 1980, 1990, and 2000

| Age Group | NUMBER OF ROBBERY ARRESTS PER 100,000 PEOPLE | | | |
	1970	1980	1990	2000
Under 15	16.7	19.4	16.6	8.1
15	139.4	211.9	196.0	88.8
16	172.9	265.5	255.0	109.6
17	189.7	292.5	268.4	135.9
18	197.5	281.2	267.0	151.1
19	194.9	242.7	225.6	134.3
20	172.2	210.6	191.2	109.8
21	165.1	196.0	180.3	94.7
22	142.1	166.2	165.7	79.8
23	121.8	155.3	155.1	67.2
24	122.0	140.2	147.8	55.0
25–29	75.8	99.0	110.8	41.7
30–34	40.4	55.5	70.7	33.8
35–39	21.9	30.0	38.9	25.1
40–44	11.6	17.1	18.6	15.9
45–49	6.2	9.7	9.1	7.6
50 and over	1.5	2.2	1.6	1.3
All ages	43.1	61.6	54.8	25.7

Sources: Rates calculated from data in Federal Bureau of Investigation, *Crime in the United States: Uniform Crime Reports,* Washington, DC: U.S. Government Printing Office, 1970, 1980, 1990, and 2000 volumes; U.S. Department of Commerce, Bureau of the Census, *General Population Characteristics: United States,* Washington, DC: U.S. Government Printing Office, 1970, 1980, 1990, and 2000 volumes.

eighteen, and their median age was twenty-three. For the four violent crimes, only 15.4 percent were under eighteen, and their median age was about twenty-seven. Suspects in violent crimes were generally older than suspects in property crimes, with 30.4 percent of property crime suspects being under eighteen and their median age being twenty-one.

Age Distribution and Crime Rates

Because arrest rates differ by age group and because this seems to reflect a difference among age groups in actual involvement in criminal activity, a society can experience an increase or decrease in its crime rate if the age distribution of its population changes. In other words, if the young have an especially high crime rate, a society with a large proportion of young people in its population at one time will have a higher overall crime rate than it would have at a different time when a smaller proportion of its population is young.

The post–World War II "baby boom" produced a significant increase in the proportion of the American population in the high-crime-rate years from fifteen to twenty-four in the 1960s; between 1960 and 1975, the size of that age group increased about six times as fast as the rest of the population. The dramatic increase in official crime rates during the 1960s is due in part to the increased proportion of the population in this high-crime-rate age group (President's Commission on Law Enforcement and Administration of Justice, 1967). (See the Using Criminology box.)

Although changing age distribution explains some of the increase in index crime rates in the United States during the 1960s and 1970s, it does not explain most of it. Instead, there was an increase in the rate at which people of every age committed crime. Looking at changes in the rate of violent index crimes from 1960 to 1970, for instance, we find that changes in the age distribution would have led us to expect a 40 to 50 percent increase in the rate of those offenses, but instead there was a 200 percent increase (Silberman, 1978). The important theoretical question thus becomes

USING CRIMINOLOGY

Can Curfews Stop Juvenile Crime?

"What if you've done your homework and you're a really good kid and you're out at a movie or something? It's, like, you're automatically guilty until you prove yourself innocent. . . . It's just so unfair and unconstitutional." (cited in Pertman, p. 1). This sixteen-year-old San Diego girl is reacting to her city's curfew law that requires her to be home by 10 P.M. during the week or face a $100 fine. Similar laws now exist in more than one thousand American communities, including three-fourths of the nation's 200 largest cities. A smaller number of cities have enacted daytime curfews to curb truancy by students during the week. Seventeen is the usual upper age limit for those restricted by curfews, but some cities set the age at fifteen or sixteen.

Curfews are aimed at curbing youth crime, particularly gang violence and drive-by shootings. Based on evidence that those under eighteen account for a disproportionate number of both offenders and victims, curfew laws seek to control potential offenders and protect potential victims by reducing opportunities for crime. These laws empower the police to disperse young people who congregate in public late at night and to question youths who are on the street after curfew. They also provide parents with legal support for restricting their children's nighttime activities.

Critics argue that curfew laws deny young people equal protection of the law, restrict their freedom of movement and association, are used in a racially discriminatory fashion, and intrude on the right of parents to

raise their children as they wish. When the courts have ruled curfews invalid, however, it has not been on these grounds, but rather because the ordinances are too vague and broad. Ordinances that specify legitimate excuses for young people to be in public after curfew have been viewed favorably by the courts.

Many municipal officials believe that curfews cut crime, but criminologists are skeptical. Research suggests that curfews might not be effective because most violent juvenile crime is not committed during typical nighttime curfew hours. National Incident-Based Reporting System data gathered by the FBI reveal that on school days juveniles are more likely to commit serious violent crime, as well as to be the victims of such crime, during the hours immediately after school closes. An evaluation of curfews in California for the period from 1980 to 1997 concluded as follows:

> The consistent result of this analysis is that curfew enforcement (even the strongest) has no effect on crime, youth crime, or youth safety no matter what the time period, jurisdiction, or type of crime measure studied (Males and Macallair, 1999: 18).

Only slightly less pessimistic were the conclusions of a study of fifty-seven cities that any effects of juvenile curfew laws are small, applicable to only a few crimes, and do not "encourage the idea that curfews help prevent juvenile crime" (McDowall, Loftin, and Wiersema, 2000: 89).

Sources: Based on Adam Pertman, "In by 10: Curfews for Minors Spur Debate," *Boston Globe,* January 17, 1996, pp. 1, 12; Mike A. Males and Dan Macallair, "An Analysis of Curfew Enforcement and Juvenile Crime in California," *Western Criminology Review* 1 (1999) (http://wcr.sonoma.edu/v1n2/males.html); Office of Juvenile Justice and Delinquency Prevention, *Violence after School,* Washington, DC: U.S. Department of Justice, November 1999; David McDowall, Colin Loftin, and Brian Wiersema, "The Impact of Youth Curfew Laws on Juvenile Crime Rates," *Crime and Delinquency* 46 (January 2000), 76–91.

what social changes, in addition to change in the age distribution of the population, produced the increase in the crime rate.

Just as an increasingly youthful population can be expected to have rising crime rates, so too should an increasingly older population have declining crime rates. Recent research indicates that the decline in property crime rates from 1980 to 1984 can be attributed largely to a change in the age structure of the population, with reductions in larceny and motor vehicle theft rates being the most influenced by the aging of the population (Cohen and Land, 1987; Steffensmeier and Harer, 1987). One study found that changes in violent crime rates were not explained by the changing age structure of the population (Steffensmeier and Harer, 1987), but another study concluded that the decline in homicide rates during the early 1980s did reflect changes in the age structure over that period (Cohen and Land, 1987).

When crime rates fell in the 1990s, some criminologists pointed to an aging population as one explanation. Change in the age structure did contribute modestly to the drop in crime rates from 1990 to 1999, accounting for 20 percent of the decline in the murder rate, 17 percent of the decline in the robbery rate, 12 percent of the decline in the burglary rate, and 8 percent of the decline in the motor vehicle theft rate (Conklin, 2003). However, the rate at which people of all ages committed crime fell dramatically during the 1990s, so factors other than change in the age structure accounted for most of the reduction in crime rates during the decade.

Age and Victimization

Adolescents and young adults have the highest rates of criminal victimization. Murder victimization rates increase with age to a peak for eighteen to twenty-one year olds, then decrease with age (Perkins, 1997). Victimization rates for rape and sexual assault, robbery, aggravated assault, and personal theft rise with age to a peak for sixteen to nineteen year olds and then steadily decline for successive age groups (Rennison, 2002).

The NCVS has found that people sixty-five and above have lower victimization rates than any other group over the age of twelve, except for personal theft. In contrast to violent crimes against younger victims, offenses against elderly victims are more likely to be committed by strangers, by armed offenders, in or near the victims' homes, and during the day (Klaus, 2000). The characteristics of the crime incidents in which the elderly are involved might explain their high level of fear of crime, which exists despite their apparently low rates of actual victimization. There might also be a sense in which the elderly do have a high rate of victimization: They may be at risk less often than younger people because they do not usually go to work, they often live in age-segregated housing (including nursing homes), and they frequently stay indoors out of fear or infirmity. If victimization rates are calculated in terms of their time at risk, the elderly's victimization rate might actually be as high as or even higher than that of younger people (Lundquist and Duke, 1982; Stafford and Galle, 1984).

Variations in Crime Rates by Race

Variations in crime rates by racial and ethnic group reflect social, cultural, and economic differences among groups. In the past, some have suggested that such variations in crime rates are due to biological differences among racial and ethnic groups, but it is now well established that any biological differences among racial and ethnic groups are unimportant in explaining differences in crime rates.

Researchers have investigated the relationship between crime rates and the racial composition of nations. J. Philippe Rushton (1995) concluded that predominantly black nations have higher violent crime rates than predominantly white nations and that Asian nations have the lowest rates. He attributed the difference between black nations and white nations to inheritable differences between the races in intelligence, sex hormones, and aggression. Critics have assailed Rushton's uncritical use of international crime data, his failure to explain variations in racial groups' crime rates across nations and over time in the same nation, his neglect of historical context, and his inattention to the social and economic correlates of racial composition. An analysis of cross-national homicide rates by Jerome Neapolitan (1998) found that race had a very small and statistically insignificant association with variations in homicide rates across nations, once those nations' income inequality, standard of living, ethnic heterogeneity, household size, urbanization, and age composition were taken into account.

Looking at cross-national research on the relationship between crime and racial or ethnic minority status, Michael Tonry (1997: 12–18) reached the following conclusions:

1. In every country, crime and incarceration rates for members of some minority groups greatly exceed those for the majority population. . . .
2. Minority groups characterized by high crime and imprisonment rates are also characterized by various indicators of social and economic disadvantage. . . .

CRIME AND THE MEDIA

Race and the Student-Murderer

Despite evidence that fewer students were killed in school in 1997 than in 1993, the media conveyed the impression that lethal violence by students was rampant from 1996 to 1999. The following cases made headlines:

- *February 2, 1996.* Barry Loukaitis, fourteen, killed three and wounded one when he fired on an algebra class in his Moses Lake, Washington, middle school.
- *February 19, 1997.* Evan Ramsey, sixteen, shot to death a student and a principal in his Bethel, Alaska, high school.
- *October 1, 1997.* Luke Woodham, sixteen, killed his mother; then he shot two students to death and wounded seven others at a Pearl, Mississippi, high school.
- *December 1, 1997.* Michael Carneal, fourteen, killed three and wounded five when he fired on a prayer group outside a West Paducah, Kentucky, high school.
- *March 24, 1998.* Andrew Golden, ten, and Mitchell Johnson, thirteen, killed a teacher and four students and wounded ten others after the victims left a Jonesboro, Arkansas, middle school when the killers set off a fire alarm.
- *April 24, 1998.* Andrew Wurst, fourteen, killed a teacher and wounded two students at a middle school dance in Edinboro, Pennsylvania.

- *May 21, 1998.* Kipland Kinkel, fifteen, killed his parents; then he shot two students to death and wounded twenty-two others in a Springfield, Oregon, high school.
- *April 20, 1999.* Eric Harris, eighteen, and Dylan Klebold, seventeen, used assault weapons and homemade bombs in an attack on their Littleton, Colorado, high school in which they killed twelve students, one teacher, and then themselves.

These murderers had certain things in common:

1. Each case involved a child who felt inferior or picked on, with a grudge against some student or teacher. . . .
2. The killers were able to easily acquire high-powered guns, and in many cases their parents helped the children get them, either directly or through negligence. . . .
3. To varying degrees, each of the attackers seemed to have been obsessed by violent pop culture. . . .
4. The student killers gave ample warning signs, often in detailed writings at school, of dramatic, violent outbursts to come. (Egan, pp. 1, 22)

The killers had something else in common: They were all white. The descriptions of these killers in the

3. In countries in which research has been conducted on the causes of racial and ethnic disparities in imprisonment, group differences in offending, not invidious bias, appear to be the principal cause. . . .
4. Seemingly neutral case processing practices, especially pretrial confinement decisions and sentence reductions for guilty pleas, operate to the systematic disadvantage of members of minority groups. . . .
5. Subcultural behaviors and stereotypes sometimes associated with minority group members often work to their disadvantage in contacts with the justice system.

Race, Arrest Statistics, and Self-Report Studies

The FBI presents arrest data for whites, blacks, American Indian or Alaskan Natives, and Asian or Pacific Islanders. FBI data do not allow us to analyze differences in arrest rates for white ethnic groups such as Irish Americans, Italian Americans, Eastern Europeans, or Jews. However, sociological research has found that crime rates for Jews, Japanese Americans, and Chinese Americans are lower than rates for the total population, whereas crime rates for African Americans and Mexican Americans are higher than rates for the total population (Wolfgang, Figlio, and Sellin, 1972; Tracy, Wolfgang, and Figlio, 1990). (See the Crime and the Media box.)

This memorial is for the Columbine High School teacher and twelve students who were killed in 1999 by Eric Harris and Dylan Klebold.

press were remarkably different from the descriptions typically used for young black and Latino males accused of murder. Luke Woodham was described as "the chubby, poor kid at Pearl High School who always seemed to get picked on," a "nerd," and "intelligent but isolated." Michael Carneal was described as "a solid B

student," and Mitchell Johnson and Andrew Golden were called "little boys." Andrew Wurst was described as a "shy and quirky eighth-grader with an offbeat sense of humor." Columbine High School students remarked on Eric Harris and Dylan Klebold's "flashes of humor, intellect, and kindness." *Newsweek* described Kipland Kinkel as follows: "With his shy smile and slight build, 15-year-old Kip Kinkel has an innocent look that is part Huck Finn and part Alfred E. Neuman—boyish and quintessentially American."

Roxbury (Massachusetts) District Court Judge Milton Wright responded, "Quintessentially American. That always means white." Sociologist Darnell Hawkins commented on these descriptions of white student-murderers as follows: "Never is an African-American kid or a Latino kid described as being an all-American kid." Characterizing young black and Latino murderers as "superpredators" while portraying young white murderers as too small, intelligent, or innocent to have committed their crimes is, according to political scientist Franklin Gilliam, "thinly veiled racial coding. They might have said this is a normal kid, but to say he's Huck Finn is a little much."

Sources: Based on Tamar Lewin, "Despite Recent Carnage, School Violence Is Not on Rise," *New York Times,* December 3, 1997, p. A16; Timothy Egan, "From Adolescent Angst to Shooting Up Schools," *New York Times,* June 14, 1998, pp. 1, 22; Steve Fainaru, "Killing in the Classroom: Many Struggle to Put Their World Together," *Boston Globe,* October 20, 1998, pp. A1, A20, A21; Zachary R. Dowdy, "Race: Who Pulled the Trigger?" *Boston Globe,* June 21, 1998, pp. E1, E3 (all quotations from Dowdy).

Ninety-eight percent of all arrests in 2001 for FBI index crimes were of whites or blacks. In that year, blacks were 12.7 percent of the U.S. population, but they accounted for 33.1 percent of arrests for index crimes. Blacks constituted 37.6 percent of arrests for crimes of violence and 31.4 percent of arrests for property crimes. For each index crime, blacks are arrested out of proportion to their numbers in the population. Table 4.2 shows the rates of arrest per 100,000 people of the same race for whites and for blacks; the third column shows the ratios of blacks' arrest rates to whites' arrest rates. Overall, blacks have an arrest rate for index crimes that is 3.3 times as great as the rate for whites.

We must be wary of using FBI arrest data, for they can distort actual involvement in index crimes by blacks and whites if the police are more likely to arrest black suspects than they are to arrest white suspects. However, most criminologists agree that arrest statistics for blacks and whites reflect a real difference between the groups in their rates of committing crimes and that the difference in arrests between the racial groups is not primarily a result of discriminatory arrest practices by the police. Chapter 13 examines racial discrimination by the police, the courts, and the prisons.

Some self-report research finds a higher frequency of all delinquent acts by blacks (Elliott and Ageton, 1980), but other studies find that blacks and whites report similar involvement in all delinquent acts (Tracy, 1987). Blacks and whites are more similar in their self-reported involvement in relatively trivial delinquent acts, but blacks seem to report committing serious offenses more often than whites (Elliott and Ageton, 1980; Tracy, 1987).

Race, Crime, and Background Variables

Differences in crime rates among racial and ethnic groups are a function of group differences in age, income, occupation, education, family background, place of residence, and other social characteristics, as well as a function of differences in opportunities to commit crime. This suggests that if blacks and whites of similar

TABLE 4.2   Rates of Arrest per 100,000 People, 2001

CRIME	WHITE RATE OF ARREST PER 100,000 PEOPLE	BLACK RATE OF ARREST PER 100,000 PEOPLE	RATIO OF BLACK TO WHITE RATE
Murder	2.0	12.8	6.4
Forcible rape	5.1	18.0	3.5
Robbery	15.0	115.2	7.7
Aggravated assault	92.5	310.0	3.4
Burglary	60.5	158.0	2.6
Larceny	233.2	701.2	3.0
Motor vehicle theft	25.8	114.0	4.4
Arson	4.3	7.4	1.7
Total index crime	438.4	1,436.6	3.3

Sources: Arrest rates are calculated using Bureau of the Census estimates for 2001 on the number of whites (227,883,000) and blacks (35,784,000) and arrest data from Federal Bureau of Investigation, *Crime in the United States, 2001: Uniform Crime Reports,* Washington, DC: U.S. Government Printing Office, 2002, p. 253.

social backgrounds are compared, differences in crime rates between the groups will be reduced or eliminated. However, to suggest that people of different races but similar social characteristics will have the same crime rate is tantamount to suggesting that there are no cultural differences between the groups that result in different crime rates. More specifically, to argue that blacks and whites with similar social characteristics will have the same crime rate is to argue that centuries of discrimination have had no long-term effects on blacks that are conducive to criminal behavior.

Wolfgang, Figlio, and Sellin's (1972) cohort study revealed that 29 percent of the whites had had police contacts as juveniles, compared with 50 percent of the blacks. Even when blacks and whites of similar social class were compared, blacks were more likely to have had police contacts. Thus, 53 percent of lower-class blacks had had police contacts as juveniles, compared with only 36 percent of lower-class whites. Thirty-six percent of higher-class blacks had had police contacts, compared with only 26 percent of higher-class whites. From those figures, we can see that blacks of the higher class were actually as likely as whites of the lower class to have had contact with the police.

Evidence suggests that blacks have higher crime rates than whites, even when individuals of similar backgrounds are compared, but that differences between the groups are reduced in comparisons of people of similar backgrounds. Research in Philadelphia found that blacks committed murder and rape at higher rates than whites with similar occupations (Wolfgang, 1958; Amir, 1971). A more recent study showed that at low socioeconomic levels blacks engaged in more violent behavior than whites, but that at high socioeconomic levels the two groups engaged in similar amounts of violent behavior (Paschall, Flewelling, and Ennett, 1998).

Race and Victimization

While pointing out that the sources of high crime rates among blacks are in the larger society, African American leaders have focused attention on the problem of black-on-black crime. Jesse Jackson has remarked, "I am rather convinced that the premier civil rights issue of this day is youth violence in general and black-on-black crime in particular. It's clear now that we must look inward to go onward" (cited in Rezendes, 1993: 1). Harvard Medical School professor Alvin Toussaint has commented,

> Yes, we can talk about the ongoing discrimination that affects our communities. But we also have to say to people: "You pulled that trigger. You committed that burglary. And you can't do it anymore because you're destroying your community." (cited in Rezendes, 1993: 4)

Blacks are disproportionately likely to be the victims of murder. In 2001, 46.9 percent of all homicide victims were black, although only 12.7 percent of the population was black. According to a Bureau of Justice Statistics report (Greenfeld and Smith, 1999), the average annual murder victimization rate per 100,000 people from 1992 to 1996 varied by racial group as follows:

Blacks	34
American Indians	7
Whites	5
Asians	5

About seven months of the six-year gap in life expectancy between blacks and whites is accounted for by the higher rate at which blacks are murdered (McClam, 2001).

Black males between fifteen and twenty-four are murdered at a rate seven times the rate for the rest of the population; indeed, murder is the primary cause of death for this group. As a result, some health officials have argued that the high murder rate of young black males should be considered a public health issue in the same way that diseases are.

Figure 4.10 shows NCVS victimization rates for 2000 for Hispanics and four non-Hispanic groups: whites, blacks, American Indians, and Asians. American Indians have the highest rates for simple assault, aggravated assault, and rape and other sexual assault. Blacks have the highest rate for robbery, and the second highest rates for the other crimes. Compared to the rates for non-Hispanic whites, the rates for Hispanics are slightly lower for simple assault and rape and other sexual assault, the same for aggravated assault, and higher for robbery.

Violent crime typically involves a victim and an offender of the same race. A disproportionately high number of all murders involve a black offender and a black victim, and most other murders involve a white offender and a white victim. In 2001, only 11.3 percent of murders crossed racial lines; three-fifths of those cross-racial murders involved a black offender and a white victim. About three-fourths of forcible rapes involve an offender and a victim of the same race, with black rapist–white victim offenses being the most common kind of cross-racial rape. The majority of robberies involve a victim and an offender of the same race, but nearly two-fifths of white victims are robbed by black offenders (Curtis, 1974; O'Brien, 1987; Whitaker, 1990; Federal Bureau of Investigation, 2002).

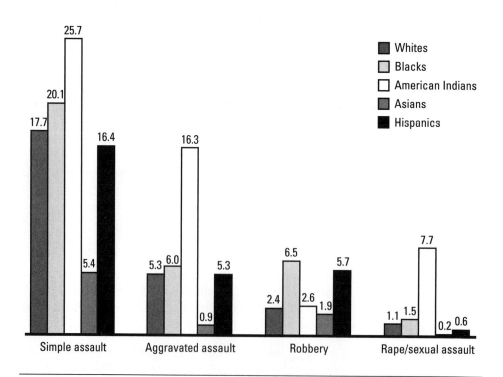

FIGURE 4.10   Victimizations per 1,000 People Age Twelve and Older, by Racial and Ethnic Group, 2000

Note: Rates for whites, blacks, American Indians, and Asians are for non-Hispanic persons.

Source: Based on Callie Rennison, *Hispanic Victims of Violent Crime, 1993–2000.* Washington, DC: U.S. Department of Justice, April 2002, p. 2.

Variations in Crime Rates by Social Class

When criminologists examine the relationship between crime and **social class**—which is defined as social standing based on economic resources, occupational prestige, political power, or lifestyle—they usually look at conventional crimes such as murder, rape, robbery, and larceny. However, the most expensive crimes are white-collar crimes, so we can conclude that the cost of crime is attributable primarily to violation of the law by people of relatively high social standing, even though "the crime problem" defined by the FBI, the media, and the public usually refers to violations of the law most often committed by the lower and working classes.

Popular wisdom is that the lower and working classes engage in more crime, or at least more of the most serious conventional crime, than does the middle class. This view has existed for centuries and characterizes societies other than the United States. People act on their assumption that there is a relationship between crime and social class: They avoid lower-class communities after dark and expect to be safer when they move from the city to the suburbs.

FBI statistics include no information on the social class of arrested suspects, nor do victimization surveys provide us with that information, because victims could not be expected to judge in a reliable way the social class of the offender. There is, however, much research that has examined the relationship of social class to crime and delinquency. Unfortunately, that research does not lead to a simple conclusion.

Social Class and Adult Crime

When we look at official measures of crime produced by the police, the courts, or the prisons, we find "a small but consistent inverse correlation of social class with street crime" for adults (Hindelang, 1983: 180). For instance, one review of forty-six studies that used arrest data found consistently higher crime rates for lower-class adults (Braithwaite, 1979, 1981).

From the few studies that have been done of adult criminality using self-report questionnaires, researchers have concluded that the class–crime link is less strong in self-report data than in official data. The self-report studies show either that the lower class has a higher crime rate than other classes or that there are no significant differences by class. No self-report study of adults has found that the middle class has a higher crime rate than the lower class (Braithwaite, 1979).

Some have attributed the difference between the relatively strong association between social class and adult crime found in official statistics and the weak or non-existent association found in self-report studies to class bias by the police and the courts. If the police are more likely to arrest a lower-class suspect than a middle-class suspect, arrest data would show that the lower class is more involved in crime, even though self-report studies might show little or no difference among the classes in actual criminal behavior. However, a review of studies of adults that have used arrest data or self-report questionnaires concluded that class bias by the criminal justice system could not explain away the strong relationship between social class and crime found in studies using official statistics. The author concluded that "[l]ower-class adults commit those types of crime which are handled by the police at a higher rate than middle-class adults" (Braithwaite, 1979: 62).

Social Class and Juvenile Delinquency

One review of studies that have examined the link between social class and juvenile delinquency found that in forty-four of fifty-three studies that used official statistics, lower-class juveniles had higher rates of delinquency than middle-class juveniles (Braithwaite, 1979). Another review of the research found a "small but consistent inverse correlation of social class with street crime" by juveniles when official data were used (Hindelang, 1983: 180).

When self-report studies rather than official data are used to look at the link between social class and juvenile delinquency, the results are not clear. One review of the research found that self-report studies provide less support for a class-delinquency link than do arrest data, but that many self-report studies show higher delinquency rates for the lower class and that none finds higher rates for the middle class (Braithwaite, 1979). Another review of self-report studies of delinquency concluded as follows: "About half of the American studies support the hypothesis of an even smaller inverse relationship between various social-class indicators and reported illegal behavior [than is found in studies using official data], and half provide no support for the hypothesis" (Hindelang, 1983: 180). The class–delinquency relationship might be weaker in self-report studies than in research based on official data because the police are more likely to stop or arrest lower-class adolescents than they are to stop or arrest middle-class adolescents in the same circumstances.

Self-report studies suggest that class differences in delinquency are most pronounced for the most serious crimes and smallest for the most trivial offenses. Serious and repetitive violations of the law seem to be most common among the lower classes (Clelland and Carter, 1980; Elliott and Ageton, 1980; Braithwaite, 1981; Elliott and Huizinga, 1983).

Self-report studies that have looked at a broader range of delinquent acts, rather than only at the most serious ones, have sometimes concluded that there is little or no association between social class and delinquency. One review of the research found a weak-to-moderate relationship between class and official data on violations of the law, but almost no relationship between class and self-reported violations of the law (Tittle, Villemez, and Smith, 1978). Other self-report studies have also found no relationship between class and delinquency (Krohn et al., 1980; Tittle and Meier, 1990). Several self-report studies of juvenile delinquency have even concluded that there is no relationship between social class and serious, repetitive violations of the law (Cernkovich, 1978a; Johnson, 1980; Krohn et al., 1980).

Contradictory evidence on the association between social class and self-reported delinquency also comes from the few studies that have compared the delinquency of people from the lowest class with that of all people of higher social standing. One self-report study that found no overall relationship between class and delinquency did find that boys from the lowest class were the most prone to delinquency. Of those boys whose fathers had been without a job and had received welfare assistance, 62 percent reported at least one delinquent act, compared with only 40 percent of the boys whose fathers had not been unemployed or on welfare (Hirschi, 1969: 72). However, another study found no significantly greater amount of self-reported delinquency—measured only by acts that would be crimes if committed by adults—among the underclass, a class that is below the poverty level, uneducated, often on welfare, and unemployed or working at low-prestige jobs (Johnson, 1980).

Methodological Problems

Several methodological problems account for some of the inconsistency in the conclusions of the research that has examined the social class-delinquency relationship. One problem is how to measure the social class of adolescents. Rather than ask them about the class of their parents, as most researchers have done, it might make more sense to tap adolescents' job aspirations or expectations of future earnings. Another problem is that by gathering data from students who are in school on the day the survey is done, researchers miss truants and school dropouts, who may be especially prone to delinquency. In addition, self-report surveys sometimes increase the number of respondents who are classified as delinquents by asking about many relatively trivial acts.

Despite methodological problems, many self-report studies find higher rates of serious and repetitive delinquency among the lower classes, and none of those studies finds higher rates of serious and repetitive delinquency among the middle class. Official arrest data show even more consistent evidence for a class-delinquency link. Moreover, for adults, arrests show a strong class-crime association, and data from the few existing self-report studies of adults reveal an association between class and crime, although a somewhat weaker one than is found in studies using official data.

We will see later that many sociological theories of crime and delinquency are based on social class, even though the relationship between class and violation of the law is still somewhat unclear. The theories rarely consider that involvement in crime and delinquency can affect an individual's class standing by reducing job opportunities or by making upward social mobility difficult; unlike sex, age, and race, the variable of social class can be both a cause and an effect of crime and delinquency (Thornberry and Christenson, 1984). One review of eight theories of crime and delinquency concludes that none of them provides an adequate rationale for predicting an inverse or negative relationship between social class and crime without bringing in untested or unsupported assumptions about what the lower class is like (Tittle, 1983). Perhaps sociologists would be on firmer ground in looking for general social processes—such as ways of neutralizing the constraints of the law—that are sometimes correlated with class, rather than treating class itself as a cause of crime and delinquency.

Social Class and Victimization

The NCVS does not use a single measure of social class, but it does gather data on indicators of class such as annual family income, education, employment status, and employment sector. Using annual family income as a measure of social class, victimization rates for rape and sexual assault, robbery, aggravated and simple assault, and personal theft generally decline with increasing income levels (Rennison, 2002).

Summary

Rates of crime vary from one country to another; by region within a country; by size of a community; from one time to another; and by sex, age, race, and social class. Theories of crime causation should help us make sense of these variations.

Cross-national comparisons of crime rates are difficult because of differences among countries' laws and crime statistics. The United States has a high homicide rate compared with other industrial nations that report crime data to the United Nations. Within the United States, the South has a high homicide rate, and the South and the West have the highest rates of property crimes.

Both FBI data and NCVS studies show that rates of index crimes are generally higher in larger communities. Shaw and McKay found that crime and delinquency are most common in neighborhoods closest to the center of the city. Geographers have mapped the residences of offenders and victims and the places where crimes occur, finding that most offenders commit crimes close to home. Immigrants frequently have crime rates no higher than, and sometimes lower than, native-born populations, in spite of perceptions by the native-born that the new arrivals are especially prone to crime.

NCVS studies show there are some seasonal fluctuations in crime rates that require explanation. FBI data show a large increase in crime rates beginning in the 1960s and a substantial decline in rates since the early 1990s. NCVS data show stable or declining crime rates since 1973.

In recent years, some kinds of juvenile delinquency have become more common among girls, but boys still outnumber girls in arrests. There is differential treatment of the sexes in the juvenile justice system, with girls less likely than boys to be processed formally if they commit acts that would be crimes when committed by adults, and girls more likely than boys to be processed formally if they commit status offenses such as running away from home.

Since 1963, there has been an increase in the proportion of females arrested for index crimes, with the greatest increase being for larceny. This may be because store detectives and the police have become more likely to treat female thieves formally rather than release them with a warning, because merchandising changes have made theft easier for women who shop, or because women have actually become more likely to steal.

In the United States, most people who commit index offenses are relatively young. Changes in the age distribution of a population over time can increase or decrease a society's overall crime rate. In general, victimization rates are higher for younger people than they are for older people, but the elderly may have a high victimization rate if we take into account their limited exposure to the risk of victimization.

Black Americans are arrested in numbers disproportionate to their numbers in the population. Arrest data seem to reflect a real difference between blacks and whites in their perpetration of index offenses, rather than police bias in the arrest of suspects of different racial groups. Self-report data also indicate that blacks are more likely than whites to commit serious offenses, but some self-report studies find that blacks and whites differ less in the rates at which they commit less serious crimes. Comparing blacks and whites of similar social backgrounds reduces the difference in their crime rates, but several studies have found that blacks have higher rates of involvement in crime even when people with the same social characteristics are compared. Blacks are more likely than whites to be the victims of both violent and property crimes. Violent crime most often occurs between an offender and a victim of the same race.

The relationship between social class and violation of the law is complex. In general, official arrest statistics show that lower-class adults commit more crimes than middle-class adults. The few self-report studies of adults find a similar though weaker association between social class and crime. Most studies of juvenile delinquency find an inverse relationship between social class and official measures of delinquency, but in some studies the relationship is not strong. Self-report studies of delinquency are mixed in their conclusions: Some show an inverse relationship between social class and delinquency, and others find no relationship. Methodological problems with self-report studies make it difficult to unravel the exact relationship between social class and violation of the law, especially among adolescents. In general, rates of victimization decline with increasing income.

IMPORTANT TERMS

| age-specific arrest rate | concentric-zone model | social class |

REVIEW QUESTIONS

1. Why do you think the homicide rate in the United States is high relative to the rates of other industrial societies?

2. What regional variations in rates of violent and property crime exist in the United States? How would you explain these variations?

3. Which kinds of communities in the United States have the highest crime rates? Why do you think this is the case?

4. What have been the trends in crime in the United States in recent decades? Why do you think crime rates have changed as they have in recent years?

5. Why are crime rates in the United States higher for men than women, for younger people than older people, for blacks than whites, and for the lower class than the middle and upper classes?

FOR FURTHER STUDY

Cross-National Variations in Crime Rates The annual Home Office report on crime in the United Kingdom can be found at www.homeoffice.gov.uk/rds/pdfs/hosb1201.pdf. For a comparison of nations' crime rates, see James Lynch's "Crime in International Perspective" (in James Q. Wilson and Joan Petersilia, eds., *Crime: Public Policies for Crime Control*. Oakland, CA: ICS Press, 2002, pp. 5–41).

Migration and Crime Two useful collections of essays are Michael Tonry, ed., *Ethnicity, Crime, and Immigration: Comparative and Cross-National Perspectives* (vol. 21 of *Crime and Justice: A Review of Research*. Chicago: University of Chicago Press, 1997) and Ineke Haen Marshall's (ed.) *Minorities, Migrants, and Crime: Diversity and Similarity across Europe and the United States* (Thousand Oaks, CA: Sage, 1997).

Annual Trends in Crime Rates Data on trends in crime rates are provided in Kathleen Maguire and Ann L. Pastore's (eds.) *Sourcebook of Criminal Justice Statistics 2001*, available at www.albany.edu/sourcebook. An examination of the reasons for the decline in crime rates in the 1990s is presented in John E. Conklin's *Why Crime Rates Fell* (Boston: Allyn & Bacon, 2003).

Variations in Crime Rates by Age Two valuable sources of information on juvenile delinquency and victimization are the U.S. Department of Justice's Office of Juvenile Justice and Delinquency Prevention (www.ojjdp.ncjrs.org) and the University of New Hampshire's Crimes against Children Research Center (www.unh.edu/ccrc).

Variations in Crime Rates by Race Callie Rennison's *Violent Victimization and Race, 1993–1998* (Washington, DC: U.S. Department of Justice, March 2001), which is based on NCVS data, is available at www.ojp.usdoj.gov/bjs/abstract/vvr98.htm.

5 Biological and Psychological Explanations of Crime

Modern criminology began with the positivist approach of an Italian physician, Cesare Lombroso. His theories of crime causation have since been found deficient, but his emphasis on the collection of data to test hypotheses about criminals became the basis of modern criminology. Much criminological research is now conducted by sociologists, but biological and psychological approaches to the study of crime causation have been important in the past and continue to be so today.

Biological Explanations of Crime

Biological explanations of crime propose that offenders differ from nonoffenders in some physiological or anatomical way. The idea of a biologically different criminal minimizes the role in crime causation of social conditions such as poverty and unemployment, and instead attributes crime to individual differences. For example, in the movie *Frankenstein* the monster apparently becomes destructive because Dr. Frankenstein's assistant stole an "abnormal" brain rather than a "normal" one to transplant into the monster's corpse.

History of the Biological Perspective on Crime

The biological perspective on crime can be traced to about 1750, but this viewpoint was most dominant at the end of the nineteenth century and beginning of the twentieth. With the rise of modern psychology and psychiatry in the early twentieth century, the biological perspective lost influence in criminology, though important work continues to be done by biological researchers.

Physiognomists and Phrenologists   Between 1750 and 1850, physiognomists and phrenologists tried to show links between criminal behavior and biological factors. Physiognomists studied facial features and sought a correlation between criminal behavior and characteristics such as the shape of the ears or the eyes. Phrenologists stressed the relationship between the external shape of the skull and an individual's propensity to engage in crime. They thought that studying the shape of the skull would allow them to tell which areas of a person's brain would dominate behavior and possibly lead to crime. Modern research indicates that certain areas of the brain do control particular types of behavior and that stimulating certain parts of the brain can incite violence, which might be socially defined as crime. However, phrenologists failed to understand the complexity of the brain and did not demonstrate any relationship between skull shape, behavioral control centers in the brain, and criminal behavior. Both phrenologists and physiognomists failed to test their theories in a methodologically sound way, but they did draw attention to the possibility that offenders and nonoffenders might differ in measurable ways.

Lombroso's Theory of the Atavism   Cesare Lombroso explored what he thought were the physically distinctive features of criminals. After examining the skull of a notorious Italian criminal, he observed:

> At the sight of that skull, I seemed to see all of a sudden, lighted up as a vast plain under a flaming sky, the problem of the nature of the criminal—an atavistic being who reproduces in his person the ferocious instincts of primitive humanity and the inferior animals. Thus were explained anatomically the enormous jaws, high cheek bones, prominent superciliary arches, solitary lines in the palms, extreme size of the orbits, handle-shaped or sensile ears found in criminals, savages and apes, insensibility to pain, extremely acute sight, tattooing, excessive idleness, love of orgies, and the irresistible craving of evil for its own sake, the desire not only to extinguish life in the victim, but to mutilate the corpse, tear its flesh and drink its blood. (Lombroso, 1911: xiv)

Lombroso theorized that criminals were **atavisms**, people "born out of time" who were similar to primitive people or lower animals in their biological makeup. This theory owed much to the influence of Darwinism at the end of the nineteenth century, but the idea that people could revert to an earlier stage of evolutionary development was not widely accepted even then.

Lombroso also erred in his ideas about what features could be inherited. For example, the tattoos he said were characteristic of criminals were obviously not inherited. Some of the features he thought were typical of offenders might have been the product of both inheritance and diet, with the latter being a function of income, education, and other social factors.

Lombroso made several important mistakes in testing his theory. He failed to select in a careful way a control group from the general population with which to compare criminals. In addition, many of the differences between criminals and noncriminals that he documented were small enough to have occurred by chance.

Lombroso's most important contributions to modern criminology were the application of measurement and the testing of hypotheses. As a result of this positivist method, his ideas on crime causation were revised, and he increasingly took social and environmental factors into account. In the final edition of his textbook on the criminal offender, Lombroso suggested that as few as one offender in three might be a born criminal. Other types were insane criminals and occasional offenders who were the products of a poor social environment. Nevertheless, the born offender remained at the center of Lombroso's work, and he never did systematic research on the social causes of criminal behavior.

Post-Lombrosian Researchers: Goring and Hooton   Several researchers built on Lombroso's ideas. The Englishman Charles Goring (1870–1919) sought to test Lombroso's theory that offenders had certain physical defects or anomalies. Goring found no significant differences between offenders and groups from the general population in skull shape, eye color, hair color, or various other physical traits. He did find what he thought was a real difference in height and weight, with offenders being shorter and lighter than nonoffenders. Still, Goring (1913: 173) concluded that "there is no such thing as a physical criminal type."

Earnest Hooton, an American anthropologist who worked on crime causation during the 1930s, criticized Goring's research. Hooton (1939) contended that criminals were the products of environmental influences on organically inferior people. However, he failed to provide a clear meaning for the idea of physical inferiority or how it might lead to criminal behavior. He offered no satisfactory evidence that "physical inferiority" was inherited rather than acquired. Moreover, Hooton's research contained important methodological problems; for instance, he did not compare offenders with a carefully chosen and random sample of nonoffenders.

Sheldon's Theory of Somatotypes   One biological theory that incorporates psychological traits is William Sheldon's theory of **somatotypes** or body types. This theory focuses on differences among individuals in embryonic development and claims that people with different body types have different temperaments that affect their propensity to engage in crime and delinquency.

Sheldon, an American psychologist and physician, developed a rating scheme to classify bodies as one of three basic types. One study found that endomorphs, who are slow, "soft," and comfort-loving, exhibited no particular tendency to be delinquent, nor did ectomorphs, who are described as lean and fragile. However, mesomorphs, described as muscular, active, and aggressive, were twice as common among delinquents as they were among the general population (Glueck and Glueck, 1950, 1956). This association between mesomorphy and delinquency might result from a propensity by the police and the courts to label as delinquent those adolescents who are most muscular, active, and aggressive.

Modern Biological Research on Crime

Modern biological approaches to the study of crime propose that there is great variation among individuals in biological strengths and weaknesses, and that individuals with certain "vulnerabilities" or "risk factors" have a greater probability of responding to stressful environmental conditions with antisocial behavior (Fishbein, 1996; Rowe, 2002). Moffitt (1993) distinguishes life-course-persistent delinquency, which purportedly has a biological basis, from adolescent-limited delinquency, which is associated with social processes of peer influence and the achievement of maturity. Adolescent-limited delinquents usually desist from crime when they reach adulthood, but life-course-persistent delinquents often continue to break the law as adults. Rather than being two distinct types, life-course-persistent delinquency and adolescent-limited delinquency are probably part of a continuum, with biological factors playing a greater or smaller role depending on the point on the continuum (Rowe, 2002). Contemporary researchers have used various strategies to test the impact on crime and delinquency of various physical traits and inherited characteristics.

Twin Studies   One potentially rewarding approach to the study of biological influences on criminal behavior is the study of twins. Identical twins develop from a single female egg and have no inherited differences. Fraternal twins develop from two eggs and do have inherited differences. Researchers can thus look at the relative impact on crime of heredity and environment by comparing the criminality of identical twins with the criminality of fraternal twins of the same sex. Evidence for genetic factors would take the form of a higher **concordance rate**, or similarity of criminal behavior, between identical twins than between fraternal twins.

The results of twin studies conducted in the United States, Japan, and Europe between 1929 and 1962 are consistent with the idea that inherited factors influence criminal behavior. The concordance rates for identical twins were between 60 and 70 percent in these studies, but the concordance rates for fraternal twins were only 15 to 30 percent. However, because of methodological problems with the studies, they exaggerated the importance of genetics (Pollock, Mednick, and Gabrielli, 1983).

In what is perhaps the best twin study to date, Karl Christiansen (1974, 1977) examined all 3,586 pairs of twins born in one area of Denmark between 1881 and 1910. He found that if one identical twin had a criminal conviction, the other twin also had a conviction in 35 percent of the cases. The rate of concordance was only 12 percent for fraternal twins. Similar results were produced by a study of twins in Norway (Dalgaard and Kringlen, 1976). In a study in Ohio, a researcher found that concordance rates for self-reported delinquency were higher for identical twins than for fraternal twins (Rowe, 1983). In general, these studies yielded smaller differences between the concordance rates of identical twins and the concordance rates of fraternal twins than early researchers had found; this was probably due to the weaker methodology of the older studies.

Studies of twins, such as England's notorious Reggie and Ronnie Kray, find that identical twins are more similar in their criminal behavior than fraternal twins.

Identical twins are more alike biologically than fraternal twins, and because identical twins look more alike, they are probably more apt than fraternal twins to have similar environments when young and to receive similar treatment by parents, relatives, peers, and teachers. As a result, we would expect identical twins to be socialized in ways that are more alike than is true of fraternal twins, and thus similar behavior by identical twins cannot be attributed solely or even primarily to hereditary factors. A review of the research on twins concludes as follows:

> No definitive conclusions can be drawn from twin studies of aggressiveness or criminal behavior because no consistent pattern of genetic influence emerges. Nevertheless, twin studies of criminal and related behaviors fairly consistently provide some intriguing evidence for a genetic effect, and genetic influences warrant continued, but more rigorous, study. (Fishbein, 1990: 45)

Adoption Studies An ideal method to test the relative importance of biological and environmental influences on crime would be to study identical and fraternal twins who are separated at birth and who never have contact again, and then compare their crime rates as adults. Because this situation is too rare to provide sizable samples for study, researchers have turned to other approaches. One that is promising is the study of adopted children, who are usually separated from their biological parents at a young age and often never see those parents again. Researchers have compared the criminality of adoptees with that of their biological and adoptive parents. These studies are not without methodological problems, particularly in measuring subjects' involvement in crime and delinquency and in ensuring that subjects have a similar duration of biological parenting.

A study of all 14,427 adoptions that occurred in Denmark from 1924 to 1947 found that children who had biological parents with criminal convictions had a greater chance of themselves being involved in repetitive property crimes, but they had no greater propensity to engage in violent crimes. Among sons raised by adoptive parents, only 13.5 percent had a criminal conviction if neither their biological parents nor their adoptive parents had a criminal conviction. If their adoptive parents had been convicted of a crime but their biological parents had not, the proportion of the sons convicted of a crime rose slightly to 14.7 percent. However, if at least one of the biological parents had been convicted of a crime and the adoptive parents had not been, 20 percent of the sons had a conviction. If both the biological and the adoptive parents had criminal convictions, then 24.5 percent of the sons also had criminal convictions (see Figure 5.1). Similar results were found for female adoptees. This research is consistent with the theory that inherited factors influence criminal behavior, because the data indicate that the criminality of a child's biological parents is a better predictor of the child's criminality than is the criminality of the child's adoptive parents. However, the researchers did not claim that the data proved that inherited traits cause crime. Instead, they cautiously concluded that inherited traits might lead some people who are raised in certain ways and who live in certain circumstances to become criminal more often than people in the same situation who lack the inherited traits (Pollock, Mednick, and Gabrielli, 1983; Mednick, Gabrielli, and Hutchings, 1987).

According to one review of adoption studies, the evidence on genetic involvement in crime causation is even stronger than those researchers asserted. Lee Ellis (1982: 57) concludes that

> to the degree that causal statements can ever be made with finality in science, the adoption studies carried out in the decade just past seem to be making the following, cautiously worded pronouncement about the involvement of genetics in criminal behavior possible: Significant amounts of the observed variation in human tendencies

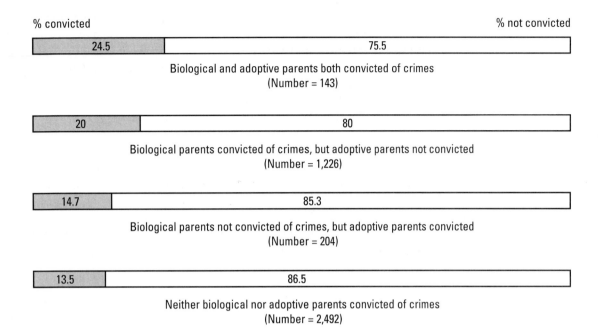

FIGURE 5.1   Percentage of Adopted Sons Convicted of Crimes, as Related to Whether Their Biological and Adoptive Parents Have Been Convicted of Crimes

Source: Based on Sarnoff A. Mednick, William F. Gabrielli, Jr., and Barry Hutchings, "Genetic Factors in the Etiology of Criminal Behavior," in Sarnoff A. Mednick, Terrie E. Moffitt, and Susan A. Stack, eds., *The Causes of Crime: New Biological Approaches*. Cambridge, England: Cambridge University Press, 1987, p. 75.

to behave criminally appear to be the result of some genetic factors, presumably operating on the functioning of the nervous system (at least for the variations observed in criminal behavior other than those describable as victimless and status offenses).

Others have been more critical of adoption studies. A reanalysis of the evidence from Denmark concluded that it pointed in the direction supporting the heredity-crime hypothesis, but that the magnitude of the association was "at best insubstantial" (Gottfredson and Hirschi, 1990: 56). An examination of thirty-eight studies found "a consistent and statistically significant association between various indices of heredity and crime," even though "the actual magnitude of the relationship was modest" (Walters, 1992: 604, 606). Furthermore, the relationship was weaker in adoption studies, which seem to be the purest way to investigate the influence of heredity on crime, than it was in either twin or family studies, which encounter more difficulty separating the effects of heredity from environmental influences.

Sex Differences   The fact that male and female crime rates differ to varying degrees from one society to another suggests that much of the sex difference in crime rates is due to social and cultural factors, but the fact that men commit more crime than women in all societies suggests that some of the difference could be the result of biological differences between the sexes.

Evolutionary psychologists explain male-female differences in murder and assault by applying Darwinian ideas of biological evolution (Daly and Wilson, 1997; Wilson and Daly, 1998). They claim that through natural selection over many generations, humans developed psychological adaptations or traits that were designed to solve problems they confronted in the environment. This process required reproductive success, and violence and aggression by men developed as one means of ensuring that success. Margo Wilson and Martin Daly (1998: 295) describe this process as follows:

> Sexual rivalry between males is endemic to the human animal. . . . Moreover, there are diverse manifestations that men around the world are inclined to perceive and treat women, in part, as productive and reproductive resources that warrant protective investments against the risk of usurpation. . . . We suggest that men's attitudes, emotions, and actions indicative of sexual proprietariness and the commoditization of women are contingent products of sexually-differentiated evolved mental mechanisms in the contexts of particular historical and cultural circumstances.

Manifestations of sexual proprietariness include a double standard that values female fidelity more than male fidelity and to some degree acknowledges the acceptability of a man's violent response to his partner's infidelity. Men are more likely than women to use violence for two reasons:

1. One man's gain is another's loss in reproductive competition for mates (women being regarded as a more crucial resource because they make a greater parental investment in the young), whereas women's reproductive competition is less for access to mates than for access to resources.
2. The paternity of a child can be mistaken, so husbands risk investing resources in raising the child of a sexual rival.

To evolutionary psychologists, then, motives of sexual rivalry and proprietariness evolved over time in a sexually differentiated way to ensure reproductive success: Men became more concerned with their partners' sexual infidelity, and women became more concerned with the allocation of their partners' resources and attentions. Coercion of women was aimed at deterring and punishing violations of men's sense of proprietary entitlement and exclusivity, thereby ensuring women's fidelity and dependence. Men's competition with sexual rivals, their efforts to control women, and women's violent responses to that coercion are thus motives in a significant proportion of murders and assaults (Wilson and Daly, 1998).

One review of research on differences in aggressiveness between males and females cites developmental studies showing that children under six do not seem to imitate the behavior of same-sexed adults (Maccoby and Jacklin, 1980; Mednick et al., 1982). However, most studies of children under six do reveal that boys are significantly more aggressive than girls; none of those studies finds more aggressiveness among girls. The data thus "suggest strongly that greater male aggressiveness is present in children before social learning can explain it. It is a likely hypothesis that greater aggressiveness in males is related to their higher levels of male sex hormones" (Mednick et al., 1982: 30). There is, however, little direct proof that male-female differences in aggressiveness are caused primarily by differences in sex hormones. One review of the research concluded as follows:

> Correlations between circulating testosterone levels and violence have been sought in a number of studies, which have employed different groups of subjects and different methods for quantifying levels of aggression and violence. These studies have ranged from the analysis of hostility questionnaires administered to normal male college students to the collection of histories of violent acts in male prisoners. Most have shown no relation between circulating testosterone and the behavioral measures, although a few intriguing studies have revealed higher testosterone levels in groups of especially violent persons, such as incarcerated rapist-murderers. (Rubin, 1987: 256–257)

Some research has pointed to the need to integrate biological and social factors in an explanation of crime, finding that testosterone has a moderately strong relationship with adult deviance, but primarily through the influence of testosterone on social integration and on prior juvenile delinquent behavior. Testosterone levels and criminal behavior are apparently more strongly associated for men who are less well integrated socially, which is indicated by lower-class status, being unmarried, and having an unstable work history (Dabbs and Morris, 1990; Booth and Osgood, 1993; Rowe, 2002).

Compared to females, males have lower activity levels of monoamine oxidase A (MAOA), a neurologically active enzyme that is controlled by genetic and hormonal factors. Lower MAOA activity levels are, in general, correlated with higher probabilities of criminal behavior and modestly associated with the following behavior patterns linked to criminality: extreme impulsiveness, childhood hyperactivity, poor academic performance, sensation seeking, and recreational alcohol and drug use. Thus, sex differences in criminal behavior could be associated to some degree with sex differences in MAOA activity levels (Ellis, 1991; Ellis and Walsh, 1997).

A few studies suggest that crime committed by women is more likely to occur in the four premenstrual days and the four days of menstruation than it is to occur at other times during the menstrual cycle (Shah and Roth, 1974; Ginsburg and Carter, 1987). **Premenstrual syndrome (PMS)**—a set of symptoms that include tension, nervousness, irritability, fatigue, headaches, cramps, and depressed moods—does not manifest itself in the same way in all women who suffer from it, and some doubt that it is a single condition. Women experiencing PMS may simply be more likely to be arrested for crimes they commit during their premenstrual and menstrual days, perhaps because their reaction time is slower then or because they are more fatigued.

Biochemical Factors and Temperament   Some violent behavior seems to be associated with defects in the neurotransmitters serotonin, dopamine, and norepinephrine. Serotonin reduces aggressiveness by inhibiting behavioral responses to emotional stimuli; violent and impulsive behavior seems to be more common among people with lower levels of serotonin. Dopamine and norepinephrine are excitatory neurotransmitters that counteract the inhibitory effects of serotonin, and so an imbalance in the activities of these neurotransmitters can produce mood disorders and aggressive behavior (Fishbein, 1996).

Some research suggests that a variant gene that influences the brain's response to dopamine might be linked to "novelty seeking," a personality trait that predisposes people to be impulsive, quick-tempered, and excitable. Other research contradicts that conclusion (Angier, 1996a, 1996b). Some sociological studies (for example, Katz, 1988) have emphasized the importance to criminals of the excitement generated by breaking the law.

Brain Dysfunctions, Attention-Deficit Hyperactivity Disorder, and Learning Disabilities   There is growing evidence that brain dysfunctions and neurological defects are more common among excessively violent people than among the general population (Fishbein and Thatcher, 1986). Many violent offenders seem to have defects in the frontal and temporal lobes of the brain that are associated with impaired self-control. The rate of epilepsy seems to be higher among delinquents than among nondelinquents, even though most epileptics are not delinquents. In spite of such evidence, researchers have been cautious in concluding that such abnormalities cause criminal behavior. One reason is that some studies, such as those examining the link between epilepsy and crime, reach contradictory conclusions (Pollock, Mednick, and Gabrielli, 1983). Another reason is that the cause-effect relationship is not clear. For example, physical abuse of a child can cause severe head injuries, including brain damage that leads to violent outbursts; but children who are the victims of such abuse can also learn to be violent by observing their parents' behavior. (See the Using Criminology box.)

Delinquents seem to be more likely than nondelinquents to have neurological problems (Fishbein and Thatcher, 1986). There is also evidence that the parents of violent delinquents have more neurological problems than the parents of nonviolent

---

USING CRIMINOLOGY

Neurological and Psychological Problems of Juveniles Condemned to Death

In November 1987, a study of fourteen death-row inmates who had been convicted of crimes committed when they were under the age of eighteen was presented to the U.S. Supreme Court. The inmates were all juveniles who had been condemned to death in the only four states that allowed Dorothy Otnow Lewis and her colleagues to carry out their research. There were an additional twenty-three inmates under sentence of death for crimes committed as juveniles in other states.

Lewis and her colleagues found the following about their fourteen subjects:

- Eight had suffered injuries to the central nervous system that were severe enough to result in hospitalization and/or an indentation of the cranium.
- Nine had major neurological impairment.
- Seven were psychotic or had been diagnosed as psychotic earlier in childhood, four had histories indicating severe mood disorders, and the other three experienced occasional paranoid ideation.
- Only two subjects had IQ (intelligence quotient) levels above 90 (which is below average), and only three were reading at grade level.
- Twelve had been brutally, physically abused, and five had been sodomized by older male relatives.

The researchers concluded that these handicaps were potential mitigating factors that might have been used to argue against imposition of the death penalty. However, the youths had little recognition of their vulnerabilities or the way they might have mitigated their punishment. Indeed, most of the juveniles tried to hide evidence of their problems, claiming that they were not crazy or retarded and concealing their parents' brutality toward them. Their parents also hid such evidence, sometimes pressuring their child's attorney to keep such information secret. In only five of the fourteen cases were any pretrial evaluations of the youths carried out, and those evaluations were usually perfunctory and yielded inadequate data on the juveniles' neuropsychiatric and cognitive functioning.

Steven Pincus, an attorney who worked on this study, concluded as follows:

This study demonstrates that people who are on death row for committing crimes as juveniles have major psychiatric problems, neurological problems, and educational and learning problems. The law says that if someone's capacity is diminished—and the capacities of these juveniles clearly are—that needs to be considered in any calculation of moral blameworthiness. (Cited in Bass, 1988: 53)

These findings were considered by the Supreme Court in reaching its June 1988 decision that it is unconstitutional to execute anyone convicted of a crime committed under the age of sixteen, unless a state's law explicitly allows for the execution of such youthful offenders. The following year the Court considered the constitutionality of executing offenders who had committed their crimes when they were between the ages of sixteen and eighteen, the age range in which most of the researchers' subjects fell. In June 1989 the Court upheld state laws that permitted the execution of offenders who had committed their crimes between the ages of sixteen and eighteen, with the majority of the Court holding that there was no societal consensus that such executions were "cruel and unusual punishment" prohibited by the Eighth Amendment. From the time of that decision until August 2002, seventeen offenders were executed for murders committed at age seventeen and one for a murder committed at age sixteen.

Sources: Based on Dorothy Otnow Lewis et al., "Neuropsychiatric, Psychoeducational, and Family Characteristics of 14 Juveniles Condemned to Death in the United States," *American Journal of Psychiatry* 145 (May 1988), 584–589; Alison Bass, "Head Injuries Found in Young Killers," *Boston Globe,* June 20, 1988, pp. 53, 55; Adam Liptak, "3 Justices Call for Reviewing Death Sentences for Juveniles," *New York Times,* August 30, 2002, pp. A1, A13. ▲

delinquents, suggesting the possibility of a genetic factor associated with adolescent violence. Violent delinquency is not inherited behavior, but children can inherit a susceptibility to stress that could lead them to engage in violence in certain situations (Lewis et al., 1979).

Some delinquents and criminals produce abnormal EEG readings of brain activity (Mednick and Volavka, 1980; Pollock, Mednick, and Gabrielli, 1983; Fishbein and Thatcher, 1986). Research suggests that the EEGs of criminals may be similar to those of normal people at younger ages, suggesting that antisocial behavior might be associated with, though not necessarily caused by, "brain immaturity" (Mednick et al., 1981, 1982; Fishbein, 1990).

Attention-deficit hyperactivity disorder (ADHD) is defined by inattention (failure to listen and to complete tasks), impulsivity (acting without thinking), and hyperactivity (restlessness and excessive motor activity). Children with ADHD are often rejected by their peers, which can lead to aggression and violation of rules. Young children diagnosed with ADHD are especially likely to engage in delinquency as adolescents and crime as adults (Moffitt, 1990; Lilienfeld and Waldman, 1990; Farrington, Loeber, and van Kammen, 1993; Mannuzza et al., 1993). There is growing agreement that the roots of ADHD are biological, with genetic predisposition, brain damage and dysfunction, and neurological immaturity being implicated as causes. ADHD is diagnosed in males four to eight times as often as in females (Barkley, 1996).

Perhaps one-fourth of children with ADHD also have learning disabilities, although estimates of that proportion range from 9 to 92 percent (Barkley, 1990; Wicks-Nelson and Israel, 1991). **Learning disabilities** are "impairments in sensory and motor functioning which lead to deviant classroom performance" (Holzman, 1979: 78). Their exact causes are unclear, but genetic factors, brain damage, neurological problems, epilepsy, and motivational problems have been suggested as causes. Learning disabilities include reading disorders (dyslexia), disorders of written expression (aphasia or dysphasia), and mathematics disorder (dyscalculia). The diagnosis of a learning disability is based on performance on an individually administered standardized test that is substantially below the expected level for an individual of a given age and grade. Learning disabilities are diagnosed in boys two to five times as often as in girls (Taylor, 1989). Children with learning disabilities are more likely than those without them to be involved in delinquency (Brier, 1989).

Some people might be more biologically predisposed than others to crime and delinquency, although many people who are predisposed that way still learn to conform to the law. Brain disorders, ADHD, and learning disabilities can predispose individuals to crime and delinquency, but those problems can also lead to rejection and stigmatization of people who seem unintelligent or unable to function socially. This rejection by itself could be conducive to violation of the law. Brain disorders, ADHD, and learning disabilities may also be reflected in poor academic performance and rejection by teachers, both of which can be conducive to delinquency. As Figure 5.2 shows, brain disorders, ADHD, and learning disabilities could directly lead to delinquency and crime, or they might increase the likelihood of delinquency and crime indirectly by leading to social rejection or academic failure.

Biology and Modern Criminology

There are several reasons that many contemporary criminologists have paid little attention to biological explanations of crime. One is that relatively little research on crime has been done by biologists and medical researchers. Some of their early work was based on a lack of understanding of the human brain and was marred by poor methodology. The political abuse of the biological approach in Nazi Germany also made this perspective suspect in the eyes of many criminologists. Some criminologists

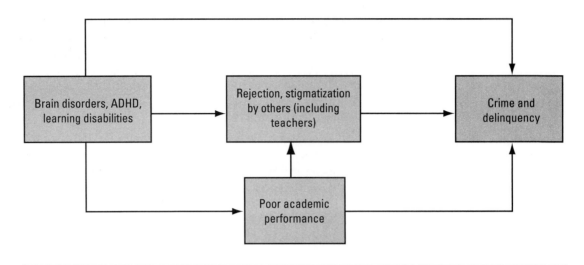

FIGURE 5.2   Possible Links of Brain Disorders, ADHD, and Learning Disabilities to Crime and Delinquency

react with hostility to the biological perspective because it is viewed as a threat to the ideology of welfare liberalism and social change to which they adhere. Heredity appears unchangeable, and a theory that stresses biological causes of crime seems to imply that efforts to reduce crime through social change are misguided. The technical nature of the language used by biological researchers has also made it difficult for those from other fields to understand their studies, so many criminologists have ignored or prematurely dismissed biological studies of crime.

Another reason criminologists have paid little attention to biological research in recent years is that this work does not seem to explain geographic, temporal, and social variations in crime rates. Biological explanations do not help us understand why crime rates vary from one nation to another, from one region to another, or among communities of different sizes. Likewise, these theories do not seem to explain changes in crime rates over time, for there is no evidence that increases and decreases in crime rates are associated with changes in biological factors. Biological factors might account for some of the difference between the sexes in crime. For example, males are diagnosed more often than females with ADHD and with learning disabilities, both of which have biological sources and are linked to crime. Biological research has not yet offered a good explanation of why crime rates peak in the late teens and early twenties and then decline with age. There is no evidence that biological differences among racial groups explain differences in crime rates among those groups; racial groups are socially defined categories rather than biologically distinguishable groupings. Finally, there seems to be no way for biological theories to account for social class differences in crime rates, for the factors on which biological researchers have focused are not associated with class standing in any obvious way.

Modern biological researchers do not dismiss nonbiological explanations of crime and delinquency, nor do they claim that all criminals and delinquents have physiological or anatomical disorders that cause them to violate the law. Instead, biological criminologists often go only so far as to say that some physical factors are associated with a propensity to crime and delinquency. Thus, genetic factors are usually seen as interacting with the familial and social environment to increase the probability that a person will violate the law, rather than seen as operating alone to cause crime and delinquency (Rowe and Osgood, 1984; Fishbein, 1990; Denno, 1990; Walters, 1992).

One criticism of biological work on crime is that inherited traits are specific, but crime is a very broad concept. Thus, for biological researchers to make progress in their search for the causes of crime, they must focus on links between specific inheritable traits and specific kinds of criminal behavior. In a sense, there cannot be an inherited predisposition to violate a socially created law, but it is possible that certain inherited predispositions might be linked to behavior such as violence that is often defined as crime.

Some criminologists have worked to develop an interdisciplinary approach that incorporates biological, psychological, and social factors (Jeffery, 1979; Mednick and Volavka, 1980; Ellis, 1982; Fishbein, 1996; Rowe, 2002). One example is a longitudinal study of crime and delinquency that followed 987 black Philadelphia residents from birth through early adulthood. This research found that biological, psychological, and social factors interact in complex ways to generate crime and delinquency, with the data suggesting that

> delinquency is related to family instability and, most importantly, to a lack of behavioral control associated with neurological and later central nervous system disorders. It appears that attention deficit disorder and hyperactivity, which are part of disciplinary problems, are associated with the learning and behavioral disorders evidenced in some members of the Biosocial Study sample. These disorders would considerably inhibit the ability of young children to create social bonds even before the school experience. Academic failure would perpetuate misconduct and impede attempts at future social bonding. Indeed, a sizable amount of research shows that children who evidence attention deficit disorder and hyperactivity are significantly more likely to retain antisocial tendencies during adulthood, a time when most individuals start to show commitments to socially desirable behavior. (Denno, 1994: 119–120)

Psychological Explanations of Crime

The idea that the criminal is somehow psychologically abnormal developed early in the twentieth century. The logic of this position is that because only certain people commit crimes, some individual trait must distinguish them from those who do not break the law.

Intelligence and Crime

Mental deficiency theories maintain that criminals either lack the intelligence to appreciate the reasons for the existence of the law and thus violate it, or are unable to control their actions or make good decisions if they are aware of the law. Nonoffenders are seen as intelligent enough to understand the law, make good decisions, and control their actions.

Research on the relationship between crime and intelligence has usually relied on IQ tests. These tests have been shown to contain cultural biases, in spite of efforts to develop unbiased tests. For instance, whites might average somewhat higher scores on IQ tests than blacks because those tests reflect the cultural biases of the whites who design the tests. As a result of such problems, critics claim that IQ tests measure social learning rather than native intelligence.

Some studies of the IQ–crime relationship have employed an inadequate research design. For example, researchers have administered IQ tests to prisoners and then compared the prisoners' IQs with those of a group from the general population. This kind of research encounters several problems. First, prisoners are not necessarily representative of all people who violate the law; indeed, prisoners might be the least competent of all offenders. Thus, researchers are often comparing *prisoners* with the general population, not *criminals* with the general population. Second, the "general population" to which the prisoners are compared includes many people who have violated the law but who are not in prison at the time of the study. As a result, researchers often end up comparing those offenders who are imprisoned with a sample of the general population that is not in prison but includes some offenders. Such a research design does not allow us to say much about what distinguishes criminals from noncriminals. A better approach would be to administer IQ tests to a randomly chosen cross section of the nation's population (including prisoners), gather evidence on that sample's involvement in crime from official arrest records and self-report questionnaires, and then examine the relationship between IQ and both officially recorded and self-reported crime.

Evidence on IQ and Crime   One study that employed a good research design to study the relationship between intelligence and delinquency concluded that if boys of the same social class are compared, delinquents generally have lower IQs than nondelinquents. Thus, a lower-class delinquent usually has a lower IQ than a lower-class nondelinquent, and a middle-class delinquent generally has a lower IQ than a middle-class nondelinquent (Reiss and Rhodes, 1961). This study also found that lower-class boys are more likely to be delinquent than middle-class boys of the same level of intelligence. Social class and intelligence are both related to delinquency.

Hirschi and Hindelang (1977) claim that sociologists regularly ignore or deny the role of individual differences such as intelligence in the genesis of crime and delinquency because "kinds of people" theories are seen as nonsociological. Their systematic review of the research literature found that there is a small but consistent and reliable difference of about nine points between the IQs of delinquents and the IQs of nondelinquents. Evidence for this difference came from studies carried out in diverse settings using different IQ tests and controlling for race and social class. They concluded that IQ is an important correlate of delinquency that seems to be as closely linked to delinquency as race and social class.

Several cohort studies have found an association between delinquency and IQ test scores. Wolfgang, Figlio, and Sellin (1972) found that the average IQ of boys who had been stopped by the police was 101, compared with an average of 108 for boys who had not been stopped. Looking at boys of the same race and social class, the researchers found that IQ scores were still three to five points lower for delinquents than for nondelinquents. An English cohort study (West, 1982) found that boys who were to become delinquent as teenagers scored an average of 95 on IQ tests at ages eight and ten, and boys who did not become delinquent during their teen years scored an average of 101 at ages eight and ten. This difference of six points showed that performance on IQ tests at a young age is associated with future delinquency.

A cohort study carried out in New Zealand examined the relationship between scores on several neuropsychological tests and delinquency as measured by police, court, and self-report data (Moffitt, Lynam, and Silva, 1994). Test scores at age thirteen were not associated with delinquency that started in adolescence, but those scores were associated with the early onset and subsequent persistence of male delinquency. Verbal skills and verbal memory were the factors most strongly linked to delinquency. The researchers concluded as follows:

> Children who have difficulty expressing themselves and remembering information are significantly handicapped. Dysfunctional communication between a child and his parents, peers, and teachers may be one of the most critical risk factors for child-

hood conduct problems that grow into persistent antisocial behavior in young adulthood. (Moffitt, Lynam, and Silva, 1994: 296)

In their controversial book, *The Bell Curve: Intelligence and Class Structure in American Life* (1994: 235), Richard J. Herrnstein and Charles Murray found that "[l]ow IQ was a risk factor for criminal behavior, whether criminality was measured by incarceration or by self-acknowledged crimes." The deeper white males had penetrated into the criminal justice system, the lower their IQ scores: Those who reported never having been stopped by the police for anything but a minor traffic violation averaged 106, those who had been booked but not convicted averaged 101, and those who had been sentenced to a correctional facility averaged 93. Herrnstein and Murray suggested that low intelligence might lead to criminal behavior by being associated with

- lack of success in school and the job market, which might lead to resentment toward society
- lack of foresight and a desire for immediate gains
- unconventionality and insensitivity to pain or social rejection
- failure to understand the moral reasons to abide by the law

They concluded that cognitive ability, rather than economic and social disadvantage, caused crime, and that policy makers should therefore develop measures to deal with cognitive disadvantage rather than focus on social problems such as poverty and unemployment.

Interpreting Research on IQ and Crime   Herrnstein and Murray's arguments generated much criticism. They were accused of using an outdated view of intelligence, of claiming that it was difficult to boost IQ scores despite evidence to the contrary, and of obliquely explaining high crime rates by blacks in terms of inherited intellectual inferiority. One critique concluded as follows:

> Their analysis exaggerates the causal importance of intelligence in criminal behavior and ignores an enormous body of research on competing predictors of crime. Their failure to consider alternative criminogenic risk factors is inexcusable not only because the research documenting their salience is readily available but also because doing so leads them to justify ill-conceived, repressive crime policies. By portraying offenders as driven into crime predominantly by cognitive disadvantage, Herrnstein and Murray mask the reality that stronger risk factors not only exist but also are amenable to correctional intervention. (Cullen et al., 1997: 405–406)

These critics acknowledged that there was a weak to modest relationship between intelligence and crime but pointed out that sociological variables such as urban residence, social class, living with one's father at age fourteen, religious participation, commitment to a work ethic, and educational aspirations outweighed intelligence in their ability to explain crime.

We do not have to choose between intelligence and sociological factors as explanations of crime, because differences in IQ between offenders and nonoffenders are consistent with some sociological theories of crime. If intelligence affects school performance and attitudes toward the school and its teachers, lower intelligence could be associated with a lower "stake in conformity," which increases the chance that an adolescent will engage in delinquent behavior.

Another interpretation of the association between intelligence and delinquency is that instead of low intelligence producing trouble in school and thus generating delinquency, it may be that lower-class status is associated with both delinquency and trouble in school. Trouble in school could lead to a failure to learn, which is then reflected in lower IQ scores, thereby producing correlations among class, IQ scores, and delinquency. Lack of motivation to do well in school might show up in the results of IQ tests, which can be seen as a measure of academic performance rather than of basic intelligence.

A structuralist interpretation of the evidence linking IQ and delinquency is that this association exists only because of specific responses by institutions such as the school to low levels of intelligence, low IQ test scores, and poor academic performance. An empirical test of this theory with self-report data revealed that structural variables— access to desirable social roles, negative labeling, alienation, and delinquent peer-group association—explained significant amounts of delinquency, and that IQ, academic aptitude, and school performance added very little to the explanation of delinquency. The researchers concluded that IQ is not causally linked to delinquency but is instead an individual characteristic that institutions may or may not reward. Consequently, it is "the institutional pattern of behavior that (a) is causally related to delinquent behavior and (b) must be altered if the frequency or type of aggregate delinquent behavior is to be reduced or changed" (Menard and Morse, 1984: 1374).

One problem with determining the relationship between intelligence and violation of the law is that intelligence probably varies considerably among different types of offenders. Sex offenders such as child molesters seem to have lower-than-average IQ levels. Embezzlers probably have higher IQ levels than the general population, because they can embezzle funds only if they have attained a position of trust in the business world, and intelligence plays a role in achieving such a position. Intelligence influences an individual's social position and thus affects the opportunities available for crime.

Personality Characteristics

Several reviews of published research have failed to find personality traits that are consistently and systematically linked to criminal behavior (Waldo and Dinitz, 1967; Tennenbaum, 1977; Arbuthnot, Gordon, and Jurkovic, 1987). When offenders' personality traits were found to differ from those of a control group or those of the general population, the differences were usually small, of questionable validity, and inconsistent with the results of other studies. A recent meta-analysis of fiftynine studies reached a different conclusion, finding several personality dimensions that were moderately associated with antisocial behavior. According to the authors, criminals are "hostile, self-centered, spiteful, jealous, and indifferent to others (i.e., low in Agreeableness)," and they "tend to lack ambition, motivation, and perseverance, have difficulty controlling their impulses, and hold traditional and unconventional values and beliefs (i.e., are low in Conscientiousness)" (Miller and Lynam, 2001: 781).

The Criminal Mind   Researchers have not yet found a single "criminal personality," but some psychologists and psychiatrists continue to search for personalities or personality traits that distinguish criminals from noncriminals. This was the thrust of a study by Samuel Yochelson and Stanton Samenow (1976, 1977). Samenow (1984: 5) has made the following claim:

> . . . I shall draw a picture for you of the personality of the criminal just as the police artist draws a picture of his face from a description. I shall describe how criminals think, how they defend their crimes to others, and how they exploit programs that are developed to help them.

It seems unlikely that all criminals—from the corporate price fixer to the sadistic rapist, from the professional burglar to the desperate addict, and from the organized crime boss to the juvenile shoplifter—would have the same personality, but that is the basis of Yochelson and Samenow's work.

In *The Criminal Personality*, Yochelson and Samenow report that in working with criminals they initially found that traditional psychiatric techniques were ineffective, and so they studied the psychology of the criminal in order to develop a workable treatment program. Their data come from interviews with 255 offenders, many institutionalized in St. Elizabeths Hospital in Washington, D.C., and the rest from referrals by the police or the correctional system. They did not compare their criminal subjects with a control group, nor were their subjects a representative sample of all offenders, so their conclusions are based on a flawed research design.

Yochelson and Samenow claim to have identified "thought patterns" that exist among all offenders, whether blacks from the ghetto or whites from the suburbs, whether grade-school dropouts or college graduates. The fifty-two "errors of criminal thinking" that form the criminal personality include the following:

- chronic lying
- a view that other people's property is their own
- unrelenting optimism
- great energy
- fear of injury or being insulted
- intense anger
- manipulativeness
- an inflexibly high self-image

Without a control group, however, there is no way to show that those personality traits are more common among criminals than among the general population.

Treating the Criminal Personality   Yochelson and Samenow then sought a way to treat people with this criminal personality. Traditional therapy seemed ineffective because the offenders were manipulative, mimicked psychiatric jargon, and faked insight into their problems. Job training did not work either, according to Samenow, who has said, "I'm all for job training, but if that's all you do, you'll simply have a criminal with job skills. And he'll use those skills to gain entry into new avenues of crime" (cited in Krost, 1982: 8).

Yochelson and Samenow developed a technique of confronting offenders with their flaws, subjecting their thoughts and actions to detailed examination, and forcing them to accept responsibility for their behavior. Much like the technique used by Alcoholics Anonymous, their approach was rigid in demanding full conformity to the rules and in being most effective for offenders who had hit "rock bottom" and saw their only options as prison, suicide, or change. By eliminating "criminal thinking" through this "exercise in self-disgust," Yochelson and Samenow hoped to create a morally responsible person.

Did their approach work? Only thirty of the 255 interviewed offenders completed the 500 hours of therapy that the program required. Of the thirty, twenty showed improvement, although precise measures of their improvement were not provided. The kind of evidence offered by Yochelson and Samenow cannot tell us whether their method works. The twenty offenders who completed treatment might have changed even without the program, and they were only a small part of the initial group of offenders and might not be representative of that group, much less of all criminals in society.

Self-Control and Crime   In *A General Theory of Crime,* sociologists Michael Gottfredson and Travis Hirschi (1990: 88) describe the personality trait of self-control as "the individual characteristic relevant to the commission of criminal acts." They argue as follows:

> In our view, lack of self-control does not require crime and can be counteracted by situational conditions or other properties of the individual. At the same time, we suggest that high self-control effectively reduces the possibility of crime—that is, those possessing it will be substantially less likely at all periods of life to engage in criminal acts. (Gottfredson and Hirschi, 1990: 89)

People lacking self-control are described as "impulsive, insensitive, physical (as opposed to mental), risk-taking, short sighted, and nonverbal, and they will tend therefore to engage in criminal and analogous acts" because they are less apt to consider the negative consequences of their actions (Gottfredson and Hirschi, 1990: 90). Gottfredson and Hirschi claim that these traits can be treated as a stable construct because they cluster together in the same people, are present at an early age, and persist over the life cycle.

Rather than providing direct evidence that offenders differ from the rest of the population in self-control, Gottfredson and Hirschi infer that criminals are low in self-control because of the nature of crime: It provides immediate gratification but little long-term benefit; it is exciting and risky; and it requires no special motivation, preparation, skill, or specialization. Their portrait of crime draws selectively from the research evidence, ignoring offenses such as insider trading that would seem to contradict their theory. They assert that the low self-control they claim is common to all offenders, from juvenile delinquents to white-collar criminals, is the product of inadequate socialization, defined as the "absence of nurturance, discipline, or training" (Gottfredson and Hirschi, 1990: 95).

Michael Gottfredson and Travis Hirschi propose that low self-control, resulting from inadequate socialization by the family, leads to criminal behavior such as the violence shown here.

Research supports Gottfredson and Hirschi's contention that low self-control is linked to criminal behavior, but also finds that criminal opportunities and situational influences on the choice of behavior need to be incorporated into a complete theory of crime (Grasmick et al., 1993; Nagin and Paternoster, 1993; Piquero and Tibbetts, 1996; Forde and Kennedy, 1997). For example, one study that found a durable relationship between self-control and crime also uncovered a "contextual effect": Residing in a community with more female-headed households was associated with more involvement in crime (Evans et al., 1997). Another study which confirmed that delinquency was associated with weak constraint (impulsivity or low self-control) criticized Gottfredson and Hirschi's theory as "simplistic psychologically" because it omitted another personality trait that was also strongly associated with delinquency: negative emotionality, the tendency to experience fear, anxiety, and anger and to break down under stress (Caspi et al., 1994: 187).

Low self-control is associated with a variety of quality-of-life measures in addition to crime. People with low self-control have poorer relationships with family and friends, less involvement in religious institutions, lower levels of educational attainment and job achievement, and more contact with criminal associates. If self-control is a trait established in childhood that endures over a lifetime, as Gottfredson and Hirschi claim, then low self-control might have the above consequences, all of which increase the chance of criminal involvement. However, the causal direction of the relationship between self-control and quality-of-life measures is unclear. For instance, low self-control might lead to more contacts with criminal associates, but contact with criminal associates could also weaken self-control (Evans et al., 1997).

Aggressiveness and Crime   One personality trait sometimes associated with crime and delinquency is the inability to tolerate frustrating situations without resorting to aggression and violence. Frustration that arises from not being able to achieve a goal can lead to aggression that sometimes takes the form of crime, either against the frustrating object or against another object (displaced aggression). There is evidence that children who are the most assertive, daring, prone to fight, quick to anger, and resistant to discipline are also the most likely to violate the law later in life (Radzinowicz and King, 1977: 89). A study done in Sweden that used teachers' ratings of boys' aggressiveness at ages ten and thirteen concluded that the most aggressive boys were the most likely to be involved in serious and repetitive crime by the age of twenty-six (Stattin and Magnusson, 1989).

Few psychologists believe that aggression follows directly and simply from frustration. Even when frustration does lead to aggression, that aggression can be channeled into acceptable activities such as athletic or academic competition rather than criminal behavior. One psychologist (Megargee, 1982) identifies the following determinants of whether an individual will respond aggressively to a situation:

1. *Instigation to aggression:* the total of all internal factors motivating the person to commit an aggressive or violent act.
2. *Habit strength:* learned preferences for the use of aggressive behavior in a particular situation.
3. *Inhibitions against aggression:* learned preferences to avoid aggression against a certain target.
4. *Stimulus factors:* environmental influences facilitating or impeding aggressive behavior.
5. *Competition:* making a choice among several responses to the situation so that the individual's needs are met in the best way.

Even a model as complex as this does not incorporate such influences on aggressive behavior as genetic predisposition, endocrinological balance, the availability of weapons, and differences in political power and economic resources. Psychologists, biologists, and social scientists who have studied aggression in recent years have recognized that the causes of aggression and violence are extraordinarily complex.

Children Who Kill   A study of homicidal behavior by children under the age of thirteen included a three year old who had held a knife to his mother's neck as she slept and a ten year old who had twice tried to kill his mother. The psychiatrist who did the study found that compared with nonhomicidal children who were also psychiatric patients, the homicidal children were more likely to have

- a history of psychomotor seizures
- attempted suicide
- fathers who had been violent to their mothers
- fathers who had been homicidal
- mothers who had been hospitalized for psychiatric reasons (Lewis et al., 1983)

Another study found two kinds of murderers under the age of sixteen. One was the "nonempathic murderer" who was incapable of seeing things from another person's perspective. Those children had histories of assaultive behavior, did not cope well with stress, and had spent their first year of life with little affection, either in an institution or with a mother who was not nurturing. One fifteen-year-old boy who had killed a six-year-old girl said, "I didn't know the girl, so why should I have any feelings about what happened to her?" (Zenoff and Zients, 1979: 547). The second type of young killer was the "sexual-identity-conflict murderer." These were boys who carried weapons because they lacked physical confidence, often as a result of being taunted as effeminate. Their mothers were dominant, and their fathers absent or passive. Sometimes their parents actually encouraged them to commit crime. One thirteen-year-old boy who had his face rubbed in the mud by another boy was told by his parents to do whatever was necessary to defend himself; he then got a large knife and stabbed his tormentor in the heart (Zenoff and Zients, 1979).

Most children who commit murder have experienced severe rejection by one or both parents, and often they have no role model in the home from whom they can learn empathic behavior. The physical abuse that many of these young murderers have suffered can produce brain dysfunctions and neurological problems that are associated with violent behavior.

Rapists and Sexual Murderers   One problem with studying the personality of the criminal is that different kinds of crime can be committed by people with very different personalities. Even the same kind of crime can be committed by people with several types of personalities. For instance, one study categorized 800 convicted rapists as follows:

1. *Exploitative rapists* (about 50 percent of all rapists): For them, rape is an impulsive and predatory act, with the victim seen only as an object for sexual gratification. The rape is often committed on the spur of the moment, and it arises out of a social situation such as a casual date. These rapists tend to see active resistance by the victim as a sexual maneuver, and this often heightens their arousal.

2. *Compensatory rapists* (about 25 percent): They are obsessed with sexual fantasies and feel very inadequate. They have fantasies that their victims will enjoy the

rape and perhaps even fall in love with them, but they also think that no woman would want to have sex with them.

3. *Displaced anger rapists* (about 20 percent): Rape expresses their displaced anger and rage. The victim represents to them a hated woman in their life, such as a mother or wife. Sex is a way of humiliating the victim, and physical resistance often increases the offender's anger.

4. *Sadistic rapists* (5 percent): Sexual feelings are linked to aggression for this type; they become more violent as they become more aroused. Their crimes are often premeditated and sometimes involve a compulsive and ritualized fantasy (Prentky, Cohen, and Seghorn, 1985).

Knowing that the perpetrators of a single crime such as rape have very different personalities can be important in developing policies to treat criminals and counsel victims. Different kinds of rapists pose different threats to society, and they may respond to different kinds of treatment. Victims who are raped by different types of offenders can have quite different experiences, and counseling them might have to take different forms. In addition, advice to women about how to react to a rapist at the time of the crime—for instance, "resist at all costs" or "comply with the offender's demands"— often assumes a single kind of rapist, and knowledge that rapists have very different personalities should make advice givers more cautious (Carter, Prentky, and Burgess, 1988).

Men who commit rape do seem to share certain attitudes and beliefs. One study found a strong association among three components of a Hypermasculinity Inventory (HMI): callous sexual attitudes, a belief that violence is manly, and an attitude that danger is exciting. Men scoring high on the HMI were likely to have a history of sexual aggression and become aroused when exposed to rape imagery (Mosher and Sirkin, 1984; Mosher and Anderson, 1986). The tendency to commit rape is also associated with younger age at first sexual intercourse, a large number of sex partners, a traditional view of gender roles, hostility toward women, a tendency to blame victims, peer-group norms supportive of sexual assault, and a strong belief in rape myths (such as, "when women say 'no' they really mean 'yes'"). These attitudes are most likely to lead to rape when a strong moral and legal framework is absent, such as in a criminal subculture or during wartime (Archer, 1994b; Pollard, 1994).

A study by the FBI's Behavioral Science Unit of thirty-six convicted sexual murderers, twenty-nine of whom had killed multiple victims, provides insight into the social background and personality of those who kill in the context of power, sexuality, and brutality. The murderers had experienced numerous family problems when they were young: alcohol and drug abuse, psychiatric problems, criminal histories, sexual problems, abuse and neglect, negative parent-child interactions, poor discipline, lack of strong role models, and frequent changes of residence. To cope with their inadequate family life and their sense of personal failure, they retreated into a sexually violent fantasy world. Their fantasies, which drove their behavior, included themes of "dominance, revenge, violence, rape, molestation, power, control, torture, mutilation, inflicting pain on self/others, and death" (Ressler, Burgess, and Douglas, 1988: 74). Their personalities were characterized by "a sense of social isolation, preferences for autoerotic activities and fetishes, rebelliousness, aggression, chronic lying, and a sense of privilege or entitlement" (Ressler, Burgess, and Douglas, 1988: 73). Their lack of empathy made it possible for them to ignore the impact of their behavior on their victims and treat them as mere extensions of their own world who existed only to gratify their desires.

Rampage Killers   In an investigation of 102 killers involved in 100 rampage homicides, which were defined as "multiple-victim killings that were not primarily domestic or connected to a robbery or gang" and were not serial or politically motivated murders, the *New York Times* concluded that "society's lack of knowledge of mental health issues" was a major factor leading to the killings (Fessenden, 2000: 20). Though the murders were often described "in a language of incomprehension— 'senseless,' 'random,' 'sudden,' 'crazy,' " they did have a logic: Nearly two-thirds of the killers had threatened violence before their rampage, and more than half of the killers had threatened specific people with harm (Fessenden, 2000: 20). Nearly half of the rampages had been precipitated by the loss of a job, and nearly one-fourth had been preceded by the dissolution of a romantic relationship.

More than half of the rampage killers had a serious mental health problem. Twenty-four of them had been prescribed medicine to control their problem, and fourteen of those had stopped taking their medication prior to the rampage. One-fourth of the killers had been diagnosed with a serious mental problem—often schizophrenia— before committing the crime, and an additional one-fourth of them had been diagnosed with such a problem after the rampage while preparing for trial. Mental problems are also suggested by the fact that none of the rampage killers got away with the crime; nearly 90 percent never even left the scene of the killings. More than half of the killers committed suicide either immediately after the rampage or later, attempted to kill themselves, or placed themselves in a situation in which they were killed by police officers or others. One killer who hanged himself in his cell after surviving his rampage left the following suicide note: "I guess I wanted to kill the person I hate most—myself. I just didn't have the courage. I wanted to die, but I couldn't do it, so I had to get someone to do it for me. It didn't work out" (cited in Fessenden, 2000: 20).

Personality Inventories   The Minnesota Multiphasic Personality Inventory (MMPI) is a personality test of 556 true-false items that have been carefully selected to distinguish average people from those who are suffering from certain forms of psychopathology. The MMPI includes ten clinical scales, three of which are especially important in distinguishing criminals and delinquents from the general population:

> *Psychopathic deviate scale:* conflict with authority and shallow personal attachments
>
> *Schizophrenia scale:* bizarre thought and affect, and withdrawal from personal contact
>
> *Hypomania scale:* unproductive hyperactivity

Delinquents and prisoners, especially those who have committed the most serious offenses, score high on these three scales when compared with the general population (Monachesi and Hathaway, 1967; Megargee and Bohn, 1979). In other words, delinquents and prisoners can be characterized as having personalities that include conflict with authority, shallow personal attachments, bizarre thought and affect, withdrawal from personal contact, and unproductive hyperactivity.

To James Q. Wilson and Richard J. Herrnstein (1985: 190), who have reviewed the research on the MMPI and crime, these results illustrate "vividly that institutionalized offenders have atypical personalities as compared to the general population" and that these three scales of the MMPI are "the major personality correlates of crime for adult criminals as well as juvenile delinquents." However, a closer look at what these scales are measuring makes this claim seem extravagant. "Conflict with authority" and "unproductive hyperactivity" can be seen as definitions of crime and delinquency rather than as personality traits that lead to crime and delinquency; these phrases describe actual behavior rather than personality traits. "Shallow personal attachments" and "withdrawal from personal contact" describe social interaction with others and fit well with a sociological theory of crime and delinquency called social control theory, which is examined in Chapter 7. Only the "bizarre thought and affect" of the schizophrenia scale seem to be psychological constructs, and we might ask, " 'Bizarre' from whose perspective? Those making and enforcing the law?"

In looking at research that used a second personality test, the California Psychological Inventory, Wilson and Herrnstein concluded that important parts of the "typical criminogenic personality" are lack of "conformity," lack of "value orientation," and lack of "social adjustment." This does not tell us much about the kind of personality apt to violate the law, because these "traits" are little more than ways of saying that an individual has engaged in behavior that violates social norms.

Antisocial Personality Disorder   The *Diagnostic and Statistical Manual of Mental Disorders (DSM-IV)* of the American Psychiatric Association (1994: 645) defines **antisocial personality disorder** as "a pervasive pattern of disregard for, and violation of, the rights of others that begins in childhood or early adolescence and continues into adulthood." This diagnosis requires an individual to have shown, before the age of fifteen, symptoms of **conduct disorder**, "a repetitive and persistent pattern of behavior in which the basic rights of others or major age-appropriate social norms or rules are violated" (American Psychiatric Association, 1994: 85). Many of the diagnostic criteria for antisocial personality and conduct disorders are, in fact, criminal and delinquent acts, including aggression against others, destruction of property, theft, and serious violations of rules.

The traits of antisocial personality disorder, which is similar to what has been called psychopathy or sociopathy, are failure to conform to social norms, deceitfulness, manipulation, impulsivity, irritability, aggressiveness, disregard for self and others, lack of empathy, cynicism, arrogance, glibness, and irresponsibility. Those with this disorder feel little or no remorse when they hurt others and do not learn easily from experience. When frustrated, they become furious and aggressive and cannot sublimate or rechannel their impulses. Because of their impulsivity, their crimes are rarely planned in much detail and often seem purposeless.

Antisocial personality disorder is more common in males than in females, perhaps six times as common (Robins et al., 1984; Kessler et al., 1994). It is also especially common among those of low socioeconomic standing and those who live in urban areas. Rates of antisocial personality disorder among whites and blacks of the same social background are similar (Kessler et al., 1994). The American Psychiatric Association (1994: 647) acknowledges that the diagnosis might be misapplied to those who have adopted antisocial behavior for self-protection and survival in threatening social contexts, warning that the label should be reserved for underlying dysfunctions within the individual rather than reactions to the immediate environment.

The prevalence of conduct disorders for those under eighteen in the general population is 6 to 16 percent for males and 2 to 9 percent for females (American Psychiatric Association, 1994: 88). About 40 percent of boys and 24 percent of girls with conduct disorders will be diagnosed with antisocial personality disorders as adults (Robins, 1986). The prevalence of antisocial personality disorder in samples from the general population is 3 percent in males and 1 percent in females, but prevalence in clinical samples ranges from 3 percent to 30 percent, and even higher in some samples of prisoners and substance abusers (Hare, Hart, and Harpur, 1991; American Psychiatric Association, 1994: 648).

Twin and adoption studies indicate that conduct and antisocial personality disorders have both genetic and environmental origins (American Psychiatric Association, 1994: 648). Those with antisocial personality disorder seem to learn tasks that are positively rewarded as well as the general population, but the general population learns well, and those with antisocial personality disorder learn poorly, those tasks that are negatively reinforced. This difference is apparently a result of lower arousal levels (measured by heart rate, skin conductance, and brain activity) in those with antisocial personality disorder, making them less fearful of punishment. Resting heart rate has predictive value; one study found that three year olds with lower rates were twice as likely as those with higher rates to be classified as aggressive eight years later (Raine, Venables, and Mednick, 1997), and another study discovered that a lower resting heart rate at age eighteen was associated with a greater chance of criminal convictions between the ages of nineteen and forty (Farrington, 1997). There is also some evidence that antisocial personality disorder is associated with a deficit in gray matter in the prefrontal cortex of the brain (Raine et al., 2000). According to Rowe (2002: 86), the

> prefrontal cortex may create our knowledge of mind—that other people are themselves thinking about us—and allow us to adjust our behavior to the needs and concerns of others. The prefrontal cortex is also the physiological basis of the executive functions of planning, or delaying the enticing impulses of the present for better outcomes in the future, and of evaluating many behavioral choices instead of one.

A Critique of the Concept of Antisocial Personality Disorder   One problem with antisocial personality disorder as an explanation for crime is that criminal behavior is actually part of the definition of the disorder, so crime is not being explained by measures of personality that are independent of criminal behavior.

Another problem is that some of the component traits of antisocial personality disorder are imprecisely defined. As a result, different psychiatrists and psychologists sometimes disagree on their diagnoses of antisocial personality disorder. This might be why researchers have found wide variation in the proportion of different samples diagnosed with the disorder, although that variation could also be due to differences in the composition of the samples.

Schizophrenia and Mood Disorders

Schizophrenia is a serious mental disorder that involves delusions, hallucinations, disorganized speech, grossly disorganized or catatonic behavior, and negative symptoms such as affective flattening and lack of speech or will. Paranoid schizophrenia is characterized by preoccupation with delusions or auditory hallucinations, but with relative preservation of cognitive functioning and affect (i.e., the absence of disorganized speech, disorganized or catatonic behavior, and flat or inappropriate affect). Paranoid schizophrenics have delusions of persecution or grandiosity, often organized around a theme, and are argumentative and angry, patronizing, and intense in their interactions with others. Another form of serious mental illness is **mood disorder,** which includes depressive disorders (unipolar depression) and bipolar disorders (manic or mixed episodes followed by major depressive episodes) (American Psychiatric Association, 1994).

Most people with these mental illnesses do not commit crime, and many offenders do not have these disorders, but there is mounting evidence of a relationship between crime and such mental problems as schizophrenia and mood disorder, especially when people with those disorders also abuse drugs or alcohol.

The "combination of prosecutory and grandiose delusions with anger" that characterizes paranoid schizophrenia sometimes leads to violence (American Psychiatric Association, 1994: 287). A study of released mental patients found that getting into fights was associated with the following beliefs: others intended to do one harm, one's mind was being dominated by forces outside one's control, and other people's thoughts were being put into one's head (Link and Stueve, 1998). Another study found that 82 percent of a sample of boys in a correctional school who had engaged in serious violence such as murder or rape exhibited symptoms of paranoia, but only 17 percent of the less violent boys in the school (those who had engaged in fist fights, set fires, or threatened others) showed such symptoms (Lewis et al., 1979).

One research design compares the prevalence of mental illnesses in a sample of convicted offenders with the prevalence of those illnesses in the general population. Research in Finland and the United States has found that schizophrenia, mood disorders, antisocial personality disorder, substance abuse, and post-traumatic stress disorders are more common among prisoners than in the general population (Eronen, 1995; Eronen, Hakola, and Tiihoinen, 1996; Jordan et al., 1996; Teplin, Abram, and McClelland, 1996).

Other researchers have compared the behavior of patients released from mental hospitals with the behavior of the general population. Using this method, a study in Sweden found that men with major mental illnesses were more than twice as likely as men without such illnesses to have been convicted of a crime, and four times as likely to have been convicted of a violent crime. Women with such illnesses were five times as likely to have a criminal record as women without such illnesses, and twenty-seven times as likely to have been convicted of a violent crime (Hodgins, 1992). Researchers in Denmark found that patients hospitalized for the treatment of mental illnesses committed a crime three to four times as often as people who had not been hospitalized for such disorders; the ratio was even higher when only violent crimes were considered (Hodgins et al., 1996). A study that used both official arrest records and self-report measures of violent and criminal behavior found that former mental patients who exhibited psychotic symptoms were more likely than nonpatients to engage in violent and illegal behavior, even though "the excess risk of violence posed by mental patients is modest compared to the effects of other factors" (Link, Andrews, and Cullen, 1992: 290). Others have also found the relationship between mental disorder and violence to be modest, even suggesting that "people with mental illnesses are more likely to be victims than perpetrators of violence" (Monahan, 1996: 1).

A recent study found that 1,000 patients discharged from mental hospitals in three American cities were no more violent than other people in the community unless they abused drugs or alcohol. Substance abuse by former mental patients increased their rates of violence fivefold, whereas substance abuse increased violence only threefold for others in the community (Steadman et al., 1998). Researchers in Finland and Denmark have also found that the higher crime rates of mental patients are associated with their higher rates of substance abuse (Eronen, 1995; Hodgins et al., 1996). Because mental patients abuse alcohol and drugs at nearly twice the rate of the general population, they are especially prone to violent behavior, most of which—85 percent in one recent study—is directed against their family and friends (Steadman et al., 1998).

Hospitalization for treatment can reduce the subsequent involvement of the mentally ill in violent behavior, and treatment for both their mental disorders and their substance abuse is especially effective in reducing violence (Steadman et al., 1998). However, many state mental hospitals have been closed, and local clinics to serve the mentally ill have not been built, so the mentally ill often remain untreated. One psychiatrist estimates that 100,000 Americans with schizophrenia receive no treatment (Dr. E. Fuller Torrey, cited in Butterfield, 1998).

Psychology and Variations in Crime Rates

Psychologists and psychiatrists have rarely tried to make sense of geographic, temporal, and social variations in crime rates. Thus, we have no reason to believe that variations in crime rates from one society to another, from one region to another, or among communities of different sizes can be explained by differences among the residents of those places in intelligence, personality traits, or major mental illnesses. Similarly, we have no evidence that variations in crime rates over time are the result of changes in any of those psychological variables. For instance, it seems unlikely that the dramatic increase in the rate of index crimes in the United States during the 1960s, or the reduction in that rate during the 1990s, was caused by short-run changes in intelligence, personality, or schizophrenia and mood disorders.

Whether psychological factors can explain variations in crime rates by sex, age, race, and social class is less clear. Males and females are socialized differently, and differences in personality traits that result from socialization might be linked to male-female differences in rates of crime and delinquency. For instance, variations between males and females in self-control explain some of the "gender gap" in crime rates (Burton et al., 1998; LaGrange and Silverman, 1999). Some of this gap might also result from differences between the sexes in the rates at which they suffer certain mental disorders. Intelligence does not seem to be a source of male-female differences in rates of crime and delinquency.

Differences in crime rates by age do not seem to be explained very well by psychological theories. Neither IQ test scores nor personality traits seem to change dramatically over the course of a lifetime for most people, but involvement in crime does vary significantly over the life cycle.

Differences in crime rates among racial groups do not seem to be easily explained by psychological theories either. On average, blacks score lower than whites on IQ tests, but those tests are widely regarded as biased against blacks because they are designed by whites. Moreover, the IQ scores of blacks can be raised significantly by education and by changing the social environment, suggesting that IQ scores are best seen as the product of the socially structured opportunities available to members of different racial groups.

Social class differences in crime rates are not explained well by psychological theories. IQ scores are lower on average for the lower classes, but this is probably due mainly to the poor quality of the schools that the lower classes attend. There might be class differences in personality traits or the frequency of major mental illnesses, but the differences have not been shown to explain class differences in rates of crime and delinquency.

Psychology and the Criminal Law

Psychological perspectives on crime have long been important in determining the legal responsibility of people who violate the law. Modern psychology questions the ability of some people to form criminal intent, a necessary element of most crimes, and the legal system sometimes relieves people of responsibility for actions that violate the law if they cannot form criminal intent. The legal system's emphasis on the individual offender focuses attention on the psychology of the lawbreaker rather than on the social environment in which the offender lives. This serves to maintain the legitimacy of the social system, because individuals rather than social conditions are blamed for crime.

Rules Determining Criminal Responsibility   One legal rule on criminal responsibility is the McNaghten rule, which was originally spelled out in a case in Great Britain in 1843, well before the advent of modern psychology and psychiatry. The McNaghten rule establishes a "right and wrong test." For defendants to prove a lack of criminal responsibility because of insanity, they must demonstrate either (1) that at the time of the crime they were under a defect of reason so as to be unable to know the nature and the quality of the act, or (2) that if they were aware of the nature of the act, they did not know the act was wrong.

The McNaghten rule raises difficult issues. It is concerned with the rational and cognitive elements of human thought, or what a defendant knows, rather than with human emotions and desires and with mental disorders. The law speaks of the "rational person," but it rarely consults modern behavioral science to determine what would be "rational" behavior for a particular person in a given situation. "Reasonable" often means what a judge thinks is reasonable in a situation, and what is reasonable for a judge earning a high income may not be reasonable for an unemployed parent of five living in poverty.

The Model Penal Code drawn up by the American Law Institute in 1955 is the basis of a rule of criminal responsibility that is widely used today. This **Brawner rule** states that a person should be found not guilty "if at the time of such conduct as a result of mental disease or mental defect, he lacks substantial capacity either to appreciate the criminality of his conduct or to conform his conduct to the requirements of the law." This rule focuses on a defendant's understanding of his or her conduct, as well as on the defendant's ability to control that conduct.

The Insanity Defense Reform Act of 1984 dropped the idea of an inability to conform one's conduct to the requirements of the law, limiting the insanity defense to situations in which "the defendant, as a result of a severe mental disease or defect, was unable to appreciate the nature and quality or the wrongfulness of his acts" (cited in Simon and Aaronson, 1988: 22). This federal law was the product of a heated public debate that followed the attempted assassination of President Ronald Reagan.

The Hinckley Case and the Insanity Defense   On March 30, 1981, John Hinckley fired four shots at President Reagan in an assassination attempt he hoped would win him public attention and the love of actress Jodie Foster. Reagan and three others were wounded. Hinckley later pleaded not guilty by reason of insanity. Under federal law, the prosecutor had to prove beyond a reasonable doubt that Hinckley was sane; the defense attorney did not have to prove beyond a reasonable doubt that Hinckley was insane. More than a year after the shooting, Hinckley was found not guilty by reason of insanity and sentenced to an indefinite term in St. Elizabeth's Hospital in Washington, D.C. The verdict caused a public outcry and much criticism by lawmakers, and led to a reevaluation of the insanity defense.

Critics of the Hinckley verdict pointed out that he had purchased a gun, stalked the president, and knew what he was doing when he fired the shots, and that those

This self-portrait shows John W. Hinckley, Jr., prior to his 1981 attempt to assassinate President Ronald Reagan.

actions indicated that he had committed the crime intentionally. Some critics did not want to allow the insanity defense to be used if a crime was committed intentionally, even if the defendant's psychological condition meant that he or she had been unable to control his or her behavior. Opponents of this view said it would reverse the development of the criminal law since the 1843 McNaghten decision.

In the five years following Hinckley's 1982 acquittal, Congress and the legislatures of thirty-nine states made more than one hundred changes in their laws on the insanity defense, although one sociologist concluded that the impact of these reforms has been negligible (Moran, 1991). A few states have abolished the insanity defense as a basis for acquittal, a reform that was allowed to stand by the U.S. Supreme Court in 1994. The reforms do not seem to have significantly affected the number of defendants escaping conviction, and defendants still have a constitutional right to argue that they did not possess the mental capacity to form criminal intent to violate the law, a basis for an acquittal (Moran, 1991).

The Hinckley verdict led to other changes in the rules of criminal responsibility. Congress and ten states shifted the burden of proof from the prosecution to the defense, so that the majority of states now require defendants to prove their insanity. Most insanity defenses are plea bargained (see Chapter 13), but in contested cases the side that has the burden of proof usually loses. Thus, if the Hinckley defense had had to prove him insane, rather than require the prosecution to show him to be sane, John Hinckley probably would have been convicted.

The Hinckley case caused eight states to adopt a verdict of "guilty but mentally ill." This did not replace the insanity defense, but instead added to it. If a defendant is found guilty but mentally ill, then the jury, the judge, or a board of mental health professionals must determine whether the defendant should be sent to a prison or to a mental hospital. Such a verdict does not require the defendant to be given psychiatric care, nor does it mitigate punishment. Critics claim that the "guilty but mentally ill" verdict avoids the difficult question of whether the defendant is criminally responsible for violating the law, and that it is impractical and perhaps unconstitutional.

The Use of the Insanity Defense   Even total abolition of the insanity defense would have little impact on the crime rate, because it is used in less than 1 percent of all felony cases, and in fewer than one-fifth of those cases are defendants acquitted on the basis of insanity (Kenneth Appelbaum, cited in Bass, 1995: 4).

There is some evidence that the insanity defense has been used more often in recent times (Caplan, 1984). One reason is that there has been growing pressure to release mental patients after shorter periods in custody. The courts have expanded the civil rights of mental patients, and psychiatrists today prefer to return patients to the community rather than institutionalize them. The law now requires that patients be released unless they are still mentally ill and dangerous; John Hinckley must have a hearing for possible release every six months. However, psychiatrists cannot predict future dangerousness very well, so vesting power in them to determine a release date seems to be asking too much of them. For example, a study of mental patients who had committed felonies found that 14 percent of those classified as dangerous by psychiatrists were rearrested for violent crimes within three years of their release, but 16 percent of those classified by psychiatrists as nondangerous were rearrested for violent crimes within three years (Cocozza and Steadman, 1978).

Another possible reason for the increased use of the insanity defense is the renewed application of the death penalty since 1977. If the alternative to an insanity plea is the risk of execution, then defendants charged with capital crimes will have a strong incentive to plead not guilty by reason of insanity. The link between the insanity plea and capital punishment can be seen in the experience of Great Britain, where the proportion of defendants found not guilty by reason of insanity declined noticeably after capital punishment was abolished in 1965 (Wilson, 1983: 185).

Those who argue for abolition of the insanity defense sometimes claim that such a change would make it possible to imprison dangerous offenders for longer periods. However, few studies have compared the length of time spent in custody for convicted criminals with the length of time spent in custody for matched samples of defendants who are found not guilty by reason of insanity. What little research has been done is inconclusive as to whether those found insane spend more or less time in custody than those found guilty of similar charges. The studies do show that defendants initially charged with more serious crimes and then found insane spend more time in custody than defendants initially charged with less serious offenses and then found insane (Steadman, 1985).

The insanity defense will remain a source of controversy. Changes in the rules of criminal responsibility may redefine the conditions under which people who violate the law can be punished, but the insanity defense will probably continue to be raised in a very small proportion of all criminal cases, so reforms in the rules of criminal responsibility are unlikely to have much effect on crime rates.

Summary

Most criminological research today is done by sociologists, but biologists and psychologists have contributed in important ways to our understanding of criminal behavior.

Early biological theories of crime—such as the theories of the physiognomists and phrenologists, Lombroso's atavism theory, and Sheldon's somatotype theory—have little empirical support and do not receive much attention today, but they were significant in the development of criminology.

Modern biological research has produced important findings that might ultimately fit into a general theory of crime. Twin studies find that identical twins, who are genetically alike, are more similar in their criminal behavior than fraternal twins, who share fewer inherited traits. These findings have been explained by environmental influences as well as by inheritance. Adoption studies seem to provide evidence for an inherited propensity to crime, with criminality being better predicted from the criminality of an adopted person's biological parents than from the criminality of that person's adoptive parents. There is mixed evidence about the effects of sex hormones on behavior. ADHD and learning disabilities seem to be correlated with involvement in crime and delinquency.

Most biologists who study criminal behavior today are cautious in their conclusions, treating inherited predispositions to certain behavior as factors that interact with environmental influences. However, because biological explanations do not seem to make sense of geographic, temporal, and social variations in crime rates, many criminologists have not paid much attention to biologists' research.

One psychological approach to the study of crime and delinquency proposes that law violators have lower levels of intelligence than people who abide by the law. Research shows a small but consistent difference in IQ levels between delinquents and nondelinquents, even when class and race are taken into account. This research has been criticized because IQ scores can be changed by environmental factors, because IQ tests are culturally biased, because structural factors determine what is made of IQ socially, and because sociological variables outweigh intelligence in their ability to explain crime.

Researchers have not found a single criminal personality type, but efforts continue to identify such a cluster of traits. It is more likely that different kinds of offenders will have different personalities; in fact, research on rape finds that there are several personality types among men who commit that offense. Most psychologists now regard aggressiveness, which seems to be linked to some crimes, as the product of many interacting factors. Antisocial personality disorder, which has both genetic and environmental origins, is also linked to criminal behavior.

Serious mental illnesses, such as schizophrenia and mood disorder, are associated with criminal behavior, though some researchers have described the association as modest. The higher crime rates of mental patients are largely due to their more frequent abuse of drugs and alcohol and the failure to treat their mental disorders and substance abuse.

There is little reason to think that psychological explanations can help us understand geographic or temporal variations in crime rates. Psychological factors might help explain variations in crime rates by sex, age, race, and social class, but there have been few systematic attempts to use psychological variables to make sense of those differences in crime rates.

Psychological perspectives on crime causation are used by the criminal justice system to determine if a defendant is criminally responsible. Several rules, most of them quite vague in their wording, have been used to determine if a defendant is not guilty by reason of insanity. The Hinckley verdict led to reform of the insanity defense rules. Acquittals because of insanity are rare, and as a result, changes in the insanity defense are unlikely to have much effect on crime rates.

IMPORTANT TERMS

antisocial personality disorder
atavism
attention-deficit hyperactivity
    disorder (ADHD)
Brawner rule

concordance rate
conduct disorder
learning disabilities
McNaghten rule
mood disorder

premenstrual syndrome (PMS)
schizophrenia
somatotype

REVIEW QUESTIONS

1. What are the major kinds of modern biological research on the causes of criminal behavior? What does that research tell us about the significance of biological factors as causes of crime?

2. Why have most modern criminologists paid less attention to biological research on the causes of crime than they have to the social causes of crime? What might be the advantages, or disadvantages, of an interdisciplinary approach to the study of the causes of crime?

3. How could biological factors explain variations in crime rates by nation, region, and size of community; over time; and by sex, age, race, and social class?

4. What is the relationship between intelligence (as measured by IQ tests) and criminal and delinquent behavior? Why might a less intelligent person be more likely to commit certain kinds of crime?

5. Is there a "criminal personality"? What personality traits might be common to all criminals, and why?

6. Is the idea of antisocial personality disorder useful in the study of crime? What types of criminals would be most likely to have this disorder? What kinds of criminals would be least likely to have this disorder?

7. What kinds of criminals do you think would be most likely to suffer from schizophrenia or mood disorder? What kinds would be least likely to have these mental illnesses?

8. How could psychological factors explain variations in crime rates by nation, region, and size of community; over time; and by sex, age, race, and social class?

9. What are the different insanity defense rules? What reforms have been made in the use of the insanity defense since the Hinckley verdict?

FOR FURTHER STUDY

Biology and Crime   Three books on the relationship between crime and behavioral genetics, evolutionary psychology, and brain chemistry are Adrian Raine's *The Psychopathology of Crime: Criminal Behavior as a Clinical Disorder* (New York: Academic Press, 1993); Diana Fishbein's *Biobehavioral Perspectives in Criminology* (Belmont, CA: Wadsworth, 2001); and David C. Rowe's *Biology and Crime* (Los Angeles: Roxbury, 2002).

Evolutionary Psychology and Crime   Martin Daly and Margo Wilson's *Homicide* (New York: Aldine de Gruyter, 1988) applies the evolutionary psychology perspective to murder.

Psychology and Crime   A helpful introduction to various perspectives on individual differences in criminal behavior is D. A. Andrews and James Bonta's *The Psychology of Criminal Conduct* (2nd ed., Cincinnati, OH: Anderson, 1998). James Q. Wilson and Richard J. Herrnstein's *Crime and Human Nature* (New York: Simon and Schuster, 1985) is a controversial study of the constitutional and developmental causes of crime. Two websites that provide links to information on psychology and the law are www.unl.edu/ap-ls, sponsored by the American Psychology-Law Society, and http://psych.athabascau.ca/html/aupr/psyclaw.shtml, sponsored by the Centre for Psychology Resources at Athabasca University in Alberta, Canada.

The Insanity Defense   Rita J. Simon and David E. Aaronson's *The Insanity Defense: A Critical Assessment of Law and Policy in the Post-Hinckley Era* (New York: Praeger, 1988) examines the roles of experts and juries in trials that raise the insanity defense and discusses changes in insanity defense rules following the Hinckley trial. Dorothy Otnow Lewis's *Guilty by Reason of Insanity: A Psychiatrist Explores the Minds of Killers* (New York: Fawcett, 1998) argues that many murderers suffered brain damage from abuse or accidents when young and later exhibited symptoms of psychosis; she claims that these factors are often ignored by the courts in determining criminal responsibility.

6 Social, Cultural, and Economic Sources of Crime

One way to explain arson is to focus on the individual who sets fires. Seeing the arsonist as a deviant—perhaps a "pyromaniac" with severe psychological problems—leads nowhere in the prevention of arson, a crime that has destroyed major parts of our cities. A much better approach is to look at the social-structural causes of arson. There is an important link between legitimate institutions—particularly banks, real estate developers, and insurance companies—and arson-for-profit schemes by gangsters, professional arsonists, landlords, and corrupt political officials. Swiss insurance companies only allow their clients to use the funds paid to cover fire losses to rebuild the same structure on the same land, whereas American insurance companies provide their clients with a motive for arson by imposing no such restriction. A cultural bias against regulating private residences means that American fire codes focus on public buildings rather than on the houses and apartment buildings where four-fifths of all fire-related deaths happen. Knowledge of the socioeconomic sources of arson can be used to curb this crime by implementing new fire codes, fixing legal responsibility for "accidental" fires on negligent people, organizing citizen-action groups, applying arson-prediction methods, revitalizing housing, changing environmental design, and regulating the banking, real estate, and insurance industries more closely (Brady, 1982; McMillan, 1995).

Social, Cultural, and Economic Sources of White-Collar Crime

Several aspects of the social structure, culture, and economic system of the United States are conducive to white-collar crime. Competition in the business world creates pressure to increase consumer demand for products and services as well as pressure to capture existing markets. The result is advertising, which sometimes goes beyond "puffing one's wares," to fraud, a crime characterized by the intent to deceive. Advertising can also stimulate demand that leads to theft when that demand is not fulfilled. Advertising fuels consumption in the American economy, but by urging people to consume and maintain an expensive lifestyle, it can also encourage larceny, robbery, and embezzlement.

Free Enterprise: Profits and Competition

The American ideology of free enterprise stresses two goals: the pursuit of profits and open competition among sellers. Each goal can be conducive to violation of the law by businesspeople.

The Pursuit of Profits   The emphasis on consumption and the use of advertising create profits for firms. Some economists have suggested that companies seek a "satisfactory profit" rather than the maximum profit and that corporations have goals other than making a profit. However, profits are basic to the corporation, even if other considerations play some role in corporate decision making.

In one study, many retired middle managers of large corporations cited the pressure to show profits and keep costs in line as the greatest pressure on middle management. About nine-tenths of the executives said that the various pressures on middle managers sometimes cause unethical behavior; about four-fifths of them said that such pressures can lead to criminal acts (Clinard, 1983).

Firms seem most likely to violate the law when the economy is unstable and their profits are declining. The drive for profits can lead to antitrust violations such as price fixing, which is the illegal setting of prices by firms acting in collusion rather than depending on the free market to determine prices. This is an offense that the federal government explicitly states it will prosecute. Profit seeking can also push businesspeople into the arms of gangsters to secure capital for investment and expansion; this sometimes leads to the takeover of legitimate businesses by organized crime. Economically weak firms sometimes try to recoup their losses by "selling out to the insurance company"; that is, they hire a "torch" to burn down the plant in order to collect the fire insurance.

In 1986, indictments were returned against several Wall Street financiers for violating federal laws against insider trading, the use of material and nonpublic information about a company to trade its stock. These investment analysts had sold or used inside information to speculate on the outcome of corporate mergers and takeovers. One of them, Ivan Boesky, was required to pay $100 million for his illegal use of such information, which had helped him accumulate nearly $2 billion in capital; he was also sentenced to a three-year prison term, of which he served twenty-two months. In 1988, the investment firm of Drexel Burnham Lambert Inc. pleaded guilty to six felony counts related to securities fraud and agreed to pay a $650 million penalty. In 1990, Michael Milken, who built that firm, pleaded guilty to violations of securities laws; in addition to paying stiff fines, he was sentenced to ten years in prison, though he spent only twenty-two months there. Milken was only thirty-nine in 1986, when his "junk bond" empire began to collapse, and four people who pleaded guilty in another case were between twenty-three and twenty-seven. One executive of a brokerage house said that the young people coming to work on Wall Street in the 1980s "all want to do things faster, more aggressively, in terms of compensation, and that is their measure of success. They get here from the business schools with all sorts of knowledge about financial instruments, but less of a sense of what's right and what's wrong" (cited in Sterngold, 1986: 36).

In 1989, the American public began to learn of enormous losses due to fraud in the savings and loan industry. Estimates of the total cost to taxpayers of bailing out the insolvent government-insured institutions range from $150 billion to $500 billion. Criminal activity in the pursuit of profits in this newly deregulated industry was involved in 33 to 80 percent of all insolvencies. Criminal behavior took the form of illegal risk taking, looting an institution's funds, and covering up fraud by manipulating an institution's records. By March 1992, 580 people had been convicted of criminal charges; 78 percent of them had received prison sentences, including Charles H. Keating, Jr., who was given a ten-year term for defrauding depositors into buying junk bonds (Calavita, Pontell, and Tillman, 1997).

In 2002, the news media featured reports of accounting fraud by large corporations such as Adelphia Communications, WorldCom, and Enron. All three filed for bankruptcy, adversely affecting the stock market and costing thousands of workers their jobs and life savings. Five Adelphia executives were arrested for looting the company's assets. The Securities and Exchange Commission charged WorldCom with fraudulently misstating its cash flow by billions of dollars in order to conceal increasing losses. One employee of Enron, a Houston-based energy company that was the largest contributor to George W. Bush's 2000 presidential campaign, pleaded guilty to conspiracy to commit wire fraud and money laundering. According to a report by a special committee of the company's board, Enron created the illusion of profitability through a series of complex transactions that apparently had no purpose other than to inflate the company's earnings and enrich its executives and favored investors, two of whom invested $5,800 each and reaped a return of $1 million in two months (Eichenwald, 2002). Arthur Andersen, which had been both Enron's and WorldCom's auditing firm, was convicted in federal court of obstruction of justice for altering an internal memorandum related to Enron's questionable transactions.

Former Enron chairman Kenneth Lay is sworn in before a U.S. Senate committee investigating the collapse of his company. Lay exercised his constitutional right and refused to answer any questions.

Competition   The second element of free-enterprise ideology is open competition among firms, which is theoretically beneficial to the consuming public because it reduces profits to a "fair" level. However, competition can also lead firms to try to capture a larger share of the market through illegal acts such as false advertising or bribery. Individual firms do not seek to maximize competition for themselves and reduce their own profits to a "fair" level. Instead, they seek to reduce the strength of their competitors and maximize their own profits. To do this, they sometimes turn to price fixing to drive competitors out of business, or steal new ideas through industrial espionage.

Competition in foreign markets sometimes involves businesses in the bribery of officials to secure contracts and establish plants. In recent years, the increased globalization of trade, the rise of multinational corporations, and the growing interdependence of nations have generated concern about white-collar crime in the international arena. Competition among the corporations of the world sometimes leads to clearly illegal behavior, such as assassinations, and sometimes into gray areas that involve unethical behavior, which may not violate existing laws. Since the passage of the Foreign Corrupt Practices Act in 1977, firms based in the United States that pay bribes to foreign officials are in violation of American law. However, only ten cases were prosecuted under that law in its first decade of existence. In 1997, thirty-four industrialized nations signed a treaty banning bribery of foreign government officials.

A Comparative Note   The failure to look at other societies can lead to an overemphasis on the competitive pursuit of profits in capitalist economies as a cause of white-collar crime. In fact, developing societies and socialist economies also experience white-collar crime when people seek to achieve goals other than profits, such as state-imposed production quotas. John Braithwaite (1988) has suggested some general causes of white-collar crime that apply to all economies. He says that white-collar crime is more likely to occur "when people in positions of responsibility are put under enormous performance pressures to achieve economic or cultural goals," "in contexts with structural blockages to legitimate means of goal attainment," and "in contexts in which illegitimate opportunities are more structurally available." White-collar crime "is less likely to occur when people in positions of responsibility are put under performance pressures to achieve economic and cultural goals by legitimate means only" (Braithwaite, 1988: 629–630).

Market Structure and Crime

Some white-collar crimes are more likely to occur in certain market structures or economic circumstances (Leonard and Weber, 1970; Kramer, 1982). Seller concentration—a situation in which a large share of the market is controlled by a few producers—might be conducive to price fixing in some industries. A small number of wealthy buyers—called buyer concentration—can give them the power to demand bribes and kickbacks from sellers. Another aspect of market structure conducive to price fixing is price inelasticity, a situation in which there will be little reduction in demand for a product if its price increases. A slow rate of growth in demand can encourage false advertising.

Product differentiation, which is the ability to distinguish one's product from a competitor's product, can give rise to false or deceptive advertising. Sometimes the opposite situation, trying to make one's product seem as much like another product as possible, leads to crimes such as copyright or patent infringement. Consumer demand for designer clothing or designer cosmetics is conducive to the counterfeiting of those products.

Deregulated markets that were once controlled by the government are ripe for exploitation by white-collar offenders. One example is the massive fraud that followed deregulation of the savings and loan industry in the 1980s (Calavita, Pontell, and Tillman, 1997). The emergence of a global economy has increased the pressure to deregulate, as nations seek a competitive edge in attracting investment by limiting their control of corporate behavior. This trend has created more opportunities for fraud; for instance, the unregulated and unlicensed offshore insurance industry has sold billions of dollars of worthless policies to Americans in recent years (Tillman, 2002).

Trust and Credit

Some business crimes stem from the economic system's reliance on trust and credit. Businesspeople have faith that others will fulfill their obligations honestly. When that trust is violated, crimes can occur. Employers sometimes violate the trust of employees and union leaders by engaging in illegal labor practices. Merchants abuse the trust of their customers when they misrepresent prices, engage in deceptive credit practices, or substitute inferior goods upon delivery. Corporate directors violate stockholders' trust when they fail to disclose information about illegal contributions to political candidates and bribes to foreign officials.

One trust relationship that is conducive to certain crimes is credit, which is given on the creditor's faith that the borrower will repay the money. Business credit fraud is sometimes planned in advance, with a new company established to defraud suppliers, or a legitimate business converted into a firm that abuses its creditors. Banks and corporations sometimes continue to extend credit to a firm even though its shaky financial condition makes it unlikely that it will be able to repay its debts. One businessperson who aspired to wealth through fraudulent credit practices was Tony DeAngelis, who borrowed millions of dollars by using as collateral for his loans salad oil that he said was stored in large tanks. His creditors trusted him, but they failed to check on the existence of the salad oil. When the tanks were found to be empty, DeAngelis defaulted on the loans and his creditors lost millions of dollars.

Corporations and Crime

Various aspects of large corporations—such as their bureaucratic structure, working conditions, and use of rationality in decision making—are conducive to crime.

Bureaucratic Structure   Bureaucratic structure can be associated with the fragmentation of responsibility and the difficulty of determining who made a particular decision. Supervisors often blame underlings for the company's violation of the law, and underlings claim that their supervisors encouraged them to break the law to meet corporate goals.

The division of tasks in a large corporation enhances bureaucratic efficiency but also makes it difficult to exercise control over business activities. The decentralization of General Electric in 1950 broke that large corporation into several relatively autonomous divisions, each of which was under pressure to show a profit. The need to stabilize profits at a high level led to price fixing, an offense that was made easier by the company's fragmentation.

Corporate crimes can result from organizational defects such as poor information flow, lack of coordination, inaccurate promotional material, failure to deal with complaints after misleading advertisements, and failure to tell sales representatives all relevant facts about a product. Top-level managers at the National Aeronautics and Space Administration and Morton Thiokol were apparently aware of the mechanical problems that caused the explosion of the space shuttle *Challenger* and killed seven astronauts in 1986, but they decided to go ahead with the launch because of a breakdown in communication with technical advisors and a willingness to accept risks that previously had been unacceptable (Boisjoly, Curtis, and Mellican, 1989).

Working Conditions   Employees may find it easier to steal from their companies if they are less loyal to them, a situation that is most likely when workers change jobs frequently. Loyalty to the firm might also be weaker, and theft from the firm more common, if union-management conflict is necessary to increase wages and benefits. Such conflict can lead workers to believe that management is not concerned with their welfare and will make concessions only grudgingly.

Dissatisfied workers who feel exploited or underpaid and executives who are frustrated by not being promoted or by an unsatisfactory salary might justify theft or embezzlement as the only way to gain the compensation they feel they deserve. Some observers believe that workers steal to increase their spendable incomes; the policy implication is that theft can be reduced by paying workers more. Another view is that because many jobs are dull, repetitive, lacking in prestige, or unchallenging, workers steal for job enrichment or to increase their self-esteem. The impersonality of the work environment in large corporations and on plant assembly lines can generate a need to create a challenge that workers can meet, and this sometimes takes the form of crime against the company. Giving workers a vested interest in the company's success and integrating them into the firm might reduce employee theft (Hollinger and Clark, 1983).

Rational Decision Making   The rational decision making of large corporations can be conducive to business crime. Given a low risk of arrest, a small likelihood of being convicted in court, and a negligible chance of a meaningful criminal sanction, corporate executives may knowingly violate the law or enter gray areas where they are aware they could be breaking the law. It might be rational, if not moral or legal, for executives to break the law if their gains are great and their risks are small. Even if the company is convicted of a crime, it will probably gain more in profits than it loses in fines, and individual executives could gain more in promotion and salary than they lose from criminal sanctions.

In the 1970s, the Ford Motor Company calculated that it would be too costly for it to modify its cars and light trucks in a way that would prevent the fuel leakage that had caused serious burns and deaths. Ford estimated it would cost $137 million to make such modifications, but those changes would save the company only $49.5 million in repairs it would be required to make and civil damages it would be forced to pay to accident victims. The $49.5 million figure was arrived at on the basis of $700 in repairs per burned vehicle, $67,000 per serious burn injury, and $200,000 per burn death. Critics allege that on the basis of such calculations, Ford decided it would be too expensive initially to fix and later to recall the Pinto, which was involved in numerous serious accidents (Cullen, Maakestad, and Cavender, 1987).

Development of New Technology

Breakthroughs in technology in the computer and telecommunications industries have given rise to new kinds of crime and provided new techniques for committing traditional crimes such as fraud and embezzlement. (See the Crime and the Media box.)

Computer crime, which is any violation of the law in which a computer is the target or the means, takes many forms, some of which are shown in Table 6.1. Computer crimes include the following:

- introduction of unauthorized data into a system
- manipulation of authorized data
- creation of unauthorized files

- unauthorized use of passwords or accounting ("hacking")
- theft of hardware, software, or computer time
- use of the computer to support criminal enterprises

"Shaving" is a crime in which someone programs a computer to round off each employee's paycheck down to the nearest ten cents and then to deposit the extra few pennies in the offender's account; one programmer made $300 a week with this scheme.

Other criminal uses of computers are associated with developments in telecommunications technology (Grabosky and Smith, 1998). "Phone phreaking" is a form of fraud in which electronic signals are used to trick a telephone company into thinking that charges for long-distance calls are being paid for by the caller. Fired employees have illegally tapped into the voice mailboxes of their former co-workers to steal confidential information. In another form of telecommunications fraud, thieves use a device, available by mail order, to pick up radio waves and record private cellular codes from telephones in passing cars. They then use a personal computer with a chip etcher to reprogram microchips with the stolen codes. By inserting a reprogrammed chip into a cellular phone, they or others can charge calls to the owner of the phone from which the code was stolen.

Several aspects of computer technology are conducive to crime. First, it is relatively easy for a knowledgeable computer programmer to hide a program or a modification within a larger program ("Trojan horses," "logic bombs," "trap doors," and "viruses") or to destroy records and leave no trail of the crime. Second, computer

CRIME AND THE MEDIA

Internet Crimes against Young People

The growth of the Internet has brought with it anxiety that young people are increasingly being exposed to the dangers of the world outside the home. Of particular concern has been the victimization of children by strangers with whom they first communicated online. These crimes include the enticement of children into sexual acts, either for profit or personal gratification, and the exploitation of children in the production and distribution of pornography. Unlike other crimes against young people, Internet crimes do not require physical contact between the victim and the offender; for example, innocent pictures of children can be digitally altered into pornographic images that are then distributed online. Such crimes can produce long-term victimization; for example, pornographic pictures can remain on a website for years. These crimes often transcend jurisdictional boundaries and involve multiple law-enforcement agencies.

A survey of a nationally representative sample of 1,501 regular Internet users between the ages of ten and seventeen by the Crimes against Children Research Center concluded that in the past year

- one in five had been sexually approached or solicited over the Internet
- one in thirty-three had been aggressively solicited (defined as being asked to meet somewhere, being called on the telephone, or being sent a letter or package)
- one in seventeen had been threatened or harassed

Only one of every four youths who had been approached sexually told a parent. Nearly half of all offenders were other young people, and one-fourth of the aggressive solicitors were females. About three-fourths of the victims were at least fourteen years of age, older than the usual victims of pedophiles. The survey uncovered no instances of adults traveling to meet and have sex with children they met on the Internet, nor did it find any cases of completed seduction or sexual exploitation.

Source: Based on Office for Victims of Crime, Office of Justice Programs, *Internet Crimes against Children.* Washington, DC: U.S. Department of Justice, May 2001.

TABLE 6.1 Categories of Computer Crime

INTERNAL COMPUTER CRIMES	SUPPORT OF CRIMINAL ENTERPRISES
Trojan horses	Data bases to support drug distributions
Logic bombs	
Trap doors	Data bases to keep records of client transactions
Viruses	
	Money laundering
TELECOMMUNICATIONS CRIMES	
Phone phreaking	**HARDWARE/SOFTWARE THEFTS**
Hacking	Software piracy
Illegal bulletin boards	Thefts of computers
Misuse of telephone systems	Thefts of microprocessor chips
	Thefts of trade secrets
COMPUTER MANIPULATION CRIMES	
Embezzlements	
Frauds	

Source: Catherine H. Conly and J. Thomas McEwen, "Computer Crime," *NIJ Reports,* January/February 1990, p. 3.

software or programs are copied relatively easily, an act the courts have treated as copyright infringement. Third, the chips used in computer hardware are small but expensive and have been a target of thieves, who sell the chips to companies that cannot purchase enough in the legitimate market. Fourth, computers emit radio waves or "compromising emanations" that can be decoded with the proper equipment. The federal government calls this the "Tempest" problem and worries about electronic espionage that might reveal secret information in computerized files.

One important aspect of computer technology is electronic fund transfers (EFTs), which include all payment systems that permit transactions or exchanges in which value is represented by electronic messages, rather than by paper such as currency or checks. **EFT crime** is any violation of the law that would not have occurred except for the presence of an EFT system. This includes crimes that involve automated teller machines (ATMs) and wire transfers from bank to bank (Colton et al., 1982; Tien, Rich, and Cahn, April 1986). In 1993, thieves collected personal identification numbers (PINs) from bank cards by rolling a bogus ATM machine into a Connecticut shopping mall; they then used the numbers to withdraw at least $50,000 from the accounts of the unsuspecting users of the machine. In 1995, three thieves used a stolen bank card to make 724 withdrawals totaling $346,770 from the victim's account.

Social, Cultural, and Economic Sources of Organized Crime

The tendency in American society to pass legislation that prohibits the consumption of widely demanded goods and services has produced vast profits for people who are willing to supply those goods and services. One example is Prohibition.

Prohibition and Organized Crime

Prior to the passage of the Eighteenth Amendment, which prohibited the manufacture, sale, and transportation of alcoholic beverages, there were gangsters in many American cities, but they were not well organized.

The efforts of religious, white, native-born Americans in small towns and rural areas to protect the dominance of their cultural values led to Prohibition in 1920. The consequence of making a widely demanded product illegal was that those willing to supply alcoholic beverages could charge higher prices than consumers had paid when those beverages were legal and in more plentiful supply. This source of great profits led to the organization of criminal gangs that distributed alcoholic beverages to meet the public's demand.

The Eighteenth Amendment was repealed during the Great Depression, partly for economic reasons. People needed the jobs that the liquor industry could provide, and the government hoped to raise more tax revenue from the legal sale of alcoholic beverages. Repeal was also a result of the unenforceability of the law and the public's reactions to the tactics used by the Prohibition Bureau. National prohibition became a thing of the past in 1933, but gangsters had become well organized as a result of this experiment in the legislation of morality.

Organized Crime after Prohibition

When Prohibition ended, gangs turned to other illegal enterprises for revenue. They became involved in prostitution, though they are not much involved in it today. Currently, the major sources of revenue for organized crime seem to be illegal drugs and loan sharking, and perhaps gambling. However, gangsters have shown ingenuity in making a profit from many different illegal activities, including bankruptcy fraud, the disposal of toxic wastes, and extortion.

Gambling   According to some scholars and law-enforcement officials, many bookies work for, or are members of, organized crime "families." However, research in New York City, where the largest number of organized crime families in the country are located, indicates that organized crime does not have a firm control over gambling and that bookies operate in a competitive market rather than as agents of organized crime. Because the gambling business is unpredictable, bookies often turn to loan sharks, who do have ties to organized crime, in order to borrow money to keep their gambling operations afloat (Reuter, 1983). Bookies thus provide a source of income for organized crime not because their profits are channeled directly to gangsters, but because they pay high interest rates to loan sharks who are members of organized crime.

Loan Sharking   Loan sharks are a major source of income for organized crime. The interest rates on their loans are illegally high and well in excess of what borrowers pay to legitimate institutions. Loan sharks thrive on the difficulties that some people encounter in getting loans from legitimate institutions. Many borrowers from loan sharks are poor credit risks who are turned down by banks and finance companies. Other borrowers need money for purposes that legitimate institutions would disapprove, such as the repayment of gambling debts or the financing of a drug deal. Loan sharks are willing to lend money to such people with less financial information or collateral than legitimate institutions require.

Many who borrow from loan sharks have difficulty repaying their loans on time. When this happens, a loan shark may threaten violence against the borrower or the borrower's family. However, a study of loan sharking in New York City found that violence and intimidation were less common than some accounts suggest, because borrowers and lenders often have close ties and because borrowers usually repay their loans in the hope that they will be able to get money from the loan shark again (Reuter, 1983).

Illegal Drugs   The money lent by loan sharks who are linked to organized crime often comes from the profits from the importation and sale of illegal drugs. Laws against the sale and possession of drugs lead to high profits for those willing to take the risk of importing and distributing drugs. John Dombrink (1988: 63) has described organized crime's involvement in the drug business as follows: "Heroin has for the longest time been viewed as an integral enterprise of traditional organized crime groups, despite protestations that narcotics trafficking was to be avoided, whereas the cocaine business has been operated by Cubans, and later Colombian 'cocaine cowboys.'"

Bankruptcy and Stock Fraud   Organized crime has sometimes taken advantage of the trust inherent in credit transactions in the business world to engage in bankruptcy fraud (DeFranco, 1973). In this crime, racketeers purchase a business that has a good credit rating or establish a "front business" with a name much like one of a respected firm. They stock up on merchandise bought on credit. They demand quick delivery, pay for initial orders with cash so as to establish good credit, and then buy to the limit on credit, excusing nonpayment because of the rapid expansion of their business or because it is the busy season of the year, the Christmas season being a favorite time for this crime. The goods they buy are appealing to consumers, can be purchased in volume, and are easy to transport and hard to trace. Office equipment, television sets, and toys are examples. The racketeers sell these goods as quickly as they can through discount houses and by mail order; they then disappear and leave their creditors with unpaid bills.

In recent years, organized crime figures, in search of new sources of income, have turned to stock fraud. In 1997, nineteen men were charged with defrauding investors of millions of dollars by bribing brokers to sell stock in a company that owned physical fitness clubs; they worked with the head of the company to inflate the stock's value and then sold their shares at a profit before prices tumbled (Raab, 1997).

Disposal of Toxic Wastes   Organized crime has shown flexibility by moving into newly profitable areas of illegal activity. For instance, the disposal of toxic waste material produced by industry has become difficult and expensive because of strict environmental protection laws. There is some evidence that garbage companies owned by organized crime have developed highly profitable, but dangerous and illegal, methods of waste disposal. One method involves mixing toxic materials with recycled fuel oil (Block and Scarpitti, 1985; Szasz, 1986).

Extortion   Organized crime has used its control of certain labor unions and the threat of violence to extort millions of dollars a year from industry. In New York City, concrete companies, some of which have ties to organized crime, overcharge construction companies about $50 million a year by threatening to withhold workers or slow down the delivery of concrete to companies that are working against deadlines. A U.S. Attorney estimated that in the mid-1980s such extortion drove up construction costs in New York City by about 20 percent, an increase that was passed on to consumers in higher rents, higher taxes for public works projects, and higher prices for goods and services (Roberts, 1985).

A virtual monopoly over the waste-removal industry makes the cost of garbage collection in New York City about 50 percent higher than it would be without organized crime's involvement, according to one economist (Reuter, 1993). This monopoly was created and maintained through the threat of violence against legitimate entrepreneurs seeking to enter the industry. For instance, according to an FBI official,

> some time ago a man . . . entered the refuse business in New York State, mortgaging his home to buy a few garbage trucks. Before long, sugar was found in the gas tanks. . . . Then someone tried to blow up a truck. One afternoon the phone rang, and a gruff voice described what the man's ten-year-old daughter was wearing that day. The voice warned that if the trucks were not sold, the girl would disappear. The business was shut down within hours. (Shenon, 1985: E4)

Organized Crime and the Economic System

Organized crime serves economic functions for some people; for example, loan sharks make money available to people who cannot borrow elsewhere. Gangsters in the United States, Japan, Russia, and elsewhere adopt the economic strategies and managerial skills of legitimate business to carry out their illegal profit-making ventures. (See the Cross-Cultural Perspective box.)

Legitimate industries sometimes serve important functions for organized crime. For instance, banks "launder" or recirculate billions of dollars in illegal profits each year to make it seem that the money comes from honest investments. The Senate Permanent Investigating Subcommittee describes this process as follows:

> A drug dealer gives a large amount of cash from drug sales to a "launderer" who dispatches "smurfs" to several banks to purchase money orders or cashier's checks.
>
> The money orders or checks are then deposited in accounts which are usually fronts for criminal activity. The money from the accounts is then wired to overseas banks, where confidentiality laws prevent disclosures of information about the account's ownership or transactions.
>
> The money can be sent back to the U.S. bank accounts controlled by the drug dealer, or it can be transferred to foreign bank accounts to purchase new drug shipments. (cited in *Boston Globe,* December 30, 1986: 10)

Increasingly, money laundering involves EFT crime, with home-banking computer programs being used to move money across international borders. Perhaps the biggest money-laundering scheme was uncovered in 1991, when bank regulators in several nations closed the Bank of Commerce and Credit International (BCCI), which had served the money-laundering needs of the powerful Colombian drug cartel. In 1994, a court in the United Arab Emirates sentenced twelve former executives of that bank to prison. Organized crime is thus supported by the actions of legitimate financial institutions, as well as made possible by the failure of those institutions to meet the demand for goods and services.

Social, Cultural, and Economic Sources of Conventional Crime

Conventional crime is influenced by the social structure, the culture, and the economic system in many ways. Modernization affects the level of a society's crime rate and the kinds of crime it experiences. Changes in the value of goods create new opportunities for crime. Unemployment and crime are related to each other in complex ways. Cultures that encourage people to strive for material success can generate dissatisfaction, which is conducive to crime among the unsuccessful.

Modernization and Crime

The process of economic development affects the amount and characteristics of crime. In general, high proportions of all of the crimes committed in economically developed societies are property crimes, because with prosperity there are many

CROSS-CULTURAL PERSPECTIVES

Japanese Corporations and the *Yakuza*

In Japan, about 43,500 gangsters known as *yakuza* have amassed wealth in ways similar to those used by the Mafia in the United States: extortion, gambling, and drug dealing. The yakuza have also dominated the sex trade and have been hired to use intimidation to collect debts, settle traffic accident disputes, force tenants from apartments, and break strikes. In the booming Japanese economy of the 1980s, the yakuza got involved in real estate development, the construction industry, and the stock market; but by 2000 a faltering economy, aggressive law enforcement, and opposition from business and community organizations had weakened the yakuza.

Linking organized crime bosses and Japanese corporations are the *sokaiya,* professional extortionists, most all of them yakuza, who blackmail executives by offering to keep secret their knowledge of the executives' sexual indiscretions or information about the company's misuse of funds or failure to negotiate certain deals. The sokaiya, some of whom once worked as corporate accountants or journalists, often own stock in the company, making it easier to gather information about the company and giving them a reason for attending annual meetings.

The sokaiya exploit a Japanese cultural trait, the desire to avoid embarrassment. They intimidate executives by threatening to use violence, disrupt annual shareholders' meetings, and publicly share embarrassing information. After they have been paid off, they suppress even reasonable questions from shareholders at annual meetings, shouting down questioners and even threatening to assault them.

The sokaiya exist because corporate officials are willing to deal with them. One extortionist has said, "People like us are told we should not exist, but the fact is that some companies seek our help and trust us, or we wouldn't still be around" (p. F6). In fact, the sokaiya are such an integral

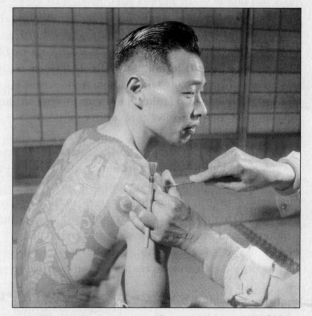

A Japanese gangster gets another tattoo, a symbol of his membership in the yakuza.

part of Japanese business that a directory of them is published, listing their addresses, telephone numbers, syndicate affiliations, and methods of operation.

The number of sokaiya declined after 1982, when corporate payoffs were outlawed. Prior to passage of this law, there were an estimated 7,000 to 8,000 sokaiya; the number in the early 1990s was down to about 1,250. Their estimated annual earnings had declined from about $800 million to about $40 million, but as many as 300 companies still paid them to suppress information.

Sources: Based on James Sterngold, "Japan Takes On the Mob, and the Mob Fights Back," *New York Times,* June 15, 1992, pp. A1, A7; James Sterngold, "Corporate Japan's Unholy Allies," *New York Times,* December 6, 1992, pp. F1, F6; Calvin Sims, "Feeling Pinch, Japan's Mobs Struggle for Control," *New York Times,* April 2, 2000, p. 6.

opportunities to steal. In less developed economies, property crimes usually make up a smaller proportion of all crimes, and violent crimes are relatively more common (Clinard and Abbott, 1973; Shelley, 1981a). The overall crime rate tends to rise with economic modernization, but some of that increase is probably due to the development of a professional police force that keeps better records. With economic development also come increases in the relative amounts of crime by juveniles and by women. In developing societies women rarely commit more than one-tenth of all crimes, but in economically advanced societies they are responsible for as many as one-fifth of all crimes (Shelley, 1981a).

Some societies have avoided high and rising crime rates as they have modernized. High rates have been avoided where traditional group ties and cultural values have been maintained; Japan and some Middle Eastern nations are examples. Control over urbanization and migration can also reduce the rate at which crime increases. Harsh treatment of criminals—including long prison sentences or capital punishment—seems to have contained the crime problem in Stalin's Soviet Union and Franco's Spain. For years, eastern European nations limited the growth of crime by redistributing income and guaranteeing jobs.

Opportunity and the Economy

Property crime rates increase especially dramatically with economic development because of growing opportunities for theft. Within developed economies, fluctuations in the value of certain goods can create new opportunities for crime. For instance, the enormous increase in the market value of gold and silver during the 1970s changed the theft patterns of burglars, who began to leave behind televisions and stereos in favor of jewelry and silverware. Street criminals began to grab gold necklaces from women's necks, injuring and in a few cases even killing their victims. This increase in the theft of precious metals had several consequences: longer waiting lists for bank safe-deposit boxes; the updating of insurance policies; the establishment of refineries to melt down stolen jewelry, coins, and silverware; and advertisements by metal dealers to buy gold and silver with "no questions asked."

Unusual crimes have developed as the value of certain goods has increased. "Bee rustling"—the theft of beehives—became a problem as the cost of a bee colony climbed from $25 to $65 between 1975 and 1982; a truckload of one hundred hives could net thieves $6,500 for one night of work. Other items that have become the targets of thieves as price and demand have risen include endangered species of cacti (which can sell for up to $15,000 apiece), colonial tombstones (which fetch as much as $3,000 each), and laptop computers (of which about 480,000 were stolen in 2001).

Unemployment and Crime

Crime rates are directly and often significantly associated with unemployment rates, but the relationship between the two rates is complex and difficult to unravel. This relationship is strongest in studies that use data from smaller units of analysis, such as census tracts within a city, rather than from larger units, such as states or the nation as a whole. Apparently, this is because statistics from smaller units are purer measures of poverty and deprivation. Unemployment rates are also more closely correlated with rates of property crime (robbery, burglary, and larceny) than with rates of violent crime (murder, rape, and assault). In addition, crime rates seem to increase some time after unemployment rates have risen, probably because accumulated deprivation is needed to produce criminal motivation (Chiricos, 1987; Land, Cantor, and Russell, 1995).

Unemployment is related to crime in various ways (Fagan and Freeman, 1999). Some crimes cannot occur unless a person is working. Embezzlement and price fixing are examples. In such cases, higher unemployment rates might reduce crime. Other offenders mix employment and crime by "moonlighting" in crime, by using a job as a front (as with a professional fence), or by using legitimate income as a stake for a crime (as in drug deals). For moonlighters, more unemployment might increase criminal activity, but for those who use a job as a front or use their income for a stake, unemployment might reduce crime. Some people, especially youths, alternate between employment and crime, and in those cases more unemployment might increase crime (Hagedorn, 1994). Other offenders are committed to crime as a source of income. They would not work even if jobs were available, so a higher unemployment rate would not affect their criminal activity. Involvement in crime can also isolate offenders from the contacts typically used to secure good jobs (Hagan, 1993).

The workplace is sometimes a setting for crime, with rates of victimization varying by occupation. Not surprisingly, police and corrections officers have the highest rates of nonfatal workplace violence. Among jobs outside the criminal justice system, driving a taxi is the most dangerous (see Figure 6.1). Between 1993 and 1999, there were about 900 workplace homicides per year; 82 percent were committed with

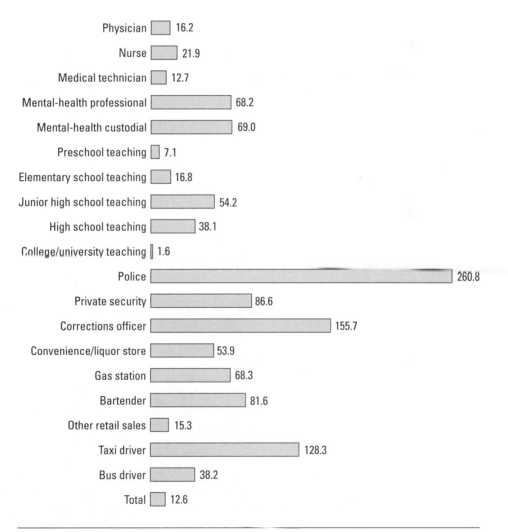

FIGURE 6.1   Number of Victims of Nonfatal Workplace Violence per 1,000 Workers, 1993–1999

Source: Based on Detis T. Duhart, *Violence in the Workplace, 1993–99.* Washington, DC: U.S. Department of Justice, December 2001, p. 4.

firearms, and 81 percent involved male victims. Eighty-four percent were committed by strangers (usually robbers), 11 percent by work associates (co-workers, former co-workers, customers, or clients), and 5 percent by intimates, relatives, or acquaintances (Duhart, 2001).

Employees who experience sudden loss of a job or conflict with a supervisor sometimes turn to violence against those thought to be responsible for their problem. The typical offender is a middle-aged white male who fears losing a job, or has lost a job, in an economy that seems to offer few opportunities for a new job and that seems to him to offer advantages to younger workers, women, blacks, and foreigners. Workers who are predisposed to blame others rather than themselves for their problems and who lack the support of family and friends are especially likely to resort to violence against supervisors when they lose their jobs, especially if they have worked many years for the same company (Fox, 2000).

There might be a difference in criminal activity between people who are working or are temporarily unemployed, and people who have been out of work for a long time or who have stopped looking for jobs. More important than finding a job is keeping a job over time, for jobs bind people to legitimate institutions and give them a "stake in conformity" that they do not want to jeopardize by involvement in crime. Criminals tend to have poorer work records and higher rates of unemployment than nonoffenders, but some research indicates that more and better job opportunities would lead some offenders, especially older ones, to select legitimate sources of income over illegal ones (Freeman, 1983; Nasar and Mitchell, 1999; Uggen, 2000). People who hold unattractive jobs that are low paying, boring, and offer little room to advance may not think they stand to lose much if they are arrested. As a result, finding a good job to which a person can feel committed over time is probably more important than simply having some job. The precipitous decline in crime rates throughout the 1990s was reinforced, if not initially caused, by an increase in the number of well-paid jobs available to young black males with a high school education or less, a demographic group with historically high rates of unemployment and crime (Nasar and Mitchell, 1999; Bernstein and Houston, 2000; Conklin, 2003).

People who are without jobs seem more likely to commit the kinds of crime that lead to imprisonment. A 1991 survey found that one-third of state prison inmates had been unemployed during the month prior to being arrested for the offense for

On December 26, 2000, computer software tester Michael McDermott, 42, murdered seven co-workers at Edgewater Technology in Wakefield, Massachusetts.

which they were incarcerated. That unemployment rate was much higher than the rate for the general population (Beck et al., 1993). In addition, offenders who are even slightly more successful at work commit fewer crimes than offenders who are less successful in the labor force (Petersilia, Greenwood, and Lavin, 1977). Some research indicates that unemployment prior to imprisonment is a strong predictor of which inmates will engage in crime at the highest rate after their release (Greenwood, 1982). An experimental study concluded that employment in the post-release period and the steadiness of that employment were associated with lower arrest rates (Rossi, Berk, and Lenihan, 1980).

One explanation of property crime by young people focuses on their lack of access to jobs that provide them with the income they need to participate in peer-group activities and to buy the clothes and other things that will win them the esteem of their friends (Phillips and Votey, 1981). However, other research indicates that adolescents who work are actually more likely to be delinquent than adolescents who do not have jobs, because those who work are less committed to school and more likely to be exposed to delinquent peers (Wright, Cullen, and Williams, 1997; Ploeger, 1997).

Recent structural changes in the economy, such as the relocation of manufacturing to suburban areas or Third World countries, in combination with the ecological concentration of poverty in ghettoes, threaten to create a permanent underclass of unemployed blacks. Discrimination in hiring and pay in the retail industry poses a formidable barrier to upward mobility for members of this underclass and reduces their attachment to the labor force. Persistent unemployment limits the development of stable households and reduces job opportunities, weakening informal social control and contributing to higher crime rates. If legitimate jobs are not available or if they pay poorly, people are more likely to turn to theft, the sale of drugs, or other income-producing crimes (McGahey, 1986; Sampson and Wilson, 1995; Baskin and Sommers, 1998).

Relative Deprivation and Crime

Even more important than poverty or unemployment as a cause of crime may be the way poor or unemployed people perceive their situation. Most poor and unemployed people are law-abiding, and the crime rates of the poor in many developing nations are lower than the crime rates of Americans, who have higher absolute standards of living. For instance, blacks in the United States have higher incomes, on the average, than black Africans, but black Americans have higher crime rates than black Africans.

What seems important, then, is people's relative standard of living. Resentment is probably more common among the poor in a wealthy nation than it is among people who have a lower absolute standard of living in a poor nation. Quetelet observed in the nineteenth century that the rural poor in Europe were generally honest, but that the urban poor who were nearer to great wealth and temptation were more prone to crime. Relative rather than absolute poverty was given as the reason for this difference (cited in Radzinowicz and King, 1977). A study of fifty-two nations found that inequality generated by economic discrimination against certain groups, such as racial and ethnic minorities, is significantly and positively related to a society's homicide rate (Messner, 1989). In the United States, growing income inequality within both black and white racial groups from 1957 to 1990 is associated with increases in the rate of homicide, robbery, and burglary arrests for each group over that time (LaFree and Drass, 1996). Crime rates are also highest in American cities where the difference between the income of the poor and the income of the rich is the greatest (Sampson, 1985, 1986; Fowles and Merva, 1996; Kovandzic, Vieraitis, and Yeisley, 1998).

The discrepancy between people's expectations and their capabilities can motivate them to violate the law. Expectations are the goods and conditions of life to which people think they are rightfully entitled, and capabilities are the goods and conditions of life they believe they can attain and maintain under the current social system. The discrepancy between the two is called **relative deprivation.** Crime is probably most common when there is much relative deprivation with regard to deeply held goals such as material success. Crime also occurs when people think they have exhausted all constructive means to reach their goals and believe that legitimate opportunities to reduce their relative deprivation are unavailable to them. The perception of being worse off than other people induces negative self-feelings that in turn increase the likelihood of committing violent and property offenses (Stiles, Liu, and Kaplan, 2000). Crime is not, however, the only reaction to a sense of relative deprivation, for relative deprivation can also lead to political action, a social movement, suicide, or alcoholism. Those who control political power often define the actions of the relatively deprived as crime, whether those actions are larceny, political protest, or terrorism.

Relative deprivation becomes greater when expectations increase or when capabilities decrease. A sudden drop in prosperity can reduce perceived capabilities, but relative deprivation more often increases because of a growth in expectations. In developing nations, the "demonstration effect" leads to a desire for a better standard of living among people who move to large cities where a wealthy lifestyle can be observed firsthand. Capabilities usually do not rise as fast as expectations, and thus relative deprivation increases and crime rates rise.

People develop their ideas about what they are entitled to not only by comparing their own social position to that of others but also by comparing their own efforts and contributions to those of others. A sense of equity exists when individuals believe that their own social position is in the same ratio to their efforts as are the social positions and efforts of others. The belief that others are getting more than they deserve relative to their efforts can lead to a **sense of inequity** that motivates people to violate the law for personal gain (Wilson and Herrnstein, 1985). An unexplored question is whether state lotteries, which produce millionaires on the basis of no more effort than the lucky selection of a few random numbers, increase a sense of inequity among the population at large.

Anomie, Strain, and Crime

In an important paper first published in 1938, Robert Merton (1968) related particular types of behavior to the social position of the people engaging in the behavior. For Merton, crime was rooted in the social system rather than intrinsic to the makeup of humans. Instead of explaining the behavior of each and every individual, he wanted to make sense of differences in rates of behavior for different groups and categories of people.

Goals and Means Merton's theory is based on a distinction between culturally defined goals and the norms that regulate the means to achieve those goals.

Goals are the valued purposes and interests that a culture holds out as legitimate objectives for all members of society. For instance, American culture emphasizes equal opportunity for all to attain the goals of wealth and power. It encourages everyone to have the same high ambition and treats the failure to achieve cultural goals as an individual failing rather than as a flaw in the social system, a belief that protects the social system from criticism. The culture's emphasis on the measurement of individual worth by material success produces a society with a built-in incentive to achieve. This has helped the nation attain a high overall standard of living, but it has also generated relative deprivation and crime among those who do not achieve the goals of wealth and power.

The second factor in Merton's theory can be described as the institutionalized means to reach the cultural goals. Norms, which define acceptable ways to reach cultural goals, are derived from the values or preferences of a society, rather than from the pure technical efficiency of the means in reaching goals. Thus, robbing a bank might be the most technically efficient way for an uneducated and unskilled person to attain material well-being, but social and legal norms define this as an unacceptable way to achieve wealth. Instead, norms emphasize hard work at a socially approved occupation over a lifetime as the appropriate way to achieve financial well-being.

Anomie and Strain

Social equilibrium exists when satisfactions accrue to people who use the institutionalized means to reach the culturally approved goals. When there is a disjunction between means and goals, **anomie**, or normlessness, results. Such a disjunction often results from the socially structured incapacity of people to use the approved means to reach cultural goals. For example, racial discrimination in education and employment makes access to the institutionalized means for achieving success difficult for black Americans. Discrimination by social class is another socially structured incapacity. Success might require a good education, which is less available to the poor, and "good manners," which are defined by the preferences of those who hold wealth and power. **Strain** is the frustration and sense of injustice that result from experiencing socially structured incapacities as low capabilities.

Socially structured incapacities might not produce anomie or strain in a society in which success goals are not held out to everyone. The relative significance of material well-being in comparison to other goals might be the same in most societies, but the absolute strength of the drive to attain material success is probably greater in the United States than elsewhere. This American "fetishism of money" is spurred by the mass media (Taylor, Walton, and Young, 1973: 94). Television shows such as *Lifestyles of the Rich and Famous* and MTV's *Cribs* strengthen the desire for luxury goods. Commercials also encourage consumers to spend money, sometimes in subtle ways. For instance, the large kitchens shown in television commercials for dish soap, scouring pads, and floor wax can be found in homes that only a small proportion of Americans can afford. Television viewers may vaguely sense being disadvantaged because the kitchens they see in television commercials are so much better than their own, and they may hope that some day they will be able to afford a home with such a kitchen.

Modes of Adaptation

Merton develops a paradigm of five **modes of adaptation** to the social structure. He looks at the ways that individuals in different social positions adapt to cultural goals and the institutionalized means to reach those goals. Table 6.2 indicates acceptance of a goal or means by a plus sign (+), rejection of a goal or means by a minus sign (–), and rejection of a goal or means and the substitution of a new goal or means by a plus-minus (±) sign.

Conformity   **Conformity** is by far the most common mode of adaptation in a stable society. This pattern involves acceptance of cultural goals (such as material wealth) and acceptance of the institutionalized means to reach those goals (such as a legitimate occupation).

Innovation   **Innovation** is the mode of adaptation most relevant to the analysis of criminal behavior. Here the goal is accepted, but means are used that society regards as unacceptable. Innovation is especially common when the goal that is sought is

TABLE 6.2   Merton's Five Modes of Adaptation

MODES OF ADAPTATION	GOALS	MEANS
I. Conformity	+	+
II. Innovation	+	−
III. Ritualism	−	+
IV. Retreatism	−	−
V. Rebellion	±	±

+ = acceptance

− = rejection

± = rejection of goals or means, and substitution of new goals or means

Source: Reprinted with the permission of The Free Press, an imprint of Simon & Schuster Adult Publishing Group, from *Social Theory and Social Structure,* Revised & Enlarged Edition by Robert K. Merton. Copyright © 1967, 1968 by Robert K. Merton.

charged with great emotion. Thus, the strong emphasis on material wealth as a sign of individual worth in the United States produces a powerful emotional investment in that goal, leading to a readiness to resort to illegal means to attain it when acceptable means are unavailable. Shoplifting in department stores is closely related to the acquisitiveness of American society and its emphasis on material symbols of success, with store goods being "dazzlingly arrayed before people who have been exhorted to desire them" (Cameron, 1964: 171).

Merton's theory of the disjunction between goals and means is general enough to apply to property crimes committed by members of all social classes. Innovation occurs when businesspeople resort to embezzlement or price fixing to attain material wealth for themselves or profits for their firms. Innovation also describes crimes such as tax fraud and larceny, which occur when the desire for more money or goods leads to violation of the law. The pressure to break the law might be greatest among the lowest classes, because they are most distant from the goal of financial security and because their access to institutionalized means to attain material success is the most limited. However, as we have seen, the relationship between social class and crime is not clear-cut, even though serious and repetitive index crimes seem to be most likely to be committed by people at the bottom of the stratification system.

The rise of some big-city political machines in the nineteenth century grew out of efforts by Irish immigrants, who found industry and wealth controlled by native-born Americans, to gain power and status for themselves. When Italians arrived some time after the Irish, they found not only that wealth was controlled by the native-born and that political power was controlled by Irish Americans but also that society's need for unskilled labor was less than it had been in earlier years. With the stimulus of Prohibition, some Italian immigrants innovated by using criminal means to achieve wealth and power (Bell, 1962). Another view attributes the involvement of Italians in organized crime not to blocked opportunities to achieve wealth and power but rather to a rational choice of crime as an easy and exciting way to get rich (Lupsha, 1981). Just as not all Irish Americans became politicians, so not all Italian Americans became gangsters, but in each case some members of an ethnic group innovated by using new means to reach societal goals. In recent years, other racial and ethnic groups—including the Chinese, Vietnamese, Jamaicans, and Colombians—have also engaged in organized crime to achieve material success.

Ritualism   Merton's third mode of adaptation, **ritualism**, holds little significance for the study of crime. Ritualists accept society's norms about appropriate means to reach cultural goals; for example, they hold regular jobs that produce steady incomes. However, ritualists scale down or give up cultural goals. They keep working but relinquish the hope of achieving material success.

Retreatism   In **retreatism**, cultural goals are abandoned and institutionalized means are also rejected. Because retreatists, such as homeless alcoholics and drug addicts, reject cultural goals and are unwilling to use accepted means to reach those goals, their behavior is often interpreted as a challenge to the goals most people hold, so it may be defined as criminal, even if there is no identifiable victim of their actions.

Rebellion   The final mode of adaptation is **rebellion.** Here, a person seeks to create a new social structure that will more effectively allow people to meet what the rebel considers appropriate goals. Rebels attack the value system of the ruling class and seek to replace it with an "ideal universal concept of justice" (Schafer, 1974: 30). Rebels' goals include the humanitarian treatment of all members of society; they oppose the exploitation of some groups to further the narrow interests of the powerful and wealthy. Rebels have an "altruistic communal motivation" for crime, rather than an egoistic motivation, and their offenses are directed toward nonpersonal goals. They try to set an example for their followers and seek publicity for their crimes. They pose a threat to lawmakers because they not only reject society's goals but also propose to replace those goals with their own. Some acts of rebellion involve conventional crimes such as vandalism, burglary, arson, and murder. Other rebellious acts, such as treason and conspiracy to overthrow the government, are defined as crimes by those who control power in order to punish people who challenge the status quo. Crimes that are officially labeled "politically motivated" or "terrorist" are punished with prison sentences longer than those for nonpolitical offenses (Smith and Damphousse, 1996).

Critique of Anomie Theory   Merton's anomie theory is quite general, but it has stimulated important theoretical work on the values of different groups and the availability of legitimate and illegitimate means to reach cultural goals. The theory's assumption that everyone accepts the same cultural goals and that everyone is encouraged to achieve those goals does not describe many societies very well. Even in the United States, anomie theory seems to apply primarily to the goal of financial success and to crimes against property; it does not explain crimes of violence very well.

One study found that income-generating crime and drug use were related to "the central variable in classic strain theory—dissatisfaction with monetary status," whether that dissatisfaction was a result of objective or subjective monetary position (Agnew et al., 1996: 698). People with less education and lower incomes were less satisfied with their monetary situation, and that dissatisfaction was associated with higher crime rates. Objective social class position thus had an indirect effect on crime. Dissatisfaction was also more common among people, regardless of their social class standing, who desired a lot of money, did not expect to make a lot of money, and felt relatively deprived. That subjective monetary position was also associated with greater involvement in crime.

General Strain Theory   Robert Agnew has proposed and tested a **general strain theory** that expands on Merton's theory. In place of anomie theory's limited focus on the blockage of access to societal goals, especially those involving monetary success, Agnew (1992: 74) proposes that a general strain theory should focus on at least three measures of strain: "(1) the actual or anticipated failure to achieve positively valued goals, (2) the actual or anticipated removal of positively valued stimuli, and (3) the actual or anticipated presentation of negative stimuli." Agnew (1992: 74) suggests that criminologists should pay attention to such dimensions of strain as its "magnitude, recency, duration, and clustering of strainful events." He spells out several cognitive, emotional, and behavioral adaptations to strain, some of which have received little attention from criminologists. Then he proposes a series of factors that determine whether an adolescent will cope with strain in a delinquent or nondelinquent fashion. These factors include temperament, intelligence, interpersonal skills, self-efficacy, association with delinquent peers, and conventional social support.

Elaborating on this theory, Agnew (2001) proposes that strain is most likely to lead to crime and delinquency when it is perceived as unjust and high in magnitude, is associated with a low level of social control, and produces pressure to cope by breaking the law. The importance of these factors leads him to conclude that crime will be no more than weakly associated with some kinds of strain, such as lack of success in school or at work, but will be more strongly associated with other types of strain, such as parental rejection, harsh and erratic discipline, child abuse and neglect, peer abuse, and discriminatory treatment.

One test of general strain theory provided qualified support for the impact of strain on delinquency and drug use, and found that delinquent peers and self-efficacy conditioned the impact of strain on such behavior (Agnew and White, 1992). In another study, such measures of general strain as poor relations with adults, dissatisfaction with friends and school, stressful life events (e.g., family breakup, unemployment, and moving), and living in a problem-ridden neighborhood were positively related to delinquency. General strain also led to delinquency by weakening conventional social bonds and increasing involvement with delinquent peers (Paternoster and Mazerolle, 1994). Other research has found that strain is most likely to generate delinquent behavior among juveniles who are high in negative emotionality and low in constraint, perhaps because those with such personality traits are "more likely to experience intense emotional reactions to strain, less able to engage in noncriminal coping, less aware of and concerned with the costs of crime, and more disposed to criminal coping" (Agnew et al., 2002: 64; see also Broidy, 2001).

Differential Opportunity and Delinquency

During the 1950s and 1960s, many cities in the United States experienced juvenile gang warfare, which involved assaults and sometimes murders. Not only did gang "rumbles" provide the basis for many newspaper, radio, and television reports, but they seeped into the popular culture in plays and movies such as *West Side Story*. During this era, criminologists focused their attention on juvenile delinquency, especially gang delinquency.

Opportunity and Gang Delinquency   One influential theory of gangs is Richard Cloward and Lloyd Ohlin's (1960) **differential opportunity theory**, which combines Merton's anomie theory with Sutherland's differential association theory (see Chapter 8).

Cloward and Ohlin follow Merton in emphasizing cultural goals and the means people use to reach those goals. According to Merton, innovation in the form of crime occurs when people lack access to the legitimate means to reach culturally approved goals and turn to illegitimate means to achieve those goals. Cloward and Ohlin add to this theory by suggesting that people's access to both legitimate and illegitimate means is socially structured. In other words, there is "differential opportunity" to reach cultural goals by legitimate means, but there is also "differential opportunity" to use illegitimate means to reach those goals.

Differential opportunity theory focuses on the discrepancy between what lower-class juveniles want and what is available to them. It assumes that "discrepancies between aspirations and legitimate chances of achievement increase as one descends in the class structure," with lower-class youths learning their goals from the larger culture but "unable to revise their aspirations downward" (Cloward and Ohlin, 1960: 86). Their lack of access to legitimate means to reach cultural goals produces intense frustration, and they search for illegitimate means to achieve cultural goals.

Cloward and Ohlin claim that two kinds of opportunities are differentially distributed. First, there are differences in access to "learning structures," which are the "appropriate environments for the acquisition of the values and skills associated with the performance of a particular role" (Cloward and Ohlin, 1960: 148). Second, there are differences in access to "performance structures," or opportunities to join with others who share a similar problem of adjustment and opportunities to gain peer approval for one's behavior. In Cloward and Ohlin's theory, delinquents must not only learn certain values and skills but must also have support for the performance of delinquent behavior once they have acquired those values and skills. According to differential opportunity theory, the social structure of a community determines the access that lower-class youths will have to both learning and performance structures.

Critique of Differential Opportunity Theory   Like Merton, Cloward and Ohlin assume that people are socialized with the desire for cultural goals but confront obstacles to reaching those goals. Cloward and Ohlin offer no evidence that lower-class gang boys are socialized to want to reach those cultural goals, and no evidence that the discrepancy between goals and legitimate means is greater for lower-class gang members than for other lower-class youths. Like Merton, Cloward and Ohlin focus on social-structural factors such as institutionalized access to opportunities rather than on individual decisions about how to act. A more complete theory might also look at the way people seek out or actually use opportunities to engage in crime and delinquency. In spite of its shortcomings, Cloward and Ohlin's theory has had a major influence on social policies, especially the Great Society programs of the mid-1960s, that have tried to reduce crime and delinquency by increasing the legitimate opportunities available to the lower classes.

Research on Illegitimate Opportunity Structures   A few criminologists have tried to identify the factors that determine access to illegitimate means to achieve goals. One study found that women's access to opportunities in the criminal underworld is blocked in various ways (Steffensmeier, 1983). Because women are excluded from criminal organizations and lack the contacts that would allow them to engage in criminal enterprises safely and profitably, they are less involved than men in most kinds of crime, and they tend to engage in criminal activity that is congruent with existing gender roles.

Research indicates that adolescents' use of illegitimate means depends on the resources available to them, such as money, a car, intelligence, and body type; these and other resources "provide the adolescent with the power and autonomy necessary to overcome the barriers to delinquency" (Agnew, 1990: 559). Access to such resources is most likely to lead to delinquent behavior among adolescents who are predisposed to delinquency, are high in perceived self-efficacy, and find themselves in situations in which the advantages of delinquency are high and its disadvantages low.

Social Class, Values, and Delinquency

Closely related to Merton's and Cloward and Ohlin's theories are two theories that emphasize social class differences in values and responses to blocked opportunities: Albert Cohen's (1955) reaction-formation theory and Walter Miller's (1958) theory of lower-class culture.

Reaction-Formation Theory   In *Delinquent Boys*, Albert Cohen (1955: 25) seeks to explain why a juvenile delinquent subculture that he characterizes as "nonutilitarian, malicious, and negativistic" is found among working-class male adolescents. His concern is only with certain kinds of delinquency: gang fights and vandalism, rather than profit-oriented theft.

Cohen describes dominant American values in much the same way Merton does: striving for success through hard work, deferring gratification, being ambitious, maintaining hope for the future, being self-reliant, respecting property, and controlling aggression. Cohen claims that working-class adolescent males pick up these values from their parents, who share middle-class values even though they are members of the working class. Adolescents also learn middle-class values from the media and from former members of the working class who have entered the middle class. The school is an important source of middle-class values such as discipline and self-reliance, and its teachers communicate middle-class values and often come from the middle class themselves. According to Cohen, working-class adolescents are at a disadvantage in school, because their background does not equip them for academic success in this middle-class setting. Because they are too young to form a family or to hold a job that pays well, working-class adolescents lack legitimate opportunities to achieve culturally approved goals.

Because they are emotionally attached to middle-class goals they cannot attain, these working-class boys must repudiate those goals. This produces a **reaction-formation**, in this case a reversal of middle-class values. For instance, the middle class favors the control of aggression, so the working-class male adolescent subculture awards prestige for the use of violence. The middle class reveres property, so the working-class gang values the senseless destruction of property. This reaction-formation, a psychological defense against the failure to achieve strongly held desires, seeks the exact opposite of middle-class goals as a way of repudiating those goals and validating the goals that replace them.

Cohen thus links a particular social class (the working class) to specific values (aggressiveness and destructiveness) that in turn lead to certain kinds of delinquency (gang fights and vandalism). The type of delinquency Cohen is interested in thus originates from a repudiation of middle-class values, rather than from conformity to working-class values.

Critique of Reaction-Formation Theory   Cohen's theory, like Merton's, requires a culture that encourages everyone to strive for the same goals, especially material success. Lois DeFleur (1970) found that Cohen's theory did not explain delinquency in Argentina. Little "nonutilitarian, malicious, and negativistic" working-class delinquency occurred there, apparently because the lowest classes were not socialized to seek middle-class goals.

Cohen's reaction-formation theory does not explain middle-class delinquency, nor does it explain why some delinquents turn away from violations of the law and leave gangs as they grow older, while other delinquents move on to become adult criminals. Cohen's emphasis on age explains why some males move out of delinquency as they gain access to other sources of prestige such as jobs and families, but his emphasis on social class does not tell us why most delinquents give up illegal behavior even though they remain members of the working class.

Lower-Class Culture Theory   Contrary to Cohen's theory that nonutilitarian, working-class male delinquency has its roots in the rejection of traditional middle-class values is the position of Walter Miller (1958). Miller proposes that gang delinquency in lower-class communities is a result of positive efforts by adolescents to achieve goals implicit in lower-class **focal concerns**, or areas of interest that elicit widespread, persistent attention and emotional involvement.

The focal concern of "trouble" refers to situations that bring unwelcome or complicating involvement with official authority. Issues of staying out of trouble and getting into trouble are of daily concern to the lower class, according to Miller. The lower class avoids illegal behavior, he says, in order to keep out of trouble, rather than because it is committed to a law-abiding way of life. The lower class seeks to avoid breaking the law but at the same time may admire those who engage in crime and delinquency.

A second focal concern is "toughness," a concern with masculinity, physical prowess, bravery, and daring. A third is "smartness," the capacity to outwit or con others and avoid being duped oneself. Through clever verbal exchanges, lower-class youths can achieve prestige by demonstrating maximum use of their mental abilities and minimum use of their physical strength. There is an apparent contradiction here, for toughness can inhibit the display of smartness and smartness can inhibit the display of toughness; both, however, are of concern to the lower class, according to Miller.

Another focal concern of lower-class culture is "excitement," the concern with thrills, risks, and the avoidance of boredom. The life of the poor may be unstimulating because of the lack of money with which to pay for leisure goods and activities, and this could be a source of the lower class's interest in exciting activities. Indeed, an early study of teenage gangs concluded that avoidance of boredom was a major reason for gang delinquency (Thrasher, 1963). The search for excitement can also lead to gambling and the use of alcohol and illegal drugs.

Another focal concern of the lower class is "fate," an interest in luck, fortune, and jinxes. The poor often feel, and with some justification, that their lives are governed by external forces over which they have little or no control. Related to this attention to external control is a sixth focal concern, "autonomy," which is the desire to be one's own master, often expressed as "no one's going to push me around."

Critique of Lower-Class Culture Theory   Miller's theory might lead us to believe that all members of the lower class, even adults, will violate the law regularly, for the theory does not distinguish between offenders and nonoffenders from the lower class in terms of their focal concerns. Unlike Cohen, who examines the sources of the values and norms of working-class male adolescents, Miller does not explain the origins of lower-class focal concerns. Neither Miller nor Cohen explains variations in values and delinquency among racial and ethnic groups. For instance, a study in San Diego found that Mexican American gangs were oriented to a local network of family and friends and emphasized the preservation of honor, whereas African American gangs were businesslike enterprises that focused on making money through illegal means (Sanders, 1994).

Delinquency and Values   Social class by itself is not a cause of crime and delinquency. Instead, violation of the law is a result of factors associated with social class, such as values, goals, and socially structured opportunities. We might thus expect delinquents from all social classes to have certain values, goals, and opportunities in common, and to differ from nondelinquents of all social classes in those factors.

One study that looked at lower-class, middle-class, and upper-class delinquency tried to explain youthful misbehavior in terms other than social class. The researcher found that commitment to values such as short-run pleasure seeking, thrills, excitement, trouble, toughness, conning, and the search for a "fast buck" was associated with self-reported involvement in delinquency; this was true for all social classes. This study also revealed less commitment to conventional value orientations such as hard work, delayed gratification, formal education, and various themes of the Protestant ethic among boys of all social classes who engaged in delinquency (Cernkovich, 1978c). This research suggests that social class is a less important predictor of delinquency than values, and that values correlate imperfectly with social class.

Some people may violate the law because they are able to "stretch" values (Rodman, 1963). They may share values with the middle class and the law-abiding, but because they are weakly attached to family, school, and work, they believe they have little to lose from violating the law. They are thus more flexible in interpreting social constraints on their behavior. For instance, one middle-class value is respect for property; a related norm is that property should not be stolen, damaged, or used without the owner's permission. This norm is adhered to by most people, but some people are able to stretch the norm by reinterpreting it to define a purse on an office desk as property that can be stolen because the owner was careless enough to leave it unattended. The stretching of norms to permit violation of the law probably occurs among members of all social classes, including poor people who shoplift and wealthy executives who engage in price fixing.

The Subculture of Violence

One theory of the origin of violent crime that uses norms and values as explanatory variables is the **subculture-of-violence theory** developed by Marvin Wolfgang and Franco Ferracuti (1982). They state that the norms shared by a group of people sometimes define violence as an appropriate response to certain circumstances. These norms have a reality of their own and influence behavior, sometimes leading people to engage in violent crime in order to conform to others' expectations. Wolfgang and Ferracuti do not explore the historical and social-structural origins of these norms in detail, but they imply that the norms originate in the social conditions of certain countries, social classes, and racial and ethnic groups. This theory is a cultural explanation of violent crime rather than a social-structural one, so it emphasizes norms, values, and beliefs rather than the social conditions that cause violence.

A **subculture** is a patterned way of life similar in some ways to but different in others from the dominant culture of a society. It includes specific standards of behavior that are learned and transmitted from generation to generation. In a subculture of violence, the norms differ from those of the dominant culture in expectations about the use of violence or aggression as a response to threats, insults, or the display of a weapon. As a result, the more integrated into a subculture of violence an individual or a group is, the greater the likelihood that the individual or group will engage in violent crime. Violence in such a subculture is rarely accompanied by guilt, because violence is not considered wrong or deviant.

Evidence of the Subculture of Violence   Wolfgang's (1958) study of homicide in Philadelphia found evidence consistent with the subculture-of-violence theory. Forty-three percent of the homicide offenders had been arrested previously for crimes against the person, and about one-fourth of the homicide victims had been arrested for crimes against the person. Whites had a murder rate of 1.8 per 100,000, and white males between twenty and twenty-four had a rate of 8.2 per 100,000. Blacks, on the other hand, had a murder rate of 24.6 per 100,000, and black males between twenty and twenty-four had a homicide rate of 92.5 per 100,000. The homicide rate for young black males was thus much higher than the rate for any other group. Wolfgang and Ferracuti later interpreted these and other data—such as Colombia's pattern of *la violencia,* in which 280,000 people were killed from 1946 to 1958—as support for their theory that among certain groups and in certain nations there exist norms favoring the use of interpersonal violence.

A subculture of violence exists among young homeless males. As children these street people learn from their abusive parents that violence is useful for imposing one's will on others, and they therefore develop values that favor violence as a way to solve interpersonal problems. Later, the strain of homelessness and poverty contributes to their high level of arousal and tendency to anger easily. Interaction with other street people spreads values favoring violence through peer socialization and the rewards that come from successfully using violence to resolve differences. Violence helps the homeless youths avoid victimization by others, thereby strengthening values supporting the use of violence for self-protection. These values heighten the youths' sensitivity to insult and perceived harm, making them more likely to resort to violence than they would be in the absence of such values. These homeless youths are especially likely to behave violently when their conflicts with others are intense, when they perceive a high level of potential harm, when the other party to the dispute is a male, and when the confrontation occurs on the street (Baron, Kennedy, and Forde, 2001).

Several criminologists have tried to explain the high homicide rates in the southern United States in terms of a subculture of violence. One method used to test the effect of cultural values on the homicide rates of different regions is to isolate the effects of economic and social factors on homicide rates and then attribute the remaining variation in rates to cultural differences, such as the norms of a subculture of violence. The problem with this approach is that it includes no direct measure of regional variations in norms and values. As a result, if the measurement of economic and social factors is inadequate or incomplete, the residual effect of cultural factors will be exaggerated. One study concluded that the economic, educational, and racial composition of the states was relatively unimportant in explaining regional variations in homicide rates and suggested that a subculture of violence explained such variations (Hackney, 1969). However, a later study that employed a more sophisticated measure of poverty found that poverty explained much of the state-by-state variation in homicide rates (Loftin and Hill, 1974). Thus, an index that better measured poverty left a smaller residual variation in homicide rates that could be attributed to a subculture of violence.

One study found that the homicide rates of metropolitan areas in the United States were influenced by the region in which the city was located and by its racial composition, even when factors such as poverty were controlled (Messner, 1983). In other words, the higher homicide rates in the southern cities, and also in the cities with larger black populations, could not be accounted for by low income alone. However, this study, like most previous ones, provided no direct measure of subcultural values.

Another study used the results of a national survey to test for the existence of a southern subculture of violence. The researchers distinguished between "violent attitudes" (such as approving of a man who punches a protester or punches a drunk who has bumped into the man and his wife) and "defensive attitudes" (such as approving of a man who punches a burglar in his house or punches a stranger who has hit his child). The researchers concluded that the violent attitudes were not associated with a regional subculture of violence, after structural differences among regions were taken into account. Defensive violence was more widespread in the South, but the researchers argued that defensive violence was not characteristic of a subculture of violence. They saw it instead as "a part of mainstream American cultural attitudes that regard violence in the protection of people and property as legitimate" (Dixon and

Lizotte, 1987: 391). Critics contend that the greater willingness of Southerners to use violence to defend themselves or their honor is in fact evidence of a subculture of violence (Ellison and McCall, 1989; Nisbett and Cohen, 1996). Dixon and Lizotte's study is an advance over previous research that had failed to measure attitudes toward violence in a direct way, but it raises another issue: Exactly how do we define a subculture of violence, and what specific attitudes about when violence should be used will demonstrate the existence of such a subculture? The precise role of the subculture of violence in explaining regional variations in homicide rates remains unclear.

Critique of the Subculture-of-Violence Theory   Some groups, regions, and countries do have high rates of criminal violence, but there is as yet no strong evidence supporting a role for the subculture of violence in the genesis of violent crime. This could be because the appropriate research design to test for this relationship has not been developed or implemented. Some researchers have inferred norms and attitudes supporting the use of violence from high rates of violent crime, and have then explained those high rates of violent crime by the inferred norms and attitudes. This circular approach provides no independent evidence that norms and attitudes supporting violence exist in groups, regions, or countries that have high rates of violent crime.

There is also no compelling evidence that either blacks or southerners hold the values of a subculture of violence (Dixon and Lizotte, 1987; Cao, Adams, and Jensen, 1997). More research on cultural differences among regions of the country might be done by carrying out surveys or by examining regional variations in preferences for art, literature, music, or sports (Messner, 1983). Even if such regional variations were found, they might not explain differences in rates of violent crime, because violence might be more closely related to the nature of social interaction in a group than it is to the group's norms and values about when violence is appropriate.

Angry Aggression and Disputatiousness   The failure to demonstrate conclusively that groups and regions with high rates of violent crime hold values that actually support violence has led some sociologists to suggest alternative explanations for violence. One theory proposes that "angry aggression" that sometimes takes the form of violent crime characterizes "the truly disadvantaged," William Julius Wilson's (1987) term for lower-class people who live in cities and experience discrimination and social isolation. Their low position exposes members of this social class to a high level of stress and limits the resources they have available for coping with the effects of that stress. The urban environment exposes the truly disadvantaged to stress, crowding, noise, and other conditions associated with a high level of arousal, which in turn is associated with a high probability of angry aggression. Racial and ethnic discrimination blocks opportunities and insults people, thereby heightening arousal and increasing angry aggression. Social isolation reinforces angry aggression by confining the truly disadvantaged to communities that have high rates of violent crime; living with the daily threat of crime exacerbates stress and angry aggression (Bernard, 1990). This theory does not propose that people value violence, but rather that certain social conditions heighten arousal, stress, and angry aggression, all of which are linked to high levels of violent crime for particular social classes, racial and ethnic groups, communities, and regions.

A similar theory proposes that differences in rates of violent crime may be explained by variations in "disputatiousness" (Luckenbill and Doyle, 1989). A dispute begins when a person defines a negative outcome of a social interaction as an injury for which the other person is to blame. After the negative outcome is defined as a grievance, the victim may demand reparation from the person who caused the injury. If that other person rejects the claim for reparation, the situation becomes a dispute. The person holding the grievance might react in a variety of ways, one of which is the use of force. Disputatiousness is the likelihood of defining an injury as a grievance and claiming reparation, and aggressiveness is the willingness to persevere and use force to resolve the dispute. When homicides occur, they are often the result of the use of force to resolve such interpersonal disputes (Luckenbill, 1977).

Other attitudes related to disputatiousness and angry aggression might also be more common in groups, communities, and regions that have high levels of violence. For example, one study found that variations in punitiveness and in emphasis placed on showing courage in interpersonal conflicts helped explain the relatively high rate of violence by the lower classes. To some extent, variations in punitiveness also explained the relatively high rate of violence by young males (Markowitz and Felson, 1998).

Gender, Crime, and Feminist Criminology

Explanations of the difference between men's and women's crime rates have long been part of criminology. Early theorists assumed innate differences between the sexes, portraying men as naturally more aggressive than women as a way of explaining why men commit so much more crime. Others have proposed that men commit more crime than women because they are socialized differently; that is, men are taught to be more aggressive, and women learn to be more passive. More recently, feminists have argued that **gender structure**—the institutional arrangements that treat men and women, and boys and girls, differently—is associated with differences between the sexes in crime. Gender structure involves a division of labor between men and women, males' domination of the power structure, and gendered differences in sexuality (Connell, 1993).

Kathleen Daly and Meda Chesney-Lind (1988: 504) describe feminist thought as having the following five characteristics:

- Gender is not a natural fact but a complex social, historical, and cultural product; it is related to, but not simply derived from, biological sex difference and reproductive capacities.
- Gender and gender relations order social life and social institutions in fundamental ways.
- Gender relations and constructs of masculinity and femininity are not symmetrical but are based on an organizing principle of men's superiority and social and political-economic dominance over women.
- Systems of knowledge reflect men's views of the natural and social world; the production of knowledge is gendered.
- Women should be at the center of intellectual inquiry, not peripheral, invisible, or appendages to men.

Feminist theories focus on gender, but they also incorporate race and social class into their explanations of behavior.

Daly and Chesney-Lind propose three major problems that gender poses for criminologists. The first is the **generalizability problem**, the question of whether theories of crime, most of which were developed to explain offending by men and tested on male subjects, can be applied to crime and delinquency by women. The second problem is the **gender ratio problem**, the issue of why males commit more crime than females. The third problem is sexism in theories of female crime and in the treatment of females by the juvenile and criminal justice systems. Daly and Chesney-Lind (1988: 517, 519) suggest that feminist criminologists should set aside the generalizability and gender ratio problems and "plunge more deeply into the social worlds of girls and women" in order to understand "crime at close range."

The Generalizability Problem

Most theories of crime and delinquency have been developed to explain males' violations of the law and have then been tested with data collected from boys or men. One explanation for this is that most criminologists have been men, and they have simply failed to acknowledge or be interested in law breaking by females. Daly and Chesney-Lind (1988: 506) believe that "criminologists should begin to appreciate that their discipline and its questions are a product of white, economically privileged men's experiences." A different explanation for criminology's neglect of women is that crime by females is less common, and less serious when it does occur, than crime by males. In 2001, 70 percent of suspects arrested for serious property crimes were males, 83 percent of those arrested for serious violent crimes were males, and 93 percent of prison inmates were males. These figures do not justify neglect of the female offender, but they do suggest that crime, especially serious violent crime, is committed primarily by males.

Theories of crime have indeed paid little attention to the female offender, often speaking of criminals as if they are all males. This deficiency is common to both the privileged white men who have developed theories of crime in the past and some of today's feminists who propose theories of "male violence" with little effort to develop a general theory of violence (Archer, 1994a; Newburn and Stanko, 1994). For example, many feminists have treated serial murder as a prototypically male phenomenon, despite evidence that 10 to 15 percent of all serial killers are women (Jenkins, 1994).

Eileen Leonard (1982) has assessed influential theories of crime such as Merton's anomie theory and found that they typically neglect female offending and cannot explain it. Merton speaks of the learning of success goals, but his theory was developed at a time when striving for financial success was something boys were more likely than girls to learn from their parents, teachers, peers, and the media. His theory would have been more complete if he had examined the goals that girls and women learned and then looked at their modes of adaptation to disjunctions between those goals and the means available to attain them.

Travis Hirschi's social control theory, examined in Chapter 7, was tested only with the data for boys, even though he collected data from both boys and girls. Wolfgang, Figlio, and Sellin's first cohort study, discussed in Chapter 1, gathered data only from boys. When a second cohort was studied, data were gathered for both boys and girls, allowing the researchers to test the generalizability of their results from the first study and thus determine if the same social processes were common to delinquency by boys and by girls.

The Gender Ratio Problem

Feminists have criticized criminologists for using the male offender as the point of comparison for assessing the female offender, claiming that the question traditionally asked about the female criminal was why she was not similar to the male criminal. The answer was often cast in sexist terms, portraying women as innately passive, unambitious, and well suited to the domestic role. Today the gender ratio problem is commonly phrased as, "Why do so many more men than women commit crime, especially violent crime?" (Messerschmidt, 1993; Archer, 1994a; Newburn and Stanko, 1994).

Male-Female Convergence?   Freda Adler's *Sisters in Crime: The Rise of the New Female Criminal* (1975) looked at the gender ratio problem in terms of the changing position of women in society, arguing that the liberation of women from traditional gender roles and their greater participation in the labor force were opening up new opportunities to commit crime, and suggesting that this would eventually produce a convergence of male and female rates. As we saw in Chapter 4, gender arrest rates have converged somewhat over time but are still far from equal, with at least four-fifths of the arrests for every serious crime except larceny being males.

Has the feminist movement increased crime by women? Those most active in the feminist movement, white women of the middle and upper-middle classes, are rarely arrested for index crimes. Most crime by women is committed by poorer members of minority groups, and they are not well represented among contemporary feminists. Moreover, research on delinquency by girls finds that violation of the law is not associated with feminist attitudes; indeed, feminist attitudes seem to inhibit property offenses and violent crimes (Giordano, 1978; James and Thornton, 1980; Figueira-McDonough, 1984).

Since the end of World War II, there has been a large increase in the proportion of women holding jobs outside the home. Some, but probably not most, of this increased involvement in the labor force is attributable to the feminist movement and the changes in gender roles that it has produced. Other social forces that have led more women to take jobs include rising rates of divorce and illegitimacy, an increase in average age at first marriage, and the perception that inflation has so eroded the family's buying power that two incomes are needed. Whatever the reasons for women's increased labor-force participation, women who hold jobs outside the home have more opportunities to commit crimes such as larceny and embezzlement. However, FBI data indicate that most arrests of females are not occupationally related; women are more likely to be arrested for passing bad checks, credit card or welfare fraud, and shoplifting rather than for employee theft or embezzlement. One study concludes that the increase in theft by women is due less to the feminist movement or increased labor-force participation than it is to changes in merchandising—such as more self-service stores or more buying on credit—that make theft or fraud easier for shoppers, a traditional female role (Steffensmeier and Cobb, 1981).

Increased participation of women in the labor force might have a more subtle effect on the crime rate of females, increasing a sense of relative deprivation or entitlement among women who are not working outside the home, or among those who are being paid less than their male colleagues for the same work. If there is a widespread perception—accurate or not—that other women are doing well financially and being fulfilled by their jobs, then women who are not working may believe that they deserve more than they have. This sense of deprivation could also develop if women, whether in the labor force or not, compare their own position unfavorably with that of men. Feminism might have raised expectations faster than reality has changed, and thus produced frustration that has led to more crime by women.

Gender Structure and Male-Female Differences in Crime   Because society is structured in terms of gender, males and females experience different types of strain. Strain theorists suggest that men more often experience financial strain, which can lead to property crimes, and severe interpersonal conflict, which can lead to violent crime. Women more often experience strain because they are subjected to high levels of social control and restricted in access to both legitimate and illegitimate opportunities. Those forms of strain can lead to self-destructive behavior such as drug use or to violence against family members. Increased financial strain for females has led to greater equality between females and males in their involvement in minor property offenses (Broidy and Agnew, 1997).

Male and female robbers have similar motivations but adapt their behavior to a gendered environment in which men are perceived as strong and women as weak.

Male robbers do not usually victimize women, because such crimes would not demonstrate their masculinity to their male peers. Female robbers, on the other hand, often victimize other women, because female victims are seen as less apt to be armed and as weaker and more easily intimidated than males. Some female robbers use men's views of women as weak, sexually available, and easily manipulated to entice men into situations that make them vulnerable to robbery. Those female robbers typically use firearms to reduce resistance by males who see all women as weak (Miller, 1998).

Gender Socialization

Male-female differences in crime, especially violent crime, are often explained in terms of differences in the way the sexes are socialized and the roles they play. Anne Campbell and Steven Muncer (1994; Campbell, 1993) reject biological explanations of sex differences in aggressiveness, claiming that men are more aggressive than women because they learn different attitudes toward aggressive behavior. Men are taught to regard aggression as a practical way to establish control over others and assume authority over the external world. Women, on the other hand, learn to regard aggression as a personal failure to control their impulses and therefore as something to avoid. This theory is consistent with some of the evidence on crime. For example, male serial killers frequently use sexual aggression to control their victims, and battered women who kill their husbands usually resort to violence only after a long period of trying to control their anger.

Feminist critics argue that some gender-socialization and gender-role explanations are simply elaborations on assumptions about innate differences between men and women and that such explanations ignore the role of power and inequality between men and women and the way that social institutions such as the state, the family, the school, and the media construct and reinforce those differences. Gender-role theory also minimizes variability in the construction of gender by implying that there is a single way to be masculine or feminine. An emphasis on socialization also suggests that males and females passively accept what they are taught, rather than actively contribute to the construction of gender (Messerschmidt, 1993).

Doing Gender

A concept that links socialization with social structure is **doing gender**, the idea that through their social behavior men develop and act out forms of masculinity, or masculinities, and that women develop and act out forms of femininity, or femininities. Ways of being masculine or feminine are learned through socialization, but they are also influenced by the situations in which people find themselves, by the resources available to them, and by social-structural factors such as the division of labor, the allocation of power, and cultural definitions of sexuality. (See the Using Criminology box.)

James Messerschmidt (1993, 1997) has explored the link between the masculinities that men enact and the crime they commit, showing that much crime by males involves behavior defined as masculine. Race, ethnicity, social class, and age determine the resources that boys and men have to construct masculinity. The situations in which they find themselves (in school, on the street, at work, or in the family) influence the ways they enact masculinity. Lower-class black adolescents might enact masculinity by carrying a gun, and upper-middle-class white teens might enact masculinity by stealing hubcaps. Adult men of the upper-middle class enact masculine scripts by engaging in competitive business practices, which sometimes lead to white-collar crime, whereas adult men of the working class demonstrate their masculinity by drinking in bars, which can lead to fights. Masculine scripts of this sort both express and reinforce the division of labor between men and women, male dominance and power, and the norm of heterosexuality. As Messerschmidt (1993: 85) writes,

> Crime by men is not simply an extension of the "male sex role." Rather, crime by men is a form of social practice invoked as a resource, when other resources are unavailable, for accomplishing masculinity. By analyzing masculinities, then, we can begin to understand the socially constructed differences among men and thus explain why men engage in different forms of crime.

Men are especially likely to enact masculine scripts when their manliness is in question and they need to establish their character. Murders and assaults by men are

USING CRIMINOLOGY

Gender and the Student-Murderer

Following the April 20, 1999, murders of twelve students and one teacher at Columbine High School in Littleton, Colorado, many explanations were offered for the behavior of Eric Harris and Dylan Klebold, the students who took their own lives after their brutal attack. Blame was placed on lax gun-control laws, violent images in the media, irresponsible parents, and cruel peers. Jackson Katz and Sut Jhally have pointedly asked, "All of these factors are of course relevant, but if they were the primary answers, then why are girls, who live in the same environment, not responding in the same way?" (p. E1) They observe that we talk about violence in a gender-neutral way when the perpetrators are male, trying to understand what it is about "the youth of America" that makes them commit such crimes. Had the student-murderers been girls, they argue, everyone would have focused on their gender as the primary factor in need of explanation.

Katz and Jhally claim that

> [t]he issue is not just violence in the media but the construction of violent masculinity as a cultural norm. From rock and rap music and videos, Hollywood action films, professional and college sports, the culture produces a stream of images of violent, abusive men and promotes characteristics such as dominance, power, and control as means of establishing or maintaining manhood" (p. E5)

When some teenage boys are rejected by their peers—whether by male athletes who ridicule them for not fit-

ting in, as in Littleton, or by a girlfriend, as in a nonfatal shooting spree a month later in Conyers, Georgia—they sometimes turn to an "equalizer," a firearm, for revenge. Easy access to guns facilitates violence in a cultural context in which male strength is defined in terms of the ability to dominate others with fear and force. Katz and Jhally claim that in the wake of violence in the schools we should be asking,

> "How does the cultural environment, including media images, contribute to definitions of manhood that are picked up by adolescents?" Or, "How does repeated exposure to violent masculinity normalize and naturalize this violence?" (p. E5)

Mona J. E. Danner and Dianne Cyr Carmody (p.107) regard the schools themselves as a source of violence, describing them as "important institutions for doing gender" in two ways: male domination of females, and higher-status male domination of lower-status males. They point out that the news media, as well as the law-enforcement officials and academics on whom the media rely, miss the real meaning of school violence when they identify the sources as individual psychopathology and easy access to firearms. Recognizing "the interpersonal and gendered dynamics behind the attacks," the classmates of the offenders and victims more accurately explain school violence in terms of the bullying of some males by higher-status ones and revenge against girlfriends by male killers (Danner and Carmody, p. 107).

Sources: Based on Jackson Katz and Sut Jhally, "Society: The National Conversation in the Wake of Littleton Is Missing the Mark," *Boston Globe,* May 2, 1999, pp. E1, E5; Mona J. E. Danner and Dianne Cyr Carmody, "Missing Gender in Cases of Infamous School Violence: Investigating Research and Media Explanations," *Justice Quarterly* 18 (March 2001), 87–114.

often efforts to reestablish a reputation after an argument, insult, or threat, particularly when there is an audience to the disrespect shown by another person (Archer, 1994b). Often men's violence against women is aimed at maintaining proprietary control over their wives or lovers, or at thwarting men who threaten that control (Polk, 1994). Men also enact masculine scripts to show others they are not feminine—indeed that they have contempt for women—when they engage in sexual assault, gay bashing, and sexual harassment.

Most murders committed by men fit one of these scenarios, but relatively few murders by women do. For instance, women rarely kill their husbands or lovers to maintain proprietary control over them. One study of women who had committed murder found that most of them had killed men after long-term provocation and abuse (Kirkpatrick and Humphrey, 1989; see also Mann, 1996). Before resorting to lethal violence, the women usually had to define their situation as life-threatening or as seriously affecting their physical or emotional well-being. Nearly all of the women had violent upbringings, frequently seeing their parents fighting, sometimes with weapons. Many of the women had been beaten, tortured, or sexually abused as children. The women had typically lost someone close to them. Those losses produced an overpowering sense of aloneness, a resentment of others, and a feeling that the world was conspiring against them, which often caused the women to withdraw from social contacts and reject help offered by others. In such circumstances, repeated abuse by a husband or lover sometimes led to lethal violence.

Power-Control Theory

John Hagan (1989: 145) and his colleagues have developed and tested **power-control theory,** which "asserts that the class structure of the family plays a significant role in explaining the social distribution of delinquent behavior through the social reproduction of gender relations." "Family class structure" is defined as "the configurations of power between spouses that derive from the positions these spouses occupy in their work inside and outside the home" (Hagan, 1989: 145). Also central to power-control theory is the idea of "social reproduction of gender relations," which refers to the "activities, institutions, and relationships that are involved in the maintenance and renewal of gender roles, in the family and elsewhere" (Hagan, 1989: 145).

Proposing that both the presence of power and the absence of control are conducive to deviance, power-control theory seeks to identify the family and social class relations most likely to lead to ordinary delinquency. The theory asks why male adolescents are more free than their female counterparts to deviate in ways defined by the state as delinquent. The answer, according to Hagan and his colleagues, lies in the greater control of girls' behavior by their parents. Both instrumental controls, such as supervision and surveillance, and relational controls, which involve ties of affiliation, are imposed more on daughters than on sons. This greater control of girls discourages them from taking risks, and because delinquency is a form of risk taking, girls are less delinquent than boys.

Power-control theory links gender and social class differences in delinquency to the structure of the family, claiming that there are critical differences between patriarchal (male-dominated) families and families that are more egalitarian. In a patriarchal family, the husband works at a job outside the home in which he has authority over others, and the wife is not employed outside the home. In an egalitarian family, both the husband and the wife work outside the home at paying jobs in which they have authority over others. Power-control theory predicts that egalitarian families will treat their daughters more like their sons, being less controlling and more encouraging of risk taking by their daughters. Patriarchal families, on the other hand, will control their daughters much more than their sons and discourage their daughters from taking risks. In this way, patriarchal families prepare their daughters for an adult life centered on the home, and egalitarian families prepare their daughters for work outside the home.

Because delinquency is a form of risk taking, power-control theory predicts that male-female differences in delinquency will be greater in patriarchal families, and in the lower and working classes where such families are most common. Male-female differences in delinquency will be less in egalitarian families, and in the middle and upper classes where those families are most common, because girls and boys in egalitarian families are both open to taking risks.

This complex theory has been subjected to several criticisms. Feminists object to the implication that participation in the labor force by mothers in egalitarian families is a cause of their daughters' delinquency, especially since female delinquency has not increased relative to male delinquency over a period when women's labor-force participation has increased significantly (Morash and Chesney-Lind, 1991). Others have argued that working at a paid job, even one with authority over others, does not necessarily translate into greater power in the home for women relative to their husbands. There is ample evidence that women working outside the home continue to do most of the domestic chores in the family, an indication of continuing patriarchy in two-worker households.

Power-control theory receives only mixed support from research studies. Work by Hagan and his colleagues in Toronto supports the theory's main points, but other studies have not supported the theory (Singer and Levine, 1988; Jensen and Thompson, 1990; Morash and Chesney-Lind, 1991). Gary Jensen (1993) claims that power-control theory adds nothing important to Hirschi's social control theory (see Chapter 7) by introducing the concept of power, and that power-control theory weakens its explanatory value by omitting such normative factors as aspirations, commitments, and beliefs, which are included in social control theory.

Women as Victims, Women as Resisters

Feminist criminologists have focused on the victimization of women by violent men, particularly in domestic assaults and forcible rapes. Critics have argued that the portrayal of women as victims, or potential victims, who need to be protected from male offenders poses a risk to the liberation of women from traditional gender roles by implying that women are not capable of being independent and equal to men (Roiphe, 1993).

Most feminist scholars believe, on the contrary, that the study of male violence against women is liberating, in that it challenges patriarchal dominance by men and empowers women. Women are capable of acting on their own behalf, despite structural pressures to remain subordinate. Pressure from feminists has produced important changes in recent years: Legal reforms have made it easier for rape victims to report their victimization, get help, and prosecute rapists; shelters have been established to house women who are leaving their abusive partners; and prisons have made changes to accommodate the gender-specific needs of female inmates.

Social, Cultural, and Economic Factors and Variations in Crime Rates

The social, cultural, and economic factors examined in this chapter help to make sense of the variations in crime rates that we looked at in Chapter 4.

Cross-national variations in crime rates seem to be due to differences among countries in social structure, culture, and economy. For instance, some white-collar crimes are more likely to occur in certain kinds of economies. Thus, price fixing occurs in the American economy as businesspeople try to enhance profits, and bribery by consumers is more common in Russia, where goods and services are in short supply. The degree to which a society relies on laws to make widely desired goods and services illegal influences the development and strength of organized crime in the society. Variations in rates of conventional crime from one society to another are attributable in part to the level of economic development, the extent of relative deprivation, and the opportunities that are available to achieve culturally approved goals.

Regional variations in crime rates can also be explained by differences in the social structure, the culture, and the economy. The subculture-of-violence theory proposes that regional variations in violent crime rates are a result of differences in norms and attitudes toward violence, though we lack strong supporting evidence for this theory.

Variations in crime rates by size of the community are also related to the factors examined in this chapter. For example, economic conditions in urban communities differ from economic conditions in small towns and rural areas, and those differences explain in part the higher crime rates of cities. In addition, the close proximity of people from different social classes in large communities can increase relative deprivation or a sense of inequity among the poor and lead to more conventional crime than occurs in the relatively more homogeneous small towns and rural areas.

Temporal variations in crime rates can be accounted for by changes in the social structure, the culture, and the economy. Changes in market conditions can increase or decrease white-collar crime. Technological breakthroughs and a growing reliance on trust and credit create new opportunities for white-collar crime. The passage of laws prohibiting the consumption of widely desired goods and services results in more opportunities for organized crime; this happened during Prohibition, and again more recently with the development of strict controls on the disposal of toxic wastes. The modernization process leads to changes in rates of conventional crime, especially rates of property crime. Conventional crimes also increase or decrease as groups experience relative deprivation, anomie, and blocked opportunities.

Variations in crime rates by sex, age, race, and social class are also related to the social structure, the culture, and the economy. For example, most white-collar crimes are committed by middle-aged or older white men of the middle or upper classes. The time needed to advance to the positions in which white-collar crime is committed means that white-collar offenders are usually middle-aged or older. White-collar offenders are usually white men, because discrimination by sex and race has closed many high-level corporate positions to women and minorities. As such discrimination is reduced, more white-collar crimes might be committed by women and minorities.

Anomie theory, differential opportunity theory, reaction-formation theory, and the theory that lower-class culture is a generating milieu of gang delinquency all account for the higher rates of serious and repetitive conventional crime among the lower and working classes. These theories help to explain the high rate of crime by young people, for young people are the most remote from the cultural goal of material success and are probably the most likely to encounter blocked opportunities. These theories also account for the high crime rates of blacks, who have had opportunities to achieve material success blocked by racial discrimination. The subculture-of-violence theory proposes that blacks' high rate of violent crime is due to a difference between their norms and attitudes toward violence and whites' norms and attitudes toward violence, but there is no compelling evidence that this is so. Many of the theories examined in this chapter do not do a good job of explaining the low crime rates of females and the high rates of males, but recently developed feminist theories have corrected this deficiency by showing how gender structure accounts for male-female differences in crime and delinquency.

We have not looked at all of the ways in which the social, cultural, and economic factors examined in this chapter can explain geographic, temporal, and social variations in rates of white-collar, organized, and conventional crime. From this brief discussion, however, we can see that social, cultural, and economic theories can be useful in explaining variations in crime rates.

Summary

This chapter has looked at the social, cultural, and economic causes of white-collar crime, organized crime, and conventional crime (with an emphasis on juvenile delinquency).

American free-enterprise ideology emphasizes profit seeking and competition. The pressure to make profits sometimes leads executives and corporations to violate the law. Efforts to outperform competitors can lead to offenses such as false advertising. Certain market conditions are conducive to white-collar crime, and trust and credit are sometimes abused. Large corporations have characteristics such as bureaucratic structure, unsatisfactory working conditions, and rational decision making that facilitate white-collar crime and employee theft. As new technology develops, opportunities are created for crime; computer and telecommunications crimes are costly offenses that have become more common in recent years.

Prohibition provided an opportunity for gangsters to become highly organized in their pursuit of profits. Since Prohibition ended in 1933, organized crime has turned to other sources of income, including gambling (according to some accounts), loan sharking, illegal drugs, bankruptcy and stock fraud, the illegal disposal of toxic wastes, and extortion.

Conventional crimes, especially property crimes, increase with economic development. Modernization also brings increased participation in crime by juveniles and by women. New opportunities for crime develop as an economy modernizes, and changes in the value of certain goods (such as precious metals) can alter patterns of crime. Employment might be more important for the social ties it provides than for the income it produces. One source of criminal behavior is relative deprivation, a condition in which people believe they are entitled to more than they can achieve by the legitimate means available to them.

Anomie theory proposes that a disjunction between cultural goals and access to legitimate means to attain those goals can lead to certain kinds of crime. Innovation occurs among those who strongly pursue cultural goals with means that are not socially approved; examples include petty theft by the poor and price fixing by corporate executives. Retreatists and rebels are often defined as criminals by those who control power.

Differential opportunity theory emphasizes access to both legitimate and illegitimate means to reach cultural goals, and claims that community social structure affects access to learning and performance structures.

Reaction-formation theory proposes that working-class male adolescents learn middle-class values, but because they are not equipped to succeed in school and at work, they reject these values and create values opposite to them. Their new values support violence and the theft and destruction of property, and this leads to "nonutilitarian, malicious, and negativistic" behavior.

The theory that delinquents react against middle-class values differs from the theory that the lower class is a generating milieu for gang delinquency. In this lower-class culture theory, delinquency is seen as conformity to the values or focal concerns of the lower class: trouble, toughness, smartness, excitement, fate, and autonomy.

The subculture-of-violence theory proposes that among certain groups and in certain areas there is a set of norms that support violent responses to particular situations. Some groups, such as young urban black males in the United States, and some regions, such as the South, do have high rates of criminal violence, but there is no strong evidence that those groups and regions have distinctive norms and attitudes that support violence or that such norms and attitudes lead to violent crime.

Feminist theories claim that gender structure is associated with low rates of crime and delinquency by females and high rates by males. The way that gender is constructed by a society's institutions influences the way that men and women do gender; male crime, especially violent crime, is often a way of enacting scripts of masculinity. Power-control theory aims to explain differences in delinquency rates between boys and girls in patriarchal and egalitarian families.

The social, cultural, and economic factors examined in this chapter can be useful in explaining geographic, temporal, and social variations in different kinds of crime.

IMPORTANT TERMS

anomie	gender structure	relative deprivation
computer crime	general strain theory	retreatism
conformity	generalizability problem	ritualism
differential opportunity theory	innovation	sense of inequity
doing gender	mode of adaptation	strain
EFT crime	power-control theory	subculture
focal concern	reaction-formation	subculture-of-violence theory
gender ratio problem	rebellion	

REVIEW QUESTIONS

1. What are the sources of white-collar crime in the United States? What policies can you suggest to reduce white-collar crime?

2. What are the major sources of income for organized crime in the United States? How do legitimate economic institutions contribute to organized crime?

3. What economic factors are conducive to conventional crime? What is the relationship between unemployment and conventional crime?

4. How does Robert Merton's anomie theory help us understand the sources of conventional crime? What are the shortcomings of the theory?

5. How do Richard Cloward and Lloyd Ohlin's, Albert Cohen's, and Walter Miller's theories of juvenile delinquency differ?

6. What is subculture-of-violence theory? Does research support this theory as an explanation of violent crime?

7. How does gender structure explain the gender ratio problem? What is the generalizability problem? What does it mean to do gender and enact masculinities? How does power-control theory explain male-female differences in delinquency in patriarchal and egalitarian families?

FOR FURTHER STUDY

White-Collar Crime   Two useful textbooks are James William Coleman's *The Criminal Elite: Understanding White-Collar Crime* (4th ed., New York: St. Martin's, 1998) and Stephen M. Rosoff, Henry N. Pontell, and Robert H. Tillman's *Profit without Honor: White Collar Crime and the Looting of America* (2nd ed., Upper Saddle River, NJ: Prentice Hall, 2002). A wide-ranging collection of essays on corporate crime is Frank Pearce and Laureen

Snider's (eds.) *Corporate Crime: Contemporary Debates* (Toronto: University of Toronto Press, 1995). The National White-Collar Crime Center's website (www.nw3c. org) provides links to information on the topic.

Organized Crime   Sources of income for organized crime are explored in Howard Abadinsky's *Organized Crime* (6th ed., Belmont, CA: Wadsworth, 2000). A recent examination of organized crime in Japan is Kenneth Szymkowiak's *Sokaiya: Extortion, Protection, and the Japanese Corporation* (Armonk, NY: M. E. Sharpe, 2002).

Crime, Employment, and Workplace Violence   Two studies of the relationship of crime to unemployment, work, and wages are Jeffrey Fagan and Richard B. Freeman's "Crime and Work" (in Michael Tonry, ed., *Crime and Justice: A Review of Research,* vol. 25. Chicago: University of Chicago Press, 1999, pp. 225–290) and Jared Bernstein and Ellen Houston's *Crime and Work: What We Can Learn from the Low-Wage Labor Market* (Washington, DC: Economic Policy Institute, 2000). Workplace violence is described in Detis T. Duhart's *Violence in the Workplace, 1993–99* (Washington, DC: U.S. Department of Justice, December 2001).

The Subculture of Violence   Richard E. Nisbett and Dov Cohen's *Culture of Honor: The Psychology of Violence in the South* (Boulder, CO: Westview, 1996) argues that southerners are more likely than residents of other regions to support the use of violence for self-protection or defense of their honor.

Gender and Crime   Two books that deal with women as offenders, victims, and criminal justice professionals are Joanne Belknap's *The Invisible Woman: Gender, Crime, and Justice* (Belmont, CA: Wadsworth,1995) and Sandra Walklate's *Gender and Crime: An Introduction* (Englewood Cliffs, NJ: Prentice Hall, 1995).

7

Social Control and Commitment to the Law

Because most people learn to abide by the law, or are at least aware that the law commands widespread respect, they can engage in crime or delinquency only after they have minimized their commitment to the law. People neutralize the power of the law by justifying their offenses to themselves and to others. People who are weakly attached to conventional institutions are already relatively free to violate the law. This chapter explores the ways that neutralization of the law and the absence of social control lead to crime and delinquency.

Neutralizing the Law

The theories of anomie, differential opportunity, reaction-formation, and lower-class culture all suggest that social forces push some juveniles into delinquency. A contrasting perspective is that delinquents exercise some free will, choosing to violate the law rather than being forced to do so by the social structure. According to this view, delinquents do not hold values that are diametrically opposed to dominant values, as reaction-formation theory suggests, nor are they members of delinquent subcultures that require them to violate the law, as differential opportunity theory and reaction-formation theory imply (Matza and Sykes, 1961; Matza, 1964).

Drift

David Matza (1964) proposes that some adolescents are in a state of **drift,** a condition of limbo between a conventional lifestyle and a criminal lifestyle with no strong attachment to either. Juveniles drift into delinquency in an almost accidental and unpredictable way through their exercise of personal choice. Becoming delinquent involves neither a compulsion to deviate nor the complete freedom to choose how to behave. Matza does not say why juveniles continue to engage in delinquency over time, nor does he indicate why they are drawn to delinquency in the first place. In other words, he does not specify the rewards of delinquent behavior.

In describing everyday delinquency rather than explaining its causes, Matza returns to the ideas of the classical school of criminology, particularly free will. He suggests that one motive for delinquency is existential in nature: Adolescents need to "make things happen" to assure themselves of their existence and their mastery over the world. For some adolescents, delinquency involves less risk of failure, and more potential gains, than schoolwork or athletics. Survey data indicate that adolescents who respond to the constraints imposed on their autonomy by parents and teachers with a sense of diminished personal control are able to assert their independence through delinquent behavior. This evidence is consistent with high crime rates during adolescence, when adult controls are greatest, and diminishing rates for people who are older and more independent (Brezina, 2000).

Delinquent, Dominant, and Subterranean Values

Part of the attractiveness of delinquency for juveniles is that it has much in common with the leisure activities of the dominant classes. Rather than see society as split into various strata with distinct norms and values—as do Cloward and Ohlin, Cohen, and Miller—Matza and Sykes (1961) examine contradictions within the dominant value system. For example, the dominant value system exhorts people to work hard and defer gratification, but it also encourages them to seek excitement and go on occasional sprees. The search for adventure is best regarded not as a deviant value but as a **subterranean value** in the dominant value system. In other words, the value is subordinate or below the surface in the dominant value system and is sought by most people only occasionally and in appropriate circumstances. Delinquents can then be seen as people who act in accordance with subterranean values in inappropriate circumstances. For instance, vandalism is tolerated, within limits, on Halloween, but people who destroy property at other times will be labeled delinquent. Matza and Sykes (1961: 717) see the delinquent not as alien to society, but as "a disturbing reflection or a caricature" of society's values. The delinquent's "vocabulary is different, to be sure, but kicks, big-time spending, and rep [reputation] have immediate counterparts in the value system of the law-abiding" (Matza and Sykes, 1961: 717). The motivational thrust behind delinquent behavior is thus normal and derived directly from conventional morality.

Evidence that delinquents have a strong bond to dominant values is the fact that they often express respect for law-abiding citizens. If delinquents held values opposed to dominant ones, they probably would regard law-abiding behavior as incorrect or immoral. Their recognition of the moral validity of dominant values suggests an attachment to the larger culture, even if that bond is broken at times.

The fact that delinquents are selective in choosing targets for offenses is additional evidence that they recognize the dominant morality. Theft and violence are often directed against people who are held in low social regard, such as prostitutes and the homeless. This suggests that delinquents can distinguish acceptable victims from those who would elicit negative reactions from the larger society.

Techniques of Neutralization

Social norms that define expected or appropriate behavior for particular situations often lack specificity as to how and when they apply. In other words, norms have flexibility and act only as "qualified guides for action" (Sykes and Matza, 1957: 666). Thus, a norm that theft is wrong might be qualified so that theft is tolerated—or even actually encouraged—if one is hungry or needs to feed one's starving children, if the victim is another criminal, or if the theft is from a large and impersonal corporation.

Individuals can avoid moral blame and maintain self-esteem while violating the law if they tell themselves and others that they had no criminal intent or that their behavior was justified. People who accept the law as legitimate find it difficult to launch frontal assaults on dominant norms, and so they remove the constraints of the law by justifying their behavior in some way. These justifications, which Sykes and Matza call **techniques of neutralization,** are tangential blows against dominant norms and help to render inoperative the social controls that would otherwise check law-violating behavior, enabling but not requiring people to break the law (Minor, 1981). These justifications make it possible for people to commit crime and delinquency without serious damage to their self-image. Deviance such as this has been described as apologetic rather than oppositional deviance (Sykes and Matza, 1957).

The five techniques of neutralization that Sykes and Matza look at are used prior to violation of the law to allow an offender who otherwise accepts the moral validity of the law to break it. Rationalizations can also be used after the crime, but there is less need to justify a crime that has already been committed than to neutralize the law that would have kept the individual from committing the crime in the first place.

Denial of Responsibility One technique of neutralization is the **denial of responsibility,** a refusal to be held personally accountable for one's actions. People sometimes claim that a criminal or delinquent act was an accident or assert that it was caused by factors beyond their control, such as a broken home, wayward friends, poverty, addiction, or drunkenness. Those who use this technique often feel acted upon by the social environment, rather than in control of their own lives. Other people might avoid crime and delinquency because they accept personal responsibility for their actions. When asked why he had not become a criminal, one nonoffender said: "I was given a certain amount of responsibility and learned to become responsible, and accept the fact that I was accountable for my actions" (cited in Rogers, 1977: 91).

To the extent that the positivist approach to the explanation of criminal behavior has seeped into the popular culture, it can be used to deny responsibility. Sociological research that shows a link between violation of the law and factors such as poverty or minority-group membership can be used by delinquents and criminals to argue that those factors forced them to violate the law, thereby absolving them of personal responsibility for their actions. Some critics have argued that the United States has become "a nation of victims," with increasing numbers of people using an "abuse excuse" to support a claim that they should not be blamed for their actions (Sykes, 1992; Dershowitz, 1994). In one case, a North Carolina jury required a psychiatrist to pay $500,000 in damages to Wendell Williamson, a former patient who had killed two men at random. Williamson, who was found not guilty by reason of insanity and confined to a state psychiatric hospital, claimed that the "murders would not have happened if Dr. Liptzin had done his job properly" and that his therapist "had more control over the situation than I did" (cited in Glaberson, 1998: A10). Following the verdict, Dr. Liptzin's attorney commented, "This is part of the attempt to shift responsibility in our society. Nobody's responsible for their own actions anymore. It's always somebody else's fault" (cited in Glaberson, 1998: A1).

Walter Miller (1974) claims that the civil rights movement of the 1950s added a "justificatory vocabulary" to traditional explanations for gang activity and other kinds of juvenile delinquency. Gang behavior was not much different in the 1960s than it was in the early 1950s, before the civil rights movement, but in the 1960s gang members were more likely to attribute their behavior to "exploitation by the power structure, restitution for past injustices, and brutalization by the system" (Miller, 1974: 233). One example of this kind of justification for crime was black activist Eldridge Cleaver's "political" defense of his rapes of white women:

> Rape was an insurrectionary act. It delighted me that I was defying and trampling upon the white man's law, upon his system of values, and that I was defiling his women—and this point, I believe, was the most satisfying to me because I was very resentful over the historical fact of how the white man had used the black woman. I felt I was getting revenge. (Cleaver, 1968: 14)

Denial of responsibility has also been used to justify white-collar crime and political corruption. In his final months in office, President Nixon blamed his advisors and tax lawyers for his problems. In his resignation speech, he blamed the press that had reported the Watergate incident and Congress that had forced him to leave office. Physicians caught defrauding the Medicaid program have blamed their patients' demands and bad advice from the welfare department for their violations (Jesilow, Pontell, and Geis, 1993). Corporate executives have asserted that their firms broke the law because their subordinates misunderstood orders or took the law into their own hands. Subordinates have responded by claiming that their supervisors told them to violate the law for the good of the company or established goals that could be met only by breaking the law (Shover, Coffey, and Hobbs, 2003). What little information we have on the denial of responsibility by white-collar criminals is usually in the form of rationalizations after their offenses have been committed. We lack evidence that these justifications are used prior to violation of the law to make it possible for white-collar offenders to reduce their commitment to the law and commit crimes.

Denial of Injury   A second technique of neutralization is the **denial of injury**, the claim by offenders that no one is hurt by their crimes, even if they technically violate the law. Nonoffenders sometimes say they do not break the law because they are able to perceive injury to others and because they are concerned about inflicting harm on others. In other words, sensitivity to others keeps some people away from crime and delinquency (Rogers, 1977). Those who violate the law are less sensitive to the effects that their behavior has on victims or regard their victims as objects or means to their own ends, rather than as individuals who suffer when victimized.

Offenders sometimes contend that victims who lose money or have property damaged can afford the losses, or that they can recover their losses from their insurance companies. Offenders often see the losses incurred by insurance companies as unreal, even though policyholders pay higher premiums to offset the costs of claims paid by the companies.

One instance of thieves' regarding their crimes as causing no real loss to anyone comes from a study of eighty-eight workers in a midwestern electronics assembly plant (Horning, 1970). Workers rationalized their theft as causing no injury by making a distinction among three kinds of property in the plant: property that belonged to the company, property that belonged to the employees, and property of uncertain ownership. Property classified as being of uncertain ownership was small, plentiful, inexpensive, and expendable, and the company did not regulate its flow within the plant. The property did belong to someone or to the company, but if workers could categorize it as being of uncertain ownership, they thought they were doing no injury if they stole it. Almost all workers reported pilfering goods from the plant, but few expressed any guilt at doing so, because work-group norms supported theft when it was confined to property of uncertain ownership and limited to what was needed for personal use. The conditions under which theft was tolerated were communicated to workers through "folktales" about thefts that had occurred in the past.

Delinquents use the denial-of-injury technique to justify their violations of the law. Car thieves say they are only "temporarily borrowing" cars, rather than permanently depriving owners of their cars. Gang fights are defined as private quarrels that are no one else's business. Sometimes delinquents and adult offenders actually claim that their crimes are socially useful, as by claiming that they are "Robin Hoods" who steal from the rich and give to the poor. For example, professional fences have justified their crimes as a way of redistributing property from wealthier neighborhoods to poorer ones (Klockars, 1974).

Criminals often say that it is appropriate to victimize certain targets, but that other targets should be avoided. The general public seems to think that theft from a large corporation is preferable to theft from the government, which in turn is better than theft from a small business. People seem to believe that large corporations can afford losses because they are insured, are highly profitable, can raise prices to compensate for their losses, and cheat customers anyway. Large corporations are also unpopular because they are seen as impersonal, inefficient, and unresponsive to the best interests of their customers and clients (Smigel and Ross, 1970: 4). This "rip-off mentality" is evident in the following statement by a safecracker:

> We [professional thieves] would never beat the average working man or anything like that. . . . When I was a young kid learning, I stole anything. But later on I became a professional and started hanging around with professionals and learned from them that you didn't steal from a home or small place of business; you only stole from a big place that could afford the loss. (King and Chambliss, 1984: 13)

Denial of injury has also been used to justify white-collar crime. A Westinghouse executive responded as follows to a question from a congressional committee about

Some thieves deny injury to their victims by claiming to be "Robin Hoods" who steal from the rich and give to the poor.

whether he knew that his meetings with other executives to fix the prices of electrical equipment were illegal: "Illegal? Yes, but not criminal. I didn't find that out until I read the indictment. . . . I assumed that criminal action meant damaging someone, and we did not do that" (cited in Geis, 1967: 144). The executive was wrong. Not only did the jail sentences served by some executives suggest that harm had been done, but the fact that plaintiffs recovered millions of dollars in civil damages from the offending companies indicated that financial harm had been done.

Denial of the Victim   A third technique of neutralization is the **denial of the victim,** the claim that a crime is justified as rightful retaliation against the victim. Offenders sometimes define victims, rather than themselves, as wrongdoers, and they use that attitude to justify their crimes.

The victimization of certain targets, such as prostitutes and shopkeepers who sell shoddy merchandise, is more likely to be socially accepted than the victimization of other targets, such as children and the elderly. Offenders often appeal to widely held ideas about valued and disvalued people to justify their acts. Individuals who recognize that victims suffer, in spite of what those victims might have done to "deserve" victimization, are more likely to avoid criminal behavior. One nonoffender says, "If there is something I want, I work for it because I don't want to hurt anyone else by trying to obtain it by other means. I always try to remember that other people have feelings too" (cited in Rogers, 1977: 92). Offenders do not seem to share this view, but instead think it is acceptable to victimize certain people. For instance, con artists and telemarketers who engage in fraud justify their behavior by the complicity of their victims, who are seen as having "larceny in their hearts" (Maurer, 1974; Shover, Coffey, and Hobbs, 2003).

Rapists justify their crimes by saying that their victims deserved to be raped because they were sexually experienced, promiscuous, or had a bad reputation, and that such women are "public property" and have no right to reject them as sex partners. Rapists also portray women as seductresses, claim that women mean "yes" when they say "no," contend that most women eventually relax and enjoy the sexual assault, assert that nice women do not get raped, and declare that they are at most guilty of a minor wrongdoing (Scully and Marolla, 1984).

Condemnation of the Condemners   Another technique of neutralization is the **condemnation of the condemners,** the assertion that it is the motives and behavior of the people who are condemning the offender, rather than the motives and behavior of the offender, that should be condemned. Actions of the condemners, including police brutality and political corruption, are used to justify an offender's violation of the law. One member of a Puerto Rican gang in Chicago decided that if the police were "going to mishandle me because they think I'm a Diamond I might as well be one" (cited in Padilla, 1992: 87). People who remain nonoffenders are able to concede the imperfection of the condemners without using it to justify their own violation of the law (Rogers, 1977).

Many kinds of offenders justify their actions by condemning the condemners. Murderers and bank robbers compare the harsh punishments they receive with the lack of punishment for politicians who send young men to their deaths in pointless wars. Fences claim that some of their best customers are judges and police officers (Klockars, 1974). Political criminals and terrorists use the corrupt and self-serving nature of the political system to justify crimes aimed at changing that system (Schafer, 1974). Justifying his Medicaid fraud, one physician condemned the program in the following words:

It's not related to reality, you know. It's done by people who are not medical people, who know nothing about the services being provided. One of the peculiarities that they do is that they make arbitrary decisions about things totally unrelated to the services you provide. They're constantly irritating and aggravating the doctors and their staff. (cited in Jesilow, Pontell, and Geis, 1993: 172)

Appeal to Higher Loyalties   A fifth technique of neutralization is the **appeal to higher loyalties,** an attempt to justify violation of the law by the demands of a group—such as a juvenile gang or a corporation—that is smaller than the whole society but that requires its members to conform to standards that might be incompatible with the law. Those who place loyalty to the larger social system and its laws above loyalty to individuals or a group are more likely to stay away from crime. One noncriminal expressed this as follows: "I am not a criminal . . . because I trust the system. I am willing to sacrifice for it. I believe in it" (cited in Rogers, 1977: 94).

Different types of offenders justify their violations of the law by appealing to higher loyalties. Juvenile delinquents rationalize their acts by peer pressure and the need not to let their friends down. Retaliating against a rival gang that invades a gang's turf or otherwise "disses" (disrespects) it is a way of demonstrating solidarity with other gang members. Police officers justify graft and corruption by the need to remain loyal to fellow officers. Physicians punished for committing Medicaid fraud cite the higher goals of serving their patients and adhering to professional standards (Jesilow, Pontell, and Geis, 1993). President Nixon's appeal to national security was an effort to justify the Watergate burglary and its cover-up by demands higher than the law. In a 1977 interview, he strongly implied that whatever the president did was not a crime because the president was above the law. Another use of loyalty to demands higher than the law was by an electrical company executive involved in a price-fixing conspiracy; he said, "I thought that we were more or less working on a survival basis in order to try to make enough to keep our plant and our employees" (cited in Geis, 1967: 144). White-collar offenders imprisoned in England used a similar argument, justifying their fraudulent activities by their financial obligations to their families, employees, clients, and creditors (Willott, Griffin, and Torrance, 2001).

Other Techniques of Neutralization   Other techniques of neutralization are also used to justify crime and delinquency (see Table 7.1). A person who uses a "defense of necessity" may justify an act by saying it is required by the circumstances; this differs from the denial of responsibility in that the offender accepts responsibility for the act while claiming it was necessary. Stealing food to feed one's starving children might be justified as a necessary act for which an offender accepts full responsibility.

TABLE 7.1   Techniques of Neutralization

1. Denial of responsibility
2. Denial of injury
3. Denial of the victim
4. Condemnation of the condemners
5. Appeal to higher loyalties
6. Defense of necessity
7. Defense of the ledger
8. Denial of the justice or necessity of the law
9. Claim that "everybody is doing it"
10. Claim of entitlement

Another technique is the "defense of the ledger," which is used by offenders who claim that the good and evil they have done balance out in their favor over time (Klockars, 1974; Minor, 1981). This technique was used by the lawyer for "junk bonds" dealer Michael Milken after Milken pleaded guilty to securities fraud and conspiracy, for which he was fined and imprisoned. The lawyer said,

> It is an enormous accomplishment for Michael to have been instrumental in finding the capital for hundreds of American corporations, which are generating jobs, providing a livelihood for hundreds of thousands of people. It is Michael's hope that in the long run history will see his violations in context and judge him not just on the basis of his lapses but on the basis of the contributions that he made to the economy and to the American people. (cited in Labaton, 1990: D1)

James William Coleman (1998) has identified several additional techniques of neutralization. One is the claim that the law being violated is unnecessary or unjust. This argument can take the form of asserting that government interference in business affairs actually hurts the public, a variation on the condemnation-of-the-condemners theme. Another technique is the claim that "everybody else is doing it too." A version of this justification is that it is not fair to condemn one offender without condemning them all. An additional technique, which is sometimes used by employee thieves, is that the offender deserves the money or that the stolen property is a "morally justified addition to wages" or an "entitlement due from exploiting employers" (Mars, 1974: 224).

Evidence on Techniques of Neutralization

Several researchers have found that techniques of neutralization play an important role in the genesis of crime and delinquency.

Embezzlement and the Techniques of Neutralization   From his study of imprisoned embezzlers, Donald Cressey concluded that people violate an employer's trust and embezzle funds when they face a nonshareable financial problem, become aware that they can solve that problem by turning the skills and opportunities of their job in a criminal direction, and can "apply to their own conduct in this situation verbalizations which enable them to adjust their conceptions of themselves as trusted persons with their conceptions of themselves as users of the entrusted funds or property" (Cressey, 1971: 30). These "verbalizations," which Sykes and Matza call techniques of neutralization, permit people to define the relationship between a nonshareable financial problem and an illegal solution to that problem in a way that makes embezzlement seem justifiable.

Cressey found that justifications were used either before or at the time of the crime; after the offense, there was no need for the verbalization. Verbalizations were often applications of general cultural values to an offender's specific situation. For example, embezzlers said the following:

> "Some of our most respectable citizens got their start in life by using other people's money temporarily."
>
> "In the real estate business there is nothing wrong about using deposits before the deal is closed."
>
> "All people steal when they get in a tight spot." (Cressey, 1971: 96)

The vagueness of some business practices made it possible for embezzlers to say they were using the money "temporarily" and to claim that they were "only borrowing," even though they took the money without the owner's knowledge and rarely repaid it.

Whereas men typically cite nonshareable financial problems arising from business miscalculations, overspending, or gambling as reasons for embezzling funds, women are more likely to neutralize the law against embezzlement by citing their responsibilities as wives and mothers, such as keeping their family together or paying for the care of a sick relative (Zeitz, 1981; Daly, 1989).

Justifications for Crime by Blacks   Another study that uncovered techniques of neutralization asked 150 black men between the ages of fifteen and thirty the following: "It is said that black men violate the criminal law more frequently than others. If this statement is true, are there any reasons you feel why such a higher violation rate exists?" (Davis, 1974: 74).

The men, who were approached on the street, said that the legal system lacked legitimacy for blacks and gave various reasons for a general "justification for no obligation" to the law by black men. More than four-fifths of the respondents thought that laws had been created by whites to control blacks, that blacks lacked equal access to participation in social institutions, and that unequal access to opportunities is unjust and indicative of hypocrisy about democratic ideals. At least two-thirds of the respondents said that racial discrimination had a long history and that whites had supported it over the centuries, that blacks were not obliged to obey the law because they had been forcibly brought to the country and had no choice in citizenship, and that blacks were not protected by the law in the same way that whites were.

For black men who find themselves in a state of drift and without a strong commitment to a conventional lifestyle, these justifications can support involvement in crime. Crime by blacks can result from grievances about unjust conditions and a subsequent lowering of respect for the law and its enforcers, with illegal activity then being accepted as a solution to those grievances. This study did not test directly for the presence of Sykes and Matza's techniques of neutralization among black criminals, but it showed that one group of streetwise black men thought that crime by blacks was a result of the ease with which blacks can neutralize the constraints of the law.

Justifying Violence   In a study of sex-related and robbery-related murders and execution-style homicides, several justifications for lethal violence were uncovered (Dietz, 1983). Street violence was justified by the need to protect oneself or one's property, the need to control others and keep them from using violence, the need to protect a reputation from personal affronts, and the need to ward off unprovoked attacks. In sex-related and robbery-related murders, offenders sometimes forced themselves to think of the victim as an object rather than as a person with feelings. The murderers also killed to prevent the victim from reporting the crime to the police and testifying in court. In execution-style homicides, "hit men" sometimes justified their crimes by saying that the victim "deserved to die" or by claiming that the murder was a "public service."

An analysis of National Youth Survey data found that few adolescents explicitly approved of violence or were indifferent to violence, but that many of them used techniques of neutralization that justified violence in certain situations. This study supported Sykes and Matza's contention that neutralizations precede delinquency: Adolescents who accepted neutralizations were more likely to engage later in violent behavior, especially fighting with their peers (Agnew, 1994).

Delinquency and Techniques of Neutralization   More evidence on the techniques of neutralization comes from a study of delinquency by Travis Hirschi (1969).

Data were gathered from interviews with California junior and senior high school students, and from school and police records. Self-reports were used to measure personal involvement in six delinquent acts: theft of property worth less than $2, theft of property worth $2 to $50, theft of property worth more than $50, auto theft, vandalism, and battery (beating someone up). The number of acts that a student admitted to formed an index of delinquency. Because few students had engaged in many delinquent acts, those who admitted to no acts were compared with those who admitted to one or more. It is questionable whether someone who has only stolen a pencil from a store should be classified as delinquent, or would be likely to be so classified by a judge, but this way of measuring delinquency was required by the data in order to explore relationships between self-reported delinquency and the acceptance of statements used to justify violation of the law.

Denial of Responsibility   Hirschi measured support for the denial-of-responsibility technique by asking students if they thought that criminals were to blame for their actions. Because few respondents—only 12 percent of the sample—said that criminals should not be held responsible for their actions, Hirschi could not use this question to measure support for this technique of neutralization.

Another indicator of support for the denial-of-responsibility technique was the following: "I can't seem to stay out of trouble no matter how hard I try." Students who agreed with this statement might be able to deny personal responsibility for their behavior and justify violation of the law. Thus, we might expect that those who agreed most strongly with this statement would be the most likely to report involvement in delinquent acts, and those who most strongly disagreed would be the least involved in delinquency. Hirschi's data show that this was the case. Sixty-three percent of the boys who strongly agreed with the statement admitted at least one delinquent act, but only 25 percent of those who strongly disagreed with the statement admitted at least one delinquent act. Those who expressed intermediate levels of agreement with the statement showed intermediate levels of self-reported delinquency. The findings provide tentative support for a link between denial of responsibility and juvenile delinquency. Michael Hindelang's (1973) study of boys and girls in rural New York state provided similar support for an association between this denial-of-responsibility item and self-reported delinquency.

Denial of Injury   Hirschi tested for the technique of neutralization called denial of injury with the following statement: "Most things that people call 'delinquency' don't really hurt anyone." Agreement with this statement would suggest greater ease in denying harm to potential victims of delinquent acts and should thus be associated with more involvement in delinquency. This was the case: 72 percent of those who strongly agreed with this statement reported at least one delinquent act, but only 31 percent of those who strongly disagreed with the statement reported a delinquent act. Hindelang's replication of Hirschi's study found similar support for a link between this statement and self-reported delinquency.

Denial of the Victim   The item Hirschi used to measure denial of the victim was the following: "The man who leaves the keys in his car is as much to blame for its theft as the man who steals it." This particular item was not related to self-reported delinquency; the percentages who admitted at least one delinquent act were similar for those who agreed and those who disagreed with the statement. Hindelang did not find support for this technique of neutralization either. Hirschi suggests that had he phrased the question as "The *sucker* who leaves the keys in his car . . . ," he might have found an association between responses to this statement and self-reported delinquency. The item Hirschi did use might have said too little about the respondent's attitude toward the victim by referring to him simply as a man.

Condemnation of the Condemners   Condemnation of the condemners was measured by asking for responses to the following: "Policemen try to give all kids an even break." Agreement should be associated with low involvement in delinquency, because those who think the police are fair should be less able to justify violating the law. The evidence supports this: 35 percent of the boys who strongly agreed with the statement admitted a delinquent act, but 58 percent who strongly disagreed with the statement reported a delinquent act. Hindelang also found an association between this statement and self-reported delinquency.

Appeal to Higher Loyalties   Hirschi could not test the technique of appealing to higher loyalties with the data he collected, nor did Hindelang ask about this technique.

Conclusion   Hirschi's and Hindelang's studies tentatively support a positive association between three techniques of neutralization and self-reported involvement in delinquent acts. Their work lends support to Sykes and Matza's theoretical ideas but does not provide a definitive test for those ideas. For instance, Hirschi's and Hindelang's data do not allow them to conclude that the techniques of neutralization were used prior to committing the delinquent acts to make it possible for the boys and girls to neutralize the constraints of the law.

Critique of Neutralization Theory

Neutralization theory implies that people who are committed to a conventional life or who have not yet engaged in deviance will be the most likely to need to use techniques of neutralization. However, one study found that the techniques were used both by youths who disapproved of deviance and therefore needed to neutralize norms, and by youths who already approved of deviance and should therefore not have needed to use neutralization techniques. Moreover, the relationship between the acceptance of neutralizing excuses and subsequent deviant behavior existed only for people who had already committed that deviant act in the past, not for people who had never violated the norm before. This suggests that techniques of neutralization might develop and be used only after people commit an initial act of delinquency or crime, and that the techniques might not precede violation of the law as Sykes and Matza suggest (Minor, 1981).

Techniques of neutralization can be used after the law is violated, when other people call into question an individual's behavior and try to label that person a wrongdoer. At that point, techniques of neutralization might help people minimize their guilt and allow them to continue to see themselves as worthy citizens (Hamlin, 1988). The accounts that people give after the fact for violating the law might, however, reflect the reasoning they engaged in before breaking the law. More research is needed to determine whether techniques of neutralization precede violation of the law to make it possible, follow violation of the law to justify it to oneself and others, or both.

Neutralization of the law is a social-psychological process by which potential offenders justify crime or delinquency by employing general arguments about when such violations are acceptable. Neutralization theory can be criticized for ignoring aspects of the social structure that make it easy or difficult to justify violations of the law. These social-structural factors have been explored in social control theory, which proposes that people who are the most weakly attached to social institutions are the freest to violate the law.

Social Control Theory

Travis Hirschi's *Causes of Delinquency* (1969), widely regarded as "one of the most important works of American criminology published in [the twentieth] century" (Greenberg, 1999: 66), presents the author's **social control theory** of delinquency. This theory proposes that people who engage in delinquency are free of intimate attachments, aspirations, and moral beliefs that bind them to a conventional and law-abiding way of life. Delinquents are not forced into delinquency so much as they are free to commit delinquent acts because they lack ties to the conventional social order. Delinquency violates other people's expectations about appropriate behavior, so if people do not care about the opinions of others, they are free to deviate from norms. Most people have deviant impulses from time to time, but whether they act on those impulses depends on their attachments to others.

Delinquents believe in the conventional order even as they violate its norms; the critical factor is the extent to which they believe they should obey norms. Hirschi (1969: 198) says that "delinquency is not caused by beliefs that require delinquency but is rather made possible by the absence of (effective) beliefs that forbid delinquency." This position is similar to Matza's notion of drift: the delinquent is midway between crime and convention, between deviance and conformity.

Social control theory does not make clear the motivations that give rise to violation of the law but rather looks at the institutions that create barriers to the expression of deviant motivations. The desire to acquire material goods, the need for social approval, and association with other law violators can all push a person to violate the law. However, if a person experiencing those pressures to violate the law is also subject to social control that results from attachment to family, school, job, and friends, that control can counteract the pressure to break the law.

The Family

One institution that is basic to all societies is the family. It socializes the young and provides surveillance over their behavior. It also controls the behavior of people of all ages who value the good opinion of other family members.

Hirschi's research shows that delinquents are much less closely attached to their parents than nondelinquents are. The critical factor is not whether the parents are always physically present to supervise the behavior of the child, but whether the parents are "psychologically present" when the child faces a temptation to violate the law. If the parents are not present in the child's mind, he or she is free to commit a delinquent act without giving any thought to how the parents might react. Nonoffenders sometimes say that they abide by the law because they take their parents' feelings into account when deciding how to act (Rogers, 1977: 37–42). Nondelinquents are also more likely to say that their parents know where they are most of the time, and this acts as a check on their behavior. By contrast, delinquents are more likely to say that their parents often do not know their whereabouts.

The closer a child's relationship with his or her parents, and the more intimate the communication with them, the less likely that child is to be delinquent. Relationships with mothers and fathers are of equal importance in controlling delinquency (Hirschi, 1969; Rankin and Kern, 1994). Through attachment to a parent, children learn to care about parental expectations. Attachment to parents is important for children of all social classes and all racial and ethnic groups.

The School

A second important institution in controlling delinquency is the school. The most academically successful students are the least likely to be delinquent, for they are most attached to the school and its teachers. Adolescents are more likely to be delinquent if they do not care what their teachers think of them. Again, the expectations of "significant others" are important in controlling delinquency. As Hirschi (1969: 127) says, "Positive feelings toward controlling institutions and persons in authority are the first line of social control. Withdrawal of favorable sentiments toward such institutions and persons at the same time neutralizes their moral force."

Hirschi's research shows that students who are not much concerned with their teachers' opinions and who dislike school also have the weakest relationships with their parents. Those adolescents are the most likely to report that they have committed delinquent acts.

The Peer Group

The third type of attachment that is important in social control theory is relationships with the peer group. Hirschi finds that delinquents are more likely to have delinquent friends than nondelinquents are. However, the relationship between friendships and delinquency is less clear-cut than the commonly assumed pattern of poor family relationships leading to attachment to peers, which then leads to delinquency. Instead, Hirschi finds that adolescents who have weak relationships with their parents tend to have weak relationships with their peers, and those closest to their parents have the greatest number of close friends.

Attachment to peers does not necessarily produce attitudes conducive to delinquency, for the more adolescents respect the opinions of their friends, the less likely they are to be delinquent. Those who are more delinquent and more likely to have delinquent friends are less likely to say their friends are worthy of respect. Contrary to the picture of the juvenile gang as a warm and supportive group similar to a family, Hirschi finds that delinquents do not have warm and intimate relationships with each other, or with anyone else for that matter.

Conventional Lines of Action and Adult Activities

Thus far, the picture that social control theory offers of the delinquent is of someone who lacks strong attachments to parents, teachers, or peers. Another link in the chain of circumstances leading to delinquency is an individual's aspirations to conventional lines of action, such as education and work. Adolescents who have such aspirations do not want to jeopardize their chances of success, and they would risk losing their "stake in conformity" by getting into trouble with the law.

Young people who do not aspire to conventional lines of action are more involved in adult activities during adolescence. Adult privileges without adult responsibilities might compensate for a bleak outlook on the future. Delinquents are more likely than nondelinquents to see their high school years and the years immediately after as the time in their lives when they will be the happiest. They are especially likely to engage in delinquency because their lack of orientation toward the future frees them from conventional pursuits such as education and a career.

As measures of involvement in adult activities, Hirschi uses the age at which an individual began to smoke cigarettes and the number of "adult activities"—smoking, drinking, and dating—in which the person is involved. Each indicator shows a significant relationship to self-reported delinquency. Thus, adolescents who began smoking before they were thirteen were the most likely to report a delinquent act; those who began to smoke between thirteen and fifteen were less likely to report a delinquent act; those who started after fifteen were even less likely to report a delinquent act; and those who did not smoke at all were the least likely to report a delinquent act. Involvement in the three adult activities was directly associated with a higher rate of self-reported delinquency. Boys who smoked, drank, and dated reported delinquent acts three times as often as boys who engaged in none of those activities (Hirschi, 1969).

According to Hirschi, adolescents who have fewer attachments to family, school, peers, and conventional lines of action are more likely to engage in delinquency because they do not feel society's rules are binding on them and do not fear the disapproval of others. This perception can be seen as a "master technique of neutralization" supported by the specific techniques of neutralization examined earlier. This theory is diagrammed in simple terms in Figure 7.1. Here four variables have direct effects on delinquency, but the four variables have no clearly specified causal relationships with one another. For instance, Hirschi finds that lack of family ties correlates with weak ties to the school, but he does not claim that one directly causes the other.

Evidence on Social Control Theory

Hirschi's study provides evidence that delinquency is associated with weak attachments to conventional institutions and lines of action. Other studies, too, support social control theory.

National Youth Surveys of Delinquency and Drug Use   Delbert Elliott, David Huizinga, and Suzanne Ageton (1985) employed self-report data from three National Youth Surveys conducted in 1977, 1978, and 1979 to develop a theoretical model that would explain delinquent behavior and drug use. This model, shown in Figure 7.2, reveals a complex pattern of interaction among variables that have both direct and indirect effects on delinquent behavior.

This model indicates that delinquent behavior is directly affected by involvement with delinquent peers, contrary to Hirschi's conclusion that delinquents have

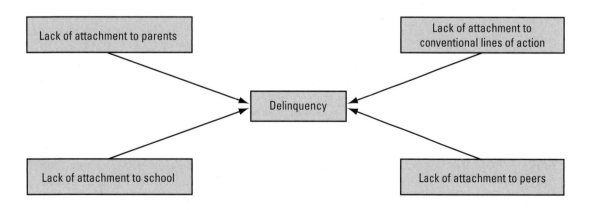

FIGURE 7.1   Hirschi's Model of Delinquency

Source: Based on Travis Hirschi, *Causes of Delinquency.* Berkeley: University of California Press, 1969.

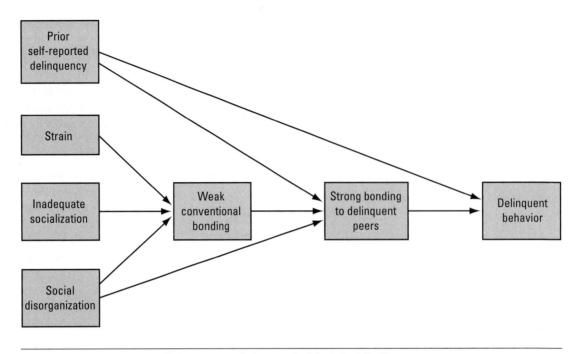

FIGURE 7.2   Elliott, Huizinga, and Ageton's Model of Delinquency

Source: Delbert S. Elliott, David Huizinga, and Suzanne S. Ageton, *Explaining Delinquency and Drug Use,* p. 146. Copyright © 1985 by Sage Publications, Inc. Reprinted by permission of Sage Publications, Inc.

weak peer ties. Delinquent behavior is also directly influenced by prior self-reported delinquency, suggesting a continuity of behavior over time and perhaps the impact of having been labeled delinquent in the past.

Weak conventional bonding means that individuals spend little time with their families and on academic matters at school, and that they express relatively little commitment to conventional norms at home and at school. This weak conventional bonding leads to strong bonding with delinquent peers, which in turn leads to delinquent behavior. However, weak conventional bonding does not lead to delinquent behavior in a direct way, but only through its impact on attachment to delinquent peers.

The arrow from prior self-reported delinquency to strong bonding to delinquent peers indicates that earlier involvement in delinquency makes it more likely that an adolescent will later associate with delinquent peers, who in turn influence the adolescent to become more involved in delinquent acts. The social disorganization of the community in which the adolescent lives might also influence attachments to delinquent peers, although there was no direct evidence of this.

Weak conventional bonding to family and to school is influenced by strain, inadequate socialization, and social disorganization of the community. Strain in the family was measured by the discrepancy between the subject's goals for family life—such as getting along with parents and holding their good opinion—and the subject's perceived realization of those goals. Similarly, strain in school was measured by the perceived discrepancy between academic goals—such as high grades and teachers' good opinions of the student—and the actual realization of those goals. Strain in the family and at school does not increase delinquent behavior directly, but instead leads to weak conventional bonding, which then produces strong bonding to delinquent peers, which in turn leads to delinquent behavior.

This model suggests that a revised version of social control theory can explain delinquency, but that variables such as inadequate socialization and social disorganization that are not part of social control theory are also important parts of a complete explanation of delinquency.

Delinquency and Crime over the Life Course

In their reanalysis of Sheldon and Eleanor Glueck's (1950) data on 500 delinquent males and 500 nondelinquent males who were followed from childhood into their forties, Robert Sampson and John Laub (1993) examined structural background factors and social control processes that influence delinquency and crime. Figure 7.3 is a model of their **life-course perspective**, which examines delinquency and crime in terms of "patterns of change and the continuity between childhood behavior and later adulthood outcomes," as well as "the social meanings of age throughout the life course, intergenerational transmission of social patterns, and the effects of macro-level events (such as the Great Depression or World War II) on individual life histories" (Sampson and Laub, 1993: 9).

Family processes of social control were found to be critically important; "low levels of parental supervision, erratic, threatening, and harsh discipline, and weak parental attachment were strongly and directly related to delinquency" (Sampson and Laub, 1993: 247). Except for family size and household crowding, structural factors did not have consistent direct effects on delinquency. Structural factors such as family disruption and poverty indirectly influenced delinquency by affecting family and school processes of informal social control, which in turn affected delinquency. Thus, "families do not exist in isolation but instead are systematically embedded in social structural contexts" (Sampson and Laub, 1993: 96).

Attachment to school had a strong effect on delinquency, independent of family processes. Peer attachments were also positively related to delinquency regardless of family and school processes, although the effect of peer relations on delinquency was less important than the effect of either family or school processes.

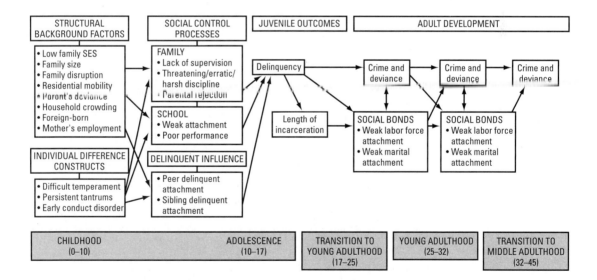

FIGURE 7.3   Sampson and Laub's Dynamic Theoretical Model of Crime, Deviance, and Informal Social Control over the Life Course of 1,000 Glueck Men, circa 1925–1975

Note: In the *Unraveling Juvenile Delinquency* design, delinquent and nondelinquent males were matched on age, race/ethnicity, neighborhood socioeconomic status, and IQ.

Source: Reprinted by permission of the publisher from *Crime in the Making: Pathways and Turning Points through Life* by Robert J. Sampson and John H. Laub, pp. 244–245, Cambridge, MA: Harvard University Press, Copyright © 1993 by the President and Fellows of Harvard College.

Sampson and Laub found that individual characteristics such as temperament and early conduct disorder were linked to family and school processes as well as to delinquency, but those individual characteristics did not significantly diminish the strong impact on delinquency of family and school processes.

Traits such as low self-control that result from family and school processes can predispose individuals from an early age to become delinquent during adolescence and criminal during adulthood. However, antisocial behavior during childhood and adolescence can also lead to adult crime by weakening the social bonds that tie individuals to institutions such as the family and the labor force. Those weakened bonds then contribute to subsequent violation of the law.

Social bonds during adulthood, such as marital attachment and job stability, by themselves have an effect on adult crime that is independent of any effects of childhood experiences. Adult experiences can thus counteract the negative effects of early childhood experiences; they can also lead adults with no previous history of delinquency to violate the law. Thus, "life-event transitions and adult social bonds can modify quite different childhood trajectories" (Sampson and Laub, 1993: 24).

Sampson and Laub's analysis confirmed their integrated theory of informal social control, which they derived in part from Hirschi's social control theory.

Delinquency and the Family   Not surprisingly, much research on crime and delinquency points to the crucial role of the family, the primary institution in the socialization and supervision of children.

Socialization   The way children are socialized by their parents is a major factor in the causation or prevention of crime and delinquency. A study that asked students why they had not become criminals found that many said that their parents had taught them right from wrong and had been models of hard work and honesty. The students said that their parents had taught them important values and that they themselves abided by the law because they believed in those values rather than because they feared punishment (Rogers, 1977). Delinquents are more likely to say that their childhood experiences with their parents were unpleasant and that they rejected their parents as models while they were young (Medinnus, 1965). In general, crime and delinquency seem to be more common in societies where young people have less contact and less identification with their parents (Bacon, Child, and Barry, 1963).

Socialization by parents is most likely to reduce the chance that children will violate the law if

- parents clearly define their expectations
- there is a close relationship between parents and their children
- parents control their reactions toward their children's rebellious behavior
- parents reward the learning of expected behavior and withhold rewards for the failure to learn that behavior (Toby, 1974)

People can also be socialized to break the law. They might learn values, norms, and skills from the members of a criminal or delinquent subculture. Few parents intentionally socialize their children to violate the law, but the failure to recognize their children's crime and delinquency as deviant and the use of ineffective methods of punishment can socialize children to break the law (Hirschi, 1983). A study of serious delinquents in Miami found that they had first been drunk at a mean age of 8.8, in four-fifths of the cases with an adult present, leading the researchers to conclude that "adults who gave children alcohol were also giving them a head start in a delin-

Children are less likely to violate the law if their parents clearly define their expectations, have a close relationship with their children, control their reactions toward their children's rebellious behavior, reward the learning of expected behavior, and withhold rewards for the failure to learn such behavior.

quent career, . . . and this earlier start meant more serious drug/crime involvement [when they got older]" (Inciardi, Horowitz, and Pottieger, 1993: 136).

A study in which observations of the family environments of boys were compared with their subsequent behavior found that mothers were especially important in insulating boys against delinquency but that fathers had a greater influence on the adult criminal activity of their sons. Mothers who were self-confident, consistently nonpunitive, affectionate, and who provided leadership reduced the chances that their sons would become delinquent. High family expectations for the son had a similar effect. To the extent that these factors influenced adult criminality, they did so indirectly through their impact on juvenile delinquency. The father's interaction with the family was less strongly associated with juvenile delinquency but had a significant impact on adult criminal behavior, with the sons being more apt to engage in criminal behavior as adults if their fathers had undermined their mother's self esteem, fought with the family, and been highly aggressive while their sons were young (McCord, 1991).

Discipline   Careful observation of interactions between children and their parents has led researchers at the Oregon Social Learning Center to conclude that some parents are ineffective in disciplining their children, in that they fail to make penalties contingent on their children's behavior in a systematic and predictable way. (See the Using Criminology box.) Children are most likely to break the law and violate social conventions when parents care too little about their children to pay attention to their actions, when they fail to supervise their children, when they do not regard their children's misbehavior negatively, and when they fail to punish their children. The failure of parents to react consistently to deviant behavior leaves children with the belief that they cannot control what will happen to themselves by their own actions. Irritable parents who sometimes apply harsh penalties or even strike out violently at their children, but at other times "natter" at their children for similar behavior, make it seem to children that the punishment they suffer is not linked to their behavior in any predictable way (West, 1982; Wells and Rankin, 1988; Larzelere and Patterson, 1990). Ineffective child rearing is cited by Gottfredson and Hirschi (1990) as the major cause of low self-control, which they see as the source of criminal behavior.

The most effective parental style of discipline for reducing criminal or aggressive behavior is an "authoritative" approach, which combines a high degree of control over children with a great amount of support and encouragement. In contrast to this, an "authoritarian" style that combines tight control with a cold and detached parental attitude often leads children to withdraw from social contact. A "permissive" style that involves nurturing and encouragement, but a failure to control, often produces children who lack self-control (Baumrind, 1978; Wilson and Herrnstein, 1985; Hay, 2001; Wright and Cullen, 2001). This permissive style was found to be common among the parents of delinquents in a longitudinal study done in England, with the researcher concluding:

> A particularly noticeable characteristic of parents of many of the delinquents in the study was carelessness or laxness in matters of supervision. They were less concerned than other parents to watch over or to know about their children's doings, whereabouts and companions, and they failed to enforce or to formulate fixed rules about such things as punctuality, manners, bedtime, television viewing or tidying up. (West, 1982: 57)

USING CRIMINOLOGY

Holding Parents Responsible for Their Children's Behavior

The public sometimes blames juvenile crime on parents who have failed to supervise and discipline their children adequately. Information that one of the teenage gunmen in the 1999 Littleton, Colorado, high school attack had a sawed-off shotgun barrel and bomb-making materials in his bedroom led the mother and father of one of the victims to sue the killer's parents. Parents of the victims of school violence in Mississippi, Kentucky, and Arkansas have also brought legal action against the parents of student-murderers.

Lawmakers have sometimes passed measures that hold parents responsible for their children's behavior. To hold a parent criminally responsible for a child's crime requires evidence that the parent intended to participate actively in the crime. Such evidence rarely exists, so the criminal law is of limited effectiveness in holding parents responsible for their children's crimes. Instead, most states rely on the civil law to impose damages on parents for the harm inflicted by their children on crime victims. A parent can be held negligent in supervising a child if there is evidence that the parent had prior knowledge that the child was going to commit a crime but failed to stop it; proving such prior knowledge is difficult. Many states, cities, and towns now have parental responsibility laws that re-

quire negligent parents to participate in counseling or educational programs. The laws sometimes impose fines or jail terms on such parents if their child fails to attend school, drinks alcoholic beverages, or vandalizes property. For example, in Louisiana parents can be fined up to $1,000 or imprisoned for up to six months for improperly supervising their children. Idaho, Indiana, and New Hampshire require parents to pay some of the costs of detaining their children in state institutions.

Critics allege that these measures are useless, politically motivated "quick fixes" aimed at a complex problem. Some find the laws intrusive or even unconstitutional and suggest that they might backfire by unfairly penalizing low-income parents who cannot afford to pay fines, or by causing conflict within families. Supporters of these laws claim that they can be a useful part of an overall strategy of forcing parents to pay more attention to supervising and disciplining their children. The police chief of Silverton, Oregon, found his town's ordinance useful, saying, "The other day I brought a kid in here for shoplifting. What does the father do when he came in? He chews the kid out for getting caught. Not for what he did. Well, now I can cite him as well" (cited in Egan, 1995: B7).

Sources: Based on Timothy Egan, "If Juveniles Break Law, Town Is Charging the Parents, Too," *New York Times,* May 31, 1995, pp. A1, B7; Peter Applebome, "Holding Parents Responsible as Children's Misdeeds Rise," *New York Times,* April 10, 1996, pp. A1, D8; William Glaberson, "Case against Parents Would Be Hard to Prove," *New York Times,* April 27, 1999, p. A20.

The way that parents discipline their children is quite likely learned from observing how they as children were disciplined by their own parents. This could explain why the children of parents with criminal records are especially likely to have criminal records themselves, for people discipline their own children in the way they were disciplined by their parents, and that style of discipline leads their children into crime just as it led them to violate the law. Parents with criminal records seem to be poor at supervising their children and are therefore unlikely to be "psychologically present" when their children are tempted to violate the law.

Broken Homes   There has been much speculation and research on the broken home as a cause of delinquency and crime. Broken homes include those that are not structurally intact for various reasons: the death of a parent, divorce, desertion, separation, and illegitimacy (in which case the family was never completed). Broken homes could have an impact on delinquency in any of a variety of ways: by producing unstable habits and personalities in young children through inadequate socialization; by failing to provide children with ties to the conventional social order that would control their behavior; by producing stress and conflict that lead children to "act out"; and by offering fewer resources and opportunities to children and thus leaving them at a disadvantage in competing with others for a good education and a desirable job (Wells and Rankin, 1986). Because families can be "broken" in different ways and because families have many kinds of effects on children, it is not surprising that research on the relationship between broken families and delinquency is inconclusive.

In addition, many studies of this relationship have employed inadequate research designs. Because broken families are more common among the lower classes and among minority groups and because those classes and groups have higher rates of officially recorded delinquency, researchers need to separate the effects of class and minority-group membership on delinquency from the effects of family structure on delinquency. For instance, some research shows that among the middle class, neither officially recorded nor self-reported delinquency is associated with coming from a broken home (Grinnell and Chambers, 1979; Richards, Berk, and Foster, 1979). Researchers need to use self-report measures to determine if there are real differences in delinquency between adolescents from broken homes and those from intact homes, because adolescents from broken homes may be more likely than adolescents from intact homes to be arrested and found delinquent in court.

The most carefully designed studies have found a weak but consistent relationship between delinquency and broken homes, with delinquents slightly more likely than nondelinquents to come from broken homes (Hennessy, Richards, and Berk, 1978; Canter, 1982; van Voorhis et al., 1988; Wells and Rankin, 1991). Analysis of National Youth Survey data found that children who are strongly attached to both parents are less likely to commit delinquent acts than children who are strongly attached to only one parent, whether that one parent is in a broken home or an intact one (Rankin and Kern, 1994). A recent study that also used National Youth Survey data concluded that changes in family relationships are related more strongly to delinquency than prior research suggests; more specifically, parents' divorce and separation early in the life course are predictive of a child's delinquency in later years, recent remarriage is associated with status offenses, and the presence of a stepparent is linked to violent offenses (Rebellon, 2002).

Separation of Children from Their Parents   One factor that might be related to delinquency is the early separation of children from parents. Regular or prolonged separation from parents during the early years could make it harder for children to develop feelings for others later, and this lack of empathy could be linked to delinquency and crime.

Some researchers have found that delinquency is especially common among the children of parents who both hold jobs outside the home (Hirschi, 1969; Austin, 1982). The negative effects on children of having both parents work might be attributable to a loss of supervision or to conflict between spouses that results from the wife's working outside the home. Another possibility is that the wife took a job to escape a problematic family situation, such as an alcoholic and unemployed husband. The problematic family situation itself, rather than the wife's working, might be the cause of the delinquency. Sampson and Laub's (1993) study of delinquency and crime over the life course found that a mother's employment had an insignificant direct effect on delinquency. The mother's employment did have an indirect effect on delinquency, through its impact on such family control processes as supervision, attachment, and discipline.

Child Abuse   The abuse of children by their parents or by other caretakers can take the form of physical abuse, sexual abuse, emotional neglect, or other intentional maltreatment. Abuse adversely affects thinking, memory, emotions, and learning by damaging the chemistry and structure of the brain. Abuse is apparently more likely to lead to violent behavior if a child has a genetic marker that produces low levels of the enzyme MAOA (E. Barry, 2002). As a result of these and other factors, abused children are more likely than children who are not abused to have trouble at school, be aggressive, have difficulty with alcohol or drugs, violate the law, and become abusing parents themselves (Gelles and Straus, 1988; Ireland and Widom, 1994).

A comparison of the criminal records of 908 people who had been officially reported to be the victims of child abuse or neglect with the criminal records of 667 people of similar social backgrounds for whom no report of child abuse or neglect had been filed concluded that being maltreated increased the chance of being arrested as a juvenile by 59 percent, the chance of being arrested as an adult by 28 percent, and the chance of being arrested for a violent crime by 30 percent. Children who had been physically abused and neglected were more likely than children who had been sexually abused to be arrested later for a violent crime (Widom and Maxfield, 2001).

A longitudinal study of 1,000 youths in Rochester, New York, found that maltreatment before the age of twelve was associated with delinquency during adolescence. The researchers used Department of Social Services records to measure child maltreatment of the following types: physical abuse or neglect; sexual abuse; inadequate supervision; and emotional, educational, or moral-legal maltreatment. Figure 7.4 shows that, compared to nonmaltreated children, maltreated ones had a higher rate of official delinquency (measured by number of official contacts with the police as a juvenile and arrests as an adult) and higher rates of minor, moderate, serious, violent, and general delinquency (measured by seven self-report interviews done every six months). These relationships persisted when sex, race/ethnicity, family disadvantage, family structure, and mobility were controlled. The children who were most extensively maltreated exhibited the highest rates of delinquency (Kelley, Thornberry, and Smith, 1997).

A study that compared the officially recorded delinquent behavior of maltreated children, nonmaltreated children, and nonmaltreated impoverished children concluded that the effect of maltreatment on juvenile delinquency has been exaggerated. The degree to which the maltreated children were more involved in delinquency than the other two samples was greatly diminished when children from the same demographic groups and family structures were compared. Moreover, most of the difference in delinquency between the maltreated children and the other two samples was due to the greater involvement of the maltreated children in status offenses. Maltreated children were no more involved in property or violent offenses than the nonmaltreated children or the impoverished children (Zingraff et al., 1993). Maltreated

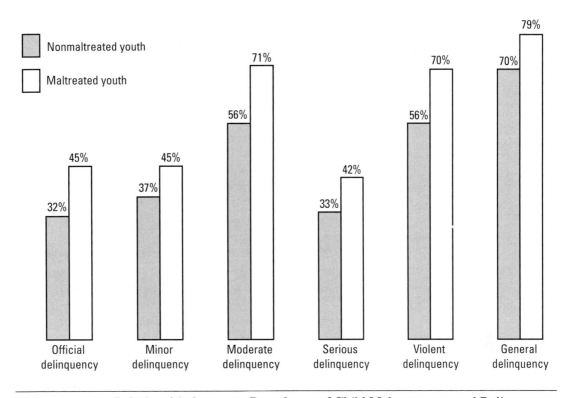

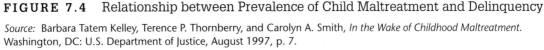

FIGURE 7.4   Relationship between Prevalence of Child Maltreatment and Delinquency

Source: Barbara Tatem Kelley, Terence P. Thornberry, and Carolyn A. Smith, *In the Wake of Childhood Maltreatment.* Washington, DC: U.S. Department of Justice, August 1997, p. 7.

children who performed adequately in school were less likely to be delinquent than maltreated children whose academic performance was poorer, suggesting that attachment to school can counteract some of the negative effects of abuse (Zingraff et al., 1994).

Family Cohesiveness   What seems most important in determining whether a child will become delinquent is family cohesiveness, which is indicated by the quality of interpersonal relationships in a family, communication between parents and children, and emotional support of the children by their parents (Hirschi, 1969; Hindelang, 1973; Poole and Regoli, 1979; Wiatrowski, Griswold, and Roberts, 1981). A study of delinquency in three cultures found less family cohesiveness, less confiding in parents, and fewer stable home situations among delinquents than among nondelinquents (Rosenquist and Megargee, 1969). Higher levels of hostility within the family were found to be associated with more deviant behavior in a study done in Mexico (Meadow et al., 1981).

The quality of family relationships might be associated in different ways with various kinds of crime. In one study, adult males who as boys had frequently been exposed to conflict and aggression between their parents were especially likely to commit violent crimes such as murder, rape, and kidnapping. Those men who as boys had lacked maternal affection and whose fathers had engaged in deviance were especially likely to be arrested for property crimes such as larceny, car theft, and burglary (McCord, 1979).

In explaining why Switzerland has relatively low rates of juvenile delinquency, Marshall Clinard (1978) focuses on the close ties and good communication between young people and adults. He suggests that Swiss adolescents often prefer interaction in mixed-age groups to interaction in peer groups, and that people of various ages often participate together in outdoor activities. Interaction of various age groups also occurs in the large Swiss army. In addition, many Swiss continue to live with their parents after they become young adults. Clinard attributes Switzerland's relatively small problem with youth crime to the culture's emphasis on harmony and compromise, which sustain close ties between people of different ages, both within and outside the family.

The family is an especially important institution in generating or preventing delinquency and crime. The structure of the family is important, but what seems most critical is the quality of relationships among family members. Harmonious relationships between parents, and between parents and children, help to prevent delinquency and crime.

Delinquency and the School   Students with low levels of academic performance are especially likely to be delinquent, to commit serious and violent offenses, and to persist in delinquency (Maguin and Loeber, 1996). Poor academic performance in high school is a strong predictor of being arrested for crime as an adult (Polk, 1980).

When academic pressure is coupled with a high likelihood of failure, adolescents come to regard school as irrelevant to their future, ungratifying, and unrewarding. They see their grades as unimportant and spend less time on homework, factors that lower their academic achievement. Their ties to the school and its teachers then weaken, and they drift into delinquency (Hirschi, 1969; Empey and Lubeck, 1971; Hindelang, 1973; Figueira-McDonough, 1987). Lack of commitment to school and lack of support for school rules are strong predictors of delinquent behavior by seventh and eighth graders (Jenkins, 1997). Nondelinquents often mention their commitment to education and their respect for their teachers' good opinions as reasons for not turning to crime. They also say that education is important to their future and that they do not want to risk their stake in conformity by violating the law (Rogers, 1977).

Evidence that weakened attachment to the school is linked to delinquency was uncovered in Wolfgang, Figlio, and Sellin's (1972) cohort study. Boys with more contacts with the police were more likely than boys with fewer police contacts to have changed schools frequently, have lower IQs, have completed fewer grades, and have a lower overall level of achievement. Another study found that delinquency was more common among adolescents who were less bonded to the school, and that this was equally true for both blacks and whites. Even though school bonding was not a powerful predictor of delinquency, it played as significant a role in delinquency as family and peers (Cernkovich and Giordano, 1992). A study of drug use and serious delinquency in Miami concluded that

> most of the serious delinquents interviewed who were still in school have little if any attachment to school. Few consider high school graduation to be "*very* important," and they assign even less importance to good grades or teachers' opinions of them. They are often absent, and, when they are in school, they are usually high on drugs. Their high rates of suspensions/expulsions suggest that school personnel view them as troublemakers. And indeed many of them are. (Inciardi, Horowitz, and Pottieger, 1993: 146)

School Organization and Delinquency   Some research suggests that the organizational context of the school can influence the amount of delinquency by its students. A study in England concluded that the schools that did the best job of keeping rates of delinquency low were the ones that had a relatively high proportion of good students and combined firm but fair discipline with rewards for good academic performance. The presence of more students who found school rewarding seemed to set the tone for the whole student body in a way that kept delinquency rates down. Teachers who treated their students in the way that parents who were effective at discipline did—that is, by using an "authoritative" style of discipline—seemed most likely to suppress delinquent behavior. For a school to keep delinquency down required parental involvement, a strong principal, and highly motivated and experienced teachers (Rutter et al., 1979).

Research in the United States has found less truancy, class cutting, verbal abuse of teachers, and student fighting in private and parochial schools than in public schools. Private and parochial schools are more likely than public ones to be characterized by clear goals, firm expectations, fair discipline, and rewards for work well done (Coleman, Hoffer, and Kilgore, 1982).

Delinquency and the Peer Group   Hirschi's conclusion that weaker peer-group ties are associated with higher rates of delinquency is challenged by other research, perhaps because Hirschi did not adequately distinguish ties to conventional peers from ties to delinquent ones. One national study found no relationship between attachment to peers and self-reported delinquency (Wiatrowski, Griswold, and Roberts, 1981), but other research has found that greater identification with peers is linked to higher rates of delinquency (Empey and Lubeck, 1971; Hindelang, 1973; Elliott and Voss, 1974; Elliott, Huizinga, and Ageton, 1985). This could be because the adolescent subculture is "oppositional" to the dominant, middle-class culture, and so closer ties to the peer group are associated with more delinquency (Elliott and Voss, 1974).

Delinquent behavior leads to delinquent peer associations ("birds of a feather flock together"), but delinquent peers also increase delinquent behavior ("rotten apples spoil the barrel"). Delinquents associate with delinquent peers, increasing the chance of more delinquency; and nondelinquents associate with nondelinquent peers, increasing the chance of more conforming behavior (Thornberry et al., 1994). An analysis of National Youth Survey data concluded that the impact of delinquent behavior on delinquent peer associations was greater than the effect of delinquent peers on delinquent behavior (Matsueda and Anderson, 1998).

One effort to assess social control theory's contention that delinquents' friendships are exploitative rather than supportive questioned nearly a thousand twelve to nineteen year olds living in a large metropolitan area. The researchers concluded that "youths who are very different in their levels of involvement in delinquency are nevertheless quite similar in the ways in which they view their friendship relations" (Giordano, Cernkovich, and Pugh, 1986: 1191). Social control theory's idea that individuals bring delinquent values to the group at the outset fits with the findings of these researchers, but they also conclude that after the group forms, mutual influence further strengthens patterns of delinquent behavior. The researchers contradict social control theory's assertion that delinquents lack attachments to their peers, finding instead that delinquents derive as many or more benefits from their friendships as other adolescents.

Peer Groups and Families   After looking carefully at the effects of parents and delinquent friends on self-reported delinquency, two researchers concluded that both had independent effects on delinquency. However, the delinquent peer group had a greater effect on delinquent behavior for adolescents who had weaker family ties than it did on the behavior of adolescents who had stronger family ties. Adolescents who had little support from their parents were more open to the influence of their delinquent peers, and adolescents who were wary of harming their good relationships with their parents were more likely to stay away from delinquent peers (Poole and Regoli, 1979).

A study of Chinese Canadian adolescent gangs concluded that they had emerged as a consequence of poor family supervision and guidance. Traditionally, the Chinese family in North America has been strong and able to insulate young people from trouble with the law, but in Canada during the 1970s this cohesive family unit was not as strong as it once was, so young Chinese Canadians turned to gangs. In part, this might have been an escape from family pressure to succeed in school, which created problems for recent immigrants who lacked the necessary language skills (Joe and Robinson, 1980).

Delinquency and Religion   One bond that could prevent delinquency but was not incorporated into social control theory is membership in organized religion. Religious activities are especially effective in inhibiting criminality because regular involvement in religious activities exposes people to moral proscriptions and makes real the threat of sanctions by enabling the "close monitoring and sanctioning of waywardness" (Evans et al., 1995: 210).

The two most commonly used measures of religiosity are salience (the importance of religion in a person's life) and attendance (the regularity with which a person goes to religious services); other measures of religiosity are denominational affiliation, the role of prayer and the study of sacred texts in a person's life, and participation in various religious activities. A review of research on the relationship between individual religiosity and criminality led Lee Ellis (1985: 511) to conclude there is "strong support and essentially no contradiction" for the following generalizations:

1. Among church members, frequent church attendees have lower crime rates than infrequent (or non-) attendees, especially in regard to victimless crimes.
2. Among church members, Jews have lower crime rates than Christians. Among Christians, Protestants have lower crime rates than Catholics.
3. Persons who believe in an afterlife with divine punishment for sins have somewhat lower crime rates than persons who lack such beliefs.

An analysis of forty studies of the religiosity–delinquency relationship revealed that three-fourths of them found that greater religiosity led to less delinquency, one found that greater religiosity led to more delinquency, and the rest showed mixed effects or no effects. The studies that had used the best research methods were the ones most likely to have found that greater religiosity was associated with less delinquency (Johnson et al., 2000). An examination of sixty studies concluded that "religion had a statistically significant, moderately sized effect on crime" (Baier and Wright, 2001: 16).

Religion is but one of a large set of influences on delinquent behavior, and one that interacts with the influence of the family, the school, and the peer group to inhibit or cause delinquency. A study that used religious salience (measured by strength of belief in the power of prayer) and religious orthodoxy as measures of religiosity found a weak to moderate relationship between religion and delinquency but concluded that religion was not a significant predictor of delinquency when compared with other factors such as the family and the peer group (Elifson, Petersen, and Hadaway, 1983). Other scholars have concluded that individual differences in the demand for arousal account for much of the association between religiosity and delinquency: Young people who demand a lot of stimulation are attracted to delinquency but bored by religious services, and young people who require less arousal are comforted by religion but avoid delinquency (Cochran, Wood, and Arneklev, 1994).

Migration and the Disruption of Social Bonds   Earlier in the book we saw that migration is sometimes associated with increases in crime rates for people who move. Increases are most likely to occur when migration from one nation to another or migration within a nation disrupts social bonds and weakens the informal control of behavior by family, school, peer group, religion, and community. One study concluded that "frequent potentially disruptive residential changes tend to undermine the individual's moral commitment to conventional norms that, in turn, increase the chances of offense" (Tittle and Paternoster, 1988: 324).

In developing nations, crime rates often increase as people become detached from traditional institutions through detribalization. Research shows that Ugandans who left their villages and moved to the large city of Kampala, especially to its slum shantytowns, were likely to have high rates of crime unless they established new social bonds in the city. Migration caused crime rates to increase by weakening attachments to groups that had traditionally controlled deviant behavior (Clinard and Abbott, 1973).

Migration might not be disruptive if the receiving community contains groups into which immigrants can be integrated or if individuals move from one place to another in groups. People who move alone and lack social ties in their new community are especially likely to become involved in crime because there is little to control their behavior. In the study of Uganda, it was relatively unimportant for migrants to the city to maintain direct ties to their village; what was important was that they form attachments to relatives and other immigrants from their village in the city to which they had moved (Clinard and Abbott, 1973). The ways that communities keep crime in check through a process of informal social control are examined in Chapter 12.

Social Bonds in Other Societies   One way to examine the usefulness of social control theory is to see whether it explains cross-national differences in rates of crime and delinquency. If social control theory is correct, we would expect the lowest rates to exist in societies characterized by close attachments to institutions. One study found that social control theory effectively explained differences in delinquency among Turkish, Surinamese, Moroccan, and Dutch males living in the Netherlands (Junger and Marshall, 1997). A study of ten nations, which were characterized by less fear of crime than existed in the United States, concluded that those nations had been able to create or maintain effective institutions of social control, especially the family (Adler, 1983). Let us look at the role of social bonds in India, China, and Japan.

India   Juvenile delinquency is relatively uncommon in India, because young people are an important part of the nation's peasant or agrarian economy. Because unskilled labor is not much in demand in advanced industrial economies such as the United States, young people must postpone their entry into the labor force, and as a result adolescent subcultures supportive of delinquency sometimes develop. In contrast, peasant economies that make use of unskilled labor integrate children and adolescents into the community from an early age. Social activities are rarely segregated by age, adolescent hangouts are practically nonexistent, and there is no adolescent subculture conducive to delinquency.

Indian society is organized in terms of role relationships that create for everyone a set of obligations to the family, the subcaste, and the community. Agricultural workers and landowners have mutual obligations that extend beyond the worker-employer relationship; employers look out for the welfare of employees and their families, and workers have obligations to employers that go beyond economic dependence. The complex network of social relationships in India makes an individual's deviance of concern to many others and creates pressure to conform to their expectations (Hartjen and Priyadarsini, 1984).

China   China, which apparently has a low rate of conventional crime, is characterized by strongly integrated groups. Chinese citizens learn an ideology of attachment to the country and to a version of communist ideology; they are thus subordinated to supraindividual concerns. The family is a strong institution that controls individual behavior, and young people spend much of their free time in state-run recreational facilities.

A study in Tianjin, China, confirmed that the family was a dominant institution that contributed to a low overall rate of delinquency. However, the strength of the family also meant that deviance within the family was strongly predictive of official delinquency status, suggesting that some families transmit deviance from generation to generation. Associating with delinquent peers also predicted delinquency status, contrary to the researchers' initial assumption that the influence of the family would overwhelm the influence of the peer group (Zhang and Messner, 1995).

The regimentation and lack of privacy in China have been compared to life in an army barracks (Butterfield, 1982). Two institutions that maintain social control by public scrutiny of behavior are the *danwei* (or workplace) and the street committee. All Chinese belong to a danwei through the school they attend or the office or factory in which they work. The danwei often provides housing, schooling, and medical care, and it must give permission to marry and to divorce. Ties to the danwei are so strong that the Chinese are more likely to be asked their danwei rather than their name if they travel to another community. The urban street committee is another institution that controls behavior, searching people's homes, recommending job assignments and housing changes, and even deciding who may have children. These and other institutions make the Chinese very sensitive to the expectations of others and help curb delinquency and crime.

Japan   The Japanese traditionally have had strong ties to their family, to the company for which they work, and to the community in which they live. Bonds to such tightly knit groups offer security and success to individuals and ensure conformity by requiring the fulfillment of social responsibilities. The group nature of Japanese society is so strong that crime rates are low even in densely populated urban areas, where we might expect social bonds to break down and crime rates to be high (Clifford, 1976).

The strength of family ties is a major reason that Japan has a low crime rate.

In Japan, individual behavior is guided by obligations to family, employer, neighborhood, and society, rather than by self-interest. Americans usually speak of their rights, but the Japanese more often think of the debts they owe to others. The social structure of Japan is similar in its group orientation to some communist nations such as China that also have low crime rates, but Japan provides striking evidence that crime is more a result of the social structure of a society than a product of its political and economic ideology. The capitalist society of Japan and the communist society of China have low crime rates because both have created and maintained social bonds that tie people to groups and institutions.

Traditional social controls have weakened somewhat in Japan in recent years. Arrests of minors for serious crimes doubled from 1990 to 1998, though even after that increase such crime was much less common than in the United States. Japan's upsurge in teenage crime has been attributed to a growing emphasis on economic success, which has led parents to spend more hours working and commuting; this has reduced the amount of time they spend with their children, leaving those children without discipline and supervision. Greater pressure to perform well academically has resulted in children spending more hours in school and on homework, so they have little time for recreation with their peers. Even their leisure-time activities isolate Japanese youths from human contact, with many of them spending hours alone in their bedrooms with video games, televisions, and computers. The consequence of these trends is diminished social control over the behavior of young people, a tendency reflected in the term applied to the growing number of troubled youths, *hikikomori,* which means the socially withdrawn (French, 1999; Moshavi, 2000).

Critique of Social Control Theory

One shortcoming of social control theory is that it does not identify the social-structural sources of motivations to break the law. Attachments to family, school, and peer group can keep people from violating the law even when other social forces—such as poverty—impel them to engage in crime and delinquency. However, a complete theory of crime and delinquency needs to explain the way that social, cultural, and economic forces produce the motivation to break the law.

Social control theory would benefit from a more dynamic analysis of social interaction. Rather than describing attachments as they are at a given time, social control theory needs to examine the way that attachments change over time. For instance, the way that parents behave at one time affects their children's actions at a later time, but those actions by the children can in turn affect the way that their parents will treat them in the future.

One criticism of social control theory is that it fails to take into account possible reciprocal relationships between social bonds and delinquency, focusing instead on the way that weak attachments lead to delinquency (Agnew, 1985). One study found that weakened attachments to family and school caused delinquency, but also that delinquent behavior reduced the strength of bonds to family and school, which in turn increased delinquency (Thornberry et al., 1991). Another study found that parental attachment did affect delinquency, but that most of the relationship between school attachment and delinquency was due to the effect of delinquency on school attachment, rather than the effect of school attachment on delinquency (Liska and Reed, 1985).

Other research suggests that social control theory oversimplifies reality when it claims that low attachment, commitment, and belief create the freedom to violate social norms. One study concluded that low attachment, commitment, and belief also increase anger and frustration, and that anger and frustration act as sources of strain that generate delinquency. Moreover, this study showed that social control variables are associated with delinquency only for individuals motivated to engage in such behavior, namely those who are high in anger and frustration and those who associate with delinquent peers (Agnew, 1993). A study done in New Zealand found that more ties to family, school, work, and partners reduced criminal behavior, whereas more ties to delinquent peers increased such behavior; however, these effects were much stronger for people with low to moderate levels of self-control than for those with high self-control (Wright et al., 2001).

Attachments to different institutions probably take on varying degrees of importance at different stages of the life cycle, and social control theory needs to identify more clearly the relative significance of bonds to different institutions for people of various ages (Agnew, 1991). One study that did this found that the causal processes identified in Hirschi's social control theory are most applicable to youths in midadolescence (about age fifteen). Attachments to parents and teachers and commitment to conventional lines of action are important "psychological anchors" to conformity for this age group. This study also found that the influence of delinquent peers was strongest for older adolescents (around age eighteen) (LaGrange and White, 1985). A different study found that the family's ability "to supervise and control developing youths is restricted by a lack of social and material resources in the communities where serious delinquency is concentrated" and concluded that because the family's impact on socialization wanes before adolescence, policy makers must look to schools, peers, and communities for ways to reduce delinquency (Fagan and Wexler, 1987: 664).

The way in which bonds to different institutions interact with one another needs to be more fully delineated. Some researchers have examined the relationships among bonds to family, school, and peer group (Empey and Lubeck, 1971; Liska and Reed, 1985; Patterson and Dishion, 1985), but we need much more information on how relationships with parents affect attitudes toward school and work, how bonds to teachers during adolescence influence adult work history, and how attachments to family and job among adults are related to involvement in criminal behavior. For instance, a young father with strong bonds to a wife and children and a strong attachment to his career might experience conflict between his loyalty to his family and his loyalty to his job. This conflict could cause frustration that leads to violence in the home or theft at work. Social control theory needs elaboration, and researchers must investigate further the complex relationships among attachments to different institutions.

Some researchers have found that empirical support for social control theory is only weak to moderate and that the evidence is at least as consistent with competing perspectives such as strain theory (see Chapter 6) and differential association theory (see Chapter 8) (Akers, 1997; Greenberg, 1999). Consequently, social control theory might best be integrated with other theories to produce a more complete explanation of crime. One possibility is a general utility-maximizing theory that combines social control theory's emphasis on the costs of criminal and noncriminal behavior with strain theory's emphasis on the gains from such behavior (Greenberg, 1999). Another possibility is John Braithwaite's (1989) reintegrative shaming theory (see Chapter 14), which brings together social control theory with labeling, subcultural, opportunity, and learning theories. A third possibility is Charles Tittle's (1995) **control balance theory**, which explains crime in terms of the ratio between the control imposed on an individual by others and the control that an individual is able to exercise over others. Adding to Hirschi's theory the idea that people have varying degrees of autonomy or command over their own destiny, control balance theory predicts that those with either a control deficit or a control surplus will engage in predatory crime.

Techniques of Neutralization, Social Control Theory, and Variations in Crime Rates

We do not now have enough evidence on the distribution of the techniques of neutralization to know whether they can account for variations in crime rates. One country might have more crime than another because its culture includes beliefs that make it easier to neutralize the law and engage in crime and delinquency. Differences in access to techniques of neutralization could also help to explain variations in crime rates by region, by size of the community, over time, or by sex, age, race, and social class. However, we have no evidence that this is so.

Social control theory does make sense of cross-national variations in crime rates, because nations that have lower crime rates seem to be characterized by stronger and more extensive bonds to family, peer group, school, community, and nation. We have little evidence that regional variations in crime rates in the United States can be explained by differences in the strength of attachments to such institutions. Variations in crime rates by size of the community might be accounted for by social control theory. Attachment to community seems weaker in larger cities than in small towns and rural areas, with interpersonal relationships in large communities often being described as weak and segmented. We lack good evidence that fluctuations in crime rates over time parallel changes in social bonds to institutions such as the family, the school, the peer group, the community, and organized religion. The increase in crime rates in the decades following World War II has been attributed in part to a decline in the legitimacy of the family, but the sharp decrease in rates in the 1990s cannot be explained by changes in family attachments, which weakened during that decade (LaFree, 1998; Conklin, 2003).

Social control theory helps explain variations in crime rates by sex, age, race, and social class. Adolescent boys probably have high rates of delinquency because they are supervised less closely than girls and preadolescent boys, two groups that have relatively low delinquency rates. Age variations in crime rates can also be explained by social control theory. Adolescents are concerned with breaking away from their parents, and this creates pressure on parents to exert less control. Adults marry, have children, take jobs, and settle down in a community; these bonds help to account for the decline in crime rates with age. Blacks' high crime rates could be due in part to their weaker attachment to jobs, with the lack of promising jobs to which they can form strong attachments being a product of racial discrimination and the poor quality of education in many public schools. The higher rates of family dissolution and illegitimacy among blacks also suggest that differences in family relationships between blacks and whites might account for some of the differences in crime rates between the groups. Finally, social class differences in crime rates might exist because poorer families tend to be larger, more likely to be broken, and more likely to experience financial strain. These factors could be associated with reduced control over deviant behavior. In addition, lower-class students might feel that they cannot win the good opinion of their middle-class teachers, or believe that education will gain them little in improved job prospects even if they do form close attachments to their teachers.

We have little research that demonstrates that variations in crime rates among different groups, regions, and countries are directly due to variations in attachments to institutions. Social control theory is, however, compatible with some of these variations in crime rates, and more research might show that this theory can explain those variations.

Summary

Most people must neutralize the hold that the law has over them before they can violate the law. People who are in a state of drift and lack strong bonds to the conventional order are free to engage in delinquency and crime, but they are not forced to do so. The values of law violators have some things in common with the dominant value system, but delinquents and criminals act on subterranean themes in the dominant value system in inappropriate situations.

Techniques of neutralization, which are used to justify delinquency and crime prior to the deviant act, include the following: denial of responsibility, denial of injury, denial of the victim, condemnation of the condemners, and the appeal to higher loyalties. These and other techniques are used by many kinds of offenders—juvenile delinquents, professional criminals, and white-collar offenders.

Evidence that these techniques of neutralization are associated with violation of the law comes from a study of embezzlers, a survey of black men interviewed on the street, a study of sex-related and robbery-related murders and contract killings, and several studies of juvenile delinquency. However, we lack good evidence that offenders use these techniques prior to violating the law, and we do not know what aspects of the social structure make it easy or difficult to justify violations of the law.

Social control theory proposes that people engage in delinquency or crime when they are free of intimate attachments to the family, the school, and the peer group, and when the aspirations and moral beliefs that bind them to a conventional way of life are weak. The absence of a "psychological presence" of parents leaves adolescents free to violate the law without being afraid of how their parents will react. Close ties between adolescents and their parents inhibit delinquent behavior, as do strong ties to schools and their teachers. Adolescents who do not aspire to conventional lines of action such as education and work but who want to engage in adult activities before assuming adult responsibilities are especially likely to engage in delinquency.

Comparisons of delinquents and nondelinquents generally support social control theory, but the interrelationship of variables is more complex than Hirschi's initial formulation of the theory suggests. The way parents socialize their children, particularly the way they discipline them, is related to delinquency and crime. If relationships between parents and their children, and between the parents themselves, are characterized by conflict or poor communication, the children are more likely to become delinquents. The relationship between broken homes and delinquency is weak but consistent. In general, more cohesive families are better able to insulate their children against trouble with the law.

Delinquents have weaker ties to schools and teachers than nondelinquents. They also do less well in their academic work.

The relationship between the peer group and delinquency is not entirely clear, but most studies find that delinquents usually have delinquent friends. Whether those friends lead them into delinquency or whether they choose those friends after violating the law is unclear.

Most research indicates that there is less delinquency among adolescents who are more religious. Religion may also interact with the family, the peer group, and the school to curb delinquency.

Under some conditions, migration disrupts social bonds and increases criminality. This occurs when traditional social bonds are broken by moving and are not replaced by other attachments that inhibit criminality.

Social control theory has several shortcomings. It does not identify the social-structural sources of motivations to violate the law. It has not yet specified the relative importance of different kinds of attachments for people of various ages. Social control theory has also failed to spell out the way that attachments to different institutions interact with one another to prevent or cause crime and delinquency.

We do not yet have enough evidence on the distribution of the techniques of neutralization to account for geographic, temporal, and social variations in crime rates. Social control theory does seem capable of explaining those variations, with attachments to institutions being weakest in those countries and among those groups that have the highest crime rates.

IMPORTANT TERMS

appeal to higher loyalties
condemnation of the
    condemners
control balance theory

denial of injury
denial of responsibility
denial of the victim
drift

life-course perspective
social control theory
subterranean value
technique of neutralization

REVIEW QUESTIONS

1. How do juvenile delinquents neutralize the restraining influence of the law on their behavior? Do white-collar criminals use similar or different techniques of neutralization before committing crime?

2. What evidence is there that people who break the law use techniques of neutralization before engaging in crime and delinquency? How could researchers further test the significance of techniques of neutralization?

3. What bonds or attachments inhibit delinquent behavior, according to Travis Hirschi's social control theory? What evidence supports that theory? What are some of the theory's shortcomings?

4. Describe a family that would be especially likely to produce delinquent children. What government policies might reduce the number of families that produce delinquent children?

5. Have other societies been more successful than the United States in creating or maintaining social bonds that keep crime and delinquency to a minimum? What do the experiences of other societies tell us about how the United States might lower its crime rate?

6. How would social control theory explain variations in crime rates from one nation, region, or community to another, and across categories of sex, age, race, and social class?

FOR FURTHER STUDY

Life-Course Perspective   Three books on crime over the life course are Robert J. Sampson and John H. Laub's *Crime in the Making: Pathways and Turning Points through Life* (Cambridge, MA: Harvard University Press, 1993), Michael L. Benson's *Crime and the Life Course: An Introduction* (Los Angeles: Roxbury, 2001), and Alex Piquero and Paul Mazerolle's (eds.) *Life-Course Criminology: Contemporary and Classic Readings* (Belmont, CA: Wadsworth, 2001).

Peer Groups and Crime   Mark Warr's *Companions in Crime: The Social Aspects of Criminal Conduct* (Cambridge, England: Cambridge University Press, 2002) reviews research on the impact of peers on crime and delinquency.

Religion and Delinquency   A recent summary of published research on religion and delinquency is Byron R. Johnson et al.'s "A Systematic Review of the Religiosity and Delinquency Literature" (*Journal of Contemporary Criminal Justice* 16, February 2000, 32–52).

8 Learning to Commit Crime

Crime arises from needs that can be met by violating the law. Because most people are attached to the legal order, or at least know that the law commands widespread respect, they must justify their criminal acts and be relatively free of bonds to the legitimate social order before they can break the law. In addition to learning techniques for neutralizing the law, criminals must learn the skills and motives that are needed to violate the law. For instance, they learn how to recognize opportunities for crime, how to reduce victim resistance, and how to find outlets for the property they steal. The degree to which such skills have to be learned varies from crime to crime. No particular skill is needed to steal an unattended purse, but finding a safe that contains a large amount of money, breaking into the building, and cracking the safe require considerable skill.

Sources of Learning to Commit Crime

Offenders learn motives and techniques for breaking the law from many sources, including the community, the peer group, the general culture, the media, sports, pornography, and correctional institutions.

The Community

Opportunities to learn to commit crime are associated with the social organization of a community. Learning about crime is easier when there are close ties and frequent interaction among people of different ages within a community. Interaction between teenagers and adult criminals, as well as between teenage gang members and preteen nonmembers, provides opportunities to engage in criminal activities under the supervision of more experienced offenders. An unusual instance of this was reported in

1993 in Los Angeles, where two adults were implicated in 175 bank robberies carried out by teenagers whom they had enlisted and coached. The adults recruited boys as young as thirteen from gangs or from those who wanted to join gangs, provided them with automatic weapons and a stolen getaway car, and paid them with money or drugs. The supervisors remained a safe distance from the bank while the teenagers carried out the robbery, often firing their weapons before speeding away.

Local criminals sometimes act as role models for young people, as we can see from the following childhood memory of one of the robbers in the 1950 Brinks holdup:

> "When I was a kid, we all knew what a big-time crook was, and most of us looked up to them. I was always working to make money from the time I could walk. You wanted money because the parents were so poor. And I had all kinds of legitimate jobs, but they didn't pay nothing. But these racket guys would drive up in those big touring cars filled with pretty girls and all the money they wanted. I remember one of them giving us kids five bucks each just to stand and watch his car while he and the girl went to eat at a restaurant. Jesus, five bucks was almost as much as my father made in a week." (cited in Behn, 1977: 60)

Criminal role models are especially influential in communities that have high rates of poverty and unemployment, because in those neighborhoods there are few adults who have been successful in legitimate careers for young people to emulate.

The Peer Group

Learning to commit crime often occurs within groups or gangs, but many adolescents learn not to be delinquent from their peers. Those who are concerned with their reputation and believe they have an investment in abiding by the law cite the influence of their peers as a major reason for not violating the law (Rogers, 1977). Adolescents who do not have a stake in conformity sometimes join gangs and learn criminal motives and skills from peers who encourage and reward violation of the law.

In gangs, adolescents gain respect for older criminals, develop specific skills such as car theft, learn to cooperate with other offenders, and become aware of fences, shady lawyers, bondsmen, and corrupt politicians and police officers (Rettig, Torres, and Garrett, 1977). One professional robber reports that he first got involved in an adult robbery gang because as an adolescent he had a reputation as a skilled car thief. Members of the gang approached him to steal a getaway car for a robbery, and he was gradually accepted into the gang on a permanent basis (Conklin, 1972).

The General Culture

People sometimes learn criminal motives from the general culture. For instance, the increase in violent crime after the end of wars is particularly dramatic in nations that were actively involved in the war, were victorious, and suffered large combat losses. The best explanation of this is that war makes violence legitimate, with people coming to believe that if their leaders can solve international disputes with violence, it is also a suitable means for resolving interpersonal differences (Archer and Gartner, 1984).

The techniques of neutralization examined in Chapter 7 are part of the general culture and are used to justify violations of the law. Embezzlers learn motives for their crimes from the general culture, justifying their offenses by the ambiguity that surrounds the ownership of money and property, and saying that they are only "borrowing the money temporarily" (Cressey, 1971).

Forcible rape is also closely linked to the values of a culture. Cultures that emphasize **machismo**—the exaggerated belief that men should be aggressive, dominant, and strong—are likely to have more rape and other violence against women than are cultures that deemphasize differences between the sexes and provide men and women with the same opportunities (Schwendinger and Schwendinger, 1983). The Cross-Cultural Perspective illustrates this with an example from Brazil. One sociologist argues that rape and violence against women would be less common if

> our culture considered it masculine to be gentle and sensitive, to be responsive to the needs of others, to abhor violence, domination, and exploitation, to want sex only within a meaningful relationship, to be attracted by personality and character rather

CROSS-CULTURAL PERSPECTIVES

Machismo and Murder in Brazil

Brazilian culture traditionally has supported the use of violence by men against women who insult their dignity. Some men have killed their unfaithful wives and lovers, even though those men expect to have an unchallenged right to engage in sex with other women. Never a formal part of the Brazilian criminal code, the "legitimate defense of honor" has been used thousands of times to win acquittals for men who have killed their wives and lovers.

In a 1979 murder trial, forty-five-year-old Raul "Doca" Street was tried for shooting and killing Angela Diniz, his thirty-two-year-old lover, after she ordered him to move out of her expensive villa so that she could replace him with someone else. She also hit him in the face with a handbag. Street's attorney justified the killing by calling the victim "a luxurious Babylonian prostitute" and "a lascivious woman," claiming that his client had suffered "a violent moral aggression" and had murdered the victim out of "legitimate defense of his honor." Women who were present inside and outside the courtroom applauded the defendant and carried signs of support for him. A jury of five men and two women convicted Street of involuntary homicide, and he was given a two-year suspended sentence and allowed to go free.

Some observers claimed that this verdict and sentence increased the number of murders of women by "affronted" men. One feminist described the months following Street's trial as "a hunting season on women." Led by a small group of militant feminists, Brazilian women became increasingly angry over the murder of women in defense of "masculine honor." They demanded a retrial of Street to show that women could not be killed merely for insulting a man's honor. Eventually, an appellate court declared that the verdict of involuntary homicide was invalid and ordered a new trial.

In the retrial, which ended in December 1981, Street was convicted and sentenced to fifteen years in prison. At the new trial, military police had to force an opening through five hundred angry feminist protesters. The atmosphere at the new trial was one of condemnation of machismo killings, rather than the supportive atmosphere at the first trial only two years earlier. Some Brazilians believe that the second verdict, and the protest over killing in defense of "masculine honor" that followed the first verdict, weakened this justification for murder. During the two weeks after the second verdict, three men who claimed that they had killed their wives to defend their honor were found guilty of murder.

Over the next decade, Brazilian women campaigned against the "legitimate defense of honor," and in 1991 the Brazilian Supreme Court finally outlawed the defense, ruling as follows:

> Homicide cannot be seen as a normal and legitimate way of reacting to adultery. Because in this kind of crime what is defended is not honor, but vanity, exaggerated self-importance and the pride of the lord who sees a woman as his personal property. (p. B16)

Sources: Based on Jim Brooke, "Feminism in Foreign Lands: Two Perspectives: Macho Killing in Brazil Spurs Protesters," *Boston Globe,* January 3, 1982, pp. A23, A24; James Brooke, "'Honor' Killing of Wives Is Outlawed in Brazil," *New York Times,* March 29, 1991, p. B16.

than by physical appearance, to value lasting rather than casual relationships. . . . (Russell, 1975: 264–265)

The Media

Today, the average American household has a television set turned on about seven hours a day. In looking at the consequences of such heavy television viewing, social scientists have focused on the large amount of violence that viewers see. A 1996 report found that violence—defined as an overt depiction of the use or threat of physical force intended to physically harm a living being—was included in 85 percent of premium cable channel shows, 59 percent of basic cable channel shows, and 44 percent of broadcast television channel shows (see Figure 8.1). Three-fourths of those who committed violent acts were not punished in the same scene, half of all victims of violence were not shown as being harmed, one-fourth of the violent incidents included a handgun, and only 4 percent of shows that contained violence also emphasized nonviolent means of resolving conflicts.

The hypothesis that violence in the media might reduce real-life violence by releasing tensions is contradicted by most studies. One review of the research literature

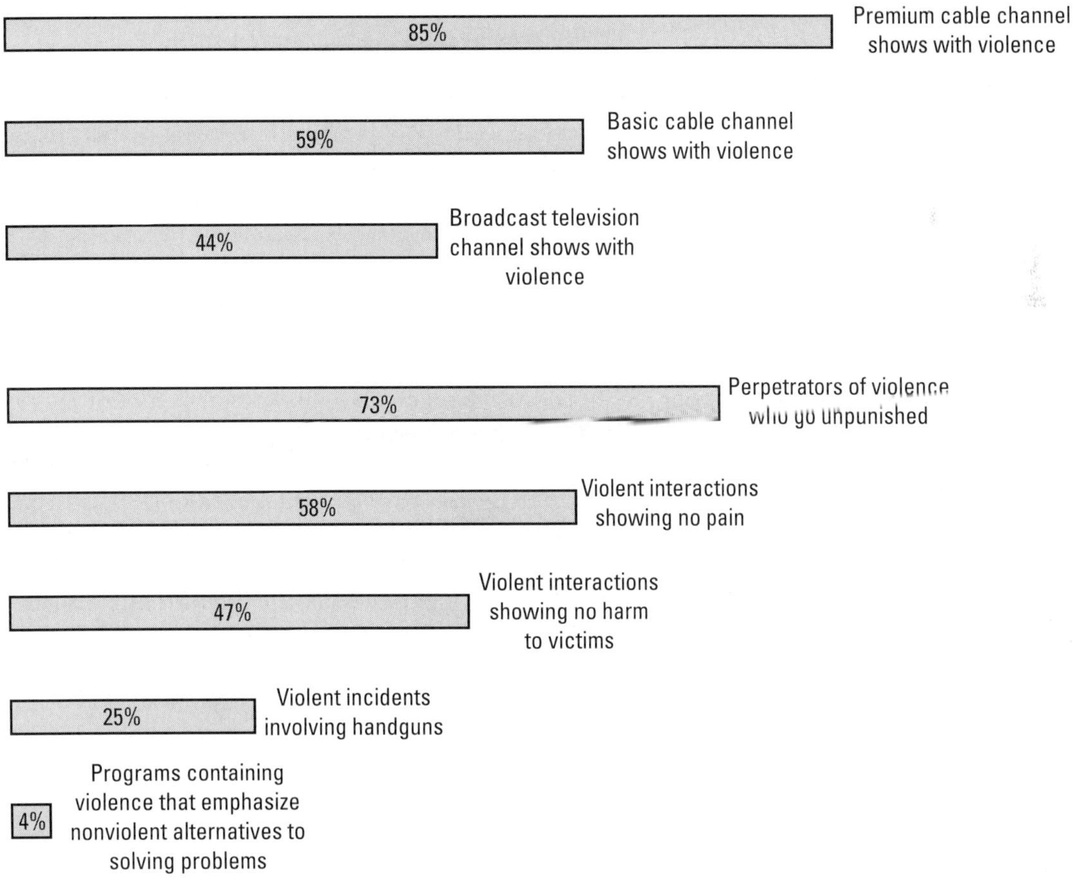

85%	Premium cable channel shows with violence
59%	Basic cable channel shows with violence
44%	Broadcast television channel shows with violence
73%	Perpetrators of violence who go unpunished
58%	Violent interactions showing no pain
47%	Violent interactions showing no harm to victims
25%	Violent incidents involving handguns
4%	Programs containing violence that emphasize nonviolent alternatives to solving problems

FIGURE 8.1   Violence on Television

Source: Based on data in Paul Farhi, "Researchers Link Psychological Harm to Violence on TV," *Boston Globe,* February 7, 1996, p. 3; Bill Carter, "A New Report Becomes a Weapon in Debate on Censoring TV Violence," *New York Times,* February 7, 1996, pp. C11, C16.

confidently concluded that viewing violence in the media has the following major effects:

1. An *aggressor effect* of increased meanness, aggression, and even violence toward others.
2. A *victim effect* of increased fearfulness, mistrust, or "mean world syndrome," and self-protective behavior (such as carrying a gun, which ironically increases one's risk of becoming a victim of violence).
3. A *bystander effect* of increased desensitization, callousness, and behavioral apathy toward other victims of violence.
4. An *appetite effect* of increased self-initiated behavior to further expose oneself to violent material. (Donnerstein, Slaby, and Eron, 1994: 240)

According to the authors,

> scholars in the field of mass media overwhelmingly support the assumption of a strong relation between televised violence and aggressive behavior. . . . These analyses support a number of conclusions. First, there is a positive association between televised violence exposure and aggressive behavior over a wide range of ages and measures of aggressive behavior. Second, exposure to violent programming not only increases aggressive behavior but is associated with lowered levels of prosocial behavior. (Donnerstein, Slaby, and Eron, 1994: 228)

One longitudinal study found that the exposure of young boys to televised violence correlated with their aggressiveness at later ages, concluding as follows: "The greater was a boy's preference for violent television at age eight, the greater was his aggressiveness both at that time and ten years later" (Lefkowitz et al., 1977: 115–116). What the boys watched on television when they were eighteen was not related to their aggressiveness at that age, possibly because television violence was no longer realistic to them or perhaps because the modeling effect occurs only earlier in life. In response to methodological criticisms of this study, one of the researchers remarked:

> Now, it could have been said that aggressive youngsters like violent programs to begin with. But because of the methodology we used to control the experiment, we were fairly certain this was a cause-and-effect relationship, with television viewing preceding the aggressive behavior. The highly aggressive youngsters who were watching nonviolent programs were significantly less aggressive by age eighteen than the youngsters who were not aggressive at eight but who had watched violent programs; they turned out to be more aggressive in the end. We later repeated the study, and found the same thing. Furthermore, the more violent the program, the more aggressive the children became. (Leonard Eron, cited in Bennetts, 1981: 25)

A follow-up study of the subjects at about age thirty found that "the violent programming they had watched was related to the seriousness of the crimes they committed, how aggressive they were to their spouses, and even to how aggressive their own kids were" (Leonard Eron, cited in Kolbert, 1994: D20).

Another longitudinal study concluded that fourteen year olds who spent more hours viewing any television programming were more likely to act aggressively at ages sixteen or twenty-two. The percentage of fourteen-year-old boys who engaged in aggressive acts at sixteen or twenty-two was 8.9 for those who watched one hour or less of television per day, but 32.5 percent for those who watched one to three hours per day, and 45.2 for those who watched three or more hours per day. For fourteen-year-old girls, the percentages engaging in aggressive acts at sixteen or twenty-two rose from 2.3 to 11.8 to 12.7 for the same categories of television viewing. The researchers controlled for childhood neglect, family income, and psychiatric disorders, but other variables they did not introduce into the analysis could account for some of the association between television viewing and later aggressiveness (Johnson et al., 2002).

The way that violence is portrayed in the media determines how much it will influence actual behavior. Its influence is greatest if those who act aggressively are rewarded or are not punished, if the aggressive behavior is shown as justified, and if the violence is portrayed as similar to real life. Media violence is also more influential when it is motivated by a desire to inflict harm, seems to produce no pain or remorse, is unrelieved or uninterrupted, is not criticized, and leaves the viewer aroused or frustrated. The impact of media violence is also greatest when the viewer is predisposed to aggressive behavior and strongly identifies with the aggressor (Paik and Comstock, 1994; Donnerstein, Slaby, and Eron, 1994).

Media attention to real acts of violence can trigger additional violence in the general population. After the assassination of President John F. Kennedy in 1963, aggravated assaults and robberies increased throughout the country. Similar increases occurred in 1966 after two widely reported crimes: the murder of eight nurses by Richard Speck and the killing of fourteen people by Charles Whitman from a tower at the University of Texas (Berkowitz and Macaulay, 1971). One study found a noticeable increase in the homicide rate after heavyweight championship boxing matches, and an especially great increase after those matches that were most heavily publicized (Phillips, 1983). News stories about violence that is rewarded, such as a championship fight, seem to be followed by a short-term increase in the homicide rate, but news accounts of violence that is punished, such as a murder for which the perpetrator is executed or imprisoned for life, seem to be followed by a short-term drop in the homicide rate. Apparently, the homicide rate is not affected by reports of violence that is neither punished nor rewarded (Phillips and Hensley, 1984).

Representatives of television networks usually emphasize those few studies that find no association between media violence and aggressiveness, and point to the methodological flaws of the many studies that find such an association. Nevertheless, the networks continue to solicit billions of dollars from advertisers on the assumption that what people see on television does influence their behavior.

In response to growing public concern about the effects of televised violence, a ratings system introduced in 1997 displayed for fifteen seconds at the start of a show a label that denoted the appropriate age group for the program (TV-Y: suitable for all children; TV-Y7: suitable for children seven and older; TV-Y7-FV: suitable for older children, with fantasy violence; TV-G: suitable for general audiences; TV-PG: parental guidance suggested; TV-14: parents strongly cautioned, may be unsuitable for children under fourteen; and TV-MA: mature audiences only, may be unsuitable for children under seventeen). Material in the program that might be considered objectionable was also rated (V: violence; S: sexual situations; L: vulgar language; D: suggestive dialogue; and FV: fantasy violence). Critics claimed that this system was confusing, that the networks did not fully comply with it, that many parents did not use the symbols to control their children's viewing behavior, and that ratings could actually attract children to shows that featured violent or sexually explicit material. By January 1, 2000, all new television sets had to contain a violence- or V-chip that would allow viewers to use this rating system to screen out programs. In mid-2001, a survey by the Kaiser Family Foundation found that 60 percent of parents did not yet have a television set with a V-chip, 21 percent had one but did not know it, 12 percent knew they had one but did not use the V-chip, and only 7 percent had one and used the V-chip to block programs (cited in Rutenberg, 2001).

Even though exposure to media violence correlates with aggressive behavior, we lack conclusive proof that it is a major cause of crime and delinquency. Aggressiveness can be expressed in various ways, including athletics, and it does not necessarily lead to violation of the law. However, for some people in certain circumstances, media portrayals of violence might contribute to delinquency and crime. For example, social control theory suggests that people exposed to media violence would be especially likely to commit crime if they lacked attachments to conventional institutions and lines of action.

Sports

There is evidence that sports contribute to the aggressiveness of both athletes and spectators. High school and college athletes in combative sports such as football and hockey anger more easily than athletes in less combative sports such as swimming. In addition, athletes in combative sports become more aggressive during the course of the season and are more likely to remain more aggressive after the season ends (Russell, 1983; Goleman, 1985). By encouraging aggressiveness and male camaraderie, organized sports denigrate femininity and encourage attitudes conducive to sexual assault. A study of National Collegiate Athletic Association Division I varsity athletes found that they were significantly more likely than other male students to commit sexual assaults on campus (Bass, 1994). Because they are usually treated more leniently by the law and by their institutions than are nonathletes, athletes are less easily deterred from committing sexual assault, theft, and illegal drug use (Golden, 1995).

Professional athletes may be even more prone to crime than collegiate ones because the wealth and celebrity of professionals can lead them to believe they are above the law. Male professional athletes have abundant opportunities for sex with female "groupies" and are encouraged to believe that all women who approach them are willing sex partners, an attitude conducive to sexual assaults against unwilling women. The high salaries of professional athletes allow them to hire the best legal counsel when they are charged with crimes; their celebrity status makes it difficult to get juries to convict them; and the publicity given to professional athletes who are charged with crimes discourages victims from pursuing cases (Benedict, 1997). In fact, many assaults committed by professional athletes on competitors, coaches, fans, and sportswriters are not even prosecuted as crimes. Latrell Sprewell's 1997 assault on basketball coach P. J. Carlesimo led to his one-year suspension by the National Basketball Association and the termination of his $25 million contract by the Golden State Warriors, but it did not lead to criminal assault charges; indeed, Sprewell joined the New York Knicks after his suspension was completed. In an apparent exception to the lenient treatment of professional athletes, Boston Bruins hockey player Marty McSorley was convicted of assaulting a Vancouver Canucks player with his stick in 2000, but he was then given the opportunity to clear the conviction from his record by successfully completing his sentence of eighteen months of probation.

Even though professional athletes are infrequently convicted, they seem to commit crimes at a high rate; an estimated one-fifth of National Football League players have been arrested for a serious crime (Benedict and Yaeger, 1998). One reason for the high crime rate of professional athletes is that they are disproportionately drawn from a demographic group that has a high rate of conventional crime: young black males from lower- and working-class backgrounds. (Because these athletes have usually attended college, a training ground for professional sports leagues, they are actually more highly educated than the average person.) Other factors reinforce the demographic propensity of professional athletes to commit crime, including the indifference of coaches, team owners, and league officials to such crime; the athletes' permissive lifestyle; an exaggerated sensitivity to challenges to their manhood and sexuality; a lowered accountability for their actions in high school and college; the

Marty McSorley of the Boston Bruins was found guilty of criminally assaulting Vancouver Canucks player Donald Brashear during a hockey game on February 21, 2000.

effects of contact sports on aggressive behavior; and the demeaning attitudes toward women common among male athletes (Benedict, 1997).

Well-known sports figures who have been targets of criminal investigations—including boxer Mike Tyson, football player Michael Irvin, and baseball player Pete Rose—are role models for young athletes, and perhaps for all young people. The message these athletes convey is that law-violating behavior is common, even expected, among athletes, and that the criminal justice system is a nuisance rather than a real threat to their careers.

Watching sporting events can make spectators more aggressive. In 1985, thirty-nine people died when British fans at a soccer game in Belgium attacked an area of the stadium where Italian fans were sitting, resulting in the unexpected collapse of a section of the stands. Latin American soccer fans have assaulted referees who make unpopular decisions, and in 1994 fans murdered a Colombian national team player after he accidentally scored a goal for the opposing team. Research shows that watching certain kinds of sporting events increases fans' hostility and aggressiveness. One study found that fans at an Army-Navy football game were more hostile after the game than before it, and that hostility increased whether the fan's preferred team won or lost, or even if the fan did not care who won the game. The largest increase in hostility occurred among fans of the winning team, apparently because they had seen aggression on the field rewarded with a victory. This study also found no increase in hostility among spectators at an Army-Navy gymnastics match—a nonaggressive sport—on the same weekend (Goldstein, 1986). Another study showed that aggressiveness increased among spectators at hockey and wrestling matches but not at swim meets, again suggesting that viewing aggression increases aggressiveness among spectators (Arms, Russell, and Sandilands, 1979).

Factors other than simple imitation of athletes' behavior contribute to spectator aggressiveness. Research indicates that fans experience changes in heart rate, brain waves, hormone levels, esteem, optimism, depression, and alienation when watching their favorite teams. In some circumstances, these changes could increase aggressiveness (McKinley, 2000). The excitement of an important game might weaken normal inhibitions against aggression, and the consumption of alcoholic beverages could reinforce that effect. Spectator violence usually involves young males, a group especially prone to violent activity in other contexts. Nationalism, unemployment, general social unrest, and the cultural context can also contribute to spectator violence, but the game itself builds up aggressiveness among spectators (Goldstein, 1983; Goleman, 1985).

The increased aggressiveness that results from watching and participating in sports does not always lead to criminal behavior, and the exact conditions under which it does so are unclear. Contact sports do heighten aggressiveness, but the way that aggressiveness is channeled—whether into criminal assaults or into loud cheering and boisterousness—is less well understood.

Pornography

There is a widely held view that people who view or read pornography are more likely to commit sex offenses because they learn to see such behavior as rewarding or because they are stimulated to act on their sexual fantasies. **Pornography** is material that is intended to arouse people sexually by portraying sexual matters in visual or verbal terms. **Obscene material** is material, often pornographic in nature, that has been declared illegal because it poses a threat to the state or to organized religion, violates common morality, has no redeeming social value, or appeals to a prurient or lascivious interest.

Even though pornographic material arouses people sexually, not everyone responds to it in the same way. Those most likely to be sexually aroused by pornography are the young, the college educated, the religiously inactive, and the sexually experienced.

Exposure to pornography rarely causes major changes in the viewer's sexual behavior, except for short-term increases in masturbation or sexual intercourse with regular partners. No effects on sexual morality have been found, nor is there consistent evidence that nonviolent pornography causes sex crimes (Goldstein and Kant, 1973; Donnerstein, Linz, and Penrod, 1987). The 1986 Attorney General's Commission on Pornography concluded that aggressiveness is heightened by pornography that is either violent or degrading, adjectives the commission asserted were descriptive of nearly all available pornography. The commission claimed that this increased aggressiveness led to sexual violence, but critics, including two members of the commission, said that social science research did not support that claim.

Contrary to what the commission's conclusions suggest, the legalization of pornography in Denmark in 1966 actually preceded a decline in arrests for exhibitionism, voyeurism, child molesting, and physical indecency with adult women. Rates of rape and other serious offenses against adult women seemed unaffected by the legalization of pornography. Falling numbers of arrests do not necessarily prove that actual criminal behavior has declined; they could simply reflect greater police or public tolerance of the behavior. However, the data are consistent with the hypothesis that the legalization of pornography reduced sex crimes in Denmark. At the very least, they suggest that the legalization of pornography did not increase recorded sex crimes (President's Commission on Obscenity and Pornography, 1970; Gagnon, 1974). Evidence from the United States, Sweden, and West Germany also supports the conclusion that the legalization or increased circulation of pornography does not increase, and can even decrease, rates of rape (Kutchinsky, 1988).

A study that looked at exposure to pornography among several groups—including the general population, regular users of pornography, child molesters, homosexuals, transsexuals, and rapists—found no clear-cut pattern of antisocial sexual activity following arousal by pornography. Erotic material was a factor in a few offenses, but sex crimes were more likely to be associated with lowered inhibitions due to alcohol consumption, rejection by wives or lovers, and interaction with peers who suggested sex crimes. Sex offenders rarely mentioned pornography as stimulating, but some of them reported being aroused by material depicting violence (Goldstein and Kant, 1973).

Several experiments have found that pornography combining sex with explicit violence against women increases aggressiveness toward females. Nonviolent erotic material does not have that effect (Donnerstein, Slaby, and Eron, 1994). However, these experiments used college students as subjects and measured aggressiveness by the subjects' administration of electric shocks and by the subjects' responses to questionnaires. We cannot generalize from these studies and say that violent pornography increases actual sex offenses among the population at large. There is some evidence that men who are already angry have their level of aggressiveness increased by exposure to hard-core pornography, but this is not the same as showing that exposure to hard-core pornography causes sex crimes among the male population at large, or even among men who are already angry (Donnerstein, Linz, and Penrod, 1987).

Exposure to pornography can weaken condemnation of rape by both men and women. One experiment found that students who were exposed to more pornographic films recommended more lenient prison sentences for convicted rapists than did students who were exposed to less pornography. Those exposed to more pornography also became more tolerant of violent forms of pornography and less supportive of equality between the sexes (Zillmann and Bryant, 1984). However, other evidence suggests that exposure to pornography does not necessarily cause such attitudes, but might instead simply reinforce and strengthen attitudes that people already hold (Donnerstein, Linz, and Penrod, 1987).

Correctional Institutions

Prisons, jails, and juvenile detention centers are sometimes described as "schools of crime" where relatively inexperienced offenders are thrown into daily contact with skilled criminals. Conversations in these settings often focus on crime, spreading criminal motives and techniques from more experienced offenders to less knowledgeable inmates, possibly increasing criminal behavior by these inmates after they are released.

There are no reliable data on the extent to which this kind of learning actually takes place. Many offenders are quite skilled in crime before they are incarcerated. There seems to be no clear relationship between the length of time inmates are imprisoned and the likelihood that they will return to crime when released (von Hirsch, 1976). Indeed, the longer inmates spend in prison, the less efficient and more out of practice they might become in the commission of crimes that require skill. Any learning of criminal motives and skills by inmates might thus be counterbalanced by the loss of efficiency that occurs with the passage of time.

To the extent that criminal motives and skills are learned in a penal institution, this seems to happen during an inmate's middle stage of confinement. Inmates are less likely to pick up skills when they are first incarcerated or when they are about to be released (Radzinowicz and King, 1977). Whether inmates learn criminal motives and skills is also related to personal characteristics. For instance, inmates who have families and plan to go straight when released are probably less likely to learn criminal motives and skills than are inmates who have no family ties and are committed to a life of crime.

The prison experience can be conducive to the formation of motives to engage in crime, with deprivations of prison life such as lack of freedom and demeaning treatment causing resentment that is later used to justify crime. Material deprivations and crowded living conditions lead to the exploitation of inmates by one another, and sometimes to assault, homicide, and homosexual rape. Because prisoners lack opportunities to make their own decisions and take responsibility for their own lives, they do not acquire the everyday skills needed to lead law-abiding lives once they are released, and this can push them back into crime after they leave prison (Cordilia, 1983).

Offenders learn the motives and skills to commit crime from a variety of sources. One theory that emphasizes the process by which people learn to commit crime through interaction with others is differential association theory.

Differential Association Theory

Edwin Sutherland introduced **differential association theory** in the 1939 edition of his criminology textbook and modified the theory in 1947. This general theory, which is presented in nine statements, aims to explain why crime rates are distributed as they are among various groups, as well as why any given individual does or does not become a criminal (Sutherland, Cressey, and Luckenbill, 1992: 88–90).

1. *Criminal behavior is learned.* Differential association theory first rejects the possibility that individual pathology or biological factors cause crime. It also denies that criminal behavior is unique to or invented anew by individuals. This assumption is questionable, for some crimes—such as one kidnapper's attempt to have ransom money delivered through a computerized bank terminal—seem to be unique to the offender. Many aspects of an offender's behavior are indeed learned from others—for example, the motives and justifications for the crime—but the criminal's specific actions can be the result of a combination of skills, ideas, and opportunities that are available only to that individual.

2. *Criminal behavior is learned in interaction with other persons in a process of communication.* This communication can be either verbal or nonverbal.

3. *The principal part of the learning of criminal behavior occurs within intimate personal groups.* The claim that crime is learned in face-to-face interaction in small groups rejects the possibility that such behavior is learned from the media. Differential association theory probably regards learning from the media as unimportant because the theory was developed before mass ownership of television. In 2000, 98 percent of all American households had television sets, 84 percent had videocassette recorders, and 67 percent had cable television. The pervasive role of the media in contemporary society would seem to require a modification of differential association theory to incorporate the effects of learning from that source (see the Crime and the Media box).

4. *When criminal behavior is learned, the learning includes (a) techniques of committing the crime, which are sometimes very complicated, sometimes very simple; (b) the specific direction of motives, drives, rationalizations, and attitudes.* Little or no skill is needed to commit some crimes; the murder of a spouse requires little skill, especially if a handgun is available, and many kinds of theft require little skill. Embezzlers have to learn "verbalizations" that allow them to use their accounting skills for illegal ends, but they do not need to learn specific techniques of embezzlement (Cressey, 1971).

5. *The specific direction of motives and drives is learned from definitions of the legal codes as favorable or unfavorable.* This statement assumes that people orient their actions toward the law; in other words, the law is not irrelevant to any individual who is deciding how to behave. Some situations are defined as favorable to violation of the law; for example, an unattended bicycle might be seen as an opportunity for theft.

However, the same situation can also be defined as unfavorable to violation of the law, with the unattended bicycle being seen as a chance to alert the owner to the risk of theft. Some people define the situation in one way, and others define it differently. The way that the situation is defined depends on the favorable or unfavorable definitions of the law that an individual has learned in the past.

6. *A person becomes delinquent because of an excess of definitions favorable to violation of the law over definitions unfavorable to violation of the law.* This statement, called "the principle of differential association," stresses contact with criminal or noncriminal definitions but does not require contact with criminal or noncriminal individuals. People can learn definitions favorable to violation of the law from law-abiding people, and they can learn definitions unfavorable to violation of the law from criminals. Parents might not violate the law but still verbally approve of theft for certain purposes (such as feeding a family) or in certain situations (such as from a large store). Parental approval of this sort will convey to children a definition favorable to violation of the law. On the other hand, a professional thief might convey to young thieves the need to avoid violence against the victims of theft. Some offenders even warn others away from behavior that they themselves engage in. For instance, heroin addicts often tell nonusers to stay away not only from heroin but also from marijuana, the drug with which many of them began.

The principle of differential association proposes that an individual holds both definitions favorable and unfavorable to violation of the law, and that it is only when definitions favorable to violation of the law exceed definitions unfavorable that a person will turn to crime. There is an obvious difficulty in measuring these definitions of the law so that an exact ratio can be calculated for any given person.

CRIME AND THE MEDIA

The How-to-Commit-Crime Manual

First published in 1971, *The Anarchist Cookbook* has now sold more than 2 million copies. This book provides detailed instructions on the production of pipe bombs and LSD and was the first in a genre of how-to commit-crime books. Available titles include *Homemade Grenade Launchers, The Ultimate Sniper, Successful Armed Robbery, 21 Techniques of Silent Killing,* and *The Ancient Art of Strangulation.* White-collar crime has not been neglected, with *How to Do Business off the Books, Biz Op: How to Get Rich with Business Opportunity Frauds and Scams,* and *Hide Your Assets and Disappear: A Step-by-Step Guide to Vanishing without a Trace* selling briskly.

The publishers of these books advertise in *Soldier of Fortune* magazine, the *National Enquirer,* and gun magazines. They claim that their customers, most of whom are young or middle-aged men, buy the books out of curiosity, but they acknowledge that some criminals might use the material to carry out crimes. However, they argue, their books are not turning people into criminals; instead, people otherwise predisposed to crime are attracted to their books.

In 1996, the families of three murder victims sued Paladin Press, the publisher of *Hit Man: A Technical Manual for Independent Contractors,* for aiding and abetting James E. Perry, a hired killer who allegedly followed twenty-seven of the book's recommendations when he murdered a woman, her disabled son, and the son's nurse. Cases of this sort have proved difficult to win in the past, but in 1999 the publisher agreed to a multimillion-dollar settlement with the plaintiffs.

Even if how-to-commit-crime books do not generate the motive to commit crime, they do make readily available methods that potential offenders can use to break the law and perhaps injure or kill more victims than they otherwise would have. Clearly, techniques of crime can be learned from the media as well as through face-to-face interaction.

Sources: Based on J. Peder Zane, "You Too Can Be a Successful Criminal!" *New York Times,* July 24, 1994, p. E2; Mary Boyle, "Publisher Sued over Manual for Murder," *Boston Globe,* July 23, 1996, p. A3; Katherine Shaver, "Murder-for-Hire Defendant Set Up, Attorney Says," *Washington Post,* March 21, 2001, p. B2.

7. *Differential associations may vary in frequency, duration, priority, and intensity.* It is the nature of associations with criminal and noncriminal patterns, rather than the mere fact of those associations, that is important. Associations that are more frequent play a larger role in the balance between definitions favorable to violation of the law and definitions unfavorable to violation of the law. Associations that endure over the longest time are the most significant in determining criminal behavior. Associations that occur earlier in life—in childhood or in adolescence—are the most important in forming definitions of the law; this is called priority. Finally, the intensity of associations is important. This means that the prestige of the source of the definition of the law and the individual's emotional reactions to the source are significant in learning definitions of the law. Thus, a young child who learns a definition favorable to violation of the law from a parent who presents that definition frequently and over long stretches of time will be more influenced in the direction of violating the law than will an adult who is exposed to a definition favorable to violation of the law by a passing acquaintance whom the adult sees infrequently and for short periods.

8. *The process of learning criminal behavior by association with criminal and anticriminal patterns involves all of the mechanisms that are involved in any other learning.* This statement reiterates Sutherland's view that crime is a form of behavior that is learned in the same way as noncriminal behavior.

9. *While criminal behavior is an expression of general needs and values, it is not explained by those general needs and values, since noncriminal behavior is an expression of the same needs and values.* Here Sutherland argues that criminal behavior cannot be explained by a general desire to accumulate property or enhance status among peers because those motives can also lead to noncriminal behavior. Only learning through differential association with definitions favorable and unfavorable to violation of the law can explain criminal behavior.

Critique of Differential Association Theory

The theory of differential association stresses the ratio of definitions favorable to violation of the law over definitions unfavorable to violation of the law. The theory might be mistaken in looking at definitions of the law in general, because individuals violate specific laws. Thus, a person might not need to hold an overall unfavorable view of the law before committing a crime; holding an unfavorable definition of one specific law could be enough.

Differential association theory examines the learning process by which people become criminals, but it does not explain why people have the associations they do. Because the theory does not tell us how the associations that expose people to different definitions of the law are distributed throughout the social structure, it does not fulfill its goal of explaining why crime rates vary among groups as they do.

Differential association theory has been criticized for holding an overly simplified view of the way that people choose models for their behavior. **Differential identification theory** proposes that the choice of models does not necessarily involve interaction with others in intimate personal groups, as differential association theory claims. Instead, differential identification theory argues that "a person pursues criminal behavior to the extent that he identifies himself with real or imaginary persons from whose perspective his criminal behavior seems acceptable" (Glaser, 1956: 440). Differential identification theory thus "allows for human choice, and stresses the importance of vocabularies of motives existing in the wider culture independently of direct intimate association" (Taylor, Walton, and Young, 1973: 129–130).

Because differential association theory looks at the individual's perception of the situation, rather than at the actual situation itself, the theory is a social-psychological rather than a social-structural one. It is not, however, a purely psychological theory because it does not consider personality traits and psychological variables to be important factors in crime causation.

One criticism of differential association theory is that it might describe how some people initially become involved in crime better than it explains why people continue in a criminal career. The direct rewards of crime—such as money, euphoria from illegal drugs, or prestige among peers—might be a sufficient cause of continued violation of the law.

Some critics argue that differential association theory is too general and imprecise to test easily or to verify fully. They claim that even if the concepts of the theory could be defined in measurable terms, an enormous amount of data would be needed to test the theory. Consider the difficulty of measuring not only all associations with criminal definitions, but also all associations with noncriminal definitions, from the time a person is conscious of the social environment. To test the theory, it would be necessary to measure how frequent all of those associations are, how long they last, how they vary in significance because of the person's age, and how the person reacts emotionally to the various sources of definitions. Although this measurement process cannot realistically be accomplished, some criminologists have found differential association theory useful, testing hypotheses derived from the theory and finding it has explanatory power (Orcutt, 1987).

Social Learning Theory   A theory that addresses some of the criticisms of differential association theory by integrating it with behavioral learning theory is **social learning theory,** first developed by Ronald L. Akers and Robert L. Burgess in 1966 and most recently reformulated by Akers in 1998. Social learning theory retains differential association theory's emphasis on learning from the people with whom an individual interacts, but it broadens the focus of Sutherland's theory by specifying the process of learning from other people and by examining the way that individuals learn from other sources. Social learning theory proposes that people learn attitudes and techniques conducive to crime in both nonsocial and social situations from positive reinforcement (rewards) and negative reinforcement (punishments) that result from their own behavior, whether that behavior is criminal or law-abiding; this process is called differential reinforcement. Thus, an absence of rewards for attending school would make criminal behavior more attractive, as would the peer esteem that results from fighting or stealing with a gang. Social learning theory also proposes that criminal behavior is learned through imitation, the process of observing and modeling others' behavior. A third learning mechanism is stimulus discrimination/generalization, with verbal and cognitive stimuli acting as cues for behavior to occur. Differential reinforcement, imitation, and stimulus discrimination/generalization operate in a process of differential association through which people learn behavioral sequences and definitions conducive to criminal behavior.

Recently, Akers (1998) has proposed a **social structure and social learning (SSSL) theory** that links the social learning process to the following social-structural variables:

- structural correlates (differential social organization), such as society, community, culture, social institutions, and region
- sociodemographic/socioeconomic correlates (differential location in the social structure), such as age, gender, race, socioeconomic status, and religion
- theoretically defined structural variables (social disorganization and conflict)
- differential social location in primary, secondary, and reference groups, such as family, peers, school, work, church, and the media

According to Akers, integrating these social-structural factors with the social learning process will make it possible to explain conforming and criminal behavior, as well as the onset, maintenance, change, and versatility or specialization of individuals' criminal behavior. It will also make it possible to explain groups' crime rates and changes in those rates over time.

Evidence on Differential Association Theory

Much of the research that is consistent with differential association theory focuses on the relationship between delinquent behavior and patterns of interaction among adolescents, demonstrating that the associates of delinquents are other delinquents and that delinquency is often a group phenomenon. Other evidence supportive of differential association theory comes from studies of professional theft, sex offenses, and white-collar crime.

Juvenile Delinquency and Differential Association Theory   Juvenile gangs stimulate and reinforce delinquency by supporting law-violating behavior and by offering protection from outsiders to gang members who break the law. A study of juvenile theft in Great Britain found that associating with other adolescents who had already stolen property was very important in leading boys to steal, especially if those associations began when a boy was quite young, continued over a long time, and involved boys who stole frequently (Belson, 1975). However, another study found that differential association theory's emphasis on priority is misplaced, because recent friendships have more impact on delinquency than do friendships formed earlier in life (Warr, 1993). Research suggests that delinquent behavior is more strongly influenced by learning from direct observation of peers' behavior than it is by learning peers' attitudes (Warr and Stafford, 1991).

Much delinquency takes place in groups, although the extent to which this is true varies with the specific offense and with the age and sex of the offender. Young shoplifters commonly steal in groups, learning attitudes and techniques from their peers, but as they get older they are more likely to steal by themselves (Cameron, 1964).

One study found that the impact on delinquency of broken homes and attachments to parents and peers was better explained by differential association theory

The associates of juvenile delinquents are usually other delinquents, and their delinquent acts are frequently committed in groups. Here two teenage girls from rival Los Angeles gangs fight while other members watch.

than by social control theory. Broken homes weaken parental supervision, which increases interaction with delinquent peers, exposure to definitions favorable to delinquency, and eventually delinquent behavior. Broken homes also contribute directly to an excess of definitions favorable to delinquency over definitions unfavorable to delinquency. Because this effect is greater for blacks than for whites, broken homes have a larger impact on delinquency among blacks (Matsueda and Heimer, 1987).

Professional Theft and Differential Association Theory   Evidence consistent with differential association theory comes from studies of professional thieves. Members of the subculture of professional thieves teach new recruits the skills that make expert theft possible, and immersion in the subculture isolates the thieves from noncriminal patterns (Sutherland, 1937; Maurer, 1964, 1974; Letkemann, 1973). The process of **tutelage**, or instruction, provides new thieves with knowledge of how to spot opportunities for theft and how to plan and carry out thefts. Burglars learn specific skills such as how to enter a building or open a safe. Robbers learn to interpret the body language of potential victims, control victims, and show self-confidence and mastery during the crime. Con artists learn to lie convincingly, size up and manipulate victims, display a winning personality, and look respectable. Young members of juvenile gangs sometimes learn techniques of car theft from older members; Coco, a member of Chicago's Diamonds gang, describes the process of tutelage by his "main man" as follows:

> Like in stealing autos, he taught me to put the screwdriver on the corner of the window; it pops the window without shattering it—no noise. He taught me how to peel the column. You peel the bottom piece, and the rod is right there. You pull up the shoehorn, and it is straight; you turn on the car; you steer the steering wheel, put the car in drive, and you're gone. That's how he taught me. He would stand by the window of the car telling me "Hurry up—do this and do that." (cited in Padilla, 1992: 121–122)

Experienced pickpockets show novices how to steal: "One thief turns out another. That is, he teaches him" (Maurer, 1964: 157). After learning that it is possible to steal from other people, pickpockets learn specific skills, practice them, and are evaluated by other thieves, refining their skills and eventually being accepted as professionals by other pickpockets. Novice pickpockets learn to look unobtrusive in public, be cautious, and use the opportunities with which they are presented. Manual dexterity is a source of professional pride for these thieves; they are expected to be able to take money from a victim if they can figure out where the victim is carrying his or her money. Pickpockets learn timing, speed, misdirection, concealment, rhythmic movement, and dexterity, blending these skills into a "single, almost instantaneous, and practically invisible act of theft" (Maurer, 1964: 41).

A study of professional thieves in a Canadian prison concluded that early involvement in juvenile delinquency is a prerequisite for an adult career as a professional criminal (Letkemann, 1973). As juveniles, the thieves learned such things as how to avoid attention when stealing and how the police would typically react to a certain crime. They usually progressed gradually from awkward juvenile theft, to learning from other thieves while incarcerated, to trial and error with new forms of theft, and then to learning from skilled thieves and from personal experience. These professional thieves learned mechanical skills, social skills such as the management of victims, and organizational skills such as planning and executing a crime. They learned these things from other prisoners, from members of their gang, and from thieves they met in bars. In this way, safecrackers learned about different styles of safes and how to break into them, information that had to be continually updated.

Sexual Aggression and Differential Association Theory   One study found a strong association between sexual aggression by males and the presence of sexually aggressive friends. The researcher measured sexual aggression by self-reports, asking subjects the following:

> It has been noted that in the course of men's and women's sexual lives together, some men on occasion make physically forceful attempts at sexual activity which are disagreeable and offensive enough that the woman responds in an offended manner such as crying, fighting, screaming, pleading, etc. Have you ever engaged in such behavior? (Alder, 1985: 312–313)

The strongest predictor of this kind of sexual aggression, which includes forcible rape as well as lesser degrees of sexual assault, was the presence of sexually aggressive friends. The men who were most likely to report engaging in sexual aggression had sexually aggressive friends, had served in Vietnam, and held attitudes legitimating sexual aggression. These findings are consistent with the learning process described by differential association theory.

Research on sexual assault on college campuses in the United States and Canada led Martin D. Schwartz and Walter S. DeKeseredy (1997) to develop the modified male peer-support model shown in Figure 8.2. This model proposes that social support from male peers is influenced by patriarchal (male-dominant) attitudes in the broader culture, in the family, and in courtship and dating practices, and by the stress that results from the fear that males will not measure up to cultural standards of masculinity. The support of male peers leads to membership in social groups such as fraternities and sports teams, to heavy alcohol use, and to the verbal and physical abuse of women. Peer groups give rise to a narrow conception of masculinity, protection of the group from outsiders through a code of secrecy, and the treatment of women as objects to gratify male sexual desires. These factors increase sexual assaults against women by "violent, irresponsible, misogynist, privileged men" who seek opportunities to prove their masculinity to themselves and their peers (Schwartz and DeKeseredy, 1997: 73). The absence of an effective threat of punishment by the criminal justice system or the university further increases the likelihood of such assaults.

White-Collar Crime and Differential Association Theory   Differential association theory is useful in explaining white-collar and computer crimes, which result from the learning of cultural goals, such as material success, and the pursuit of those goals through illegal means. (See the Crime on Campus box.)

Because there is no enforceable code of business ethics to limit the pursuit of material success to legal means, definitions unfavorable to violation of the law are not readily learned in the world of business. Those who are most assimilated into a business organization seem to be the most likely to violate the law, and those new to the world of business are less apt to do so because they are more influenced by the definitions unfavorable to violation of the law that they have brought with them from the outside world. A study of attitudes toward bribes and payoffs made by businesspeople to foreign officials found that experienced executives who were enrolled in business school programs were more tolerant of such bribes and payoffs than were undergraduate business students who lacked experience in the world of business (Jensen, 1976). This suggests that business experience is conducive to the learning of definitions supportive of bribes and payoffs. Whether these definitions lead to actual violation of the law depends on factors such as exposure to definitions unfavorable to violation of the law and the presence of opportunities to break the law.

Learning from superiors and colleagues in the company is probably a more important determinant of business crime than is the personality of the individual. A

FIGURE 8.2   The Modified Male Peer-Support Model of Sexual Assault

Source: Martin D. Schwartz and Walter S. De-Keseredy, *Sexual Assault on the College Campus: The Role of Male Peer Support,* p. 46. Copyright © 1997 by Sage Publications, Inc. Reprinted by permission of Sage Publications, Inc.

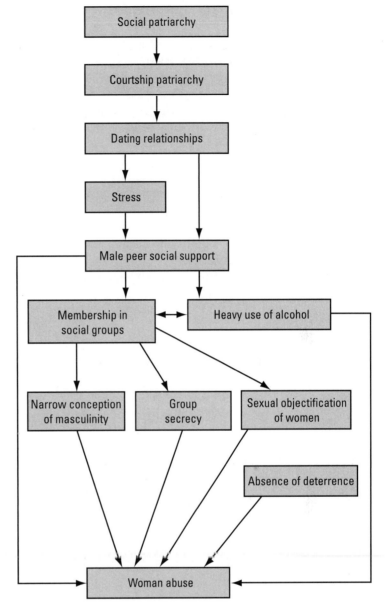

former head of the Securities and Exchange Commission's Division of Enforcement stated this bluntly: "Our largest corporations have trained some of our brightest young people to be dishonest" (Stanley Sporkin, cited in Kohlmeier, 1976: 53). Social pressure to violate the law was described as follows for fraudulent activity by the Equity Funding Corporation of America: "Corporations can and do create a moral tone that powerfully influences the thinking, conduct, values, and even the personalities of the people who work for them. The tone is set by the men who run the company, and their corruption can quickly corrupt all else" (Blundell, 1976: 46).

Differential association theory fits much of what we know about white-collar crime. Businesspeople learn definitions favorable to violation of the law, such as loyalty to the corporation over loyalty to the law. In addition to techniques of neutralization that are conducive to violation of the law, the learning process involves the segregation of businesspeople from the law-abiding public, making them relatively immune to public criticism and limiting their exposure to definitions unfavorable to violation of the law. Ties to the law-abiding public are weakened and dependence on the corporation is strengthened by the common practice of regularly moving young executives from one region to another.

Evidence against Differential Association Theory Differential association theory does not explain all crimes. For instance, some check forgers who operate alone apparently lack the associations with criminal patterns required by differential association theory (Lemert, 1953). Other crimes are evidently invented anew by offenders who have not experienced the learning process proposed in differential association theory.

Offenders who are not part of a criminal subculture or do not have ties to other criminals might lack exposure to the patterns and associations needed to learn criminal motives and skills. One study found that shoplifters often had no contact with a criminal subculture or with other criminal patterns. Few of those who were apprehended had prior convictions, most were "respectable" people who were employed or were housewives, many did not live in poor neighborhoods, most took inexpensive merchandise with little resale value, and many were ignorant of the arrest process (Cameron, 1964). These characteristics suggest a lack of contact with a subculture that could have provided the shoplifters with criminal motives and techniques.

Research showing that delinquent peers exert more influence on children who are antisocial and have low self-control than they do on children who are prosocial and have high self-control also raises questions about the general applicability of differential association theory and its dismissal of personality traits (Wright et al., 2001).

Conclusion Research on various forms of crime is consistent with differential association theory, but there is no direct proof of the theory as it is formally stated. In

---

CRIME ON CAMPUS

Computer Crime and Differential Association Theory

A self-report survey of undergraduates at a major southern university focused on students who were in departments that had high levels of computer usage and who had broad knowledge of computer applications and were thus likely to know how to commit computer crimes. One-third of the students admitted to having pirated software during the previous year; one of every eight admitted to having done so in the previous month. One-sixth of the students admitted to having gained illegal access to browse or change information; one in twenty had done this in the previous month.

The threat of punishment had little influence on student involvement in computer crime. Only 7 percent of the students had been caught for illegal computer activity, and only 13 percent had friends who had been caught. Laws against computer crime did have an educa-

tive effect; students who said that they would not commit computer crime because it was against the law were the least likely to commit such offenses.

The strongest predictor of computer crime was differential association with others who presented definitions favorable to violation of the law. Students were most likely to engage in software piracy or illegal access if they had friends who had committed computer crimes. Siblings, parents, and professors who offered students pirated software and condoned or even advocated computer crimes were also influential. Students who used computer bulletin boards most frequently were the most likely to try to gain illegal access, perhaps because bulletin boards often post passwords to restricted governmental and corporate computer systems.

Source: Based on William K. Skinner and Anne M. Fream, "A Social Learning Theory Analysis of Computer Crime among College Students," *Journal of Research in Crime and Delinquency* 34 (November 1997), 495–518.

other words, there is no concrete evidence that different kinds of offenders initially became criminals because of an excess of definitions favorable to violation of the law over definitions unfavorable to violation of the law. To demonstrate this would involve a measurement task that might be impossible. It would also require comparisons of offenders with samples from the general population who did not become offenders.

The Labeling Perspective

Since Edwin Lemert's (1951) pioneering work on the labeling of deviant behavior, much attention has been directed to the way that individuals are affected by being treated as deviants. The labeling approach is a general perspective on deviance that has been applied to mental illness, drug abuse, and even stuttering. Because crime and delinquency are forms of deviant behavior, this perspective should help us understand some of the causes of law-violating behavior.

The **labeling perspective** assumes that people first violate a norm by chance or for unexplained reasons. This initial act of deviance, called **primary deviation**, sometimes elicits reactions from others. Those reactions often take the form of stereotyping and rejecting the deviant. For instance, one study suggests that offenders are treated more harshly in court if they fit the stereotype of a "normal primitive," an image of lower-class blacks and other minorities whose limited education, lack of job skills, orientation to the present, possession of weapons, and immaturity are thought to predispose them to violence (Swigert and Farrell, 1976, 1977). Another stereotype is of lower-class delinquents, who are thought to violate the law because of blocked opportunities, poor education, or other defects of the social structure. This contrasts with the stereotype of middle-class delinquents, who are said to violate the law because of a temporary lack of commitment to adult roles and values, a view that relies on social-psychological factors and social control theory (Cernkovich, 1978b). Ideas about why different types of people break the law influence the way those people will be treated by the criminal justice system.

Differences in norms about parental supervision of the sexual activity of sons and daughters can lead to the labeling of one sex but not the other as delinquent, even though the behavior of both sexes is the same. Many girls brought into juvenile court are there for reasons related to their "adult" sexual activities. By contrast, the boys with whom they were sexually involved are rarely labeled delinquent for the same behavior.

People who engage in socially disapproved behavior are disvalued as individuals. Their status as deviants sometimes becomes a **master status;** that is, other aspects of their behavior are submerged in their social identity as deviants. The labeling perspective directs attention away from the causes of primary deviation, or rule breaking, and focuses instead on the people and institutions that have the power to label behavior deviant. The processing of rule breakers by institutions such as prisons and mental hospitals keeps deviants at a distance from the rest of society. Deviant acts would occur even if there were no such institutions, but the deviant acts' "nature, distribution, social meaning, and implications and ramifications are significantly influenced by patterns of social reaction" (Schur, 1969: 115). The labeling perspective assumes that a major cause of continued deviant behavior is the way that people who initially violate norms are treated by lawmakers, police officers, judges, psychiatrists, and others who have the power to affix the label "deviant." Deviant behavior that is a product of this labeling process is called **secondary deviation.**

Labeling and Self-Concepts

One way the labeling of deviant behavior leads to secondary deviation is through the effects of the label on the self-concept of the person who has been labeled. People who violate the law and are arrested by the police and tried in court can have their conceptions of themselves altered and come to think of themselves as criminals or delinquents. Court appearances have been called "status-degradation ceremonies" in which people accused of violating the law are recast as unworthy persons (Garfinkel, 1956). These people then reject other people and become hostile to society in order to maintain their self-esteem. Being labeled criminal or delinquent in court can thus produce a self-fulfilling prophecy, so that people behave in ways consistent with their altered self-concepts. In other words, once they are labeled criminal by the police, the courts, and the prisons, people continue to behave as criminals.

The labeling perspective suggests that the first time youngsters engage in minor vandalism or petty theft, they think little of it. If they are arrested, brought to court, and treated as delinquents, they will come to think that they have done something drastically wrong and that perhaps they are unworthy people. As a result, they begin to associate with others who have also been labeled as troublemakers, and this leads them into more serious delinquency. A study of adolescent shoplifters found that those who had been exposed to the police by store officials were more likely to engage in subsequent shoplifting than were adolescent shoplifters who had not been subjected to the police (Klemke, 1978). This is consistent with the labeling perspective's assumption that officially processing a deviant will amplify or increase deviance.

Rather than engage in more deviance because of being labeled, some people who are labeled deviant react by changing their behavior to conform to social expectations. The fact that many juveniles who are arrested are apprehended only once can be interpreted to mean that the status-degradation ceremony that occurs in juvenile court persuades some of them to avoid delinquency in the future. This is probably most likely to occur for first-time offenders with the following characteristics:

They have a stake in conformity.

They are sensitive to others' evaluations of themselves.

They are labeled in private rather than in public.

They are not committed to a delinquent or criminal career.

They are able to remove the label with good behavior in the future (Thorsell and Klemke, 1972).

Self-Concepts and Containment Theory   Self-concept plays an important role in the **containment theory** of crime and delinquency (Reckless, 1978). This theory proposes that people are insulated to various degrees against pressures to commit deviant acts by "external" and "internal" factors. External containment results from attachments to family, community, and other parts of the social structure. Internal containment is composed of the following "self" components:

1. A favorable image of self in relation to other persons, groups, and institutions.
2. An awareness of being an inner directed, goal oriented person.
3. A high level of frustration tolerance.
4. Strongly internalized morals and ethics.
5. Well developed ego and superego. (Reckless, 1978: 189)

Greater strength of internal or external containment will reduce vulnerability to crime and delinquency, but "the inner containment is the more important in the mobile, industrialized settings of modern society" (Reckless, 1978: 189).

People who abide by the law see themselves as accountable for their actions. They feel good about themselves and behave accordingly, taking into account the hypothesized reactions of others before they act. This is much like what Hirschi calls the "psychological presence" of parents and authority figures. Noncriminals feel vulnerable if they deviate from the law, and they fear the loss of material rewards and the good opinion of others (Rogers, 1977: 64–68).

There is evidence that delinquents have poorer self-concepts than nondelinquents and are more likely than nondelinquents to believe that they will break the law, not finish school, and be unsuccessful. Delinquents are less likely than nondelinquents to be committed to long-range goals, and they are more likely to strive beyond their means, be impulsive, have a short time perspective, and feel unable to control themselves (Jensen, 1973; Reckless, 1973). One study concluded that self-rejection—as measured by self-derogation, perceived lack of socially desirable attributes, and perceived rejection by parents and teachers—had a strong direct effect on junior high school students' disposition to deviance, which was measured by disaffection from family, school, and the conventional community. That disposition to deviance in turn had a strong direct effect on deviant behavior, including many acts that might lead to being labeled delinquent (Kaplan, Martin, and Johnson, 1986).

Parents, teachers, and friends influence the part of the self that is a "reflected appraisal" of how significant others evaluate a rule violator. Previous delinquent behavior also affects self-concepts, directly as well as indirectly through its influence on parents' appraisals of the rule violator. Furthermore, the self-concepts of rule violators have a major effect on their future delinquent behavior (Matsueda, 1992).

Not all research finds a strong relationship between self-concept and violation of the law (Farrell and Nelson, 1978). One study concluded that self-esteem has a negligible impact on subsequent delinquency, but that involvement in delinquency does lower subsequent self-esteem to some extent (McCarthy and Hoge, 1984). Another study found that delinquent behavior enhances self-esteem among youths with either very low or very high self-esteem, but that adolescents with normal levels of self-esteem do not have their self-esteem improved and can even have it hurt by involvement in delinquency (Wells, 1989). A third study found that low self-esteem increases neither delinquent behavior nor association with delinquent peers; however, association with delinquent peers, but not delinquent behavior, does enhance self-esteem (Jang and Thornberry, 1998).

Rejecting the Label   An individual's self-concept is a product of many influences. It is affected by the reactions of others, but it is also the result of choice and reflection by the individual. A label attached by the criminal justice system can alter a person's self-concept, but the individual can also reject or fight the label. Self-concepts are constructed in an active way: The opinions of others are considered and sometimes incorporated into the self-concept, but those opinions can also be rejected as inconsistent with a person's idea of himself or herself (Scimecca, 1977).

Conventional Criminals   Conventional offenders sometimes disavow the label "criminal." Professional fences see themselves as decent people who perform socially useful functions (Klockars, 1974). Robbers claim that they are "not too dishonest" because they steal from their victims in a direct way, rather than sneaking around in a house at night to commit a burglary (Inciardi, 1975). Many shoplifters disavow the label of criminal when first caught, but the threat of prosecution usually forces them to redefine themselves as offenders. This happens because they fear exposure and lack support for a noncriminal definition of self (Cameron, 1964).

White-Collar Criminals   White-collar offenders often believe that because few of them are arrested, convicted, and imprisoned, they are not "real criminals." This view is shared by some law enforcers. The head of the Antitrust Division of the U.S. Department of Justice expressed this nicely in 1940:

> While civil penalties may be as severe in their financial effects as criminal penalties, yet they do not involve the stigma that attends indictment and conviction. Most of the defendants in antitrust cases are not criminals *in the usual sense*. There is no inherent reason why antitrust enforcement requires branding them as such. (cited in Sutherland, 1949, 1983: 54; emphasis added here)

White-collar criminals frequently see their offenses as "technical violations of government regulations" and are thus able to maintain a noncriminal self-concept, even when labeled criminal in court. A General Electric vice president, who was on his way to jail after a conviction for price fixing, said to the press: "All of you know that next Monday, in Philadelphia, I will start serving a thirty-day jail term, along with six other *businessmen,* for conduct which has been *interpreted* as being in conflict with the *complex* antitrust laws" (cited in Geis, 1974: 273; emphasis added here). This convicted offender disavowed the label of criminal, something that is easiest for law violators who do not fit the stereotype of the typical criminal, are treated with leniency by the courts, and enjoy the support of their families, friends, and colleagues (see also Willott, Griffin, and Torrance, 2001).

The Effects of Labeling on Self-Concepts   Some research suggests that the effects of official labeling on the self-concepts of delinquents and criminals might not be as great as the labeling perspective proposes. One study found that labeling by law enforcers had no major effect on self-satisfaction, identification with other delinquents, or future commitment to delinquency (Hepburn, 1977). A cohort study found that being labeled once as a delinquent did not necessarily transform a person (Polk, 1980).

The effects of labeling vary from individual to individual. One study found that the self-concepts of lower-class white delinquents are more influenced by a juvenile court appearance than are the self-concepts of other delinquents (Ageton and Elliott, 1973). Delinquents' self-concepts might be less influenced by official sanctions than by the frequency and seriousness of their illegal acts. In other words, their self-concepts could be grounded more in their actual behavior than in official reactions to that behavior, with the police and the courts validating their self-concepts rather than applying totally new labels.

Even if official labeling affects a person's self-concept, it does not necessarily increase that person's delinquent or criminal behavior, for there is no strong evidence that changes in self-concepts cause changes in law-violating behavior. Moreover, any effects that labeling has could fade over time. In sum, official labeling by the juvenile and criminal justice systems might not have the dramatic effects suggested by the labeling perspective. It is possible, however, that there are effects of labeling that are subtle and complex or that occur only over long periods, so researchers might not yet have uncovered all of the effects of stigmatizing people as criminals and delinquents.

Labeling and Opportunities

A second effect of labeling—in addition to its possible effects on self-concepts—is harm to the social relationships of people who are labeled by the criminal or juvenile justice system. Even if his or her self-concept does not change, a person may experience difficulty in relationships with parents, friends, teachers, or potential employers if those people react negatively to the label of delinquent or criminal.

One study of adolescent boys sought to determine if juvenile court intervention had reinforced their deviance by producing spoiled identities or by harming their relationships with people who viewed them with mistrust and suspicion because of their official status as delinquents (Foster, Dinitz, and Reckless, 1972). In general, the boys did not believe that their contact with the law had created major problems for them in their social relationships. They perceived no negative effects on their friends' attitudes toward them. Few of the boys thought that being in trouble with the law would cause them any special problems at school because they would be protected by the secrecy of juvenile court records and by their ability to separate their out-of-school life from their role as student. The boys believed that their court experiences would not influence their parents' attitudes toward them, other than simply confirming attitudes that their parents already held.

The boys in this study thought that their contact with the courts might have some negative effects in two areas: their relationships with the police and their relationships with future employers. About half of the boys said that the police would be more likely to keep an eye on them because they had been to court, but they thought this problem could be solved by convincing the police that they had given up delinquency. Nearly half of the boys believed that future employers might hold their court appearances against them, but many thought that this liability would be unimportant if they avoided encounters with the law in the future. The boys also counted on the secrecy of juvenile court records to minimize their problems with future employers.

This study concluded that the labeling perspective overemphasizes the effects on the individual of stigmatization by the juvenile courts. Such labeling might actually close legitimate opportunities or harm social relationships, but the boys in this study did not generally perceive this to be the case. However, nearly half of the boys had been involved with the juvenile justice system before, and a study of the impact of their first court appearance might have found more dramatic effects on their social relationships.

Even though more than half of the boys in this study thought their appearance in juvenile court would not hurt them with future employers, there is evidence that job opportunities are lost when potential employers learn about a person's problems with the law (Erickson and Goodstadt, 1979). Even the knowledge that a job applicant has been acquitted of charges makes some employers less willing to offer that person a job (Schwartz and Skolnick, 1962). Longitudinal research in London reveals that youths labeled by the juvenile justice system are more likely than youths not so labeled to associate with delinquents, develop a deviant identity by engaging in antisocial behavior, and underachieve in education and at work (De Li, 1999). The law in the United States now prohibits employers from asking about arrests, limiting them to questions about actual criminal convictions. Until recently, juvenile court records were sealed or kept secret so that job opportunities would not be denied to those who had gotten into trouble at a young age, but many states have loosened their rules on the confidentiality of juvenile records, especially for offenders who have committed serious crimes.

Labeling and Subcultures

In addition to the effects of labeling on self-concepts and social relationships, labeling people "delinquent" or "criminal" can push them into subcultures in which they learn criminal motives and skills in the way described by differential association theory. Learning from the subculture can affect an offender's self-concept, even if labeling by the police or the courts did not have that effect. Thus, a woman convicted of prostitution might be approached by a pimp, a drug dealer, or a gangster who sees her

FIGURE 8.3 The Labeling
Perspective

FIGURE 8.3 The Labeling
Perspective

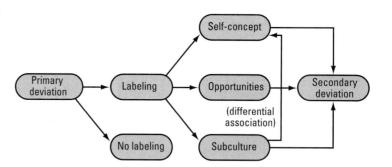

spoiled identity as making her vulnerable to exploitation. By pushing an offender into a subculture, labeling makes reintegration into society difficult and increases the probability that people will repeat their crimes.

Critique of the Labeling Perspective

Figure 8.3 shows the labeling perspective in schematic form. The perspective proposes that primary deviation, or rule breaking, sometimes leads to labeling of the rule breaker. This can affect the individual's self-concept and opportunities and drive the person into a subculture. In the subculture, the individual can experience a change in self-concept through differential association with deviant norms, values, and behavior patterns. In these ways, the labeling process increases secondary deviation.

The labeling perspective has some shortcomings. It does not tell us why some people engage in primary deviation and others do not break rules or do so infrequently. The labeling perspective helps us understand what society makes of primary deviation, but it tells us little about rule breaking that is not socially labeled. The perspective fails to make clear the conditions under which labeling will alter self-concepts, restrict opportunities, hurt social relationships, and drive deviants into subcultures. It also does not specify when a label will be accepted by a rule breaker and when a deviant will reject or disavow a label. Furthermore, there is little empirical evidence that labeling by the criminal justice system actually increases crime or delinquency (Braithwaite, 1989). Experiences with the criminal justice system sometimes deter potential offenders, and some offenders who are labeled and then commit more crime might have committed more crime even if they had not been labeled. The labeling perspective is useful in directing our attention to social processes that might, under some circumstances and for certain kinds of people, reinforce tendencies to violate the law, but it is not a fully developed and empirically verified theory of crime and delinquency.

Rewards and Risks of Crime

Differential association theory claims that people turn to crime when their attitudes become supportive of crime—that is, when their definitions favorable to violation of the law outweigh their definitions unfavorable to violation of the law. The labeling perspective suggests that being processed by the criminal justice system changes self-concepts and social relationships and pushes people into criminal subcultures. A third approach sees criminal behavior as learned and reinforced through the intrinsic rewards and risks that it offers to offenders.

Reward-Risk Models of Criminal Behavior

One reward-risk model we have already looked at is social learning theory, which incorporates the ideas of Sutherland's differential association theory into a broader theory proposing that people learn from rewards and punishments in both social and nonsocial situations. In recent years, several related reward-risk models have been proposed by political scientists, psychologists, economists, and sociologists.

Crime as Choice   In *Crime and Human Nature*, political scientist James Q. Wilson and psychologist Richard J. Herrnstein claim that people choose preferred courses of action and that their behavior is governed by its consequences. They argue that if the rewards (or benefits) of crime are great and its risks (or costs) small, and if the rewards (or benefits) of a noncriminal way of life are comparatively small and its risks (or costs) relatively great, people will choose to violate the law. According to Wilson and Herrnstein (1985: 44), "The larger the ratio of net rewards of crime to the net rewards of noncrime, the greater the tendency to commit crime." Table 8.1 shows some of the many risks and rewards of criminal activity. Money is one of the rewards from property crimes, but many of the rewards from crime are noneconomic, including excitement and challenge, satisfaction in carrying out a difficult crime, prestige in the eyes of other offenders, and the chance to be one's own boss.

Wilson and Herrnstein argue that the impact of the rewards and risks of both crime and noncrime on the behavior of individuals is associated with several characteristics of those rewards and risks. Rewards and risks that are more certain will influence behavior more than rewards and risks that are less apt to be experienced. Rewards and risks experienced in the present will alter current behavior more than rewards and risks that will not be experienced for a long time. In addition, the more reinforcement (rewards and punishments) a person is receiving at any given time, the less impact any additional reward or punishment will have. Finally, people consider not only what they might gain from crime or noncrime, but also what others will gain from comparable efforts.

The Rational-Choice Perspective   The **rational-choice perspective** emphasizes offenders' strategic thinking, or the ways that they process information and

TABLE 8.1   Rewards and Risks of Crime

REWARDS (BENEFITS)	RISKS (COSTS)
Money	Anxiety before and after a crime
Property for personal use or to sell	Injury or death
Self-determination of work hours	Loss of freedom if arrested and incarcerated
Excitement, challenge, relief from boredom	Threatening social environment in prison
Sense of accomplishment	Difficulty of sustaining a criminal career in middle age
Social identity	Lack of medical insurance and retirement benefits
Peer respect	Shame at being labeled a criminal
Camaraderie with other offenders	
Preservation of individual and collective honor	
Expression of anger against the victim	
Domination of the victim	

evaluate opportunities and alternatives. It stresses calculated decision making, arguing that offenders choose how to act after determining the likely payoff from a particular kind of behavior. This perspective looks in detail at specific crimes, because different offenses meet different needs and because there is considerable variation from one offense to another in the situational context of decision making and in the information that must be considered. This perspective focuses on the processes by which individuals initially decide to violate the law, choose to continue in a life of crime, and eventually opt to desist from crime. Not all people calculate rewards and risks in the same way; some of the many factors that affect the choices people make are age, marital status, group ties, social class background, opportunities for legitimate careers, attitude toward work, willingness to use violence, preferred lifestyle, identity, and values (Shover, 1996). For example, the way that robbers and burglars perceive opportunities for crime and make decisions to commit crime is influenced by their interaction with others and their improvised responses to the situations they encounter (Hochstetler, 2001).

The rationality of persistent property offenders is limited: They do not formally calculate the risks associated with theft, nor do they thoughtfully consider legitimate alternatives to crime. Instead, their decisions to commit crime are affected by lower- and working-class values such as autonomy, toughness, and excitement; by their lack of opportunities for legitimate careers; by their low aspirations; and by their desire to gain the respect of others. Their decisions to steal are made in the context of a lifestyle characterized as "life as party," meaning that they seek the "enjoyment of 'good times' with minimal concern for obligations and commitments that are external to [their] immediate social setting" (Shover, 1996: 93).

Persistent property offenders believe they are unlikely to be arrested and think that if they are imprisoned it will be for a short time. They approach their first prison term with some fear, but soon learn they can survive incarceration, and even gain the respect of their peers for doing time. Young offenders typically see imprisonment as a temporary setback, vowing to be more careful the next time they commit crime. Conversations with other inmates change the way thieves calculate rewards and risks, making money a more important goal and teaching them the penalties they can expect for different offenses (Shover, 1996).

The Seductions of Crime   Some of the rewards and risks of crime cannot be easily incorporated into a perspective that treats offenders as reasoning decision makers. The rewards of challenge, excitement, and domination of victims are unlikely to enter into an offender's rational calculations about the payoff from a particular crime, nor are risks such as anxiety about being caught or the shame of being labeled an offender apt to be carefully weighed.

In *Seductions of Crime: Moral and Sensual Attractions in Doing Evil*, sociologist Jack Katz (1988) considers the subjective appeal of crime to offenders. He argues that people would not commit crime if they rationally considered its rewards and risks. For example, few robbers make much money from their crimes, and most of them end up in prison. Analyzing self-reports by his students, Katz found that shoplifting was valued more for the "sneaky thrills" it offered than for the property that was stolen. Describing the attraction of shoplifting and other crimes, Katz (1988: 312) writes:

> Follow vandals and amateur shoplifters as they duck into alleys and dressing rooms and you will be moved by their delight in deviance; observe them under arrest and you may be stunned by their shame. Watch their strutting street display and you will be struck by the awesome fascination that symbols of evil hold for the young men who are linked in the groups we often call gangs. If we specify the opening moves in muggings and stickups, we describe an array of "games" or tricks that turn victims

into fools before their pockets are turned out. The careers of persistent robbers show us, not the increasingly precise calculations and hedged risks of "professionals," but men for whom gambling and other vices are a way of life, who are "wise" in the cynical sense of the term, and who take pride in a defiant reputation as "bad."

Katz (1988: 216) argues that offenders actively create the forces that impel them to break the law, saying that the

> causes of crime are constructed by the offenders themselves, but the causes they construct are the lures and pressures that they experience as independently moving them toward crime. By dissipating the proceeds of their crimes, stickup men, regardless of the social position from which they start, create an environment of pressures that guide them back toward crime.

Shoplifters sometimes endow the things they steal with a kind of magical power over themselves, as is suggested in the following recollection by a woman in her thirties:

> A gold-plated compact that I had seen on a countertop kept playing on my mind. Heaven knows I didn't need it, and at $40 it was obviously overpriced. Still, there was something about the design that intrigued me. I went back to the counter and picked up the compact again. At that moment, I felt an overwhelming urge. (cited in Katz, 1988: 55)

This theft was sensually rewarding for the offender, even though her thinking cannot be described as rational decision making. In addition to providing immediate emotional rewards, thefts such as these are also influenced by factors to which Katz pays little attention, such as the age and gender of the thief, the strain resulting from lack of economic opportunities, and even the physical layout of department stores (McCarthy, 1995).

Reward-Risk Models and Self-Control   Reward-risk models that emphasize situational influences on criminal behavior might seem to be incompatible with theories that stress individual traits (for example, low self-control) that are established in childhood. A study by Daniel Nagin and Raymond Paternoster (1993) of college students' self-reported involvement in drunk driving, theft, and sexual assault found support for both kinds of theories and concluded that there was no incompatibility between them. All three forms of criminal behavior were strongly associated with low self-control, even after the researchers took into account prior behavior, situational aspects of the crime, and perceived rewards and risks of committing crime. The researchers also found support for reward-risk models: The intention to break the law was influenced by the accessibility and vulnerability of the target, perceptions of the sanctions apt to result from breaking the law, and the pleasure derived from committing crime. The anticipated rewards from committing the crime turned out to be more important than the perceived costs of committing the crime in predicting the intention to break the law, apparently because rewards are more immediate and risks are more uncertain and remote in time. Nagin and Paternoster concluded that there was support for both reward-risk models of criminal behavior and predispositional theories such as low self-control theory, and that both kinds of theories are needed to understand fully the sources of offending. They suggested that people with low self-control are oriented to the pursuit of pleasure in the present and lack commitment to conventional lines of action—such as education, a career, and lasting social relationships—that provide long-term rewards. As a consequence, they have little to lose when they break the law.

The Rewards and Risks of Crime

Before looking in detail at the rewards and risks of specific kinds of crime, we will consider the rewards and risks of crime in general.

Rewards   Many offenders find that the rewards of crime justify their violation of the law. Some of them believe that the income they derive from crime is more certain and more substantial than the income they could earn from the legitimate jobs available to them (Fagan and Freeman, 1999). However, even if all offenders were paid the amount they realize from their criminal activities, many of them would continue to violate the law because of the noneconomic rewards of crime. One study concluded that the behavior of habitual offenders is reinforced by the intrinsic rewards they derive from their crimes, specifically "(1) the neurophysiological high such acts produce and (2) the symbolic meaning of the behavior as it relates to self-concept and identity formation" (Wood et al., 1997: 335). Offenders "reported that when performing crime—particularly violent crime—they were pumped up, experienced a substantial high, and felt they could do anything they wanted. They also felt intensely alive and had a sense of accomplishment" (Wood et al., 1997: 360).

One noneconomic reward of criminal behavior, the challenge of violating the law and getting away with it, is important in many computer crimes:

> A general characteristic of computer programmers is their fascination with challenges and desire to accept them. In fact, they face the great challenge of making computer systems do their bidding day in and day out. Telling a programmer that a computer system is safe from penetration is like waving a red flag in front of a bull. The challenge of an unauthorized act often overshadows the question of morality. (Parker, 1976: 47–48)

One example of this "electronic machismo" involved Robert Morris, the son of an important federal computer security official (Hafner and Markoff, 1991: 153). Attracted to the challenge of beating supposedly secure computer systems, Morris set in motion a "virus" that eventually slowed down or stopped 6,000 systems.

Another important noneconomic reward from crime is excitement. The author of a study of the criminal mind concludes that "thinking about the crime is exciting. Committing the crime is exciting. Even getting caught is exciting. Trying to figure out a way to beat the rap is exciting" (Stanton Samenow, cited in Serrill, 1978: 90). A study of adolescent shoplifters found that equal numbers stole for instrumental reasons (i.e., reasons related to the product of the crime, such as money) and for expressive reasons (i.e., reasons related to emotional needs fulfilled by committing the criminal act, such as excitement) (Klemke, 1978). One young woman described the rewards of committing robberies as follows:

> Yeah, we'd cut outta school and hang for a while. But then we'd get bored and look for something exciting to do. We'd go to the park and stick people up, see their faces, see how surprised they were. Sometimes we'd go into stores and stick them up. Then we'd take the stuff we got and go and party. (cited in Baskin and Sommers, 1998: 104)

One study treated middle-class delinquency as a form of play, claiming that it serves needs similar to those served by other forms of leisure: adding interest to the daily routine, providing entertainment, learning new techniques and skills, and learning social rules (Richards, Berk, and Foster, 1979). Even white-collar criminals find breaking the law exciting; one insider trader describes his motivation as follows:

Something deep inside me forced me to try to catch up to the pack of wheeler-dealers who always raced in front of me. . . . It was only in time that I came to view myself as an insider trading junkie. I was addicted to the excitement, the sense of victory. Some spouses use drugs, others have extramarital affairs, I secretly traded stocks. (Levine, 1991: 390)

What makes violating the law fun for some people? Perhaps breaking rules set by other people is satisfying because it gives the rule breaker a feeling of autonomy. Sometimes the physical activity involved in a criminal or delinquent act is intrinsically pleasing, or perhaps the consequences of the act are gratifying in some way. For instance, there might be an aesthetic element involved in vandalism, with vandals enjoying the visual, auditory, and tactile sensations resulting from their "creative conversion" of material things (Allen and Greenberger, 1978). The fun or "kicks" derived from crime are often short-lived, and this can lead to continued criminal activity. Some thieves claim that stealing is hard work with little thrill about it, and some say they are very tense while committing their crimes, but many offenders seem to be motivated by the challenge, excitement, and relief from boredom that they derive from criminal activity.

Some crime is motivated by a desire to preserve individual or collective honor. Trying to maintain one's self-image when insulted by another person can lead to homicide (Luckenbill, 1977). A study of Chicano gang violence found that preservation of the gang's collective honor and the self-esteem of its members often led to gang violence (Horowitz and Schwartz, 1974).

Repetitive property criminals report that they are motivated to steal by rewards in addition to money but say that their desire for "quick, easy money" is the primary reason they commit crime. Rewards such as excitement, sense of accomplishment, peer respect, vengeance, and control over victims are usually latent by-products of their crimes rather than primary motivational factors (Tunnell, 1992).

Risks The primary risk associated with crime is the threat of arrest, conviction, and imprisonment. Offenders often plan their crimes to minimize this risk, but most people who continue in crime for any significant amount of time are eventually arrested. They are turned in by informants, caught because the police happen to be near the scene of the crime, or arrested because of police investigative work. The probability of arrest for any given crime is relatively low, with the overall clearance rate for index crimes in 2001 being only 19.6 percent, but the chance of being arrested for at least one crime, if many crimes are committed, is quite high. If an offender has an 80 percent chance of escaping arrest for a given offense, the chance of escaping any arrest if two such crimes are committed is only 64 percent, the chance of not being arrested at all if three offenses are committed is 51 percent, the chance of no arrest if ten offenses are committed is only 11 percent, and the chance of no arrest if the offender commits twenty crimes is only 1 percent. In other words, the chance of not being arrested for a single crime is quite high, but the chance of never being arrested over the course of a criminal career is quite small. As a result, most criminal careers are eventually interrupted by arrest.

Continued criminal activity might make offenders more expert, thereby minimizing their chance of being arrested, but with continued success many offenders become overconfident and careless. Because chance plays an important role in determining whether an offender will be arrested for a given crime, an offender's luck will eventually run out if he or she continues to break the law.

Conventional Property Crimes The conventional property offenses of robbery, burglary, car theft, and arson involve many risks, but they also offer rewards in addition to money and excitement. Professional thieves mention satisfaction in a job well done, the leisure time between jobs, being their own boss, the nonroutine nature of theft, and the intrinsic satisfaction of stealing (Sutherland, 1937). For those who lack the education and skill to get a good job, the choice of property crime as a source of income might seem rational.

Robbery   A study of "casual robbers" in the United States found that they stole to buy drugs and clothing, to maintain or enhance their standing among their peers, and to create a more exciting life. Their "adventurous deviance" was more rewarding because it was risky, but they did try to keep their risks to a "manageable level" (Lejeune, 1977: 125).

Other robbers are more systematic in their crimes. For instance, two robbers who committed nearly two hundred crimes in an eighteen-month period decided to engage in robbery in a very calculating way. They had some money but lacked good job prospects and disliked the manual labor available to them. They wanted to make money quickly and decided on crime, which they saw as a business with risks and rewards like any other job. They spent four days in a public library doing research to find the best way to get money quickly and safely. After examining crime statistics, including the amounts stolen and the chances of arrest and conviction, they decided on armed robbery because it was direct and did not require them to convert property into cash. To reduce the risk of being injured by victims or the police, they carried firearms (Jackson, 1969). Few offenders select their crimes in such a deliberate fashion, but these robbers considered the rewards and risks of crime in a way that is consistent with the rational-choice perspective on crime.

Burglary   Few burglars commit their crimes primarily for excitement and thrills, though some mention those as secondary rewards. For most burglars, money is the primary motivating factor. One study found that residential burglars respond both to the amount and probability of illicit gain and to the amount and probability of punishment, but that perceptions of financial rewards influence their decisions to commit burglary more than perceptions of the risks of punishment do (Piquero and Rengert, 1999). Burglars typically attribute their crimes to a pressing financial need, which they define in terms of the streetlife value of "keeping the party going." Their proceeds are most likely to be spent on illegal drugs or status-enhancing clothes, although some of them report using their profits to pay for food, shelter, and clothing for their children. Many burglars claim that they would give up crime if they were offered a good job or if all of their financial needs were met, but those circumstances are unlikely to develop for most burglars (Reppetto, 1974; Cromwell, Olson, and Avary, 1991; Wright and Decker, 1994).

Car Theft   Car theft has multiple motives. Some thieves steal cars for joyriding—to have a good time and enjoy prestige in the eyes of their peers. Others steal cars for short-term transportation because of situational pressures for rapid mobility or the lack of other ways to get around. Some car thefts are for transportation over longer periods; these thieves keep stolen cars for personal use for a while. Cars are sometimes stolen to commit other crimes, such as burglaries and robberies, because stolen cars cannot be traced to the offenders. Amateur thieves strip cars of their tires or batteries; well-organized professionals steal cars, repaint them, and ship them out of state or out of the country for sale.

Arson   There are also multiple motives for arson. Some arson is thought to be motivated by "pyromania"—a supposed psychological abnormality in which the "firebug" derives pleasure from seeing things burn. Another motive for arson is revenge against rival gang members or the inhabitants or owners of a building. Others seek to profit from arson through fraud; landlords burn buildings they cannot rent or pay taxes on, and manufacturers suffering economic hardship "sell out to the insurance company" by burning a plant and collecting the insurance. Arsonists also burn buildings because others have paid them to or because they want to steal and sell copper tubing or plumbing from the abandoned building.

White-Collar Crime   For white-collar offenders, the risks are relatively small: Few of them are convicted of a crime, and those who are usually are treated leniently by the courts. Perhaps the major risk they face is the loss of reputation. The instrumental nature of white-collar crime lends itself to a careful calculation of the costs and benefits of violating the law. For instance, in Chapter 6 we saw that in marketing the Pinto, the Ford Motor Company carefully considered the costs it would incur in legal actions resulting from burn injuries and deaths and from burned vehicles. After determining that those costs were less than the cost of modifying the vehicles, Ford went ahead and produced dangerous automobiles (Cullen, Maakestad, and Cavender, 1987).

Drug Use   Drugs such as marijuana, cocaine, and heroin provide rewards in the form of physiological effects on users and profits for importers and dealers, but there are significant costs associated with drugs as well.

The effects of heroin are sufficiently strong that some first-time users do not need to learn from others how to enjoy the drug; one book on heroin is titled *"It's So Good, Don't Even Try It Once"* (Smith and Gay, 1972). Other new users do need to learn to experience the effects of heroin as pleasurable. A study of addicts in Baltimore concluded that pleasurable sensations were the primary reason that addicts continued to use heroin. Nearly all of the addicts wanted to get high every day, even though lack of money and commitment to a conventional lifestyle kept some of them from getting high more than two or three times a week (McAuliffe and Gordon, 1974). Another study found that 84 percent of a sample of regular heroin users described their first use of the drug in terms of euphoria and ecstasy, though 38 percent were nauseated and 31 percent vomited after injecting the drug for the first time. This study concluded that the search for euphoria was an important motivator for heroin use, but not the primary reason for addiction. Instead, the addicts sought "calmness, stability, peace of mind, and even serenity, that fall short of transporting the user to a euphoric state" (Hanson et al., 1985: 88).

The sale, possession, and use of heroin, cocaine, and marijuana are criminal, but illegal drugs are associated with crime in other ways as well. State and federal laws prohibit the possession, without a prescription, of the hypodermic syringes used to administer heroin, leading some users to share needles, even though there is a substantial risk of contracting the HIV virus or hepatitis from contaminated needles. Drug users also engage in crimes that are secondary to their addiction to pay for expensive drugs, which are costly because they are illegal. Because drug users are frequently socially disadvantaged, they are often unable to afford drugs on the income derived from the legitimate jobs available to them. As a result, heroin and cocaine users often turn to crimes such as shoplifting, stealing from cars, burglary, robbery, con games, gambling, and prostitution (McAuliffe and Gordon, 1974; Hanson et al., 1985; Inciardi, Horowitz, and Pottieger, 1993). A study carried out in Miami found that nearly all addicts committed crimes to get money with which to buy drugs; nearly half of them used money from legitimate jobs, and about one-fifth of them used income from public assistance. Only one-eighth of the male addicts, but nearly one-third of the female addicts, got money for drugs from family and friends (Inciardi, 1979).

Users of illegal drugs typically increase their criminal activities after becoming addicted, but most of them also committed crimes before they started using drugs. Here a teenager smokes a crack pipe.

Between 50 and 80 percent of all heroin addicts engage in crime before becoming addicted, indicating that they experience the rewards of crime even before starting to spend the proceeds of their crimes on heroin (Greenberg and Adler, 1974; McGlothlin, Anglin, and Wilson, 1978; Inciardi, 1979). Addicts do increase their criminal activities greatly after becoming addicted (Anglin and Speckart, 1988; Chaiken and Chaiken, 1990). When addicts enter treatment or kick their habits, their criminal behavior decreases, but it remains greater than it was before becoming addicted, suggesting that the rewards of crime are still sought when crime is no longer necessary to support their drug use (Cushman, 1974; Stephens and Ellis, 1975).

Critique of Reward-Risk Models

Reward-risk models often fail to indicate exactly how potential offenders weigh the various benefits and costs of criminal and noncriminal behavior. For instance, how does an offender calculate the probability of arrest, or balance a small chance of a prison sentence against a high probability of making a small financial gain? Reward-risk models also seem to work better for some offenders (such as white-collar criminals) than for others (such as child molesters).

Reward-risk models have paid too little attention to the sources of people's methods of evaluating rewards and risks. For example, people who have little stake in conformity might think that a small financial gain is worth the risk of arrest. Others with a greater stake in conformity might think that even the possibility of a large financial gain is not worth a small risk of arrest. Reward-risk models need to spell out in detail the actual process of considering rewards and risks, the reasons that people balance rewards and risks differently, and the way that the social structure influences the assessment of rewards and risks.

Learning Theories and Variations in Crime Rates

The learning theories examined in this chapter suggest some ways that geographic variations in crime rates might be explained. If there are geographic differences in the definitions favorable and unfavorable to violation of the law to which people are exposed, differential association theory might explain variations in crime rates by nation, region, and size of the community. Geographic variations could also be due to cross-national, regional, or community differences in the groups that control power and label behavior criminal. For instance, the difference between the United States and Great Britain in rates of drug addiction and secondary crimes associated with addiction has been attributed to the definition of drug addiction as a crime in the United States and as a medical problem in Great Britain (Schur, 1962; Judson, 1974). Another possible explanation of geographic variations in crime rates is that people in different places might balance rewards against risks differently. For instance, if people living in one country have a low stake in conformity, they might be willing to take more risks to gain the rewards of crime than people elsewhere who have a greater stake in conformity. To date, however, there is little direct evidence that such cross-national, regional, or size-of-community variations in crime rates can be explained by the learning theories explored in this chapter.

Learning theories do not seem to explain temporal variations in crime rates very well. For differential association theory to explain changes in crime rates, it would have to tell us why an increasing or decreasing number of people have an excess of definitions favorable to violation of the law over definitions unfavorable to violation of the law. The theory does not make clear why that might happen and thus does not do a very good job of explaining changes in crime rates. Labeling theory would suggest that the kind of behavior defined or treated as criminal fluctuates over time as certain groups gain power or change their views about the kind of behavior that is threatening to them. However, there have been few efforts to use the labeling perspective to explain temporal variations in crime rates. Similarly, there have been few attempts to use reward-risk models to explain changes in crime rates, although the way people evaluate and balance rewards and risks might change over time in ways that would explain increases or decreases in crime rates.

Learning theories can make sense of variations in crime rates by sex, age, race, and social class. Differential association theory suggests that exposure to criminal and noncriminal definitions of the law varies by social group, with males, young people, minority groups, and the lower classes being the most likely to commit crime because they are the most likely to be exposed to an excess of definitions favorable to violation of the law over definitions unfavorable to violation of the law. This explanation does not tell us why differences in definitions of the law are distributed in society in this way, nor is there much direct evidence that those groups actually differ in their exposure to definitions favorable and unfavorable to violation of the law. The labeling perspective suggests that one reason official crime rates are higher among certain groups is that those groups lack the power to define what kind of behavior will be treated as criminal. The high crimes rates of young people, minorities, and the lower classes could thus be explained by the tendency for crime to be defined by older people, dominant racial and ethnic groups, and the middle and upper classes. This approach would not explain the higher crime rate of males, because for the most part it has been men who have written and enforced criminal laws. Reward-risk models might explain variations in crime rates by suggesting that people with different characteristics evaluate the rewards and risks of criminal and noncriminal behavior differently, though there is little direct evidence that this is so.

In sum, learning theories might explain geographic, temporal, and social variations in crime rates, but there have been few explicit attempts to use those theories to make sense of such variations.

Summary

People learn skills and motives to commit crime from various sources. The social structure of some communities is conducive to learning criminal and delinquent behavior. Many delinquents become involved in violation of the law by learning from peers and from older adolescents in gangs. People also learn criminal motives and techniques from the general culture. Watching violence on television and viewing or participating in certain sports can increase aggressiveness, but whether these activities lead directly to criminal behavior is less certain. Exposure to pornographic material does not seem to cause men to commit sex offenses, but violent pornography could have this effect on people who are otherwise predisposed to commit such crimes. There is little solid evidence that correctional institutions act as "schools of crime," but some sociologists believe that interaction among inmates is a source of criminal motives and skills.

Differential association theory proposes that crime and delinquency are learned through face-to-face interaction. Techniques and motives are learned from definitions of the law in favorable or unfavorable terms. People violate the law when definitions favorable to violation of the law exceed definitions unfavorable to violation of the law. These definitions result from associations with criminal and noncriminal patterns that differ in frequency, duration, priority, and intensity.

Research on juvenile delinquency is consistent with differential association theory: Much delinquency occurs in groups, and delinquents interact frequently with other delinquents. Professional thieves are often introduced to crime through tutelage by experienced thieves. Differential association theory also fits much of what we know about white-collar crime, though the theory has not been rigorously tested. Business offenders might be exposed to definitions favorable to violation of the law within the company, and they can be isolated from definitions unfavorable to violation of the law.

The labeling perspective proposes that some people who engage in primary deviation, or rule breaking, are labeled delinquent or criminal by institutions such as the police and the courts. This can change an individual's self-concept, close off opportunities, alter social relationships, and push people into subcultures. This leads to secondary deviation, or repeated rule breaking by those who see themselves as criminals or delinquents. There is mixed evidence about the actual effects of labeling on self-concepts, and changes in self-concepts do not necessarily lead to more violation of the law, but delinquents seem to have poorer self-concepts than nondelinquents. It is not clear that labeling closes off opportunities for all labeled deviants, but some adult offenders seem to have their job opportunities reduced. Labeling can push delinquents and criminals into a subculture, leading to a changed self-concept and more crime as a result of differential association with definitions favorable to violation of the law.

Crime offers offenders various rewards or benefits and produces certain risks or costs for them. The major risk that most crime poses is the possibility of arrest and punishment. Rewards vary from crime to crime. Monetary gain is a primary reward, but challenge, excitement, and autonomy are other benefits derived from criminal activity. Some offenses, such as arson and car theft, provide different kinds of rewards to different offenders. Reward-risk models focus attention on the factors that motivate offenders, but they can exaggerate the rationality of criminal activity. These models need to provide more details on the exact way that offenders consider the rewards and risks of crime, and they need to look at the influence of the social structure on the way that people balance rewards and risks.

Differential association theory, the labeling perspective, and reward-risk models might explain geographic, temporal, and social variations in crime rates, but so far there have been few attempts by researchers to show how learning theories explain these variations.

IMPORTANT TERMS

containment theory	master status	secondary deviation
differential association theory	obscene material	social learning theory
differential identification theory	pornography	social structure and social
labeling perspective	primary deviation	learning (SSSL) theory
machismo	rational-choice perspective	tutelage

REVIEW QUESTIONS

1. What are the sources from which people learn to commit delinquency or crime? What sources other than those discussed at the beginning of this chapter can you identify? Which sources have the greatest impact on delinquents and criminals?

2. What is differential association theory? What are the advantages and shortcomings of the theory? For which kinds of criminal behavior does this theory work best? For which kinds is it least applicable?

3. How does the labeling perspective suggest that official labeling affects crime and delinquency? What does this perspective contribute to our understanding of law-violating behavior? What are the shortcomings of this perspective?

4. What are some of the reward-risk models of criminal behavior? What are the rewards and risks of different kinds of crime? How could crime be reduced by increasing the risks of criminal behavior or by increasing the rewards of noncriminal behavior?

5. How would the three theoretical perspectives examined in this chapter—differential association theory, the labeling perspective, and reward-risk models—explain variations in crime rates by country, region, size of community, sex, age, race, and social class?

FOR FURTHER STUDY

The Media and Crime   Television's portrayal of crime is examined in Stephen M. Chermak's *Victims in the News: Crime and the American News Media* (Boulder, CO: Westview, 1995) and Mark Fishman and Gray Cavender's (eds.) *Entertaining Crime: Television Reality Programs* (Hawthorne, NY: Aldine de Gruyter, 1998).

Social Learning Theory   Ronald L. Akers's *Social Learning and Social Structure: A General Theory of Crime and Deviance* (Boston: Northeastern University Press, 1998) integrates differential association theory with general behavioral principles and applies the resulting social learning theory to crime and delinquency.

Rational-Choice Perspective   A wide-ranging collection of essays on decision making by different types of offenders can be found in Derek B. Cornish and Ronald V. Clarke's (eds.) *The Reasoning Criminal: Rational Choice Perspectives on Offending* (New York: Springer-Verlag, 1986).

Seductions of Crime   Jack Katz's *Seductions of Crime: Moral and Sensual Attractions in Doing Evil* (New York: Basic Books, 1988) is an innovative exploration of the ways that murderers, robbers, gang members, and shoplifters experience crime.

9 Opportunities and Facilitating Factors

Crime requires a social structure conducive to violation of the law, weakened commitment to the law through techniques of neutralization or detachment from conventional institutions, and the learning of criminal motives and skills. However, crime cannot be committed unless there are opportunities to break the law. The first section of this chapter looks at the way people's everyday behavior creates opportunities for crime. Then, the way that offenders select their targets is examined. The final section investigates three factors that are often associated with crime, even if they do not actually cause it: alcohol, drugs, and firearms. These facilitating factors increase the chance that a situation will lead to crime.

Routine Activities Theory

Routine activities theory sees crime as a function of people's everyday behavior. This approach focuses on three elements: motivated offenders, target suitability, and guardianship. Earlier chapters examined the factors that motivate offenders to commit crime. Target suitability refers to the form and value of property, the visibility and accessibility of targets, and the vulnerability of property and people to victimization. The third element is guardianship, the degree to which targets are protected from victimization. The routine activities approach proposes that crime occurs when motivated offenders are present near suitable targets that are not adequately protected. This approach can be used to explain variations in crime rates among groups, forecast trends in crime rates, understand the spatial distribution of crime, and plan future needs for criminal justice services and personnel (Cohen and Felson, 1979; Cohen and Cantor, 1981; Messner and Tardiff, 1985; Felson, 1998).

The routine activities approach suggests that the presence of an abundance of goods that can be stolen will be associated with a high rate of property crime. In fact, economically developing societies do experience rising rates of theft (Clinard and Abbott, 1973). A study of Sweden's crime rates from 1950 to 1979 found that theft increased as more goods became available and concluded that the increase was better explained by changes in opportunities for theft than by changes in income inequality (Stack, 1982).

Guardianship is measured by the extent to which people in the course of their daily behavior do, or do not, protect property and individuals from crime. Long-term changes in patterns of behavior seem to have reduced guardianship and thus increased crime rates. These changes include the following:

- a large increase in the proportion of women holding jobs outside the home
- an increase in the proportion of all households that have only one person
- more frequent and longer vacations

On the other hand, burglaries might have decreased since 1980 because recreational activity has become more home-centered.

The routine activities approach makes sense of the spatial distribution of crime. An analysis of more than 300,000 calls to the Minneapolis police department found that relatively few "hot spots" in the city accounted for most of the calls; half of the calls came from only 3.3 percent of the city's addresses and intersections (Sherman, Gartin, and Buerger, 1989). The hot spots in which motivated offenders, suitable targets, and inadequate guardianship converged to generate crime included a large discount store near a poor neighborhood, a large department store, convenience stores, bars, and a public housing apartment building. Another study found that crime was more common on residential blocks in Cleveland that had taverns and cocktail lounges. This effect on crime was greatest when the recreational liquor establishments were in areas characterized by anonymity and little guardianship (Roncek and Maier, 1991).

Routine activities theory can explain a wide variety of deviant actions by individuals as well as aggregate crime rates. Analysis of data from a national survey of eighteen to twenty-six year olds found that criminal behavior, dangerous driving, illicit drug use, and heavy alcohol consumption were strongly associated with "time spent in unstructured socializing with peers in the absence of authority figures" (Osgood et al., 1996: 637). Lack of structure makes more time available for deviant behavior, the presence of peers makes deviance easier and more rewarding, and the absence of an authority figure reduces social control. The researchers describe the routine activities of people with different characteristics as follows:

> [I]ndividuals in the most deviant structural condition—18-year-old males with D grade-point averages whose parents have graduate or professional degrees—typically go riding in a car for fun 110 times per year, visit informally with friends 200 times, go to 40 parties, and spend 170 evenings out for fun. In contrast, 26-year-old females who had A grades in high school and whose parents had grade school educations typically go riding in a car for fun 9 times, visit with friends informally 25 times, go to 6 parties, and spend 53 evenings out for fun. (Osgood et al., 1996: 652)

The researchers concluded that much of the relationship between deviant behavior and the variables of sex, age, and socioeconomic status was accounted for by such differences among groups in routine activities.

At first, researchers who used routine activities theory employed demographic variables such as sex, age, race, and social class as indicators of people's daily behavior. More recently, researchers such as Osgood et al. (1996) have used direct measures of

Deviant behavior by young people is more likely if their leisure time is unstructured, peers are present, and authority figures are absent.

people's lifestyles and behavior patterns, rather than assuming how people with different social background characteristics will behave. (See the Crime on Campus box.) One study that measured exposure to the risk of victimization with data on the nature and quantity of people's activities outside the home found that routine activities theory predicted variations in property crime rates better than it predicted variations in violent crime rates (Miethe, Stafford, and Long, 1987). However, an analysis of Canadian victimization data showed that variations in violent crime were associated with lifestyle factors (Kennedy and Forde, 1990). In contrast to these studies, researchers who analyzed data from six Atlanta neighborhoods concluded that direct measures of routine activities were not strongly predictive of victimization. For instance, the amount of time that residents were away from their homes did not affect the chances that their homes would be targets of crime (Massey, Krohn, and Bonati, 1989).

A Critique of Routine Activities Theory

Recent research suggests that routine activities theory needs to be revised to incorporate additional variables associated with exposure to the risk of victimization. For instance, by limiting the communities in which people can live, the economic system and the housing market increase the proximity of some people to offenders and thus increase their exposure to the risk of victimization (Garofalo, 1987; Sampson and Lauritsen, 1990).

Terance Miethe and Robert Meier (1994) have developed a model that integrates routine activities theory with theories of victimization, criminal motivation, and social context. They propose that routine activities theory explains the production of opportunities for crime, that traditional theories identify the factors that motivate offenders, and that more attention should be paid to the situational context in which motivated offenders and criminal opportunities come together. Contextual factors that they find to be important in explaining crime rates and risks of victimization include a neighborhood's income level, unemployment rate, residential mobility, ethnic heterogeneity, and number of single-parent households.

Lifestyle theory proposes that individuals who commit violent and property crimes, abuse drugs and alcohol, spend more time on the street, and associate with deviant peers are themselves exposed to a high risk of victimization (Jensen and Brownfield, 1986; Sampson and Lauritsen, 1990; Lauritsen, Sampson, and Laub, 1991; Hoyt, Ryan, and Cauce, 1999; Dobrin, 2001). For example, research in Denver and Pittsburgh shows that youths who have been seriously injured as the result of an assault or a robbery are more likely than youths who have not been the victim of such a crime to participate in gang or group fights, carry weapons, commit serious assaults, sell drugs, and associate with delinquent peers (Loeber, Kalb, and Huizinga, 2001).

Targets of Crime

The crime-generating process examined in previous chapters—the social-structural pressure to commit crime, the neutralization of the law, and the acquisition of criminal motives and skills—is necessary but not sufficient for the commission of crime. Without an opportunity, there will be no crime.

CRIME ON CAMPUS

Routine Activities and Criminal Victimization

Researchers have applied routine activities theory to the criminal victimization of college students. In doing so, they have relied on behavioral rather than demographic measures of students' lifestyles.

A survey of 1,513 college students at nine institutions by Elizabeth Ehrhardt Mustaine and Richard Tewksbury found that to predict a student's risk of larceny victimization, it was less important to know how often the student was away from his or her place of residence than to know where the student went and what he or she did when out in public. Students' risk of theft victimization was strongly associated with the following:

- participation in illegal activities such as smoking marijuana and threatening others
- social activities such as dining out frequently, belonging to many organizations, leaving home often for studying, and playing on public basketball or tennis courts
- living in neighborhoods with high levels of crime and noise

- taking self-protective measures such as owning a dog or installing extra locks on doors

From their research on 3,472 college students at twelve institutions, Bonnie S. Fisher and her colleagues concluded that property crime and violent crime are associated with different lifestyle factors. Risk of property victimization was increased by proximity to crime, target attractiveness, exposure, and lack of guardianship. Students who lived in all-male or coed dormitories were more likely to be victims of theft on campus than students who lived off campus or in all-female dormitories. Students who spent more time on campus and more money on nonessential items had higher levels of theft victimization. Living in a fraternity or sorority reduced the risk of theft victimization, perhaps because other members guarded property when a student was away. Risk of violent victimization—a relatively rare event on campuses— was more common among students who routinely partied on campus at night and among those who used recreational drugs.

Sources: Based on Elizabeth Ehrhardt Mustaine and Richard Tewksbury, "Predicting Risks of Larceny Theft Victimization: A Routine Activity Analysis Using Refined Lifestyle Measures," *Criminology* 36 (November 1998), 829–857; Bonnie S. Fisher et al., "Crime in the Ivory Tower: The Level and Sources of Student Victimization," *Criminology* 36 (August 1998), 671–710.

There is a nearly unlimited number of targets for crime. What is important is the way these targets are perceived by potential offenders. A robber might see a bank with both a front and a rear entrance, a nearby expressway, and weak security as an excellent opportunity for a bank holdup; law-abiding citizens will view the same bank simply as a place to deposit and withdraw funds. One thief comments on the process of spotting opportunities for crime as follows:

> An underworld education makes a lot of difference to a man. In every way. Say you're a legitimate businessman and you're taking a ride in an automobile with a man that's a loser, that's been in the rackets for years. Like me. . . . I see an attractive young woman stepping out of a big restaurant. It's about one-thirty in the afternoon. She has a thick envelope under her arm and she's walking toward the bank. That doesn't mean anything to you. But to me it means she's bringing money to the bank. I'm gonna get back and check on her, see if she does that every day, it might be worth grabbing. As we ride along for eight or ten blocks, I've seen a half dozen things that are not legitimate and you have seen nothing but the ordinary street scenes. A man that's a thief, whenever he's moving around, will recognize a hundred opportunities to make a dollar. (Martin, 1952: 182–183)

The target selected by an offender depends in part on the specific skills the offender possesses. Some criminals specialize in or prefer one kind of offense, but most are quite versatile. Even experienced professional thieves usually "hustle" for crime opportunities rather than seek specific targets. They read newspapers, swap information with other thieves and fences, and keep their eyes open for crime targets. Specialization would force them to pass up lucrative opportunities.

Property Crimes

Thieves consider several factors in choosing targets for their crimes. The form of the property to be stolen is important, as is the value of that property. Target vulnerability and the likelihood of victim resistance are also considered.

Form of the Property   The form of the property to be stolen is important. Most thieves will have to avoid computers as targets for crime because they lack the necessary skills, but assets in the form of computerized data are vulnerable to theft by computer operators who have the necessary skills. Some observers have suggested reducing theft by eliminating cash and replacing it with computerized assets, thereby making property inaccessible to many thieves, at least until they develop computer skills.

Most thieves steal cash or property, with the property either being used personally or converted into cash or drugs. Conversion of stolen property into cash requires access to a fence, a receiver of stolen goods who pays the thief one-tenth to one-third of the retail value of the stolen merchandise. Young burglars often steal goods that they dispose of among their acquaintances, but older and more experienced burglars are more likely to steal goods that they convert into cash with fences (Reppetto, 1974). Amateur shoplifters ("snitches") often take small, easily concealed goods for personal use. Professional shoplifters ("boosters") steal more expensive items and sell them to fences or to jewelry stores and clothing shops that are primarily legitimate retail outlets (Cameron, 1964).

The conversion of property into cash is time-consuming, an important consideration for offenders who require cash immediately, such as thieves who are heroin addicts looking for a fix. Selling stolen goods to a fence can be risky as well as inconvenient, because the police can trace stolen property back to the thief through the fence. For these reasons, some offenders prefer the direct theft of cash from victims and turn to robbery. Robbery has the important advantage over other forms of theft of providing offenders with immediately usable assets that cannot be traced back to them. Robbery also requires relatively little preparation in most cases, and there is an abundance of potential targets. Robbers often claim that burglary is more trouble than robbery because it involves entry into a house or building, a search for valuable goods, the physical labor of carrying the goods from the building, and the conversion of those goods into cash. Robbery is faster and more direct, and it provides readily usable assets, but it also involves the risks of violent confrontation with and identification by the victim.

Value of the Property   Thieves who commit robbery, burglary, and other types of theft consider which victims they can get the most money from with the least effort and risk. Pickpockets usually select their "marks" or victims by criteria such as sex (men being thought to carry more money), age (older people being thought to carry more money), and race (whites being thought to carry more money) (Maurer, 1964). For robbers, the holdup of a commercial establishment such as a supermarket or a bank will typically net more money than the robbery of an individual on the street. Burglars have to locate the money or valuable property once they enter a building, even if they have chosen a potentially lucrative target.

Offenders usually choose victims on the basis of general expectations about how much money or property they will get. Sometimes they are more systematic in calculating their profits in advance, especially if the crime involves elaborate planning and substantial risk. One gang of jewelry store robbers regularly sent its "straightest-looking" member into a store a few days before a planned crime in order to examine the jewelry and decide whether the robbery was worth the trouble and risk it would involve. The gang would then steal only the most valuable jewelry and fence it with a receiver of stolen goods in a different state. The members of the gang had a very good idea of how much they would gain from a particular holdup. Another robber secured information about the number of employees working for a firm and the approximate amount earned by each worker; his robbery of the company on payday netted him an amount very close to his estimate (Conklin, 1972).

The amount of money a given target will yield is often calculated in detail by professional thieves, who seek as large a "score" as possible while keeping risks to a minimum. By contrast, opportunistic thieves look for smaller gains and are less methodical in assessing what they will get from a theft. Still, even opportunists consider what they are likely to get from potential victims. They observe how expensively potential victims are dressed and watch to see who "flashes a large wad of bills." Sometimes they try to improve their odds of a large score by stealing on paydays and on days when welfare checks are delivered.

Vulnerability of Victims

A major factor that criminals consider in choosing targets is the vulnerability of their victims. Check forgers believe some stores are more willing to accept checks from strangers and are therefore easier to victimize. For instance, supermarkets are seen as easy "marks," but men's clothing stores are thought to be relatively invulnerable to check passing (Jackson, 1969). Shoplifting is also easier in certain stores. Stores that emphasize self-service seem to accept shoplifting as a cost of doing business. Managers may even think that if shoplifting is infrequent, their merchandise is not attractive enough or accessible enough to customers (Cameron, 1964).

Opportunistic robbers—typically young, male members of minority groups who operate in gangs—tend to choose victims who are elderly, female, and alone. In other words, they seek victims who are vulnerable because of their age, sex, or lack of company, even though these victims usually carry less money than other potential victims. Because opportunists often lack experience and skill in committing crime, they place greater emphasis on victim vulnerability and the minimization of risk than they do on the size of the score. In contrast, professional robbers have a broader conception of vulnerability. For them, a vulnerable target is one from which they can steal after planning and preparation. For example, the 1950 Brinks robbery was directed against a target that would be seen as invulnerable by most robbers, but careful observation by the thieves showed that the Brinks office lacked adequate security and was vulnerable to theft (Behn, 1977).

Obstacles to theft sometimes turn offenders away from particular targets. Exact-fare requirements on buses can reduce robberies of bus drivers but lead thieves to steal from the stores or newspaper stands that make change for bus riders. Since 1940, there has been an increase in bank security, including the installation of electronically controlled doors and cages, alarm systems, and closed circuit television. These measures have eliminated sneak theft from banks, a crime in which thieves go behind a counter, grab money from a till, and run from the bank (Inciardi, 1975).

In a study of residential burglary by Thomas Reppetto (1974), nearly one hundred convicted burglars were shown slides of buildings and asked to pick the type of target from which they usually stole. They were then asked why they chose a particular building. The burglars emphasized easy access and the appearance of affluence in selecting targets. The type of information they most wanted before committing a burglary was whether there were occupants in the building. They also wanted to know if there was a burglar alarm and what valuables were available (see Figure 9.1). The importance of occupancy is shown by the fact that the more hours of the day a dwelling was unoccupied, the greater the chance it would be burglarized. Offenders learned whether anyone was home primarily by observing the dwelling, but sometimes they made telephone calls, questioned neighbors, or looked for signs of non-occupancy such as piles of newspapers or mail. They learned if there were valuables to be stolen by peeping in windows and by tips from friends and fences.

A study of active burglars in St. Louis found that even though they committed their crimes to meet what they defined as pressing financial needs, they were still cautious in assessing the costs and benefits of breaking into different buildings. Many of them had a target in mind before they felt a need for money. They learned of potential targets by knowing a dwelling's occupant, who was usually a casual acquaintance, neighbor, or drug dealer rather than a relative or friend; by observing a dwelling, its occupants, and their possessions for a time prior to the break-in; and, less commonly, by receiving inside information about a target from a "tipster," friend, or criminal associate (Wright and Decker, 1994).

Thieves try to minimize their risks by selecting targets that are not likely to be under police or neighborhood surveillance. They prefer targets that are isolated from the view of passersby, whether the police or private citizens. Even those who rob commercial establishments try to conceal themselves from public view during the crime, picking establishments that are set back from the street or positioning themselves inside the building so as to be invisible from the street. Lookouts are often stationed outside the building to report any threat of intrusion.

Robbers use nonverbal cues to assess the vulnerability of potential victims. A study that asked inmates who had been convicted of violent attacks on strangers to rate people who had been videotaped while walking on the street found that the people who were rated "easy to mug" by the inmates showed distinctive body movements that signaled that they would be good targets:

Specifically, the most muggable people tended to take strides that were of unusual length, either too short or too long. Instead of walking heel to toe, they walked

FIGURE 9.1 How Burglars Select Their Targets, Percentage of Burglars Giving Each Response

Source: Based on data from Thomas A. Reppetto, *Residential Crime.* Cambridge, MA: Ballinger, 1974, pp. 16, 105.

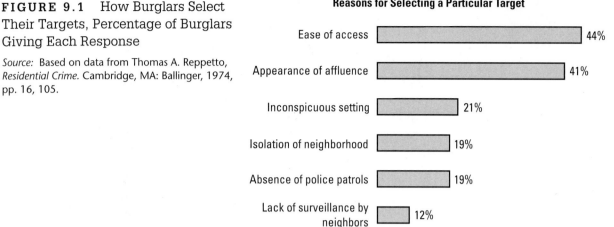

Reasons for Selecting a Particular Target

Ease of access — 44%
Appearance of affluence — 41%
Inconspicuous setting — 21%
Isolation of neighborhood — 19%
Absence of police patrols — 19%
Lack of surveillance by neighbors — 12%

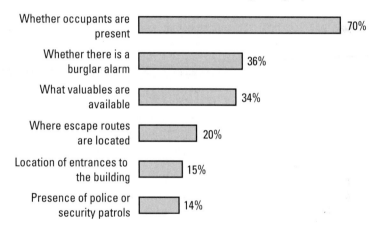

Information Wanted before Committing a Burglary

Whether occupants are present — 70%
Whether there is a burglar alarm — 36%
What valuables are available — 34%
Where escape routes are located — 20%
Location of entrances to the building — 15%
Presence of police or security patrols — 14%

flat-footed. Instead of swinging their left arm while striding with their right foot, they moved their left arm and left foot, then right arm and right foot together. Instead of the usual figure 8-like sway of upper body and lower body, the most muggable people seemed to move their torsos at cross purposes to the bottom half of their bodies.

And instead of moving "posturally" (letting the movement start from within the body core), potential victims seemed to move "gesturally" (moving from one part of the body, an arm for instance, as though the movement started outside the body). Indeed, the most muggable people seemed to walk as though they were less in touch with their bodies. (study by Betty Grayson, described in Foreman, 1981: 20–21)

These movements were more important to offenders in choosing victims than were age and sex. Muggers read movement as an indicator of vulnerability, although they did not seem to do this consciously.

Serial murderers also select their victims on the basis of perceived vulnerability. They rarely kill people who are their equals in physical strength and intellect, instead choosing victims they see as weak, helpless, and easy to overpower and control. Most of the victims of serial murderers are either young women or children (Hickey, 2002).

Victim Proneness   One measure of vulnerability is the frequency with which people are victimized repeatedly. There is a **victim proneness** among certain "hot

Non Sequitur © 1996 Wiley Miller. Dist. by Universal Press Syndicate. Reprinted with permission.

dots" because of their personal characteristics, social situation, physical location, and relationship to offenders (Pease and Laycock, 1996). Victim proneness can be a result of the following factors:

1. *Precipitation or provocation:* The victim does or says something that causes an offender to violate the law.

2. *Instigation or perpetration:* The victim actively encourages a crime or takes criminal action against another person.

3. *Facilitation:* The victim places himself or herself at risk by deliberation, recklessness, or negligence.

4. *Vulnerability or invitation:* Some people are unusually susceptible because of personal attributes, social status, or entry into a risk-filled situation.

5. *Cooperation:* The victim is a party to a consensual crime such as gambling or prostitution.

6. *Attractiveness:* Affluence will often attract offenders.

7. *Impunity:* Offenders can expect that the victim will not report the crime to the police or testify in court, perhaps because the victim is also breaking the law (Sparks, 1981, 1982).

Past victimization is a good predictor of subsequent victimization, often by the same offender. The more victimizations an individual has experienced, the greater the chance that he or she will be victimized again (Hoyt, Ryan, and Cauce, 1999; Menard, 2000; Wittebrood and Nieuwbeerta, 2000). The British Crime Survey found that 4 percent of victims suffered about 44 percent of the crimes uncovered in the study. Research on domestic violence in England showed that only 7 percent of 1,450 households suffered 43 percent of reported domestic violence incidents over a twenty-five-month period (Pease and Laycock, 1996). Whatever makes victims vulnerable to crime in the first place continues to make them vulnerable, and whatever measures they take to reduce their vulnerability seem to have little effect. This phenomenon of repeat victimization has policy implications, suggesting that crime prevention measures should focus on people who have been victimized in the past.

Victim Precipitation

Victim precipitation means that the person who suffers eventual harm from a crime plays a direct role in causing the crime to be perpetrated. One clear case of a victim-precipitated murder involved an incarcerated offender who reported that he had regularly used a knife to hold up drugstores because "a knife is quieter than a gun." A few months after the interview, he used a homemade knife to attack another inmate, who took the knife away and stabbed the attacker to death (Conklin, 1972).

Victims who act in particular ways with regard to potential offenders can create opportunities for crimes where none existed before. A man who enters a bar, picks an argument with another customer, and draws a knife in a sense contributes to his own murder if the other person responds by killing him with a handgun. This might not absolve the murderer of legal responsibility, but it could mitigate the punishment.

One definition of victim precipitation suggests that much information is needed to assess the role of the victim in the causation of a crime:

> Victim precipitation occurs when the offender's action in committing or beginning to commit a crime is initiated after and directly related to an action (be it physical or verbal, conscious or unconscious) on the part of the victim. The offender perceives the victim's behavior as a facilitating action (including temptation, invitation) to the commission of the crime. The action of the victim might be said to have triggered the offender's behavior. (R. A. Silverman, cited in Curtis, 1974: 96)

There is a continuum from deliberate provocation by the victim, to some involvement by the victim, to little or no victim contribution. The intent of the offender must be considered on a continuum from deliberate premeditation, to some intent, to none at all. Victim precipitation exists when offenders have little or no intent to commit a crime and victims clearly provoke them to commit a crime. Real-life situations are usually less clear-cut. Information on the interaction between the offender and the victim, and the state of mind of each, is difficult to get after a crime has been committed, especially if one participant is murdered. Witnesses might describe how the crime developed, but it is often difficult to gather data on the perceptions and expectations of the participants.

Murder   About one murder in four is victim-precipitated (Wolfgang, 1958; Curtis, 1974), although one study found that 38 percent of a sample of homicides were caused in part by the victim (Voss and Hepburn, 1968). Victims of victim-precipitated murders are especially likely to be male and black and to have prior criminal records. Female murderers are more likely than male murderers to be involved in victim-precipitated murders, because female murderers have often been provoked by their male victims.

In a study of interaction between offenders and victims prior to murder, about half of the seventy cases were found to involve prior hostility or physical violence between the offender and the victim (Luckenbill, 1977). Homicides were not usually one-sided events in which a passive victim was attacked by the murderer. In nearly two-thirds of the murders, the victim initiated the interchange, the offender stated an intent to harm the victim, and the offender then killed the victim. The interaction among the offender, the victim, and the audience to the murder can be analyzed in the following stages:

1. The offender first feels personally injured by the victim's behavior, which can be intentional or unwitting. This might include physical or verbal insults, gestures, or refusal to comply with the offender's wishes.

2. The offender then seeks to restore "face" by retaliating, expressing anger or contempt, or casting the victim as an unworthy person.

3. The victim next reacts to the offender's behavior by defining violence as the appropriate solution to the disagreement.

4. The offender interprets the victim's behavior as intentional noncompliance with his or her wishes.

5. Commitment to violence develops and actual violence is made more likely by the presence of weapons.

6. The offender "drops" the victim and then flees, voluntarily stays at the scene, or is involuntarily held at the scene by witnesses (Luckenbill, 1977).

Another study looked at the interaction leading to 159 incidents of homicide and assault and found similar patterns of behavior. Physical violence typically followed an "identity attack," a failure to influence the antagonist, threats, and sometimes efforts at evasive action or mediation. Offenders retaliated in an effort to reestablish a favorable identity, and the situation escalated into assault or murder. Each individual responded to the other's actions and the implications of those actions for his or her well-being and honor. Consequently, it was difficult to classify violent crime as offender-precipitated or victim-precipitated. Victims often acted aggressively, but they attacked less often and were more likely to take evasive action than were the offenders. Efforts at mediation and evasion suggested that offenders and victims did not share norms supporting violence as the appropriate response to an identity attack (Felson and Steadman, 1983).

The interactional dynamics of homicides committed by single offenders differ from those of homicides committed by multiple offenders. Single-offender murders typically involve character disputes that evolve during a single interaction into a fatal confrontation. Multiple-offender homicides that are related to another felony are usually unplanned, often being the by-product of a robbery or burglary that "goes bad," rather than the result of a character dispute. Multiple-offender homicides that do not involve another felony usually develop over time from disputes over business or status; these murders are often planned, with a final decision to kill being made prior to the lethal interaction (Cheatwood, 1996).

Forcible Rape   The cultural stereotype that rape victims contribute to their own victimization reflects the mistaken belief that rape is primarily a sexual act rather than a violent crime, even though victims experience rape as violence rather than sex. The widely held view that some victims provoke rapists, and even enjoy the act, is used to defend rapists' actions as justifiable, excusable, or understandable. Violent pornography contributes to this view (Donnerstein, Linz, and Penrod, 1987).

The idea that rape is often a victim-precipitated crime overlooks an important difference between rape and homicide. In the events leading to a homicide, the lives of both the eventual victim and the eventual murderer are usually at risk. However, in a confrontation between a rapist and a woman, only the woman is at risk. Thus, most murders are symmetrical in terms of the risk of being killed, but rapes are asymmetrical in terms of risk.

Nevertheless, the view that rape victims precipitate their own victimization persists. Many people regard placing oneself in a risky situation—for instance, hitchhiking alone or telling dirty jokes in a bar—as a form of victim precipitation. A study of jurors in rape cases concluded that their decisions were frequently based on the reputation and social life of the victim. Jurors were especially likely to acquit defendants whose victims were sexually active, drank, or used drugs (LaFree,

1989). There are now "shield laws" to prevent defense attorneys from questioning rape victims about their sex lives, but attorneys have developed strategies to plant in jurors' minds the idea that a victim leads an unchaste and nontraditional life, and jurors seem to respond by "blaming the victim" for the crime and exonerating the defendant.

One researcher concluded from his study of rape in Philadelphia that 19 percent of the cases were victim-precipitated, in that the victim had actually agreed to have sexual relations with the offender—or had been thought to have agreed to this by the offender—but had retracted before the act, or had not reacted "strongly enough" when the suggestion of sex was first made by the offender. This researcher also categorized rapes as victim-precipitated if they were preceded by "risky situations marred with sexuality," such as a woman's using "indecent" language or gestures or behaving in a way that could be taken as an invitation to sexual relations (Amir, 1971). Application of this extremely broad definition of victim precipitation led the researcher to conclude that nearly one rape victim in five contributes to her own victimization, even though "contribution" here seems to encompass anything outside a very restricted range of puritanical behavior.

Using a different definition of victim precipitation of rape, a seventeen-city survey of violent crime found that only 4 percent of rapes were victim-precipitated, 83 percent were not, and 13 percent could not be classified easily or accurately (Curtis, 1974). In this study, rape was defined as victim-precipitated if a female agreed to sexual relations and clearly invited them verbally or by gestures but then retracted before the act.

Crimes against Property   Theft can be precipitated by property owners. Individuals who leave their homes vacant while on vacation, allow mail and newspapers to accumulate, and leave windows and doors open while away provide potential burglars with obvious signals that the dwelling is an easy target. People who leave car keys in the ignition facilitate car theft, because a thief does not even have to possess the skill to start the car without a key. Similarly, leaving property where it can easily be stolen encourages theft. A study of crime in Uganda found that immigrants to a large city from small villages brought with them a tradition of leaving property unguarded, thus encouraging theft. In the village, thieves could be observed and recognized, so the tradition of leaving property unguarded did not lead to theft there. In the city, similar informal controls were absent, so the tradition frequently led to theft (Clinard and Abbott, 1973).

Offenders who lack a strong commitment to crime as a way of life might break the law when they happen upon easy opportunities to gain something with little risk. Sometimes they are drawn into crime because of victim precipitation. Thus, marginally committed offenders might steal unattended property, enter an empty house through an open window, or attack someone who insults them.

Facilitating Factors: Alcohol, Drugs, and Firearms

Three factors that often are present when crimes are committed, but do not actually cause crime, are alcohol, drugs, and firearms. The high frequency with which these factors are present during crimes suggests that they are **facilitating factors** that increase the chance that a situation will lead to criminal violence or theft.

Alcohol and Crime

Alcohol use and crime are strongly associated with one another. A 1997 survey found that 37 percent of state prison inmates and 20 percent of federal prison inmates reported that they had been under the influence of alcohol at the time of the offense for which they were incarcerated (Maguire and Pastore, 1999: 508). Such self-reports can be questioned as to their validity, because inmates might try to diminish their personal responsibility for violating the law by blaming it on the effects of alcohol. Moreover, the percentage of inmates who report being under the influence of alcohol at the time of their offense tells us little about the contribution of alcohol to crime unless we also know what percentage of the total population is under the influence of alcohol at any given time.

Alcohol is present in a significant proportion of homicides and assaults, and a smaller proportion of rapes, according to studies that have used official crime statistics. A survey of homicides in the seventy-five largest counties in the United States found that alcohol was present in 47 percent of the victims and 64 percent of the defendants (Dawson and Langan, 1994). A survey of convicted murderers in state prisons found that alcohol was implicated in nearly half of their homicides. Only the offender had been drinking in 25 percent of the crimes, only the victim in 10 percent of the crimes, and both had been drinking in 14 percent of the murders (Greenfeld, 1998).

CRIME ON CAMPUS

The Role of Alcohol and Drugs

A 2002 report by the National Institute on Alcohol Abuse and Alcoholism's Task Force on College Drinking concluded that the annual toll of drinking for American college students is enormous: 70,000 alcohol-related sexual assaults, 600,000 alcohol-related assaults, and 1,445 alcohol-related deaths from injuries and accidents, about three-fourths of them the result of car accidents.

A 1989 survey of 1,857 students found that since enrolling in college 8 percent had committed crimes and one-third had been victims of crimes but had never committed any. What was intriguing was the extent to which alcohol and drugs were associated with both criminal offending and criminal victimization. Students who reported committing crimes were more likely than either victims or nonoffenders/nonvictims to be heavy users of drugs and alcohol. Those who reported committing multiple offenses reported heavier use of drugs and alcohol than offenders who reported committing a single offense. The six students who admitted to sex offenses were the heaviest drug and alcohol users. The students who used alcohol and drugs the most had the greatest chance of being either an offender or a victim. Victims were heavier users of drugs and alcohol than nonvictims, and students who were victimized more than once reported heavier drug and alcohol use than those who were victimized just once (Bausell, Maloy, and Sherrill, 1990).

A 1992 Canadian survey showed that male college students who drank twice or more per week and whose friends supported emotional and physical partner abuse were more than nine times as likely as men with none of these characteristics to report that they had committed sexual abuse. The men who had peer support for partner abuse and who used alcohol were apparently more likely to see women who drank or used drugs as acceptable targets for sexual assault (Schwartz et al., 2001).

Much of the alcohol use that occurs on campus is "binge drinking," defined in one study as five consecutive drinks for men or four consecutive drinks for women. A 2001 survey found that 49 percent of male students and 41 percent of female students had engaged in binge drinking at least once in the previous two weeks. Twenty-five percent of the males and 21 percent of the females had engaged in binge drinking three or more times in the previous two weeks. Binge drinking was more common among white students (50 percent) than among Hispanic (34 percent), Asian (26 percent), or black (22 percent) students. It was more common among residents of fraternities and sororities (75 percent) than among students who lived in dormitories (45 percent) or

Alcohol also seems to play a role in various sex offenses. The Philadelphia study of forcible rape found that alcohol was present only in the victim in 10 percent of the cases, only in the offender in 3 percent of the cases, and in both the offender and the victim in 21 percent of the reported rapes (Amir, 1971). A common pattern for incest is an unemployed man with an absent wife and an available daughter (or, less commonly, stepdaughter), along with a pattern of heavy drinking by the man (Gebhard et al., 1965). Physical and social isolation of the family and tension within the marriage are also conducive to incest. These conditions are especially likely to lead to incestuous behavior if the strong norms against it are neutralized by the heavy consumption of alcohol. Other sex offenses, such as child abuse and child molestation, are also associated with alcohol use (McCaghy, 1967, 1968). Most studies have found that alcohol is present in 40 percent or more of all sex offenses (S. Greenberg, 1981).

Explaining the Alcohol–Crime Relationship   Several explanations have been offered for the relationship between alcohol use and crime. (See the Crime on Campus box.) One explanation is that alcohol reduces inhibitions and triggers law-violating behavior in some people. The reduction of inhibitions from alcohol consumption is suggested by the results of a study of homicide in Philadelphia, which found that murders in which alcohol was present involved more violence and brutality than did murders in which neither the offender nor the victim had been drinking (Wolfgang, 1958).

---

off campus alone or with a roommate (55 percent). Other researchers have found that fraternity and sorority leaders engage in binge drinking even more often than fraternity and sorority members who are less involved in those organizations.

Several measures have been proposed to reduce the abuse of alcohol by college students, including enforcing the minimum drinking age, increasing the price of alcohol, and limiting the number of bars and liquor stores near campuses. Another approach is "social norming," an effort to convey the impression that campus drinking is less common than research on binge drinking suggests, in the hope that such a message will establish a standard of moderate alcohol use by students.

Campus crime is closely associated with the use of drugs and alcohol, and especially with binge drinking.

Sources: Based on Carole R. Bausell, Charles E. Maloy, and Jan Mitchell Sherrill, *The Links among Drugs, Alcohol, and Campus Crime,* Towson, MD: Campus Violence Prevention Center, Towson State University, January 1990; Jeffrey R. Cashin, Cheryl A. Presley, and Philip W. Meilman, "Alcohol Use in the Greek System: Follow the Leader?" *Journal of Studies on Alcohol* 59 (January 1998), 63–70; Martin D. Schwartz et al., "Male Peer Support and a Feminist Routine Activities Theory: Understanding Sexual Assault on the College Campus," *Justice Quarterly* 18 (September 2001), 623–648; Henry Wechsler et al., "Trends in College Binge Drinking during a Period of Increased Prevention Efforts: Findings from 4 Harvard School of Public Health College Alcohol Study Surveys: 1993–2001," *Journal of American College Health* 50 (March 2002), 203–217; National Institute on Alcohol Abuse and Alcoholism, retrieved from www.collegedrinkingprevention.gov.

Another piece of evidence that is consistent with this disinhibition explanation comes from a study of robbery, which found that alcohol was present in 71 percent of the crimes committed on the spur of the moment but in only 44 percent of the planned crimes (G. D. Wolcott, cited in Petersilia, Greenwood, and Lavin, 1977: 81). Research conducted at college parties concluded that heavy alcohol consumption reduced students' perceptions of the risks of crime, diminished their moral condemnation of criminal behavior, and made crime seem more desirable to them. These changes might account for the relationship between alcohol use and crime (Lanza-Kaduce, Bishop, and Winner, 1997).

A second explanation of why alcohol use is linked to crime is that people who are actively involved in a life of crime rely on alcohol to reduce their anxiety or build up their courage for crimes they plan to commit (Collins, 1981a, 1981b; Tunnell, 1992). However, nearly one-third of jail and prison inmates drank on a daily basis, not just before committing crimes (Greenfeld, 1998). Because many offenders are heavy drinkers even when not engaging in crime, they probably do not drink just to build up their courage. It is more likely that they are problem drinkers who occasionally commit crimes when their inhibitions are reduced by alcohol.

A third explanation of the association between alcohol use and crime is that groups have norms about how people under the influence of alcohol should behave. Among some groups, drunkenness is seen as a "time out" from conventional demands. In this situation of relaxed behavioral standards, aggressive or even criminal behavior might be tolerated or expected. There is little research on differences among groups in their norms about "drunken comportment," but if such differences exist, they would help explain why alcohol use and crime are associated with each other in different ways for different groups (MacAndrew and Edgerton, 1969).

We do not yet have enough research to tell us exactly why alcohol use is associated with crime. More studies are needed to make clear "(1) the role of alcohol in the criminal situation, (2) the prevalence of alcoholism among criminals, and (3) the criminal history of alcoholics" (S. Greenberg, 1981: 106–107).

Drugs and Crime

Earlier in the book, we saw that many kinds of drug use are defined as crime, and that the need to support a drug habit can lead to secondary crimes. Drugs can also facilitate crime by reducing inhibitions or clouding a user's judgment, much as alcohol does.

Drug use among criminals is extensive. In 1997, 33 percent of state prison inmates and 22 percent of federal prison inmates reported that they had been under the influence of an illegal drug at the time of the offense for which they were incarcerated (Maguire and Pastore, 1999: 508).

The Arrestee Drug Abuse Monitoring (ADAM) program uses voluntary and anonymous urine specimens from samples of arrestees to test for the presence of cocaine, opiates, PCP, marijuana, amphetamines, methadone, methaqualone, benzodiazepines (Valium), barbiturates, and propoxyphene (Darvon). About two-thirds of the adults and more than half of the juveniles who were arrested in 1998 in the thirty-five cities with ADAM programs tested positive for at least one drug. In that same year, the National Institute of Justice began to help the governments of several other countries develop ADAM programs. In England, 59 percent of arrestees at five sites tested positive for one or more drugs, compared to a rate of 68 percent at five matched sites in the United States (National Institute of Justice, 1999; Taylor and Bennett, 1999).

Drug use is clearly associated with greater involvement in other criminal activities. According to the 1991 National Household Survey on Drug Abuse, there is a high correlation between drug use, especially cocaine use, and being booked for property and violent crimes (Harrison and Gfroerer, 1992). Heroin addicts in California prisons and jails report that they commit more than ten times as many thefts, robberies, and burglaries as nondrug-using inmates. Addicts in Baltimore commit four to six times as many crimes during periods of heavy drug use as they do when they are relatively drug-free (Graham, 1987).

Explaining the Drugs–Crime Relationship   The greater amount of drug use by offenders does not tell us the reason for the association between drug use and crime. Paul J. Goldstein (1985) suggests that drugs can generate criminal behavior in the following ways:

1. Drugs have *psychopharmacological* effects such as paranoia, excitability, irrationality, and loss of self-control that can lead to assaults and murders.
2. The *economic-compulsive need* to raise money to pay for expensive drugs can lead to predatory crimes such as robberies and burglaries.
3. The *systemic* nature of the drug trade can lead to violence among those involved in the sale and use of drugs.

The psychopharmacological effects of some drugs increase the likelihood that a user will become an offender or a victim. Marijuana and heroin typically reduce aggression, but heroin can increase irritability, and perhaps violence, during withdrawal. Cocaine does not necessarily make users more violent, but it can do so in some circumstances. Smoking crack cocaine quickly produces intense euphoric effects but results in dysphoria shortly thereafter, leading to "missions" to get the money to pay for additional hits. Crack can also lead to paranoia and flawed judgment, generating arguments and assaults. Less frequently used drugs such as amphetamines and PCP have psychopharmacological effects that can increase violent behavior.

The economic-compulsive explanation of the drugs–crime connection assumes that people who use expensive drugs need more money than they can raise from legitimate sources. Users earn money by selling drugs, carrying drugs from one place to another for dealers, steering buyers to dealers, or performing other tasks associated with the distribution of drugs. Some users, especially heavy consumers of expensive drugs, rely on income-producing property crimes such as robbery. However, because criminal behavior starts before drug use about as often as drug use precedes criminal behavior, and because variations over the life course in drug use are not strongly associated with changes in criminal activity, the causal significance of the economic-compulsive need for money to pay for drugs is questionable (Chaiken and Chaiken, 1990; Menard, Mihalic, and Huizinga, 2001).

Systemic factors associated with the drug subculture are conducive to crime. Violence is useful in marketing drugs, because dealers lack recourse to the legal means to enforce their agreements, encounter intense competition from one another, and need to impose discipline on lower-level dealers. Violence also occurs in robberies of drug dealers and in disputes with customers over the price and quality of drugs. To gain an edge in the dangerous drug market, participants often arm themselves with powerful firearms, a situation conducive to assaults, robberies, and homicides (Johnson, Golub, and Fagan, 1995; Grogger, 2000; Ousey and Lee, 2002).

In addition to the ways that drug use can generate criminal behavior, criminal behavior can also lead to drug use. Offenders who plan to commit crimes sometimes use drugs to deal with the stress of violating the law, confronting a victim, and evading the police. Robbers, burglars, and other thieves often spend the proceeds of their crimes on illegal drugs (Shover, 1996).

Firearms and Crime

In 1996, 68 percent of murders in the United States were committed with firearms, four-fifths of them handguns. In contrast, only 7 percent of murders in England and Wales in 1996 were committed with firearms, and the per capita homicide rate there was only one-sixth that of the United States (Langan and Farrington, 1998). (See Figure 9.2.) A cross-cultural examination of lethal violence concluded as follows:

> Current evidence suggests that a combination of the ready availability of guns and the willingness to use maximum force in interpersonal conflict is the most important single contribution to the high U.S. death rate from violence. Our rate of assault is not exceptional; our death rate from assault is exceptional. (Zimring and Hawkins, 1997: 122–123)

With about 250 million firearms, a third of them handguns, in private hands in the United States, and two-fifths of all homes containing at least one firearm, there is a good chance that one will be present at the scene of a bitter argument or a fight. If a firearm is used during an altercation, murder is a likely result. Assaults with a firearm are much more likely to result in death than assaults with a knife or without a weapon. According to one study, firearm assaults are fatal about 13 percent of the time, knife attacks are fatal about 3 percent of the time, and attacks with hands, fists, and feet are fatal only 1.7 percent of the time (Morris and Hawkins, 1970). Other research finds that firearm assaults lead to death two to five times as often as attacks with knives (Wright, Rossi, and Daly, 1983). Because guns are the most deadly weapon, their easy availability is associated with higher homicide rates (Cook, 1983; Sloan et al., 1988).

Firearms are also used in rapes, aggravated assaults, burglaries, and robberies. In 1996, 40 percent of robberies in the United States were committed with firearms, compared to only 5 percent of all robberies being committed with firearms in England and Wales (Langan and Farrington, 1998). (See Figure 9.3.) Instead of using firearms to demonstrate their toughness and masculinity, robbers employ guns for instrumental purposes—to acquire money more easily and with less resistance, to pro-

---

FIGURE 9.2 Types of Weapons Used in Murders, 2001

Source: Based on data from Federal Bureau of Investigation, *Crime in the United States, 2001: Uniform Crime Reports.* Washington, DC: U.S. Government Printing Office, 2002, p. 23.

FIGURE 9.3   Types of Weapons
Used in Robberies, 2001

Source: Based on data from Federal Bureau of Investigation, *Crime in the United States, 2001: Uniform Crime Reports.* Washington, DC: U.S. Government Printing Office, 2002, p. 35.

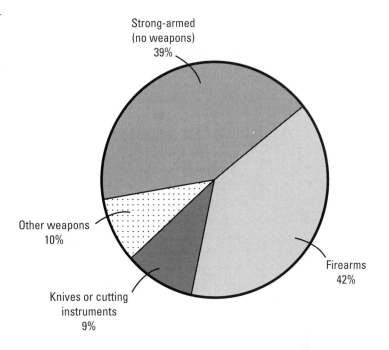

Strong-armed
(no weapons)
39%

Other weapons
10%

Firearms
42%

Knives or cutting
instruments
9%

tect themselves from armed victims, and to ensure a safe escape from the scene of the crime (Sheley and Wright, 1995; Desroches, 1995). Paradoxically, the use of firearms by robbers might prevent violence, because victims are less likely to resist offenders who carry guns (Conklin, 1972; Block, 1977). When a victim does resist, the robber often increases the level of intimidation by cocking the pistol, holding it to the victim's head, or using it as a blunt instrument to hit the victim. Sometimes, of course, a firearm is used to shoot a victim, and then the robbery produces serious injury or death. Victims who resist armed robbers are about three times as likely to be injured seriously as victims who do not resist (Block, 1977, 1981).

Firearm violence by young people remained about the same between 1976 and 1984, but it increased dramatically from 1984 to 1993, before dropping from 1993 to 1997. From 1985 to 1993, firearm homicides by ten to seventeen year olds tripled while nongun homicides by this age group showed no change (Snyder, Sickmund, and Poe-Yamagata, 1996; Fox and Zawitz, 1999). Jeffrey Fagan and Deanna Wilkinson (1998) have attributed the high level of firearm usage by young people to an "ecology of danger," which includes street gangs, expanding drug markets, high rates of adult violence, and norms that call for carrying and using firearms in order to survive and earn respect. Alfred Blumstein (1995) has attributed the increase in firearm violence by young people after 1984 to the growth of the market in crack cocaine, arguing that juveniles were recruited to make that growth possible and were provided with guns to protect themselves in the dangerous drug trade. Gun ownership then diffused to young people who were not involved in the drug trade, both for self-protection and for status enhancement, with the increased number of guns in the hands of young people leading to higher levels of violent crime. Gary Kleck (1997: 73–74) has rejected Blumstein's argument, asserting that there is "no empirical basis for believing that increases in gun possession or a 'diffusion' of guns into the larger community of inner-city youth was responsible for the gun homicide increases in the 1985–1991 period."

A 1991 survey found that 86 percent of a sample of male inmates of juvenile correctional facilities and 30 percent of a sample of male inner-city high school students had owned a gun at some time. The inmates and students rarely bought guns from retail outlets, but instead got them through purchase or trade from friends, family members, or street sources such as thieves and addicts. They preferred sophisticated firearms to small, cheap ones, saying that the characteristics they wanted in a gun were firepower, quality construction, difficulty in tracing the weapon, ease of shooting, and accuracy. Guns of this sort were readily available, usually for $100 or less. Those most likely to own firearms were drug dealers (not those who simply used drugs) and gang members, especially those who belonged to highly structured gangs. These drug dealers and gang members lived in a dangerous world in which they were visible to and threatened by others, so they saw firearms as necessary for survival. Those who committed the greatest number of crimes and the most serious ones usually carried firearms most of the time, not just when they were planning to commit crimes (Sheley and Wright, 1995; see also Wright and Rossi, 1986).

Explaining the Firearms–Crime Relationship   The easy availability of firearms facilitates crime in several ways. Access to a gun can make the difference between wanting to hurt someone and actually committing a violent crime. The presence of a weapon during an argument can escalate the level of violence, producing a murder when an assault would have occurred if no firearm had been present. Firearms give some robbers and rapists the courage to commit crimes that they would otherwise have avoided. Tight restrictions on the ownership of firearms in Japan have been cited as one reason for that society's low rate of violent crime. On the other hand, Switzerland has widespread private ownership of firearms but no tradition of using guns to settle interpersonal disputes, and it has a low rate of criminal violence (Clinard, 1978). One assessment of research on the relationship between firearms and crime concluded that there was "little or no conclusive evidence to show that gun ownership among the larger population is, per se, an important cause of criminal violence" (Wright, Rossi, and Daly, 1983: 137).

Firearms might even deter potential offenders from crime. For example, a robber might think twice about holding up a store in which the owner had shot another thief the week before. Overall, however, there is little evidence that citizen ownership of firearms directly deters crime (Green, 1987; McDowall, Lizotte, and Wiersema, 1991). Gun ownership might have an indirect effect on crime by making people feel more secure and affecting their behavior in ways that keep crime rates low, for instance, by encouraging a storekeeper who feels safer to stay open at night, thereby providing informal control over nearby sidewalks and streets. On the other hand, firearms that people keep for self-protection are often stolen by burglars, who use them for illegal purposes or sell them to other criminals (Wright, Rossi, and Daly, 1983; Wright and Rossi, 1986; Sheley and Wright, 1995).

Assuming that more guns in the hands of citizens will reduce crime, the majority of states now have laws that require law-enforcement agencies to issue permits to carry handguns to qualified citizens, which usually means anyone who does not have a criminal record or a history of mental illness. However, these laws have apparently had little effect on the prevalence of carrying firearms, and their impact on crime rates is uncertain (Ludwig, 2000). Lott and Mustard's (1997) analysis of counties with and without permissive concealed-carry laws concluded that those laws had reduced homicides, rapes, and aggravated assaults by 5 to 8 percent but had increased property crimes by 3 percent. Kleck (1997) doubts that the decline in violent crime uncovered by Lott and Mustard was due to any deterrent effect of what was probably only a small increase in the legal carrying of firearms, believing that the decline in violent crime simply coincided with the implementation of concealed-carry laws. Controlling for variables ignored by Lott and Mustard, Black and Nagin (1998) found that the only meaningful impact of concealed-carry laws was an increase in assault rates. A similar study by Ludwig (1998) discovered a small but statistically insignificant tendency for concealed-carry laws to increase rates of adult homicide victimization. Ludwig (2000: 410) concluded that "concealed-carry laws are as likely to cause crime to increase as to decrease, though this evidence is far from definitive."

How often do gun owners use their weapons against criminals? Victimization survey data indicate that victims use firearms to defend themselves against robberies, assaults, and burglaries about 80,000 times each year (Cook, 1991). A 1993 national survey concluded that defensive gun use was much more prevalent, estimating that civilians use firearms to protect themselves against crime 2.1 to 2.5 million times each year; the crime being defended against is usually a burglary, an assault, or a robbery (Kleck and Gertz, 1995). A methodological critique of both of Kleck and Gertz's study and the victimization survey estimated that the actual number of defensive gun uses each year is between 256,500 and 1,210,000 and called for further research to provide a more precise count (Smith, 1997). More information is also needed on the specific circumstances of defensive gun uses; one study found that some of these situations actually involve offensive behavior by people with criminal histories (Wells, 2002).

Crime and firearms might also be related in another way. Crime generates fear, which can lead people to arm themselves. Gary Kleck (1997: 75) concludes from surveys of why people own firearms that "most owners of guns in general, and long guns in particular, own them primarily for recreational reasons unrelated to crime, but about half of handgun owners, and some long gun owners as well, own guns mainly for protection." Victimization experiences and fear of crime are not strongly linked to firearm ownership, but a low level of citizen confidence in the ability of the criminal justice system to control crime is associated with more gun ownership (Young, McDowall, and Loftin, 1987). The people who are most likely to own firearms for protection are male, were socialized into a gun culture when young, hold punitive attitudes toward criminals, believe their neighborhood has a relatively high level of crime, and do not believe that their neighbors will protect them against criminals (Cao, Cullen, and Link, 1997).

Firearms owned for protection against criminals are often used to inflict injury on innocent people. One study found that when the sex, age, and race of household members, their use of illicit drugs, and their history of domestic violence were taken into account, having a firearm in the home nearly tripled the chance that someone living there would be murdered. Half of the victims were killed following a dispute that involved a romantic triangle or some other type of altercation or quarrel; and three-fourths of them were killed by a relative or someone they knew (Kellermann et al., 1993).

Gun Control and Crime Rates   Most laws aimed at controlling the criminal use of firearms take one of two forms: Either they are designed to prevent people with criminal records or criminal tendencies from acquiring guns, or they try to deter offenders from using firearms by requiring additional penalties for crimes committed with guns (Wright and Rossi, 1986). More radical solutions, such as the confiscation and destruction of all handguns, or a constitutional amendment explicitly limiting the right to bear arms, have not been publicly debated.

There is mixed evidence as to whether crime can be reduced by controlling access to firearms. One study that compared five states with strong gun-control laws to five states with weak laws found that the states with the strong laws had lower homicide rates. In those states, a smaller proportion of the homicides that did occur were committed with firearms (Criminal Division, U.S. Department of Justice, 1968). Although this study suggests that strong gun-control laws might reduce the homicide rate, the results can also be interpreted to mean that the states that were able to pass strong gun-control legislation were the states in which people were more opposed to the use of firearms to begin with or were the states in which firearms were relatively unimportant to residents. Thus, both the low murder rate and the gun-control law could have been products of a nonviolent, anti-weapons attitude on the part of the state's residents. That attitude, rather than the law itself, might account for a low homicide rate.

One type of law aims to control the possession and use of firearms by the general public. For example, the Bartley-Fox law, implemented in Massachusetts in 1975, required a one-year jail sentence for anyone carrying an unlicensed firearm. The law had some effect in reducing homicides and robberies with firearms but researchers concluded that it was the publicity about the intent of the law, rather than the severity or certainty of the sanctions that were actually imposed, that produced this reduction in firearm crimes (Pierce and Bowers, 1981).

A strategy tried by some states, including Michigan and Florida, requires judges to impose an additional prison term on offenders convicted of a serious crime in which they used a firearm. A study in Detroit found that crime rates declined after implementation of a two-year mandatory additional penalty for the use of a firearm in a serious crime, but it concluded that the decline did not seem to be attributable to the new law. The decline began before the law was implemented, and unarmed violent crime as well as crime with firearms showed a decrease. The law's lack of impact was attributed to the fact that "offenders were not responsive to a mandatory two-year increment in sanctions for offenses which already carry maximum sentences much greater than two years" (Loftin, Heumann, and McDowall, 1983: 310). Thus, the law did not increase the perceived certainty or perceived severity of punishment in a significant way. The law would have affected rates of murder, robbery, and assault only if offenders who used weapons in those crimes placed relatively little value on the use of weapons, and this apparently was not the case. The fact that Detroit's population was heavily armed when the law was passed probably meant that offenders placed great value on being armed because of the high probability that they would encounter armed resistance from their victims (Loftin and McDowall, 1981; Loftin, Heumann, and McDowall, 1983).

Research has not demonstrated that gun-control laws requiring mandatory jail sentences for anyone carrying an unlicensed weapon or for anyone using a firearm in a serious crime have long-term effects on the use of firearms in crime. Sometimes "mandatory" penalties are not imposed. Either the police do not arrest everyone who carries an illegal firearm, or judges fail to impose the required sentence. Even if the criminal justice system imposed the mandatory penalty, it is not clear that felons would give up their firearms.

An experiment carried out in Kansas City, Missouri, offers evidence that aggressive police patrols aimed at taking guns away from people who illegally possess them can reduce crime. A special patrol specifically looked for opportunities to conduct legal searches of cars or pedestrians for firearms; opportunities included curfew violations and traffic stops for driving a stolen car, using high-beam lights, or running a stop sign. This directed patrol, which concentrated on "hot spots" where many gun-related crimes had been reported, increased the number of gun seizures in the target area by 65 percent, while crimes committed with firearms there dropped by 49 percent. Neither gun seizures nor gun crimes changed much in a comparison area a few miles away where there was no patrol aimed at seizing firearms, and there was no apparent displacement of gun crimes from the area with the directed patrol to neighboring areas. Both homicides and drive-by shootings were significantly reduced in the target area but did not decline in the comparison area (Sherman and Rogan, 1995; Sherman, Shaw, and Rogan, 1995). Research done in Indianapolis also found gun patrols to be effective: Homicides in a target area fell from eleven a year earlier to one during the experimental phase, even though homicides increased by 53 percent in the city as a whole over that time (McGarrell, Chermak, and Weiss, 1999; McGarrell et al., 2001).

Implemented in 1994, the federal Brady Handgun Violence Prevention Act was designed to prevent felons from purchasing handguns from federally licensed dealers by mandating a five-day waiting period between initiation of a purchase and delivery of the weapon. From 1994 through 2001, 840,000 applications for firearm transfers were rejected; this number represented 2.2 percent of all applications filed (Bowling et al., September 2002). Gun-control advocates cite these figures as evidence that the Brady Act has prevented hundreds of thousands of potential offenders from acquiring guns, but others argue that people who cannot buy guns legitimately have little difficulty getting them from illicit sources.

The Debate over Gun Control   Despite the uncertain effects of gun-control laws, most Americans support stronger laws than we now have. A May 2000 Gallup Poll found that 62 percent of Americans wanted stricter laws covering the sale of firearms, 31 percent thought the laws should remain the same, only 5 percent thought they should be made less strict, and 2 percent had no opinion (Polling the Nations, 2000).

Gun-control laws in the United States are relatively weak not because of lack of public support, but because of the power of the National Rifle Association (NRA), which a 1999 *Fortune* magazine survey ranked second in political clout among all lobbying groups in the country, trailing only the American Association of Retired Persons (Milligan, 2000). This well-financed organization of 3.8 million members can mobilize its supporters to write to members of Congress to oppose any gun-control legislation that is being considered. Many NRA members are "single-issue" voters who will vote against candidates who favor tougher gun-control laws. Because most voters who support tougher gun-control laws will not vote for or against candidates solely because of their stand on gun control, NRA members pose a more significant threat of lost votes to candidates, and thus many politicians vote against gun control out of fear of alienating the opponents of stronger gun-control laws.

Several lobbyist groups—such as the Center to Prevent Handgun Violence and the Violence Policy Center—now fight for stronger gun-control laws. However, these organizations are hampered by lack of funds, small memberships, and well-organized opposition from the NRA and the firearms industry. The efforts of these gun-control advocates have been strengthened by support from several police organizations.

The debate over gun control continues. Three-fourths of Americans think they have a constitutional right to own firearms, even though the U.S. Supreme Court has denied the existence of any such individual right since 1939. The Second Amendment prefaces the phrase, "the right of the people to keep and bear arms, shall not be infringed" with the rationale for that right: "A well-regulated militia, being necessary to the security of a free state . . . " The handguns involved in murders and robberies are not designed for military or collective use, nor do their owners buy them for that purpose. Since the late 1990s, however, some legal scholars and judges have argued that the intent of the Second Amendment may well have been to guarantee individuals the right to keep and bear arms. U.S. Attorney General John Ashcroft supported this position in a letter to the NRA in 2001 and reiterated it the following year in a Justice Department brief to the U.S. Supreme Court. He also took a stance against gun control when he denied access to Justice Department records by the FBI in its effort to determine if anyone detained following the September 11th terrorist attack had recently bought a firearm.

Another argument against more gun control is that the criminal justice system cannot keep firearms out of the hands of potential offenders, and even if it could, this might not produce any net reduction in violent crime. In one survey, four-fifths of imprisoned felons thought they could get a firearm within a few days of being released from prison, even though the law prohibits convicted felons from acquiring firearms. That study also found that if cheap handguns were banned, the most serious felons would get a bigger gun or use a sawn-off shotgun rather than not carry a firearm (Wright and Rossi, 1986). Consequently, Gary Kleck (1997) recommends that lawmakers should never place restrictions on less deadly weapons, such as cheap handguns, without also restricting access to more deadly weapons, such as assault rifles. Such measures only encourage offenders to substitute more powerful firearms for less deadly ones.

Evaluating the research on the effectiveness of gun-control laws, Kleck (1997: 377) found that most studies were poorly done and that the better the research was on technical grounds, the more likely it was to show that "most types of gun control have no measurable net effect, for good or ill, on rates of most types of crime and violence." However, he points out the following important exceptions to that generalization, offering hope that legal measures might reduce firearm crimes:

1. Licensing and permit laws, i.e., measures with background checks, appear to reduce rates of homicide and perhaps suicide.
2. Bans on gun possession by criminals may reduce robbery and aggravated assault.
3. Bans on possession by mentally ill persons appear to reduce homicide and perhaps suicide.
4. Local licensing of gun dealers may reduce robbery, aggravated assault, and suicide.
5. Mandatory penalties for unlicensed gun carrying may reduce robbery.
6. Discretionary add-on penalties for committing crime with a gun may reduce homicide, robbery, and rape. (Kleck, 1997: 377)

Beginning in 1998, cities such as Chicago, New Orleans, and Los Angeles brought lawsuits against gun manufacturers, distributors, and shops for producing and marketing an unsafe product and violating public nuisance laws by making firearms available to criminals, thereby imposing excess costs on the cities' law-enforcement agencies, fire departments, and public hospitals. Plaintiffs argued that manufacturers had produced more firearms than legitimate buyers could purchase, and thus knowingly or recklessly made weapons available to criminals. The city of Chicago claimed that these excess firearms flowed from gun shops in the suburbs into the hands of criminals in the city. States with strict gun-control laws argued that excess weapons available in states with weak gun-control laws—especially Florida, Georgia, South Carolina, and Texas—were purchased and shipped to their states, where they ended up in the hands of offenders. The goal of these lawsuits was to reduce the number of guns available to criminals by imposing financial costs on those who manufacture and distribute firearms. So far, plaintiffs have been thwarted by court dismissals and by state legislation granting gun manufacturers immunity from lawsuits.

Summary

This chapter has looked at the way offenders seek suitable targets that are not protected by owners or bystanders. Opportunities for crime are a function of people's everyday behavior, according to routine activities theory.

Criminals consider various aspects of potential targets for crime: the form and value of property, and the vulnerability of victims. Some victims are more prone to victimization than others because they have characteristics or play roles that make them especially vulnerable.

Sometimes a victim precipitates an offense, contributing to his or her own victimization. Homicide victims are often the first to use abusive language or force in an interaction that culminates in murder. Rape victims sometimes enter risky situations, though this does not absolve rapists of legal responsibility for their crimes. Owners of property precipitate crimes by leaving their property unguarded and vulnerable to theft.

Alcohol and drugs sometimes facilitate crime. There is an association between alcohol use and crime, with many offenders being under the influence of alcohol when they violate the law. Similarly, many offenders are under the influence of illegal drugs when they engage in crime. More research is needed to determine the precise manner in which drugs and alcohol are associated with the commission of crime.

In the United States, many offenses are committed with firearms. Guns facilitate crimes such as murder and robbery. Assaults with firearms are more likely to produce death than are attacks with other weapons, so the presence of a firearm makes murder a more likely outcome of an altercation. However, some countries, such as Switzerland, have relatively low crime rates despite widespread ownership of firearms. There is little persuasive evidence that gun-control laws can significantly reduce crime. Mandatory penalties are often not applied, and additional penalties for the use of a firearm in a serious crime do not seem to deter most offenders. The debate over gun control continues, with a majority of Americans favoring stronger laws.

IMPORTANT TERMS

facilitating factors

lifestyle theory

routine activities theory

victim precipitation

victim proneness

REVIEW QUESTIONS

1. What is routine activities theory? What aspects of criminal behavior does it try to explain? What research supports routine activities theory? What modifications to the approach are needed to fit the findings of researchers?

2. How do the form and value of property and the characteristics of victims influence the ways that property offenders select their targets?

3. What is victim precipitation? How does this concept help us to understand violent crime and property crime?

4. What are the three facilitating factors examined in this chapter? How would you explain the association between crime and each of the facilitating factors?

5. What does research tell us about the effectiveness of gun-control legislation in preventing crime? What kind of a gun-control law might reduce violent crime?

FOR FURTHER STUDY

Routine Activities Theory   Three books that look at the relationship between criminal behavior and patterns of daily activity are Terance D. Miethe and Robert F. Meier's *Crime and Its Social Context: Toward an Integrated Theory of Offenders, Victims, and Situations* (Albany: State University of New York Press, 1994), Marcus Felson's *Crime and Everyday Life* (3rd ed., Thousand Oaks, CA: Pine Forge Press, 2002), and Vincent F. Sacco and Leslie W. Kennedy's *The Criminal Event: Perspectives in Space and Time* (2nd ed., Belmont, CA: Wadsworth, 2002).

Alcohol and Crime   The National Institute on Alcohol Abuse and Alcoholism's website (www.collegedrinking prevention.gov) provides links to research on campus drinking and its relationship to criminal behavior.

Drugs and Crime   Information on drugs and crime is available on the websites of the National Criminal Justice Reference Service (http://virlib.ncjrs.org/DrugsAnd Crime.asp) and the Bureau of Justice Statistics (www. ojp.usdoj.gov/bjs/drugs.htm). International issues are dealt with on the United Nations Office of Drug Prevention and Crime Control's website (www.undcp. org).

Firearms and Crime   Gary Kleck's *Targeting Guns: Firearms and Their Control* (New York: Aldine de Gruyter, 1997) is a comprehensive study of the relationship between guns and crime. The pro–gun-control position is presented on a website sponsored by the Center to Prevent Handgun Violence and the Violence Policy Center (www.cphv.org). The anti–gun-control position is presented on the NRA's website (www.nra.org).

10 Criminal Careers

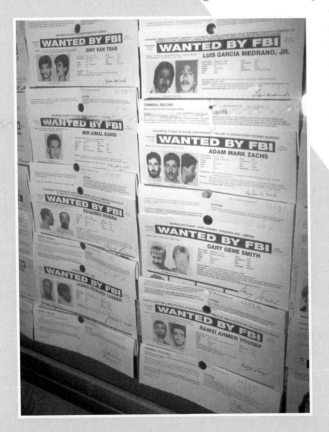

A career is a "sequence of movements from one position to another in an occupational system made by an individual who works in the system" (Becker, 1973: 24). A **criminal career** is not an "occupation" as we commonly understand that term, but a sequence of crimes over time can be analyzed much like a career in a legitimate occupation, for both involve skills, tasks, and commitment. As long ago as 1893 it was recognized that "correct statistics of offenders can be developed only by a study of the total life histories of individuals" (Otto Kobner, cited in Petersilia, Greenwood, and Lavin, 1977: 2–3).

Even though criminal careers are similar to legitimate careers in some ways, there are also important differences between them. Legitimate careers develop within stable contexts, such as a corporation or a law firm. Criminal careers usually develop in less formal contexts. For instance, robbers' and burglars' careers develop outside stable organizational settings. In addition, criminal careers often lack the well-defined sequence of stages and the pattern of upward mobility that frequently characterize legitimate careers. Although some legitimate workers do not experience these changes during their careers, and some offenders do gain in status over their lifetimes, there is probably less upward mobility in deviant careers than in legitimate ones. Careers in crime are less structured and perhaps more dependent on individual initiative in seeking out rewards than are legitimate careers. Moreover, criminal careers develop in secrecy from established authorities, whereas legitimate occupations have the support of social institutions (Luckenbill and Best, 1981).

Criminal careers can be studied by examining the autobiographies of individual offenders. These accounts reveal much about the subjective states and actual experiences of certain offenders, but they might not be representative of all criminals. Another approach is to develop conceptual typologies, or categorizations, of criminal careers. Arrest statistics have also been used to study the careers of offenders, but because relatively few crimes lead to arrest, the data might tell us more about contacts with the criminal justice system than about actual involvement in criminal behavior.

Knowledge of criminal careers has practical value. Understanding why offenders get involved in a life of crime can lead to policies that prevent criminal careers from developing. Knowing why career offenders "retire" from crime can generate programs that hasten their departure from crime. The fact that relatively few career criminals account for a large proportion of all of the crime that occurs suggests that the punishment and treatment of career offenders might have a significant impact on the crime rate.

Theoretical Perspectives on Criminal Careers

Criminologists disagree about the importance of studying criminal careers. Those who support such research argue that different factors might explain why people start to commit crime, why they persist in crime, and why they stop committing crime. For instance, lack of a legitimate job might push a person into crime, but access to such a job later in a criminal career might not lead that person out of crime (Blumstein et al., 1986; Blumstein, Cohen, and Farrington, 1988). The opposing position is that research on criminal careers is of little value, because the tendency to engage in crime changes predictably over the life cycle, and thus criminal behavior at one time correlates strongly with criminal behavior at another time. Proponents of this position point to evidence that offenders neither specialize in crime nor commit increasingly serious crimes as they grow older (Gottfredson and Hirschi, 1990). In response, those who support criminal career research argue that some offenders do have long-term careers in crime, and that offenders differ among themselves and over time in the frequency with which they engage in crime.

Some researchers have employed a **temporal boundary conception of the criminal career**, looking at the age at which criminal activity begins, the length of time over which it occurs, the kinds of crime an individual commits, and the age at which criminal activity ceases. Age of onset is the year at which criminal activity begins, and age of termination is the year at which it ceases. The length of time between age of onset and age of termination is the duration of the career. Persistence is the continual engagement in criminal activity throughout a career, and desistance is the causal process leading to the termination of criminal activity, with crime switching—the change from one type of crime to another—often characterizing a career (LeBlanc and Loeber, 1998; Laub and Sampson, 2001).

In contrast to the temporal boundary conception of the criminal career is the dynamic conception of **developmental criminology**, which studies changes in offending within individuals over time. Developmental criminology acknowledges both continuity and change over time, explaining patterns of offending in terms of the life transitions experienced by individuals and the developmental processes of activation, aggravation, and desistance. Activation is the process through which criminal activities are initiated and stimulated, and through which offending increases over time in frequency (acceleration), continuity (stabilization), and variety (diversification). The second process, aggravation, involves a sequence in which offending behavior escalates or increases in seriousness. The third process, desistance, or the cessation of offending behavior in part or altogether, is characterized by reductions in the rate of offending (deceleration), the diversity of offending behavior (specialization), or the seriousness of offenses (de-escalation). Movements along these developmental sequences are called trajectories or pathways (LeBlanc and Loeber, 1998).

Researchers have tried to determine whether crime is better explained by this developmental theory, which proposes that different factors give rise to delinquency and crime at various stages in the life cycle, or by a **criminal propensity theory**, which claims that crime is a result of causal traits such as self-control that remain relatively constant over the life course. One study that supported the developmental model found that low verbal ability, hyperactivity, and negative/impulsive personality were more strongly related to antisocial behavior by children than they were to the same behavior by adolescents; adolescent antisocial behavior was more strongly associated than childhood antisocial behavior with peer delinquency. In addition, childhood antisocial behavior was strongly predictive of later convictions for violent crime, whereas adolescent antisocial behavior was more strongly associated with later convictions for nonviolent offenses (Bartusch et al., 1997). Another study that supported the developmental theory concluded that processes such as improved parenting, increased commitment to school, and reduced association with delinquent peers lowered the chance that boys who were oppositional during childhood would engage in delinquency and drug use during adolescence (Simons et al., 1998). These and other studies suggest that developmental processes explain changes in offending behavior over time better than antisocial traits such as low self-control do.

Analyzing Criminal Careers

An analysis of criminal careers requires attention to the social conditions that influence the development of recurrent criminal activity. Labeling by the criminal justice system can affect an individual's life chances and make criminal behavior more likely. Criminal careers can be understood in terms of an individual's alternation between legitimate work and criminal activities. Attention must also be paid to the way that people are recruited into criminal careers, especially the way that involvement in juvenile delinquency is linked to adult criminal careers.

Career Contingencies

Criminal careers depend on various **contingencies,** or factors that determine movement from one criminal role to another, or from one crime to another (Becker, 1973). For instance, organized and professional crime primarily involves males, even though sex segregation in the underworld varies from one crime group to another. Women are at a disadvantage in being recruited into crime groups, in the criminal career paths available to them, and in their access to opportunities for learning criminal skills and gaining the rewards of crime. Gender-role socialization and patterns of parental surveillance of boys and girls also limit females' access to certain criminal careers (Hoffman-Bustamante, 1973; Steffensmeier, 1983). Women who do commit crime seem to be more likely to stop offending and remain crime-free for longer than men in similar situations, but why that is the case is not yet clear (Uggen and Kruttschnitt, 1998).

One career contingency is apprehension for violating the law. People who break the law, are arrested by the police, and are convicted in court might later engage in crime because of the social contacts they make while incarcerated. Experience with the criminal justice system can also contribute to a criminal career by causing bitterness or by closing off job opportunities. However, offenders might commit even more crimes if they were not arrested and convicted, because successful crimes could reinforce their law-violating behavior by providing them with rewards.

Being arrested is a career contingency that can increase social interaction with other criminals, embitter offenders, and close off job opportunities.

Short-run rewards of peer prestige and money can create a "mobility trap" for juvenile delinquents, who gain immediate prestige and property at the cost of long-term upward mobility if they are expelled from school, are socially stigmatized, or become known to the police as offenders (Wiley, 1967). Evidence of this mobility trap comes from a study of Puerto Rican youths in Chicago (Padilla, 1992). Seeing no future for themselves in school or the kinds of jobs an education would lead to, they turned to gangs as an alternative source of income. Over time, car theft and drug dealing did not prove rewarding but instead limited the youths' access to conventional jobs.

A study of month-to-month variations in the self-reported criminal activity of convicted felons identified several "local life circumstances," or contingencies, that were associated with offending. During the months that the felons were using illegal drugs, their chances of committing a crime increased sixfold. Heavy consumption of alcoholic beverages also increased offending, especially property crimes. Living with a wife reduced criminal behavior, but living with a girlfriend was associated with higher levels of crime. Attending school significantly reduced involvement in crime. Working was weakly related to offending, decreasing assaults but unexpectedly increasing property crimes. These findings indicate that "local life circumstances can change criminal careers by modifying the likelihood of offending *at particular times*" (Horney, Osgood, and Marshall, 1995: 670; emphasis in original).

The Labeling Perspective

The labeling perspective focuses on the development of deviant careers, including careers in crime. People who break rules repeatedly and are labeled deviant by others sometimes organize their lives around deviant behavior. What begins as casual experimentation with rule breaking becomes a deviant career, or "a whole sequential process in identity formation" (Rettig, Torres, and Garrett, 1977: 192). For example, negative labeling by parents and peers increases the chance that delinquents will continue in a delinquent career, apparently by affecting their perceptions of how other people see them (Matsueda, 1992; Smith and Brame, 1994).

Most people who break the law repeatedly are eventually arrested and convicted. As criminals say, "If you want to play, you have to pay," or "If you can't do the time, don't do the crime." Earlier in the book we saw that the chance of avoiding arrest for any given crime is good, but the chance of never being arrested if one commits many crimes is small. Offenders who are more skilled might go longer without an arrest, but eventually they "take a fall."

Because the legal system deals more harshly with some people than with others, it acts as a contingency that influences the development of delinquent and criminal careers. For instance, the police react to suspects on the basis of the seriousness of the offense, the individual's demeanor, the complainant's preferences, and the requirements of the police department (Piliavin and Briar, 1964; Black, 1980). The arrest, conviction, and imprisonment of an individual might be more likely if he or she is seen as a member of a criminal subculture who is likely to continue to commit serious crimes, rather than perceived as someone who violated the law because of poor judgment or situational pressures (Cloward and Ohlin, 1960). Reactions to defendants by the criminal justice system might be based on valid assumptions about the likelihood that different kinds of people will continue in a life of crime, but these reactions also elicit patterned and persistent behavior. In other words, the label "criminal" can structure other people's responses to the offender; some people, for example, will refuse to hire an ex-convict. Responses of this sort then act as contingencies that influence the development of a criminal career (Sampson and Laub, 1993; Bushway, 1998).

The "Zigzag Path": Criminal Careers and Legitimate Pursuits

Criminal careers vary considerably. One study of thieves found that most followed a "zigzag path" back and forth between criminal and noncriminal pursuits (Glaser, 1974). Offenders would commit crimes, go to prison, try to get a job when released, and often return to crime later. Contacts with other criminals and the difficulty of finding a good job often made a return to crime the "path of least resistance" (Rettig, Torres, and Garrett, 1977: 4). The effects of situational factors such as peer influence and financial need were mediated in part by the ex-convict's commitment to a criminal career or commitment to a legitimate career, but tempting situations sometimes drew even those who were committed to a conventional way of life back into crime. People who are committed to a conventional way of life do engage in less crime than people who are committed to a criminal career, even if they do not stay away from crime altogether (McAuliffe and Gordon, 1974).

Success at crime can lead to continued criminal activities, and success in legitimate pursuits can lead to a continuation of those activities. Once people have engaged in crime and escaped arrest, they might think that the risk of negative consequences from crime is small and the rewards are great. Even if they are caught the first time, they may receive only a "slap on the wrist" in court and believe the chance of a harsh sanction is small. Serious failure in either criminal activities or legitimate pursuits can lead people to shift to the other form of behavior. Thus, losing a job might push a person into crime, and being arrested might lead someone else to look for a legitimate job.

During the course of his career as a physician in Manchester, England, Harold Shipman murdered at least 215 of his patients, many of them elderly women. He was convicted of fifteen of those murders in January 2000.

Recruitment into a Criminal Career

Recruitment into a criminal career often begins during adolescence, with early delinquency frequently being a prerequisite for an adult career in theft and violence. While still in their teens, future career offenders learn criminal skills and motives, what a criminal way of life involves, and how the police react to different crimes. Access to criminal careers seems to be greater in communities where there are close ties between adolescents and adult criminals who act as role models and communicate to the adolescents the values and skills necessary to commit crime. Access to criminal careers is also greater where there are stable relationships between people with conventional values and people with criminal values (Cloward and Ohlin, 1960). In such communities, a delinquent subculture is more likely to develop, and involvement in this subculture increases the likelihood of entry into an adult criminal career.

Adult offenders must also learn criminal skills and motives. For example, to move from various forms of hustling into a specialty as a professional fence, one career criminal had to acquire considerable knowledge about merchandise, including what he should pay for it and how much he could sell it for. This fence also needed "ability, energy, ingenuity, and certain persuasive skills," as well as a willingness to deceive both the buying public and the thieves who sold to him (Klockars, 1974: 177). To become a buyer of stolen goods required a modest amount of capital, the skill to purchase goods, the opportunity to buy goods for less than their retail price, a regular source of supply, a predictable demand for goods, and the ability to avoid arrest and imprisonment. The fence also needed a convincing front that would keep the police away but still attract customers looking for low prices.

Career criminals are recruited from various settings. Sutherland (1937) found that professional thieves had rarely been amateur thieves in slum areas but instead came from legitimate occupations and severed their ties to the legitimate world after a period of unemployment. They spent time in bars and hotels where professional thieves gathered. Bartenders, taxi drivers, bellhops, and waiters who worked in the social world of the professional thief sometimes entered a life of crime by taking tangential roles in the commission of crime (Inciardi, 1975). Often they began by playing a small part in one crime and were called on later for more important roles in other offenses, gradually acquiring the skills and status of a professional thief. Others became career criminals by applying specific job skills to crime; for example, a printer might become a counterfeiter, or a locksmith might become a safecracker.

Typologies of Criminal Careers

One way to analyze criminal careers is to construct a **typology**—or set of categories—of offenders and their patterns of criminal activity. Such a typology is developed from criteria that a criminologist thinks are important in distinguishing one criminal career from another. This kind of typology assumes there is some specialization among offenders in the sorts of crime they commit.

One typology of "criminal role careers" was derived from information about the offense itself, the interactional setting of the behavior (alone or with others), the offender's self-concept and attitudes, and the pattern of crime over the offender's lifetime (Gibbons, 1992). Also taken into account were an offender's class and family background, peer-group associations, and contacts with law-enforcement agencies. The criminal role careers, twenty in one version of the typology, included "professional thieves," "naive check forgers," "embezzlers," "aggressive rapists," and "opiate addicts." However, because research shows that most offenders are versatile and do not specialize in a particular type of crime, many of them cannot be said to have a distinct kind of criminal role career (Hartjen and Gibbons, 1969; Shover, 1973; Petersilia, 1980).

Another way to develop a typology of offenders is to categorize them by the specific combinations of offenses they commit over time. A survey of adult male inmates in three states identified ten types of offenders by the combination of offenses they had committed. Chaiken and Chaiken (1984) found that these ten types differed in their rates of committing crime, their persistence in crime, and their personal characteristics. Table 10.1 shows these ten offender types and the kinds of crimes they committed. Chaiken and Chaiken gave the most attention to the first type, the violent predatory offender. This kind of offender engages in robbery, assault, and drug dealing, and sometimes burglary and other thefts. The violent predatory offender commits a disproportionate amount of all of the crime committed, is usually quite young, has been arrested frequently, began to commit crime at an early age, rarely has any family obligations, and has an irregular employment record. Violent predatory offenders are difficult to identify from official records, because they are young and the juvenile records that would indicate their heavy involvement in criminal activity are often unavailable to probation officers, prosecutors, judges, and researchers.

Delinquent Careers

Criminal careers can be studied by looking at lifetime patterns of delinquency and crime for a sample of individuals born in the same year. A cohort study of this sort was conducted by Wolfgang, Figlio, and Sellin (1972) in a project described in Chapter 1. They used school, police, court, and draft board records to study males who were born in 1945 and lived in Philadelphia from their tenth through their eighteenth birthdays. Tracy, Wolfgang, and Figlio (1990) later replicated this study, using the same methods to study a cohort of males and females who were born in 1958 and lived in Philadelphia from their tenth through their eighteenth birthdays. These Cohort I and II studies made it possible to examine past contacts with the juvenile justice system but did not allow the researchers to question individuals and administer self-report questionnaires to learn about offenses that never came to the attention of the police and the courts.

TABLE 10.1 Ten Offender Types by Combinations of Offenses Committed

GROUP	ROBBERY	ASSAULT[a]	BURGLARY	THEFT,[b] FRAUD, FORGERY, CREDIT CARD CRIMES	DRUG DEALS	PERCENTAGE OF STUDY SAMPLE[c]
Violent predators (robber-assaulter-dealers)	+	+	?	?	+	15
Robber-assaulters	+	+	?	?	0	8
Robber-dealers	+	0	?	?	+	9
Low-level robbers	+	0	?	?	0	12
Mere assaulters	0	+	0	0	0	5
Burglar-dealers	0	??	+	?	+	10
Low-level burglars	0	0	+	?	0	8
Property and drug offenders	0	??	0	+	+	6
Low-level property offenders	0	0	0	+	0	8
Drug dealers	0	0	0	0	+	6

Note: + = Group member commits this crime, by definition.

0 = Group member does not commit this crime, by definition.

? = Group member may or may not commit this crime. Analysis shows that nearly all members of the group do.

?? = Group member may or may not commit this crime. Most don't.

[a]Assault includes homicide arising out of assault or robbery.

[b]Theft includes auto theft.

[c]Percentages add to 87%. The remaining 13% did not report committing any of the crimes studied. Some serious crimes (e.g., rape, kidnap) were not included in the self-report survey. Respondents with missing data (150 out of 2,190) were excluded in calculation of percentages.

Source: Marcia R. Chaiken and Jan M. Chaiken, "Offender Types and Public Policy," *Crime and Delinquency,* vol. 30, no. 2 (April 1984), 198. Copyright © 1984 by Sage Publications, Inc. Reprinted by permission of Sage Publications, Inc.

Chronic Offenders

A **chronic offender** is a person who has violated the law frequently. Criminologists define "frequently" in various ways, with some classifying offenders as chronic if they self-report three or more serious crimes, and others requiring nine or more convictions (Loeber, Farrington, and Waschbusch, 1998).

Wolfgang, Figlio, and Sellin found that a relatively small proportion of the boys in Cohort I accounted for a large proportion of all of the cohort's contacts with the police. Defining chronic offenders as juveniles who had had five or more contacts with the police, they found that the 6 percent of the boys who were chronic offenders accounted for 52 percent of all of the cohort's police contacts. Nonchronic offenders, who had had two to four contacts with the police, were 12 percent of the cohort but accounted for 32 percent of the cohort's police contacts. If the nonchronic and chronic groups are combined into a category of "career delinquents," that is, juveniles with more than one police contact, the 19 percent of Cohort I classified as career delinquents accounted for 84 percent of the cohort's police contacts.

Other research confirms Wolfgang, Figlio, and Sellin's finding of a high concentration of police contacts among a small proportion of the cohort. Tracy, Wolfgang, and Figlio found that the 7.5 percent of Cohort II classified as chronic offenders (five or more police contacts) accounted for 61 percent of all of the cohort's contacts with the police and 68 percent of all contacts for FBI index crimes. A study in Racine, Wisconsin, found a similar concentration of police contacts among a small percentage of three different cohorts: 5 to 7 percent of each cohort accounted for more than half of all of the cohort's nontraffic police contacts, and 8 to 14 percent of each cohort accounted for all of the cohort's felony arrests (Shannon, 1988). A study in London found that the 6 percent of a cohort categorized as chronic offenders (six or more convictions before the age of twenty-five) accounted for about half of all convictions recorded for the cohort (Blumstein, Farrington, and Moitra, 1985). A study in California produced a similar result: The 7 percent of the cohort classified as chronic adult offenders (three or more arrests between ages eighteen and twenty-nine) accounted for 67 percent of the cohort's arrests (Tillman, 1987).

Recently, Rolf Loeber, David P. Farrington, and their colleagues defined a type of offender similar to the chronic offender, the **serious and violent juvenile (SVJ) offender.** SVJ offenders are juveniles who have committed one or more of the following crimes: homicide, voluntary manslaughter, rape or attempted rape, robbery, aggravated assault, arson of an occupied building, or kidnapping. SVJ offenders are usually male and have early behavioral problems such as trouble at school (poor attitude, low achievement, truancy, suspension, expulsion, and dropping out), substance abuse, precocious sexual behavior, and mental health problems. SVJ offenders start committing delinquent acts earlier and persist longer in that behavior than non-SVJ offenders. The vast majority of chronic offenders are SVJ offenders, and they account for more than half of all serious crimes by juveniles (Loeber and Farrington, 1998).

Patterns of Delinquent Careers

Wolfgang, Figlio, and Sellin examined several issues related to delinquent careers. They discovered that boys who had one contact with the police and then had no more contacts usually had engaged in relatively trivial offenses the first time. However, boys with at least two police contacts were more likely to have been stopped the first time for a relatively serious offense that involved injury, theft, or damage.

Of the boys in Cohort I with at least one police contact, 54 percent were stopped a second time. Of those stopped a second time, 65 percent went on to a third contact with the police, and of those with three or more contacts, the chances of being stopped an additional time ranged from 70 to 80 percent. In other words, the likelihood of never again being stopped by the police for delinquency is greatest after the first contact; after a second contact, the chance of continuing in a delinquent career is greater. Another study found even higher "transition probabilities" among a sample of adults arrested for violent crimes; the chance of being arrested again after any given arrest was about 80 percent, whatever the individual's prior arrest history (Miller, Dinitz, and Conrad, 1982).

Juveniles who are first stopped by the police at a very young age are more likely to have another police contact than are juveniles whose first contact with the police comes at a later age. Early age at first contact is also associated with a long career in crime and delinquency, a rapid development of that career, and involvement in serious offenses (Wolfgang, Figlio, and Sellin, 1972; Miller, Dinitz, and Conrad, 1982; Tracy, Wolfgang, and Figlio, 1990; Loeber et al., 1991). Early contact with the police could indicate a serious behavioral problem that is conducive to a criminal career, or early police contact might subject individuals to a labeling experience in juvenile court that closes off legitimate opportunities, breaks conventional bonds, and pushes them into lives of crime. Research has not determined if past and future criminal behavior are correlated because prior participation alters individuals and their behavior, or because certain individual characteristics that have a stable association with criminal behavior persist over time (Nagin and Paternoster, 1991; Nagin and Farrington, 1992a, 1992b).

Most studies of juvenile delinquents find little tendency for them to specialize in certain types of offenses. The Philadelphia cohort studies found only "a weak propensity toward offense type specialization" (Wolfgang, Figlio, and Sellin, 1972: 249). Other cohort studies have also found no clear pattern of offense specialization among delinquent youths (Lab, 1984; Shelden, Horvath, and Tracy, 1989) and no marked tendency for offenses to escalate in seriousness over the course of delinquent careers (Datesman and Aickin, 1984). A study in Columbus, Ohio, of boys and girls arrested at least once for a violent crime concluded that even violent juvenile offenders do not tend to specialize in the kinds of crime they commit, and that they do not progress from less serious to more serious offenses during their criminal careers (Hamparian et al., 1985). Another study of juvenile offenders did find a "small but significant degree of specialization superimposed on a great deal of versatility," with about 20 percent of juveniles identifiable as specialists (Farrington, Snyder, and Finnegan, 1988: 483).

The Philadelphia Cohort I study found that the time between police contacts became compressed over the course of an individual's delinquent career. The average time from first contact to second contact was sixteen to eighteen months. However, the average time from second contact to third contact was only ten months, and the average time from the third to the fourth contact was only eight months. The interval continued to decrease with each additional police contact, so that the average time between contacts after the twelfth one was only about three months. A similar compression of time between police contacts as the criminal record lengthens has been found for adult offenders (Miller, Dinitz, and Conrad, 1982). It is unclear whether this compression results from increased criminal or delinquent activity once a career begins or whether it occurs because the police are more likely to arrest people they have come to think of as troublemakers.

Delbert Elliott (1994) used longitudinal data from the National Youth Survey (NYS) to look at the careers of those reporting that they had committed serious violent offenses, defined as aggravated assaults, robberies, and rapes that involved injury or a weapon. Elliott found that the prevalence of such crimes was greater, the age of onset younger, and race differences smaller than indicated by studies based on official records. Compared to those studies, the NYS self-report study provided more evidence that careers escalate in terms of frequency, seriousness, and variety of offenses. The NYS study did support some of the conclusions of previous research based on official records: The general pattern of progression involved diversification rather than specialization in certain offenses; the proportion of all crimes reported in a given year that were serious violent offenses was small; serious violent offenders were less than 5 percent of the sample but accounted for 83 percent of all index offenses reported by the sample; and early age of onset of serious violent offending predicted continuity of that behavior into adulthood (Elliott, 1994).

Juvenile Delinquency and Adult Criminal Careers

Wolfgang, Thornberry, and Figlio (1987) studied police contacts up to the age of thirty for a 10 percent sample of the original Philadelphia cohort of boys. The probability of being stopped by the police before age eighteen was .35; that is, thirty-five of every one hundred males in Cohort I had contact with the police as a juvenile. The probability of any contact with the police from age ten to age thirty for the 10 percent sample from the original cohort was .47. Thirty percent of the sample had a police contact between eighteen and thirty.

The likelihood of police contact as an adult for a person who had been stopped by the police as a juvenile was .51, but the probability of contact as an adult if a person had not been stopped as a juvenile was only .18. Thus, a male with a juvenile record was nearly three times as likely as a male without a juvenile record to have a police contact as an adult. The juvenile offenders who were most likely to go on to have long and serious adult criminal careers were those who had their first police contact at an early age, had a large number of police contacts, had been stopped for serious offenses, and had specialized by offense type. Adult offenses were, on the average, much more serious than offenses committed as juveniles. Unlike juvenile offenses, those committed as adults escalated in seriousness over the course of a criminal career (Wolfgang, Thornberry, and Figlio, 1987; Tracy and Kempf-Leonard, 1996).

Using data from the Philadelphia Cohort II study, Kempf-Leonard, Tracy, and Howell (2001) classified juveniles as chronic delinquents (five or more police encounters), violent delinquents (a record of homicide, rape, robbery, aggravated assault, or aggravated sexual intercourse), and serious delinquents (a record of any violent offense, burglary, theft, motor vehicle theft, arson, or vandalism more than $500). Table 10.2 shows that the likelihood of having an adult criminal record by the age of twenty-six varied with the kind of delinquent career an individual had. Adult criminal activity was most likely for those whose juvenile delinquency was serious, violent, and chronic.

An English cohort study reached conclusions similar to those of the Cohort I and II studies, finding that 61 percent of boys who were convicted of delinquent acts were eventually convicted of crimes as adults, whereas only 13 percent of boys who were not found delinquent went on to be convicted as adults. Boys who were convicted of delinquent acts at the earliest ages were the most likely to become persistent adult offenders, but nearly one-fourth of the adults who had two or more convictions had never been found delinquent. There was little offense specialization by the age of twenty-one, although there was some continuity in aggressive behavior over time (Farrington, 1979).

The study of the Columbus, Ohio, cohort of juveniles arrested for violent offenses found that 59 percent of them were arrested at least once for an adult felony by the time they reached their mid-twenties. The youthful violent offenders who

TABLE 10.2   Likelihood of an Adult Criminal Record

	PERCENTAGE HAVING AN ADULT CRIMINAL RECORD
Nonchronic delinquents with no serious offenses	32
Serious delinquents	48
Violent delinquents	53
Chronic delinquents	59
Serious and chronic delinquents	63
Violent and chronic delinquents	63

Source: Based on Kimberly Kempf-Leonard, Paul E. Tracy, and James C. Howell, "Serious, Violent, and Chronic Juvenile Offenders: The Relationship of Delinquency Career Types to Adult Criminality," *Justice Quarterly* 18 (September 2001), 449–478.

were most likely to be arrested for a felony as an adult were male, had been arrested for a violent index offense as a youth, had first been arrested at age twelve or less, and had been committed to a state juvenile correctional facility (Hamparian et al., 1985). However, about two-fifths of this cohort of youthful violent offenders did not go on to be arrested for serious crimes as adults, although some probably committed offenses for which they were not arrested.

Using data on delinquent and nondelinquent males who were followed from childhood into their forties, Sampson and Laub (1993) found that whether a man engaged in crime was significantly influenced by his adult social bonds, regardless of any propensity to antisocial behavior that might have existed during his childhood and adolescence. Adult marital attachments and job stability can thus counteract, at least to a degree, the influence of childhood or adolescent experiences. In terms of the life-course perspective employed by Sampson and Laub, an event such as getting married or taking a job can be a "turning point" or "transition" that redirects an individual's long-term "trajectory" or line of development away from continued involvement in crime.

It is not too surprising that many juvenile offenders do not go on to commit crimes as adults, because often their delinquent acts would not be crimes if committed by adults. There is no reason to expect that a fifteen-year-old boy apprehended for underage drinking or skipping school will commit robbery or burglary as an adult, or even as an adolescent. Researchers have found weak or nonexistent relationships between such status offenses and serious acts of delinquency (Rojek and Erickson, 1982; Kelley, 1983; Shelden, Horvath, and Tracy, 1989). Because juvenile delinquency includes status offenses as well as acts that would be crimes if committed by adults, juvenile delinquents cannot be seen simply as criminals who happen to be under the age at which people are legally treated as adults.

Even juvenile delinquents who do commit serious crimes often realize that the chance of a harsh punishment increases greatly when they become adults. They might know that their juvenile records will usually be kept secret and that they will start with a clean slate when they reach adulthood. These considerations lead some juvenile offenders to avoid breaking the law when they become adults. Other juvenile offenders settle down when they become adults, taking full-time jobs, getting married, and having children. These changes take them away from the street life and the gangs that are conducive to criminal activities and reduce their motivation to engage in crime.

There is, nevertheless, a relationship between juvenile delinquency and adult criminal careers. Some attribute this relationship less to the continuity of behavior over time than to the effects of the juvenile and criminal justice systems on young people (Wolfgang, Figlio, and Sellin, 1972). This position has led some criminologists to support **radical nonintervention**, a policy of minimizing official reaction to delinquency to prevent the labeling that could drive juveniles into adult criminal careers (Schur, 1973). A different view is that adolescent offenders who represent the most serious threats to society are the most likely to be labeled delinquent, and it is they who are the most likely to go on to engage in crime as adults, even without official intervention when they are young. To date, researchers have not provided persuasive evidence of whether the relationship between juvenile delinquency and adult criminal careers is a result of labeling, a result of continuity of behavior over time, or some combination of the two.

Criminal Careers of Robbers

One way to look at criminal careers is to examine the lifetime criminal and noncriminal experiences of a single type of offender. Petersilia, Greenwood, and Lavin

(1977) used this approach to study forty-nine men who were serving sentences in a California prison for armed robbery and who had been in prison at least once before. They used self-reports of criminal activity as well as official data on arrests and convictions to trace the careers of these habitual offenders.

Career Patterns

The armed robbers had been incarcerated an average of half of their criminal careers, and they averaged about twenty years from their first self-reported offense until their current incarceration. Collectively, the forty-nine robbers reported 10,505 offenses over their careers, an average of 214 per offender. They had moved from crimes such as auto theft and burglary when they were juveniles to more serious offenses such as robbery when they became adults. The average age at first arrest was fifteen; 29 percent had begun significant criminal activity by twelve, 75 percent had started by fifteen, and 90 percent had started by eighteen. Over their careers, the average amount stolen in a crime was about $250, and their average annual income from crime was only a few thousand dollars.

There was no strong tendency toward crime specialization among these offenders; they often switched from one offense to another. Other studies support this finding of little specialization over the course of a criminal career (Petersilia, 1980; Peterson and Braiker, 1981; Rojek and Erickson, 1982; Kempf, 1987; Britt, 1994). One study of thieves involved in commercial burglary and truck hijacking found considerable versatility in the choice of crimes (Gibbs and Shelly, 1982). A study of offenders chosen because they had been arrested for a serious violent crime found that 93 percent of them showed "no discernible pattern of violence" in their arrest histories (Miller, Dinitz, and Conrad, 1982: 59).

The armed robbers were more likely to be arrested for any given crime as adults than they were as juveniles; arrest rates were calculated in terms of number of arrests per self-reported crime. Why they became less successful in avoiding arrest as their criminal careers progressed is not clear. Few of them believed they were watched more carefully by the police because of their prior record. They might have become careless over time, perhaps because their experience made them overly confident.

These robbers continued to commit crimes after earlier releases from prison because they had difficulty getting good jobs, lacked financial resources, and continued to interact with other offenders. A criminal record can be an impediment to securing a good job, but even more important might be the offender's lack of job skills and experience. The jobs these career criminals found were often low-paying, menial jobs with little or no chance for advancement. The ex-convicts who managed to get good jobs had lower offense rates than those who found poor-paying jobs or no jobs at all.

Planning Crimes

Relatively few of the armed robbers did much planning of their crimes. One-fourth did no planning or preparation at all, about half did very little planning, and one-fourth planned their crimes to some extent. Planning was more common when the offenders were young adults or adults than when they were juveniles, but even planning by adults was quite limited. Offenders typically included in what plans they did make the location of the crime, the presence of police patrols, when money would be present, whether there was an alarm on the premises, where a getaway car would be stolen, what disguise (if any) to wear, and how to escape from the scene of the crime.

As the habitual armed robbers got older, they increasingly operated alone. This allowed them to keep the profits of their crimes for themselves and reduced the risk that a partner would be arrested and cooperate with the police. Some offenders used fences or drug dealers to meet certain needs, but in general they relied on others less as they got older.

Use of the Stolen Money

While the armed robbers were juveniles, their crimes tended to fulfill expressive needs, such as peer approval, revenge, hostility, excitement, and a sense of being grown up. Over the course of their criminal careers, financial needs became relatively more important (Petersilia, 1980). The increased importance of financial needs suggests that economic assistance or a job that pays well might draw some older criminals away from crime and into a conventional way of life.

In a survey of male California inmates who were serving time for felonies, researchers discovered that 47 percent reported that economic distress was an important reason for their crimes. Offenders who cited this reason reported fewer violent offenses than inmates who said they had other motivations for their crimes. Thirty-five percent of the felons reported that their desire for high times motivated them to commit crime; these offenders reported the most frequent commission of offenses. Finally, 14 percent of the inmates reported that bad temper was an important reason for their crimes, which were frequently violent. These three motivations for crime—economic distress, a desire for high times, and bad temper—were statistically unrelated to one another (Peterson and Braiker, 1981).

Intensive and Intermittent Career Criminals

Petersilia, Greenwood, and Lavin's research on armed robbers led them to distinguish between two kinds of career criminals: intensives and intermittents (see Table 10.3). **Intensive offenders** engage in criminal activity that begins at an early age and is sustained over time, consciously planned, persistent, skilled, and frequent. In contrast, **intermittent offenders** engage in irregular and opportunistic crimes with low payoffs and great risks and do not think of themselves as professional criminals. Intensive criminals see themselves as career criminals, have a specific goal for their crimes (such as supporting high living or a drug habit), and try to avoid arrest. Compared with the intermittent offender, the intensive criminal steals more money in each crime and is more likely to injure the victim. Intensives commit relatively serious

TABLE 10.3   A Comparison of Intensive and Intermittent Offenders

INTENSIVES	INTERMITTENTS
crime began at an early age	started crime at somewhat later age
criminal behavior sustained and consciously directed	criminal behavior irregular and opportunistic
pre-crime planning	little pre-crime planning
juvenile crimes committed alone	juvenile crimes committed with partners
self-concept as career criminal	no self-concept as career criminal
profitable burglaries committed	unprofitable burglaries committed
unlikely to be well employed	likely to be better employed
more likely to injure victims	less likely to injure victims
more violence in personal lives	less violence in personal lives

Source: Based on Joan Petersilia, Peter W. Greenwood, and Marvin Lavin, *Criminal Careers of Habitual Felons.* Santa Monica, CA: Rand, 1977.

crimes and engage in crime often; the intensives in this study admitted to an average of fifty-one crimes per year, compared with an average of only five self-reported offenses per year for the intermittent offenders (Petersilia, Greenwood, and Lavin, 1977).

The survey of male felons in California prisons estimated that the average incoming prisoner had committed about fourteen serious crimes per year during the three years prior to his incarceration. However, this average conceals the fact that most inmates had committed few offenses, and a small number had committed many. More than half of the inmates had committed fewer than three offenses per year while on the street, but the most criminally active of the inmates accounted for more than sixty serious offenses per year (Peterson and Braiker, 1981). In Chapter 14, we will see that the high rate of crime by intensive offenders has been the basis of programs that focus the criminal justice system's resources on the apprehension, conviction, and imprisonment of career criminals.

Criminal Careers of White-Collar Offenders

Little research has been done on the criminal careers of white-collar offenders, because most criminologists have assumed that they are one-shot offenders whose "career" is limited to a single crime. Two recent studies have shown that this assumption is wrong.

Weisburd, Waring, and Chayet (2001) used data from presentence investigation reports and FBI arrest records to study a sample of offenders convicted in federal courts of economic crimes that involved fraud, deception, or collusion. At the time of their crime, nearly all of the offenders were employed in a white-collar job; their jobs were not of uniformly high prestige, but they were considerably better than the jobs typically held by street criminals. About one-third of the white-collar offenders had been arrested at least once before the arrest that led to their inclusion in the study, and about one-third had been arrested at least once since that arrest. Repeat offending and a high frequency of offending were more common among street criminals than in the sample of white-collar offenders, but the white-collar offenders were surprisingly likely to have been arrested repeatedly. The age of onset of criminal activity, as measured by first arrest, was about thirty-five for the white-collar offenders, much higher than for street criminals, most of whom are first arrested during their teens. The duration of the white-collar criminals' careers was long relative to those of street criminals, though the number of crimes the white-collar offenders committed during their careers was comparatively small. White-collar offenders usually continue to commit crime well into adulthood, long after most street criminals have abandoned crime. Neither white-collar criminals nor street criminals seem to specialize in crime, and both types usually desist from crime as they mature, though white-collar offenders typically desist at older ages.

Low-frequency white-collar offenders, who had been arrested only once or twice, were more conventional than chronic white-collar offenders, who had been arrested three or more times. The low-frequency offenders did not fit the stereotype of a street criminal. The majority of them were married, owned homes, and had a stable work history; one-third of them had a college degree. Some of the low-frequency offenders were classified as "crisis responders" whose crimes were "situational responses to real stress or crisis in their professional or personal lives." Often they had taken advantage of a position of trust to steal (Weisburd, Waring, and Chayet, 2001: 58). Other low-frequency offenders were "opportunity takers" whose crimes were the result of a desire to exploit a criminal opportunity that suddenly materialized. In contrast to these two types of low-frequency offenders, chronic white-collar offenders were more likely to be unconventional. They were less likely to own homes, be married, and have a high level of educational attainment and more likely to have had problems in school and with alcohol or drugs. Lower-frequency chronic offenders were described as "opportunity seekers." They were relatively conventional in background and behavior but looked for chances to commit crimes or create situations conducive to crime, and their involvement in crime was longer-term than suggested by the stereotype of a one-shot white-collar offender. Higher-frequency chronic offenders were dubbed "stereotypical criminals." Since childhood, their lives had been characterized by low self-control, instability, deviance, and recurrent criminal activity. Weisburd, Waring, and Chayet's research convincingly demonstrates that white-collar offenders do not conform to a single career type.

In their interviews with forty-seven telemarketers who had been convicted of federal crimes, Shover, Coffey, and Hobbs (2003) found that thirteen had a criminal record prior to the offense that had led to their inclusion in the study. Most of them had committed their first offense when older than is usual for street criminals, though they were similar to street criminals in their persistent use of alcohol and drugs. The telemarketers described their family backgrounds as traditional and financially comfortable. Their educations were also conventional; nearly half had gone to college, though only five had a four-year degree. Many said that as children they had more interest in money than their siblings, and most began to work at a young age. As adolescents, they had answered advertisements to do sales work or had been introduced to such work by their peers. Few had a profession that offered a chance for advancement and financial security prior to working in telemarketing. Many mentioned the challenge of selling to others by telephone, their skill at doing so, and the pleasure they derived from making a sale. Their work entailed limited responsibilities, flexible and short hours, and little need for advanced education or training. Often they moved from job to job, and some eventually became managers. Later many went out on their own to strike it rich; most said that their annual income was between $100,000 and $250,000, and five said they earned more than $1 million a year. Some of the older offenders had a lifestyle centered on their family, but more of them filled their ample leisure time with drug use, gambling, and partying, much like conventional property offenders.

Leaving a Life of Crime

In Chapter 4, we saw that the rate of arrest for index offenses declines with age; only 15.6 percent of all suspects arrested in 2001 for index crimes were over the age of forty. Later we will see that programs to rehabilitate offenders have been, for the most part, ineffective. Criminals apparently "retire" from criminal careers as they get older for reasons that have little to do with treatment programs. **Exiting** is the successful disengagement from a previous pattern of criminal behavior. What conditions or contingencies promote the change from criminal activities to noncriminal pursuits?

A Model of the Exiting Process

Neal Shover (1985, 1996) studied the exiting process through interviews with ordinary property offenders. Most of these men had a high degree of identification with crime as a means of livelihood but had been unsuccessful at this pursuit, either making little money from their crimes or spending much time in prison. Figure 10.1 shows the model of the exiting process that Shover derived from his research.

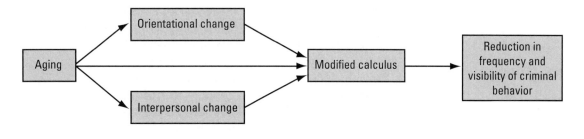

FIGURE 10.1   Shover's Model of the Exiting Process

Source: Neal Shover, *Aging Criminals.* Beverly Hills, CA: Sage Publications, 1985, p. 118. Reprinted by permission of Neal Shover.

As offenders get older, they experience both orientational change and interpersonal change. Change in orientation involves four elements:

1. *A new perspective on the self.* Offenders become more critical of their past behavior and more detached in evaluating how they behaved when younger.

2. *A growing awareness of time.* Offenders see time as a diminishing resource, viewing life in terms of the number of years they have left rather than in terms of how many years they have been alive. Offenders begin to plan how to use the rest of their lives. Sometimes this change is related to a fear of dying in prison.

3. *Changing aspirations and goals.* Offenders reduce their expectations of material well-being and assign greater priority to good relationships with others, a peaceful life, and a legitimate job.

4. *A growing sense of tiredness.* Offenders come to fear injury or death to a greater degree and become more wary of betrayal by crime partners. They feel they have slowed down relative to other offenders and inmates and must be careful of being victimized by them. Offenders also grow weary of fighting the more powerful criminal justice system.

In Shover's model, change in interpersonal relations is also important to the exiting process, with this change involving two components:

1. *Ties to another person.* Offenders seek mutually satisfying relationships with members of the opposite sex or with members of their family.

2. *Ties to a line of activity.* This typically involves finding a satisfying job, which provides direct rewards to offenders and reinforces their noncriminal identity. A job occupies their time, leaving little time for criminal activity.

According to Shover, these orientational and interpersonal changes lead to a "modified calculus," an alteration in the offender's balancing of the rewards and risks of criminal behavior. Persistent thieves increasingly see crime as producing "only penury interspersed with modest criminal gains that are depleted quickly in sprees of partying, and repeated imprisonment" (Shover, 1996: 139). This changed calculus then leads either to a reduction in the frequency and visibility of criminal activity so as to keep risks to a minimum, or to exiting from a criminal career altogether.

A study of previously incarcerated serious offenders by Shover and Thompson (1992) generally supports this model of exiting. Desistance from crime increased with age and education; it also increased as expectations for gaining friends, money, autonomy, and happiness through criminal behavior decreased. Desistance was not affected by income from legitimate work or by perceived risk of legal punishment.

Additional support for Shover's model comes from interviews with nineteen men nearly seventy years old who had desisted from crime because of "a combination of individual actions (choice) in conjunction with situational contexts and structural influences linked to important institutions" (Laub and Sampson, 2001: 48). Critical "turning points" that were the result of personal decisions influenced by institutions such as the family, the economy, and the military had provided the men with new scripts for future behavior. They had actively participated in creating new identities as family men or hard workers that were incompatible with continued criminal activity. Marriage and a job had attached them to others, structured their time, and reduced opportunities for crime by separating them from their peers.

Reasons for Leaving a Career as a Professional Thief

Evidence from biographical and autobiographical accounts of professional thieves suggests various motives for leaving a life of crime. Thieves might give up crime if they violate the code of the criminal subculture and are ostracized by other thieves; if they become inefficient as a result of fear, drugs, alcohol, or increasing age; if they can no longer find other thieves to work with them; or in rare cases if they make a "big score" (Sutherland, 1937). Thieves might also leave a criminal career if a long prison term shocks them into reforming, if they take a legitimate job, or if they marry into the legitimate world (Inciardi, 1975; Shover, 1983, 1985). Over time, thieves sometimes realize that the financial rewards of a legitimate job outweigh the financial rewards of crime, for few thieves ever make much money from crime (Petersilia, Greenwood, and Lavin, 1977; Katz, 1988).

Whatever their reasons for retiring from crime, professional thieves who do so of their own volition and who still retain their skills at theft may be seen as "retired" professional thieves rather than as new members of the conventional world (Sutherland, 1937). Thieves who leave criminal careers do not always regret their past behavior, often reflecting nostalgically on the excitement and scores of the past. They sometimes retain a "latent criminal identity," an affinity for others who are involved in crime (Irwin, 1970: 202). Some former thieves do not break their bonds with criminals and never become fully integrated into the conventional world. Exiting from crime can thus be seen as a change in criminal identity from a manifest to a latent form.

Reasons for Leaving a Career in Violent Crime

Interviews with women in New York City who had committed violent felonies (robberies, assaults, and homicides) led Deborah R. Baskin and Ira B. Sommers to conclusions consistent with Shover's model of the exiting process. They described the women's desistance from violent crime as a process that involved "recognition of problems associated with criminal participation (e.g., socially disjunctive experiences), restructuring of the self, and maintenance of the new behaviors and integration into new social networks" (Baskin and Sommers, 1998: 140).

The women were motivated to give up violent crime for a more conventional way of life because of their social isolation and their sense of leading hopelessly futile lives filled with pain, stress, and the hardships of street life. Prior to leaving her career in violent crime, one woman complained, "I'm 34 years old. I ain't no young woman no more, man. Drugs have changed, life styles have changed. Kids are killing you now for turf" (cited in Baskin and Sommers, 1998: 129). A twenty-seven-year-old woman echoed these sentiments, observing simply, "You get tired of bein' tired, you know" (cited in Baskin and Sommers, 1998: 129).

To stop committing violent crime, and to disengage from those with whom they had associated while pursuing their criminal careers, the women usually turned to treatment programs to find social support for a noncriminal way of life and a new identity as an ex-con or an ex-addict. Those who successfully left a life of violent crime were eventually able to become independent of the treatment group and build a conventional life by renewing relations with their children, making new friends, continuing their education, and acquiring job skills.

Reasons for Leaving a Career as a Drug Dealer or Smuggler

In her in-depth study of upper-level drug dealers and smugglers, most of whom trafficked in marijuana and cocaine, Patricia Adler (1993) found that about 90 percent of those she had observed and interviewed had decided to get out of the business. Early in their criminal careers, they had seen their drug dealing as temporary. As they grew aware of the restrictions and sacrifices imposed by a deviant career, and as they tired of life as a fugitive, they decided to abandon this career. What had once been a novel form of activity had become routine, exhausting, dangerous, and isolating.

However, these drug dealers and smugglers were bound to their careers by the rewards of money, drugs, and sex; by their commitment to a deviant career; and by the difficulty of finding another way to earn a good income. As a consequence, they oscillated between a deviant career and a legitimate way of life, often for years after they had decided to leave the deviant career. They moved out of dealing and smuggling temporarily, and then back into the drug business, a process described as "phaseout and re-entries" (Adler and Adler, 1983: 201).

More than ten years after her initial fieldwork, Adler was able to locate thirteen of her original sample of sixty-five dealers and smugglers. All thirteen had left their careers in the drug trade. Their reintegration into conventional society, which was achieved by fits and starts and to varying degrees, was influenced by factors associated with their lives before, during, and after their involvement in dealing and smuggling. Predealing and presmuggling factors that influenced reintegration included the age at which they had first engaged in illicit behavior, the social class into which they had been born, and the legitimate interests and skills they had developed before entering deviant careers. Factors during the time they were involved in the drug trade that affected later reintegration into society included the extent to which they had continued to be involved in the legitimate occupational world, the relationships they had maintained with people not involved in crime, the entrepreneurial skills they had developed as dealers and smugglers, and the organizational sophistication of their illicit operations. Reintegration was also influenced by factors associated with their post–drug-trade lives, including their access to legitimate jobs, their relationships with people who could help them adjust to conventional society, and their adaptability to the organizational world (Adler, 1993).

Exiting and Theories of Crime Causation

Theories of crime causation examined in earlier chapters suggest why some offenders leave a life of crime. A complete theory of criminal behavior should be able to explain why some people break the law and others do not, and also why some people who engage in crime eventually disengage from a criminal career. In fact, the correlates of desistance from delinquency are similar to the correlates of initial involvement in delinquency (Loeber et al., 1991). Here we look at some of the implications of different theories of crime causation for the process of exiting.

Differential Association Theory   Differential association theory would explain exiting by a change in a career criminal's ratio of definitions favorable to violation of the law over definitions unfavorable to violation of the law. In other words, just before leaving a criminal career, an offender should interact more with others who provide definitions that are not favorable to continued criminal activity or should interact less with people who are sources of definitions favorable to violation of the law.

There is no research that directly supports or refutes this explanation of exiting. However, this explanation is questionable, because many offenders probably decide to leave a criminal career while in prison, where their exposure to definitions favorable to violation of the law is great and where they are relatively isolated from definitions unfavorable to violation of the law. Some inmates might decide to exit because they are exposed to law-abiding values held by a correctional officer, a social worker, a visiting family member, or even another inmate who decides to go straight.

Another problem with using differential association theory to explain exiting is Sutherland's proposal that associations are more important if they occur early in life (the priority factor). This would suggest that an older career criminal would require very intense and frequent exposure to definitions unfavorable to violation of the law to change the ratio of definitions in a way that would lead to exiting. In a few cases, this might occur through religious conversion.

The Labeling Perspective   The labeling perspective offers a better explanation of why career criminals continue to commit crime than of why they abandon a life of crime. As criminal careers develop, the label "criminal" or "ex-convict" is more firmly affixed by the criminal justice system and the public. A criminal record, sometimes even an acquittal, signifies to the rest of the world a continuing intention to do social harm. There is little reason to change that label as long as an individual is involved in crime, so we would not expect a change in the label to precede the abandonment of a criminal career. Even an offender who decides to terminate a life of crime faces continued labeling as an ex-convict and must deal with closed-off job opportunities and social contacts. More support from the criminal justice system and from the people with whom the ex-convict interacts would make exiting easier.

Exiting sometimes involves deviance-disavowal by an offender or the relabeling of an offender by others. One form of relabeling is **certification**, the social verification by the criminal justice system or by conventional people that an offender has been rehabilitated. Certification eases the transition from a criminal career to membership in the conventional social world (Meisenhelder, 1977).

Anomie and Differential Opportunity Theory   Theories that focus on anomie and differential opportunity would suggest that exiting is caused either by increased access to legitimate means to reach socially approved goals or by reduced aspirations. There is some evidence that changes in aspirations are associated with the decision to abandon a criminal career. Research indicates that securing a job that holds promise for career advancement is important to exiting, but this research fits better with social control theory than with anomie or differential opportunity theory, because the bond to the conventional order provided by a job seems to be more important than the income produced by the job (Meisenhelder, 1977; Shover, 1983, 1985).

Social Control Theory   Social control theory suggests that a career criminal will "retire" when he or she forms bonds or attachments to conventional people and institutions. Just as adolescents who lack ties to family, school, peers, or a job are the most likely to become delinquents, so older offenders should be more likely to move out of crime when they form such conventional attachments.

Social control theory offers the most convincing explanation of the process of exiting. Exiting usually requires the acquisition of meaningful bonds to the conventional social order, a process opposite to the one that social control theory claims will generate delinquency. Thieves leave a life of crime as they form attachments to a life of conformity and develop a reluctance to give up those new bonds by risking further imprisonment. One important tie to the conventional order is a job that has the potential for advancement and that is perceived as meaningful and economically rewarding. A good job shifts a criminal's attention from the present to the future, and it provides a solid basis for the construction of a noncriminal identity. It also changes an individual's daily routine in ways that make crime less likely (Meisenhelder, 1977; Shover, 1983, 1985).

Good personal relationships with conventional people such as a spouse, a partner, children, or peers create bonds to the social order that an individual wants to protect. These people will then be "psychologically present" if the individual faces situations that offer a temptation to violate the law. Family members and partners also provide a place of residence, food, and help in the development of everyday skills such as paying bills and scheduling time. Because the development of quality social bonds is gradual and cumulative, desistance from crime is often gradual and cumulative (Laub, Nagin, and Sampson, 1998). One study suggests that the decrease in crime after marriage is less a result of the social control offered by the marital bond than a product of the reduced exposure to delinquent peers that follows marriage (Warr, 1998).

Other bonds that can lead people away from crime include involvement in organized religion and activities such as sports and hobbies. However, attachments of this sort are usually less important in the exiting process than ties to jobs and family members. One study found that the quality and strength of two types of social bonds formed during adulthood, job stability and marital attachment, were strongly predictive of desistance from crime (Sampson and Laub, 1993).

Exiting and the Correctional System

Correctional treatment programs are designed to rehabilitate offenders, but researchers have suggested that the conditions necessary for exiting are largely outside the control of the correctional system (Meisenhelder, 1977; Petersilia, 1980). One study, however, found that for convicted sex offenders who were on probation, a combination of court-mandated treatment and a stable work history sharply increased desistance from sex crimes, as measured by official reports (Kruttschnitt, Uggen, and Shelton, 2001).

Some critics have argued that the correctional system can impede the process of exiting. In prison, inmates learn patterns of behavior opposite to the ones they need to leave a criminal career. They depend on the prison administration for their material needs, but after release they must rely on themselves to meet those needs. In prison their time is structured for them, and often they are idle; after release, they must learn to structure their time to keep themselves from drifting back into crime. Prison life is easier for inmates who do not spend much time thinking about their future, but outside prison they must develop personal goals. In sum, changes produced by prison often hinder offenders who might otherwise leave a life of crime (Cordilia, 1983).

In order to leave a life of crime, a released inmate must "keep out of the old bag," a way of life that involves the commission of felonies and a high likelihood of arrest and conviction (Irwin, 1970). The "old bag" offers excitement and glamour, but also physical danger and the risk of a return to prison. Some observers believe the only way to leave a criminal career is to stay away from all criminal behavior, a view

Good personal relationships with conventional spouses, children, and peers create bonds to the social order that people want to protect. These attachments make it easier for inmates to leave a life of crime.

similar to the claim by Alcoholics Anonymous that alcoholics cannot drink at all without risking a relapse.

An ex-convict's first few weeks on the street after release are especially critical. During that time, the individual must become reaccustomed to the outside world, which has a faster pace and less routinization than life in prison. Often a released offender feels like a foreign traveler during the first few weeks on the street (Irwin, 1970).

As the ex-convict develops bonds and as time passes, the motivation to stay away from crime increases. The longer the individual stays away from crime, the less the chance that he or she will return to crime. Conversely, the greater a person's past involvement in crime and the longer a person's criminal career, the less the chance of abandoning a life of crime (Glaser, 1979).

The successful termination of a criminal career seems to require detachment from other offenders and from a criminal subculture, and attachment to a conventional way of life that usually involves a family, law-abiding friends, and a job that holds promise for the future. The process by which offenders detach themselves from one way of life and become attached to another is not yet fully understood, but more research on this process could reveal as much about the causes of crime as do studies that focus on the way that people become involved in crime in the first place.

Summary

Individual acts of law breaking cumulate over time into a criminal career, which is both similar to and different from a legitimate career.

Certain contingencies influence the development of a criminal career. An individual's sex can close off access to some illegitimate occupations. Another important contingency is contact with the criminal justice system, which can influence the course of a criminal career through the labeling process. Offenders often alternate in a "zigzag path" between criminal activities and legitimate pursuits. Frequently they are recruited into criminal careers from a delinquent subculture or from occupations close to the underworld.

Typologies can be useful in developing theories to explain different patterns of criminal behavior. One potentially fruitful approach is to develop typologies that categorize offenders by the combination of crimes they commit over time.

Studies of delinquent careers find that a small number of offenders account for a very large proportion of all contacts with the police in any cohort. The chance of being stopped again by the police increases as police contacts increase in number. People who have contact with the police while very young are especially likely to have further contacts. Delinquents show little inclination to specialize in one type of crime; this is true of adult career criminals as well. The time between police contacts becomes compressed as a delinquent career lengthens, indicating either increased delinquent activity or more attention to known offenders by the police. People who have police contacts as juveniles have a much greater chance of being stopped by the police as adults than do people who have no police contacts as juveniles. This could be because of the effects of labeling on young offenders, or because of a continuity of law-violating behavior over time.

Most offenders do not plan their crimes in much detail. As they grow older, criminals increasingly commit their crimes for instrumental rather than expressive purposes. Intensive career criminals commit many more crimes than intermittent offenders do. These intensive offenders also engage in more planning and are more skilled and persistent in their criminal activity. As a result, they account for a disproportionately high percentage of all serious crimes.

Career criminals exit or retire from a life of crime for many reasons, but the exiting process usually involves a growing detachment from other offenders and a criminal subculture, and a growing attachment to a conventional way of life that includes a family and a job. Different theories of crime causation would explain exiting in different ways, but social control theory seems to make the most sense of the data we now have on the exiting process. The correctional system seems to play a relatively minor role in the process of exiting.

IMPORTANT TERMS

certification	developmental criminology	serious and violent juvenile
chronic offender	exiting	(SVJ) offender
contingency	intensive offender	temporal boundary conception
criminal career	intermittent offender	of the criminal career
criminal propensity theory	radical nonintervention	typology

REVIEW QUESTIONS

1. What is a criminal career? How does a criminal career differ from and how is it similar to a legitimate career? What contingencies influence the development of criminal careers? What is the "zigzag path" followed by some criminals?

2. What is a chronic offender? What factors are associated with chronic offending?

3. What is the relationship between juvenile delinquency and adult crime?

4. What factors cause offenders to leave a life of crime? Does the correctional system play an important role in getting career criminals to "go straight"? How would differential association theory, the labeling perspective, anomie and differential opportunity theory, and social control theory explain the process of exiting a criminal career? Which theory explains exiting most convincingly?

FOR FURTHER STUDY

Analysis of Criminal Careers   Three important studies of criminal careers are Richard P. Rettig, Manual J. Torres, and Gerald R. Garrett's *Manny: A Criminal Addict's Story* (Boston: Houghton Mifflin, 1977), Neal Shover's *Great Pretenders: Pursuits and Careers of Persistent Thieves* (Boulder, CO: Westview, 1996), and David Weisburd, Elin Waring, and Ellen Chayet's *White-Collar Crime and Criminal Careers* (Cambridge, England: Cambridge University Press, 2001).

Leaving Criminal Careers   Two useful sources on the exiting process are Neal Shover's *Aging Criminals* (Thousand Oaks, CA: Sage, 1985) and John H. Laub and Robert J. Sampson's "Understanding Desistance from Crime" (in Michael Tonry, ed., *Crime and Justice: A Review of Research,* vol. 28. Chicago: University of Chicago Press, 2001, pp. 1–69).

11 The Organization of Criminal Behavior

Crime is commonly regarded as the behavior of individuals, a view reinforced by crime statistics that emphasize the personal traits of arrested suspects. This individualistic perspective on crime permeates the criminal justice system: The insanity defense recognizes an offender's mental state as the basis for a not guilty finding, and treatment programs are person-oriented. Criminology has been heavily influenced by this attention to the individual offender: Biological and psychological explanations, learning theories, and criminal career research all focus on the behavior of individuals.

Because criminology in the United States has been embedded in sociology, a discipline that studies groups and organizations, the predominance of this individualistic orientation is surprising. This chapter looks at criminal behavior as a collective or socially structured activity and examines the way that criminal groups and organizations develop, function, and persist.

Criminologists disagree about the extent to which criminal behavior is organized. Gottfredson and Hirschi claim that because criminals are low in self-control and pursue immediate pleasure, they are unlikely to participate in long-term, cooperative criminal enterprises. They argue that whatever organization is found among offenders is "imposed and maintained from without." In other words, any apparently organized criminal activity is the result of "a post hoc interpretation by scholars or law-enforcement officials to account for a series of events that otherwise has no inherent structure or coherent purpose" (Gottfredson and Hirschi, 1990: 203).

Others disagree with Gottfredson and Hirschi, asserting that although not all criminal behavior is organized, some of it certainly is. Part of the disagreement about the extent to which criminal activity is organized is a result of different ideas about what it means for behavior to be "organized," so we first need to consider what sociologists mean when they speak of organization.

The Meaning of Organization

Social structure is a recurrent, stable pattern of interaction among people. Within a system of patterned relationships that form a social structure are statuses (positions), roles (expected behaviors associated with those statuses), norms (standards of expected behavior), and sanctions (responses to violations of those norms). Social structure, which is the form or shape that social relationships take, can be distinguished from the actual people who are interacting at any given time. For instance, the organizational chart of a corporation, which describes the company's social structure, can be identical at two different times even if the actual people filling the statuses or positions in the corporation change.

One kind of social structure is a **group**, a set of relationships among people who interact on a face-to-face basis over time. Through communication among its members, a group develops common values, norms, and an identity or sense of "we-feeling." Members of a group are interdependent, being aware of and responding to one another. In other words, a group is more than an **aggregate** of people who happen to be in the same place at the same time but who do not interact much and have

CROSS-CULTURAL PERSPECTIVES

Terrorism and the al Qaeda Network

Osama bin Laden's al Qaeda, which was responsible for the September 11, 2001, terrorist attacks on the World Trade Center and the Pentagon, is an international network whose organization and membership have been difficult to document. Sworn al Qaeda members are estimated to number between 200 and 300, with 3,000 to 35,000 additional militants trained by, or allied with, the core group forming cells in perhaps sixty nations. According to Jean-Louis Bruguière, a French judge specializing in the investigation of terrorist organizations, "For these groups, there are no borders. They may consider it better or easier to have explosive materials in some countries and support bases in other countries, electronic matters in others, and financial support—forged papers, or forged credit cards and so on—in still others" (cited in Erlanger and Hedges, p. B4). The structure of al Qaeda is constantly shifting. According to Bruguière, "We may have a grasp of some cells, what they did, but we can't use this knowledge for the future. Everything changes. If you have good knowledge of the network today, it's not operational tomorrow. I compare these networks to AIDS. It's a virus. It's a moving shape. It's impossible to grasp it and to destroy it" (cited in Erlanger and Hedges, p. B4). Intelligence indicates that the war in Afghanistan dispersed al Qaeda members around the world and resulted in an alliance of locally based, ideologically oriented terrorist groups that are even more loosely held together than they were before September 11th.

Al Qaeda members are recruited in various ways: Some have been enlisted during Muslim pilgrimages to holy sites in Saudi Arabia, others by Islamic radicals in French prisons, and yet others through mosques and dissident groups in Great Britain. Recruits are sent to terrorist training camps and then join "sleeper cells" in countries as widespread as Singapore, Indonesia, the Philippines, Germany, Spain, England, Canada, and the United States. They rely on the latest in communications technology, talking on cell phones and sending messages by e-mail and through Internet chat rooms. That same technology has been used to trace their activities, often after their missions have been completed. Members of al Qaeda cells limit their interaction with neighbors and even violate their fundamentalist Islamic beliefs to appear more like those around them, for example, by shaving their beards and drinking alcohol. They mask their identities with false documents, often procured in Spain and Belgium. To support themselves, they hold jobs or commit profitable crimes such as credit card fraud and extortion. They get financial support from al Qaeda's leaders for their terrorist acts; the September 11th attacks reportedly involved about $500,000 in such support, some of which was sent from the United Arab Emirates and Germany. To undercut al Qaeda's ability to finance terrorism, soon after the attacks the U.S. government froze the assets of some financial institutions, charities, businesses, and individuals that had apparently funded al Qaeda, though the amount of money affected seems to have been only a small portion of the organization's assets.

Of the nineteen plane hijackers who died on September 11th, fifteen were natives of Saudi Arabia. Most no sense of common identity. A group has a character of its own, apart from the behavior of its members, and it influences the behavior of its members, for example, by pressuring them to conform to shared norms. For this reason, studying groups that engage in crime, such as delinquent gangs or organized crime families, provides more knowledge about criminal behavior than just studying individual offenders.

Groups are characterized by **networks**, or ties among individual members. Networks exist among as well as within groups, with several juvenile gangs or several Mafia families sometimes tied to one another in a larger social structure. Loose networks also exist among the parties to a criminal transaction, such as the sale of illegal drugs or the fencing of a stolen painting. The participants in these transactions cannot be called a group because they do not interact regularly on a face-to-face basis, but their criminal activity is organized in the sense of being structured or patterned. (See the Cross-Cultural Perspective box.)

Primary groups, such as the family and the peer group, are small groups that have warm and personal relationships among their members. Members treat each other as whole people, rather than in terms of the specific roles they play, and they work together for shared goals. Primary groups are relatively permanent, and

came from poor villages, though their families were of relatively high social standing in those villages. Their mission was apparently initiated in Hamburg, Germany, at least two years earlier. Funds to support the terrorists and their mission began to arrive in the United States more than a year before the attacks. One terrorist had lived in California since 1996, and others arrived in the country in 1999 and 2000. The hijackers formed a well-coordinated group that had three levels, described by investigators as follows:

Mr. [Mohamed] Atta, considered the mastermind, and three other leaders who chose the dates for the attack and flew the planes; a support staff of three who helped with the logistics of renting apartments, securing driver's licenses and distributing cash to the teams that would take the four planes; and beneath them, 12 soldiers, or "muscle," whose main responsibility seems to have been restraining the flight attendants and passengers while the leaders took over the jets' controls. (Zernike and van Natta, p. A1)

Though al Qaeda is a loosely organized international network, when its members undertake a specific mission, they require a more tightly organized social structure.

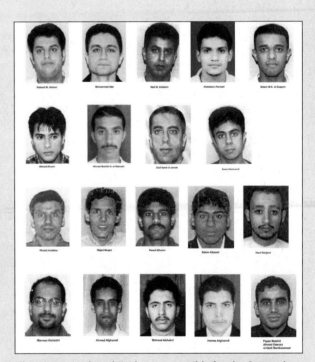

The nineteen plane hijackers responsible for the September 11, 2001, terrorist attacks on the World Trade Center and the Pentagon included four leaders, three logistical support staff, and twelve soldiers or "muscle."

Sources: Based on Edward Rothstein, "A Lethal Web with No Spider," *New York Times,* October 20, 2001; Steven Erlanger and Chris Hedges, "Terror Cells Slip through Europe's Grasp," *New York Times,* December 28, 2001, pp. A1, B4; Kate Zernike and Don van Natta, Jr., "Hijackers' Meticulous Strategy of Brains, Muscle and Practice," *New York Times,* November 4, 2001, pp. A1, B6; David Johnston, Don van Natta, Jr., and Judith Miller, "Qaeda's New Links Increase Threats from Far-Flung Sites," *New York Times,* June 16, 2002, pp. 1, 10; Douglas Frantz, "Al Qaeda Evolves into Looser Network, Experts Say," *New York Times,* October 15, 2002, p. A12.

members who leave are not easily replaced. Whether juvenile gangs fit this image of a primary group has been debated by criminologists for years.

In contrast to primary groups, **secondary groups** are characterized by less emotional, less intimate attachments. Members who leave are replaced without much difficulty, and individuals are treated in terms of the roles they play for the group rather than as complete people. The group exists to achieve some common goal, but its members have other goals as well, so their commitment to the group is less intense than that of primary group members.

A large, complex secondary group that is deliberately created to achieve certain goals is called a **formal organization.** These organizations, which include corporations and universities, are characterized by a division of labor, which is a set of interrelated and specialized tasks coordinated with one another through clearly defined lines of authority and channels of communication. Members of formal organizations are treated impersonally in terms of the tasks they perform for the organization; from the point of view of the organization, they can usually be replaced with little difficulty. A **bureaucracy** is a formal organization that is rationally organized to pursue goals in an efficient manner. It has a complex division of labor, is rigidly hierarchical, relies on written records, requires specialization of its members, formally defines the expected behavior of its members, promotes them on the basis of how well they perform their assigned tasks, separates the world of work from the personal lives of its employees, and is not owned by those who work for the organization (Weber, 1979).

Some sociologists seem to have dismissed the idea that crime is organized behavior because it rarely, if ever, fits the image of a bureaucracy. However, organizations of criminals do exist and can be described as varying along the following dimensions:

> . . . the *complexity* of their division of labor, including the number of members, the degree of stratification, and the degree of specialization of organizational roles . . .
>
> . . . their *coordination* among organizational roles, including the degree to which rules, agreements, and codes regulating relationships are defined and enforced . . .
>
> . . . the *purposiveness* with which they specify, strive toward, and achieve their goals (Best and Luckenbill, 1994: 11–12; emphasis added here)

Criminal organizations that are more complex, coordinated, and purposive offer their members a greater capacity for complex operations, more socialization into the ways of the organization, more elaborate services, and more security from external social control. Members of the most highly developed criminal organizations are usually the most actively involved in crime themselves (Best and Luckenbill, 1994).

Rather than being structured in complex, tightly coordinated, and highly purposive formal organizations, much criminal behavior is organized less formally in groups and networks in which offenders interact in predictable ways to carry out crime. This chapter investigates the extent to which juvenile delinquency, conventional crime, organized crime, and white-collar crime are organized activities.

Juvenile Gangs

The degree to which juvenile gangs are organized is a matter of dispute. This disagreement stems in part from the different types of gangs that criminologists have studied. For instance, drug-dealing gangs are probably more tightly organized than gangs that hang out on a street corner just to socialize. Gangs that have been around longer are probably more organized than newly emerging ones. The site of a study can also affect the conclusions reached about gang organization. Research indicates that few delinquents belong to gangs in Miami (Inciardi, Horowitz, and Pottieger, 1993) but that many delinquents in San Diego do (Sanders, 1994).

The Unorganized Gang

Gottfredson and Hirschi (1990) claim that researchers have not produced convincing evidence that juvenile gangs have leaders and formal structures. They assert that "serious" studies have shown that male adolescent gang members cannot identify their leaders and resist efforts by others to do so. These gangs are unorganized, being no more than informal friendship networks, and their members neither like one another much nor feel very committed to the group. Participation in the gang is variable, and there are no rules of attendance. Moreover, much of the gang's activity is not truly group behavior but is instead simply the result of the presence of multiple adolescents in the same place at the same time; what seem to be groups are really aggregates. The presence of many adolescents in one place makes delinquent activity more likely, because there is safety in numbers, immunity from sanctions, and diffusion of responsibility. Gottfredson and Hirschi (1990: 207) conclude that "the reports of juveniles themselves are suspect as a source of information about the structure of gangs" and that "gangs are not structured in ways suggested by the classical image."

Lewis Yablonsky (1966) presents a similar picture of violent juvenile gangs. He suggests that because juvenile gangs engage in different activities, the degree to which a gang is organized will depend on the kind of behavior in which it specializes and the importance of group structure to that activity. **Social gangs** have a group identity, a relatively permanent structure, informal leadership based on popularity, and intimate interaction among members. **Delinquent gangs** have a "tight primary group structure" and are organized to carry out specific profitable crimes (Yablonsky, 1966: 145).

Yablonsky devotes most of his attention to the **violent gang**, a fighting gang that emerges spontaneously to defend a territory against rival gangs, often resorting to violence over trivial provocations. Leaders are described as self-appointed manipulators of younger members. Yablonsky characterizes the members of violent gangs as psychopaths who are unable to empathize with their victims or develop intimate bonds to others, including other gang members. Membership is fluid and participation is unpredictable; usually there is a small core of active members and a larger number of marginally involved participants. Gang members often speak of a large "pseudomembership" and an extensive network of allied gangs, but both are fictitious. Yablonsky (1966: 224) refers to violent gangs as "near groups" that are in a "partial state of organization." They are more organized than collectivities such as mobs and crowds but have less permanence and cohesion, a less well-defined division of labor, fewer shared norms, and less clearly spelled out role expectations than social gangs and delinquent gangs. Violent gangs do not need a tight organization to engage in episodic street fighting, whereas delinquent gangs that engage in systematic theft or drug trafficking require more structure to be successful.

William Sanders (1994) defines gangs in terms of their willingness to use deadly force to defend territory, attack other gangs, steal money, or engage in other group-related criminal activities. From his research in San Diego, Sanders concludes that gangs do not have strong leaders or hierarchical structures; instead, gang leadership is informal, derived from friendship cliques, and based on age, gender, and reputation. Gang cohesiveness is rooted not in hierarchical organization, but rather in loyalty to and identification with a neighborhood and its "homeboys." Sanders disputes Yablonsky's contention that gang members are incapable of forming intimate social bonds, but he supports Yablonsky's claim that the violent gang lacks a tight organizational structure.

From their research on juvenile gangs in St. Louis, Scott Decker and Barrik van Winkle (1996: 116) concluded that rather than being formal organizations, the gangs were "loosely confederated groups of neighborhood residents." Gang roles were not clearly defined, the primary distinction being between real gang members and those who were less committed to the group. Members could identify gang leaders, but leadership was informal and varied over time and from one situation to another. Members were able to describe gang rules, but those rules were rarely written down or enforced through a formal process. About half of the members said their gang held no meetings, and the other half described gang meetings as informal gatherings of some of the members.

The Organized Gang

In his classic study *The Gang* (1963), originally published in 1927, Frederic Thrasher described gangs as coming together spontaneously at first, then becoming integrated through conflict with other gangs and with the community at large. These gangs have some of the features of formal organizations: an identity as a group, members' commitment, stability, exclusivity, and an internal structure with distinct statuses and roles.

Some research fits Thrasher's picture of the gang better than it fits the image of the gang as an unorganized aggregate. For example, a comparison of two gangs in Chicago and two in San Diego found that although the four gangs varied in degree of formal organization, one of the Chicago gangs that had been in existence for a long time was quite organized. That gang, the Gangster Disciples, had clearly defined leadership roles and responsibilities and distinct roles for gang members; one member described those roles as "King, . . . Board of Directors, the Generals, and First Captains. The rest is just the membership, the enforcers" (cited in Decker, Bynum, and Weisel, 1998: 403). The Gangster Disciples held regular meetings, although those meetings were not businesslike or devoted to achieving specific goals. It also had a written constitution with clearly defined rules. The Gangster Disciples thus had "many characteristics of emerging organized crime groups" and had "moved well be-

Some criminologists claim that juvenile gangs are highly organized groups, while others believe that those gangs are just loose aggregates of young people. Here members of the Bloods gang flash their sign.

yond the rather disorganized, informal quality" of most urban gangs (Decker, Bynum, and Weisel, 1998: 423).

The Organization of Street Gangs   A study of thirty-seven street gangs in New York, Los Angeles, and Boston also refutes the claim that juvenile gangs are no more than loosely structured collectivities. Instead, Martín Sánchez Jankowski (1991: 314) concludes that gangs

> are collectives in which the interaction of individuals, both leadership and rank and file, is organized and governed by a set of rules and roles. In short, they are organizations. Unlike other organizations, though, gangs function without a bureaucracy and this has tended to obscure their other organizational characteristics. . . . Ultimately, the fact that gangs have not been understood as organizations has crucially impaired our understanding of their behavior.

He suggests that some sociologists have downplayed the extent to which gangs have an organizational structure because they have observed groups that were either in a pregang stage or in a state of dissolution.

Gangs, as Jankowski sees them, are organized social systems that are closed to the public and keep much of their business secret from outsiders. However, because organizational survival is a major concern of gangs, they must deal with the external environment, gaining the support or at least avoiding the active antagonism of local residents and establishing links to local government, the criminal justice system, and the media. Concern for organizational survival also influences the gang's recruitment of new members, its provision of leadership, its development of rules to govern members' behavior, and its offering of incentives for members to continue to participate in the gang. Survival depends on the ability of the gang to meet its members' needs, which include entertainment, protection, and material well-being. Gangs allow their members to pursue personal goals, but they also try to bind them to the group through self-interest, moral incentives, and a code of behavior.

Gangs recruit members in several ways. Some use an approach similar to that of college fraternities, having a party or circulating information in the community to attract new members. Another recruiting strategy is to persuade local residents that they have an obligation to join the gang to help their community. Coercion is a third strategy, one used when a gang feels it has to increase in size rapidly. This happens when a gang expands its control to new territory, when it is defending itself against a rival gang's efforts to take over its territory, or when a new gang is formed.

According to Jankowski, to function efficiently gangs need formal leadership structures, defined roles for leaders and for rank and file members, and codes of behavior. One kind of leadership structure, which he labels "vertical/hierarchical," has three or four authority positions: a president, a vice president, a warlord, and sometimes a treasurer. Each officer has assigned duties and responsibilities; for instance, the president sets short-term goals, plans the gang's operations, and metes out rewards and punishments to members. This leadership structure is adopted by gangs that value control and efficiency in their efforts to amass material resources, gangs that are growing or taking over new territory, and gangs that need such a structure to compete successfully with other organizations, including the police.

The "horizontal/commission" type of leadership structure has several offices that are not ranked in a hierarchy; instead, officers are more or less equal in authority and share responsibilities. This leadership structure is found in gangs that are less concerned with accumulating material resources than with protecting their communities and families, so there is not much need to maximize organizational efficiency. Cultural constraints, such as emphasis on family and unwillingness to submit to authority, make it difficult for some gangs to develop a vertical/hierarchical authority structure.

The third kind of authority structure identified by Jankowski is the "influential" model, an informal structure in which charismatic individuals influence gang activities even though they have no formal titles or offices. This structure is common in small gangs, in gangs whose members see participation as a transitional stage to adult roles that will soon take them away from the gang, and among people who object to a formalized authority structure. Members of this third type of gang see it as a way to build friendships they can rely on as adults; the influentials are the members who have traits that the others admire, such as loyalty to friends and community, fighting ability, and generosity.

All but one of the gangs studied by Jankowski had a cohesive organization that was the product of efforts to establish internal social control. One mechanism for establishing order was a code that defined appropriate behavior for fights among members, for interaction with women who were relatives and partners of gang members, and for getting along in the gang's clubhouse. Some gangs had rules against heroin use, even though they tolerated the use of marijuana, cocaine, and alcohol. There were also rules about how changes in leadership were to be made, how certain behavior should be punished, and how leaders were to exercise power.

The Gang as a Business Enterprise   Felix Padilla used biographical and observational methods to document the criminal activity of a Puerto Rican street gang in Chicago. Padilla (1992: 3) described the Diamonds as a "business establishment" that operated as a "street-level drug-dealing enterprise." The gang had "its own culture, logic, and systematic means of transmitting and reinforcing its fundamental business virtues."

The Diamonds began as a fighting gang that spent much time smoking marijuana; it did not become a drug-dealing operation until the late 1970s. A 1971 Illinois law that created harsh penalties for adult drug dealers led dealers to turn to juveniles for help in distributing drugs, because those under the age of eighteen were not subject to the new sanctions. Eventually, the members of youth gangs recognized the money they could make by systematically organizing the drug trade in their neighborhoods. These enterprises were stimulated by the burgeoning demand for drugs, especially cocaine, during the 1970s. The Chicago drug trade flourished in the early 1980s with the development of an unusual organizational structure: a peaceful settlement that divided the city's gangs into two "gang nations" or alliances, with the expectation that disputes and violence would not occur among members of the same nation. This agreement was designed to reduce the gang violence that had been common in the 1970s, but the new structure also facilitated the development of stable enterprises that distributed illegal drugs, because it offered local gangs security against competitors from outside their neighborhoods.

The Diamonds were a collective enterprise that had a distinctive ideology aimed at improving the well-being of its members: Success was to be achieved not as individuals, as urged by the dominant American ideology, but rather through collective effort. Working in crews of three or more protected members against rival gangs, street criminals, and the police. The gang was supported by an ethnic community that provided a base of drug customers who were faithful to Diamond drug dealers, partly because the customers knew they could trust the dealers to provide high-quality drugs. Sometimes the Diamonds used a network of friends in the community to raise money to buy drugs to sell. Members of the community also helped gang members by refusing to provide information to the police. Belonging to the Diamonds thus offered members both a safe turf on which to sell drugs and a committed clientele.

The "hierarchical occupational structure" of the Diamonds was "an ordered arrangement of power, prestige, authority, and information" (Padilla, 1992: 111). The structure included a small number of drug suppliers and distributors, a larger number of cocaine and marijuana dealers, and several kinds of thieves. The suppliers and distributors (or "mainheads") were role models for those lower in the organization. There were few of them, and movement to that level in the gang was limited. Those who did move up to that position usually had to organize a new section of the gang in a different territory. The mainheads bought large amounts of drugs and then hired other gang members to sell the drugs on the street. The street-level dealers either bought drugs from the suppliers with their own money or were "fronted" the drugs by the suppliers and sold the drugs for a small commission. These dealers regarded the gang as "their primary form of employment" (Padilla, 1992: 13). Newer and younger members of the Diamonds stole for profit, often being directed in their criminal activity by older members. They operated in crews of three or four, often targeting cars, and turned over much of what they got to the gang as a way of proving their commitment to the group.

Padilla's and Jankowski's studies indicate that contemporary juvenile gangs are organized groups, even though they do not have the characteristics of a formal organization or a bureaucracy. Gangs are social structures in the sense that they have recognized leaders and identifiable, if fluid, memberships that interact over time. Gangs also have a sense of group identity, as is evident in their having a name, wearing "colors," and spraying their turf with graffiti. In sociological terms, gangs are more than aggregates; they are groups that engage in organized criminal activity (Office of Juvenile Justice and Delinquency Prevention, November 2000).

Conventional Crime

Most conventional crimes are not committed by organized gangs of professional criminals, but those gangs do account for some of the largest losses due to robbery, burglary, larceny, and fraud. Networks of thieves and smugglers are often organized on a temporary basis to take advantage of a particularly lucrative opportunity; this is true for both the stolen art trade and the illegal drug trade. Even conventional crimes of violence sometimes take an organized form.

Professional Theft

A **professional thief** is a skilled offender who is committed to crime as an occupation and thinks of himself or herself as a criminal. Professional crime is described by Mary McIntosh (1975: 12) as

> a relatively distinct occupational sphere [which] has its own patterning and continuity, whereas amateur activities, being only part-time, are much more influenced by a variety of circumstances, often peculiar to the individual criminal. Professional crime is thus distinguished not by its scale, or degree of turpitude or efficiency, but by its organizational differentiation from other activities.

Certain technical problems must be solved to engage in crime successfully, and organizations of professional criminals are designed for the efficient solution of those problems. According to McIntosh (1975: 24), the criminal underworld is an occupational community that serves the following functions for its members:

> It creates and develops the culture that establishes norms of working behaviour and appropriate work orientations; it provides people with contacts that help them in their careers, and referees who will vouch for their skills and character; it transmits

information about new problems and techniques; it helps members in hard times; it offers congenial sociability to people whose hours of work, income, and even presence in the free world are irregular; it keeps trade secrets and does not betray members to outsiders.

Professional thieves sometimes work alone, but often they get together with other thieves to carry out specific crimes. The social organization of the underworld provides professional criminals with the contacts needed to find accomplices to help them carry out a particular criminal project. These networks of professional thieves, which are formed in high-crime communities and in bars and clubs, provide information about targets of theft and about fences who are willing to buy stolen goods at the best prices, and they offer some protection against arrest. Four kinds of organizations of professional thieves are picaresque, craft, project, and business organizations (McIntosh, 1975).

Picaresque Organization   A **picaresque organization** is a relatively permanent gang under the leadership of a single person, who sometimes relies on the support and advice of a few officers. Rank in this kind of organization determines a member's share of the profits, with shares decided before crimes are committed. This type of organization, which is characteristic of pirates and brigands, became less common after politically centralized states established control over the places where these criminals had traditionally found sanctuary.

Craft Organization   A **craft organization** develops "highly skilled routines for taking small amounts from a large number of victims" (McIntosh, 1975: 35). In these small and relatively permanent groups of two or three petty thieves or confidence tricksters, each member plays a well-defined role in the specific type of crime that the group commits. Pickpocketing, shoplifting, counterfeiting, and cheating at gambling produce profits that are shared equally among the members. Skills are often passed on by members of a subculture that has refined its techniques over the years. Typically, at least one member of the group acts as a lookout, and the person who actually steals the goods quickly passes them to an accomplice in order to avoid being apprehended with the loot.

Project Organization   A third type of criminal organization is the **project organization**, which brings together several criminals to commit one or a series of acts of robbery, burglary, fraud, or smuggling. Because these offenses are more lucrative than the kinds of crimes committed by craft organizations, their potential victims usually have taken measures to protect themselves against loss. These crimes are more complex and less routine than petty forms of theft, so they require skill, planning, and innovation.

Project crime does not usually involve a permanent organization of thieves, and those groups that do persist are usually in a state of flux, with thieves dropping out of "the life," moving, going to prison, or being replaced. A team assembled for a particular crime often breaks up after dividing the profits. Nevertheless, project organizations engage in structured criminal activity, even if the structure resembles a group more than a formal organization.

For any given project, specific tasks must be allocated to members of the group. Some individuals have specialties, such as defeating electronic security systems or breaking into safes, but most offenders are quite versatile. The 1950 Brinks robbery involved eleven thieves who had various skills, even though the crime probably could have been committed more efficiently with a smaller group (Behn, 1977). Even though the roles in a project organization might be interchangeable, it is necessary to coordinate the actions of the participants so that the group will function smoothly and carry out the tasks required for completion of the crime. Gangs of burglars often have one person act as a lookout while the others enter a building, break into a safe or otherwise locate valuable property, and carry the loot away. Often one member of a robbery gang is assigned to act as a "wheel man," stealing a car or license plates to enable the thieves to avoid identification. This person sometimes acts as a "peek man" or lookout for the gang, although other gang members might also perform that function.

In project organizations, percentage shares or flat fees are determined before committing a crime. Some participants might be paid a flat fee for carrying out specific functions, such as stealing a getaway car or carrying messages. Tipsters who provide information about lucrative targets are often paid a flat fee. One robber who preyed on drug dealers because they were vulnerable and could not easily report their victimization to the police paid a tipster for guiding him to local dealers (Conklin, 1972). Flat fees and other expenses are deducted from the proceeds of the crime, and those who actually commit the theft divide the rest on some predetermined basis.

After completing a theft, offenders sometimes require the services of fences and fixers. They sell the stolen merchandise to a fence, who pays as little as possible for the goods and then profits from their resale. Fences sometimes direct thieves toward particular targets or place orders for specific items. Another part of the professional thieves' network is the fixer, sometimes a lawyer, who contacts victims, the police, or judges in an effort to have charges dismissed. Today this is apt to be done by offering to return the victim's property or compensate the victim for dropping charges; in the past, outright bribery of law-enforcement officials was more common (Sutherland, 1937; King and Chambliss, 1984).

One indicator of the group character of professional thieves, however they are organized, is their use of **argot** or cant, a specialized language that creates solidarity by differentiating them from outsiders. Argot is used when the offenders interact with other members of the underworld, but usually not when dealing with the straight world, because use of argot would then identify them as deviants. The argot that is used is closely linked to the kind of crime being committed. For instance, pickpockets in craft organizations use an elaborate argot in which different pockets and different means of taking wallets are given slang terms; the "stall" in the "whiz mob" picks out a "mark" and "steers" that potential victim into a position where the "tool" can take the wallet (Maurer, 1964).

The picture of professional thieves painted by "Chic Conwell," a thief interviewed by Edwin Sutherland (1937) in the 1930s, needs modification today. Conwell described thieving gangs as having an esprit de corps, or a "we-feeling" that provided the thieves with group support, and a code of behavior that required mutual aid, payment of debts to other thieves, and honest dealings with other thieves. This kind of loyalty seems a thing of the past, if it ever was common. One thief reports that there "is no loyalty among thieves today. There's no such thing at all. They have absolutely no loyalty. They'll beat one another to the money, you know, anything they can, they'll beat one another for their girls, or anything" (King and Chambliss, 1984: 78). The fact that groups of professional thieves are characterized by internal conflict and impermanence does not mean that they are not organized. The completion of individual crimes, or a series of offenses, often requires the development of a project organization, even if it does not persist for long.

Art Theft   Second only to the drug trade in profitability among international crimes, art theft is enormously costly; for example, an estimated $200 million worth of art was stolen from Boston's Isabella Stewart Gardner Museum on March 18, 1990. Most art theft is probably committed by project organizations, groups that are assembled to commit a specific theft and that use established networks to distribute the stolen art. However, one investigation of the black market in art regards it as more organized than this, describing it as "a tightly organized business operation which is all the more efficient for being excellently camouflaged within the honest trade" (Burnham, 1975: 37). History even provides examples of bureaucratically organized art theft. Napoleon Bonaparte looted art treasures throughout Europe, taking his director-general of museums on his campaigns, specifying what was to be stolen, and shipping the stolen treasures back to France. Adolf Hitler also engaged in systematic art theft, planning to use the stolen objects to turn his boyhood home in Austria into a pantheon of "Aryan" art. Hermann Goering used a government organization called Einsatzstab-Reichsleiter Rosenberg to loot art treasures, many of which became part of his personal collection, and Dr. Hans Posse used the Nazi party, the army, and the SS to steal art for the German state.

The way that art theft is organized is closely linked to the location of the objects to be stolen. Art in museums is easy to locate but difficult to steal, usually requiring elaborate planning by burglars and, occasionally, robbers. Works of art in private collections are more difficult to learn about. Some thieves attend public exhibitions to determine who has lent particularly valuable works, and others enlist the help of a domestic employee of a noted art collector.

Once valuable art is located, thieves must gain access to it. They might recruit into their gang a museum guard, an electronic security system specialist, an employee of the person who owns the art, or even a member of the owner's family. These insiders are either paid a flat fee or share in the profits of the theft in exchange for information about what art is available and how to steal it.

Most thieves have to find someone to buy the stolen art, which is often unique and well known, though several connoisseur-thieves have stolen art just to have it for themselves. Some art thieves work on commission, stealing objects that a dishonest collector or dealer orders in advance or expresses an interest in having. Other thieves have returned stolen art for a ransom. Thieves sometimes hire a restorer to alter a piece; this is often done with religious artifacts, antique furniture, and other objects

An FBI agent, the Peruvian ambassador to the United States, and the director of an archaeological museum in Peru examine a golden "backflap" worn as part of a Moche ceremonial costume following the stolen artifact's recovery by the FBI.

not valued for their uniqueness. For paintings and sculptures, thieves might pay someone to fabricate bills of sale or letters attesting to the past presence of the piece in a well-known collection. They have also paid dishonest dealers or other thieves to buy the stolen art at an out-of-the-way country auction, thereby giving the object a history of having been legitimately sold in a public place.

Art thieves often move the stolen art out of the country after a theft, making it harder for law-enforcement agents to solve the crime. The international movement of stolen art involves highly developed criminal networks, with organized crime syndicates that distribute illegal drugs reportedly using the same networks to move stolen art. For instance, the movement of antiquities looted from the Turkish countryside to art galleries in Munich, Germany, involves an established network that is apparently engaged in drug trafficking as well. Less organized groups of thieves have paid diplomats and airline employees to carry stolen art out of the country. Stolen art is moved by circuitous routes to countries where collectors have the money and the willingness to buy it and where local laws are protective of those who buy such art (Conklin, 1994).

One project organization moved a collection of recently unearthed Moche treasures from Peru to California, where they were sold to dealers and collectors. Antiquities dealer David Swetnam, who eventually served four months in a federal prison camp for his role in the smuggling of the antiquities, convinced his American backers to invest $80,000 in the purchase of the artifacts. He then contacted Fred Drew, a former American diplomat living in Lima, Peru, and a central player in a well-organized Peruvian network of grave looters, intermediaries, and dealers. Swetnam mailed Drew the money in a series of checks for less than $10,000 each, so as to avoid having to fill out currency transaction reports. Drew then purchased textiles, ceramics, and gold and silver pieces that the looters had taken from the Sipán tomb and sold to local dealers. Drew hired an expediter with reported ties to the Medellín drug cartel to ensure the safe export of the treasures from Peru to England; the expediter was paid 5 percent of the value of the property, half of which he used to bribe customs officials. In England, an accomplice of Swetnam named Michael Kelly, who was both a British citizen and a resident of the United States, used the recent death of his father as a cover for shipping three trunkloads of the treasures to the United States. The shipments were accompanied by a letter claiming that the pieces had been collected by Kelly's father in the course of his travels around the world during the 1920s, prior to Peru's passage of a law prohibiting trade in its cultural property. In the United States, Swetnam created a convincing front as a well-to-do art dealer, living in a California mansion where his wife, formerly a maid there, was house-sitting for the owner. He entertained potential clients at cocktail parties and luncheons, conveying the impression that he owned the house. Eventually, this international smuggling network was broken up when Michael Kelly reported it to U.S. Customs agents (Kirkpatrick, 1992).

Drug Smuggling and Dealing

Much drug smuggling and drug dealing is carried out not by highly structured and enduring organized crime gangs, such as Mafia families, but rather by project organizations put together for a particular deal. Patricia Adler (1993) found that marijuana smugglers in southern California had to establish a relationship with a broker who would get the drug to them from the producers in the country in which it was grown, usually Mexico. Brokers sometimes supplied the marijuana producers with the equipment to harvest a crop, a place to cure it, and a place to package it. Cocaine smugglers had to establish ties to a foreign supplier, typically in Colombia. This was usually done through referrals in a more formal manner than that used by marijuana smugglers to establish ties to brokers, because cocaine suppliers operated more secretively and in a more organized fashion than marijuana brokers. Smugglers who brought the drugs into the United States by air had to hire a pilot. They also needed to recruit drivers to move the drugs to safe locations and partners to help distribute the drugs.

Adler (1993: 63) characterizes the world of southern Californian drug smugglers and dealers as "a system of social organization which patterns the relationships of its members." She describes this world as a series of concentric circles (see Figure 11.1), with smaller circles representing closer relationships and larger circles representing relationships that are less close. Interaction among partners was intense and involved mutual trust. One kind of partnership was the crew, a stable group of individuals who could perform the specific tasks necessary to smuggling drugs. The head of the crew provided emotional and financial support to the other members and settled differences among them. More common than crews were groups of dealers and smugglers that were less enduring but more flexible; often these groups engaged in several deals, then dissolved. Crews and groups had a division of labor in which specialists played certain roles, and their members agreed before a deal to some profit-sharing arrangement.

Connections in the drug world were important for carrying out drug transactions and often endured for some time. One kind of connection was a supplier; both dealers and smugglers tried to minimize the number of suppliers they used. A second connection was a circle, a group of four to ten members who dealt with a similar quantity of drugs and usually bought and sold among themselves. Smugglers and dealers were also connected to their customers, but customers were less highly valued than suppliers because they were more numerous and easier to replace.

Less close than a dealer's or smuggler's relationships with partners and connections were their networks, acquaintanceships, and *umwelt*. Networks were made up of friends in the drug world with whom dealers and smugglers did not usually do business, but with whom they shared common interests and lifestyles. Members of networks offered one another advice and information, sometimes lent each other money, and were used to check on the trustworthiness of someone who might become a busi-

FIGURE 11.1   The Social Organization of Drug Smuggling and Dealing

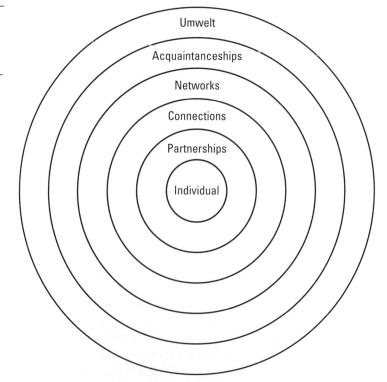

ness associate. Acquaintanceships were ties to people the dealers and smugglers knew socially but had no business dealings with; there was always a possibility of doing business in the future, but these relationships were primarily social in nature. The final circle of this organized social world was an umwelt, "a world of relationships that are based not on concrete knowledge but on reputation," that is, on knowledge of what others were doing and how trustworthy they were (Adler, 1993: 77).

Adler found that the illicit drug market in southern California was not monopolized by a criminal syndicate. Instead, it involved competition among numerous enterprises of different degrees of organization and durability. Even though the drug market as a whole was not tightly organized, the activities of smugglers and dealers were structured in ways that made it possible for them to import and distribute drugs. Groups of smugglers and dealers had some degree of cohesion and a division of labor, and their members were committed to a life of crime; they were project organizations of professional criminals. These groups were more flexible and independent, and less centralized and formally structured, than organized crime syndicates such as Mafia families. Groups of smugglers and dealers rarely lasted long enough to grow large; besides, greater size would have increased the chance of their being detected by the police. Rather than being regulated by corruption and violence, as are illegal markets dominated by Mafia-type groups, the world of dealers and smugglers was regulated informally by the allocation of prestige in the form of reputation. Instead of a formal organization, a peer subculture recruited and socialized new members of the drug trade, teaching them job skills, argot, the norms of the trade, and justifications for violating drug laws (Adler, 1993).

Violent Crime

Most violent crime is not highly organized, but there are exceptions; for example, Murder Incorporated was a gang of professional contract killers that operated in the 1930s and 1940s. Violence can even be bureaucratically organized, as was the case with the genocidal policies of the Nazis. The Cross-Cultural Perspective box shows how the crime of forcible rape was used as a conscious policy of terrorism in Bosnia in the 1990s. Rape and sexual slavery were used in a similar way in 1999 in East Timor before and after its vote for independence from Indonesia (Mydans, 2001).

Sometimes violent crime is socially structured in less formal ways, with individuals who share values and attitudes joining together to commit crime. Gang rape is committed by men who interact over time and share attitudes toward women that are conducive to sexual assault (Alder, 1985; Sanday, 1990). Some violent hate crimes are committed by white supremacist groups that are organized to carry out such acts. In these cases, there is more than simply an aggregate of individuals who are low in self-control; there is an identifiable group of interacting individuals who share common attitudes toward their victims and join together to commit crime on a systematic basis.

Organized Crime

The fourth kind of professional criminal organization identified by Mary McIntosh is the **business organization,** a permanent structure that profits from extortion and the provision of illegal goods and services. Here we follow common usage and refer to this kind of structure as organized crime, even though much criminal activity that is not called organized crime is still organized behavior. Organized crime is syndicated crime, the violation of the law on a large-scale basis by ongoing, tightly structured groups devoted to the pursuit of profit through criminal means. What distinguishes organized crime from other types of structured criminal activity are the durability and complexity of syndicates, which have some of the traits of formal organizations: a division of labor, a hierarchical authority structure, and coordination among various statuses. Members of organized crime groups are paid regularly or given a share of the organization's illegal profits. To remain successful, these groups must enjoy immunity from arrest, which they try to do through corruption of law-enforcement agents. They must also thwart efforts by competitors to take over their businesses, which they often accomplish through the use or threat of violence. Violence and demands for loyalty are used to ensure that members of the organization continue to work on its behalf.

McIntosh argues that barriers to entry into the four types of professional criminal activity are associated with the optimum size of the organization needed to carry out crime successfully. Entry into professional crime is harder when the optimum size of the firm is larger; for example, entry into syndicated crime is more difficult than entry into craft or project crime. This is because large-scale criminal organizations require more skill, specialization, training, and coordination, and creating such a structure is more difficult than putting together a craft or project group.

CROSS-CULTURAL PERSPECTIVES

Rape in Bosnia

In 2001, three former Bosnian Serb soldiers were convicted of rape by a United Nations tribunal in the Hague; two were also found guilty of sexual slavery. They were given prison sentences ranging from twelve to twenty-eight years. This was the first time that organized sexual assault by itself had been designated a war crime; according to a spokesperson for the prosecutor, the decision meant that "rape can be a crime against humanity, that it is an instrument of terror" (cited in Cullen, p. A26).

All parties to the war in Bosnia engaged in sexual abuses, but the Bosnian Serbs were the primary offenders, raping an estimated 20,000 Muslim women in 1992 and 1993, after which reports of such assaults declined significantly. The Serbs used rape as part of their policy of "ethnic cleansing," a practice that began when their troops established military command of an area. That command was then taken over by local auxiliary forces who knew the people in the area; they marked the homes of non-Serbians and ordered them to wear white armbands. Non-Serbians were then locked up, beaten, and raped or murdered. Following the rapes, officers arrived and offered residents the official documents they needed to move elsewhere, leaving the area free for Serbs to settle.

Concentration camps were built specifically for the purpose of sexually abusing women. There the victims were repeatedly raped, often by several men; they were also beaten, shot, and stabbed. Rapes were committed as sadistically as possible, often in front of members of the victim's family. Mothers and daughters were raped at the same time, and children as young as twelve were sexually assaulted. In some cases, soldiers forced Muslims to rape members of their own families. These assaults led to serious deterioration in the physical and psychological health of the victims; many suffered depression, and some attempted or committed suicide.

Rape victims who became pregnant often had to bear the children because they were locked up until it was too late to have abortions; many of these infants were abandoned. Pregnant rape victims who were free to do so sought abortions at local hospitals, often quite late in their pregnancies. Some women were raped repeatedly until they became and stayed pregnant, with one rapist telling his victim, "Now you will bear a little Serb." The rape victims were treated with contempt by the authorities and even by members of their own families. The stigma of having been raped reduced the chance that these women would marry and have children in the future.

Sources: Based on Mladen Loncar, "Rape as 'Ethnic Cleansing,'" *New York Times,* January 10, 1993, p. 74; Marlise Simons, "For First Time, Court Defines Rape as War Crime," *New York Times,* June 28, 1996, pp. A1, A6; Marlise Simons, "Bosnian War Trial Focuses on Sex Crimes," *New York Times,* February 18, 2001, p. 4; Kevin Cullen, "UN Court Establishes Rape as a War Crime," *Boston Globe,* February 23, 2001, pp. A1, A26.

Gottfredson and Hirschi (1990) dispute the claim that a significant amount of crime is committed by rationally structured gangs that work together efficiently and competently over long periods of time. They argue that organized, long-term pursuit of goals by criminals is inconsistent with evidence that offenders lack self-control and are untrustworthy, unreliable, and uncooperative. The organizations that do exist, they say, are ephemeral, with few lasting long enough to achieve their goals. Other scholars disagree, presenting evidence that organized crime groups do exist and do engage in profitable criminal activities over time.

The Mafia in the United States

Sociologists have reached different conclusions about the extent to which Italian American Mafia crime families are organized, at both the local and the national levels. They have described these crime groups as formal organizations, as kinship structures, as patron-client relationships, and as business enterprises.

The Mafia as Formal Organization   Law-enforcement agents and some sociologists see Mafia families as rationally designed, highly structured formal organizations that operate much like modern bureaucracies. Entry into these organizations is tightly controlled, specific jobs are assigned to the members, and illegal profits are pursued in an efficient and systematic manner.

At the head of such a Mafia family, depicted in Figure 11.2, is a boss who has absolute authority over the other members. Below the boss in the hierarchy are an underboss who acts as chief deputy and assistant, a staff of counselors or advisors, lieutenants who act as buffers between the higher echelons and the lower-level workers, and soldiers who operate illegal and sometimes legitimate enterprises for the family. According to sociologist Donald Cressey (1972: 36, 38), for this organization to function there must be an enforcer who "makes arrangements for killing and injuring (physically, financially, or psychologically) members, and occasionally nonmembers"; a corrupter who "bribes, buys, intimidates, threatens, negotiates, and sweet-talks himself into a relationship with the police, public officials, and anyone else who might help 'family' members secure and maintain immunity from arrest, prosecution, and punishment"; and a corruptee who is a public official, usually not a member of the organized crime family, and who can wield influence on behalf of the organization's interests.

Law-enforcement officials have sometimes claimed that Mafia families in the United States are organized in a national confederation led by a commission of powerful bosses. In 1986 in New York City, eight defendants were convicted of operating a national commission that decided which illegal enterprises to pursue, determined which families would control different criminal activities in particular geographic areas, and settled disputes among families. In 1998, law-enforcement officials announced that the formerly powerful commission of Mafia bosses was probably defunct, not having met in nearly two years (Raab, 1998). Some criminologists believe that the Mafia was never organized at the national level, pointing to internal inconsistencies in the testimony that gangsters have offered as proof of such organization (Hawkins, 1969), and citing research that has found no evidence that local crime groups are controlled by a national commission (Ianni, 1972; Chambliss, 1978). A study of Chinatown gangs in New York City also found no support for "the assertion made by some observers that a well-organized, monolithic, hierarchical criminal cartel, sometimes referred to as the 'Chinese Mafia,' exists in the United States and in many other nations" (Chin, 1996: 123).

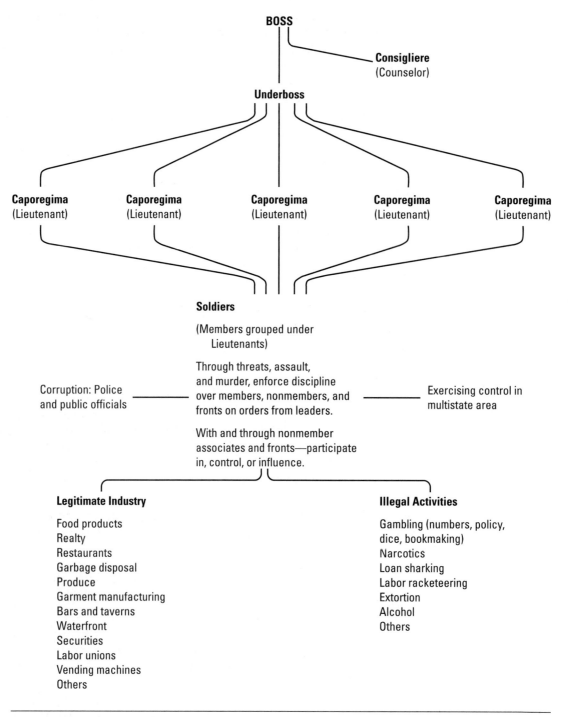

FIGURE 11.2   A Mafia Family

Source: President's Commission on Law Enforcement and Administration of Justice, *Organized Crime.* Washington, DC: U.S. Government Printing Office, 1967, p. 9.

The Mafia as Kinship Structure   Based on his participant-observation study of one organized crime family, Francis Ianni (1972: 9) concluded that Mafia families are "a form of social organization patterned by tradition and responsive to culture," a form more like a kinship structure than a formal organization. He found that a code of conduct governs the behavior of family members: Be loyal to the larger family rather than to nuclear families within it, act like a man, do nothing to disgrace the family, and do not discuss family business with outsiders. Ianni (1972: 154) described the organizational structure of this crime family as follows:

1. The family operates as a social unit with social organization and business functions merged.
2. All leadership positions, down to the "middle management" level, are assigned on the basis of kinship.
3. The higher the position in the organization, the closer the kinship relationship.
4. Leadership positions in the family are assigned to a central group of fifteen family members, all of whom have close consanguineal or affinal relationships which are reinforced by fictive godparental relationships as well.
5. Members of this leadership group are assigned primarily to either legal or illegal enterprises, but not both.
6. Transfer of monies from illegal to legal and back into illegal activities takes place through individuals rather than companies and is part of the close kin-organization of the family.

In addition to claiming that individual crime families are organized around principles of kinship, Ianni also argues that Mafia families in different cities are linked together by intermarriage. He points out that of the more than sixty bosses participating in the 1957 meeting in Apalachin, New York, nearly half were related by blood or marriage, and many others were related by fictitious kin roles. Ianni (1972: 172) describes Italian American crime families as "actually a number of lineages linked together into a composite clan," asserting that the universality of clan organization and its shared behavior has led some observers to conclude erroneously that there is a highly structured national or even international Mafia conspiracy. In fact, says Ianni (1972: 153), the various crime groups "have no structure apart from their functioning" and are not a nationally organized cartel.

The Mafia as Patron–Client Relationships   Joseph Albini (1971) regards Mafia families in the United States and Italy as hierarchical systems of power held together by a series of complex patron–client relationships among crime family members and between crime family members and people in legitimate society. Patrons look out for the best interests of their clients, and the clients repay their patrons with loyalty and service. Patron–client relationships are embedded in kinship networks, creating a complex structure for organized crime, but not one that can be described as a formal organization. Organized crime changes as the relative power of patrons changes and as new kinship ties are formed. This fluidity is functional for crime families, allowing them to adapt in ways that maintain organizational efficiency, meet new public demands for goods and services, and thwart law enforcement. In this patron–client model, influential crime family bosses, who have been described as members of a national ruling commission, are seen instead as powerful patrons who serve other members of organized crime, for instance, by intervening in disputes among family members.

The Mafia as Business Enterprise   Another view of organized crime is that all entrepreneurs develop organizations to carry out the tasks necessary for producing and marketing goods and services. What distinguishes organized crime from legitimate enterprises is simply the illegality of the goods and services in which it deals (Smith, 1978). Both illegal and legal enterprises must adapt to changes in the market to grow and to remain profitable, and both legal and illegal markets are characterized by competition and by alliances among entrepreneurs.

Economist Peter Reuter (1983) concluded that none of the three illegal markets in New York City that he studied—loan sharking, numbers betting, and bookmaking—was controlled by the Mafia, and that each was best characterized as a competitive market with many entrepreneurs. He suggested that an illegal monopoly would be vulnerable to attack by law enforcement, and that the involvement of many law-enforcement agencies in the fight against organized crime made it impossible to corrupt all of the agencies that would have to be neutralized for a single criminal enterprise to dominate an illegal market. A more recent analysis concludes that Reuter gave too much attention to economic forces such as efficiency and competition in structuring New York City's numbers gambling market and slighted the important role of corruption and police participation in shaping that market (Liddick, 1999). Even if Reuter was correct in concluding that the three illegal markets he studied were not monopolized by the Mafia, various organized groups (including Mafia families) are involved in the business of supplying illegal goods and services there. Organized groups of criminals do exist within illegal markets that are not organized in the sense of being dominated by a single crime group such as the Mafia.

Whatever the basis of their organization, individual crime families seem to be highly structured. However, the strength of some crime groups, particularly Mafia families, has been weakened in recent years by enforcement of the Racketeer Influenced and Corrupt Organizations (RICO) Act (see the Using Criminology box).

USING CRIMINOLOGY

RICO and Organized Crime

In 1970, the federal government passed the Racketeer Influenced and Corrupt Organizations Act, commonly known as RICO. This law prohibits the operation of an enterprise that shows a pattern of racketeering and allows for the prosecution of all members of a criminal organization if any member commits two or more specified crimes as a part of that organization's work. Membership in such an organization is thus defined as a crime, allowing prosecutors to show in court how organized crime families are structured and how they go about their daily business.

RICO was not used regularly against organized crime until 1981, when the U.S. Supreme Court ruled that the law was not restricted to cases involving organized crime's infiltration of legitimate businesses but could be used against any criminal racketeering scheme. RICO defines racketeering in broad terms and provides for the forfeiture of assets and for a twenty-year prison term.

The law has been used successfully to prosecute organized crime leaders in New York, Boston, Los Angeles, New Orleans, and Cleveland. Attorneys for organized crime figures have complained that the broad nature of RICO allows for the prosecution of many defendants for

crimes committed by only a few, and they have argued that charges brought under RICO are difficult to defend against. Business executives have criticized RICO for being too broadly written, claiming that this results in the use of the law to bring civil actions against legitimate corporations in fraud cases. These executives argue that such cases were not the original intent of RICO and that the law should be limited to traditional forms of racketeering such as loan sharking and illegal gambling. G. Robert Blakey, a law professor who wrote the law when he was on the Senate staff, disagrees: "The law addresses the crimes of organizations. If organizations act like racketeers, we should call them racketeers" (cited in Muro, p. A28). In 2000, a federal judge allowed plaintiffs to use RICO to sue the Los Angeles Police Department for allowing its officers to plant evidence and beat people. In 2002, four men alleged in court that the Cardinal and Archdiocese of Los Angeles had engaged in criminal racketeering by not removing a priest who had sexually abused them as boys and by not reporting that priest's behavior to the police.

Sources: Based on William F. Doherty, "RICO—A Broad Tool for Prosecutors," *Boston Globe,* February 28, 1986, p. 9; Mark Muro, "Some Say RICO Is Reaching Too Far," *Boston Globe,* March 26, 1989, pp. A25, A28.

New Forms of Organized Crime

In recent years, ethnic and national groups other than Italian Americans have developed organizations to pursue profits through illegal means (see Table 11.1). Much of

TABLE 11.1   A Comparison of Ethnic/International Organized Crime Factions

ETHNIC GROUP	ORIGINS	EXEMPLARS	NOTABLE ILLICIT ACTIVITIES	NORTH AMERICAN LOCALES	COMMENTS (UNIQUE OR NOTABLE CHARACTERISTICS)
Chinese (tongs, Triads, street gangs)	17th-century China	Wo, 14 K	Gambling, extortion, drug trafficking, robbery, prostitution, murder, arms dealing, racketeering	California, New York	■ Tongs and street gangs possess many of the characteristics we used to define organized crime groups
Japanese Yakuza	7th-century Japan	Yamaguchi Gumi	Weapons trafficking (to Japan), methamphetamines trafficking (to Japan), murder, gambling, extortion, bookmaking	California, Hawaii	■ All Yakuza gangs are highly structured/hierarchical ■ Legitimate activities include banking and real estate ■ Annual revenue estimated to be $32 billion
Colombian drug traffickers	Colombia has a long history of social banditry	Medellín and Cali cartels	Cocaine trafficking	New York area, Miami, Los Angeles, Houston	■ Complex infrastructures employ about 24,000 according to one estimate ■ Criminal activities limited to those associated with the drug trade
Vietnamese gangs	Arrival of immigrants in U.S. in the 1970s	Born to Kill	Extortion, prostitution, auto theft, arson, gambling, armed robbery	Chicago, New Orleans, Houston, Washington, D.C., Los Angeles, Boston	■ Not a major problem compared to other ethnic organized crime groups ■ Closely linked to Chinese organized crime ■ Considered to be the most ruthless of Asian groups

(continued)

TABLE 11.1 Continued

ETHNIC GROUP	ORIGINS	EXEMPLARS	NOTABLE ILLICIT ACTIVITIES	NORTH AMERICAN LOCALES	COMMENTS (UNIQUE OR NOTABLE CHARACTERISTICS)
Jamaican posses	Kingston, Jamaica. Came to U.S. in mid-1970s	Shower Posse, Spangler Posse	Cocaine (crack distribution), firearms trafficking, money laundering, fraud, robbery, kidnapping, murder, auto theft	New York, Miami, Los Angeles, San Francisco, Detroit, Philadelphia, Dallas, Washington, D.C., Chicago, Houston	■ One of the most violent organized crime groups in the country ■ 40 posses in the U.S. have 22,000 members ■ Control 30 to 40 percent of U.S. crack trade
Russian Mafia	Emigrés arrived in large numbers in the 1970s	Odessa Malina, Organizatsiya	Marketing illegal goods (drugs, weapons, stolen cars), extortion, forgery, loan sharking, racketeering, gasoline bootlegging (#1 activity)	New York, New Jersey, Philadelphia, Los Angeles, Chicago, Baltimore, Dallas, Cleveland, Phoenix, Toronto	■ Perestroika reforms coupled with economic mayhem fueled a tremendous growth in new forms of organized crime

Source: From *Organized Crime in America,* by D. J. Kenney and J. O. Finckenauer. Copyright © 1995. Reprinted with permission of Wadsworth, an imprint of the Wadsworth Group, a division of Thomson Learning. Fax 800-730-2215.

this activity involves networks that buy illegal drugs in other countries, ship them to the United States, and distribute them to users; most prominent are the Colombians in the cocaine trade and the Chinese in the heroin trade. Drug trafficking is not the only source of profit for emerging organized crime groups; they have also been involved in extortion, gambling, prostitution, and the smuggling of illegal immigrants.

Organized crime is well entrenched in the Chinatowns of large American cities. Highly structured crime groups in these communities can be traced to the mid-1800s, when organizations known as tongs were formed to assist and protect immigrants from China. In addition to their legitimate functions, the tongs became involved in gambling and prostitution. During the 1970s, the tongs formed alliances with gangs of young immigrants who had recently come from Hong Kong. From their association with the tongs, the gangs receive protection, legal assistance, and respect in the community. In exchange, the tongs use the youth gangs for intimidation, for example, to guard their gambling establishments and houses of prostitution. The youth gangs also engage in extortion, "protecting" shop and restaurant owners from violence by the gangs themselves in exchange for weekly payoffs. They also rob people who frequent local gambling dens and massage parlors (Kifner, 1991).

According to the U.S. Immigration and Naturalization Service, every year about 100,000 Chinese pay between $15,000 and $50,000 to be smuggled into Western nations, with about 10 percent of that number entering the United States. Profits from this enterprise are estimated to be about $3 billion a year (Lakshmanan, 2000). A study based on interviews with human smugglers in the United States and China describes their activity as a project organization in which familial networks and social contacts are used to assemble the resources needed to carry out a smuggling operation. The organizations are small and flexible and have a carefully defined division of labor, but they are not hierarchically structured, and they are usually disbanded after completion of a specific operation, with the smugglers blending into conventional society (Zhang and Chin, 2002).

For their passage to the United States, the illegal immigrants make an initial payment of at least $1,500, usually raising the money by selling personal and family possessions. The immigrants get forged passports and counseling when they arrive in the United States. Their relatives there sometimes pay the balance, but more often the immigrants themselves go to work for several years as indentured servants to pay off the balance. They work long hours at low wages in miserable conditions in restaurants, laundries, and garment factories; some women have been forced to work as prostitutes in Chinatown brothels. To collect the balance of the fare, smugglers have threatened violence against the immigrants and their families, sometimes kidnapping the immigrants and releasing them only when their relatives pay a ransom for their release (Myers, 1993; Treaster, 1993).

There is evidence that Chinese Triads, highly organized secret societies that date to the seventeenth century, are a major force in the international heroin trade. One study of a drug ring uncovered a complex conspiracy in which each person had a designated task to carry out. Some participants knew other members of the conspiracy, but some did not. Those involved in the drug ring were either members of Triads or had Triad connections, but the researcher found no evidence of any direct role played by a Triad organization in the operation of the drug ring. He concluded as follows:

> [D]ifferent structures appear to exist at the various levels of the heroin trade and include production, export, import, and local distribution. There is no denying that there is significant involvement of ethnic Chinese at all these stages or that distribution is facilitated by this common ethnicity, but there is no evidence supporting any overall organizational control or coordination. (Dobinson, 1993: 383)

To prove involvement by a criminal organization, Dobinson seems to require evidence of a higher level of control and coordination than is usually characteristic of either criminal enterprises or their legitimate counterparts. Highly organized multinational corporations buy raw materials from local producers, and they rely on independent stores around the world to sell their finished products. These corporations are still formal organizations, even if they do not control every stage of the process of production and distribution. In similar fashion, international drug traffickers often contract out the distribution of the drugs they import to local criminal groups rather than become involved in that risky enterprise themselves. Dobinson's research does provide evidence of structured criminal activity: an enduring group of individuals who coordinate the performance of the tasks necessary to make a profit through illegal means.

White-Collar Crime

Gottfredson and Hirschi's (1990) general theory of crime contends that white-collar crime is uncommon, simple in its techniques, condemned by business culture, and committed by people with characteristics similar to those of conventional offenders. Disagreeing with all aspects of this description, Gary Reed and Peter Cleary Yeager (1996: 377) argue that white-collar offenders are not simply people with low self-control who pursue self-interest, but rather that their motivations and the opportunities they exploit are "socially constructed in a broad institutional context that emphasizes profit making and in organizational contexts that privilege success and survival." Much white-collar crime is condoned or even encouraged, rather than condemned, by business culture. This type of crime is frequently quite complex, impeding detection by law-enforcement agents. White-collar criminals often break the law on behalf of their company or work group, rather than pursue a narrow self-interest. There is also ample evidence that white-collar crime, especially corporate law breaking, is not rare.

Rather than investigating the actions of groups and organizations that engage in white-collar crime, researchers have usually focused on individual white-collar offenders who violate the law in an organizational setting by using organizational resources. Business enterprises established for criminal purposes would be classified as organized crime groups rather than white-collar offenders. Kitty Calavita, Henry Pontell, and Robert Tillman (1997: 173) argue that much of the fraud committed in the savings and loan industry during the 1980s more closely resembled organized crime than white-collar crime, because it was "premeditated, motivated by personal gain, organized by networks, continuous, and facilitated by the participation of public officials."

White-collar criminals sometimes create structures within or across formal organizations in order to violate the law. Wayne Baker and Robert Faulkner's (1993) innovative analysis of three price-fixing conspiracies in the heavy electrical equipment industry during the 1950s found that the structure of illegal networks is the result of a need for concealment, unlike the structure of networks in legal business activities, which is the result of a need for efficiency. Illegal networks that have low information-processing requirements (i.e., relatively little need for data, knowledge, and intelligence with which to execute a sequence of tasks) tend to be decentralized, because they can be run acceptably, if not most efficiently, in that way. However, illegal networks that have high information-processing needs tend to be centralized, because face-to-face interaction among top executives is needed to carry out complex tasks and to make difficult decisions in secret.

Deal making in the securities industry also depends on "[c]omplex networks of relationships and information exchanges" (Reichman, 1993: 66). A central player in these networks is the investment banker, who mediates the flow of assets between sellers and buyers. Illegal insider trading occurs when people with access to nonpublic information that has value beyond a specific deal tip others in their network to trade on the basis of that information. It is difficult to police insider trading because "the direct evidence of illegal trades is often embedded in sophisticated inter-organizational networks that lie beyond traditional means of surveillance and information access" (Reichman, 1993: 87).

Some kinds of white-collar crimes require more organization than others. In a study of white-collar offenders convicted in federal courts, Weisburd et al. (1991) found it useful to differentiate crimes by their degree of organizational complexity: Offenses were rated as more complex if they were patterned, used organizational resources, involved more coconspirators, and occurred over longer periods. The most complex crimes they studied were antitrust violations and securities fraud; the least complex were bank embezzlement, credit fraud, and tax fraud. Between those extremes in organizational complexity were mail fraud, false claims, and bribery. More research is needed to determine the extent to which white-collar offenders who engage in crimes of varying degrees of complexity develop group structures to enable themselves to break the law.

Summary

Criminologists have given less attention to organized criminal activity than they have to the behavior of individual offenders. Some have argued that crime is rarely committed by groups or organizations that endure over time. Crime by tightly structured bureaucracies is probably uncommon, but much crime is committed by criminals who belong to groups and organizations that have crime as their major goal.

The extent to which a juvenile gang is organized depends on its purpose. One study found that violent or fighting gangs are not as highly structured as delinquent and social gangs. Gangs involved in the highly competitive drug trade are especially likely to be well organized. Research indicates that many juvenile gangs do have a structure: identifiable leaders, strategies for recruiting and socializing new members, defined statuses and roles, and codes of behavior.

Most conventional crime is probably not committed by groups and organizations, but some of it is. Professional thieves sometimes come together in project organizations, groups assembled to commit one or a series of crimes of robbery, burglary, fraud, or smuggling. These groups assign specific tasks to their members in order to carry out crimes smoothly, agreeing on the distribution of the proceeds before committing a crime. Project organizations sometimes pay nonmembers a flat fee to steal a car, carry messages, or point out lucrative targets. Art theft is a costly crime that is often done by project organizations, which are put together from international networks of thieves, smugglers, intermediaries, and dealers. Project organizations also smuggle and deal drugs, with crews and groups assembled for particular deals. Even violent crime is sometimes organized, with groups and even nations systematically murdering or raping designated victims.

Some criminologists argue that organized crime is not highly structured at the national level, and that it is even weaker at the local level than law-enforcement agents claim. Other criminologists assert that organized crime groups have a structure, but they have different ideas about the basis of that structure; organized crime has been seen as a formal organization, a kinship structure, and a set of patron-client relationships. Organized crime groups have also been analyzed as business enterprises that differ from legitimate ones only in the illegality of the goods and services in which they deal.

Little research has been done on the relationships that exist among white-collar offenders, but there is evidence that informal networks develop among people who engage in such white-collar crimes as price fixing and insider trading.

IMPORTANT TERMS

aggregate	formal organization	project organization
argot	group	secondary group
bureaucracy	network	social gang
business organization	picaresque organization	social structure
craft organization	primary group	violent gang
delinquent gang	professional thief	

REVIEW QUESTIONS

1. What is social structure? What are aggregates, groups, formal organizations, and bureaucracies?

2. In what sense are juvenile gangs organized? What kinds of juvenile delinquency are most likely to give rise to an organized gang?

3. What are the four kinds of organizations of professional thieves in Mary McIntosh's typology? To what extent can groups that engage in art theft and groups that engage in drug smuggling and dealing be characterized as project organizations?

4. What are the different views about the organizational basis of the American Mafia? What kind of evidence would support or refute each position?

FOR FURTHER STUDY

Juvenile Gangs   Three studies of juvenile gangs are Martín Sánchez Jankowski's *Islands in the Street: Gangs and American Urban Society* (Berkeley: University of California Press, 1991), Felix M. Padilla's *The Gang as an American Enterprise* (New Brunswick, NJ: Rutgers University Press, 1992), and William B. Sanders's *Gangbangs and Drive-Bys: Grounded Culture and Juvenile Gang Violence* (New York: Aldine de Gruyter, 1994). The results of the National Youth Gang Survey can be found at the website of the Office of Juvenile Justice and Delinquency Prevention (http://ojjdp.ncjrs.org).

Art Theft   The social organization of art theft is discussed in Sidney D. Kirkpatrick's *Lords of Sipán: A True Story of Pre-Inca Tombs, Archaeology, and Crime* (New York: Morrow, 1992) and in Chapter 5 of John E. Conklin's *Art Crime* (Westport, CT: Praeger, 1994). Two useful websites on art theft are sponsored by the International Foundation for Art Research (www.ifar.org) and the Art Loss Register (www.artloss.com/Default.asp).

Organized Crime   New forms of organized crime are described in Dennis J. Kenney and James O. Finckenauer's *Organized Crime in America* (Belmont, CA: Wadsworth, 1995) and William Kleinknecht's *The New Ethnic Mobs: The Changing Face of Organized Crime in America* (New York: Free Press, 1996).

12 | Community Reactions to Crime

Toward the end of the nineteenth century, the French sociologist Emile Durkheim (1895/1933: 73) defined crime as behavior that shocks the sentiments found in all "healthy" consciences. According to Durkheim, those sentiments are intensely held and specific to particular situations, and are the basis of criminal codes. Crime is thus behavior that offends a shared sense of what is valued and worth pursuing, and punishment is a reaction to that behavior. Durkheim claimed that because people are brought together in their opposition to acts that violate the law, crime actually enhances social solidarity within a community.

One reaction to crime is **social control**, a process that brings about conformity to society's norms and laws. **Formal social control** includes efforts by the police, the courts, and correctional institutions to produce conformity to the law; we examine those agents of the criminal justice system in Chapter 13. **Informal social control**, or the reactions of individuals and groups that bring about conformity to norms and laws, includes peer and community pressure, bystander intervention in a crime, and collective responses such as citizen patrol groups. There is reason to believe that the amount of formal social control varies inversely with the amount of informal social control; that is, the agents of the criminal justice system exercise more control when informal social control is weaker (Black, 1976).

Donald Black (1983) has argued that some criminal behavior functions as informal social control, with both violent crime and property crime sometimes being the result of efforts to engage in self-help, correct injustice, and pursue justice against perceived wrongdoers. Murders in which people kill because they feel insulted by their victims, vandalism in which youths destroy school property because of hostility toward teachers who have hurt their self-esteem, and theft from stores that overcharge customers can be seen as efforts to correct serious wrongs perpetrated by others—that is, as efforts to exercise informal social control over unjust actions.

Contrary to Durkheim's idea that informal responses to crime enhance community solidarity, one common reaction to crime, fear, is more likely to undermine solidarity and thereby reduce social control. Before looking at the ways that individual and collective responses to crime might informally control law-violating behavior, the consequences of the fear of crime are examined.

Fear of Crime

Fear of crime became so widespread in the United States during the 1960s and 1970s that in 1978 the National Institute of Law Enforcement and Criminal Justice listed "fear" along with "crime" on its research agenda of problems in need of federal support. Noting the "unusual elevation of a psychological construct to the level of a major social problem," Rosenbaum and Heath (1990: 222) characterized the period from 1968 to 1977 as the "war on crime" and the following decade as the "war on the fear of crime."

Individual property crimes have modest effects on fear, though they might have a large cumulative effect because they are relatively common. A relatively small percentage of American adults, perhaps 3 percent, are injured in crimes of violence during any given year. Why, then, is the fear of crime so pervasive?

Conversations with relatives, friends, and neighbors who have been crime victims generate fear. This "vicarious victimization" seems to predict an individual's level of fear better than his or her own victimization experiences (Lavrakas, 1982). The mass media heighten fear, especially among heavy television viewers who live in high-crime areas and especially if the reported crime is gruesome, local, and without apparent motive (Rosenbaum and Heath, 1990). People who watch more reality-based police shows believe that the prevalence of crime is greater, and this makes them more fearful (Flanagan and Longmire, 1996; Oliver and Armstrong, 1998). One study concluded that the "issue is not whether media accounts of crime increase fear, but which audiences, with which experiences and interests, construct which meanings from the messages received." The researchers found that "the construction of fear from the messages of television news [was] limited to middle-aged white women," because white women were most often the victims of crimes reported on television in the market they studied (Tallahassee, Florida) (Chiricos, Eschholz, and Gertz, 1998: 310).

Fear of crime is also associated with weak ties to a community, a sense among residents that they cannot control what is happening in their neighborhood, a lack of powerful local organizations, the absence of knowledge about effective ways to prevent crime, and a perception of disorder or incivility ("signs of crime") in the area. These signs of crime include gangs of teenagers hanging out on street corners, drug addicts and prostitutes in doorways, abandoned and burned-out buildings, signs of vandalism such as graffiti and broken windows, and people urinating in public (Lewis and Salem, 1986; Skogan, 1990; Taylor, 2001). Wilson and Kelling's (1982) **broken windows theory** proposes that disorder of this sort gives rise to crime. Skogan (1990) found that perceptions of disorder were linked to robbery rates, and that the relationship persisted after accounting for the effects of neighborhood residential stability, poverty level, and racial composition. In reanalyzing these data, Harcourt (2001) found that the association between disorder and robbery vanished when he eliminated the data from five adjoining areas in Newark, New Jersey. Furthermore, the associations between disorder and four other crimes (rape, burglary, physical assault,

The broken windows theory claims that vandalism, graffiti, and other signs of physical and social disorder give rise to serious crime.

and purse snatching) disappeared after controlling for neighborhood characteristics. Harcourt (2001: 78) concluded that Skogan's data did not support the broken windows theory that reducing disorder would curb crime; other researchers agree with this conclusion (Sampson and Raudenbush, 2001; Taylor, 2001).

Changes in the fear of crime do not always reflect changes in crime rates. Figure 12.1 shows that fear of walking alone at night increased from 1967 to 1975, a period over which violent crime rates nearly doubled. However, fear remained steady from 1975 to 1992, despite a big increase in violent crime rates over that time. Violent crime has dropped significantly since 1992, and fear of crime has also fallen. Fear of crime was at about the same level in 2001 as it had been in 1967, even though the violent crime rate was twice as high in 2001.

Kenneth Ferraro (1995) distinguishes the fear of crime, which is emotional, from the perceived risk of crime, which involves a cognitive judgment. Using data from a national survey, he finds that fear of crime is a product of the perceived risk of victimization, which in turn reflects actual risk as measured by official crime statistics. Ferraro finds that women are more fearful than men, despite women's lower rates of victimization (except for rape); he attributes this to the effect that women's fear of rape has on their fear of other kinds of crime. Ferraro also shows that when gender and community of residence are taken into account, older people are no more fearful of crime than younger people. From his research, Ferraro concludes that fear of crime is, for the most part, based on realistic assessments of the risks that people have of becoming crime victims.

Warr and Ellison (2000) propose that not all fear of crime is personal and not all precautions that people take are for self-protection. Using survey data, they find that most fear of crime is altruistic, a fear that other members of one's household will be victimized, and that this kind of fear is often more intense than fear for one's own safety. A husband is more likely to fear the victimization of his wife than a wife is to

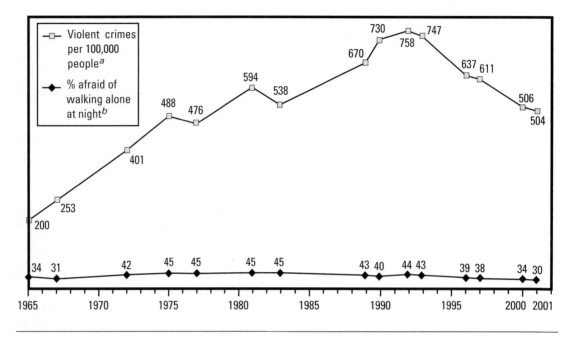

FIGURE 12.1   Fear of Walking Alone at Night and Rates of Violent Crime, 1965–2001

[a]Rates per 100,000 people for total violent crimes (murder and nonnegligent manslaughter, forcible rape, robbery, and aggravated assault) reported to the FBI.

[b]Responses to Gallup Poll question: "Is there any area near where you live—that is, within a mile—where you would be afraid to walk alone at night?"

Source: Based on data from Kathleen Maguire and Ann L. Pastore, eds., *Sourcebook of Criminal Justice Statistics 2000,* Tables 2.40, 3.120, retrieved from www.albany.edu/sourcebook.

fear for her husband's safety. Indeed, husbands are frequently more concerned for their wife's safety than for their own, whereas wives more often fear for their personal safety. These results are probably due to a fear of sexual assaults on women. Mothers are only slightly more fearful than fathers that their children will be the victims of crime. Both mothers and fathers are somewhat more concerned for the safety of their daughters than their sons, again reflecting a fear of rape. Men are especially likely to combine concern for their spouse with anxiety for their children. The common pattern among women is a combination of concern for their own safety and that of their children. Altruistic fear probably extends beyond one's immediate household, but there are no survey data to document this.

Consequences of the Fear of Crime

Fear of crime causes people to lock their doors and windows, install expensive alarm systems and bright lighting, engrave identification numbers on their possessions, enroll in self-defense classes, and buy firearms, watchdogs, electronic beepers, and cellular phones. A national survey in 2001 found that as a result of their concerns about crime

32 percent of Americans kept a dog for protection.
32 percent had special locks installed in their home.
23 percent had a burglar alarm installed in their home.
21 percent had bought a gun for protection.
17 percent carried Mace or pepper spray.

17 percent had taken a self-defense course.

11 percent carried a gun for defense.

9 percent carried a knife for defense. (Saad, 2001: 9)

Money spent on such protective measures could escalate to the point that it exceeds losses from the crimes those measures are intended to prevent.

Some people stay home rather than venture outdoors because they fear being raped, robbed, or assaulted. When they do go out, they do so only during daylight hours or when accompanied by others. At night, they use their cars to travel short distances or take cabs to avoid walking on unlit streets. Fear leads people to avoid certain neighborhoods, which then become even more deserted and dangerous. People give up visiting the library, attending meetings, and using local parks. They even forfeit income from overtime work that would require them to return home after dark. Some people respond to their fear of crime by moving to communities that seem safer.

Fear of rape restricts women's freedom of movement. Children and adolescents who are raped often stay out of school for some time; they may even transfer from schools to avoid questions and social discomfort. Adult rape victims often need outside help in homemaking and parenting, because of either physical injury or psychological distress. Some adult victims quit their jobs or stay away from work for a time in order to avoid having to talk about the rape (Burgess and Holmstrom, 1976; Gordon and Riger, 1989).

The fear of crime often becomes generalized to a fear of the streets, especially in communities that have high crime rates. As Jane Jacobs (1961: 30) has said, "When people say that a city, or part of it, is dangerous or is a jungle what they mean primarily is that they do not feel safe on the sidewalks." The public nature of the streets and sidewalks evokes a fear of strangers who are encountered there. As one observer notes: "The street is public, and the public display of tabooed behavior threatens to make it part of daily life. Openness gives such behavior an actuality and carries the threat of public acceptance and approval" (Rhodes, 1972: 36).

Fear and Trust   Social life, especially in large cities, requires a faith that others will abide by the law. Crime, even nonviolent offenses such as burglary, can reduce that trust. Imagine how the couple in the following incident felt:

> It was in Briarcliffe, N. Y., where a young couple went to dinner one evening at a local restaurant, and returned to find their car apparently stolen. After reporting it to the local police, they returned to their home and the next morning were surprised to see the car in the driveway, with an envelope on the windshield.
>
>   "There was an emergency and we had to borrow the car," the note read. "Please excuse the inconvenience, but perhaps these two theater tickets will make up for it." The couple, surprised but pleased, told the police that their car had been returned, and the next Saturday used the theater tickets.
>
>   When they returned that night, they found that their house had been completely looted. (Andelman, 1972: 49)

The burglars used the trust most people feel to their advantage. Probably the victimized couple became less trusting of strangers and maybe even of their neighbors. This crime was not a violent one; the impact on interpersonal trust might well be even greater for victims of rape, robbery, or assault.

A dramatic example of the harmful effects of the fear of crime occurred in Atlanta, Georgia, between May 1979 and July 1981, when twenty-nine black youths disappeared. All but one were later found murdered. During this time, young blacks in the city were traumatized by their fear that they would be the next victim. Tests showed that children became less verbal and more withdrawn, a change that was greatest in the neighborhoods where the murder victims had lived. Children became more mistrustful of strangers; even interviewers had a difficult time approaching them. The children also suffered a decline in self-esteem and self-confidence, became more hostile toward others, fought more at school, and carried weapons to defend themselves. Nightmares became more common. Fear of the dark, fear of school, fear of being left alone, and fear of being outdoors increased. Participation in sports and organized youth programs declined. Parents sometimes exacerbated these fears by being overprotective, an understandable response (Prugh, 1981; Rawls, 1981; Stuart, 1981). When Wayne B. Williams was arrested for some of the murders and eventually convicted of two of them, the murders stopped and tensions abated.

One crime that had long-term effects on the victims was a bizarre kidnapping in Chowchilla, California, in 1976. A school bus with twenty-six children was hijacked, and the children were buried underground in a truck trailer for sixteen hours. Eventually, they dug their way out. Nearly five years later, those children, who were between five and fourteen when the kidnapping occurred, still showed effects. They experienced nightmares, feared ordinary things such as cars and dogs, and manifested an "on guard" mistrust of everyone. Some blamed themselves for their own victimization. They had distorted senses of time, thought, and perception. Adults experiencing stress of this sort often use denial as a defense mechanism, but the children did not. They faced the reality of the event and the threat that it posed for them. Most of them continued to fear another kidnapping, even five years later (Timnick, 1981).

One response to dramatic crimes against children has been the development of school programs, books, and videocassettes to teach children self-defense techniques and a wariness of strangers. Critics suggest that such efforts might exacerbate the insecurities felt by children and their parents and instill a deep-seated suspicion of all strangers. This suspicion of strangers can be seen in changes in Halloween trick-or-treating over the years, with many parents restricting their children's activities to school parties or ringing the doorbells only of people known to the parents. Despite the paucity of documented cases of harm to children on Halloween, fear of being given poisoned candy or an apple containing a razor blade persists.

Fear and Community Ties   One study of community responses to crime concluded that

> collectivities will unite and react to crime if there is a community able to identify itself as insiders and if an opposing group of outsiders (in a sociological rather than geographical sense) can be identified. [This perspective] does not argue that solidarity will be increased within a geographical area where there are few crosscutting ties and where individuals feel no sense of community. (Podolefsky and DuBow, 1981: 10)

The heterogeneity of many American communities and the high rate of geographic mobility of Americans mean that in many communities the conditions necessary for a unified response to crime do not exist.

Fear of crime can have severe consequences for a community, including the following:

1. Physical and psychological withdrawal from community life.
2. A weakening of the informal social control processes that inhibit crime and disorder.
3. A decline in the organizational life and mobilization capacity of the neighborhood.
4. Deteriorating business conditions.

5. The importation and domestic production of delinquency and deviance.

6. Further dramatic changes in the composition of the population. (Skogan, 1986: 215)

These changes can in turn lead to even higher crime rates in the community.

Fear of crime generates suspicion and mistrust in homogeneous small towns as well as in heterogeneous urban communities. In his book *In Cold Blood,* Truman Capote (1965) reports that a common reaction to the brutal murder of a family of four in Holcomb, Kansas, was suspicion of longtime friends and neighbors. A woman who owned a local café remarked:

> One old man sitting here that Sunday, he put his finger right on it, the reason no-body can sleep; he said, "All we've got out here are our friends. There isn't anything else." In a way, that's the worst part of the crime. What a terrible thing when neighbors can't look at each other without kind of wondering! Yes, it's a hard fact to live with, but if they ever do find out who done it, I'm sure it'll be a bigger surprise than the murders themselves. (cited in Capote, 1965: 70)

Others in the town concurred. For instance, the brother of one of the victims said, "When this is cleared up, I'll wager whoever did it was someone within ten miles of where we now stand" (cited in Capote, 1965: 88). When two outsiders to the community were apprehended, "the majority of Holcomb's population, having lived for seven weeks amid unwholesome rumors, general mistrust, and suspicion, appeared to feel disappointed at being told that the murderer was not someone among themselves" (Capote, 1965: 231). Many refused to believe that the two strangers had committed the murders. The café owner said, "Maybe they did it, these fellows. But there's more to it than that. Wait. Some day they'll get to the bottom, and when they do they'll find the one behind it. The one who wanted Clutter out of the way. The *brains*" (cited in Capote, 1965: 231; emphasis in the original).

These reactions do not indicate that people always unite in response to crime, even in homogeneous and closely knit communities where the offenders are outsiders. Instead, dramatic crimes and persistently high crime rates seem more likely to breed mistrust, insecurity, and weakened attachment to the community.

Informal Control of Crime

Because only 1 or 2 percent of all serious crimes are reported to the police and lead to arrest, conviction, and imprisonment, the formal sanctions of the criminal justice system are probably less important than informal sanctions such as group censure and bystander intervention in controlling criminal behavior. Loss of esteem in the eyes of relatives and peers might be a more significant cost for an offender than a court's judgment that a crime has been committed. For instance, white-collar offenders are apparently affected more by accusation and indictment than by a criminal conviction. Concern for the good opinion of friends, relatives, and neighbors is a strong force controlling deviant behavior in Japan, where an internal "social policeman" induces conformity out of fear of losing face.

Community and Informal Social Control

By creating fear and mistrust, crime weakens community solidarity and diminishes informal social control. This can in turn increase crime as interpersonal pressures on potential offenders to abide by the law are attenuated.

Mechanical and Organic Solidarity   Simple preindustrial societies, such as tribal groups, are characterized by more intimate relationships and more social integration than are modern industrial societies. In simple societies, primary groups such as the family and the peer group are relatively stronger than they are in complex societies. These simple societies are held together by what Durkheim (1895/1933) called **mechanical solidarity**, a unity based on shared values and norms and on the similarity of functions performed by all members of the society. Children in these societies learn shared values and norms through face-to-face interaction. This socialization process perpetuates the collective conscience over generations.

In larger and more complex societies, primary groups are relatively weaker, and secondary groups such as corporations, labor unions, and schools become more important. Interpersonal relationships are less intimate, and people carry out very different tasks in their daily lives. Complex societies are integrated by **organic solidarity**, a unity based on an interdependence of functions, much as in a complex biological organism. In modern industrial societies, the collective conscience is less strong than it is in simple societies, so legal institutions develop to control behavior. The overall severity of formal sanctions is less in complex societies, as normative diversity increases and some acts that are violations of the collective conscience in simpler societies are redefined as private matters (Durkheim, 1895/1933; Green and Allen, 1981–82). However, legal sanctions are still invoked against people who violate intensely held values and norms.

Small Towns and Large Cities   Related to the idea that informal social control is stronger in simpler societies is the notion that informal control is greater in small towns than in larger cities. If informal social control is indeed stronger in small towns, it would help explain a fact discussed in Chapter 4: Crime rates tend to be lower in smaller communities.

In general, there is probably less informal social control in large cities than in small towns. The large size of the city means that residents have a difficult time distinguishing strangers from residents, and the heterogeneity of the city means that neighborhoods often include a variety of values and norms. Urban residents encounter many people on a day-to-day basis and have to screen out some of the input they receive in order to prevent "informational overload" (Milgram, 1970: 1462). The multitude of demands on city dwellers generates "norms of noninvolvement" that lead to mistrust of strangers, a desire for privacy, and withdrawal from social interaction (Milgram, 1970: 1463). Urban residents are more likely than the residents of small towns to deal with others in terms of the roles they play rather than on a personal basis. Thus, urban residents probably will be concerned only with paying for their groceries at a supermarket checkout counter, but small-town residents might ask the local grocer how his sick wife is feeling or how his children are doing in school.

A study of reactions to crime in cities, suburbs, small towns, and rural areas in Missouri found that large-city residents were the most likely to think that crime would occur in their community. Those people were also the most likely to say that their neighbors would not call the police about a burglary they witnessed. A majority of the residents of all communities believed their own community was safe, but city dwellers were the least likely to feel that way. When asked what made their own community safe, more residents of rural areas and small towns than residents of suburban and urban areas mentioned informal controls, such as a social network in the community that would lead bystanders to intervene in a crime. In comparison to the residents of small towns and rural areas, people in the suburbs and cities were more likely to say that crime in their community was kept in check by formal agents of control such as the police. Urban residents were thus the most likely to expect crime, and they relied more on formal than on informal means to control crime in their community (Boggs, 1971).

Differences among Urban Communities   In developing nations, the process of migration from tribal villages to large cities sometimes reduces informal control over deviant behavior. For instance, in Liberia

> the effectiveness of tribe and family as agents of social control has always depended upon the cohesiveness of the particular unit. In the urban areas, this cohesiveness increasingly gives way to individualism and the vacuum created by the decline in family and tribal authority has only been filled by the impersonal sanctions of the law. (Zarr, 1969: 194)

A comparison of two communities in the city of Kampala, Uganda, found that the area with less crime had greater social solidarity, more interaction among neighbors, more participation in local organizations, less geographic mobility, and more stable family relationships (Clinard and Abbott, 1973). There was also greater cultural homogeneity and more emphasis on tribal and kinship ties in the community with the lower crime rate. These conditions alleviated the anonymity that recent migrants to the city might otherwise have felt. Crime in the community with the lower rate was also prevented by strong primary group ties among residents, which made strangers to the area conspicuous.

Surveys carried out in England and Wales found that communities with weaker social organization had higher rates of crime and delinquency. One indicator of weak organization was the presence of unsupervised teenage peer groups such as gangs. These groups were more common in communities that had higher rates of crime and delinquency. The high-rate communities were also characterized by two other indicators of weak social organization: sparse friendship networks and little participation by residents in local organizations (Sampson and Groves, 1989). Evidence that local social networks can informally control crime also comes from a study of sixty urban communities in the United States, which found that neighborhood solidarity, as measured by the percentage of a community's residents who got together once a year or more with their neighbors, was strongly associated with a community's rates of burglary, motor vehicle theft, and robbery (Bellair, 1997).

A study of 343 Chicago neighborhoods reached a similar conclusion: Variations across communities in rates of violence were strongly associated with differences in **collective efficacy**, which was defined as "social cohesion among neighbors combined with their willingness to intervene on behalf of the common good" by "supervising children and maintaining public order" (Sampson, Raudenbush, and Earls, 1998: 918, 919). Collective efficacy was influenced by concentrated disadvantage, immigration concentration, and residential stability, but it was a community's collective efficacy rather than its demographic composition that directly influenced its level of violence. Communities that were most cohesive socially were the most effective at realizing informal social control.

Feeling unsafe in an urban neighborhood means not having a sense of security when in public places such as streets, sidewalks, and parks (Jacobs, 1961). Fear leads to the desertion of these public places, thus weakening informal controls that would check crime if people were there. The presence of people on the street creates surveillance of public places and attracts the attention of others to the streets, thereby reducing opportunities for crime. Fewer people on the street means less patronage of local businesses, which can cause shopkeepers to close early or move their businesses to other neighborhoods. A study of slum neighborhoods in Chicago found "impersonal domains" that were deserted and seen as dangerous at night, even though informal control over deviance was maintained in those areas during the day by businesspersons and their customers (Suttles, 1968).

This evidence suggests a crime-generating cycle in which responses to crime actually increase the crime rate. In this model, fear of crime reduces interaction in public places, which decreases informal social control there; this leads to an increase in actual and perceived crime rates, which can further reduce interaction in public and begin the cycle anew. In contrast to this crime-generating model is a crime-reducing model suggested by routine activities theory. A study that used National Crime Victimization Survey data from twenty-six cities concluded that robbery increased fear, decreased interaction, and undermined community solidarity. However, instead of increasing crime in the neighborhood by reducing informal social control, the reduction in social interaction actually decreased crime, apparently by restricting opportunities for robbery. By limiting people's daily activities to their homes, fear apparently kept the amount of crime lower than it would have been had people spent more time outside their homes (Liska and Warner, 1991).

Defensible Space and Informal Social Control

Informal control of criminal behavior can be enhanced through architectural design. Architect Oscar Newman (1973, 1996) claims that citizen involvement in crime prevention is needed and that it is possible to construct residential complexes that deter crime by creating **defensible space**, the subdivision and design of housing to allow residents to distinguish stranger from neighbor. The design of housing can reinforce or create opportunities for surveillance of a building and its surrounding grounds by eliciting from residents a feeling of territoriality and a sense of proprietary interest in the protection of the community.

A survey of residents of New York City housing projects found that more than half felt unsafe. Newman (1973: 92) claimed that this sense of insecurity had important consequences: "Fear, in itself, can increase the risk of victimization through isolating neighbor from neighbor, witness from victim, making remote the possibility of mutual help and assuring the criminal a ready opportunity to operate unhampered and unimpeded." Project residents were less threatened by crime if they knew more of their neighbors, and they were more likely to know their neighbors in housing projects where architectural design facilitated interaction.

Housing design can foster interest in nearby areas, thus creating informal control over behavior there. Crime might be reduced by making the interior spaces of large buildings more visible to people outside the buildings. Design can define private and semiprivate space near and within buildings. For example, the area enclosed by an L-shaped building often becomes the focus of surveillance and informal control by residents of the apartments that face the enclosed area, especially if the building is only a few stories high. Apartment clusters also create zones of influence by residents if shared areas are defined as private and are carefully watched. When children play in hallways or on playgrounds near a building, parents will watch those areas to protect their children from strangers. Filling the space around housing projects with play equipment, benches, or athletic facilities can attract people and attention, and keep children near home where they will be watched by their parents and neighbors.

Newman (1973: 59) states that residents of housing projects will feel safer if they can "see and be seen, hear and be heard, by day and night." Surveillance deters crime, and it reduces anxiety by creating an image of a safe environment. People who feel less anxious will spend more time in public places, thereby increasing surveillance and the informal control of behavior. Surveillance must be backed up with a willingness to intervene in a crime, either personally or by alerting the police, or mere observation will have little effect. If potential offenders believe that they will be seen committing a crime but will not be interfered with or reported to the police, they will not be affected much by surveillance.

The defensible space model is supported by research on public housing projects in the United States and Great Britain and by studies of residential blocks in the United States (Taylor and Harrell, 1996). Public housing sites with more defensible space characteristics have greater control by residents over outdoor areas and less fear and victimization among residents (Newman and Franck, 1982). Fear is lower in settings that offer fewer places for potential offenders to hide and that make it easier for legitimate users to survey an area and escape if necessary (Fisher and Nasar, 1992).

Revising the Defensible Space Model A flaw in Newman's defensible space model is that it pays attention to physical design features but slights or ignores social variables. For instance, the model ignores the demographic characteristics of the people who live in a housing area. Thus, a project that includes many teenagers and many elderly people probably will have a higher crime rate than a project limited to the elderly, whatever the defensible space design of each project. Research in Australia found that the association between public housing and crime was a result of the allocation of economically disadvantaged people to public housing rather than a result of the design of that housing (Weatherburn, Lind, and Ku, 1999). In addition to minimizing the impact of the demographic characteristics of public housing residents, Newman's model pays little attention to such social aspects of housing areas as neighborhood stability, residential mobility, employment rate, and racial integration. According to some critics, Newman's conception of defensible space lacks social reality (Taylor, Gottfredson, and Brower, 1980; Booth, 1981).

Another problem with the model is that the built environment can affect the crime rate either by encouraging residents to take action against potential offenders who violate the defensible space or by reducing opportunities for crime through controlled access or "target hardening" (for example, locks and bars on doors and windows). To test the idea of defensible space, it is necessary to separate those two processes. An evaluation of a defensible-space measure that closed off streets in a Dayton, Ohio, neighborhood concluded that the subsequent reduction in crime was attributable more to diminished opportunities for nonresidents to commit crime than it was to any impact that the street closings had on residents' social cohesion or territoriality (Donnelly and Kimble, 1997).

If the design of a built environment impedes informal social control, the area might attract more police officers, thereby enhancing formal control. Researchers would then need to separate any crime-reduction effects of formal control from those that might result from the informal control generated by defensible space design (Gillis and Hagan, 1982).

Defensible space theory needs to take into account research on human territoriality. A revised model would pay more attention to barriers deterring access by unwanted outsiders, territorial markers showing that an area is cared for, and signs of incivility indicating that social order in an area has disintegrated. This revised model would look at the way sociocultural characteristics affect territorial behavior. For instance, culturally homogeneous neighborhoods probably exert more territorial control than heterogeneous ones. A revised model would look not only at physical design but also at the traits of people who might exercise territorial control and the ways that social networks are formed and affect territorial control (see Figure 12.2). In addition, defensible space theory needs to incorporate evidence on the ways that features of the physical environment affect the perceptions and behavior of offenders (Taylor and Gottfredson, 1986; Taylor and Harrell, 1996).

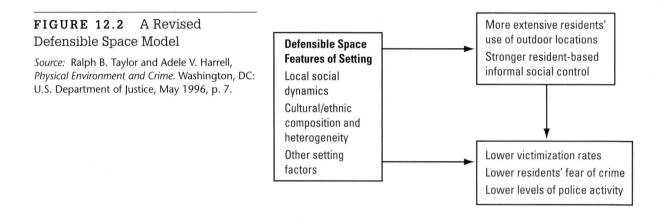

FIGURE 12.2   A Revised
Defensible Space Model

Source: Ralph B. Taylor and Adele V. Harrell,
Physical Environment and Crime. Washington, DC:
U.S. Department of Justice, May 1996, p. 7.

Individual Response to Crime

Informal control of crime depends not only on the surveillance of public places by the residents of a community but also on the willingness of those people to take action if they see a crime in progress. The combination of cooperative surveillance and willingness to intervene has been called **protective neighboring** (Schneider and Schneider, 1978). Protective neighboring seems to be more common among people with higher incomes, long-term residents of a community, and homeowners. Just as crime and delinquency are less common among people who have a stake in conformity, so it seems that efforts to control crime and delinquency are also more common among people who have a stake in conformity. The Crime and the Media box looks at one effort to get more people involved in the fight against crime.

The most common action people take in response to a crime is to call the police to report it, but sometimes victims respond directly by taking action against offenders. A controversial case involving the right of victims to use deadly force against offenders occurred in 1984 in New York City, where Bernhard Goetz, a white man, shot four black youths on the subway because he feared he was about to be robbed when one of the youths asked him for five dollars. Goetz was cleared of all attempted murder and assault charges in 1987, but he was convicted of the felony of illegal possession of a firearm. He was sentenced to one year in jail but was released after eight months. Supporters of the jury's acquittal of Goetz on the most serious charges applauded its apparent willingness to allow potential crime victims to defend themselves against their attackers. Critics said that the jury's lenient treatment of Goetz opened the way for vigilante justice and posed a threat to young black men from whites who are afraid of crime. In 1996, a civil jury awarded $43 million to Darrell Cabey, who had been paralyzed and brain-damaged by one of Goetz's shots, but Goetz's financial situation made it unlikely that Cabey would see much of that money.

Bystander Responses to Crime

Occasionally, bystanders respond to a crime in progress by intervening. Such a response is probably least likely where fear of crime leads people to withdraw from social contacts, stay home at night, and avoid strangers. This kind of behavior minimizes the likelihood that anyone will be around to witness a crime. Fear also makes those people who are on the street more likely to adopt a self-protective stance and less likely to intervene personally in a crime.

The issue of bystander response to emergencies such as crime has been called the **Good Samaritan problem** (Ratcliffe, 1966). The crime that most dramatically brought this problem to public attention was the 1964 murder of Kitty Genovese in Queens, New York. This crime occurred in a middle-class neighborhood that had a relatively low crime rate. A man attacked Kitty Genovese at about three o'clock in the morning when she was returning from work. She screamed, and lights went on in nearby apartments. People looked out and one witness shouted at the assailant to leave the woman alone. The assailant left but soon returned. Again lights went on and again the assailant left. When he returned a third time, he killed Miss Genovese. The three attacks took place over a period of about thirty-five minutes, and at least thirty-eight witnesses knew of the violence. When the witnesses were later asked about their failure to take action, some said they had been too tired to do anything and others said they had not wanted to get involved.

At first, social scientists were unable to provide a convincing explanation of the bystanders' failure to help the victim. Letters to the newspapers suggested printing the names of the nonresponsive witnesses. Others blamed the police, saying that

CRIME AND THE MEDIA

Crime Stoppers

Crime Stoppers, a program started in Albuquerque, New Mexico, in 1976, unites the news media, law-enforcement agencies, and the community in an effort to reduce serious crime. "Dead-end" crimes that the police have been unable to solve are reported in the media, and citizens are encouraged to call in tips to help solve the crimes. Because of the fear of retaliation, callers are guaranteed anonymity. They are paid for their information if it leads to an arrest and an indictment. The tipster is given an identification number on the telephone and collects the reward at a prearranged place. Money for the rewards is donated by private businesses and individuals. Some cities have also raised funds through telethons and public appeals.

As of December 31, 2002, the 1,149 Crime Stoppers programs around the world that had reported statistics to Crime Stoppers International had cleared 917,596 cases, paid $60,258,852 in rewards, and recovered $5,443,570,914 worth of property and narcotics. What is not clear is whether Crime Stoppers reduced crime rates in cities that had programs. Deterrent effects are probably limited, because the solved cases are only a small percentage of all serious offenses in those cities.

About two-thirds of the anonymous tips are from criminals and people associated with criminals, which suggests that Crime Stoppers might disrupt relationships between offenders and their accomplices, friends, and relatives by creating a fear among offenders that people close to them will turn them in for a reward.

Home page of Crime Stoppers International: www.c-s-i.org/index2.html

The size of a reward is not related to a tipster's satisfaction with Crime Stoppers or to his or her willingness to participate in the program again. However, the payment of some reward seems essential to the program's success in getting people to report crimes. This raises the question of whether citizens should be paid to do their civic duty of reporting crime to the police. Another concern is whether the desire to collect reward money might entice some people to make false accusations or intrude on their neighbors' privacy.

Sources: Based on Dennis P. Rosenbaum, Arthur J. Lurigio, and Paul J. Lavrakas, "Enhancing Citizen Participation and Solving Serious Crime: A National Evaluation of Crime Stoppers Programs," *Crime and Delinquency* 35 (July 1989), 401–420; Crime Stoppers International, retrieved from www.c-s-i.org.

New Yorkers were afraid of the police and were therefore unwilling to call them in an emergency. What was puzzling was that no help was forthcoming from a group as large as thirty-eight; had only one or two people observed the crime, it might have been possible to point the finger at a few heartless individuals. Many commentators concluded that something must be wrong with society as a whole. Several gave apathy as the cause of the problem, concluding that people just no longer cared about their fellow citizens.

Reactions to Emergencies   How do people respond when faced with a crime or other emergency that requires action? Lawrence Zelic Freedman (1966) suggests that their initial response is often fear of being hurt and fear of reprisals. Often witnesses cannot fit the unusual event into any familiar category of past experience. The witnesses to the Genovese murder might have failed to take action because the crime seemed "totally incongruous in a respectable neighborhood," creating "a sense of unreality which inhibited rational action" (Milgram and Hollander, 1970: 208).

Before witnesses take action, they must clearly define the situation as an emergency that requires personal intervention. Emergency situations are often ambiguous to witnesses; several witnesses to the Genovese murder interpreted it as a "lovers' quarrel." Witnesses often fail to respond appropriately, denying to themselves that anything so unusual could be happening in their presence. What appears to be apathy might in fact be massive inhibition or paralysis of consciousness resulting from internal conflict. Freedman (1966: 175) claims that in response to emergencies,

> apathy and indifference are the least likely primary psychic vectors. . . . The sequence as I see it is, first, the intense emotional shock—characterized predominantly, but not exclusively, by anxiety; second, the cognitive perception and awareness of what has happened; third, an inertial paralysis of reaction, which as a non-act becomes in fact an act; and fourth, the self-awareness of one's own shock anxiety, non-involvement which is followed by a sense of guilt and intrapsychic and social self-justification.
>
> I do not assume that these things happen in such neat sequence. For all practical purposes they seem to occur simultaneously.

Witnesses sometimes justify their inaction by claiming that the victim and the offender must know one another, which might indeed be the case. Bystanders are more likely to intervene in assaults between strangers than to offer help when it seems that the assault involves a married couple (Shotland and Straw, 1976). Witnesses are also more likely to intervene if they believe that the victim is totally innocent and if they can identify in some way with the victim. On the other hand, witnesses find it easier to tolerate the victimization of disvalued people such as prostitutes and skid-row alcoholics. If a witness's identification with a victim is slight, the chance that the witness will assist the victim is low (Blumenthal et al., 1972).

Experimental Studies of Bystander Response   Social-psychological experiments have cast light on the reasons that witnesses to emergencies help under some conditions but not others. According to Bibb Latané and John Darley (1970), neither public apathy nor the absence of norms requiring assistance explains bystander nonresponse. In a series of experiments, they clarified the characteristics of situations that are conducive to bystander intervention. The situational determinants of bystander assistance were so strong that differences among the personalities of witnesses paled in significance as influences on their behavior.

Before bystanders will intervene, they must make a series of decisions. A negative decision at any point means they will not help the victim. They must notice the situation and define it as an emergency. Then they must determine that they have a personal responsibility to do something. If they think the situation is none of their business, they will not help. Bystanders must also decide what kind of aid to offer—personal intervention, or calling the police or an ambulance. Finally, they must decide how to implement the course of action on which they have decided (Latané and Darley, 1970).

One reason for the public's condemnation of the nonresponsive bystanders in the Genovese murder was the failure of a large number of witnesses to help. The commonsense assumption is that if there are more people around, the chance that at least one will help should be greater. However, social-psychological research demonstrates that the presence of others at the scene of an emergency actually inhibits helping behavior. People might be embarrassed to help for fear that their assistance will turn out to be unwanted or unneeded. When no witness in a group of bystanders immediately offers help, others might assume their own interpretation of the situation as one requiring aid is wrong. If help were needed, would not someone already have offered it? People in groups take cues from others, and if no one helps they might reinterpret the event. This has been referred to as **pluralistic ignorance:** Witnesses in a group fail to help because they interpret the failure of other witnesses to help as meaning that no help is needed (Latané and Darley, 1970).

Witnesses who are alone when they observe a crime or an accident are more likely to help than witnesses who are in groups of two or more. Lone witnesses are more likely to seek information about the situation, to help the victim through their own efforts, and to report the situation to someone else who can provide assistance. A witness who is accompanied by another person is more likely to help a victim if that witness is personally acquainted with the second witness than if the second witness is a stranger. This is probably because personal knowledge breaks down pluralistic ignorance by making communication between witnesses more likely. However, pairs of witnesses who know one another are less likely to help victims than are witnesses who are alone. One reason for this is that there is no **diffusion of responsibility** when there is only one witness present (Latané and Darley, 1970). Diffusion of responsibility occurs in groups of witnesses because people can say to themselves that someone should act but that it need not be themselves, since other potential helpers are present. Especially when a victim's cries for help are not directed toward a specific bystander, people who witness an emergency can soothe their consciences by claiming that someone else should help or that others are equally responsible if no one helps. Indeed, the larger the group of bystanders, the more responsibility is diffused and the less likely it is that help will be offered.

One experiment that found that bystander intervention is more likely when responsibility is focused on a particular bystander was conducted on Jones Beach, Long Island. A "victim" placed a blanket near another bather, turned on a radio, and a short time later said to the bystander, "Excuse me, I'm going up the boardwalk for a few minutes. Would you watch my things?" This committed the bystander to watching the radio. Other bystanders were only asked for a match and were thus not committed to watching the radio. In a few minutes, a "thief"—who was actually part of the experiment—picked up the radio, which was playing loudly, and walked away with it. A third participant in the experiment observed the reactions of bystanders. Only four of the twenty uncommitted witnesses who later said they had noticed the theft tried to stop the thief, but nineteen of the twenty committed bystanders made an effort to stop the thief. Prior contact between the victim and the bystander had focused responsibility on the committed bystanders to take some action when the theft occurred (Moriarity, 1975).

Other aspects of the situation also affect the likelihood of bystander assistance to a victim. Familiarity with the location is important; help is probably more likely to be given if witnesses are in their own neighborhood than if they are in a strange neighborhood. Bystanders also consider the risks of providing help; they might be less willing to help if a weapon is present or if there are several offenders rather than one. Offering help might be a function of the other activities in which a witness is engaged at the time. For instance, help is probably more likely to be given if a witness is standing on the street doing nothing than if a witness is rushing to a doctor's appointment or a job interview (Darley and Batson, 1973).

Bystanders who are self-assured, feel good about themselves, or have specialized training in first aid, life saving, or medical and police techniques are especially likely to help others. People who seek training in such skills could be more inclined to help to begin with, or they might learn an ethic of helping behavior as they learn those skills. A study of thirty-two people who had intervened in actual crimes of violence or theft found that all but one were men, and that they tended to be above average in height and weight and were usually larger than the offenders they confronted (Geis, 1981). Perhaps size and sense of competence led more men than women to risk intervening when they encountered a crime in progress.

Would Kitty Genovese Be Helped Today?   On the twenty-fifth anniversary of the Genovese murder, an article in the *New York Times* declared that "there are enough recent examples of people coming to each other's aid to argue that New Yorkers are not hard as rocks" (Martin, 1989: 29). The detective who led the Genovese investigation stated, "People are more willing to come forward now." Edward Koch, then mayor of the city, declared, "Today the likelihood of a crowd averting its eyes and not going to the defense of someone in trouble is much less" (cited in Martin, 1989: 29).

None of those optimistic assertions relies on any empirical evidence. Indeed, they ignore a wealth of research that suggests that a victim confronting the same situation faced by Kitty Genovese could expect no different response from onlookers today. In 1987 in Manchester, New Hampshire, a twenty-one-year-old mother of two, on her way home from a friend's party at 4 A.M., was grabbed by a man, dragged shrieking across the street, and then raped, beaten, choked, and robbed. An estimated two dozen people heard the attack, and at least three people witnessed the attack. The only person to call the police was a security guard and former Marine, a man who fit the profile of the kind of bystander most likely to take action. This man's statement after the rape should be taken with as much skepticism as the optimistic statements by New Yorkers that things had improved since the Genovese murder. He said, "The next time something like this happens, I think you'll see a lot more action" (cited in Hohler, 1987: 44).

Collective Response to Crime

People sometimes band together in a collective response to crime, working for a political candidate who promises "law and order," meeting to plan a crime-prevention program, or organizing a civilian patrol group to perform tasks that they think the police are not doing adequately. "Place managers" such as storekeepers, security guards, homeowners, and building managers who are present every day in a community contribute more to the control of local drug and disorder problems when they develop collective solutions to such problems than when they respond as individuals by intervening in a crime or calling the police (Mazerolle, Kadleck, and Roehl, 1998).

A Historical and Comparative Perspective

Collective response to crime has a long history. Ancient Roman plebeians engaged in community self-help when they threw alleged offenders from the Tarpeian rock. Early Germans raised a hue and cry, took up arms, blew horns, chased suspects, and occasionally lynched them. "People's police" sometimes had to be restrained from attacking innocent people in the former Soviet Union. In China, people informally police their communities, and Africans in tribal villages sometimes impose harsh punishment on suspected criminals. Since the early 1990s, vigilantism in response to an ineffectual criminal justice system has been reported in Great Britain, South Africa, Nigeria, Cambodia, Haiti, Venezuela, Colombia, Argentina, and other countries. The Cross-Cultural Perspective box gives an example from urban Brazil.

Vigilante activity has occurred in the United States for more than two centuries. The first recorded activity was in the 1760s in South Carolina, where a group called the Regulators sought to bring order to communities in the Back Country. The Regulators apparently reduced crime, but they violated the due process rights of suspects. They elicited much hostility and eventually were disbanded when they began to mete out severe punishment, select victims rashly, and even supervise the morals and family life of law-abiding citizens.

Vigilante groups on the American frontier developed in response to a perceived lack of social order, rather than in response to specific crimes. Because the new frontier communities often lacked the resources to hire law-enforcement officials, were usually far from towns that could provide those officials, and were near open spaces to which suspects could flee, frontier vigilante groups sometimes developed as a way to establish social control over crime and bring stability to the community.

The leaders of many vigilante movements in the West were young men from the East who sought power and prestige and wanted to establish an orderly community in which they could pursue their ambitions. The rank-and-file members of those vigilante movements were often drawn from the middle classes, and the lower classes provided most of the targets of the movements.

Vigilante organizations in the West ranged in size from a dozen to as many as 8,000 participants; usually they had a few hundred members. Most groups lasted only a few weeks, but some endured for over a year. In nearly half of the recorded vigilante movements, there was at least one execution of an alleged offender, usually after a brief and formal—but extralegal—"trial."

Vigilantes traditionally espoused popular sovereignty, the right of the people to wield power in their own best interests (Brown, 1969). They also supported the idea that people had the right to revolt against established authority if it failed to maintain order. Vigilante groups sought to preserve and protect the life, liberty, and property of their members and the other residents of the community, and in this sense their extralegal efforts to preserve civil order were conservative (Little and Sheffield, 1983).

Some vigilante movements were socially constructive, dealing with specific problems of disorder and then disbanding; these movements usually represented the consensus of the community. By contrast, socially destructive vigilante movements encountered stiff opposition and produced community strife. Movements became socially destructive when they failed to exercise control over violent or sadistic members. The possibility that vigilante movements, including civilian patrol groups in today's cities, might become battlegrounds for personal and group conflicts rather than represent genuine community consensus is one reason to distrust such movements. Such consensus is difficult to establish in large and heterogeneous cities.

Urban Patrol Groups

Vigilante groups on the American frontier developed to provide social control of deviant behavior. Just as the western frontier was in transition from wilderness to settled territory, so can the transition from a small preindustrial city to a heavily industrialized urban center be understood as a kind of frontier. In Great Britain during the eighteenth and nineteenth centuries, urbanization and industrialization created a kind of frontier, a transition between social forms that left growing cities without effective law enforcement. Just as vigilante groups emerged in the American West, so did private "prosecution societies" develop in English cities. These prosecu-

CROSS-CULTURAL PERSPECTIVES

Lynchings in Brazil

Rising crime rates in Brazil have elicited a variety of public responses. More Brazilians are carrying weapons, rarely wearing jewelry or expensive clothes on the street, and avoiding places where they might be robbed or kidnapped. Most cars have alarms and secret locks, and drivers do not stop for red lights for fear of being robbed. The number of cars that had bulletproof glass installed increased from 1,000 in 1999 to 4,000 in 2000, even though this procedure costs as much as a new car.

The Brazilian market for all private security measures grew by 50 percent from 1995 to 2000, to an estimated $2.5 billion. Much of this money was spent on registered and unregistered private security guards, who were four times as numerous as civil and military police officers in 2000. Many Brazilians have moved from houses to apartment complexes that are protected by armed guards, neighbors have joined together to pay for guards to patrol their communities, and those who can afford to do so have hired personal bodyguards.

Perhaps the most dramatic response to Brazil's crime problem is citizen involvement in the lynching of suspected offenders. These lynchings are a response to the widely held view that the criminal justice system is ineffective in controlling crime. One lynching is described as follows:

Osvaldo Otavio Pires was brought handcuffed into Elio's bar in the Jardim Guanhambu slum on the outskirts of São Paulo at about 8 A.M. on April 2. Over 100 men, women and children had gathered in the small wooden building to await his arrival.

Mr. Pires, 33 years old, was thrust onto a bench facing the crowd and the handcuffs were removed.

He was allowed to smoke a cigarette and drink a glass of rough liquor, but no one moved when he asked to see his two small children. Witnesses recalled that his hands were trembling.

Mr. Pires, long feared in Jardim Guanhambu, then heard an array of charges of armed assault brought by people filling the bar. After 20 minutes, participants in the meeting later told reporters, a voice was heard to say, "All those in favor of death raise their hands." Dozens of arms were lifted; apparently no one objected.

Mr. Pires was pushed out of Elio's Bar and the crowd fell on him with sticks, poles and stones. Once he lay dead in the dusty street, the police were called. When they arrived, they took the names and addresses of 43 people who said they had joined in the lynching. No arrests were made. (Riding, p. 1)

Over time, the nature of the crimes committed by lynching victims has changed. One official remarks, "In the past, lynchings were restricted to heinous crimes—rapes of children or sadistic murders. Now a lynching can be sparked by the theft of a wallet" (cited in Brooke, p. 6). A study of fifty-six lynchings found that 58 percent of the victims had been suspected of theft and 18 percent of sexual assault.

Lynchings in Brazil have been attributed not only to the fear of crime and an ineffective criminal justice system but also to the nation's extraordinarily high rate of unemployment and underemployment, the low incomes of those who are working, the failure of the stagnant economy to offer people any hope, and the attention given to violence by the mass media.

Sources: Based on Alan Riding, "Brazilians Turn to Lynchings to Fight Soaring Crime Rate," *New York Times,* April 15, 1984, pp. 1, 12; James Brooke, "Lynching Increases in Brazil's Shantytowns," *New York Times,* November 3, 1991, p. 6; Kenneth Rapoza, "Rising Crime Has Brazilians Turning to 'Vigilante' Security," *Boston Sunday Globe,* August 12, 2001, p. A11.

tion societies sought to make the criminal justice system more accessible and more effective. They supported the rule of law and rarely meted out sentences on their own (Little and Sheffield, 1983).

One contemporary civilian patrol group that has received much attention is the Guardian Angels. Formed in 1978, this organization is made up primarily of young Hispanics and blacks who patrol subway stations and subway cars in groups in order to deter robbery, assault, and rape. Guardian Angels are trained in karate, resuscitation methods, and the legal requirements for arrests. Curtis Sliwa, founder of the Angels, announced in 1992 that early in the group's existence he had fabricated six incidents to draw favorable public attention to his group and to counteract opposition from the police. By 1992, the Angels had been reduced to "little more than a security force for a block of midtown [Manhattan] restaurants, its membership and activities greatly exaggerated, its patrols, in their trademark red berets and T-shirts, converging only on highly publicized situations" (Gonzalez, 1992: B1).

There is little evidence that the Guardian Angels were ever very effective in preventing crime. Even when the streets seemed safer because of their presence, the Angels may simply have been displacing crime to other locations or to times when they were not around. One study in New York City found that Guardian Angel patrols apparently did not affect either the amount of crime on the subways or the level of fear felt by riders, nor did they change passengers' willingness to assist one another (Kenney, 1987). Another study found that the Guardian Angels in San Diego did not reduce violent crime but might have had a small impact on property offenses. Nevertheless, 60 percent of the citizens who knew that the group patrolled their neighborhood reported feeling safer as a result (Pennell et al., 1989).

Patrol groups face several problems (Marx and Archer, 1971, 1972). To sustain the interest of their members and the support of the community, they need to make the crisis to which they are responding continuously felt. They need a charismatic leader to inspire confidence in their members and in the residents of the community. Patrol groups need to be formally organized, and they require financial support. They have a better chance of survival if they have an ideology that states positive, specific goals; vague targets such as crime and disorder do not seem to sustain patrol groups for long. These groups are most effective in limited and well-defined settings, such as housing projects and rock concerts, where there are homogeneous populations separated from other people by clear boundaries. Even if all of these conditions are met, patrol groups face difficulties:

> Self-defense groups often lack a clear mandate from the groups they wish to serve and their legal position regarding the use of force and citizen arrests is ambiguous. They may have trouble defining their task. The tendency of the groups to lack the resources for recruiting, screening, and training appropriate manpower and for sustaining motivation beyond that which stems from a deeply felt crisis (along with the degree of autonomy some groups have) may contribute to ineffectiveness and abuses. And even if internal problems are solved, the groups may face harassment from the police. (Marx and Archer, 1971: 68)

Urban patrol groups serve important symbolic and participatory functions for their members. They enhance the self-esteem and sense of power of those who are involved, leading patrol-group members as well as other community residents to think they can do something about crime. If people believe the patrols are effective in making the streets safer, even if they are not, people may be more willing to use the streets at night.

The surveillance provided by patrol groups is likely to be more effective than unorganized surveillance by community residents in deterring crime, because the chance that a member of a patrol group will take direct action is greater than the chance that a private citizen will intervene personally or call the police. Patrol groups can thus create surveillance, stimulate interaction in public places, and help reduce crime by supporting formal control agents and by increasing informal control by local residents.

Neighborhood Watches

Crime-stopping groups such as Neighborhood or Block Watches, which are sponsored by law-enforcement officials in about 2,500 communities, "share information about local crime problems, exchange crime prevention tips, and make plans for engaging in surveillance ('watching') of the neighborhood and crime-reporting activities" (Rosenbaum, 1987: 104). A 1985 survey found that only 9 percent of Neighborhood Watch groups reported that informal surveillance of the streets was their sole activity. Other common activities included property engraving, household security surveys, crime tip hotlines, the improvement of street lighting, block parenting, and more general activities related to the community's physical environment (Garofalo and McLeod, 1989).

Unlike frontier vigilantes, Neighborhood Watch groups operate in a context in which there is already a fully developed system of law enforcement. They seek to supplement the police rather than to replace them, and they are usually sponsored by a local law-enforcement agency. These groups might improve police-community relations by providing opportunities for contacts between the police and law-abiding citizens. Police support for Neighborhood Watch groups acknowledges that the police cannot solve the crime problem by themselves, and this can foster a more realistic image of the police.

Neighborhood Watch groups share information about crime problems and crime-prevention methods and engage in surveillance and crime-reporting activities.

Research shows that Neighborhood Watch groups have had no more than modest success in reducing crime, with the crimes most likely to be prevented being residential burglaries and theft from the immediate vicinity of homes (Garofalo and McLeod, 1989). According to one review of the research, "neighborhood crime prevention programs have been unable to set in motion the social interaction, territoriality, surveillance, and other behaviors that theoretically are expected at the block or neighborhood level" (Rosenbaum, 1988: 375). Furthermore, the difficulty encountered by Neighborhood Watch groups in keeping their members involved over time suggests that sustained reductions in crime could be even harder to achieve than short-term reductions. Many of the groups' activities are onetime measures, such as engraving property and household security surveys, and the activity level of many groups is low, with 40 percent not even holding regularly scheduled meetings (Garofalo and McLeod, 1989).

Community Crime-Prevention Strategies

In the mid-1980s, the appearance of crack cocaine aroused community action directed at changing the behavior of local drug dealers and users. In New York City, the leaders of black churches held all-night vigils as a part of their battle against crack. In Boston, drugs in general were the target of a group called Drop a Dime, which encouraged citizens to phone tips to its statewide hotline and report local drug problems to the police. Drop a Dime organizers set up block associations to swamp the police with complaints about drug problems, and they sponsored prayer sessions and temporary occupancy of vacant buildings used by drug dealers to attract the attention of the police and the press.

Perhaps the most dramatic action against drug dealers occurred in Detroit, Miami, and other cities where enraged citizens burned down "crack houses." Objecting to the open sale of drugs from the curb and frightened by the gunfire of rival dealers, two residents of a previously quiet Detroit neighborhood burned down a crack house. In court the men admitted to setting the fire, but a jury quickly acquitted them. A local newspaper found that 87 percent of its readers thought the arson was justified (Wilkerson, 1988).

One effective way to fight neighborhood drug problems is the enforcement of drug house abatement laws. These measures, which typically enjoy strong community support, pressure property owners to clean up or close down buildings used by drug dealers by defining those buildings as nuisances and threatening the owners with civil action. This process depends on local residents to provide law-enforcement agents with information about where drug trafficking is occurring. Even if the enforcement of drug house abatement laws only displaces the problem, it does disrupt the local drug trade by making it harder and riskier for customers to find dealers, and it reduces signs of disorder in the community. Community policing, which is discussed in Chapter 14, is a potentially effective measure that enlists local residents in cooperative efforts with the police to drive drug traffickers from the neighborhood or out of business. The organized citizen groups that sometimes grow out of community policing make it difficult for drug traffickers, driven from a community by police sweeps or the enforcement of drug house abatement laws, to return to the neighborhood where they had been doing business (Davis and Lurigio, 1996).

A study of thirty-six urban neighborhoods found that drug problems stimulate confrontational tactics by local residents rather than undermine organized community action. Contradicting some earlier research, this study found that confrontational responses to local drug problems were most common in poverty-stricken and minority neighborhoods with high crime rates. The prior existence of block clubs and other broad-based community organizations was found to encourage confrontational responses (Skogan and Lurigio, 1992).

Neighborhoods that are more successful in securing resources to fight crime from local governments and police departments have lower rates of household and personal victimization. That benefit is greater for disadvantaged communities than for prosperous ones (Vélez, 2001). The individuals who participate in patrol groups and other community efforts to fight crime are drawn to those organizations less by their fear of crime than by a general desire to improve neighborhood life (Lavrakas and Herz, 1982). Most effective community crime-prevention efforts develop from neighborhood organizations that have a general orientation toward revitalizing the community or providing services for local youths (Lewis and Salem, 1981, 1986). Neighborhood Watch and similar programs are most successful when they are part of multi-issue, general-purpose community groups rather than when they focus exclusively on crime (Lewis, Grant, and Rosenbaum, 1988; Garofalo and McLeod, 1989; Skogan, 1990).

The idea that crime-prevention organizations can be created in high-crime communities that need them but do not have them was tested in Chicago and Minneapolis. Although many residents of the neighborhoods in which block clubs and other crime-prevention measures were developed knew of and initially participated in the programs, the programs did not reduce fear of crime or increase crime reporting. The programs also failed to increase neighborhood solidarity, interaction among residents, watchfulness, or daily activities that might reduce crime. Because the programs in Chicago and Minneapolis were run by professionals, were highly visible, and got a good initial response, their lack of success cannot be attributed to a failure to implement the programs properly. It simply is difficult to get the residents of high-crime communities to participate in crime-prevention organizations, unless those organizations have emerged spontaneously from within the community and are concerned broadly with neighborhood improvement rather than narrowly with the reduction of crime (Skogan, 1990). Some observers believe that these latter factors came into play in certain cities in the 1990s and contributed to the decline in crime rates during that decade. For instance, Boston's success in curbing juvenile gang violence was widely attributed to collaboration among a group of black clergy called the Ten-Point Coalition, the Catholic Archdiocese, local voluntary organizations, the school department, the police, and probation officers.

Summary

Fear can contribute to crime by undermining community solidarity and weakening informal social control. This fear, which is not always rationally related to the actual risk of victimization, causes people to stay home, restrict their travel when they do venture outdoors, and spend money on measures they hope will protect them from crime. By reducing interpersonal trust, fear can diminish the informal control of behavior in a community.

Informal control of crime is most effective when interaction is common and the surveillance of behavior is possible. Those conditions are more common in small towns than in large cities. In large cities, where crime rates are often high, people frequently assign the task of crime prevention to the formal control agents of the criminal justice system. There is, however, much variation among urban communities, with people most willing to play an active role in crime prevention in socially integrated and stable neighborhoods.

The defensible space model maintains that architectural design can increase citizen involvement in the crime-prevention process by encouraging people to exercise control over the territory in which they live. This process might reduce some kinds of crime in certain housing situations, but overall the evidence that defensible space can have a major impact on crime is not strong. A revised defensible space model that takes into account the social characteristics of residents and the way people form networks might describe more accurately the means by which informal control can curb crime.

For informal social control to be effective in reducing crime, people must be willing to call the police or intervene in a crime. The Good Samaritan problem arises when witnesses fail to take action of this sort. Nonresponse to observed crimes is a product of the ambiguity of some crime situations, a sense of unreality when watching a crime in progress, pluralistic ignorance that results from thinking that if no one else is helping it must be because no help is needed, and a diffusion of responsibility among witnesses. Other factors that can affect the chance that a bystander will intervene include whether the person feels self-assured or is trained in offering assistance.

Collective action in response to crime has a long history, dating as far back as the 1760s in the United States and even earlier elsewhere. Vigilante groups in the American West sought to create order in the absence of a criminal justice system, taking on responsibility for preserving life, liberty, and property from suspected criminals. Today, urban patrol groups operate in the context of a functioning, but often ineffective, criminal justice system. Citizen involvement in crime prevention is usually not a direct result of the fear of victimization but is instead related to the characteristics of community residents and the presence of organizations broadly concerned with neighborhood improvement.

IMPORTANT TERMS

broken windows theory	formal social control	organic solidarity
collective efficacy	Good Samaritan problem	pluralistic ignorance
defensible space	informal social control	protective neighboring
diffusion of responsibility	mechanical solidarity	social control

REVIEW QUESTIONS

1. How is fear of crime related to actual risk of victimization? What effects does fear of crime have on people's daily behavior, on their trust in others, and on community ties?

2. What are the differences between informal social control and formal social control? How do communities exercise informal control? In what kinds of communities is informal control most likely to be effective in keeping crime in check?

3. What is defensible space? How might buildings and communities designed to enhance defensible space reduce crime? Does research support the defensible space model?

4. Under what conditions will witnesses to a crime take action to help the victim? Under what conditions will they fail to act?

5. How do contemporary urban patrol groups differ from vigilantes in the American West? How effective do you think modern patrol groups are in keeping urban crime rates down?

6. What are Neighborhood or Block Watches? How might they reduce crime in a neighborhood? Can they be effective in communities with high crime rates?

FOR FURTHER STUDY

Fear of Crime   The meaning of fear, the way it is defined by the news media, and its use by various organizations and institutions are examined in David L. Altheide's *Creating Fear: News and the Construction of Crisis* (Hawthorne, NY: Aldine de Gruyter, 2002).

Disorder and Crime   Three perspectives on the relationship between disorder and crime are Wesley G. Skogan's *Disorder and Decline: Crime and the Spiral of Decay in American Neighborhoods* (Berkeley: University of California Press, 1990), George L. Kelling and Catherine M.

Coles's *Fixing Broken Windows: Restoring Order and Reducing Crime in Our Communities* (New York: Free Press, 1996), and Bernard E. Harcourt's *Illusion of Order: The False Promise of Broken Window Policing* (Cambridge, MA: Harvard University Press, 2001).

Collective Responses to Crime   Two websites that provide information on community responses to crime are sponsored by Crime Stoppers International (www.c-s-i.org) and the National Neighborhood Watch Program of the National Sheriffs' Association (www.usaonwatch.org).

13 The Criminal Justice System

Every modern society has a criminal justice system that exercises formal social control by meting out punishment to offenders. This system also shapes offenders' behavior. Labeling by the police, the courts, and the correctional system can contribute to the development of criminal careers, but arrest and conviction also keep people from violating the law by instilling in them a fear of punishment. A prison sentence might also reduce crime by cutting an offender's ties to accomplices, by causing criminal skills to grow rusty, or by pushing an inmate into treatment. On the other hand, a prison sentence could contribute to crime by creating a desire to strike back at society, by reducing ties to conventional people, or by exposing an offender to other criminals. Thus, the criminal justice system prevents crime in some ways but contributes to it in others.

This chapter examines three components of the criminal justice system: the police, the courts, and the prisons. The following chapter looks at the principles on which this system is based. One such principle is deterrence, the notion that the threat of sanctions can prevent crime by creating a fear of punishment in those who might break the law. A second principle is incapacitation, which assumes that crime can be prevented by locking up offenders. A third principle is retribution, the idea that offenders deserve to suffer for the harm they have caused and that their punishment should be in proportion to that harm. A fourth basis for the criminal justice system is rehabilitation, which proposes that criminal sanctions should aim to reform convicted offenders so that they will not commit crime in the future.

The effectiveness of the criminal justice system in meeting the goals of deterrence, incapacitation, retribution, and rehabilitation depends on coordination among the various agencies of law enforcement. Critics have claimed that the American criminal justice system is not really a system at all, in the sense of being a set of agencies that are coordinated with one another, seek the same goals, and try to implement a single policy to deal with crime. There are important linkages among the police, the courts, and the prisons, as we can see in Figure 13.1, but these agencies do not form a unified system. When we speak of a criminal justice system, we are talking about different law-enforcement agencies and the linkages among them rather than about a single, well-integrated system.

The criminal justice system has been described as a funnel or sieve that sorts out cases. Only some of all crimes that are committed are reported to the police, and many of those that are reported do not produce an arrest. Arrested suspects sometimes have the charges against them dropped or are acquitted in court. Of those who are convicted and sentenced, many are not sent to prison. The funnel or sieve effect that characterizes the criminal justice system is one of **case attrition**, with cases being sorted out as they proceed through the system, and relatively few crimes ending with a perpetrator's conviction and imprisonment.

The cost of the American criminal justice system is enormous and has grown in recent years, primarily because of the system's increasing reliance on imprisonment. Imprisonment is an expensive form of punishment; the construction of each new maximum-security prison cell costs about $70,000, and the average annual maintenance cost for a prisoner is about $25,000. In 2001, there were 1,406,031 inmates in state and federal prisons, 631,240 inmates in local jails, 3,932,751 adults on probation (court-ordered supervision), and 732,351 adults on parole (supervised release from jail or prison) (Bureau of Justice Statistics, 2003). The lower cost of probation and parole has led some critics to argue for more use of these alternatives to incarceration.

In 1999, American justice system expenditures totaled $147 billion. Police departments accounted for 45 percent of that amount. Judicial and legal services accounted for 22 percent of the expenditures, and corrections for 33 percent of the total. Most of these costs were incurred at the local rather than state or federal level; 51 percent of the total was spent by local (city, town, or county) agencies, 34 percent by state agencies, and 15 percent by the federal government (Gifford, 2002).

The Police

The police serve multiple functions. They maintain order in public places, resolve interpersonal disputes, and provide social services. They are also the first formal line of defense against crime, for only if the police arrest suspects will the rest of the criminal justice system come into play in trying, convicting, and punishing offenders.

History of the Police

For centuries, societies have had some kind of a police force, an armed group of specialists who keep order and deal with violations of the law. The first modern police force was organized in London in 1829 by Sir Robert Peel, with officers nicknamed "bobbies" after their founder. This police force differed from earlier law-enforcement units in being full-time, paid, uniformed, and organized for the city as a whole. Standards of literacy and character were established, and recruits were trained to perform their duties (Bayley, 1983).

Public police forces have existed in the United States since the seventeenth century, but it was only in Boston in 1837 that the first modern police force was organized along the same lines as London's department. By the 1870s nearly all large American cities had their own police force, which provided all citizens, rather than

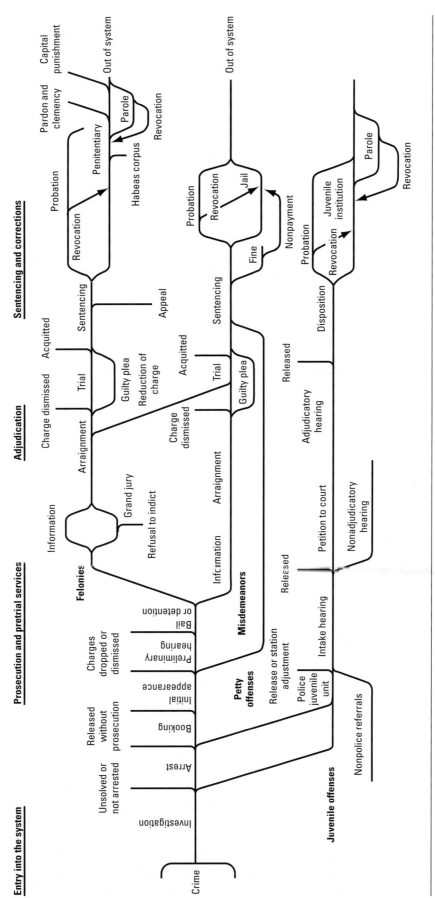

Entry into the system   **Prosecution and pretrial services**   **Adjudication**   **Sentencing and corrections**

FIGURE 13.1   A Model of the Criminal Justice System

Source: Bureau of Justice Statistics, *The American Response to Crime.* Washington, DC: U.S. Department of Justice, December 1983, pp. 2–3. Adapted from the President's Commission on Law Enforcement and Administration of Justice, *The Challenge of Crime in a Free Society.* Washington, DC: U.S. Government Printing Office, 1967.

just wealthy ones, with criminal investigation services. Urbanization had weakened the informal social control provided by families and neighbors, and the police were needed as a formal means of controlling deviance. Another important factor in the rise of American police forces was the threat to the social order posed by mob violence in nineteenth-century cities (Bayley, 1983).

Marxist criminologists regard the police in a capitalist society as a tool used by the bourgeoisie to maintain a social order that is profitable to themselves and that exploits laborers (Spitzer, 1981; Harring, 1983). Marxists have shown how capitalists historically have used the police to quell collective action by organized labor. They have also pointed to the unequal treatment by the police of suspects from disadvantaged social classes and racial and ethnic groups. Nevertheless, members of all social classes agree on the need to punish those crimes to which the police devote most of their attention: murder, rape, assault, and theft. Those crimes are the subject of police activity in socialist and communist societies as well as in capitalist ones.

There is evidence that the criminal justice system responds to perceived threats to the social order. One study found that a city's police expenditures are associated with its racial composition and with the level of black mobilization activity in the city. Cities with larger black populations spend more on police salaries, operations, and capital expenditures than do cities with proportionally fewer blacks. In addition, cities with more political activity by blacks have higher rates of police capital expenditures. One explanation of these findings is that police expenditures increase when minorities are seen as a threat to the dominant racial group (Jackson and Carroll, 1981). Another study, using data from 1950 to 1980, found a moderate to strong relationship between a city's racial composition and the strength of its police force only in the South prior to 1970. This relationship was weak outside the South, except for the period from 1960 to 1970 (Greenberg, Kessler, and Loftin, 1985). Another indication that the police respond to perceived racial threat is evidence that the rate at which officers kill blacks is associated with the size and growth of a city's black population; police killings of blacks are reduced when a city has a black mayor (Jacobs and O'Brien, 1998).

Police Abuses of Authority

The conflicting demands under which the police operate sometimes lead them to abuse their authority. For example, departmental pressure on officers to use their initiative and be efficient in solving cases can lead to the violation of due process rights, such as illegal seizure of evidence or coercion of a confession. Laws that define victimless crimes such as gambling, possession of drugs, and prostitution require the police to make arrests for consensual crimes in which the participants do not define themselves as victims; in such cases, the police sometimes find it easy to justify taking a bribe not to make an arrest. Stressful work conditions can increase police sensitivity to challenges to their authority and make brutality against citizens more likely. The camaraderie of the police subculture encourages retaliation against those who assault or kill fellow officers. Police abuses of their authority thus seem to be structurally induced, rather than the product of personality flaws in individual officers.

Discretion   Discretion is the use of judgment to decide what action to take. The police clearly possess delegated discretion, such as the power to decide when to issue a traffic ticket. Unauthorized discretion is that which the police exercise but for which they do not have authority, such as making decisions based on a suspect's race or sex (Skolnick, 1994). The way the police exercise discretion helps define the limits of permissible behavior. They regard some offenses as mere nuisances and decide to warn individuals rather than make arrests, but they have less freedom in dealing with serious crimes and usually make arrests in those cases.

One situation in which the police exercise discretion is the domestic dispute. The police traditionally have dealt with arguments or assaults between people who live together by making a judgment about the possible consequences of either arresting someone or trying to settle the dispute by mediating between the parties. An officer might judge that an arrest in a domestic disturbance will heighten conflict in the household over the long run, or the officer might believe that the complainant will not press charges in court. In such cases, the officer may choose not to make an arrest. Officers may make an arrest if they think the conflict will flare up again as soon as they leave. Critics have protested this use of police discretion, claiming that many wives are repeatedly abused by their husbands because the police are reluctant to make arrests. This is true, but so is the officer's contention that many women refuse to help in prosecuting their husbands, often out of fear, and that arrests can exacerbate tensions in the household. The following chapter examines research on the deterrent effects of different police responses to domestic violence.

In deciding whether to arrest someone, officers take into account a suspect's prior record, but they also assess the suspect's character by noting his or her group affiliations (including membership in a gang), age, race, hairstyle, dress, and demeanor. Demeanor includes how contrite the suspect is about the offense, how much respect he or she shows the officer, and how afraid of possible sanctions the suspect seems to be (Piliavin and Briar, 1964; Black, 1980). One national survey found that half of all officers thought that the police are more likely to arrest a suspect who shows "a bad attitude" (Weisburd and Greenspan, 2000). Some studies show that hostile demeanor does influence police behavior (Klinger, 1996; Worden and Shepard, 1996; Engel, Sobol, and Worden, 2000), but other research suggests that demeanor does not independently affect the chance that the police will arrest a suspect (Klinger, 1994).

Use of Force   One decision that is difficult for a police officer to make is whether to use force against a citizen, a decision that must be made quickly and often under stressful and ambiguous circumstances. In *Tennessee* v. *Garner* (1985), the Supreme Court ruled that the police cannot use deadly force "unless it is necessary to prevent the escape and the officer has probable cause to believe that the suspect poses a significant threat of death or serious physical injury to the officer or others" (cited in

Whether to use force and how much force to use are decisions that police officers must make quickly and often under stressful and ambiguous circumstances.

Tennenbaum, 1994: 244). The use of deadly force to stop fleeing felons who are un-armed and nonviolent was thus declared unconstitutional. This decision significantly reduced police homicides by curtailing the use of deadly force against fleeing felons and by leading police departments to adopt guidelines that decreased other kinds of police shootings as well (Tennenbaum, 1994).

A survey of police officers from 121 departments revealed that most of them condemned the illegal use of force and thought that extreme cases of such abuse were uncommon. However, quite a few officers believed that procedural rules limited their effectiveness: 31 percent said that they were not allowed to use as much force as was often needed to make an arrest; 43 percent said that following the rules was not al-ways compatible with getting their job done; and 25 percent said that it was some-times acceptable to use more force than legally allowable to control someone who was assaulting an officer. Twenty-two percent of the respondents said that officers in their department sometimes used more force than necessary to make an arrest, and 15 percent acknowledged that their fellow officers sometimes reacted to verbal abuse with force. Few respondents thought that their colleagues were more likely to use physical force against blacks and other minorities than against whites (11 percent) or more likely to use force against poor people than against middle-class people (14 per-cent). Two-thirds of the respondents said that an officer who reports another's mis-conduct is apt to be ostracized, and half said it was not unusual for an officer to ignore improper conduct by fellow officers (Weisburd and Greenspan, 2000).

Observational data gathered in Indianapolis, Indiana, and St. Petersburg, Florida, revealed that use of force by the police is often a response to legal considerations such as safety concerns and the suspect's resistance. Disrespect by a suspect did not in-crease the likelihood that an officer would use force, but inexperienced and less educated officers were more apt to resort to force. Suspects' characteristics were asso-ciated with the likelihood that they would be subjected to force: Those who were male, nonwhite, poor, and young were especially likely to be treated forcefully (Ter-rill and Mastrofski, 2002).

Racial Discrimination   There is mixed evidence on whether the police discrim-inate against minority groups. The complexity of this issue can be seen in a study based on data collected in Boston, Chicago, and Washington, D.C., by observers who rode in police cars and systematically observed police behavior (Black and Reiss, 1970; Black, 1980). The researchers found that the police were much more likely to arrest a black juvenile suspect than a white juvenile suspect. However, two factors other than racial discrimination seemed to explain this difference. One was that more of the black juveniles were stopped for serious crimes, and the police acted on the le-gal basis of seriousness of the offense in arresting more of the black suspects. Second, most complaints about black juveniles came from black adults, and they were more likely than white adults who complained to the police about white juveniles to de-mand that the police make an arrest, rather than merely warn the juvenile. In mak-ing arrest decisions, the police were thus responding to the seriousness of the crime and the preferences of the complainant, rather than to the race of the suspect.

Much research, especially that done outside the South in recent years, finds that the race of the suspect is a less important influence on the police arrest decision than factors such as the seriousness of the offense, prior criminal record, demeanor, and the socioeconomic status of the neighborhood in which a police encounter occurs. However, even when other variables are taken into account, some studies find that race remains as a factor that influences the disposition of a case.

If the police discriminate by race, black offenders would stand a greater chance of being arrested than white offenders who committed the same offense. We can test this possibility for the crime of robbery, which involves a face-to-face confrontation between offender and victim. If the police "overarrest" black robbers, the proportion of all arrested suspects who are blacks would be higher than the proportion of all robbers that victims report to be blacks. However, a study of robbery in Boston showed that the police actually "underarrested" black robbers in comparison to white robbers. In the first six months of 1964, 55 percent of all robbers were blacks, according to victims, but only 44 percent of all suspects arrested for robbery were blacks, suggesting that black robbers had a smaller chance than white ones of being arrested for their crimes. The data for 1968 show a similar pattern (Conklin, 1972). A study of robbery in Milwaukee, Wisconsin, found that the percentage of all arrested robbery suspects who were blacks was about the same as the percentage of all robbers identified as blacks by victims (Pruitt and Wilson, 1983). Neither of these studies supports the contention that the police are more likely to arrest black suspects than white suspects, at least for the crime of robbery. A study that used victimization survey data and FBI arrest data concluded that there was "virtually no criminal justice selection bias for either rape or robbery but there [was] such bias for assault, especially aggravated assault" (Hindelang, 1978: 101).

The observational study of the police carried out in Boston, Chicago, and Washington, D.C., in the mid-1960s uncovered a significant amount of prejudice among the police, with about three-fourths of the officers classified as very prejudiced or considerably prejudiced against blacks on the basis of spontaneous comments. This study found that prejudice, an attitude, was not necessarily associated with discrimination, which is behavior. The observers saw forty-four cases of police assault on citizens during seven weeks of round-the-clock observation; in many of these assaults no suspect was arrested. They found a higher rate of undue force used against whites than against blacks. Black and white officers used violence with about the same frequency, and usually against members of their own race, something that reflected the areas to which the officers were assigned. The police might have been less likely to use violence against blacks during this period because of the threat of urban riots, many of which occurred between 1965 and 1968. The civil rights gains of blacks might also have convinced some officers that police abuses would be reported and lead to trouble for them. In addition, officers might have adjusted their behavior in the presence of observers in order to avoid the appearance of discrimination, although they apparently did not adjust their verbal comments to avoid the impression of racial prejudice (Reiss, 1971).

One way in which the police possibly discriminate by race is in the shooting of civilians. However, a study of police shootings in Chicago between 1974 and 1978 found that if rates of being shot by the police were calculated for blacks, Hispanics, and whites by dividing the number of shooting victims of each group by the number of people of that group arrested for serious crimes, whites were actually somewhat more likely to be shot than blacks and Hispanics, although differences among the groups were small. Rates were calculated in this way to account for group differences in involvement in the kinds of situations most likely to lead to police shootings (Geller and Karales, 1981). A study of police shootings in Memphis, Tennessee, did find that the police were more likely to shoot blacks than whites, even if group differences in criminal activity were taken into account (Fyfe, 1981). The evidence thus suggests that police discrimination against blacks in the use of force exists in some cities but not in others. Differences in the relative power of blacks, the organization of the municipal police department, and the department's administrative directives could account for such city-to-city variations in the use of force by the police (Fyfe, 1981; Waegel, 1984).

On March 3, 1991, three white Los Angeles police officers brutally beat Rodney King, a black man, in the presence of a white sergeant while twenty-three other law-enforcement officers watched. As many as twenty local residents witnessed the attack, and one of them recorded it with his video camera. King, who had a criminal record, had been stopped after a high-speed car chase; some of the officers later said that he had resisted arrest and seemed to be reaching for a weapon. None of his behavior justified the violent response by the police: They kicked, bludgeoned, electrically shocked, and hog-tied him, then they dragged him to the side of the road until an ambulance arrived. In a trial that took place in another county, four officers were acquitted of assault charges by a jury that had no black members. After the acquittals, a riot broke out in Los Angeles; fifty-two people were killed and more than $1 billion worth of property was damaged or destroyed. The officers who had been acquitted were then indicted on federal charges of violating King's civil rights. In 1993, two of them were acquitted and two were found guilty; the convicted officers were sentenced to two and a half years in prison.

Sociologist Jerome Skolnick has commented on the King beating as follows: "It is highly unlikely that this is unrepresentative of Los Angeles police. Two people can go crazy, but if you have ten or twelve people watching them and not doing anything, this tells you that this is the normal thing for them" (cited in Mydans, 1991: B7). Skolnick and James Fyfe (1993) claim that such brutality is partly the result of an attitude that officers learn on the job, namely, that they are engaged in an all-out war on crime. Many officers see themselves as "ghetto gunslingers," outsiders to the communities they patrol, who must use force to maintain respect and enforce the law. Skolnick and Fyfe also fault some police administrators for being insulated from effective constraints on their power and reluctant to take strong action against brutal officers and their supervisors. Even though it is difficult to document police brutality, due to a code of silence among officers and because allegations of brutality are investigated by the police themselves, Skolnick and Fyfe believe that brutality has declined over the past fifty years.

In the late 1990s, several cases of racial discrimination by the police attracted national attention. One was the May 1999 confession by New York police officer Justin Volpe, during the course of a trial in which four fellow officers broke the traditional "blue wall" of silence to give testimony against him, that in August 1997 he had rammed a stick in Abner Louima's rectum and then thrust it in his face, in an effort to humiliate and intimidate the recently arrested black man. He then warned Louima, "If you tell anybody about this, I'll find you and kill you" (cited in Barstow, 1999: A1). A second case involved well-publicized protests at New York police headquarters against four white officers who had fired forty-one shots at Amadou Diallo in 1998, killing the innocent black man, whom they had incorrectly identified as a suspect in a crime and erroneously thought had a gun.

Another instance of discrimination involved evidence that New Jersey state troopers had been using race as a criterion for deciding which motorists to stop for drug searches, a practice prohibited by court decisions and one that led to the 1998 shooting of three unarmed black and Hispanic men in a van. This case focused national attention on **racial profiling**, the assumption that an individual is more likely to violate the law if he or she is a member of a particular racial or ethnic group. This issue was largely limited to allegations of discrimination against blacks and Hispanics prior to September 11, 2001. After the terrorist attacks, the use of racial profiling against Arab men aroused concern, but also widespread support, because all nineteen hijackers responsible for the attacks fit that description. There was even evidence that blacks were more likely than whites to regard the profiling of Arab men as potential terrorists as acceptable (Scales, 2001). According to law-enforcement agents, the higher probability of illegal acts by people with certain racial or ethnic characteristics justifies greater suspicion, and hence more aggressive action. The black police chief of Los Angeles once remarked, "It's not the fault of the police when they stop minority males or put them in jail. It's the fault of the minority males for committing

Abner Louima, speaking at a news conference, was the victim of a brutal assault by New York City police officers in August 1997. One officer confessed to the attack and another was convicted of the crime.

the crime. In my mind it is not a great revelation that if officers are looking for criminal activity, they're going to look at the kind of people who are listed on crime reports" (Bernard Parks, cited in Goldberg, 1999: 53–54). In the opinion of civil libertarians, however, targeting an entire group for the acts of a few of its members violates the constitutional guarantees to equal protection of the law and freedom from unreasonable searches and arrests. Racial profiling is therefore unjustifiable, even on the grounds of more effective law enforcement (Glaberson, 2001).

Sex Discrimination Research indicates that the police respond differently to male and female defendants. A study in a midwestern city found that from 1948 to 1976, police disposition of males and females became more similar for juvenile and adult misdemeanors and for adult felonies, but that males and females continued to be treated differently for juvenile status offenses and juvenile felonies. Overall, treatment of males and females became more alike over time, but sex discrimination had not disappeared by the mid-1970s, with female status offenders continuing to receive more lenient and paternalistic treatment even in the 1970s (Krohn, Curry, and Nelson-Kilger, 1983).

A study that covered the period from 1934 to 1979 found that sex differentials in arrests had diminished in most offense categories, with the largest changes occurring in the 1960s and 1970s. Women showed the most significant increases in arrests for petty property crimes—such as larceny, fraud, and forgery—and for vagrancy and disorderly conduct, which were often related to prostitution. The researchers concluded that the narrowing of the sex differential had not yet produced a convergence of male and female arrests. This narrowing seemed to be due to changes in law-enforcement practices and changes in FBI statistical coverage of a larger part of the nation, as much as or even more than it was due to changes in actual behavior by men and women. The following factors accounted for the increases in arrests of females:

1. A decline in chivalry and sympathy for female defendants.
2. A possible increase in the surveillance of women because of growing attention to crime by women.
3. Increased social and legal pressure to administer the law in a nondiscriminatory way.
4. Professionalization and bureaucratization of the police.
5. Improvements in police recording practices, including a greater likelihood of recording a suspect's sex.
6. Changes in welfare agencies, leading to more prosecution of crimes such as fraud and larceny (Steffensmeier and Cobb, 1981).

The Clearance Rate

To measure their effectiveness in dealing with crime, the police use a **clearance rate**, the proportion of offenses that they solve to their satisfaction. Many cleared cases lead to arrest, prosecution, and conviction, but the police also classify as cleared some cases that do not produce an arrest. Sometimes an offender cannot be arrested because he or she is deceased, out of the country, or in prison in another state. For example, a man who kills his wife and then commits suicide would leave the police with no one to arrest for the murder, but they would still call the homicide cleared. In other cases, the police strongly believe they know who committed a crime but lack the evidence to make an arrest. Often those crimes are classified as cleared.

There are problems with relying on clearance rates to measure the effectiveness of the police. Because the police themselves decide when a case is cleared, they can classify cases as cleared to make themselves look good. This might mean that the actual offender in a crime that is erroneously marked cleared will no longer be hunted by the police. Such "false clearances" could reduce the deterrent effect of the law. Another difficulty with clearance rates is that a crime committed by several offenders will be marked cleared with the arrest of a single suspect, an action that exaggerates police effectiveness in apprehending criminals. Departmental pressure to clear cases can lead to illegal police actions to get suspects to do things for which they can be arrested. Critics see this as illegal entrapment, but supporters justify it by saying that only people predisposed to crime will be drawn into it.

One study of the role of police detectives in solving crimes concluded that their efforts were as important as the investigative work of patrol officers in solving robberies and burglaries. Within the police department, robbery and burglary cases were divided into three categories:

1. Cases that could not be solved with a reasonable amount of effort.
2. Cases that are solved by circumstances, requiring only the arrest of a suspect and the development of the case for prosecution.
3. Cases that could be solved with a reasonable amount of effort.

Many robberies and burglaries were not even assigned to detectives for investigation because there were few or no leads or because the case was solved by circumstances, but of those cases that were assigned to detectives, many were solved by investigation. The investigation process included interviews with witnesses and informants, discussions with other police officers, and an examination of the department's files. Interviews with victims led to few arrests (Eck, 1984).

An examination of homicide cases in four large American cities revealed that some factors associated with the likelihood that a case would be cleared were outside the control of the police but that the following factors that they could control increased the chance that a case would be solved:

- The first officer to arrive at the crime scene was quick to notify the homicide unit, the medical examiner, and the crime lab.
- That officer tried to identify and locate witnesses and secure the crime scene.
- Three or more detectives were assigned to the case.
- A detective arrived at the crime scene quickly.
- Computer checks were run on victims, suspects, witnesses, and firearms (Wellford and Cronin, 2000).

A detective's decision to investigate a victim's complaint about the theft of property is affected by the characteristics of the victim and the crime. Detectives are most likely to spend time in a follow-up investigation if there is some evidence that might help them solve the crime. In burglary cases, victims living in well-to-do communities receive more attention from police investigators than victims living in poor communities. Minority-group members who are burglary victims are slightly less likely than white victims to receive favorable treatment by police investigators. Police activity in follow-up investigations of violent crimes is influenced by the willingness of the victim to aid in the prosecution of the case (Bynum, Cordner, and Greene, 1982).

A study of reported burglaries found that a southern sheriff's department was more likely to use evidence technicians to dust for fingerprints when entry into the building involved force or when the property that had been stolen was "a marker of the self." Jewelry, silver, and firearms were items that recalled the past or had special personal significance for victims, and the sheriff was more likely to make special investigative efforts when such property had been taken. Dusting for fingerprints rarely led to an arrest, but it helped to foster good public relations and restore the victim's peace of mind (Stenross, 1984).

The police are more likely to investigate complaints about crimes that are serious, provide evidence, occur in well-to-do neighborhoods, have a victim who is willing to prosecute, and involve the loss of property with personal significance. As a result, police work introduces contingencies into an offender's career, with offenders who commit certain kinds of crime being especially likely to be arrested and processed by the courts.

Criminal Courts

In the United States, because suspects are presumed innocent from the time they are arrested until they are found guilty or innocent in court, they have a right to be free pending disposition of the charges against them. At the initial appearance or preliminary hearing, bail is set, charges are considered, and suspects are informed of their right to counsel and right to remain silent. Felony charges based on probable cause that a suspect has committed a crime are formally stated in an indictment issued by a grand jury, a group of citizens that considers evidence presented by a prosecutor in a closed hearing, or in an information filed by a judge. The defendant is then formally arraigned in court, where the charges are read, the defendant responds with a plea (guilty, not guilty, or *nolo contendere* [no contest]) or stands mute, bail is reviewed, and a trial date is assigned. A district attorney prosecutes the defendant, a defense attorney helps the defendant get acquitted or secure the most lenient sentence possible, and a judge or jury decides guilt or innocence. Often a defendant pleads guilty in return for an agreed-on sentence that is less than the one that might result from a trial. Judges sometimes give very different sentences to offenders who have similar criminal records and have been convicted of similar offenses. Some defendants appeal their convictions to a higher court, which considers whether mistakes were made in the legal processing of the case; if there were errors, the appellate court can order a new trial or, less commonly, the release of the defendant.

The Bail System

The **bail system** is designed to ensure that defendants will show up to face the charges against them when their trial is scheduled, while allowing them to remain free until the trial takes place. To do this, an amount of money is set that must be deposited with the court before the defendant can be released. Because bail requires suspects to pay money, it discriminates against those who cannot afford the amount set for their release, so jails that hold suspects awaiting trial are usually filled with poor defendants.

Defendants awaiting trial are released in several ways. Some are released on their own recognizance, a promise to appear for trial. Others gain their release by placing with the court an amount of cash equal to the bail set by the judge, or by giving the court something equal in value to the amount of bail, such as a savings account passbook or a real estate deed. Because most defendants have little money or property, a system of bail bonding agents has developed in the United States to help defendants gain their release.

Bonding agents write a bail bond, a kind of insurance policy, which guarantees the court that they will pay the full amount of the bail if the defendant fails to appear for trial as scheduled. In return for this guarantee, the bonding agent charges the defendant a nonrefundable fee to write the bond. Bonding agents make it easier for defendants to gain their release, but they do not seem to improve the chance that defendants will show up for trial and they cost defendants much money. They have also been involved in corrupt practices. As a result, some states have replaced bonding agents with a system that allows defendants to gain their release by depositing with the court a sum of money that is returned when their case is disposed of, even if they are found guilty.

Preventive Detention

Long delays from arrest until trial provide opportunities for defendants who are released on bail to commit crimes. Concern with such bail crimes led to demands for **preventive detention**, a system that holds some defendants without bail. This system, which is common in Europe, was implemented in Washington, D.C., in 1971 but rarely used thereafter. Preventive detention was authorized for the federal court system in 1984. In many states, judges are allowed to consider whether a defendant is dangerous to others in making a decision to release the defendant prior to trial. Even where preventive detention is not specifically authorized, judges can set very high bails for defendants they believe will endanger the safety of others or commit bail crimes. These defendants are held in jail when they cannot afford to make bail.

Critics claim that preventive detention violates the Eighth Amendment's right to have a reasonable bail set. In 1987 the U.S. Supreme Court rejected that argument, declaring preventive detention legal if a prosecutor could show that freeing a defendant would endanger the community. Another objection to preventive detention is that it imprisons people for acts they might commit if they were released, and accurately predicting the behavior of pretrial releasees is difficult (Angel et al., 1971; Fagan and Guggenheim, 1996).

Preventive detention could contribute to criminal careers, if defendants who are held in jail cannot consult with their attorneys and contact witnesses to develop a defense. Preventive detention could set in motion a cycle in which suspects thought to be dangerous are denied bail, are then more likely to be convicted as a result of being held in jail, and thus have a worse criminal record that is then used to hold them without bail the next time they are arrested. The denial of bail can also cause defendants to lose their jobs, force their families to go on welfare, sever their bonds to the conventional order, and even make criminal behavior by their children more likely.

Prosecutors

Prosecutors, or district attorneys, are usually lawyers who are elected to office. Often they see themselves as independent of public control, while still serving the public, and they regard themselves as lawyers whose behavior should reflect the standards of the legal profession. They bring charges against defendants and try to ensure that justice is done. They are concerned with all aspects of the case and interact with police officers, defense attorneys, judges, jurors, witnesses, victims, and defendants.

Prosecutors measure their success by a conviction rate, just as the police measure their effectiveness by a clearance rate. Some prosecutors blame the police when they fail to get convictions, claiming that the police are more concerned with clearing cases than with presenting cases that can produce convictions. In response, the police accuse prosecutors of being too willing to reduce charges from felonies to misdemeanors just to secure convictions, rather than using the resources of the district attorney's office to convict suspects on more serious charges. Prosecutors do screen cases brought by the police to find the ones most likely to produce convictions. They are not necessarily concerned with getting judges to mete out the harshest possible sentences to convicted offenders, being more concerned with fairness than with getting the longest possible prison term or getting a conviction in a case in which the evidence does not warrant it (Neubauer, 1974).

Defense Attorneys

The American criminal justice system is based on an adversarial model or "fight theory," which assumes that the correct verdict will emerge if a prosecutor presents the best case against, and a defense attorney presents the strongest case for, the defendant. In fact, many more cases are settled by guilty pleas by defendants than by trials using this adversarial model. Defense attorneys are an integral part of the court system, interacting cordially with prosecutors and judges rather than behaving in an antagonistic manner. Good relationships with other court personnel make plea bargaining easier and help defense attorneys get trial dates postponed when necessary. The close relationship of defense attorneys to other court personnel dilutes the adversarial nature of the American criminal justice system, which seems designed to produce the most expeditious processing of cases (Blumberg, 1979).

Defendants learn at their arraignment of the charges against them and the maximum penalties for the crimes with which they are charged. The threat of a very long sentence, which few defendants actually receive, makes them eager to seek the assistance of defense attorneys. Defense attorneys act as counselors who interpret the law for their clients and try to keep them out of court. The expertise of defense attorneys is important in getting defendants the lightest possible sentence—the "normal" penalty or "going rate"—in exchange for a guilty plea. When cases are tried before a judge or a jury, defense attorneys try to get their clients acquitted, convicted on the least serious charge, or sentenced as leniently as possible (Neubauer, 1974).

U.S. Supreme Court decisions in *Gideon* v. *Wainwright* (1963) and *Argersinger* v. *Hamlin* (1972) guaranteed free counsel to any indigent defendant facing the threat of incarceration in a felony or misdemeanor case. Poor defendants are provided with legal counsel through public defender organizations or through the assignment of lawyers by the courts.

Judges

In lower criminal courts, where most criminal cases are first heard, one of the judge's primary functions is to ratify agreements between defense attorneys and prosecutors about the sentences that defendants will receive for pleading guilty. When cases go to trial, judges act either as decision makers or as supervisors of the proceedings when cases are tried before juries. Perhaps the most important function for the judge is the sentencing of convicted offenders.

Judges are supposed to sentence offenders on the basis of legal criteria: the nature of the crimes for which they have been convicted, and perhaps their criminal records. Criminologists are concerned that judges' sentences might be influenced by extralegal factors such as race, sex, and age. The actual role of legal and extralegal factors in determining sentences is examined later in this chapter.

Juries

The jury system has been criticized for giving a group of amateurs who lack legal training the power to make decisions that dramatically affect defendants' lives. It has also been defended as an important democratic institution that involves the average citizen in the process of defining and meting out justice. However, no more than 5 percent of all felony cases that are prosecuted involve jury trials, because guilty pleas account for most convictions.

A landmark study of the American jury asked judges to fill out questionnaires about the jury trials over which they had presided. In about four-fifths of the cases on which data were collected, judges said that jurors had reached the same verdict they themselves would have reached. In the remaining cases, juries were much more likely to acquit defendants when judges said they would have convicted them, rather than to convict defendants whom the judges would have acquitted. The jurors seemed to require more proof to find guilt beyond a reasonable doubt than did the judges, and so juries can be said to be "defendant-friendly." The judges thought the juries performed quite well, considering the evidence carefully and taking longer to reach verdicts in cases the judges thought were the most difficult from a legal point of view (Kalven and Zeisel, 1966).

In contrast to this study's conclusion that juries were more lenient than judges, another study found that juries were significantly more likely than judges to convict defendants (Levine, 1983). This study of more than 58,000 felony trials concluded that after the 1950s there was a growth in public conservatism regarding crime that accounted for the increasingly harsh treatment of defendants by juries. Since this researcher's methods differed from those of the earlier study, we must be cautious in attributing differences between the conclusions of the two studies to actual changes in jury behavior over time.

Plea Bargaining

More than 85 percent of all felony convictions in American courts are the result of guilty pleas (Smith, 1986). **Plea bargaining** is an informal but structured process of negotiation in which a prosecutor and a defense attorney agree on a guilty plea and a sentence that the prosecutor will recommend to a judge. Because defendants can request trials or delays, which are costly and time-consuming for the court, prosecutors are often willing to agree to a reduced charge or a light sentence in exchange for a guilty plea. Because prosecutors have the power to go to trial and ask for a severe sentence, defendants are frequently willing to plead guilty and accept a penalty less than the one they might receive if convicted in a trial (Rosett and Cressey, 1976; Maynard, 1984).

One study found that judges sentenced defendants to longer terms if they asked for trials than if they pleaded guilty. Judges seemed to adopt the position that if a defendant took some of the court's time to have a trial, which is of course the defendant's legal right, then the judge would take some of the defendant's time by meting out a longer prison sentence (Uhlman and Walker, 1980). A second study confirmed that defendants who were convicted after trials received harsher sentences than defendants with similar characteristics who faced the same charges and pleaded guilty (LaFree, 1985). A third study concluded that although more defendants convicted after trials were incarcerated than was true for defendants who pleaded guilty, the difference was not evidence that plea bargaining was coercive. Instead, the difference in incarceration rates for the two groups was attributable to two factors: (1) Some of the defendants who pleaded guilty would not have been convicted if they had gone to trial, and (2) cases in which pleas were negotiated had characteristics different from cases in which convictions followed trials (Smith, 1986).

Critics of plea bargaining claim that it induces innocent defendants to acquiesce to a guilty plea in order to get a more lenient sentence than they would if they demanded a trial and were found guilty by a judge or a jury. Critics also complain that plea bargaining goes on behind closed doors, therefore keeping the process from public view and making abuses more likely. In addition, some critics claim, a defendant cannot be sure that a judge will hand out an agreed-on sentence after the defendant pleads guilty in court. Because the sentences given out as a result of plea bargaining usually fall far short of maximum sentences so as to induce defendants to plead guilty, some critics allege that offenders are punished much less harshly than justice demands, thereby undermining the deterrent and incapacitative effects of punishment.

Supporters of plea bargaining argue that court resources would have to be multiplied many times to process all criminal cases if plea bargaining were not used to resolve most charges. Supporters claim that plea bargaining does provide just sentences—that is, penalties proportional to the harm caused by offenders—even if those penalties fall short of the legal maximum. They point out that the actual penalties given out by the courts are much longer in the United States than in other Western democracies and that plea bargaining keeps punishment from being even harsher than it already is (Rosett and Cressey, 1976).

Probation

One penalty that judges sometimes impose on convicted offenders is **probation**, a form of supervised release. Probation originated in the work of a Boston shoemaker named John Augustus, who in 1841 began to supervise offenders and report on them to the court. In 1878 Massachusetts became the first state to pass a probation law; today all states and the federal government provide probation for some offenders. Probation is much less expensive than incarceration, and as a result there are many more offenders on probation than in the nation's jails and prisons.

Probation is designed to offer convicted offenders treatment outside prison where they can maintain ties to conventional society. Judges, with the help of probation officers who present them with presentence reports, try to select for probation those offenders who are the best risks to avoid committing crime. In addition to providing probationers with services, this system aims to control behavior through surveillance by probation officers to whom offenders have to report regularly. However, many probation officers are so overburdened with cases that they have little time to supervise their clients or provide them with services.

Sentence Disparity

A major problem with American courts is **sentence disparity**, the difference in the criminal sanctions handed out to people who are convicted of similar offenses and who have similar criminal records. For instance, there is significant variation in sentences from one state to another, from one city to another, and from one judge to another in the same city. A defendant's race, social class, and sex can also influence sentencing.

Race and Sentencing   The fact that blacks constitute about half of all inmates in American jails and prisons, while being only 12.7 percent of the population, has led some critics to blame the imprisonment of so many blacks on racial discrimination by the criminal justice system.

Much research has been done on the role of race in the sentencing of offenders, particularly for capital offenses, but scholars differ in their interpretations of the results. Some have argued that it is the greater involvement of blacks in crime that explains the high proportion of inmates who are blacks. Different studies have estimated that 76 to 90 percent of the discrepancy between the proportion of blacks in the general population and the proportion of blacks in jails and prisons is attributable to black-white differences in arrests (Blumstein, 1982, 1993; Langan, 1985; Crutchfield, Bridges, and Pritchford, 1994). The 10 to 24 percent of the discrepancy that is unexplained by arrest differentials might be due to racial discrimination, but it could also be the result of using legally relevant criteria for sentencing, such as prior criminal history or seriousness of the offense. Two studies dispute the conclusion that no more than 24 percent of the racial disproportionality in prisoners is due to discrimination, estimating that for Pennsylvania as much as 42 to 52 percent of the disproportionality cannot be explained by differences in legally relevant criteria for sentencing. This indicates that there may be more racial discrimination in the decision to incarcerate than is suggested by research that has used national data for aggregated offenses (Hawkins and Hardy, 1989; Austin and Allen, 2000).

When legally relevant criteria are taken into account, usually race greatly diminishes in importance, and sometimes even disappears, as an influence on sentencing decisions. One review of published research found that of twenty-four studies of sentencing that took a defendant's prior criminal history into account, only two found evidence of racial discrimination (Kleck, 1981, 1985). Another research review concluded that although there was some evidence of subtle and indirect effects of race on sentencing decisions, the weight of the evidence supported the following conclusion:

> When restricted to index crimes, dozens of individual-level studies have shown that a simple *direct* influence of race on pretrial release, plea bargaining, conviction, sentence length, and the death penalty among adults is small to nonexistent once legally relevant variables (e.g., prior record) are controlled. For these crimes, racial differentials in sanctioning appear to match the large racial differences in criminal offending. Findings on the processing of adult index crimes therefore generally support the NDT [no discrimination thesis]. (Sampson and Lauritsen, 1997: 355)

One study that supported this conclusion looked at offenders convicted in California of assault, robbery, burglary, theft, forgery, and drug offenses. The researchers found that race was not a factor in sentencing once type of offense, prior record, and legal procedural variables (such as having a private attorney) were taken into account. This absence of racial discrimination was true for each of the six crimes, for the decision to place on probation or imprison a convicted offender, and for the decision about length of sentence (Klein, Turner, and Petersilia, 1988).

Because decision making in the juvenile justice system is more discretionary than sentencing in the criminal courts, there is a greater likelihood of racial discrimination in the processing of juveniles. A study in Florida concluded that although the impact of race on the sentencing of juveniles was less than the impact of legally relevant criteria, blacks were "more likely to be recommended for formal processing, referred to court, adjudicated delinquent, and given harsher dispositions than comparable white offenders" (Bishop and Frazier, 1988: 258). A study in five counties concluded that black and Hispanic youths were more likely than white juveniles to be detained at three different decision points, even when juveniles who were from similar social backgrounds and who were charged with similar offenses were compared (Wordes, Bynum, and Corley, 1994). Research in a western state showed that race affected the sentencing of juvenile offenders indirectly: In classifying, assessing, and recommending punishment, probation officers attributed offending by white and black offenders to different causes, blacks' delinquency more often being attributed to attitudinal and personality problems, and whites' delinquency more often being attributed to social environmental factors. Those attributions influenced probation officers' assessments of the risk that a juvenile would reoffend and thus affected the sentences they recommended (Bridges and Steen, 1998).

Criminologists have also uncovered some evidence of discrimination in the treatment of adult offenders. For instance, in Florida blacks were more likely than whites to be sentenced as habitual offenders, even when comparing defendants who had similar criminal records and who were facing charges of similar seriousness. Habitual offenders were required to serve at least 75 percent of their sentence, as opposed to the 40 percent typical of all offenders in the state. Differential treatment was greatest for defendants charged with drug offenses and property crimes, and least for defendants charged with violent and weapons-related crimes (Crawford, Chiricos, and Kleck, 1998).

The role of race in sentencing is complex, varying with the type of crime, the racial composition of the offender–victim dyad, the offender–victim relationship, and social contextual factors such as the racial composition and socioeconomic status of the community. Research in Detroit found that the decision to charge suspects in sexual assault cases was influenced by prior offender–victim relationship and by the victim's age, character, and behavior at the time of the assault. The charging decision was not influenced by the strength of the evidence or the seriousness of the crime (Spears and Spohn, 1997). Compared to whites charged with sexually assaulting whites, blacks charged with sexually assaulting whites were actually more likely to have charges dismissed and less likely to be convicted. The racial composition of the offender–victim dyad did not affect the decision to incarcerate offenders, but it did affect sentence length, with blacks who assaulted whites receiving the longest prison terms (Spohn and Spears, 1996). The researchers concluded that if they had simply looked for the direct effects of race on sentencing, they "would have missed these subtle and more interesting interactive effects" (Spohn and Spears, 1996: 678).

A study in Pennsylvania found that seriousness of the crime and prior criminal record were the main determinants of sentencing decisions but that demographic variables also influenced those decisions. More specifically, race influenced sentences for younger males but not sentences for older ones, with young black males being treated more harshly than other groups. Sex had the largest direct effect on sentencing, followed by age, and then race. However, the direct effects of these individual variables were smaller than the impact of various combinations of the variables. Interviews indicated that court officials treated young black men most harshly because they were "perceived as dangerous, committed to street life, and less reformable than women and older offenders," and because they were seen as better able to spend time in prison and as less remorseful and more recalcitrant than other categories of offenders (Steffensmeier, Ulmer, and Kramer, 1998: 787).

Analyses of Pennsylvania and federal court data revealed that offense seriousness and criminal history accounted for most of the differences in sentences meted out to defendants. After those legal criteria were taken into account, however, race and ethnicity still had a small to moderate effect on sentencing: Hispanic defendants received harsher penalties than black defendants, and black defendants were punished more severely than white defendants. The inclusion of more information on the cases, defendants, and court procedures might have reduced the apparent impact of race and ethnicity on sentencing, but the studies raised concern about the unequal application of the law (Steffensmeier and Demuth, 2000, 2001).

A useful distinction is between "direct" discrimination—in which race or ethnicity plays a part in the sentencing decision, even after taking into account seriousness of the crime and prior criminal record—and "organizational" discrimination, in which economically disadvantaged people are more likely to be convicted or to receive a long prison term because they cannot afford to be released on bail or to hire a private attorney. Organizational or economic discrimination might not be based directly on race, but it affects the way blacks are treated by the criminal justice system, because they have lower incomes, on average, than whites, and are thus more affected by organizational discrimination (Lizotte, 1978; Unnever, 1982). Thus, some of what appears to be racial discrimination is actually a result of disadvantages more likely to be suffered by blacks, such as poverty, lack of job skills, unemployment, low levels of education, and residence in blighted urban areas. The relationship between direct discrimination and organizational discrimination is complex and has important consequences for social policy. Evidence of direct racial discrimination would require civil rights remedies, but evidence of organizational discrimination would point to the need for policies to alleviate the burden of poverty for people of all races.

Race and the Sentencing of Drug Offenders

The War on Drugs waged by the Reagan and George H. W. Bush administrations led to the incarceration of many more blacks, despite the fact that during that time there was little increase in the proportion of all suspects arrested for index crimes who were blacks. In 1979, 32 percent of suspects arrested for index crimes were blacks, and in 1992 the percentage was 35. Over that time, however, the proportion of offenders admitted to state and federal prisons who were blacks rose dramatically, from 39 percent to 54 percent. This increase was a direct result of more prison sentences for drug offenders; from 1980 to 1993, the proportion of state and federal prison inmates who were incarcerated for a drug crime rose from 8 percent to 26 percent. The increased number of inmates serving time for drug offenses was disproportionately black; 22 percent of drug arrests in 1979 but 40 percent of drug arrests in 1992 were of blacks. Michael Tonry (1995: 49) has shown that blacks "are arrested and confined in numbers grossly out of line with their use or sale of drugs," and argues that the War on Drugs has been destructive to poverty-stricken black neighborhoods.

Discrimination against poor black women also characterizes the recent prosecution of drug offenders, with increasing numbers of pregnant drug users being prosecuted for crimes such as child abuse, endangering an unborn child, and even distributing drugs to a minor (the fetus). One study found that about 15 percent of both white and black women who were pregnant used illicit drugs, but black women were ten times as likely to be reported to the authorities as white women, and poor women were more likely to be reported than those with higher incomes (Kolata, 1990).

Recognizing that drug laws sometimes discriminate against blacks, a Minnesota judge in 1990 declared unconstitutional a state law that punished first-time users of crack cocaine with four years in prison but first-time users of powder cocaine with probation. Lawmakers said they had singled out crack for harsher punishment because of its potency, cheapness, and devastating effects, but statistics for 1988 showed that 92 percent of all arrests for possession of crack were of blacks, whereas 85 percent of all arrests for possession of cocaine in powdered form were of whites (*New York Times,* December 29, 1990). In *United States* v. *Armstrong* (1996), the Supreme Court ruled that similar evidence in federal cases—blacks being 90 percent of convicted crack offenders but only 30 percent of powder cocaine offenders—was not sufficient to prove racial discrimination. The Court said that a defendant had to show that similarly situated defendants (e.g., blacks and whites charged with possession of crack) had been treated differently by the courts. In 2002, the U.S. Department of Justice supported a 5.4 to 1 ratio in the length of the sentences meted out for possession of five grams of crack and possession of five grams of powder cocaine by arguing that crack is distributed and used differently and is more closely associated with violent crime. The department argued that the harsher penalties for crack benefit minority communities where that form of cocaine is more commonly used by acting as a deterrent to the sale and use of the drug. One critic responded, however: "The government is pretending to be protecting the minority community. But its harsher enforcement of crack has never worked out that way" (cited in Lewis, 2002).

Race and Capital Punishment

The major reason that the U.S. Supreme Court declared the states' death penalty laws unconstitutional in the 1972 case of *Furman* v. *Georgia* was that the application of those laws had shown an excessive degree of arbitrariness, especially in the more frequent use of capital punishment for black defendants. Since 1972, three-fourths of the states have enacted new death penalty laws to satisfy the criteria established by the Supreme Court, but those new laws have not eliminated racial discrimination in the use of capital punishment.

Research has consistently shown that the race of the victim influences "the likelihood of being charged with capital murder or receiving the death penalty, i.e., those who murdered whites were found to be more likely to be sentenced to death than those who murdered blacks" (U.S. General Accounting Office, 1997: 271). This differential treatment suggests that the legal system places greater value on the lives of whites than on the lives of blacks. In the 1987 case of *McCleskey* v. *Kemp,* the Supreme Court upheld the constitutionality of the death penalty despite evidence that killers of whites are given the death penalty more often than killers of blacks.

Until 1977, forcible rape was a capital offense in some states, but in that year the Supreme Court ruled in *Coker* v. *Georgia* that the death penalty could not be imposed for rape. Before that decision, there was much racial discrimination in the administration of the death penalty for rape, with black males convicted of raping white females in the South especially likely to be executed (Kleck, 1981). One study finds that black men accused of raping white women still receive harsher penalties than either white men who rape white women or black men who rape black women. Rapes of black women by white men rarely come to the attention of the courts. It thus appears to be the race of the victim, or a combination of the race of the victim and the race of the offender—rather than the race of the offender alone—that is most important in determining how convicted rapists will be sentenced (LaFree, 1980).

Much of the research on the death penalty that has found past discrimination in rape cases, and past and current discrimination in homicide cases, relies on data from the South. In part this is because all southern states, but only some nonsouthern states, have the death penalty; and in part it is because southern states have meted out capital punishment much more often than other states that have death penalty laws. Since 1977, when executions were resumed after a ten-year hiatus, four-fifths of all executions have occurred in southern states. One study found that outside the South, black homicide defendants actually seem less likely than white ones to be sentenced to death and less likely to be executed if they are sentenced to death (Kleck, 1981).

Social Class and Sentencing   Some research supports conflict theory's contention that people of lower socioeconomic status fare worse in the criminal justice system than people of higher social standing. One study found social class bias in the court dispositions of juveniles charged with such status offenses as truancy and running away. For conventional offenses against person and property, the evidence of bias by social class was less clear-cut (Carter and Clelland, 1979). Another study found that juries' decisions were influenced by the socioeconomic status of the defendant (Adler, 1973). Research using data from Chicago courts showed that length of sentence was influenced by a defendant's occupation. This unequal treatment was largely a result of poor defendants' inability to afford pretrial release on bail and a private attorney, the absence of which made it less likely that they would mount a successful defense (Lizotte, 1978). Court-appointed lawyers are often overburdened with cases and cannot devote as much attention as private attorneys to the preparation of a defense.

Other researchers have concluded that social class has no strong and consistent impact on sentencing. A study of adult prisoners discovered that sentence severity was not associated with socioeconomic status, when prisoners with similar prior records and demographic characteristics were compared (Chiricos and Waldo, 1975). A review of research on discrimination in the criminal justice system concluded as follows: "Over 80 percent of both racial and socioeconomic studies fail to support differential processing hypotheses" (Williams, 1980: 222).

Sex and Sentencing   Boys referred to the juvenile justice system for acts that would be crimes if committed by adults have traditionally been treated more harshly than girls referred for the same behavior. For status offenses, however, girls have been more likely to be formally processed, detained, and institutionalized. Some researchers have argued that gender discrimination in the juvenile justice system has declined in recent years, but others claim that discrimination persists in more subtle forms. For example, there is evidence that girls and boys who are first-time status offenders are treated in a comparable manner but that girls who are repeat status offenders are treated more harshly than boys who are repeat status offenders, indicating that female status offenders continue to be treated more protectively (Johnson and Scheuble, 1991; Bishop and Frazier, 1992). Another study found that although boys and girls are treated similarly in the early stages of the juvenile justice system, once legally relevant factors are taken into account, at disposition girls are sanctioned more harshly than boys for relatively minor offenses such as running away from home (MacDonald and Chesney-Lind, 2001).

Differential leniency toward women has been found in some research on the sentencing of conventional offenders. Some criminologists claim that women who exhibit behavior that is socially defined as appropriate for women are especially likely to be treated leniently. Thus, older white women who are apologetic and submissive are less apt to be treated severely by the criminal justice system than women who are young, black, and hostile toward authorities. Similarly, women who are more economically dependent on their husbands might be treated more leniently than women who are economically independent, perhaps because judges think that the courts need to exert less formal social control over women who are informally controlled by the men on whom they depend economically (Kruttschnitt, 1982). Greater leniency toward women might also occur if judges believe that women are led into crime by men and are unlikely to violate the law on their own, or if they think that women are less dangerous or more easily rehabilitated than men (Steffensmeier, 1980).

One review of the research on the differential treatment of men and women in the criminal justice system concluded that women were more likely than men to be released on their own recognizance (without bail) but that when bail was set, there seemed to be no difference by sex in the amount at which it was set. Sex did not seem to make a difference in the decision to prosecute a defendant, nor were there differences by sex in the use of plea bargaining or in the likelihood of being convicted. At the sentencing stage, there was a small but consistent differential leniency toward female defendants, even when variables such as prior criminal history and the nature of the offense were taken into account (Nagel and Hagan, 1983). These findings of no differences by sex in prosecution, plea bargaining, or conviction, but a difference by sex in the sentencing of convicted offenders, were confirmed by a study done in Dade County, Florida (Curran, 1983).

Research on sentencing in Pennsylvania concluded that "the primary determinants of judges' imprisonment decisions are the type or seriousness of the crime committed and the defendant's prior record, not the defendant's gender (or, for that matter, age, race, or other background/contextual variables)" (Steffensmeier, Kramer, and Streifel, 1993). Men were slightly more likely than women to be incarcerated, but interviews with judges indicated that this difference was usually either a result of the application of legally relevant criteria or a result of considerations that might not be legally relevant but seemed justified, such as pregnancy, responsibility for the care of young children, or demonstration of remorse. There were negligible differences by sex in the length of imposed sentences. The researchers suggested that they might have found more gender neutrality in sentencing than earlier studies because over time the courts had become more bureaucratic and more concerned with equal application of the law, or perhaps because they had controlled for offense seriousness and prior record more rigorously in their study.

Kathleen Daly and Rebecca Bordt's (1995) review of published research showed that 45 percent of thirty-eight studies that took into account a defendant's prior record found that women were treated more leniently than men, 26 percent of those studies uncovered no effect of sex on sentencing, and 26 percent found mixed effects. Daly (1994) concluded from her own research on convicted felons in New Haven, Connecticut, that women were less likely than men to be incarcerated and that women's terms of confinement were shorter than men's. However, her comparison of pairs of female and male felons matched by statutory offense, prior criminal record, age, race and ethnicity, and pretrial release status showed that the women had committed less serious crimes and had been less centrally involved in the commission of the crimes. Daly concluded that what initially appeared to be greater leniency in the sentencing of women was not due to gender bias but was instead warranted by the nature of the crimes the women had committed.

From 1970 to 2001, the percentage of state and federal prison inmates who were females increased from 2.9 percent to 6.7 percent (Beck, Karberg, and Harrison, 2002). Much of this increase was due to harsher penalties for drug offenders, a significant proportion of whom were women. Because most prisoners are men, insufficient attention has been paid to the development of programs to meet the needs of female inmates, including drug treatment, mental health services, gynecological and obstetric care, educational and vocational training, parenting skills courses, and transportation so that their children can visit them (Morash, Bynum, and Koons, 1998).

An inmate in the North Carolina Correctional Center for Women in Raleigh reads to her visiting daughter in a room designed to allow women to leave their cells and behave as mothers.

Sex and Capital Punishment   In his concurring opinion in *Furman* v. *Georgia* (1972), Justice Thurgood Marshall suggested that women are treated more leniently than men in capital cases. Chivalrous treatment has been used to explain why the percentage of suspects arrested for murder and nonnegligent manslaughter who are females (12.5 percent in 2001) is greater than the percentage of new prison admissions under sentence of death who are females (0 percent in 2001) and the percentage of executed offenders who are females (4.5 percent in 2001) (Snell and Maruschak, 2002).

Elizabeth Rapaport (1991) challenges the chivalrous-treatment explanation for the underrepresentation of women in capital cases. She shows that the death penalty is usually applied to offenders convicted of predatory murders and felony murders (murders committed during the course of a rape, robbery, burglary, auto theft, or other felony). Only 6.2 percent of all suspects arrested for felony murders from 1976 through 1987 were women, much less than the 14.3 percent of all murder and nonnegligent manslaughter suspects who were women. Other characteristics of the murders most likely to result in a death sentence also reduce the chance that women who kill will receive the death penalty: Females are less likely than males to kill strangers, to have a prior record of violence, and to kill multiple victims. Rapaport concludes that it is the kinds of murders that women commit and their criminal records, rather than chivalrous treatment by the legal system, that account for the infrequency of death sentences for women. She also argues that by singling out predatory murders and murders of strangers as the crimes most deserving of capital punishment, and by treating as less serious those murders that occur in domestic settings (the kind most apt to be committed by women, but also the type most likely to take the lives of women and children), the law reflects patriarchal values that attach more opprobrium to violence in the commercial sphere and between nonintimates than to violence in the domestic sphere.

The Prisons

No more than 1 or 2 percent of all serious crimes lead to the imprisonment of an offender, but most people who commit many crimes eventually end up in jail or prison. Prison sentences probably deter some people from crime, but the certainty of punishment is low in the present-day United States.

History of Prisons

For centuries, jails and prisons were places to hold people before they were punished for their crimes, rather than places of punishment for convicted offenders. People were locked up until they could be executed, pilloried, or subjected to other forms of suffering. Today, defendants are held in city or county jails until they are tried in court. Those who are found guilty are given a criminal sentence such as a fine, time on probation, a term in a state or federal prison or a local correctional institution, or the death penalty.

In the late eighteenth century, the Quakers in Philadelphia developed a use for prisons different from the earlier practice of holding people until they were punished. The Quakers believed that even the worst offenders could be saved, and they sought to do this by requiring offenders to serve long periods in total silence in prison, hoping this would lead prisoners to reflect on their mistakes and see the correct way to behave. These institutions were called penitentiaries, because the Quakers thought that inmates would grow penitent about their crimes while reflecting on their lives.

In the nineteenth century, prison reformers developed an institution at Auburn, New York, that used a different philosophy of punishment: Put prisoners to work and teach them to become law-abiding by instilling in them the work ethic. Since then, inmates have often been put to work, though usually only for part of each day and often at menial and poorly paid tasks.

In contrast to the view that prisons originally had a humanitarian impulse behind them is the view that they were and continue to be weapons of class conflict, a tool used by the powerful and the wealthy to control the "dangerous classes" (Foucault, 1978; Ignatieff, 1978; Rothman, 2002).

The Prison Population

A 1997 report by the Sentencing Project found that there were 600 prisoners for every 100,000 people in the United States. Among the other nations surveyed, only Russia had a higher rate (690). Western European nations' rates ranged from 55 to 125, and Japan's was only 37 (Mauer, 1997). Furthermore, the use of incarceration has increased dramatically in the United States in recent years, with the number of state and federal inmates per capita more than tripling since 1980 (see Figure 13.2).

Figure 13.3 shows criminal justice expenditures in seven countries in euros per recorded crime, thus standardizing for variations in crime rates across the countries. Per crime expenditures on the police in the United States are comparable to those of Canada and the United Kingdom, much less than those of Austria, and somewhat greater than those of Sweden, France, and the Netherlands. Expenditures on prosecution and sentencing are much greater in the United States than in the other six countries, indeed more than twice as high as in all other countries but Austria. The United States differs even more drastically in prison expenditures, spending more than three times as much per crime on incarceration as all other nations except Canada. In sum, after taking into account cross-national differences in crime rates, the United States is comparable to the other nations in spending on the police but devotes much more money to the prosecution and incarceration of offenders. These differences might be due to greater punitiveness in the United States, but they could also be due to the country's higher rates of violent crimes, which mandate greater court and prison expenditures.

One analysis of cross-national differences in imprisonment underscored the difficulty of making comparisons, showing that the usual comparison of jurisdictions in terms of number of inmates confined on a particular day or average number of prisoners over a whole year conceals cross-national variations in prison admissions, sentence lengths, pretrial detainments, and parole revocations (Young and Brown,

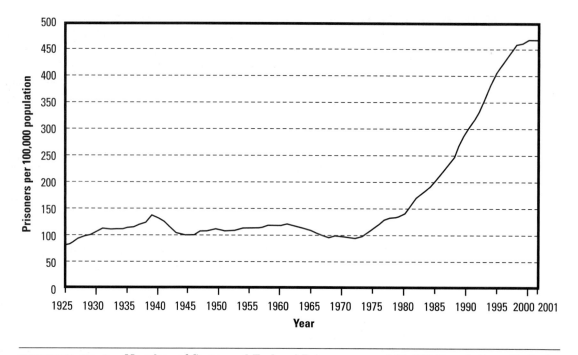

FIGURE 13.2   Number of State and Federal Prisoners per 100,000 Population, United States, 1925–2001

Source: Based on data from Kathleen Maguire and Ann L. Pastore, eds., *Sourcebook of Criminal Justice Statistics 2001,* Table 6.23, p. 494, retrieved from www.albany.edu/sourcebook.

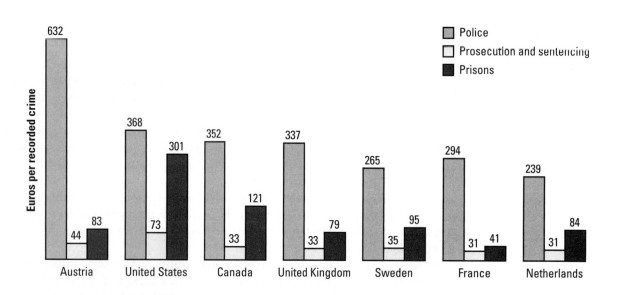

FIGURE 13.3   Expenditures on Criminal Justice System in Euros per Recorded Crime, 1998 Prices

Source: Based on data in Frans van Dijk and Jaap de Waard, *Legal Infrastructure of the Netherlands in International Perspective: Crime Control.* The Hague, Netherlands: Ministry of Justice, June 2000, p. 9.

1993). Typically, jurisdictions that have higher rates of prisoners per capita impose longer sentences rather than send more offenders to prison. This study found that cross-jurisdictional differences in prison populations were not primarily a result of differences in crime rates, nor were they mainly due to a nation's prison capacity or its unemployment rate. Cross-national differences in rates of imprisonment were instead associated with differences in public attitudes toward punishment. These punitive attitudes were in turn related to egalitarianism:

> Countries that have a highly individualistic and competitive ethos, premised on notions of meritocracy and equal opportunity, and have substantial gaps between rich and poor are likely to be comparatively severe in their penal outlook. Countries that have highly developed welfare systems and a less materialistic reward structure are likely to be comparatively mild. (Young and Brown, 1993: 41–42)

Another study reached a different conclusion, finding that although the United States has the highest incarceration rate among industrialized democracies, it is not obviously more punitive than those nations. The likelihood that a homicide offender will be sentenced to prison is similar in the United States and the other democracies, though American murderers are given longer sentences and serve more time behind bars. The long sentences for homicide offenders, in combination with the high homicide rate in United States, account in part for the country's high incarceration rate. The tendency to imprison other violent offenders is also similar in the United States and other democracies, but the discrepancy between the United States and those countries in actual time served increases as the level of violence decreases. The fact that more robberies in the United States are committed with firearms probably accounts for some of this discrepancy. Offenders convicted of property and drug crimes in the United States are more likely to be incarcerated and to serve longer terms than offenders convicted of those crimes in other democracies. Overall, "differences between the United States and other nations [in punitiveness] are less than commonly believed and are more crime-specific" (Lynch, 2002: 41).

Parole

Both prison crowding and the high cost of incarceration can be reduced by releasing inmates before they complete their full sentences. They can then be supervised on the street and sent back to prison if they violate the conditions of their release. This system is called **parole.**

State parole boards meet regularly to review inmates' progress toward rehabilitation and to determine whether they can be safely released if certain conditions are met. Parole board decisions cause anxiety and bitterness in prisoners, who often see the decisions as arbitrary. One study found that the most annoying thing to inmates about serving time in prison was never knowing when they would be released. Fifty-two percent mentioned this problem, and only 12 percent mentioned the next most commonly voiced complaint: being treated like a child by the prison staff (Kassebaum, Ward, and Wilner, 1971).

If a parole board decides to release an inmate, it specifies the conditions of release, which typically include a steady job, staying away from known offenders, and avoiding the use of alcohol and illegal drugs. The parolee is required to meet regularly, perhaps once or twice a month, with a parole officer to discuss problems of adjustment and signs of progress. Parole officers frequently know about violations of parole conditions but usually do not send inmates back to prison for minor infractions. Instead, parole officers "save" those infractions so that if a major one occurs, such as arrest for a new crime, their decision to revoke parole and send the parolee back to prison can be justified with a list of infractions.

Not all inmates who leave prison are paroled. Some "wrap up" their sentence, that is, complete their full sentence in prison. The use of parole has been restricted in response to criticisms that the granting of parole is arbitrary and violates due process rights and that the behavior of parolees is difficult to predict and monitor. By the end of 2001, the federal prison system and fifteen states had abolished parole, and five other states had prohibited its use for certain violent offenders. Even where parole is used, inmates must serve a minimum part of their sentence before they are eligible for release. From 1990 to 1999, the proportion of all inmates released from prison who were paroled dropped from 39 to 24 percent (Bureau of Justice Statistics, 2002).

Critics argue that changes in the use of parole have had negative consequences. Requiring inmates to serve their full sentence contributes to prison crowding and increases the cost of new prison construction. Offenders who cannot be paroled have less incentive to reform while in prison and cannot be required to report to parole officers or to participate in treatment programs after they are released, perhaps causing them to return to crime at higher rates than was true for earlier generations of ex-convicts. In some states parole officers now return higher proportions of those inmates who are paroled to prison for violating the conditions of their release. In 1980, 17 percent of inmates admitted to state prisons were parole violators, but in 1999 that proportion was 35 percent (Gonnerman, 2002).

The Victim in the Criminal Justice System

The American criminal justice system includes procedural rights designed to protect defendants against the power of the state. Some people complain that this emphasis on defendants' rights neglects "victims' rights." Critics also complain about the slowness of the legal process, which costs victims and witnesses time and money to sit in court hallways awaiting trials.

In recent years, more attention has been paid to the victims of crime. Every state now has a statute or constitutional amendment that gives certain rights to crime victims. Systems of compensation and restitution have been developed to repay victims for their losses. District attorneys have come to realize that cases cannot be prosecuted successfully without cooperative victims and witnesses. Judges have increasingly considered the impact of crimes on victims before sentencing offenders, and parole boards sometimes listen to victims before releasing inmates. One scholar concludes that "what the 'victims' movement,' however defined, has achieved within a short space of time can only be described as remarkable, and there are few signs of a waning of enthusiasm" (Maguire, 1991: 420). For a contrasting picture of the victim's role in the criminal justice system, see the Cross-Cultural Perspective box.

Compensation

Compensation is a system by which a state repays victims for their financial losses or physical injuries. Under this system, it is not necessary to arrest and convict an offender for a victim to be compensated, nor does a convicted offender have to be financially solvent for the victim to be repaid for his or her losses. Most states now provide compensation for victims, but many programs are not well funded or well publicized.

Compensation has been justified in several ways. Some say that the state has an obligation to protect the welfare and safety of its citizens, so that when it fails to prevent crime, it should pay victims for their losses. Another rationale for compensation is that it prevents victims from becoming angry at the criminal justice system and alienated from the political system (Schafer, 1968; Stookey, 1981). Even though compensation programs are aimed at improving public attitudes toward the criminal justice system and the government, research indicates that administrative obstacles to securing compensation and the inadequate rewards provided to victims engender more discontent toward the legal system among applicants for compensation than exists among people who do not apply for compensation (Elias, 1983, 1984).

Compensation programs must deal with the problem of the victim's contribution to the crime. Victims sometimes precipitate a crime or contribute to their own victimization, and in such cases the state might choose not to compensate the victim. For instance, someone who first uses force against another person and then ends up badly injured in a fight might not be compensated if the state compensation board found that the crime would not have occurred without the victim's initiating actions.

Restitution

A system of **restitution** requires offenders to make monetary payments or provide services, either to the victim or to the community at large. Relatively few criminal courts have used restitution extensively, but growing concern for victims' rights has led more judges to require offenders to repay victims for their losses.

CROSS-CULTURAL PERSPECTIVES

Rape and Adultery in Pakistan

Zafran Bibi says that while her husband was in prison for murder, she was raped repeatedly by her brother-in-law as she was working in the fields and alone at home. Her complaints to the brother's parents were ignored. She got pregnant and gave birth to a daughter. She was then charged with committing *zina,* breaking Pakistan's strict Islamic laws that forbid any sexual contact outside marriage. Virtually all those punished for adultery under these laws are women. The judge who sentenced Ms. Zafran said that her baby was proof of zina; indeed, by accusing her brother-in-law of rape, she had admitted to engaging in sexual intercourse outside marriage. According to the judge, "This left no option to the court but to impose the highest penalty." Ms. Zafran was sentenced to die by stoning, a punishment that had been carried out in other cases of zina. After public protest and a de-

Once sentenced to death by stoning for committing adultery, Zafran Bibi was released after a court dismissed her case in June 2002.

mand by the nation's president that the sentence be overturned, the court accepted changed testimony from Ms. Zafran and her husband and freed her.

Rape is a crime in Pakistan, but it is not a defense to a charge of zina, and it is difficult to prove in court. Human rights groups estimate that perhaps half of all women there who report that they have been raped are charged with adultery. Rape defendants commonly claim that the woman consented to sex, and the law requires four male Muslims of good repute to testify that they saw the rape occur in order to sustain a charge of rape that will exonerate a woman of zina. Not only do Pakistani women who are raped lack the legal protections and resources that have gradually become available in the United States, they are actually punished as criminals.

Sources: Based on Seth Mydans, "In Pakistan, Rape Victims Are the 'Criminals,'" *New York Times,* May 17, 2002, p. A3; Seth Mydans, "Sentenced to Death, Rape Victim Is Freed by Pakistani Court," *New York Times,* June 8, 2002, p. A4.

Some claim that restitution makes offenders take responsibility for their behavior and thus helps rehabilitate them. Others claim that offenders who repay their victims might stop feeling guilty for their crimes and therefore be more likely to continue to commit crime. However, by easing public hostility toward offenders, restitution could reduce the isolation of offenders from conventional society and make it easier to reintegrate them into society after they are released from prison. Restitution could also lighten the burden on taxpayers if it replaced a system of state compensation (Deming, 1976; Barnett, 1977; Bridges, Gandy, and Jorgenson, 1979).

One study found that restitution was more likely to be used as a condition of probation for adult offenders when the judge could quantify the harm that had resulted from the crime, rather than when the offender was considered a "good risk." The majority of the offenders who were ordered to pay restitution paid most of what they owed, but two-fifths of them paid less than half of their obligation. Making restitution reduced the chance that an offender would be rearrested, a benefit that was greatest for offenders who were the most integrated into the community (that is, the most likely to be married, employed, and older) (Outlaw and Ruback, 1999).

The Changing Role of the Victim

Many states have implemented programs to help the victims of crime, including compensating them for their losses and requiring offenders to make restitution. Victims have been given a greater voice in the sentencing of offenders, although offenders are usually allowed to respond to victims' statements. In some jurisdictions, victims must be notified of hearings and trials and informed when an inmate is being considered for parole or escapes from prison.

District attorneys have started to pay more attention to the role of the victim in the criminal justice system. They can help to deal with a victim's fear of retaliation by the offender, frustration with delays in court, and intimidation by a defense attorney's cross-examination. District attorneys can also impress on victims and witnesses the importance of testifying in court. In some jurisdictions, victims have even been included in plea bargaining conferences with the district attorney, the defense attorney, and the defendant. One study found that victim-witness programs in prosecutors' offices contributed in an important way to keeping victims informed about the progress and outcome of cases, and that crime victims expressed more satisfaction with the criminal justice system when they knew the outcome of a case and thought they had influenced that outcome (Forst and Hernon, 1985).

Few judges learn directly from victims about the impact crime has had on their psychological well-being, physical condition, and financial situation. Usually, judges learn about this only from presentence reports prepared by probation officers, who draw on secondhand information from police reports, medical records, and victims' discussions with prosecutors. Some courts have introduced **victim impact statements,** detailed written reports based on interviews with victims about how a crime affected them (Forst and Hernon, 1985). One study of sexual assault cases found that victim impact statements had little influence on the sentences that judges imposed, beyond the effects one would expect from legally relevant variables such as seriousness of the crime and prior criminal record. This study found much agreement between the sentences recommended by victims and the actual sentences, which could produce a placebo effect, with victims being satisfied with the outcome of a case because they believe they have influenced the sentence, even if the sentence would have been the same without their recommendation (Walsh, 1986). A second study also found that legally relevant factors explained most of the variation in sentences but concluded that victim impact statements influenced the sentences that judges handed out by improving their knowledge of the harm suffered by victims (Erez and Tontodonato, 1990). In 1991, the U.S. Supreme Court reversed a ruling it had made only four years earlier and permitted jurors to use victim impact statements to help them determine whether convicted murderers should be sentenced to death.

Today, nearly all states permit victims to appear at parole board hearings or file written statements with parole boards, in order to make known their wishes about whether a prisoner should be released. Many victims do not make their wishes known, either fearing retaliation or not wanting to dredge up unpleasant memories about the crimes committed against them.

Those who oppose the use of victim testimony to parole boards and victim impact statements in court fear that those reforms might introduce public pressure or vengeance into proceedings that should be dispassionate. They claim that uneducated offenders might be punished more severely if they are confronted with articulate victims who demand long sentences. These critics assert that sentencing and parole should be based on an offender's threat to society and behavior while in prison, not on a victim's wishes.

Supporters of these reforms argue that they draw victims into the criminal justice system, thereby providing criminal justice administrators with a new perspective. They also claim that to the extent that such reforms increase satisfaction with the criminal justice system, they improve the chance that victims will report crimes and aid in the prosecution of defendants in the future, which in turn could help to deter crime.

How effective have victims' rights laws actually been? A survey of victims in two states with strong laws and two states with weak laws concluded that victims in the states with strong laws were more likely to be notified of the progress of their cases, informed of their rights as victims, and told about available services. They were also more likely to exercise the rights they had and more likely to view the criminal justice system favorably. However, a substantial number of victims in the states with the strong laws were still dissatisfied with the legal system, and many of them were never informed about the progress of their cases or told of their rights and the services available to them. The researchers concluded:

> Strong legal protection . . . appears to be a necessary but not a sufficient condition for ensuring the protection of crime victims' rights, because a host of intervening factors, such as knowledge, funding, and enforcement, mediates the actual 'delivery' of victims' rights. (Kilpatrick, Beatty, and Howley, 1998: 2)

Summary

The criminal justice system aims to dispense justice and reduce crime. In doing so, it also influences the development of criminal careers. This system has been described as a funnel or sieve that sorts out cases as they pass from the police through the courts and to the prisons.

The police were first formally organized at the municipal level in the nineteenth century. The police exercise both delegated and unauthorized discretion. The use of discretion is influenced by an officer's perception of the likely consequences of an arrest or a warning, by the community in which an offense occurs, by a suspect's demeanor, and sometimes by race and sex. The police measure their effectiveness with a clearance rate, the proportion of offenses they solve to their satisfaction.

Suspects arrested by the police have the right to have bail set at a reasonable level, but this system discriminates against the poor. Preventive detention has been proposed as a way to reduce bail crimes, offenses committed between the time of release and the disposition of the original charge.

Prosecutors, who bring criminal charges against defendants on behalf of the state, measure their effectiveness by conviction rates. Defense attorneys try to get their clients acquitted, or at least get them the lightest possible sentence. Because many defendants are poor, defense attorneys are often appointed and paid for by the state. Prosecutors and defense attorneys theoretically engage in a "fight" or adversarial process, out of which the truth is supposed to emerge. In practice, they more often engage in plea bargaining over guilt and an appropriate sentence in order to save the time and resources of the court. Judges then ratify the negotiated plea and sentence, treating defendants more leniently for speeding up the processing of cases. Judges preside over trials, but their most important function is the sentencing of convicted offenders. Juries also try cases, but no more than 5 percent of all felony cases in the United States are disposed of in this way. Convicted offenders are sentenced in a variety of ways, one of which is probation, a form of supervised release.

One problem with the courts is sentence disparity. Legal criteria are usually the basis of judges' sentences, but race sometimes plays a role in the sentencing of offenders. This can be due to direct racial discrimination, but often it is a result of organizational or economic discrimination that affects minorities more because of their lower incomes. Criminal justice procedures rather than direct racial discrimination account for most of the disparity in sentences among racial and ethnic groups, but in capital cases murderers who kill blacks are punished less severely than murderers who kill whites. Some research indicates that defendants of lower socioeconomic standing fare worse in the criminal justice system than those of higher standing. The sex of a defendant can also make a difference, with women sometimes treated more leniently than men.

Prisoners are sometimes released on parole prior to the expiration of their sentence. They are then supervised in the community to help them become rehabilitated.

Victims are playing an increasingly important role in the criminal justice system. Compensation programs and penalties of restitution are designed to repay victims for their financial losses and physical suffering. Some victims now testify in court about the sentence they believe is appropriate for an offender, and some of them appear before parole boards to say whether they think an offender should be released. The criminal justice system might function more efficiently if it counseled victims and tried to incorporate them more into the system.

IMPORTANT TERMS

bail system	parole	restitution
case attrition	plea bargaining	sentence disparity
clearance rate	preventive detention	victim impact statement
compensation	probation	
discretion	racial profiling	

REVIEW QUESTIONS

1. Why do the police sometimes use excessive force? To what extent do the police discriminate on the basis of race and sex?

2. What purpose does bail serve in the American criminal justice system? What is preventive detention?

3. What is plea bargaining, and why is it so common in U.S. courts? Who participates in negotiating a guilty plea and a sentence for a defendant?

4. What is sentence disparity? To what extent does it characterize the sentencing of blacks in both capital and noncapital crimes? To what extent does it exist for members of different social classes? To what extent does it exist for males and females, both in juvenile court and in criminal court?

5. What is the trend regarding the number of prisoners in the United States? What accounts for this trend?

6. In what ways have victims been increasingly incorporated into the criminal justice system? What are the advantages and disadvantages of this increased role for victims?

FOR FURTHER STUDY

Police   The way police officers see themselves and their relationships with the public, the courts, the media, and departmental administrators is described in John P. Crank's *Understanding Police Culture* (Cincinnati: Anderson, 1998). The use of force by the police is the focus of Jerome H. Skolnick and James J. Fyfe's *Above the Law: Police and the Excessive Use of Force* (New York: Free Press, 1993).

Criminal Courts   The home page of the Bureau of Justice Statistics (www.ojp.usdoj.gov/bjs/welcome.html) provides links to reports and statistics on the courts, sentencing, and corrections. Links to material on the death penalty can be found at the Cornell Death Penalty Project's website (www.lawschool.cornell.edu/lawlibrary/death/default.htm).

Prisons   The increasing use of incarceration to deal with crime in the United States and the impact of this "get tough" approach on African Americans are explored in Marc Mauer's *Race to Incarcerate* (New York: New Press, 1999). A critical examination of the way that the American criminal justice system benefits the well-to-do and the powerful is Jeffrey Reiman's *The Rich Get Richer and the Poor Get Prison: Ideology, Class, and Criminal Justice* (6th ed., Boston: Allyn & Bacon, 2001).

14 Deterrence, Incapacitation, Retribution, and Rehabilitation

Modern criminal justice systems are based on several rationales. One is that the threat of punishment dissuades potential offenders from breaking the law. Another is that locking criminals up keeps them from victimizing more people. A third view is that those who violate the law deserve to be punished. Still others claim that the function of the criminal justice system is to reform offenders through treatment. This chapter explores these four rationales for punishment.

Deterrence

Crime increased dramatically in eastern Europe after the demise of communism. A senior Polish police official remarked, "Now that Poland has a government that the people support, you might think there would be less crime. But for some people, freedom means greater freedom from moral responsibility. Not everyone feels this way, but there is a segment that is easily tempted by crime" (cited in Greenhouse, 1990: 20). The domestic policy advisor to the president of the former nation of Czechoslovakia observed, "People lost what was a major commodity here. Fear of the police" (cited in *New York Times*, December 18, 1991: A21).

Deterrence is the inhibition of criminal activity by state-imposed penalties. When people perceive the threat of punishment to be weakened, as they did in eastern Europe, often crime rates rise. Deterrence is a utilitarian rationale for punishment—that is, it is based on the idea that punishment should be used to prevent crime.

Specific deterrence occurs when individuals who are punished for a particular crime do not commit that crime again because their risk-reward calculations have been altered by the punishment. They have learned that the risk is greater than they thought, so the rewards become relatively less attractive, leading them to avoid crime in the future.

General deterrence is the inhibition of the desire to engage in crime among the general population through the punishment of certain offenders. Most research focuses on general deterrence rather than on specific deterrence. One report even defines deterrence as the inhibiting effects of sanctions on the criminal activity of people other than the punished offender (Blumstein, Cohen, and Nagin, 1978).

The **marginal deterrent effect** of punishment is the extent to which crime rates respond to incremental changes in the threat of sanctions. Increasing the rate at which the police arrest offenders from 0 to 100 percent would undoubtedly deter many criminals, but increasing the arrest rate from 20 to 22 percent would probably have little or no impact. Similarly, most research indicates that capital punishment is no more effective a deterrent than life imprisonment.

Cesare Beccaria (1738–1794) and Jeremy Bentham (1748–1832) argued that the punishment of criminal acts can deter potential offenders by making the negative consequences of crime greater than its rewards. Writing in the eighteenth century, Beccaria (1764/1963: 42) stated that the goal of crime prevention should be pursued with punishments "which will make the strongest and most lasting impression on the minds of men, and inflict the least torment on the body of the criminal." He believed that punishment should be as certain as possible and as harsh as necessary to deter potential offenders, but that "all beyond this is superfluous and for that reason tyrannical" (Beccaria, 1764/1963: 43). For Beccaria, punishment should be consistent with the principle of retribution or just deserts, a principle examined later in this chapter.

For much of the twentieth century, the notion of deterrence was ignored or held in disrepute by social scientists, because positivists focused on individual and social pathologies as causes of crime. After the publication of an influential paper by the Norwegian law professor Johannes Andenaes in 1952, there was a rebirth of interest in deterrence.

Assumptions about Behavior

The deterrence model assumes that people engage in an act only after carefully and rationally considering its costs (or risks) and its benefits (or rewards). Punishment supposedly induces compliance with the law, because people fear punishment and do not want to risk their stake in conformity. In the deterrence model, the rationale for punishment is to affect future behavior, rather than to inflict pain that offenders might deserve because of their past actions; the latter is the retribution or just deserts rationale for punishment.

The deterrence model assumes free will or voluntarism, suggesting that people choose how to behave, even if they are limited in their choices by social, psychological, and biological factors. However, not all behavior is governed by careful consideration of costs and benefits; much of it is unplanned or habitual. Internalized values and beliefs, sometimes referred to as "conscience," also guide behavior. Behavior is sometimes avoided because people lack the skill or opportunity to commit an act.

Some offenders try to minimize risks by planning their crimes, and they select targets according to what they hope to gain. Even the most rational offenders, however, often lack good information on the actual risks of arrest and conviction, and on what they might gain from a particular crime. Moreover, many offenders act on impulse.

Deterrence and Other Effects of Penalties

A criminal penalty might act as a negative inducement that discourages people from engaging in behavior that violates the law, but deterrence is not the only effect of punishment. The very existence of a criminal penalty indicates moral condemnation of the behavior and a corresponding support for other values; people learn these attitudes through socialization and formal education. The law has an "eye-opener effect," directing attention to punished acts and inviting reflection on the reason those acts are condemned (Andenaes, 1974). The actual punishment of offenders makes credible the threat of a sanction and helps convince people that the government is serious in its effort to deter crime. Punishment also keeps people in line by convincing them that those who violate the law will gain no advantage over those who abide by the law.

One analysis suggests that three distinct forces operate independently and have additive effects on keeping crime in check:

1. Moral commitment, or internalized legal norms.
2. Social disapproval, or fear of informal sanctions by peers.
3. Threat of legal punishment, or fear of physical and material deprivation from legally imposed sanctions (Grasmick and Green, 1980).

Usually, only the third factor is called deterrence.

These three factors interact with one another. Subjective appraisals of social disapproval and the threat of punishment affect criminal behavior, but involvement in crime can alter perceptions of social disapproval and the threat of punishment. Criminal activity can show an offender that the consequences of breaking the law are not serious, lead an offender to a moral reassessment of norms, or provide the opportunity for an offender to learn an accomplice's values (D. Greenberg, 1981). Testing the effects of the three inhibiting factors thus requires a model like the one depicted in Figure 14.1. Research that tested a model like this found that internalized normative constraints, or moral commitment, was the best predictor of later delinquency. Perceptions of the threat of both informal and formal sanctions added significantly to the model's ability to explain subsequent delinquency. There was also evidence that the threat of sanctions might compensate for weak internalized constraints in inhibiting delinquency (Bishop, 1984). Another study concluded that informal threats

FIGURE 14.1 A Model of Crime-Inhibiting Factors

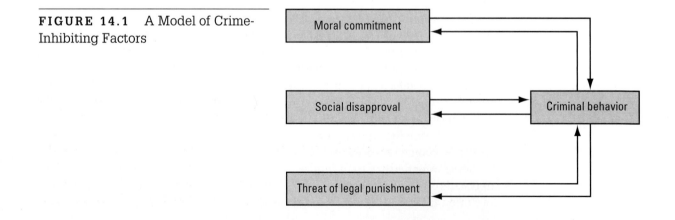

such as social disapproval and moral commitment inhibit drunk driving more effectively than the threat of formal sanctions (Green, 1989a, 1989b). A third study found that perceived certainty of punishment deterred marijuana use but that peer behavior was an even more important influence on that behavior (Paternoster, 1988). Research also demonstrates that strong moral inhibitions reduce corporate crime and that when moral inhibitions are weak, threats of legal punishment and social disapproval can deter such behavior (Paternoster and Simpson, 1996).

Deterrence and the Criminal Act

William Chambliss (1969) suggests that some crimes are more easily deterred than others. Instrumental or goal-oriented behavior, such as theft, is more easily deterred than expressive behavior that results from the inner needs of an offender, such as a violent outburst that leads to murder. The distinction between instrumental and expressive acts is not always easy to make. For instance, a juvenile gang member might commit a robbery in order to feel a sense of mastery over others (an expressive need), rather than to acquire property (an instrumental goal). Chambliss also links deterrence to the offender's commitment to a life of crime: Offenders who are highly committed to a life of crime are more difficult to deter than offenders who are not committed to crime as a way of life. The kind of offender least apt to be deterred is one with a high commitment to crime as a way of life and whose offenses result from expressive needs. On the other hand, instrumental crimes by offenders who are not highly committed to a life of crime are the easiest to deter because these offenders are likely to consider the possible rewards and risks of committing a crime.

Deterrence and Conventional Crime   Some conventional offenders, such as robbers and burglars, commit crimes without carefully assessing risks; doing so might reduce their confidence in being able to carry out the crime and might keep them from committing the crime at all. Risk taking can even make breaking the law exciting and thus rewarding to the offender. Offenders might assess risks differently from the way that the general population does. One robber described his feelings prior to his first mugging as follows: "I was scared, but it was exciting. You see, the whole thing, I was scared and excited. And I knew, you know, I had a fifty-fifty chance of either getting away or getting caught. But I figured that was the chance I was going to take. I wanted to get the money" (cited in Lejeune, 1977: 129). This robber clearly overestimated the chance that he would be caught, which was probably no more than one in eight. Most people would not commit a robbery if they thought the chance of being arrested was one in two, but some robbers will take that risk.

Harsher penalties may not deter persistent property offenders, because those criminals focus on the rewards they expect from their crimes but rarely give much thought to the risks they are taking. To the extent that they think about the chance of being arrested, chronic property offenders underestimate the length of time they will serve in prison. They are not much threatened by the possibility of imprisonment, especially if they have already served time and know they can easily survive in prison (Tunnell, 1992; Shover, 1996). Young minority-group members from urban ghettos might even regard prison as a "shelter from the storm" where they are provided with a place to live, food, clothing, medical care, remedial education, and job training, things to which they lack access in the outside world (Butterfield, 1992).

Deterrence and White-Collar Crime   Because white-collar criminals usually have little commitment to crime as a way of life and typically engage in instrumental acts, some criminologists have suggested that their crimes should be easy to deter (Conklin, 1977; Braithwaite and Geis, 1982). Charles Moore (1987) suggests that although individual white-collar offenders might be deterred by the threat of punishment, corporate offenders are not easily deterred.

Several retired middle-level executives in one study cited the threat of government sanctions as a major deterrent to illegal corporate behavior, singling out the effects of legal action against antitrust violators (Clinard, 1983). In one case, when the government filed a complaint for price fixing against bakery companies for colluding on prices, and when civil suits for treble damages were threatened, price fixing stopped and the price of bread dropped (Block, Nold, and Sidak, 1981). However, a study of white-collar offenders convicted in federal courts found that although imprisonment might have adversely affected the personal lives or job opportunities of the offenders, it had no marginal deterrent effect over the experience of arrest, conviction, and a sentence other than prison (Weisburd, Waring, and Chayet, 1995). Few white-collar offenders receive any criminal sanction at all, for several reasons: It is expensive and time-consuming to prosecute them; they often have the best attorneys; it is difficult to prove intent to defraud; and the laws they are accused of violating are complex and subject to various interpretations. As a result, more severe penalties will probably have little deterrent impact on white-collar crime unless there is a substantial increase in the certainty with which those penalties are imposed.

Deterrence and the Sanctioning Process

People have imperfect knowledge of the maximum penalties for various crimes, but their perceptions of the severity of sanctions, the certainty with which they will be administered, and the promptness of punishment all influence their choice of behavior.

Severity of Punishment   Criminal behavior can be deterred by harsher sanctions, but there is not enough research on marginal deterrence to know how much crime is prevented by a specific increase in punishment. Harsh penalties are costly, and sometimes they backfire. In early nineteenth-century Great Britain, where over two hundred crimes could be punished with the death penalty, juries often acquitted defendants rather than send them to the gallows for relatively trivial offenses.

Research in Chicago showed that juvenile delinquents who were punished more severely were arrested less often after they were punished. For instance, offenders who were removed from their community and incarcerated for an indefinite time on an involuntary basis and with custodial supervision showed a greater drop in their rate of arrest after release than did juveniles who were removed from the community for a specified period and placed in a noncustodial and voluntary program. The mildest penalties—supervision and probation—did not significantly reduce arrest rates (Murray and Cox, 1979). A study of a cohort of males in Racine, Wisconsin, found that arrest was more likely than release without arrest to deter future criminal conduct, ending the criminal careers of novice offenders and reducing crime by experienced ones (Smith and Gartin, 1989).

Research on adult arrestees discovered that their perceptions of the severity of punishment increased after their experiences with the criminal justice system and that harsher penalties raised their perceptions of severity more than lighter penalties. However, a heightened sense of the severity of sanctions does not necessarily lead an individual to avoid criminal behavior; it can also produce a sense of injustice that leads to more crime (Apospori and Alpert, 1993).

An examination of corporations that had been charged with serious antitrust violations found that the severity of formal sanctions had a greater deterrent effect on repeat offending than did either the certainty or the promptness with which the sanctions were applied. However, the deterrent impact of sanctions was a less important influence on corporate behavior than the motivations and opportunities for offending, the culture and structure of the firm, and the climate of the industry and the general economy (Simpson and Koper, 1992).

Certainty of Punishment   Perhaps more important than the maximum statutory penalty for a crime or the severity of the sentences actually meted out is the certainty of some punishment for the crime. For example, one study revealed that residential burglars' decisions to commit crime were more influenced by perceived risk of arrest than by the severity of the threatened sanction (Decker, Wright, and Logie, 1993). Similarly, a survey of college students concluded that certainty of punishment was more important than severity of the sanction in deterring drinking and driving behavior (Nagin and Pogarsky, 2001). More than two centuries ago, Cesare Beccaria (1764/1963: 58) wrote, "The certainty of a punishment, even if it be moderate, will always make a stronger impression than the fear of another which is more terrible but combined with the hope of impunity." Thus, a 100 percent chance of a one-year prison term might deter more crime than a 5 percent chance of a twenty-year sentence.

The exact combination of certainty and severity that will maximize deterrence is unknown. A certain sentence of a $10 fine or a day in jail will probably deter few robbers, because they will think that crime pays if the costs are that low. Similarly, the low certainty of any punishment for white-collar crime probably limits the deterrent effect of even those laws that permit harsh penalties. According to one estimate, a convicted antitrust violator is less likely to be imprisoned than someone who violates a migratory bird law (Yoder, 1978). However, a 5 percent chance of being executed would probably deter instrumental crimes by people with little commitment to crime as a way of life; thus, the effect of a very severe penalty would offset the low certainty of punishment.

In 1973, New York state increased the severity of penalties for major drug dealers, who were to be sentenced to a minimum of fifteen years and a maximum of life in prison. This law did not curtail heroin trafficking, nor did it reduce property crimes associated with heroin addiction (Joint Committee on New York Drug Law Evaluation, 1978). Although the law increased the severity of sanctions, it did not increase the certainty of punishment. Many defendants avoided severe sanctions through plea bargaining. Those who were unable to plea-bargain to their satisfaction demanded trials, causing a backlog in the courts that delayed punishment, which can also reduce the deterrent effect of punishment (Wilson, 1983).

It is not clear that certainty of punishment can easily be increased. Doing so would require better citizen reporting of crime, more complete recording of offenses by the police, higher arrest rates, higher rates of prosecution, or higher conviction rates. These changes cannot be made without greater expenditures, reorganization of law-enforcement agencies, or infringement on defendants' constitutional rights.

Promptness of Punishment   The promptness with which sanctions are administered can also affect criminal behavior. If an offender is punished soon after committing a crime, both the specific deterrence of that individual and the general deterrence of the public may be greater than if the offender is not punished until months or years later. The closer in time a negative reinforcement (or legal sanction) is to a crime, the more likely it is that the behavior eliciting the negative reinforcement will be avoided.

Types of Punishment   Little is known about the relative deterrent effects of imprisonment, restitution, fines, probation, and other sanctions. Marginal deterrence is often examined by focusing on the reduction of crime that results from using more of one type of penalty, rather than from using a different kind of penalty.

An experiment sponsored by the Police Foundation in Minneapolis in 1981 and 1982 tested the impact of three different sanctions on men accused of domestic violence: arrest, mediation or advice, and ordering the man to leave the home for eight hours. Officers chose one of these methods at random to deal with "moderate" domestic violence, a simple assault that did not produce severe or life-threatening injury. Suspects were followed up for six months to determine if violence recurred; both official data and victims' reports were used. The results suggested that arrests deter moderate domestic assaults. Only 10 percent of the arrested men were involved in a new official report of domestic violence within six months, compared to 19 percent of those receiving mediation or advice and 24 percent of those who had been ordered from the home. Victim self-reports also indicated that arrest was a more effective deterrent than either mediation or being ordered from the home (Sherman and Berk, 1984; Berk and Newton, 1985).

The heavily publicized Minneapolis Domestic Violence Experiment led most urban police departments to implement mandatory or preferred arrest policies for domestic assaults. These policies were also developed in response to pressure by feminists, a growing interest in crime victims, police concern with the violence they suffered while investigating domestic assaults, and successful lawsuits against municipal governments for police failure to protect the victims of domestic violence.

Because the conclusion that arrest was an effective deterrent of domestic violence was based on a single experiment, the National Institute of Justice funded six replications of the Minneapolis study to determine if its results held for other jurisdictions as well. These replications called into question the generalizability of the Minneapolis experiment's findings, concluding that arrest had no greater long-term deterrent effect on domestic violence than mediation or separation (Dunford, Huizinga, and Elliott, 1990; Sherman et al., 1991; Hirschel and Hutchison, 1992; Sherman, 1992b, 1992c). Critics have suggested that the authors of the original study failed to disseminate the generally negative results of the replication studies with as much enthusiasm as they promoted the original finding that arrest deters domestic assault (Binder and Meeker, 1993).

The exact combination of severity, certainty, promptness, and type of sanction that will maximize deterrence for different kinds of crimes is not known, but these factors are important influences on the effectiveness of punishment in reducing crime.

Deterrence and the Criminal Justice System

Scholars studying deterrence have traditionally focused on the circumstances in which the threat of punishment deters crime. Economists have raised the problem of **simultaneity:** Sanctions might reduce crime, but the crime rate also affects the sanctions meted out by the criminal justice system. An inverse relationship between crime rates and the certainty of punishment—that is, lower crime rates when punishment is more certain—might exist because the threat of sanctions reduces crime, but it could also exist because a high crime rate reduces the certainty of sanctions, for example, by overburdening the police or the courts. Thus, the crime rate could affect the certainty of punishment as much as the certainty of punishment affects the crime rate (Blumstein, Cohen, and Nagin, 1978). This simultaneity of causation should be kept in mind when considering the possibility that criminal sanctions deter crime.

Deterrence and the Police   Do cities with larger police forces have less crime? How is the risk of arrest associated with the crime rate? Which police tactics are most likely to reduce crime? These are important questions for researchers, because the American people and their lawmakers often turn to the police to deal with crime.

Researchers disagree over whether increases in police strength actually reduce crime rates, but politicians and the public often call for more officers when rates begin to rise.

Deterrence and Size of the Police Force   Does increasing the resources or the numbers of the police significantly reduce crime? Some researchers have found that increases in police strength lead to decreases in crime rates (Marvell and Moody, 1996; Levitt, 1997; Corman and Mocan, 2000), but others have found that within the range of officers per capita that exists in the United States, cities with larger police forces do not have lower crime rates than cities with smaller police forces (Loftin and McDowall, 1982; Greenberg, Kessler, and Loftin, 1983; Cameron, 1988; Karmen, 2000; Conklin, 2003). After reviewing twenty-seven studies of the relationship between police strength and violent crime, Eck and Maguire (2000: 214) concluded that there was no "consistent body of evidence supporting the assertion that hiring more police is an effective method for reducing violent crime."

Large variations in the number of police officers per capita might affect crime rates in certain situations. Police saturation of an area sometimes occurs for a short time, and it can reduce crime, but this policy is not feasible over the long run. A study of eighteen police crackdowns—sudden increases in the numbers of officers, sanctions, or threats of arrest—found that fifteen showed an initial deterrent effect, although this effect usually decreased after a short time. Five studies found that the deterrent effect continued even after the police crackdown had ended. The evidence of an initial deterrent effect that usually decreases quickly and a residual deterrent effect in some cases suggests that police crackdowns might be most effective if they are of limited duration and are rotated from area to area (Sherman, 1990).

At the other end of the spectrum, the presence of very few police officers might cause crime rates to rise. Several American cities have experienced widespread looting during blackouts, a time when the resources of the police are overtaxed. When the Nazis arrested the Danish police in 1944, rates of robbery, burglary, and larceny rose dramatically despite harsher penalties for those offenders who were caught and convicted (Andenaes, 1974). On the other hand, a study of eleven cities that have had police strikes found little evidence that the strikes significantly affected crime rates (Pfuhl, 1983).

Deterrence and Risk of Arrest   Politicians and the public commonly assume that the police deter crime through arrest, even though the rate at which the police solve crimes is quite low. The numbers in Figure 14.2, the percentages of index crimes

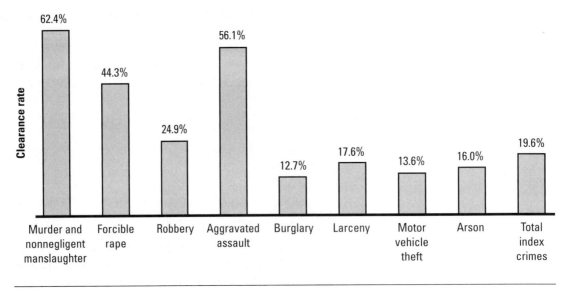

FIGURE 14.2 Clearance Rates of FBI Index Crimes, 2001

Source: Based on data from Federal Bureau of Investigation, *Crime in the United States, 2001: Uniform Crime Reports.* Washington, DC: U.S. Government Printing Office, 2002, p. 222.

cleared by arrest in 2001, overestimate the chance that an offender will be arrested, because many crimes are not reported to or recorded by the police. Even though arrest rates are higher for violent crimes than for property crimes, violent offenses are probably harder to deter, because they are often expressive in nature and occur in private settings to which the police have little access. Crimes against property are probably more likely to involve some consideration of risks and rewards, but they are solved infrequently and are thus not easily deterred.

Can the police deter crime by increasing the risk of arrest? Some researchers have found an inverse relationship between clearance rates and crime rates; in other words, the more crimes the police solve, the fewer crimes of that sort there are (Tittle and Rowe, 1974; Logan, 1975; Wilson and Boland, 1976; Yu and Liska, 1993). Another study found no consistent evidence that higher clearance rates reduce crime rates (Greenberg and Kessler, 1982).

Deterrence and Police Patrol Tactics   Police patrol cars increase the area that the police can cover, and increased mobility enhances the likelihood that officers will be at or near the scene of a crime when it occurs. However, patrol cars isolate the police from the public, cutting off a source of information that can be used to maintain order, prevent crime, and arrest suspects.

One study that sought to determine whether police patrol has a deterrent effect was conducted in Kansas City, Missouri, in 1972 and 1973 (Kelling et al., 1974). The number of patrol cars was doubled in five areas of the city, the number remained the same in five areas, and in five areas all patrol cars were taken off duty and reassigned to other areas (although they did answer calls for help). The fifteen areas were matched by crime rate, characteristics of residents, and number of calls to the police. This experiment found that changes in police patrol practices in the fifteen areas had "little value in preventing crime or making citizens feel safe" (McNamara, 1974: iii). There were no significant differences among the areas in rates of offenses reported to the police, rates of crime reported in victimization surveys, citizen fear of crime, or citizen satisfaction with the police. One critic thought these negative results were unsurprising, because crime is concentrated in certain "hot spots," whereas patrol cars are widely dispersed, so there is little chance that the police will encounter crime while on routine patrol (Sherman, 1992a).

The Kansas City experiment found no evidence of a **displacement effect**, a change in the pattern of crime without a reduction in the total amount of crime. Crime can be displaced from one target to another, one area to another, or one kind of offense to another (for instance, a burglary instead of a robbery). Displacement also refers to changes in a criminal's tactics and changes in the times at which crimes are committed (Hakim and Rengert, 1981; Barr and Pease, 1990). Visible police patrols could alter patterns of crime, but the Kansas City study found no evidence of such displacement as a result of variations in police patrol tactics. There is, however, evidence from other research that the police sometimes displace crime from one area to another where there are fewer officers or patrol cars, or from a time when there are more officers around to a time when the police are less likely to be present (Reppetto, 1974).

If more patrol cars do not prevent crime, can increased numbers of officers on foot do so? A study in Flint, Michigan, found a small reduction in total crime in areas that had foot patrols, though the patrols had no impact on burglaries and larcenies (Trojanowicz, 1983). Other researchers have concluded that foot patrols do not reduce serious crimes (Kelling et al., 1981; Bowers and Hirsch, 1987; Esbensen, 1987). Overall, greater numbers of foot patrol officers do not seem to produce consistent and substantial decreases in crime.

Most research on the deterrent effects of the police has looked at clearance rates or at the number of officers on patrol. Even more important may be what the police do while on patrol. An experiment in San Diego found that robbery, burglary, theft, auto theft, assault, sex crimes, malicious mischief, and disturbances were reduced by an aggressive patrol strategy that included field interrogations. These "street stops" apparently changed perceived risks of apprehension, even though they did not increase the actual number of arrests (Boydstun, 1975). Other studies have found that aggressive policing, as measured by the number of traffic violation citations and disorderly conduct infractions, is associated with lower robbery rates, though not with lower burglary rates (Wilson and Boland, 1978; Sampson and Cohen, 1988).

The number of officers in a neighborhood can be increased or decreased through **directed patrol**, the strategic redeployment of existing resources based on analysis of crime statistics. In a study carried out in Minneapolis in 1988 and 1989, 110 crime hot spots were chosen on the basis of frequent calls to police. Fifty-five control hot spots continued to get the same attention from the police they had been receiving, and fifty-five experimental hot spots got two-and-a-half times as much patrolling as usual. The experimental areas showed a significantly greater decline in serious crimes than the control areas (Sherman and Weisburd, 1995). In another study, extra attention by the Kansas City, Missouri, police to hot spots where gun crimes had occurred in the past resulted in more gun seizures and a marked decline in the number of gun crimes in those areas (Sherman and Rogan, 1995).

Many law-enforcement experts now advocate **community policing**, an approach based on the idea that officers in patrol cars are too isolated from the community and that there needs to be more contact between the police and the people they serve. Community policing is based on four principles:

1. Organizational decentralization and a reorientation of patrol in order to facilitate communication between police and the public.
2. A commitment to broadly focused, problem-oriented policing.
3. Police respond to the public when they set priorities and develop their tactics.
4. A commitment to helping neighborhoods solve crime problems on their own, through community organizations and crime-prevention programs. (Skogan and Hartnett, 1997: 6–8)

The programs and tactics common to community policing are foot or bicycle patrols, small neighborhood substations, crime newsletters, surveys to measure citizens' satisfaction, organization of neighborhood meetings, development of community organizations, conflict resolution programs, organization of youth activities, drug education, truancy prevention, neighborhood cleanups, and building demolition (Bratton and Kelling, 1993; Skogan and Hartnett, 1997). The extent and impact of community policing are difficult to assess because of disagreement over the precise meaning of the term and because there are few methodologically sound studies of its impact on crime (Taylor, Fritsch, and Caeti, 1998; Eck and Maguire, 2000). One recent study of 164 American cities did conclude that community policing was associated with neither lower levels of violence nor the reduction in violence over time (MacDonald, 2002).

Problem-oriented policing, which assumes that the police should deal with the underlying conditions that generate crime, shares with community policing an emphasis on cooperating with citizens to attack local crime problems. Crime statistics, officers' experiences, and information from people in the community are used to identify and analyze problems, develop and implement responses, and evaluate the impact of the responses. The goal is to solve specific problems rather than merely establish good relations with the community. Several studies suggest that problem-oriented policing can be effective, but this approach needs to be introduced more widely and evaluated more rigorously to determine if it can significantly reduce crime rates (Spelman and Eck, 1987; Braga et al., 1999; Eck and Maguire, 2000).

Deterrence and the Courts   There is an inverse relationship between crime rates and the risk of conviction: Lower crime rates are associated with higher conviction rates (Blumstein, Cohen, and Nagin, 1978). The issue of simultaneity again arises: A lower risk of conviction might increase the crime rate, but a higher crime rate can make convictions less likely. A high crime rate would reduce the risk of conviction if prosecutors drop cases because they lack the resources to bring all suspects to trial or if they lose cases because of hasty preparation. A high crime rate could also increase reliance on plea bargaining in order to ease the court's workload; this might produce more guilty pleas but fewer convictions on the most serious charges.

Deterrence and the Prisons   Higher incarceration rates reduce crime rates in subsequent years through a combination of deterrence and incapacitation, even after the reciprocal effect of crime rates on incarceration rates is taken into account (McGuire and Sheehan, 1983; Cappell and Sykes, 1991; Marvell and Moody, 1994). Marvell and Moody (1997: 220) conclude that "prison expansion . . . is probably the major reason why homicide declined after 1990." Spelman (2000) estimates that the decline in the violent crime rate from 1973 to 1997 would have been 27 percent less had the prison population not expanded. An important question is whether the cost of reducing crime through incarceration is worth the benefits: Rosenfeld (2000) estimated that averting a single homicide in the early 1990s required the imprisonment of 670 additional prisoners at a cost of $13.4 million.

One strategy that has been tried as a deterrent to delinquency is a "shock sentence," with offenders being given "a taste of the bars" to keep them from further wrongdoing. Scared Straight is a program that brings young people into prison to listen to inmates talk about the unpleasantness of prison life. Violence and homosexual rape are described in graphic terms to scare the young people away from a life of crime. This Juvenile Awareness Project was initiated at Rahway State Prison in New Jersey in 1976 and was the basis of a television documentary broadcast nationally in 1979 and shown again with follow-up reports in 1987 and 1999. The original show claimed that the program kept more than 80 percent of its participants from getting

Boot camps such as this one in Oregon try to deter offenders from crime through harsh discipline, rigorous exercise, and strenuous work.

into trouble with the law again. However, systematic research shows that Scared Straight and other prison visitation programs actually increase delinquency and crime by their participants (Finckenauer, 1982; Petrosino, Turpin-Petrosino, and Finckenauer, 2000). This is because some participants are drawn to the sense of community provided by the prison, emulate the hardened offenders they encounter during the program, or strive to meet the challenge provided by the offenders.

An approach popular with politicians and the public is the **boot camp**, a military-style program designed to scare youthful offenders away from crime by subjecting them to harsh discipline, rigorous exercise, and strenuous work. Some camps provide drug treatment, educational programs, and vocational training, but the emphasis is on deterrence rather than rehabilitation. There is no evidence that boot camps keep their graduates from returning to crime, nor do they reduce prison crowding or cut prison costs. Indeed, the use of boot camps for offenders who would otherwise have been placed on probation can actually increase correctional costs (Morash and Rucker, 1990; MacKenzie, 1993; Peters et al., 1997). By 2003, some states had eliminated or scaled back their boot camp programs.

Deterrence and Capital Punishment   In a 2002 Gallup Poll, 72 percent of Americans favored the death penalty for convicted murderers, 25 percent opposed it, and 3 percent answered "don't know." Support for capital punishment is greater among men than women, among whites than blacks, among people with higher rather than lower incomes, and among Republicans than Democrats (Polling the Nations, 2002; Maguire and Pastore, 2002: 141).

The way in which the public is asked its opinion about capital punishment influences the results of a survey. For instance, the 2002 Gallup Poll found that support for the death penalty dropped to 52 percent when respondents were given a choice between capital punishment and life imprisonment without possibility of parole; the latter penalty was favored by 43 percent of the public, and 5 percent had no opinion (Polling the Nations, 2002). Fewer people support the execution of juvenile murderers than the execution of adult murderers, and the majority prefer life in prison without the possibility of parole over capital punishment for juvenile offenders (Moon et al., 2000b). One study asked respondents in Florida whether they would support the death penalty in seventeen homicide scenarios, rather than asking whether they favored or opposed capital punishment in general. The results showed both strong support for capital punishment and variation across types of murders in willingness to apply it: 82 percent of the respondents thought that capital punishment was appropriate for some offenders but not for others, 13 percent thought it was appropriate for all offenders, and only 5 percent thought it was inappropriate for all offenders (Durham, Elrod, and Kinkade, 1996).

A major justification for capital punishment is that it deters crime, but faith in this deterrent effect is more widespread among the general public than among criminologists. A 1991 survey of the American public found that 51 percent of Americans believed that capital punishment deterred murder, and 41 percent thought that it did not. In contrast, a survey of sixty-seven past presidents of national criminology associations found that only 12 percent thought that the death penalty deterred murder, and 84 percent thought that it did not (Radelet and Akers, 1996).

There is a direct association between support for the death penalty and the belief that it is a deterrent, but it is not clear that people support the death penalty just because they believe it deters crime. A study of Californians found that most based their support for or opposition to the death penalty on symbolic or ideological grounds, rather than on a set of reasoned beliefs. Nearly all of the 59 percent of the sample who supported the death penalty believed it was a better deterrent than life imprisonment, but two-thirds of those supporters said they would favor capital punishment even if it had no deterrent effect. Nearly all of the 31 percent of the sample who opposed the death penalty believed it had no marginal deterrent effect over life imprisonment, but three-fourths of them said they would continue to oppose the death penalty even if it proved to be a much better deterrent than life imprisonment (Ellsworth and Ross, 1983).

Scholars have done much research on the deterrent effect of capital punishment. Some have compared the homicide rates of states that have the death penalty with the homicide rates of states that do not have the death penalty. Others have examined the murder rates in a state before and after its abolition of capital punishment to determine if that change affected its murder rates. Another method has been to look at murder rates in an area just before and just after executions to see if executions affect the murder rate. Most research has found no evidence that either death penalty laws or actual executions deter homicide (Peterson and Bailey, 1988, 1991; Cheatwood, 1993; Sorensen et al., 1999). One cross-national study found that abolition of the death penalty was followed by a drop in the murder rate more often than by the increase that deterrence theory predicts (Archer, Gartner, and Beittel, 1983). (See the Cross-Cultural Perspective box.)

A few studies have found that capital punishment deters homicide. One frequently cited paper that used econometric techniques estimated that each execution deters as many as eight homicides (Ehrlich, 1975). A second econometric study estimated that each execution prevents up to eighteen murders (Layson, 1985). Critics argue that the methodological shortcomings of these studies invalidate their conclusions (Blumstein, Cohen, and Nagin, 1978; Fox and Radelet, 1989). Two studies showed that well-publicized executions produced short-term reductions in homicides (Phillips, 1980; Stack, 1987); but other research found no evidence of such short-term reductions (McFarland, 1983; Bailey and Peterson, 1989). Most researchers believe that there is no long-term reduction in homicides after even highly publicized executions (Zeisel, 1982; Bailey, 1990; Peterson and Bailey, 1991).

The bulk of the evidence is consistent with the conclusion that capital punishment does not deter those crimes for which it has been used in the United States—forcible rape (until 1977) and homicide. There are reasons for the absence of a deterrent effect. Rapists and murderers do not usually reflect much on the consequences of their behavior before acting. Murder often occurs between people who are intimately involved with one another, and the emotion that characterizes such relationships can interfere with a careful assessment of the costs of violating the law. Lack of prompt punishment also reduces any general deterrent effect that the death penalty might have; the average time from imposition of a death sentence to actual execution was about twelve years for murderers executed in 2001. Another consideration is that because capital punishment statutes apply only to specific kinds of murder (for example, felony murders, premeditated murders, extremely brutal slayings, and murders of police or correctional officers), those laws are unlikely to deter all types of murder.

Capital punishment in the United States also lacks certainty, with most murderers not sentenced to death and most who are sentenced to death never executed. From 1977 through 2001, the FBI recorded 509,702 murders and nonnegligent manslaughters and 479,324 arrests for those crimes. During that time, 6,363 people

CROSS-CULTURAL PERSPECTIVES

Capital Punishment in China

In 2001, China began its third Strike Hard campaign to deter crime and inspire public confidence in the government. Like the 1983–1986 campaign, in which an estimated 30,000 death sentences were meted out, and the 1996 campaign, the new crackdown relied heavily on the use of capital punishment. Since 1983, the number of executions in China has exceeded the total for the rest of the world. Sixty-eight crimes can be punished with death in China, among them twenty-eight nonviolent offenses, including embezzlement, tax fraud, smuggling, and organizing prostitution.

The new Strike Hard campaign was the result of a loosening of the strict morality of Maoism, the development of a market economy, and increased corruption among local law-enforcement and political officials who protect gangsters. China has traditionally relied on the public, organized by the Communist party in neighborhood committees, to keep crime in check, but that informal control has eroded in recent years. The small number of police officers per capita in the country, limited police budgets, and arrest and conviction quotas have given rise to harsh, highly publicized campaigns to convince the public that crime can be controlled. The police make mass arrests, with suspects either forced to confess or convicted after quick trials. Appeals are rapidly exhausted and many

are executed, an estimated 5,000 in 2001 alone. The time from arrest until execution is usually a few months, during which time the condemned rarely see family members. Often the condemned are paraded through the streets on open trucks before being executed with a bullet in the back of the head in a public place. Sometimes their organs are removed and sent to nearby hospitals for transplantation.

There has been widespread support for the Strike Hard campaigns. A 1995 survey found that fewer than 1 percent of the Chinese people wanted to abolish the death penalty; more than 90 percent thought there should be more executions. One college student voiced his support as follows: "I think there are very, very few cases of innocent people who are executed, and, anyway, that's better than letting some criminals get away to harm other people. In China, the interests of the nation or the community are always more important that the interests of the individual" (cited in Smith, December 26, 2001, p. A10).

According to Chinese academics, the Strike Hard crackdowns have not had any long-term impact on crime. Instead, criminals lie low until the campaign ends and the police return to their usual methods. China's crime rate began to rise soon after the 1996 campaign ended, and by September 1997 it was back to the level that had prevailed before the crackdown.

Sources: Based on Craig S. Smith, "China Justice: Swift Passage to Execution," *New York Times,* June 19, 2001, pp. A1, A10; Craig S. Smith, "Chinese Fight Crime with Torture and Executions," *New York Times,* September 9, 2001, pp. 1, 8; Craig S. Smith, "China's Efforts against Crime Make No Dent," *New York Times,* December 26, 2001, pp. A1, A10; Erik Eckholm, "Order Yields to Lawlessness as Maoism Recedes in China," *New York Times,* May 29, 2002, pp. A1, A6.

were admitted to prison under sentence of death and 749 were executed. About one-third of those sentenced to death were removed from Death Row by being retried or resentenced, having their death sentence commuted, or dying before they were executed (Snell and Maruschak, 2002).

Incapacitation

Incapacitation is the custodial control of convicted offenders so that they cannot commit crimes against the general public. Incapacitation assumes that offenders will commit a certain number of crimes over a given time if they remain in society, and that those crimes can be prevented by incarcerating the offenders for that time.

James Q. Wilson (1983) argues that incapacitation will work if three assumptions are correct:

1. Some offenders are repeaters.
2. Offenders who are taken off the street are not immediately and completely replaced by other offenders.
3. Prison does not increase crime by changing inmates in ways that offset the reduction of crime from incapacitation.

Wilson suggests that the first assumption is clearly correct. The second one is plausible for certain offenses. Replacement occurs in organized crime families, and to some extent among prostitutes, drug dealers, and white-collar offenders. It is less likely for offenders who engage in domestic violence and conventional crime. Wilson acknowledges that the third assumption is debatable but suggests that the "schooling" effect of prison probably does not outweigh its incapacitative effect.

Estimating the impact of incapacitation on crime rates is difficult. Because we do not know how many offenses different criminals will commit in a given period of time, it is hard to determine how much crime will be prevented by locking up offenders. Offenders who are at the end of their criminal careers might have stopped committing crime soon even if they had not been imprisoned; for them, incarceration will have little incapacitative effect.

Selective Incapacitation

Selective incapacitation is a policy that aims to separate high-risk offenders from low-risk ones and hold only those who are the most likely to be dangerous if released.

Peter Greenwood (1982, 1984) has devised a system that would separate offenders who should get "incapacitating" prison sentences from those who can be released or placed in alternative programs. Using interviews with incarcerated robbers and burglars, he discovered that the offenders who had committed the most crimes had the following characteristics:

1. An earlier conviction for the same offense.
2. Imprisonment for more than half of the two years prior to the current arrest.
3. A conviction before the age of sixteen.
4. Previous commitment to a juvenile institution.
5. Use of heroin or barbiturates during the previous two years.
6. Use of heroin or barbiturates as a juvenile.
7. Unemployment for half or more of the preceding two years.

Robbers who had four or more of these characteristics had committed an average of thirty-one robberies per year while on the street, compared with an average of only two robberies per year for those who fit one or none of the criteria. Greenwood's seven-item scale also predicted self-reported offending by a sample of New Orleans inmates (Miranne and Geerken, 1991).

Greenwood claims that implementation of his system of selective incapacitation would allocate the limited amount of prison space more efficiently and reduce crime rates. Other researchers have found that the crime-reduction potential of his system is less than he suggests and that the prison population would have to increase dramatically to achieve even a modest reduction in crime (Visher, 1986; Bernard and Ritti, 1991).

Critics claim that many errors would be made if Greenwood's scale were used to predict which offenders should be incapacitated: Many of those locked up would not have returned to crime if they had been released (Cohen, 1983; von Hirsch, 1984; Decker and Salert, 1986). Greenwood's response to this criticism is that judges and parole boards now decide on sentences and release dates on the basis of their best guesses about future behavior, and a selective incapacitation policy would simply allow them to use available data efficiently to make their decisions (Greenwood, 1982, 1984).

One objection to selective incapacitation is that penalties should reflect the seriousness of an offender's crime rather than his or her prior record, and Greenwood's system does not base punishment on the amount of harm done (von Hirsch, 1984). Critics have also opposed selective incapacitation systems that use predictive criteria over which offenders have no control. Of Greenwood's seven criteria, only unemployment might be seen as a factor over which offenders have little or no control, as in times of high unemployment. However, it could also be argued that unemployment often reflects voluntary behavior by offenders.

Career Criminal Programs

District attorneys' offices around the country have established units to prosecute career criminals who repeatedly commit felonies. These programs concentrate resources on suspects who have prior records of serious crimes in order to incapacitate them as quickly and as long as possible. To do this, career criminal programs encourage cooperation between prosecutors and the police, screen defendants for priority prosecution, assign experienced lawyers to top-priority cases, reduce the caseloads of prosecutors assigned to top-priority cases, have the same prosecutor stay with a case until it is disposed of, assign all cases involving a defendant to the same prosecutor, have a senior prosecutor monitor the progress of top-priority cases, and minimize plea negotiation (Chaiken and Chaiken, 1991).

Career criminal programs have increased conviction rates, incarceration rates, and the length of sentences by modest amounts. A New York state program that focused on offenders who had at least one prior felony conviction and were currently charged with a major crime led to the conviction of more than 95 percent of the defendants; nearly four-fifths of those who were convicted were sentenced on the highest charge they faced (Fowler, 1981). The federally sponsored Habitual Serious and Violent Juvenile Offender Program, initiated at thirteen locations in 1984, focused on young people who had prior convictions for serious offenses and who were charged with homicides, robberies, forcible sex offenses, assaults, or burglaries. Experienced prosecutors paid special attention to cases involving these youths, and victims and witnesses were offered special assistance. The program succeeded in prosecuting cases differently from the way they had been handled before, and correctional commitments increased at all sites (Cronin et al., 1988; Office of Juvenile Justice and Delinquency Prevention, 1988).

"Three Strikes and You're Out"

Between 1993 and 1995, twenty-four states and the federal government enacted "three strikes and you're out" laws that required the long-term incarceration of offenders repeatedly convicted of serious crimes. These three-strikes laws were widely supported, with 86 percent of a national sample questioned in 1994 favoring the policy and only 12 percent opposing it (Maguire and Pastore, 1995: 176). However, rather than demanding a sentence of twenty-five years to life for every three-time felon, the public actually favors three-strike laws that target the most serious criminals and can be applied with flexibility (Applegate et al., 1996).

California enacted a three-strikes law in 1994, establishing a sentence of twenty-five years to life for a third felony conviction and a sentence double the prescribed one for a second felony conviction. Critics alleged that it would cost taxpayers billions of dollars to lock up additional offenders and that rising correctional costs might lead to reduced funding of educational and environmental programs (Greenwood et al., 1994). Three-strikes laws encourage offenders who are facing a third felony conviction to use violence against the police to avoid arrest. Defendants facing a third felony conviction often refuse to negotiate pleas that will result in long prison sentences, resulting in court backlogs as more trials are required. Jails have filled with defendants awaiting trial under three-strikes laws, and inmates serving time for misdemeanors have been released to make space for them. Some felons have challenged earlier convictions and have succeeded in having them stricken from their record so that they lack the three convictions necessary for an incapacitating sentence.

Three-strikes laws do not seem to reduce crime, partly because their provisions are rarely invoked, except in California. An assessment of that state's law concluded that it had failed to reduce rates of serious crime and petty theft, once prior trends in crime rates were taken into account (Stolzenberg and D'Alessio, 1997). The three-strikes law had little impact because serious offenders had already been getting long sentences prior to passage of the law, juvenile offenders (who account for much serious crime) were unaffected by the law, and those subject to the law were older offenders whose criminal activity was already diminishing. Moreover, many more second- and third-strike convictions were for nonviolent crimes (such as drug possession and burglary) than for serious violent offenses (such as murder and rape).

Retribution

In 1996 two boys, aged twelve and thirteen, were sent to Illinois's maximum-security juvenile prison for murdering a five-year-old boy by dropping him from a fourteen-story building two years earlier. The boys had to remain in state custody for at least five years, but they must be released at the age of twenty-one. Also in 1996, a federal judge sentenced the former treasurer of the nation's Episcopal Church to a five-year prison term for stealing $2.2 million from the church. The prison sentence, which exceeded federal standards for this type of crime and offender, was accompanied by a judicial order that the fifty-two-year-old woman repay the embezzled funds to the church.

How much punishment do offenders deserve for their crimes? (See the Crime on Campus box.) The **retribution** or **just deserts** theory proposes that offenders should be punished because they deserve to suffer for the harm they have caused and that their punishment should be proportional to that harm and to their own blameworthiness. This theory assumes that offenders freely choose to break the law and know that punishment might result from their actions. Retribution is oriented toward behavior that offenders have already engaged in, rather than toward their future conduct or the conduct of potential offenders. Retributivists suggest that offenders should be punished because they have gained an advantage over others by their crimes, and only punishment can restore a balance among all citizens.

Retribution differs from **vengeance**, which is private and personal and not imposed by an established authority such as the state. In contrast, retribution requires an authority with the acknowledged right to sanction convicted offenders (Armstrong, 1971). Whereas vengeance is motivated by the desire to be gratified or compensated for a loss, retribution is justified by the need to enforce the law and maintain social order (van den Haag, 1975).

Retribution is commonly associated with *lex talionis,* the principle of "an eye for an eye, a tooth for a tooth," which was expressed in the Code of Hammurabi in the eighteenth century B.C. To take this rule literally, a person who blinded another person would be blinded in return. Being made to pay a small fine would be an unjustly lenient sentence, and execution would be an unjustly severe penalty. Retributivists claim that offenders should be punished because they deserve to suffer but that

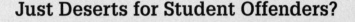

CRIME ON CAMPUS

Just Deserts for Student Offenders?

Colleges and universities have their own quasilegal judiciary systems in which panels of administrators, faculty, and students consider complaints of sexual assault and harassment. The courts have upheld the right of colleges and universities to administer justice in this way, even if they do not provide defendants with the due process rights they would have in a criminal court, as long as the schools carefully follow their own written disciplinary procedures. The campus judiciary system has been described as "a kind of parallel judicial universe where offenses as serious as arson and rape can be disposed of discreetly under the same student conduct codes that forbid sneaking into a university dance without a ticket" (Bernstein, p. 1).

Victimized students have the right to file charges with local police departments and pursue justice through the courts. Most campus police forces have arrest power and can refer suspects to the district attorney or to university administrators, but many crimes are not reported to the campus police. Instead, dormitory residents and administrators who learn of crimes encourage victims to pursue justice through the campus disciplinary system. This permits the school to avoid publicity and maintain its reputation, and it leads to swifter action than the courts can offer. Because universities lack the power to fine or in-

carcerate offenders, the most severe sanction students face is expulsion from school. Campus justice might be swifter and more certain than that provided by the legal system, but administrative sanctions are usually less severe than those handed out by the courts.

In recent years, some schools have reformed their disciplinary systems. In 2000, Columbia University made it easier for the victims of sexual assault to file complaints with the campus judiciary system, something they had been reluctant to do for years. Under the new system, described by the university's lawyer as educational rather than punitive, disciplinary hearings would be conducted informally without lawyers, and defendants would not be accorded such constitutional protections as the right to face their accusers and the right to question witnesses. Two years later, reforms of a very different sort were made by Harvard University, which raised the standard of proof it would require before investigating a sexual assault complaint and thus increased the chance that charges would be dismissed because of the absence of physical evidence, eyewitnesses, or other independent corroboration that a crime had been committed. Students whose complaints were dismissed would be referred to a district attorney or to the university's confidential mediation process.

Sources: Based on Nina Bernstein, "With Colleges Holding Court, Discretion Vies with Fairness," *New York Times,* May 5, 1996, pp. 1, 16; Patrick Healy, "College's Discipline Policy a New Flash Point," *Boston Globe,* November 20, 2000, pp. A1, A6; Patrick Healy, "Harvard to Require More Proof in Sex Cases," *Boston Globe,* May 8, 2002, pp. A1, A20.

they should be punished only in direct proportion to the harm they have caused. The idea of making punishment proportional to the seriousness of the crime makes mercy possible, "because to be merciful is to let someone off for all or part of a penalty which he is recognized as having deserved" (Armstrong, 1971: 36).

Retribution theory claims that people who violate the law are blameworthy and deserve moral disapproval for their acts. This disapproval is seen as the basis for punishment, even if the punishment does not serve a socially useful function such as deterring people from crime or rehabilitating offenders. This contrasts with the deterrence perspective, which aims to control crime by punishing offenders so that they or others will not commit crime in the future. The principle of retribution also differs from the rehabilitation perspective, which seeks to reform criminals so that they will not again make the incorrect decision to break the law.

If the only goal of punishment were to deter people from crime, innocent people might be punished, as long as the public believed they were actually guilty. A very severe penalty administered with certainty could also have a strong deterrent effect; for example, a thirty-year prison term for petty theft might deter stealing. The usual objection to punishing the innocent and to very harsh penalties is that those penalties are unjust. This idea of the "justness" of penalties is the essence of the retribution rationale.

If rehabilitation were the only goal of punishment, people identified as potentially dangerous might be imprisoned and treated even before they were convicted of a crime. If there were no effective treatment for serial killers, the rehabilitation rationale would require that they not be imprisoned at all. If there were an effective treatment method that could fully reform a petty thief with a thirty-year prison sentence, such a penalty might be justified in terms of rehabilitation. The usual objection to penalties such as these is that they are fundamentally unjust. Indeed, if there were general agreement that a six-month prison term is a just penalty for petty theft, keeping a petty thief locked up for even one month longer would seem improper to retributivists, even if the thief were rehabilitated by the extra month in prison and other people considering theft were deterred by that extra month (von Hirsch, 1976).

Retributivists assert that deterrence and rehabilitation are secondary goals of punishment; the primary justification for punishment is thus that offenders deserve to be punished in proportion to the harm they have inflicted on the victim and on society. Others suggest that deterrence and rehabilitation should play a part in determining sentences. One philosopher says that "a modified retributive theory is perfectly possible, one which only uses retributive considerations to fix some sort of upper limit to penalties and then looks to other factors to decide how much and what sort of pain shall be inflicted" (Armstrong, 1971: 38–39). A just deserts model might set an upper limit, a lower limit, or a range of penalties, with considerations of deterrence, incapacitation, and rehabilitation determining where within those limits the actual punishment falls (Morris, 1981; Wilson, 1983). Strict retributivists disagree with this approach, claiming that penalties should be proportional to the seriousness of the current offense and that other considerations should not play a role in determining punishment (von Hirsch, 1981, 1985).

A System of Just Deserts

A workable system of retribution or just deserts would require the rank ordering of crimes by their relative seriousness and the rank ordering of punishments by their relative unpleasantness. Seriousness of crimes and unpleasantness of penalties are not objective facts, so these rankings have to be based on subjective evaluations. Researchers would then need to link these two scales so that crimes of specific degrees of seriousness would be associated with penalties of particular levels of severity.

The Seriousness of Crimes   A scale that ranks offenses by seriousness might be based on the amount of harm caused by a crime and on the blameworthiness of the offender, with harmfulness and blameworthiness combined into a single measure of the seriousness of the crime (Bedau, 1977):

Seriousness = Harmfulness + Blameworthiness

Harmfulness of Crimes   Thorsten Sellin and Marvin Wolfgang's (1964) pioneering study found widespread agreement about how crimes should be ranked. They showed that various components of a crime, such as amount of injury to the victim and amount of monetary loss, could be assigned scores, with a summary score then derived for the offense. This made it possible to rank crimes by their harmfulness and to state how much more serious one crime was than another.

Table 14.1 shows the values assigned to the various elements of a crime incident. A robbery in which the victim suffered minor injuries and lost $300 when verbally threatened would have an overall score of 6, the sum of 1 point for minor injury, 3 for the theft of $300, and 2 for verbal intimidation in connection with a theft. A robbery in which there was no injury to the victim but a loss of $5 as a result of verbal

TABLE 14.1   Seriousness Scores for Elements of Crimes

ELEMENTS OF THE CRIME	SCORE VALUE
Minor injury to victim	1
Victim treated and discharged	4
Victim hospitalized	7
Victim killed	26
Victim of forcible sexual intercourse	10
Intimidated by weapon, add	2
Intimidation of persons in connection with theft, etc. (other than in connection with forcible sex acts):	
Physical or verbal only	2
By weapon	4
Forcible entry of premises	1
Value of property stolen and/or damaged:	
Under $10	1
$10–$250	2
$251–$2,000	3
$2,001–$9,000	4
$9,001–$30,000	5
$30,001–$80,000	6
Over $80,000	7
Theft of motor vehicle (recovered, undamaged)	2

Source: Thorsten Sellin and Marvin E. Wolfgang, *The Measurement of Delinquency*, p. 298. Copyright © 1964 by John Wiley & Sons, Inc. This material is used by permission of John Wiley & Sons, Inc.

intimidation would receive a score of 3, the total of 0 points for no injury, 1 for the loss of $5, and 2 for verbal intimidation in connection with the theft. We can thus say that the first robbery was twice as serious as the second one.

Sellin and Wolfgang's scoring system allows for a more meaningful measurement of crime than is possible just by counting the number of incidents. The difference between a bank robbery in which a guard is seriously injured by an armed offender who steals $10,000 and a schoolyard robbery in which a child gives up lunch money because of a verbal threat would not show up in the FBI's UCR statistics, because each event would be counted as one robbery. Sellin and Wolfgang's scoring system would emphasize the difference between the incidents. The bank robbery would be scored 16, the sum of 4 points for the use of a weapon in connection with the theft, 7 for injury to the guard, and 5 for the theft of $10,000. The schoolyard robbery would be scored 3, the sum of 1 point for the theft of less than $10 and 2 for verbal intimidation connected with the theft.

The National Survey of Crime Severity, conducted in 1977, asked people to rank 204 illegal acts. There was significant agreement on the ranking of the crimes by people with different social characteristics, although victims assigned somewhat higher severity scores than nonvictims, blacks and other minorities assigned lower severity scores than whites, and older people ranked thefts with large losses as more severe than did younger respondents. In ranking crimes, people took into account the ability of victims to protect themselves, the amount of injury and loss, the relationship of the offender to the victim, and the kind of business from which property was stolen (Bureau of Justice Statistics, October 1983; Wolfgang et al., 1985).

Research that yielded a seriousness ranking of crimes similar to the one produced by the National Survey of Crime Severity employed data on victim injury rates, jury awards in personal injury cases, crime-related death rates, estimates of the financial value of life, and out-of-pocket expenses borne by crime victims. This research concluded that violent crimes were more costly to victims than the national survey indicated (Cohen, 1988).

There is considerable cross-cultural consensus on the ranking of crimes. A study of India, Indonesia, Iran, Italy (Sardinia), Yugoslavia, and the United States found substantial agreement on the perceived harmfulness of various deviant acts and on the amount and type of punishment thought to be appropriate for each act (Newman, 1976). Other research shows that offense rankings are similar in the United States, Canada, Norway, Finland, Sweden, Denmark, the Netherlands, Great Britain, and Kuwait (Scott and Al-Thakeb, 1977; Kvålseth, 1980; Evans and Scott, 1984).

Blameworthiness of Offenders   One form of retribution theory claims that penalties should be imposed only for the harm caused by the crime; this position would ignore the offender's blameworthiness. Another form of retribution theory holds that because offenders should be punished as they deserve, their blameworthiness must be considered in determining their sentences (von Hirsch, 1992).

Blameworthiness can be measured in different ways. One is to consider motivation or mental state: Did the offender act intentionally or negligently? Another way is to look at the circumstances of the crime. An offender who is involved in a victim-precipitated crime or who is an unwilling or peripheral participant in a crime might be treated as less blameworthy than someone who plans and carries out a crime alone. Offenders could also be regarded as more blameworthy if they victimize strangers rather than intimates (Blum-West and Hembroff, 1982; Hembroff, 1987; Hamilton and Sanders, 1988).

Usually blameworthiness is measured by the number and seriousness of an individual's prior convictions, the assumption being that a crime is more serious if an offender has committed other crimes in the past. Another view is that a first-time offender warrants a "discount" from the usual penalty for a crime. Using prior record as a basis for sentencing raises the following difficult questions:

1. Should judges consider prior arrests, prior convictions, or prior sentences?
2. Should the seriousness of prior crimes be taken into account?
3. Should juvenile records be considered?
4. Should the relationship between prior offenses and the current offense be considered?
5. Does it matter if a defendant was on probation or parole at the time of the current offense?
6. Should the amount of time between the last prior offense and the current one be considered?
7. How long should prior offenses count against a defendant?
8. Should prior offenses eventually be expunged from the record used to sentence an offender? (Roberts, 1997)

An important problem with using prior arrests or convictions to indicate blameworthiness is that doing so can lead to "a cyclic reconfirmation of criminality" (Farrell and Swigert, 1978: 451). More specifically, research showing that lower-class suspects are more likely than middle-class suspects to be arrested, convicted, and severely punished for the same crime suggests that the use of prior records to indicate blameworthiness and determine penalties can lock lower-class offenders into criminal careers.

The Unpleasantness of Penalties   A retributive system of punishment requires data on how people perceive the relative severity of penalties. For example, how do people perceive the relative unpleasantness of a sentence to a state prison, a term in a county jail, a fine, and probation? We also need to know the perceived unpleasantness of an increment of a particular kind of penalty. For instance, do people think that a ten-year prison sentence is twice as severe as a five-year sentence?

There is general agreement on how unpleasant criminal sanctions are. Probation is undesirable because it imposes restrictions on offenders; they are required to report regularly to probation officers, and their mobility and privacy are restricted. Fines are disagreeable because they deprive offenders of property; they are a relatively lenient form of punishment because they do not disrupt ties to family and job as imprisonment does, but they do discriminate against people who cannot afford to pay. Imprisonment deprives offenders of freedom of movement and contacts with the outside world. Restraint on freedom of movement is subject to many gradations, with the amount of time and the institution in which an offender is confined indicating the severity of the penalty.

There is some research on the equivalence of different penalties. In one study, people equated one year in a local jail with six months in a state prison, eight years on probation, or a fine of about $3,000 (Erickson and Gibbs, 1979). In another study, prison inmates said they would be willing to accept the following as equivalent to one year in a medium-security prison: five months in a county jail or boot camp, ten months of electronic monitoring, fifty months of regular probation, nine months of intensive supervision probation, seven months of day reporting, nine months in a halfway house, 145 days of intermittent incarceration, a fine equal to 171 days of pay, or 1,160 hours of community service (Wood and Grasmick, 1999). These figures indicate that the inmates saw some sanctions as more burdensome than a year in prison. Indeed, the only two sanctions they regarded as less punitive were community service and regular probation. These studies suggest that eventually it might be possible to convert different penalties into a common quantitative measure of perceived severity. Such a measure could be used to compare judges and jurisdictions in terms of the severity of penalties given. It might even be used to have convicted offenders choose from a list of equivalent penalties.

Linking Penalties to Crimes   Developing a scale that measures the seriousness of crimes or the unpleasantness of penalties is easier than determining how severe a penalty should be administered to a person who commits an offense of a particular degree of seriousness. An early effort to do this was a proposal by the Committee for the Study of Incarceration that four sentence levels be used for offenders convicted of crimes of varying degrees of seriousness (as measured by the harmfulness of the offense and the number and seriousness of the offender's prior convictions). The committee recommended the following: Minor offenses should be punished with warning-and-release or intermittent confinement (for example, for a few Saturdays); intermediate-level offenses usually should be punished with intermittent confinement; serious offenses (lower range) should be punished with jail or prison terms of less than eighteen months; and serious offenses (upper range) should be punished with incarceration for one-and-a-half to three years. There would be no prison sentences over five years, except for certain murders and a few cases involving exceptional circumstances. Fines were avoided because of the difficulty of equalizing fines for people with different incomes (von Hirsch, 1976).

The recommendations of the Committee for the Study of Incarceration were not derived from research. Studies that first develop one scale ranking penalties by severity and another ranking offenses by seriousness, and then ask people to propose specific penalties for different crimes, would be a better basis for a system of just deserts. Efforts to link crimes and penalties in this way have encountered obstacles; some research has found a close match between perceived seriousness of crimes and perceived severity of penalties, but other research has found no straightforward relationship between the two variables (Hamilton and Rotkin, 1976; Hamilton and Rytina, 1980; Samuel and Moulds, 1986). One study found that in recommending penalties, whites are more likely to consider a crime's seriousness, whereas blacks are more likely to consider an offender's characteristics and the circumstances of the crime (Miller, Rossi, and Simpson, 1986).

When the public is asked to recommend sentences in the way that judges do— that is, by taking into account the circumstances of the crime, the characteristics of the offender, the kinds of sanctions available, and the cost of sentencing alternatives—its recommendations for punishment approximate those of judges (Thomson and Ragona, 1987). People are most punitive toward offenders who appear to have committed their crimes intentionally, seem unrepentant, and have committed crimes before. These offenders are seen as especially likely to repeat their crimes, because they do not acknowledge the moral validity of the law.

Retribution and the Criminal Justice System

Considerations of just deserts have always played an important role in the American criminal justice system, but that role has increased in recent years.

Retribution and the Police   One way to determine the goals of the police is to look at their organization and their use of resources. Police departments include detectives and squads that specialize in the investigation of the most serious offenses (e.g., homicide), and they allocate more resources to the investigation of crimes that rank high on the scale of seriousness. Retributive considerations also influence the way the police respond to apprehended suspects, with arrest and prosecution more likely than release if the offense is a harmful one and the suspect has a criminal record and thus seems blameworthy.

Retribution and the Courts   Retribution is a consideration in district attorneys' decisions about how to prosecute defendants and in judges' decisions about how to sentence convicted offenders, and it has been the impetus for changes in the handling of juvenile offenders.

Prosecutors' Decision Making

Prosecutors assume that the defendants against whom they bring charges are guilty and should be punished appropriately by the criminal justice system. To save the court's time and ensure a conviction, prosecutors pressure defendants to plead guilty. Because the plea to which a district attorney will agree is based on the harmfulness of the offense and the defendant's criminal record, offenders are usually punished according to the principle of just deserts.

One study of prosecutors' attitudes toward different offenses produced unexpected results. Prosecutors thought that white-collar crime was very serious, equivalent to offenses such as kidnapping and rape and more serious than the theft of a similar amount of money by a conventional offender. The amount of money stolen in a crime was not seen as an important consideration in determining the seriousness of an offense, because the amount of money available to be stolen was a matter of chance. In addition, whether an assault victim died was seen as partly due to chance, so manslaughter was viewed as only slightly more serious than aggravated assault (Roth, 1978). These considerations are not written into the criminal code, but prosecutors use them to determine appropriate penalties.

In contrast to this study, another survey found that most prosecutors did not regard white-collar crime as a serious problem, even though they believed that tougher penalties could deter it. They said that they were more likely to act against white-collar offenders if their crimes involved substantial harm and a large number of victims, had been committed deliberately or negligently, had victims who wanted to prosecute, and had not been dealt with by other agencies (Benson, Cullen, and Maakestad, 1990).

The relatively lenient treatment of white-collar criminals is not primarily due to lack of prosecutors' support for tough penalties or their empathy for high-status offenders. Instead, leniency is a function of the difficulty of detecting and prosecuting white-collar crimes (Shapiro, 1990). Prosecutors claim, with justification, that public pressure to enforce drug laws has drained away resources that they might have used to deal with white-collar crimes (Benson, Cullen, and Maakestad, 1990).

Judges' Decision Making

In considering how much punishment a convicted offender deserves, judges are primarily influenced by the crime that has been committed and the offender's prior record, although extralegal factors such as race, income, sex, and age can affect sentencing. One review of sentencing concluded that only 7 to 10 percent of all sentences in the United States reflect "arbitrary or idiosyncratic judicial behavior" and that most sentences can be predicted from legal factors such as harmfulness of the crime and blameworthiness of the offender (Silberman, 1978: 292). As court personnel have become more professional and the courts more bureaucratized, these legal factors have become even more important in the sentencing of offenders (Pruitt and Wilson, 1983).

Until the 1980s, states relied primarily on **indeterminate sentencing**, a system in which legislators establish long maximum sentences for different crimes, and judges can impose any penalty up to the maximum. Sentences are often a range of years to be served in prison, such as five to twenty years. Actual release dates are set by parole boards, based on the board's view that an inmate has been rehabilitated.

Many states still use indeterminate sentencing, and most of them retain parole release, but in the 1980s and 1990s some states and the federal government adopted **determinate sentencing.** Some states now use both determinate and indeterminate sentencing. Determinate sentencing systems use fixed terms of imprisonment, which can sometimes be reduced by credit for good behavior while incarcerated. Reducing the amount of good-time credits an inmate can earn is one way that sentences have been made more determinate in recent years. Another way is to introduce **mandatory minimum sentences,** which require certain offenders to be sentenced to at least a specified amount of time in prison. A form of determinate sentencing first used in 1984 is **truth-in-sentencing,** which requires offenders to serve a certain percentage (usually 85) of their sentence in prison. Forty states had passed truth-in-sentencing laws by early 1999, largely in response to a 1994 federal law that made funds for prison construction contingent on passage of such a law for violent offenders.

Determinate sentences have also been implemented by sentencing commissions that use **sentencing guidelines** to define a range of penalties for offenses of a given degree of harmfulness committed by offenders of a specific degree of blameworthiness (usually measured by prior criminal record). Under such a system, a sentence can depart from the range required by the guidelines only in extraordinary circumstances, which the judge must specify in writing. Defendants can appeal sentences above the upper limit, and prosecutors can appeal sentences under the lower limit (Austin, 1998; Ditton and Wilson, 1999).

The vast majority of penalties handed out by judges in states that use sentencing guidelines have fallen within the required ranges. Most sentences that depart from the guidelines have been less severe than the mandated penalties. Sentences outside the prescribed ranges have usually been a function of prior criminal history and offense type and severity; but women, whites, and those who plead guilty have been especially likely to be favored by mitigating departures. Nevertheless, determinate sentencing laws have reduced disparities in sentences by sex, race, and urban-rural residence (Stolzenberg and D'Alessio, 1994; Kramer and Ulmer, 1996).

Sentencing guidelines implemented in the federal courts in 1987 were aimed at reducing sentence disparity, enhancing deterrence by increasing the certainty of punishment, and creating greater proportionality between the seriousness of crimes and the severity of sanctions. The federal guidelines work as follows:

1. Crimes are classified into forty-three offense levels, each of which has a range of prison sentences in terms of months (see Table 14.2). For example, level 43 crimes (which include first-degree murder and aircraft hijacking resulting in death) receive life in prison; level 25 offenses (which include the production of pornography through sexual exploitation of a minor) are given sentences of 57 to 137 months; level 17 crimes (which include burglary of a residence) receive sentences of 24 to 63 months; and level 8 offenses (which include insider trading) receive sentences of 0 to 24 months). The score on the 43-point scale is determined by taking a "base offense level" and adjusting it upward or downward according to the circumstances of the crime, such as amount of financial loss and use of a weapon.

2. Federal judges then place the offender in one of six criminal history categories, based on points assigned for prior sentences (especially imprisonment) and whether the current offense was committed while under another sentence or within two years of release from prison.

3. Judges next consult a grid (Table 14.2) that is six columns by forty-three rows. Each of the 258 cells contains a range of sentences (for example, 37 to 46 months in prison for an offender convicted of a level 17 offense who scores in category IV in criminal history points). The range can be disregarded only in very limited circumstances. The four

TABLE 14.2 United States Sentencing Guidelines

SENTENCING TABLE (IN MONTHS OF IMPRISONMENT)
Criminal History Category (Criminal History Points)

Offense Level	I (0 or 1)	II (2 or 3)	III (4, 5, 6)	IV (7, 8, 9)	V (10, 11, 12)	VI (13 or more)
Zone A						
1	0–6	0–6	0–6	0–6	0–6	0–6
2	0–6	0–6	0–6	0–6	0–6	1–7
3	0–6	0–6	0–6	0–6	2–8	3–9
4	0–6	0–6	0–6	2–8	4–10	6–12
5	0–6	0–6	1–7	4–10	6–12	9–15
6	0–6	1–7	2–8	6–12	9–15	12–18
7	0–6	2–8	4–10	8–14	12–18	15–21
8	0–6	4–10	6–12	10–16	15–21	18–24
Zone B						
9	4–10	6–12	8–14	12–18	18–24	21–27
10	6–12	8–14	10–16	15–21	21–27	24–30
Zone C						
11	8–14	10–16	12–18	18–24	24–30	27–33
12	10–16	12–18	15–21	21–27	27–33	30–37
Zone D						
13	12–18	15–21	18–24	24–30	30–37	33–41
14	15–21	18–24	21–27	27–33	33–41	37–46
15	18–24	21–27	24–30	30–37	37–46	41–51
16	21–27	24–30	27–33	33–41	41–51	46–57
17	24–30	27–33	30–37	37–46	46–57	51–63
18	27–33	30–37	33–41	41–51	51–63	57–71
19	30–37	33–41	37–46	46–57	57–71	63–78
20	33–41	37–46	41–51	51–63	63–78	70–87
21	37–46	41–51	46–57	57–71	70–87	77–96
22	41–51	46–57	51–63	63–78	77–96	84–105
23	46–57	51–63	57–71	70–87	84–105	92–115
24	51–63	57–71	63–78	77–96	92–115	100–125
25	57–71	63–78	70–87	84–105	100–125	110–137
26	63–78	70–87	78–97	92–115	110–137	120–150
27	70–87	78–97	87–108	100–125	120–150	130–162
28	78–97	87–108	97–121	110–137	130–162	140–175
29	87–108	97–121	108–135	121–151	140–175	151–188
30	97–121	108–135	121–151	135–168	151–188	168–210
31	108–135	121–151	135–168	151–188	168–210	188–235
32	121–151	135–168	151–188	168–210	188–235	210–262
33	135–168	151–188	168–210	188–235	210–262	235–293
34	151–188	168–210	188–235	210–262	235–293	262–327
35	168–210	188–235	210–262	235–293	262–327	292–365
36	188–235	210–262	235–293	262–327	292–365	324–405
37	210–262	235–293	262–327	292–365	324–405	360–life
38	235–293	262–327	292–365	324–405	360–life	360–life
39	262–327	292–365	324–405	360–life	360–life	360–life
40	292–365	324–405	360–life	360–life	360–life	360–life
41	324–405	360–life	360–life	360–life	360–life	360–life
42	360–life	360–life	360–life	360–life	360–life	360–life
43	life	life	life	life	life	life

Source: United States Sentencing Commission, *2001 Federal Sentencing Guideline Manual.* Washington, DC: United States Sentencing Commission, November 2001, p. 335, retrieved from www.ussc.gov/2001guid/Sentntab.pdf.

lettered zones correspond to instructions about appropriate penalties. For example, probation is authorized for Zone A and for Zone B under specified conditions. The guidelines eliminate parole, with time served equaling the full sentence minus time off for good behavior while in prison.

There is substantial agreement between the sentences prescribed by these guidelines and those preferred by the American public (Rossi and Berk, 1997).

More flexible sentencing guidelines that use fewer offense categories have been successful in several states, but the federal system is widely regarded as a failure. Judges claim that the system forces them to dispense unreasonably harsh penalties, especially to the drug offenders who have been crowding the federal prisons in recent years. Judges have complained that the sentencing guidelines take away their discretion and give it to prosecutors, who influence sentences by the seriousness of the charges they bring against defendants. Court backlogs have been attributed to the guidelines, which discourage plea bargaining because the sentence is based on actual offense behavior rather than on the crime to which a defendant pleads guilty. The guidelines have been attacked for being too complex and too mechanistic, leading to excessively severe penalties that do not take into account such offender characteristics as family ties and employment record (Margolick, 1992; Tonry, 1996). There is also evidence that the federal guidelines have not eliminated sentence disparity. One study found that ethnicity, sex, educational level, and citizenship status continue to affect the sentences meted out to drug offenders (Albonetti, 1997).

Michael Tonry (1996) proposes that a just sentencing system would have no mandatory minimum sentences but would include noncustodial penalties that are intermediate between prison and probation. In his model, a sentencing commission would create and monitor sentencing guidelines, which would be compatible with existing correctional resources and facilities. Custodial penalties would include maximum terms of confinement for all offenses and minimum terms for the most serious ones. For minor crimes, judges would choose among noncustodial penalties. For more serious offenses, they would choose between noncustodial penalties and terms of full or partial confinement. Within established guidelines, judges would impose the least punitive and intrusive sentence appropriate to the case.

Juvenile Justice   Considerations of just deserts have led to reforms in the handling of juvenile offenders in recent years, because of the growing belief that there is a lack of proportionality between the harm caused by juvenile offenders and their blameworthiness, on the one hand, and the way that they are treated by the juvenile justice system, on the other hand. Those who support harsher penalties for young offenders claim that the juvenile justice system created a century ago to deal with truants and petty thieves is no longer adequate for dealing with today's young murderers and drug traffickers.

All states now allow or require some juveniles accused of serious crimes to be tried in criminal court as adults, where they can be punished more severely than in juvenile court. However, even states that use specific criteria to identify "dangerous" juveniles for treatment as adults "single out many juveniles whose records do not appear to be very serious and fail to identify many juveniles whose records are characterized by violent, frequent, and persistent delinquent activity" (Osbun and Rode, 1984: 199). One study concludes that there is no evidence that juveniles remanded to adult criminal court are the most dangerous and intractable delinquents, nor is there evidence that trying juveniles as adults enhances public safety (Bortner, 1986). Moreover, transferring juveniles to criminal court apparently leads them to commit more frequent and more serious crimes and return to crime more quickly after release than is true of offenders who are dealt with by the juvenile justice system (Bishop et al., 1996; Winner et al., 1997).

Some states no longer require the records of juvenile court proceedings to remain "sealed" or secret, so those who frequently break the law as juveniles are no longer necessarily dealt with as first-time offenders when they are arrested as adults. Criminal justice agencies and some employers now have greater access to juvenile records. The impact of juvenile records on sentencing is not yet clear, but one study concluded that even if such records are available, they do not always affect sentencing. A prior juvenile record had little impact if there was a clear predisposition for or against incarceration; it influenced the sentence only when the decision was less clear-cut (Greenwood, 1986).

Retribution and the Prisons   The blameworthiness of the offender and the harmfulness of the crime largely determine the kind of institution to which an offender is sent, with maximum-, medium-, and minimum-security institutions limiting prisoners' freedom of movement and isolating them from the outside world to varying degrees. In the mid-1990s, considerations of just deserts were the basis for reforms in several states that were aimed at making prison life harder for inmates. Alabama briefly revived the chain gang, and other states took away televisions and radios, stereos and computers, weight-lifting equipment, and basketball courts.

Because sentences in some states cover a range of years—for example, five to ten years for a robbery—the decision about how long an inmate stays in prison is made by the parole board rather than the court. Decisions about when prisoners are to be released are predictable to a large degree from the harmfulness of the offense for which they have been imprisoned, their prior criminal record, and their conduct while in prison. In other words, the decision about how much of a court-imposed sentence is actually served is based largely on retributive considerations, even though the decision is supposed to be based on whether an inmate has been rehabilitated.

Retribution and Capital Punishment   As we saw earlier in this chapter, public support for the death penalty is based partly on the belief that it is a deterrent, although many supporters say they would favor it even if it had no deterrent effect. Rather than focusing on the utility of the death penalty, many people believe that justice requires people who commit certain heinous crimes to be deprived of their own lives.

The death penalty has been both supported and opposed on religious grounds. The Roman Catholic Church historically accepted the right of the state to execute people convicted of serious crimes, but more recently the death penalty has been redefined as inconsistent with Catholic theology because execution lacks utility and dignity, fails to contribute to the common good, discriminates against the poor and minorities, and undermines an ethic of life (Beristain, 1977; Zorea, 2000). In 1983, Pope John Paul II became the first pope to criticize capital punishment. In a 1999 Mass in St. Louis, he urged American Catholics to oppose the death penalty, a message followed three days later by the governor of Missouri's grant of clemency to a triple murderer who was scheduled for execution. Protestant leaders in the United States have opposed capital punishment since 1957, denying that the state has the right to execute offenders and seeing capital punishment as "a contradiction of both the values of our Christian traditions and the principles of humane government" (cited in Franklin, 1982: 30).

Opponents of the death penalty claim that even if certain offenders deserve to die, a civilized society should not execute them. They argue that it is immoral for the state to take a human life as a form of punishment and that doing so "cheapens the value of human life" and might even encourage others to kill.

Supporters of the death penalty outnumber opponents by nearly three to one in the United States, but protesters such as these are vocal in their opposition to capital punishment.

Those who favor capital punishment do not always agree about when it is appropriate to put offenders to death. Few Americans would support capital punishment for thieves, but thieves were executed in eighteenth- and nineteenth-century England. Likewise, there is little support in the United States for using the death penalty for economic crimes such as currency violations and profiteering, but more than sixty Iraqis were executed for those offenses in Iraq in 1992. On the other hand, many Americans would favor the death penalty for someone who brutally murdered several children, assassinated the president, or engaged in a lethal terrorist attack.

The Eighth Amendment to the Constitution prohibits "cruel and unusual punishment," and although the Supreme Court has never ruled that capital punishment by itself is cruel and unusual, it has ruled that the death penalty is cruel and unusual punishment for the crime of forcible rape (*Coker* v. *Georgia* [1977]). In *Furman* v. *Georgia* (1972), the Supreme Court struck down the states' death penalty statutes because they had been administered in an excessively arbitrary way. Four years later the Court approved a new kind of law that it thought would be fairer: A defendant's guilt or innocence would be determined in a criminal trial, and then in a separate proceeding a judge or a jury would consider the death penalty as a possible sentence. Looking at the harmfulness of the offense and the blameworthiness of the defendant, a judge or jury could choose the death penalty only if there were aggravating circumstances defined by state law and no mitigating circumstances counteracting those aggravating factors. The introduction of specific aggravating and mitigating factors was an attempt to be fair to defendants while retaining the principle of retribution. The Court's interpretation of the constitutionality of the death penalty continues to evolve; two decisions in 2002 made capital punishment illegal when the defendant is retarded and when the factual determinations leading to a death sentence are left to a judge rather than a jury.

The American public strongly supports capital punishment, but there is little support for the death penalty in the intellectual community. Two exceptions are Walter Berns (1979) and Ernest van den Haag (1975), both of whom have argued that the death penalty is a deserved and appropriate penalty for some crimes. They believe that justice requires capital punishment, which reinforces the moral order and is a reasonable expression of community outrage at the violation of important values.

For example, one man remarked that the execution of his brother's killer nine years after the murder "was an extraordinary relief. I don't know how to explain it. It relieved the grief. This has been an overriding obsession for all of us" (cited in Joyce, 1984: A18). Opponents of the death penalty point out that retribution simply requires a punishment proportional to the crime, not any specific form of punishment such as the death penalty (Bedau, 1980).

Those seeking to abolish the death penalty argue that when an error is made and an innocent person is executed, there is no way to rectify the error as there is with other penalties. One study found that two-thirds of the death sentences that were fully reviewed by the courts from 1973 to 1995 were overturned on appeal because the police or the prosecutor had withheld evidence, the defense attorney had acted incompetently, or the judge had issued incorrect instructions to the jury. Eighty-two percent of the defendants whose convictions were reversed received sentences less than death when they were retried, and 7 percent were found not guilty (Liebman, West, and Fagan, 2002). An earlier study documented twenty-five cases since 1900 in which Americans had been executed despite serious errors in the legal process (Radelet, Bedau, and Putnam, 1994). What is unclear, however, is whether any factually innocent person has ever been put to death in the country. Critics of the two studies claim that the discovery of wrongfully imposed death sentences simply shows that the criminal justice system is extremely careful in reviewing capital cases; they point out that nearly everyone who has been executed has acknowledged his or her guilt. Only one possibly wrongful conviction has led to execution since the death penalty was reinstated with new safeguards in the 1970s, and there is disagreement as to whether that condemned man was actually innocent. Some proponents of capital punishment argue that even if there have been a few mistakes in the more than 7,000 executions since 1900, the criminal justice system is quite reliable. Opponents sometimes respond that the execution of even a single innocent person warrants abolition of the death penalty. Doubt about wrongful convictions and executions, perhaps in combination with the lowest murder rates in more than three decades, has reduced support for capital punishment in recent years. Illinois Governor George Ryan declared a moratorium on executions in 2002, a measure with which 53 percent of Americans agreed (Polling the Nations, 2002). In January 2003, he pardoned four inmates on Death Row and commuted the remaining 167 death sentences to life imprisonment or less.

Support for and opposition to the death penalty are based to a large extent on considerations of just deserts. Even if there were irrefutable evidence that the death penalty does or does not deter crime, the ultimate decision about its use would be based on values concerning the sanctity of human life and the requirements of justice.

Rehabilitation

Rehabilitation is the restoration of criminals to a law-abiding way of life through treatment. More specifically, rehabilitation is the result of any planned intervention focused on the offender that reduces criminal activity, whether that reduction is achieved by changes in personality, abilities, attitudes, values, or behavior. Excluded from rehabilitation are the effects of fear and intimidation—or specific deterrence—and the maturational effects that cause older offenders to stop committing crime (Sechrest, White, and Brown, 1979).

One early approach to rehabilitation was that of the Quakers, who recommended silence, reflection, and the isolation of inmates in their own cells, where they worked, ate, and read the Bible. A different approach was used in the New York state prison at Auburn, where inmates slept alone in their cells but silently worked, ate, and worshipped together during the day. Post–Civil War reformers suggested giving offenders the incentive of early release to motivate them to reform, and the indeterminate sentence was introduced. Progressives of the early twentieth century supported indeterminate sentences, presentence reports that judges could use to individualize sentences, treatment in the community rather than in prison, and parole release for offenders who seemed likely to stay away from crime. The positivist approach of the newly developing behavioral sciences, especially sociology and psychology, supported this therapeutic model by focusing on the causes of crime (Cullen and Gilbert, 1982). Rehabilitation was the dominant perspective in the American criminal justice system from the 1920s to the 1970s, when attacks on the therapeutic model led to a search for alternative ways of dealing with offenders.

The rehabilitation model assumes that the causes of human behavior can be identified by scientific study and that treatment based on knowledge of those causes should be aimed at changing the offender's behavior "in the interests of his own happiness, health, and satisfaction and in the interest of social defense" (Allen, 1971: 318). The principle underlying rehabilitation is to return "the offender to society not with the negative vacuum of punishment-induced fear but with the affirmative and constructive equipment—physical, mental and moral—for law-abidingness" (Wiehofen, 1971: 261).

Seeing rehabilitation as a required function of punishment, the courts have guaranteed inmates access to treatment programs. Because inmates sometimes feel degraded and dehumanized when treatment is forced on them, some have argued that they should also have the right to refuse treatment. As one ex-convict said,

> The whole point of the psychological diagnosis is to get [the inmate] to go for the fact that he's "sick," yet the statement he's sick deprives him of his integrity as a person.
>
> Most prisoners I know would rather be thought bad than mad. They say society may have a right to punish them, but not a hunting license to remold them in its own sick image. (cited in Mitford, 1973: 104)

The deterrence perspective regards offenders and potential offenders as rational decision makers who will stay away from crime if the threat of punishment is great enough. Those who commit crime presumably think the threat of punishment is outweighed by the rewards of crime. The rehabilitation perspective, on the other hand, sees those who violate the law as defective and in need of treatment, rather than as rational decision makers who knowingly take risks when they break the law.

In contrast to the rehabilitation perspective, retribution theory proposes that if penalties are specific and just, offenders can retain their dignity while paying for their crimes. Retribution does not necessarily lead to harsher penalties than rehabilitation. Indeed, the rehabilitation model can lead to longer sentences, which are justified by the need to cure inmates.

Rehabilitation and the Criminal Justice System

The belief that offenders' behavior can and should be changed has had a significant impact on American criminal justice, especially during the three decades following World War II.

Rehabilitation and the Police   Rehabilitation is not generally considered a police function, because the police deal with people suspected, rather than convicted, of breaking the law, and it would seem to violate the legal principle that suspects are to be presumed innocent until proved guilty if the police were to try to rehabilitate suspects. Nevertheless, the rehabilitation perspective influences the way the police deal with suspects. For example, in exercising discretion an officer might think that one suspect will avoid crime in the future if subjected to the shock of arrest and a court appearance, while believing that another will be more likely to stay away from crime if sent home to his or her family.

The police are most likely to consider the possibility of rehabilitation in dealing with juveniles. They might not arrest a young suspect if he or she will enroll in a counseling or training program. They sometimes work out an informal agreement with juvenile troublemakers and their parents or guardians to report to the police regularly, attend school, make restitution, and maintain a neat personal appearance. Measures such as these can spare the juvenile the legal stigma of court appearance and institutionalization.

Rehabilitation and the Courts   **Pretrial diversion** programs allow a district attorney to recommend to a judge that a criminal proceeding be suspended while a suspect participates in treatment. Pretrial diversion can keep suspects from acquiring criminal records and criminal identities. If a suspect is not arrested again while enrolled in a diversion program and seems to be profiting from the program, the judge at the suggestion of the district attorney can "file" the case—that is, not charge the suspect and eventually dismiss the case.

Juvenile courts use pretrial diversion on the assumption that the labeling effects of a court appearance might do more harm than good to young people. One study that looked at status offenders—juveniles charged with acts that would not be crimes if committed by adults—found no difference in the likelihood of rearrest for those processed formally by the juvenile courts and those placed in diversion programs. The data supported neither labeling theory's contention that diversion is better nor deterrence theory's claim that court processing will keep status offenders from getting into trouble again (Rausch, 1983). Another study also concluded that diversion had no significant effects on status offenders' behavior or attitudes but warned that competition among community-based programs for diverted juveniles could "widen the net" of the juvenile justice system and lead to the processing of more juveniles (Rojek and Erickson, 1981–82). Other scholars have concluded that diversion is more promising than other juvenile correctional programs and that widening the net does not seem to harm juveniles (Binder and Geis, 1984; Lab and Whitehead, 1988).

The sentences to which district attorneys and judges agree in exchange for guilty pleas are partly a product of their beliefs about the kinds of sentences that are most likely to rehabilitate offenders. Some criminologists regard plea bargaining as an essential first step in the rehabilitation process, because it forces defendants to take responsibility for their actions. Others claim that plea bargaining makes defendants cynical about the criminal justice system and thereby impedes their rehabilitation.

Judges' sentencing decisions depend on their beliefs about rehabilitation, as well as on their beliefs about retribution and deterrence. Judges weigh the likely effects on an offender of paying a fine, making restitution, or spending some time on probation. They consider the potential benefits of the various treatment programs available in the community and in correctional institutions. In reality, judges usually have few sentencing alternatives, because prisons do not differ much in their treatment programs, and many offenders cannot be fined or placed on probation because the law prohibits it or because the judge's or the public's sense of just deserts would not allow it.

Rehabilitation and the Prisons   Although indeterminate sentencing was based on the humanitarian belief that inmates should be released as soon as they are cured, indeterminate sentences actually lengthened the time served by prisoners. In 1900, the inmates at Indiana State Prison, sentenced under the recently introduced indeterminate-sentence system, served an average of six months and twenty-three days more than inmates committed to the same institution for the same crimes in 1890, when a system of definite sentences was in effect (Mitford, 1973). The time served by inmates also increased when the California correctional system introduced rehabilitation (American Friends Service Committee, 1971). Indeterminate sentences can sometimes lead to the incarceration of more offenders, because it is assumed that they are being helped. The principle of rehabilitation thus acts as a "highly efficient control mechanism," even though its original justification was humanitarian (Irwin, 1974: 975).

In many states, a parole board determines when an offender serving an indeterminate sentence is ready to be released, deciding how much of a sentence is to be served behind bars and how much is to be served in the community under the supervision of a parole officer. In deciding when to release an inmate, a parole board considers the offense for which the offender was sent to prison, the inmate's criminal record, the number of disciplinary reports filed against the inmate while incarcerated, and the treatment programs in which the inmate has participated. Participation in treatment programs and number of disciplinary reports indicate the extent to which an offender is rehabilitated; the original offense and the criminal record, as well as the number of disciplinary reports, are retributive considerations. The conditions of parole are designed to help rehabilitate the released offender: Stay away from known criminals, hold a steady job, support a family, and avoid the use of alcohol and drugs. However, the heavy caseload of most parole officers means that ex-convicts get little assistance in developing a law-abiding way of life and avoiding a return to crime.

Types of Treatment

Treatment programs aimed at rehabilitating offenders take many forms. Some deal with individuals and others with groups. Some seek to alter personality and others only to change behavior. Some equip offenders with vocational skills or educational credentials, while others try to cure drug addiction or alcoholism.

Individual Therapy, Casework, and Cognitive-Behavioral Programs

Individual therapy carried out by psychiatrists, psychologists, or psychiatric social workers is based on the assumption that offenders are emotionally troubled people who need to solve the psychological problems that have caused them to commit crime. Psychotherapy is unlikely to be effective because most therapists manipulate and control verbal behavior rather than try to change overt actions directly. Another problem is that because psychotherapy is usually done inside the prison, rather than in the environment in which crime actually occurs, any beneficial effects that it has may not carry over to behavior in the outside world. Moreover, few prisons provide therapy that is intensive enough to have much impact on inmates.

In some prisons, social workers provide inmates with counseling that is intended less to help them understand their motivations than to help them cope with the specific problems they face. This **casework** approach is oriented toward getting inmates to realize they can change, showing them how to solve problems of daily living, teaching them how to adapt to reality, and informing them of community resources that can help them to reform.

Cognitive-behavioral programs seek to change what and how offenders think in order to alter their behavioral choices, especially their decision to commit crime. These programs try to reinforce conventional attitudes and behavior and to eliminate attitudes that are conducive to crime, including the techniques that offenders use to justify violation of the law. This form of treatment also tries to change offenders' reasoning by developing skills they can use to deal with their anger and impulsiveness (Cullen, 2002).

Group Counseling   **Group counseling** allows several inmates to be treated at the same time and at low cost, especially if correctional officers are used as group leaders. Groups are also led by psychotherapists and by people who have been specially trained in guided-group interaction. Inmates in these groups discuss their feelings and attitudes in an effort to create mutual acceptance and support.

Family Intervention   Some programs, especially those focused on juvenile offenders, treat the whole family rather than just the individual who has broken the law. Some **family intervention** programs seek to improve communication and the expression of feelings, but others try to change patterns of behavior within the family and alter the way that parents manage their children.

Education and Work Programs   Many prisons offer educational programs that help inmates work toward a high-school equivalency degree or take courses for college credit. Some correctional systems make it possible for inmates to leave prison on a daily basis to take courses outside.

Prisons put inmates to work producing goods for sale to outsiders or maintaining the institution, but these jobs rarely provide skills that can be used to find attractive employment after release. Work-release programs try to ease reentry into society by allowing inmates to be released during the day to work at jobs outside the prison.

Behavior Modification   **Behavior modification** or behavior therapy tries to shape conduct by rewarding desirable actions (for example, with money) and by punishing undesirable ones (for example, by withdrawing institutional privileges). This form of treatment does not regard criminal behavior as a symptom of underlying personality flaws that must be corrected but sees it instead as a problem that has to be dealt with directly.

A major question about behavior modification is whether changes produced in inmates will persist after they are released. A review of twenty-four treatment programs of this sort concluded that virtually all of them succeeded in modifying the

Job training might help inmates become reintegrated into society after they are released. Here a woman in an Alabama prison is learning to repair electronic equipment.

behavior of the institutionalized offenders, most of whom were juveniles. Only four programs followed offenders after release, and only one found a lasting and significant effect of the program (Ross and McKay, 1978). There is thus little reason to believe that behavior modification programs within institutions significantly change how offenders act after they are released.

Milieu Therapy   **Milieu therapy** is a treatment method that introduces the idea of rehabilitation into all aspects of an institution, including relations between inmates and staff. This treatment method employs casework and group counseling, stresses inmate responsibility and self-determination, and creates a warm and supportive climate for change.

Does Rehabilitation Work?

It would be surprising if treatment programs were effective at rehabilitating offenders, because most programs are poorly funded, inadequately staffed, and available to a limited number of inmates. The skills learned in prison industries are often inapplicable to the outside world. For instance, there is little demand for the skill of manufacturing license plates, because many states manufacture all license plates in their prisons.

Recidivism Rates   The extent to which offenders are helped by a treatment program is often measured by a **recidivism rate.** This rate is calculated by taking the percentage of offenders who, during a specific period of time after their treatment has ended, are arrested and convicted of new offenses or have their punishment made more restrictive because they have failed to meet the conditions of a less restrictive sentence. The recidivism rate of inmates released from prison is often calculated by adding the number of ex-prisoners who are arrested for new crimes and the number who are sent back to prison because their parole is revoked, and then dividing the total number of "failures" by the total number of released inmates. Thus, if one hundred inmates are released from prison, and within three years eighteen of them are back in prison because they have been convicted of new crimes, and another thirty-three are back in prison because their parole has been revoked for a suspected new crime or for violation of parole conditions, the recidivism rate would be 51 percent for the three-year period.

Recidivism rates vary from study to study. In some jurisdictions, parole is revoked quickly, and so those communities have high recidivism rates. Where parole officers are more tolerant of violations of parole conditions, recidivism rates are lower. The length of the follow-up period also affects the recidivism rate; the longer the period after release, the higher the recidivism rate. A study of 272,111 prison inmates in fifteen states found that within three years of their 1994 release, 67.5 percent had been rearrested for a new offense and 51.8 percent had been returned to prison, either for violating the conditions of their release or for a new crime. Three-year recidivism rates were higher for ex-prisoners who had more prior arrests: 40.6 percent for those with one prior arrest, 47.5 percent for those with two, 55.2 percent for those with three, and 82.1 percent for those with sixteen or more. Recidivism rates were also higher for men, blacks, and younger offenders than for women, whites, and older offenders (Langan and Levin, 2002).

A major problem in using rearrest data to measure recidivism is that many crimes that ex-convicts commit are not reported to the police or do not lead to an arrest if they are reported. For instance, a study of convicted rapists and child molesters found that they admitted to two to five times as many sex offenses as they had been arrested for. Because of the low rate of reporting sex offenses to the police and the difficulty of making arrests for such crimes, recidivism rates are poor measures of the degree to which sex offenders have been rehabilitated (Groth, Longo, and McFadin, 1982).

Other Measures of Treatment Effectiveness   In addition to recidivism rates, the effectiveness of treatment has also been measured by changes in personality, attitude, and behavior, including the way that ex-convicts function in the community, on the job, in school, and within the family.

Rather than designate ex-convicts as "successes" or "failures" on the basis of whether they remain crime-free after release, it might be better to measure the degree to which a program reduces criminal behavior. A program could be considered a partial success if it lengthens the time from release until the time ex-convicts commit new crimes. Thus, a program whose graduates remain crime-free for two years but then return to crime would be regarded as more successful than a program whose graduates return to crime within a month of their release. A reasonable goal for a rehabilitation program is to reduce the number and seriousness of the crimes committed by its participants, even if they are not kept from criminal activity altogether.

Experimental Design and Treatment Effectiveness   Inmates released from prison might not return to crime because they are deterred by the fear of more punishment, because they have matured while in prison, or because they have been rehabilitated. The proper way to isolate the effect of treatment from the other effects of imprisonment is to assign inmates randomly to a group that receives treatment (an experimental group) or to a group that does not receive treatment (a control group). If treatment is effective, those in the experimental group will show a lower recidivism rate (or some other kind of improvement) than those in the control group. The difference between the groups can be attributed to treatment, because chance determined the group to which an inmate was assigned, and the inmates in both groups presumably had similar experiences in prison except for their exposure or lack of exposure to treatment. Experiments of this sort are expensive and difficult to implement, but the failure to carry out well-designed evaluation research means that treatment programs that are both costly and ineffective will continue.

The Amenability Issue   Complicating research on rehabilitation is the possibility that certain kinds of offenders are suited to treatment of a particular sort, with other types of offenders not benefiting from the same treatment. This **amenability issue** might arise in evaluating a treatment program in which 50 percent of the participants avoided recidivism and 50 percent returned to prison. Those who did not return to prison might have been amenable to the treatment they received, and those who returned to prison might not have been amenable to the same treatment. Randomization in the evaluation of treatment programs avoids some of this difficulty but leaves unanswered the question of whether inmates with specific characteristics might be matched to particular treatment methods to produce higher rates of success. More research is needed on which kinds of offenders are best suited to different forms of treatment (Sechrest, White, and Brown, 1979).

The Effectiveness of Treatment Methods   Lipton, Martinson, and Wilks (1975) systematically examined 231 treatment programs conducted between 1945 and 1967. Each program used an independent measure of participants' improvement and a comparison of an experimental group of treated offenders with a control group of untreated ones. Martinson (1974: 25) has summarized the findings of this review as follows: "With few and isolated exceptions, the rehabilitative efforts that have been reported so far have had no appreciable effect on recidivism." He wrote that the data reviewed

> are the best available and give us very little reason to hope that we have in fact found a sure way of reducing recidivism through rehabilitation. This is not to say that we found no instances of success or partial success; it is only to say that these instances have been isolated, producing no clear pattern to indicate the efficacy of any particular method of treatment. And neither is this to say that factors *outside* the realm of rehabilitation may not be working to reduce recidivism—factors such as the tendency for recidivism to be lower in offenders over the age of 30; it is only to say that such factors seem to have little connection with any of the treatment methods now at our disposal. (Martinson, 1974: 49)

Lipton, Martinson, and Wilks uncovered little evidence that treatment programs that prepared inmates for life outside prison through education, vocational training, or the development of social skills had any appreciable impact on recidivism rates. There was little evidence that individual or group counseling reduced recidivism, nor was there any evidence that milieu therapy worked. Existing evidence also failed to show that recidivism was affected by either length of sentence or type of institution in which a sentence was served.

Other evaluations of treatment programs have reached conclusions similar to those of Lipton, Martinson, and Wilks. An examination of one hundred programs found that rehabilitative effects were "slight, inconsistent, and of questionable reliability" (Bailey, 1966: 157; see also Robison and Smith, 1971; Greenberg, 1977). An updating of Lipton, Martinson, and Wilks's study carried out for the National Academy of Sciences concluded not only that nothing yet tried had proved effective but also that the earlier study might even have been too generous in assessing the benefits of treatment programs (Sechrest, White, and Brown, 1979). A survey of the research on juvenile treatment programs found that of forty-eight studies that compared experimental and control groups and tested the statistical significance of their findings, only fifteen showed that the experimental group fared better than the control group. The authors concluded as follows: "Based on these statistics, it is hard to reaffirm rehabilitation" (Lab and Whitehead, 1988: 77).

One assessment of prison treatment programs found that not only were there low rates of participation in work, vocational training, mental health programs, drug and alcohol treatment, and parent counseling programs but also that the programs that were available reinforced the gender inequality that existed in the world outside prison. Men in prison were rarely offered parental training that might induce them to take greater responsibility for their children. Incarcerated women worked at the low-paying, menial jobs available to women in the larger society: cleaning, cooking, and secretarial work. Neither women nor men had access to programs that would help them find financially rewarding jobs after they were released (Morash, Haarr, and Rucker, 1994).

Reaffirming Rehabilitation

Some criminologists seek to reaffirm rehabilitation, pointing out that critics who have concluded that treatment is ineffective have actually uncovered programs that have positive results (Cullen and Gilbert, 1982; Andrews et al., 1990a, 1990b; Palmer, 1994). For instance, Lipton, Martinson, and Wilks found that about half of the sixty-five programs in their sample that had used the best research designs had achieved positive results (Palmer, 1975). In a follow-up study of more recent treatment programs, Martinson (1979) concluded that some of the programs lowered recidivism rates in certain circumstances. A review of ninety-five correctional programs carried out between 1973 and 1978 found that some had beneficial results under certain conditions; family intervention strategies were especially effective. An examination of about four hundred experimental studies of juvenile treatment programs found that two-thirds of them benefited the experimental group and one-third benefited the control group, although the differences between the groups were not always statistically significant (Lipsey, 1991).

One evaluation of treatment programs defined "appropriate correctional service" as that which focuses on high-risk offenders and criminogenic needs and matches clients' needs and learning styles to types of treatment. The authors concluded that appropriate treatment reduces recidivism rates by about 50 percent and that there is "a reasonably solid clinical and research basis for the political reaffirmation of rehabilitation" (Andrews et al., 1990a: 384). A critique of this study claimed that the concepts of "risk," "need," and "responsivity" to appropriate treatment had been defined in ways that served to confirm the researchers' pro-rehabilitation views (Lab and Whitehead, 1990).

Criminologists seeking to reaffirm rehabilitation claim that critics of the treatment approach use especially rigorous methodological standards in evaluating programs and are thus led to conclude that nothing works. One "treatment destruction technique," or way of making even positive results seem questionable, is to raise alternative explanations for positive findings, thereby casting doubt on the conclusion that the program itself had a beneficial effect. Another method of attacking positive results is to show that the criterion of success is inadequate. Parole revocation, for example, might be criticized as a criterion of success because the decision to revoke parole is highly arbitrary and thus an unreliable measure of an ex-convict's readjustment to society. Yet another treatment destruction technique is to claim that even if a program seems to work, it might not work for everyone. Methodological criticisms such as these are valid, but those seeking to reaffirm rehabilitation assert that the application of such high standards minimizes the beneficial effects that treatment programs have achieved and makes it unlikely that any program will ever be declared an unqualified success (Gottfredson, 1979).

From his analysis of the research on the effectiveness of correctional intervention, particularly programs aimed at juveniles, Ted Palmer (1994: xviii) discovered that some forms of treatment programs have substantial positive effects, although no single type of program was "simultaneously very successful and widely applicable." The most effective approaches were behavior therapy, cognitive or cognitive-behavioral (social-skills) training, life-skills or skill-oriented (education and vocational) programs, family intervention, and multimodal programs. Ineffective methods included individual and group counseling, diversion, confrontation (such as the Scared Straight program), and areawide delinquency-prevention programs. Palmer claimed that a multiple-intervention strategy is most likely to reduce recidivism and improve adjustment, and he called for more systematic evaluation of such programs, especially with experimental methods. Francis T. Cullen's (2002: 266) review of the research led him to conclude that the

> evidence is reasonably clear about what treatment programs are most successful in reducing recidivism: interventions that are based on social learning or behavioral principles, are structured rather than nondirective, seek to build human capital in offenders, and use more than one treatment modality to address the multiple problems that offenders may be experiencing. In contrast, interventions that are loosely structured, are based on psychoanalytic or client-centered therapy, and/or that target for change factors unrelated or weakly related to recidivism (e.g., self-concepts) do not have meaningful effects on recidivism.

Reintegrating the Offender into Society

Criminals in the United States are usually stigmatized and cast out of society for violating the law, and little effort is made to reintegrate them after they are punished. In Japan, on the other hand, efforts are made to reintegrate offenders into social networks after sanctions have been applied. The difference between the societies is the result of an American cultural attitude that regards criminals as enemies of society versus a Japanese attitude that emphasizes role obligations and social solidarity (Hamilton and Sanders, 1992). John Braithwaite (1989) suggests that crime might be reduced in the United States through an approach similar to Japan's. Instead of ostracizing criminals, he proposes a process of **reintegrative shaming**, in which expressions of community disapproval of the offender's behavior would be followed by gestures of reacceptance of the offender by the larger law-abiding community. This process "communicates respect for the person as well as disapproval of that person's deed" (Braithwaite, 1995: 193–194). China's *bang-jiao* is an example of a neighborhood-based effort aimed at rehabilitating young offenders by accepting them back into the community and providing them with support and services (Zhang et al., 1996).

Restorative justice is a recent approach that seeks to repair the damage caused by criminals and reintegrate both offenders and victims into the community. This approach

> focuses on restoring the health of the community, repairing the harm done, meeting victims' needs, and emphasizing that the offender can—and must—contribute to those repairs.
>
> Restorative justice condemns the criminal act, holds offenders accountable, involves the participants, and encourages repentant offenders to earn their way back into the good graces of society. (National Institute of Justice, 1998: 10)

In victim–offender reconciliation programs (VORPs), victims and offenders meet with trained mediators to resolve their differences and develop a method to achieve justice. Family group conferencing (FGC), developed in New Zealand and used in Australia, involves a discussion of the crime and what can be done to repair the harm it has caused. Participants include victims and offenders, their families and support groups, and sometimes arresting officers, defense attorneys, and other community representatives. Another strategy is the victim–offender panel (VOP), which brings together victims and offenders who have been involved in a particular kind of crime, though not the same criminal event. The goal of all of these programs is to "empower participants, promote dialogue, and . . . encourage mutual problem solving" (van Ness and Strong, 1997: 89). Reparative measures such as restitution and community service are used to heal the community. Reintegrative measures seek to reduce the stigmatization of both offenders and victims and make them fully participating members of the community once again. In addition to helping offenders understand the effects of their crimes on victims, these practices seem to make them less likely to repeat their crimes.

From his analysis of Community Reparative Board meetings in Vermont, David Karp (2001) concluded that neither "restorative justice" nor "harm" was clearly defined, making repair of the damage caused by crime difficult and opening the way for retribution. Different sanctions were often meted out to offenders convicted of the same crime; this disparity resulted from the difficulty of the sanctioning task rather than from prejudice and discrimination. About 85 percent of the reparative agreements required apologies, restitution, or community service.

Reintegration of the offender is important, but it is necessary to consider the kind of community into which the offender is being reintegrated. Community-based correctional institutions and work- and education-release programs can help offenders maintain ties to a community that is characterized by crime-generating conditions rather than by positive social forces. What is really needed are programs in the community that help offenders develop a stake in conformity and form conventional social bonds.

More attention should be given to the adjustment problems faced by ex-convicts. On leaving prison, they have to support themselves financially, cope with parole restrictions, and stay away from their former life of crime (Irwin, 1970). They want to gratify their desires and meet certain goals when they leave prison, but their lack of resources and unfamiliarity with the outside world often make this difficult. Providing ex-convicts with a place to live and new clothing can ease their transition from prison to the outside society. An important aspect of this transition is finding and keeping a job that offers hope for future advancement. One thief describes the following predicament faced by many ex-convicts: "During the last month [since release from prison] I have had at least forty invitations from thieves to go out stealing with them, but I have not had a single suggestion from a legitimate person about how I could make some money honestly" (cited in Sutherland, 1937: 188). Providing ex-convicts with good jobs when unemployment rates are high can be difficult, particularly if honest, unemployed workers think that ex-convicts have an advantage over them. Motivating ex-convicts to search for work and keep a job can be a problem, both because their lack of job skills means that only unrewarding jobs are available to them and because they often have unrealistically high expectations.

The Future of Rehabilitation

Some former advocates of rehabilitation have abandoned it, while others seek to reaffirm it. Critics argue that treatment has not proved effective, but defenders of rehabilitation point to programs that have had positive results. Critics claim that the indeterminate sentence and the ineffectiveness of treatment programs have lengthened sentences and extended the criminal justice system's control over offenders. Defenders assert that rehabilitation is the most humane justification for punishment and the only one that "obligates the state to care for an offender's needs or welfare" (Cullen and Gilbert, 1982: 247).

Diminished faith in rehabilitation has led some criminologists, lawmakers, and citizens to argue that until treatment is shown to be effective, punishment should be based on the principle of just deserts (McCorkle, 1993; Logan and Gaes, 1993). They argue that offenders found guilty of crimes serious enough to warrant imprisonment should be incarcerated for fixed terms under humane conditions. Voluntary treatment could be provided, with the clear understanding that participation will not affect the length of the sentence or the conditions of release. Until recently, most treatment had been provided under a system of indeterminate sentences, with participation affecting the time and terms of release, so it is uncertain whether treatment under a just deserts system would be more effective than it has been so far. Treatment might be more effective under a just deserts system, because programs would be populated only with inmates who sincerely wanted to change.

Rehabilitation became a less dominant justification for punishment after the mid-1970s, as lawmakers introduced sentencing reforms based on retribution, incapacitation, and deterrence. Nevertheless, many criminologists continue to advocate rehabilitation, and treatment remains an important goal of all correctional systems.

Summary

The deterrence perspective assumes that criminal activity can be inhibited by state-imposed punishment, because offenders rationally consider the risks and rewards of crime before acting. Sometimes this assumption is correct, but not all offenders act with deliberation. Specific deterrence is the impact of a penalty on the offender who is punished, and general deterrence is the effect of penalties on the behavior of the general public. Marginal deterrence refers to the greater impact of one penalty rather than another.

Instrumental acts are probably easier to deter than expressive crimes, and offenders who are not committed to crime as a way of life are easier to deter than those with a commitment to crime. Severity of punishment is probably less important in deterring crime than certainty of punishment, and punishment is more effective if administered promptly. The type of sanction also influences the degree to which criminal behavior will be deterred.

The deterrent impact of the police, the courts, and the prisons is difficult to determine, because of the problem of simultaneity; that is, crime rates affect the way that the criminal justice system functions, just as the actions of the criminal justice system influence crime rates. The size of a police force has little or no impact on a city's crime rate, but what the police do while on patrol can affect the crime rate. There is little reliable evidence that capital punishment deters the crimes for which it has been used; the low certainty and lack of promptness of this penalty make it unlikely to prevent crime.

Incapacitation is the policy of locking up offenders to prevent them from committing crimes that affect the general public. Selective incapacitation is a system of predictive restraint that uses evidence of past behavior to imprison those convicted offenders who seem most likely to commit more crime if allowed to go free. Career criminal programs that concentrate the resources of district attorneys' offices on convicted felons have had a modest impact on crime. A currently popular form of incapacitation is the "three strikes and you're out" policy.

Retribution or just deserts theory claims that only the guilty should be punished and that their penalties should be proportional to the harm caused by their crimes and their blameworthiness. A system of just deserts would include a scale to measure the seriousness of crimes and a scale to rank the severity of punishments; seriousness is determined both by the harmfulness of the act and the blameworthiness of the offender. People generally agree on the ranking of crimes by seriousness and on the ranking of penalties by severity, but there is little research that links the two scales.

Retribution plays an important role in the American criminal justice system. The police show that they consider some offenses to be more serious than others in the way they allocate their resources. Prosecutors take into consideration the harmfulness of the crime and the blameworthiness of the defendant in negotiating guilty pleas and deciding which cases to prosecute with the greatest vigor. Judges use just deserts considerations in deciding how to sentence offenders. Retribution has been introduced into the juvenile justice system in recent years, with juveniles accused of certain crimes now tried as adults. The death penalty is often supported or opposed on grounds of just deserts.

The idea that punishment should rehabilitate offenders was dominant in the American criminal justice system from the 1920s until the mid-1970s, when considerations of just deserts, incapacitation, and deterrence became relatively more important. The police exercise discretion in part on the basis of ideas about what kind of response is most likely to keep a suspect away from crime in the future. In court, pretrial diversion is sometimes used to prevent labeling, which could push defendants into a life of crime. Plea bargaining and sentencing are influenced by ideas about what kind of punishment is most likely to reform an offender. Indeterminate sentences and parole are products of the idea that offenders should be released only when they are rehabilitated.

Treatment programs include individual therapy, casework, cognitive-behavioral programs, group counseling, family intervention, education and work programs, behavior modification, and milieu therapy. Efforts to measure the success of such programs often employ recidivism rates; other criteria of success include indicators of improved offender functioning in the community, in the family, or at a job. Research on rehabilitation is complicated by the amenability issue, the idea that some kinds of offenders are suited only to certain types of treatment. Evaluations using experimental and control groups have not proved that any type of treatment consistently reduces criminal behavior, but some programs have had positive results. Recent years have seen an increase in the popularity of the restorative approach, which seeks to repair the harm caused by offenders and to reintegrate offenders and victims into the community. Reintegration of offenders is important, but attention must be paid to the kind of community into which they are being reintegrated. Rehabilitation will continue to be an important part of the American criminal justice system, but it is now a less influential perspective than it once was.

IMPORTANT TERMS

amenability issue
behavior modification
boot camp
casework
cognitive-behavioral programs
community policing
determinate sentencing
deterrence
directed patrol
displacement effect
family intervention
general deterrence

group counseling
incapacitation
indeterminate sentencing
individual therapy
just deserts
lex talionis
mandatory minimum sentence
marginal deterrent effect
milieu therapy
pretrial diversion
problem-oriented policing
recidivism rate

rehabilitation
reintegrative shaming
restorative justice
retribution
selective incapacitation
sentencing guidelines
simultaneity
specific deterrence
truth-in-sentencing
vengeance

REVIEW QUESTIONS

1. What assumptions does the deterrence model make about human behavior? What is meant by specific, general, and marginal deterrence? How important are severity, certainty, promptness, and type of punishment in deterring criminal behavior?

2. Do the police deter crime? How important are size of the police force, risk of arrest, and patrol tactics in deterring crime?

3. What are selective incapacitation, career criminal programs, and "three strikes and you're out" laws? Are these policies likely to reduce crime?

4. What is retribution? How are the seriousness of crimes and the unpleasantness of penalties measured? How can scales measuring seriousness of crimes and unpleasantness of penalties be linked?

5. How does the idea of retribution influence the police, the courts, and the prisons?

6. Which influences attitudes toward capital punishment more, a desire to deter murder or a desire for retribution? Does the death penalty deter murder?

7. What is rehabilitation? What assumptions does it make about offenders? How does this perspective

influence the performance of the police, the courts, and the prisons?

8. How effective have treatment programs been in rehabilitating offenders? What is a recidivism rate?

What other measures of program effectiveness have been used?

FOR FURTHER STUDY

Deterrence   The effects of various policing methods on crime rates are detailed in John E. Eck and Edward R. Maguire's "Have Changes in Policing Reduced Violent Crime? An Assessment of the Evidence" (in Alfred Blumstein and Joel Wallman, eds., *The Crime Drop in America.* Cambridge, England: Cambridge University Press, 2000, pp. 207–265).

Incapacitation   The effects of prison on crime rates are examined in William Spelman's *Criminal Incapacitation* (New York: Plenum, 1994) and "What Recent Studies Do (and Don't) Tell Us about Imprisonment and Crime" (in Michael Tonry, ed., *Crime and Justice: A Review of Research,* vol. 27. Chicago: University of Chicago Press, 2000, pp. 419–494).

Retribution   Andrew von Hirsch's *Past or Future Crimes: Deservedness and Dangerousness in the Sentencing of Criminals* (New Brunswick, NJ: Rutgers University Press, 1985) presents the just deserts rationale for punishment. The United States Sentencing Commission maintains a website at www.ussc.gov.

Rehabilitation   An investigation of the evidence that treatment works can be found in Francis T. Cullen's "Rehabilitation and Treatment Programs" (in James Q. Wilson and Joan Petersilia, eds., *Crime: Public Policies for Crime Control.* Oakland, CA: ICS Press, 2002, pp. 253–289).

15 | Solving the Crime Problem

T his chapter first looks at three ideological positions and their implications for reducing crime and then traces the politics of crime in the United States since the mid-1960s. Finally, three strategies for solving the crime problem are examined: reforming the criminal justice system, minimizing the opportunities for crime, and dealing with the causes of crime.

Ideological Approaches to Solving the Crime Problem

Three general ideological orientations toward the crime problem are the conservative approach, the liberal approach, and the radical approach. Each position includes assumptions about the causes of crime and the appropriate ways to reduce it.

The Conservative Approach

The **conservative approach** seeks to preserve the status quo from criminals, who are seen as challengers to the social order. Conservatives worry about the high costs of crime and the criminal justice system. They focus on conventional crimes such as the FBI's index offenses. White-collar crime and political corruption are ignored, denied, or even justified.

Conventional crime is attributed to the lower and working classes, who are thought to be improperly socialized or irresponsible. Crime is said to be caused by the defective family structure of the poor and by the failure of their families to inculcate in children the values appropriate to a law-abiding life. Conservatives' concern with the permissiveness and immorality of groups that have high rates of conventional crime has a long history. For example, in nineteenth-century Paris crime was attributed to the "dangerous classes," a term synonymous with the lower and working classes (Chevalier, 1973).

The conservative solution to the crime problem is to encourage conformity to the standards supported by legitimate authorities. The means to do this include the improvement of family life, better discipline, more self-control, and harsher and more certain penalties. Because conservatives are ideologically opposed to the intrusion of the government into the home, even into homes that produce criminals, they rarely give much attention to programs to strengthen the family or teach parents better ways to instill law-abiding values in their children. Conservatives speak of "family values," but their proposals for reducing crime stress deterrence, incapacitation, and just deserts. They call for a larger and more efficient police force, a higher conviction rate in court, less use of probation and parole, longer prison sentences, and more capital punishment. Conservatives are often willing to abridge the procedural rights of defendants, and indeed the rights of the entire population, in order to increase the chances of arrest, conviction, and punishment.

The Liberal Approach

The **liberal approach** holds that crime can be reduced by policies that attack its underlying causes. Liberals claim that people are the products of the social and economic system in which they live. Inequality of income and power and the lack of opportunities increase the probability that more members of disadvantaged groups will engage in behavior defined as criminal by those who hold power.

Liberals believe society can be reformed in ways that will reduce crime, but they reject the idea that a full-scale revolution is required. They point to white-collar crime and political corruption as evidence that members of all social classes break the law, but they focus on conventional crimes by the lower and working classes, which they attribute to poverty and discrimination. They propose that educational and vocational training, welfare assistance, job opportunities, antidiscrimination laws, and community organization can reduce crime. Liberals usually believe that the primary function of criminal penalties should be rehabilitation.

The Radical Approach

A third perspective on the crime problem is the **radical approach.** This viewpoint focuses on crime by both the underprivileged and the privileged and attributes crime by both to the conditions of a capitalist society. Radicals point to evidence—such as some self-report studies—indicating that crime is more evenly distributed among the social classes than is suggested by official crime statistics. Group differences in crime rates are then attributed to the differential handling of the groups by the criminal justice system, rather than to actual differences in their criminal behavior. The "crime problem" is regarded as a socially defined product of selective crime recording, media attention, and differential treatment by the criminal justice system.

The radical approach focuses more on white-collar crime and political corruption than do the conservative and liberal approaches. Conventional criminals are seen as victims of a capitalist system, rather than as offenders against society. Radicals shift attention from the criminal offender to the social and economic system that defines certain behavior as criminal and pushes people into crime by failing to meet their needs. The radical perspective emphasizes justice rather than crime and looks at the negative consequences of values such as competition and material success.

Radicals offer few specific solutions to the crime problem, other than calling for the construction of a new and fundamentally different social system, one vaguely described as communist or socialist. Whether such a society has ever existed, now exists, or can be created in the future is open to question; radicals rarely describe in detail the alternative society that might keep crime to a minimum.

Attitudes toward the Causes
and Prevention of Crime

What do Americans believe are the causes of crime, and how do they think crime can be reduced? Can their attitudes be characterized as conservative, liberal, or radical?

Figure 15.1 shows the results of a 2000 Gallup Poll that asked a national sample to evaluate the importance of several causes of crime. Two of the three most commonly cited reasons—lack of moral training in the home and the absence of fathers in the homes of young people—are closely identified with the conservative approach, but another factor often cited by conservatives—the decline of religion—was chosen by only 32 percent of the sample. The three least frequently mentioned reasons—lack of good jobs for young people, racism in American society, and the poor quality of schools—are usually identified with the liberal approach. Another factor identified with this approach, the availability of guns, was mentioned by 40 percent of the sample. Figure 15.1 suggests that Americans see crime as the product of multiple causes and that those they believe are most important are the ones most often cited by conservatives. However, many people also mention the causes of crime favored by liberals, and the largest number attribute crime to the use of drugs, a factor not clearly identified with either the liberal or conservative approach.

Question: "Next, I'm going to read some reasons that have been given as the causes of crime in this country. While some people view all of these as important causes of crime, we'd like to know which factors you think are the most important. As I read each item, please tell me whether you think it is a critical factor, a very important factor, a somewhat important factor, or not an important factor."

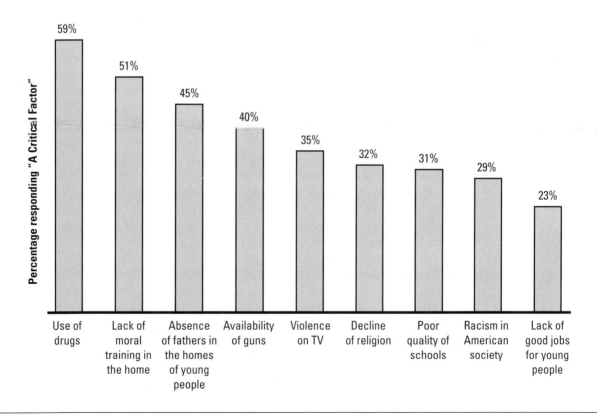

FIGURE 15.1   Attitudes toward the Causes of Crime, 2000

Source: Based on Gallup Poll data in Kathleen Maguire and Ann L. Pastore, eds., *Sourcebook of Criminal Justice Statistics 2001,* Table 2.43, p. 128, retrieved from www.albany.edu/sourcebook.

A recent review of survey data describes Americans' attitudes toward punishment and corrections as ideologically diverse and multifaceted. Americans on the whole prefer, or at least accept, "get tough" responses to crime. However, they are willing to accept less punitive measures, especially if given a good reason to do so, such as the benefits gained from community service or restitution. For example, many conservatives and moderates now support programs to find jobs for the increasing number of inmates being released from prison, a solution traditionally associated with the liberal perspective. Americans believe that rehabilitation should be one goal of the criminal justice system, especially for juvenile offenders, but that young people who commit serious crimes should be punished as harshly as adult offenders. The mixed goals of the correctional system favored by Americans have been described as follows: "Do justice, protect society, and reform offenders" (Cullen, Fisher, and Applegate, 2000: 60).

The Politics of Crime

Since the 1960s, crime has been a major political issue, often used most effectively by "law-and-order" politicians who have adopted a conservative approach.

The President's Commission on Law Enforcement and Administration of Justice

Index crime rates began to rise dramatically in the mid-1960s. One of the earliest political reactions to this increase was President Lyndon Johnson's 1965 appointment of the President's Commission on Law Enforcement and Administration of Justice, which Johnson asked to "deepen our understanding of the causes of crime and of how society should respond to the challenge of the present levels of crime" (President's Commission on Law Enforcement and Administration of Justice, 1967: 2). The seventeen volumes published by the commission in 1967 included many proposals to deal with crime, but little new information about the causes of crime. Because most of the commission's members were lawyers, police administrators, judges, and correctional officials, it is not surprising that the commission's recommendations emphasized reform of the criminal justice system.

The conservative approach to crime reduction was stressed by the commission. The first sentence of the summary chapter of its final report stated that "America can *control* crime" (President's Commission on Law Enforcement and Administration of Justice, 1967: 279; emphasis added here). The commission did give passing attention to the liberal approach:

> [C]rime flourishes where the conditions of life are the worst, and . . . therefore the foundation of a national strategy against crime is an unremitting national effort for social justice. Reducing poverty, discrimination, ignorance, disease and urban blight, and the anger, cynicism or despair those conditions can inspire, is one great step toward reducing crime. *It is not the task, indeed it is not within the competence, of a Commission on Law Enforcement and Administration of Justice to make detailed proposals about housing or education or civil rights, unemployment or welfare or health.* However, it is the Commission's clear and urgent duty to stress that forceful action in these fields is essential to crime prevention, and to adjure the officials of every agency of criminal justice— policemen, prosecutors, judges, correctional authorities—to associate themselves with and labor for the success of programs that will improve the quality of American life.

(President's Commission on Law Enforcement and Administration of Justice, 1967: 279; emphasis added here)

Why the commission thought its broad mandate from the President to devise a national policy to reduce crime allowed it to avoid detailed proposals about the social causes of crime is a puzzle.

The commission recommended federal support for the following: criminal justice planning at the state and local level, the education and training of criminal justice personnel, the development of coordinated national information systems, and technological research and development. The implementation of these proposals might have produced a more streamlined and better-funded system of criminal justice, but there is little evidence from criminological research that such changes would have reduced crime.

The Law Enforcement Assistance Administration

The work of the commission led to a 1968 law, the Omnibus Crime Control and Safe Streets Act, which established the Law Enforcement Assistance Administration (LEAA) in the United States Department of Justice. LEAA's goals were to stimulate comprehensive criminal justice planning at the state and municipal levels and to improve law enforcement through direct grants and support for research and development. At first, most of LEAA's funds were spent on the police, sometimes for such controversial purposes as establishing a computerized file of "suspected subversives" and purchasing an armored personnel carrier for use during riots. Over time, funds were increasingly used for correctional programs rather than for police crime-control measures. In 1971, President Richard Nixon announced a war on crime and increased LEAA's funding, raising expectations that the agency would reduce crime. When crime rates continued to rise in the 1970s, LEAA was attacked as ineffective and wasteful and for not having an overall guiding philosophy behind its disbursement of funds. LEAA was unable to demonstrate convincingly that it had reduced crime, and it was dismantled in 1981.

Experts disagree about what LEAA accomplished. A study based on interviews with federal officials concluded that LEAA's impact was primarily negative: It helped weaken the belief that capital punishment was a deterrent; it undermined faith in rehabilitation as a solution to the crime problem; and it showed that the crime rate would not be reduced by such changes in police methods as saturation patrolling, faster response time, and more education for officers (Cronin, Cronin, and Milakovich, 1981). Others have seen more benefits from LEAA's efforts, including the following:

- sting operations that recovered stolen goods and arrested thieves and fences
- witness assistance programs that made it easier to prosecute cases
- a program to prosecute white-collar crime that recovered ten times as much in fines and restitution as it cost
- career criminal programs that gave priority to the prosecution and punishment of serious offenders
- correctional reforms that built new facilities and created prerelease programs (Gordon and Morris, 1985)

LEAA was also able to get criminal justice agencies to work together, and more than 70 percent of the programs it sponsored were continued by the states in some form.

The 1968 and 1972 Presidential Elections

Crime was the major domestic issue in the 1968 presidential election, with the Vietnam War being the major foreign policy concern. Two of the candidates, Richard Nixon and George Wallace, were ardent and vocal advocates of a law-and-order approach that was based on the conservative belief that crime could be reduced by strengthening the criminal justice system. Nixon and Wallace claimed that the Democrats, incumbents for eight years, had been "soft" on street crime, ghetto rioting, and campus violence. The Democratic candidate, Hubert Humphrey, did not support such violence, but Nixon and Wallace were able to parlay the issue of "crime in the streets" into millions of votes in November. Many voters switched their traditionally Democratic votes to the Republican party or the American Independent party because of the crime issue.

The burglary of the offices of the Democratic National Committee at the Watergate complex occurred in 1972, the year of another presidential election. The power of the office of the presidency was great enough to allow President Nixon to cover up this crime until he was reelected. Ironically, surveys show that a major reason for his victory in 1972, as well as in 1968, was the law-and-order vote (Gallup, 1972). People who would otherwise have voted for the Democratic candidate, Senator George McGovern, voted for Nixon because of his opposition to crime in the streets. Nixon resigned in 1974 after a congressional committee voted bills of impeachment against him for obstruction of justice and other illegal acts.

The Crime Issue during the Reagan Administration

Crime was not the major issue in the 1980 and 1984 presidential elections, but President Ronald Reagan made occasional use of the issue during his time in office. In a speech before the International Association of Chiefs of Police in 1981, he incorporated several recommendations made by the Attorney General's Task Force on Violent Crime (U.S. Department of Justice, 1981). He called for capital punishment, the use of mandatory prison terms for people convicted of using handguns during felonies, and the denial of bail for defendants who were likely to commit more crime if released. He called crime "ultimately a moral dilemma," rather than simply a question of more funds for the criminal justice system, and said that the war on crime would be won only when truths such as right and wrong, individual responsibility, and swift and certain punishment for wrongdoing take hold. He criticized social scientists, social workers, and psychiatrists who assert that poverty, disadvantaged childhoods, and a bad environment lead to crime, claiming instead that crime is a way of life that some people consciously choose, not because they are "seeking bread for their families" but because they "are driven crazy with desire for stuff they'll never be able to afford." Reagan believed that criminals commit crime because it is easy and not very risky, and because they believe they are entitled to what they steal.

In October 1984, Reagan signed into law the Comprehensive Crime Control Act, which he had recommended but which was also the product of bipartisan efforts in Congress. This law was wide-ranging in its reforms, but because it applied just to federal law, under which only 5 percent of all criminal defendants are tried, it had little impact on the nation's crime problem. The law introduced preventive detention on the federal level in order to reduce bail crime. It led to the elimination of parole for federal prisoners and created a committee that in 1987 established sentencing guidelines designed to limit judicial discretion and reduce sentence disparity. The law restricted the insanity defense to people who were unable to appreciate the wrongfulness of their acts. It also created a victim-compensation program, expanded federal jurisdiction over credit card fraud, made it easier for the government to seize the illegal profits of drug dealers and organized criminals, and lengthened penalties for drug dealers and repeat offenders.

The Reagan administration waged a "War on Drugs" that emphasized law enforcement rather than education, treatment, and research. For example, the 1986 Anti-Drug Abuse Act allocated $1.7 billion to fight drugs. Twelve percent of that amount was for drug education, 22 percent was for treatment and research, and most of the remainder was for federal and state law-enforcement agencies. The burgeoning of the prison population since the early 1980s has been the direct result of the Reagan administration's policy of arresting and incarcerating more drug offenders (Tonry, 1995).

The 1988 Presidential Election and the George H. W. Bush Administration

In his 1988 campaign for the presidency, Vice President George H. W. Bush effectively used the crime issue to help defeat Massachusetts Governor Michael Dukakis. Bush embarrassed Dukakis by accepting an endorsement from the Springfield, Massachusetts, police union. Dukakis's weak response to a question during a presidential debate about how he would react to the rape of his wife reinforced the perception that he was soft on crime. Most important were the Bush campaign's advertisements about a rape and assault committed by convicted first-degree murderer Willie Horton while he was on furlough from a Massachusetts prison. Dukakis was attacked by Bush for his willingness to furlough convicted murderers, even though the federal prison system and every state system also used furloughs, with most systems even furloughing murderers. Because Horton was black and his rape victim white, Democrats accused the Bush campaign of using the crime issue in a racially divisive way.

As did his predecessor in office, President Bush focused on the drug problem. One unsuccessful strategy was his April 1989 appointment of "drug czar" William Bennett to oversee a comprehensive attack on drug crime in Washington, D.C. This plan included construction of a new prison, use of National Guard troops to do clerical work so that police officers would be freed for street duty, and raids on crack houses. A year and a half later, it was clear that these measures had been ineffective; drugs were still cheap and plentiful, and drug-related murders continued at a record pace. Bennett quit his job as director of National Drug Control Policy in November 1990.

The 1992 and 1996 Elections and the Clinton Administration

The crime issue was frequently discussed by George H. W. Bush and Bill Clinton during the 1992 presidential campaign, but it was not a decisive issue. Because Democrats had been on the defensive on the crime issue since the 1960s, Clinton's ability to portray himself as being at least as tough on crime as Bush was a kind of victory. Clinton supported capital punishment, a national police corps, a ban on some semiautomatic weapons, and a waiting period for the purchase of handguns. He attacked Bush for his inaction on handgun legislation and for his lack of support for increased funding of state and local law-enforcement agencies. Clinton secured the endorsements of several police organizations to counteract Bush's endorsements from other police groups. Overall, neither candidate gained a strong advantage over the other on the crime issue.

In his first term, Clinton continued to stake his claim to being tough on crime. He supported and signed the Violent Crime Control and Law Enforcement Act of 1994, which provided money for additional police officers, expanded the number of federal crimes covered by the death penalty, banned the sale and possession of many assault weapons, and funded new research and evaluation efforts by the National Institute of Justice. Later, Clinton chided Republicans for being soft on crime when they sought to repeal the ban on assault weapons.

As in 1992, neither candidate in the 1996 presidential election had a clear advantage on the crime issue. Republican Bob Dole called for more prison construction, abolition of parole for violent offenders, harsher punishment for juvenile offenders, drug testing for inmates, and less violence in the movies. Dole's charge that juvenile drug use had increased during Clinton's first term was answered by Clinton's assertion that during that time crime rates had declined and tens of thousands of felons had been kept from buying firearms as a result of the Brady law. Clinton's victory was partly a result of his ability to neutralize Dole on the crime issue. Clinton did this by regularly supporting such measures as curfews for teenagers, school uniforms, a national registry of sex offenders, expansion of the death penalty, and a computerized system to track gun dealers who sell firearms to juveniles.

A federal law passed in 1996 required the U.S. attorney general to produce an independent review of the effectiveness of crime-prevention measures sponsored by the U.S. Department of Justice. This review had to employ rigorous scientific methods to determine which programs decreased factors that led to delinquency and crime and which programs increased factors that protected against delinquency and crime. Assessing more than five hundred programs that had been evaluated using minimum scientific standards, a group of University of Maryland criminologists concluded that many programs were ineffective but that others were promising; they characterized the programs listed in Table 15.1 as effective in reducing crime and delinquency.

The 2000 Presidential Election and the George W. Bush Administration

After weeks of recounts and court battles over who won the state of Florida, Texas Governor George W. Bush narrowly defeated incumbent Vice President Al Gore for the presidency. The 2000 campaign, which was remarkable for Gore's failure to capitalize on the unprecedented decline in crime rates during his eight years in office, focused on three major crime issues: the violent content of popular entertainment, the death penalty, and gun control. Gore spoke against the entertainment industry's marketing of violent films, video games, and music to young people, and he even suggested the possibility of federal regulation of the industry. He was, however, sharply criticized by Bush for attending a Beverly Hills fund-raiser a few days later and for accepting millions of dollars in contributions from people in the industry. Both candidates supported the death penalty. Gore said he was open to review of the death penalty in light of evidence that errors had been made in its administration, but he opposed a moratorium on its use by the federal system. Bush took a stronger stance, arguing that the death penalty saves lives and that he was certain that all ninety-eight people who had been executed in Texas while he was governor had been guilty and had had full access to the courts. The crime issue that most clearly divided Bush and Gore was gun control. As governor, Bush had signed into law measures that allowed Texans to carry concealed firearms and made it difficult for cities and counties

TABLE 15.1   Effective Ways to Prevent Crime

FOR INFANTS
Frequent home visits by nurses and other
   professionals

FOR PRESCHOOLERS
Classes with weekly home visits by preschool
   teachers

FOR DELINQUENT AND AT-RISK PREADOLESCENTS
Family therapy and parent training

FOR SCHOOLS
Organizational development for innovation
Communication and reinforcement of clear,
   consistent norms
Teaching of social competency skills
Coaching of high-risk youth in "thinking skills"

FOR OLDER MALE EX-OFFENDERS
Vocational training

FOR RENTAL HOUSING WITH DRUG DEALING
Nuisance abatement action on landlords

FOR HIGH-CRIME HOT SPOTS
Extra police patrols

FOR HIGH-RISK REPEAT OFFENDERS
Monitoring by specialized police units
Incarceration

FOR DOMESTIC ABUSERS WHO ARE EMPLOYED
On-scene arrests

FOR CONVICTED OFFENDERS
Rehabilitation programs with risk-focused treatments

FOR DRUG-USING OFFENDERS IN PRISON
Therapeutic community treatment programs

Source: Lawrence W. Sherman et al., *Preventing Crime: What Works, What Doesn't, What's Promising.*
Washington, DC: U.S. Department of Justice, July 1998, p. 1.

to sue gun manufacturers. Gore, on the other hand, advocated longer sentences for crimes committed with firearms, photo licenses for new handgun owners, and a ban on cheap handguns. The National Rifle Association enthusiastically supported Bush, with one of its officers remarking that if Bush were elected, "we'll have . . . a president where we work out of their office" (cited in Mintz, 2000: A9).

Several kinds of crime occupied the Bush administration during its first two years. First, the September 11th attacks shifted the FBI's focus from conventional and organized crime to terrorist activity. The long-term ramifications of this change are not clear, but it is consistent with a recommendation made in 1999 by both U.S. Supreme Court Chief Justice William H. Rehnquist and an American Bar Association task force that the federal government should reduce its involvement in fighting crime. Second, U.S. Attorney General John Ashcroft took the official position that the Second Amendment guarantees all Americans an individual right to bear firearms. It is uncertain whether this view, which conflicts with the Supreme Court's most recent decision on the issue, will eventually prevail. Third, revelations of widespread accounting fraud led Bush to advocate change in the way the federal government deals with corporate crime. Some critics argued that his proposals, made in a speech on Wall Street on July 9, 2002, were neither as specific nor as extensive as needed, perhaps because the Republican party traditionally opposes government regulation of business. Others noted that prior to the 2000 election both Bush and Vice President Dick Cheney had themselves been involved in accounting irregularities much like those that Bush was promising to end. Soon after Bush's speech Congress passed a law, which Bush signed, that enacted stronger measures than the president had originally suggested: a board to regulate the accounting industry, a broadened basis for prosecuting corporate offenders, and harsher penalties for executives and auditors who break the law. Whether this law actually leads to harsher and more certain penalties and deters corporate crime remains to be seen.

Crime and the Criminal Justice System

Many proposals for reducing crime seek to reform the criminal justice system by redefining the kinds of behavior over which the law should have jurisdiction or by changing the way that the police, courts, and prisons operate.

Overreach of the Criminal Law

Some critics claim that the criminal justice system could be more effective if it gave up jurisdiction over certain kinds of behavior. This assertion that efficiency is hindered by the "overreach" of the criminal law is often applied to victimless crimes, those offenses that are consensual and lack a complaining participant. Retributivists believe that acts that harm no one should not be punished. Others think that the limited resources of the criminal justice system could better be applied to conventional crimes than to victimless crimes such as gambling and prostitution.

Proposals to reduce the overreach of the law by decriminalizing drugs are based on the following five assumptions:

1. Citizens have the right to be protected from state interference in behavior that causes no societal harm.
2. Addicts should be offered treatment rather than prosecuted as criminals.
3. The criminalization of drugs has not stopped drug use.
4. The resources used to prosecute drug offenses could better be used to deal with more serious crimes.
5. The criminalization of drugs leads to secondary crimes committed to support expensive habits (Farr, 1990).

By reducing the price of drugs, legalization might undercut the illegal drug trade as well as minimize the user's need to commit crime to support a habit.

Critics of decriminalization claim that if drugs were legal, more people would use them, because drugs would be less expensive and more readily available. Defenders of decriminalization reply that education and treatment could deal with any such increase in drug use, but critics of decriminalization say that we do not have reliable evidence that education and treatment can curb drug use. Critics of decriminalization also point out that there will always be a need for some controls on drugs, such as age limits on access to drugs similar to current laws that restrict the purchase of alcohol. If there were such age limits on access to drugs, those under the legal age would continue to provide a market for drug dealers. Opponents of decriminalization also argue that many addicts committed crimes before they started using drugs and would probably continue to commit crimes even if the price of drugs dropped as a result of decriminalization. Opponents also suggest that drugs would have to be decriminalized selectively; the consequences of open access to crack would be quite different from the consequences of open access to marijuana.

The Police

Politicians and the public often claim that putting more police officers on the street will help solve the crime problem. Even if the presence of an officer does prevent an offender from committing a crime against a particular target, the offender can easily wait until the officer leaves or find another target. Street patrols might change the type of crime that an offender commits; for instance, a criminal might burglarize a house rather than rob a pedestrian.

A study by the Police Foundation concluded that rather than measure officers' productivity by the number of arrests they make, police administrators would contribute more to the reduction of crime if they weighed the net impact of each arrest. Arrests of chronic criminals, who might commit five or more serious offenses per week, contribute more to curbing crime than arrests of occasional offenders. A weighted clearance rate that takes this into account would focus more attention on apprehending career criminals and would thus be a better way of measuring the performance of individual officers (Martin, 1986; Martin and Sherman, 1986).

Crime might also be reduced if the police established better relationships with the community and increased public trust so that more crimes were reported. Offenders might then realize that their crimes would be more likely to be reported and that they would therefore be more likely to be arrested. However, it is not clear that the reporting of crime can be increased enough for potential offenders to think that they face a significantly greater threat of punishment.

Law-enforcement strategies to reduce firearms violence try to curb the illegal acquisition of guns, the illegal possession and carrying of guns, and the improper or careless use of guns (Office of Juvenile Justice and Delinquency Prevention, 1999). Evaluations of measures designed to achieve those goals have not uncovered a single effective remedy, but some law-enforcement officials believe that comprehensive strategies that use multiple measures might reduce firearms violence.

Federal Law Enforcement   The federal government's policy of dealing with drug use relies heavily on policing the nation's borders to prevent the importation of drugs. This approach has increased the amount of drugs confiscated at the borders, but even the increased amount that has been seized is a small proportion of the drugs that importers try to bring into the country. Importers typically increase their activity to compensate for what they lose to law-enforcement agents. A 1994 Rand study recommended cutting the funds allocated to law enforcement for fighting the cocaine traffic, after concluding that treatment of abusers of the drug is a much more cost-effective strategy for curbing cocaine use (Rydell and Everingham, 1994).

Despite concern about the accuracy of the FBI's National Crime Information Center 2000's records and their threat to privacy, a national clearinghouse for information on crime is an important tool for law enforcement. Local police officers can get rapid responses to their inquiries about whether a car is stolen or a suspect they are questioning is wanted outside their state. The importance of a nationally coordinated system can be seen in the results of an FBI study showing that half of all offenders are arrested in more than one state during their criminal careers, with 18 percent being arrested in three or more states (Kelley, 1976). (See the Using Criminology box.)

The Courts

The primary way that the courts might reduce crime is by increasing the certainty of punishment, but it is not clear that certainty can be increased significantly without infringing on the constitutional rights of defendants or greatly expanding the resources of the criminal justice system.

Making Prosecution Easier   Because laws against sex offenses such as rape and child molestation have historically included impediments to prosecution and conviction, certainty of punishment might be increased by reforming those laws. For example, until recently rape victims were often asked in court about their past sexual conduct, making it seem that they, rather than the accused, were being tried. States now have "shield laws" to protect rape victims from this kind of cross-examination.

Another reform that has made the prosecution of rape defendants easier is the division of this crime into several degrees of sexual assault, with different penalties for each of the three or four degrees of the offense. This makes it easier to get a conviction for sexual assault from a jury that believes that mitigating circumstances do not warrant the severe penalty previously attached to the single type of forcible rape.

Prosecuting Organized Crime   Legal reform and increased funding have made it possible for the federal government and local district attorneys to prosecute the leaders of organized crime more successfully. The federal Racketeer Influenced and Corrupt Organizations law (RICO) has been an effective tool for prosecuting defendants who engage in a series of crimes. This law also permits the victims of financial fraud, either by organized crime or by white-collar offenders, to bring civil suits for

USING CRIMINOLOGY

Profiling the Serial Killer

An increase in murders by offenders who were strangers or had unknown relationships to their victims led the FBI's Behavioral Science Unit to conclude that there was an epidemic of serial murder in the country in the late 1970s and early 1980s. To assess the motives of serial murderers, defined as offenders who kill four or more victims over a period of at least seventy-two hours, and to establish linkages among the crimes committed by those murderers, the FBI developed a profiling system for law-enforcement agents to use in focusing their investigative efforts.

The FBI's system uses crime-scene and forensic evidence, preliminary police reports, and information about victims to develop a picture of the killer's personality, characteristics, and motives. The FBI distinguishes between the crimes and crime scenes of "organized" and "disorganized" serial murderers. Organized killers plan their crimes, target strangers, personalize their victims, demand submission from their victims, use restraints, transport and hide their victims' bodies, remove weapons from the crime scene, and generally leave behind crime scenes that show their overall control and their desire to avoid detection. Disorganized murderers commit their crimes spontaneously, know their victims or the locations of their crimes, depersonalize their victims, engage in sudden violence, make little use of restraints, commit sexual acts after their victims die, leave bodies in plain view where they commit their crimes, leave weapons or other evidence at the crime scene, and leave behind sloppy crime scenes.

These features of organized and disorganized homicides and crime scenes purportedly correlate with distinctive personal traits, or profile characteristics, of the serial

murderers. Organized serial murderers were inconsistently disciplined when young, had a high birth order, had fathers with stable work histories, are intelligent and socially and sexually competent, hold skilled jobs, use alcohol at the time of their crimes, live with partners, have cars in good condition, maintain control during their murders, and follow the news of their crimes. Disorganized serial murderers have the opposite traits.

Critics question the accuracy of these profiles and doubt their usefulness in apprehending serial killers. The profiles are based on interviews with thirty-six male sexual homicide offenders, but 10 to 15 percent of serial killers are females, and not all male serial killers are sexual homicide offenders. As a result, the profiles do not describe many serial killers, such as "black widows" (women who kill their husbands or other relatives, often for insurance money) and "angels of mercy" (women and men who work in hospitals or nursing homes and take the lives of patients there). The arrest of two black men—forty-one-year-old John Allen Muhammad and seventeen-year-old Lee Boyd Malvo—for ten sniper murders in the Washington, D.C., suburbs in October 2002 confounded profilers, most of whom had predicted that the killer would turn out to be a lone white man in his twenties or thirties.

FBI agent Paul Lindsay has expressed skepticism about the usefulness of profiling, asking, "I mean, how many serial killer cases has the FBI solved—*if any*?" (cited in Jenkins, 1994: 71). Many cases have used FBI profilers to no avail. In some cases, law enforcers have shown "linkage blindness" in failing to recognize that several murders were committed by the same offender. Erroneous information or incorrect inferences have also led treble damages. More use of undercover agents and informers, the pooling of resources by law-enforcement agencies, more concentration by the FBI on narcotics crimes, and the exchange of immunity and a new identity for a witness's testimony have all increased the prosecution and conviction of organized crime leaders. Even though critics of these policies contend that imprisoned gangsters are simply replaced from within the organized crime "family" and that organized crime is not much affected by law-enforcement efforts, by the 1990s prosecutors had succeeded in weakening the Mafia.

Prosecuting White-Collar Crime   Federal, state, and local agencies lack the resources to prosecute many white-collar crime cases, and those that are prosecuted usually require years of investigation, so certainty of punishment is low and penalties are not promptly administered. The penalties for corporate offenders also seem

The arrests of Lee Boyd Malvo (left) 17, and John Allen Muhammad, 41, for ten sniper murders in the Washington, D.C., suburbs in October 2002 surprised profilers, most of whom thought that the crimes had been committed by a lone white man in his twenties or thirties.

law-enforcement agents astray, delaying apprehension of the real killer and leading to more lost lives. In one case,

a profile on a criminal suspect told investigators the man they were looking for came from a broken home, was a high school dropout, held a marginal job, hung out in "honky tonk" bars, and lived far from the scene of the crime. When the attacker was finally caught, it was learned the psychological assessment was 100 percent wrong. He had not come from a broken home, he had a college degree, held an executive position with a

respected financial institution, did not use alcohol, and lived near the scene of the crime (Goodroe, 1987: 31).

Despite such problems, FBI agents regularly recount cases in which their clever deductions resulted in the apprehension of serial killers. Consequently, FBI profilers enjoy an almost mythological status, one that is reinforced by their heroic portrayal in newspaper and magazine articles and in commercially successful films and novels, most notably Thomas Harris's *The Silence of the Lambs.*

Sources: Based on C. Goodroe, "Tracking the Serial Offender," *Law and Order,* July 1987, pp. 29–33; Robert K. Ressler, Ann W. Burgess, and John E. Douglas, *Sexual Homicide: Patterns and Motives,* New York: Lexington Books, 1988; Philip Jenkins, *Using Murder: The Social Construction of Serial Homicide,* New York: Aldine de Gruyter, 1994.

too lenient to deter white-collar crime. Fines are often minuscule compared with a corporation's total assets, and executives who are fined are often paid back by the company. Few executives are imprisoned, and when they are it is usually for a short term in a minimum-security prison. Punishment might be a more effective deterrent if fines were heavier, more offenders were incarcerated, and recidivists were prohibited from securing government contracts. Negative publicity about violations of the law could also affect corporate behavior, because firms are concerned with their public reputations (Fisse and Braithwaite, 1983). In extreme cases, an offending corporation might even be taken over by the federal government or prohibited from doing business.

Juvenile Courts   The search for solutions to the crime problem often focuses on young people, because many arrested suspects are juveniles, and juvenile delinquents are more likely than nondelinquents to go on to commit crime as adults.

Some have proposed that instead of incarcerating juveniles in reformatories, which should be reserved for those who repeatedly commit serious offenses, most young offenders should be placed in group homes in communities other than those in which their families live. These group homes can provide surrogate families for juveniles whose own families are conducive to crime. Another proposal is to treat the entire family of the youthful offender, rather than isolate the juvenile for treatment, because the problems of delinquents often stem from poor relationships within their families.

Juvenile court records could be made more accessible than they now are, so that adults with histories of serious offenses as juveniles could be sentenced as persistent criminals rather than first-time offenders when they initially appear in adult criminal court. Others have suggested that the age at which adolescents can be prosecuted as adults should be lowered, although researchers have found that this does not significantly reduce the crime rate and may even increase it.

The Prisons

A 1993 Canadian government report on crime prevention noted that "the United States affords a glaring example of the limited impact that criminal justice responses may have on crime," observing that "[i]f locking up those who violate the law contributed to safer societies, then the United States should be the safest country in the world" (cited in Proband, 1993: 2).

Because there is no compelling evidence that incarceration reduces crime through rehabilitation, some criminologists have argued that prison sentences should be based on the principle of just deserts. Treatment could be optional during a fixed period of confinement. Whenever possible, pretrial diversion and sanctions of warnings or probation might be substituted for imprisonment, which is expensive. Offenders who seem unlikely to commit more crimes might be left in the community where they can maintain ties to their families and jobs, but predicting which offenders are likely to commit more crimes is difficult, and leaving offenders in the community continues to expose them to the influences that led them to break the law in the first place.

Support for the idea that incarceration might reduce crime comes from the fact that the rapid expansion of the U.S. prison population during the 1990s was paralleled by a steady decline in crime rates. Even if locking up more offenders reduces crime, the reduction is bought at a high price; one study estimates that each crime that California's three-strikes law averts costs $16,300 (Greenwood et al., 1994). Incarceration that cuts crime in the short term can increase it in the long run, devastating the lives of inmates who are unable to adjust to society after they are released.

Situational Crime Prevention

A second general strategy for solving the crime problem—in addition to relying on the criminal justice system to deter, incapacitate, and rehabilitate—is **situational crime prevention.** This involves opportunity-reducing measures "(1) directed at highly specific forms of crime (2) that involve the management, design, or manipulation of the immediate environment in as systematic and permanent a way as possible (3) so as to increase the effort and risks of crime and reduce the rewards as perceived by a wide range of offenders" (Clarke, 1992: 4). Influenced by the concepts of defensible space, crime prevention through environmental design, and problem-oriented policing, situational crime prevention includes the following:

1. *Techniques to increase the offender's effort* such as target hardening (e.g., locks on steering columns and tougher glass), access control (e.g., gates and identification badges), deflection of offenders (e.g., closing off streets), and control of facilitators (e.g., firearms).

2. *Techniques that increase the offender's risks* such as entry/exit screening (e.g., border searches and merchandise tags), formal surveillance (e.g., security guards and burglar alarms), surveillance by employees (e.g., bus conductors and park attendants), and natural surveillance (e.g., defensible space design and Neighborhood Watches).

3. *Techniques that reduce the offender's rewards* such as target removal (e.g., removable car radios and reduced use of cash), property identification (e.g., property marking and stolen car location devices), removal of inducements (e.g., cleaning up graffiti and gender-neutral phone listings), and rule setting (e.g., drug-free school zones and library checkout procedures) (Clarke, 1992).

Situational crime prevention has been criticized for displacing rather than preventing crime, but some research has identified measures that have reduced crime without obvious displacement (Clarke, 1992).

Law-enforcement measures to reduce violence include searches of students to prevent them from bringing weapons into schools.

Target Hardening

One way to reduce opportunities for crime is to make it more difficult for an offender to carry out a crime against a particular target, a policy called **target hardening**. This includes the installation of bars and locks on doors and windows, the use of spotlights, the purchase of guard dogs, and the use of alarms. These measures might reduce the chance that the target-hardened building will be burglarized, but a burglar who is motivated to steal might simply move to another, less well protected target.

An instance of target hardening that curbed bank robbery was the installation in New York City banks during the early 1980s of bulletproof Plexiglas shields to protect tellers, who could press an alarm button and ignore the robber's demands. According to police officials, these barriers were installed in about half of the city's banks and were partly responsible for a decline in bank robberies in the city from 848 in 1979 to 447 in 1982. The robbery rate at banks with protective shields was one-fourth that of the robbery rate at banks without the barriers (Buder, 1983).

Target-hardening measures have been proposed as a way to curb computer crime. Traditional safeguards against unauthorized access to computerized information include passwords and other electronic "locks," but these measures have been neutralized by "hackers" and by experienced computer operators who guess or steal passwords to gain access to information. Another way of making computers safer is encryption, a method that translates information into code so that someone who gains access to the information cannot interpret its meaning.

Self-Protective Measures

Some self-protective measures are much like target hardening, for they are aimed at making it harder for offenders to perpetrate a crime successfully against an individual. People buy firearms after urban riots and during crime waves in the belief that gun owners will be less likely to be victimized, or more able to resist successfully if they are attacked or robbed. They also buy dogs, carry Mace, and take karate lessons to reduce their risk of victimization.

One study asked a sample of Seattle residents whether, at least two years prior to the interview, they had taken any of the following precautions to prevent crime: locking doors and leaving lights on when not at home, asking neighbors to watch the house, installing extra locks or a burglar alarm, having a dog or a weapon in the home, and belonging to a Block Watch program. Those who had taken the most precautions were the least likely to have experienced a burglary. The risk of being the victim of vandalism or property theft was not affected by taking such precautions. Safety measures taken by one person did not displace crime to nearby targets, nor did they reduce their neighbors' risk of being victimized (Miethe, 1991).

Informal Social Control

Opportunities for crime might be reduced by increasing informal social control over criminal behavior. This could be accomplished through defensible space architecture, although research indicates that this method is of limited value. Another measure is improved street lighting, which makes public places more visible and draws more people to those places, thereby enhancing informal control. There is, however, little research showing that crime can be reduced by better street lighting.

Another way to improve surveillance is to increase people's perception that the streets are safe and that uncivil behavior in their community is rare. Programs that eliminate signs of decay that might create the impression of a dangerous community—including graffiti, broken windows, open prostitution, panhandling, and loitering on street corners—could reduce crime by enhancing informal social control if they manage to draw more people to the streets. For informal social control to be effective, people must act against criminals by intervening in a crime or by reporting it to the police.

Community Crime Prevention

Another strategy of situational crime prevention involves community organization. In 1976 a project was undertaken to reduce robbery and burglary in an area of Hartford, Connecticut, in the hope that changes in the community would reduce fear of crime and thereby enhance informal social control. This project altered the physical features of the community by changing roads to cul-de-sacs and one-way streets in order to reduce motorist traffic and define the neighborhood more clearly in a visual sense. A neighborhood police team was organized, and better communication was established between the community and the police. A formal neighborhood organization was also developed to deal with local problems.

In an evaluation of this project published six years later, the researchers concluded that making the neighborhood more residential had changed the degree to which people exercised informal control over the area and the way they felt about their neighbors. Strengthening informal control had also helped reduce residents' fear and concern about crime. The evaluators of the Hartford project concluded that increased informal control does not by itself necessarily reduce robbery and burglary but can curb crime if it is accompanied by aggressive and effective police practices (Fowler and Mangione, 1982).

Dealing with the Causes of Crime

Trying to reduce crime by relying on the criminal justice system is like relying on therapeutic rather than preventive medicine to deal with disease. Sick people do need help, but research into the causes of disease can lead to more effective treatment methods and even suggest ways to prevent the disease from occurring in the first place. A search for the causes of a disease might be more costly in the short run than using traditional methods to treat the disease, but the long-term benefits of a successful search for the causes of the disease are greater. Similarly, finding the causes of crime and attacking them is a more efficient way to reduce crime than waiting for crimes to occur and then using traditional methods to deal with offenders. The ineffectiveness of the criminal justice system in dealing with crime is suggested by James Q. Wilson, a recognized authority on crime and criminal justice, who says, "I doubt that a criminal justice system which I designed and I ran would have more than a small impact on the total crime rate" (cited in McCain, 1984: 2).

There is popular support for policies that focus on the causes of crime. A 2000 Gallup Poll found that to reduce the crime rate, 68 percent of Americans favored the use of more resources to attack the social problems that lead to crime, only 27 percent favored the use of more resources for law enforcement, and 5 percent had no opinion (cited in Maguire and Pastore, 2002: 128). Unfortunately, the causes of crime are not easily eradicated; as Gabriel Tarde said more than a century ago, "If the tree of crime, with all its roots and rootlets, could ever be torn out of our society, it would leave a vast abyss" (cited in Radzinowicz and King, 1977: 84). Even though social conditions are not easily changed, the solution to the crime problem lies in policies that deal with its underlying causes. Because social and economic factors distinguish societies with high crime rates from those with low ones, making countries with high crime rates more like those with low ones is a useful strategy for reducing crime.

Economic Factors

Usually countries undergoing economic development experience major increases in their crime rates, but neither China nor Japan has had that experience. China has apparently avoided high crime rates through careful social planning that has been implemented by an authoritarian regime. This has provided a full-employment economy in which people are trained and given rewarding jobs. Until recently, most Japanese workers were employed by the same company for life, with employers taking a great interest in the welfare of their employees. Job mobility has increased in Japan, but employee turnover is still less common there than in the United States.

The United States needs policies that create stable and meaningful jobs and provide retraining and job counseling when needed. At the national level there is no clear relationship between the unemployment rate and the crime rate, but many people who commit conventional crimes are without job skills and are unemployed. Perhaps even more important, they lack the social bond to the conventional order that work provides. Job training is more likely to foster the development of such a bond if it includes socialization in job-related skills as well as in the techniques of the work; job-related skills include promptness, cooperativeness, and willingness to take orders (Cook, 1975). Measures that reduce job turnover and encourage loyalty to an employer also foster a worker's stake in conformity. Even more important than an ex-convict's getting a job is keeping one over time and becoming habituated to a work routine.

Nations with low crime rates commonly have less relative deprivation than nations with high rates. In China, control of the media has limited citizens' access to information about the standard of living of the rest of the world, thereby minimizing the "demonstration effect" that can increase expectations beyond the current

Policies that increase the number of stable and meaningful jobs can reduce crime by fostering attachment to the conventional social order.

level of well-being. The absolute level of economic well-being in a nation might be a less important influence on crime than relative deprivation, the gap between current economic well-being and economic expectations. The Chinese are absolutely deprived compared with Americans, but crime is relatively uncommon in China because expectations there have not been increased by constant exposure to higher standards of living.

In contrast to China, Americans at all economic levels are exposed to great wealth and are exhorted to work hard to achieve material success, which is seen as an indicator of individual worth. Thus, Americans who have higher absolute standards of living than most Chinese often see themselves as relatively disadvantaged compared with other Americans. These perceptions can generate both conventional property crime and white-collar crime. Policies that reduce the American culture's emphasis on material well-being as a sign of personal worth might reduce crime, but those policies could also undercut the motivation to pursue material success through legitimate channels and thus harm the economy by lowering the demand for consumer goods.

The Process of Social Change

Crime might be curbed by policies that minimize the disruptive effects of social change. China and Japan have both experienced internal migration and urbanization, trends commonly associated with rising crime rates. In China, migration from rural areas to large cities is carefully planned so that those who move are provided with jobs in their new communities. Japan has urbanized without increased crime rates, apparently because group pressures to conform continue to exist, and are perhaps even enhanced, in large cities. Switzerland has also avoided a high crime rate through a slow process of urbanization that has minimized the disruption of individual lives.

Countries that have experienced social change without substantial increases in their crime rates, such as China, Japan, and Switzerland, have managed to maintain traditional attachments to relatives, friends, neighbors, and others who encourage conformity to the law. This is consistent with social control theory, which proposes that crime and delinquency are less common when people have a stake in conformity and are concerned with the good opinion of those close to them.

Political Factors

China's political ideology is conducive to a low crime rate. Before the Communist Revolution in 1949, China was composed of relatively autonomous regions; today it is a more integrated nation that commands its citizens' loyalty. People are attached to an institution with authority—the state—and this bond reduces their motivation to commit crime for selfish reasons.

Japan is similar in some ways, even though its political ideology is very different. As in China, the Japanese are subordinated to the nation, the family, and the community, as well as to the company for which they work. The Japanese are greatly concerned with the good opinion of other nations and censure behavior that brings shame on the country in the eyes of the rest of the world.

Because crimes are often committed to improve the situation of the offender, crime rates will be low where people learn supraindividual goals and high where people learn to pursue individual goals. It is difficult to suggest policies that would reduce the American culture's emphasis on individualism and increase its emphasis on national goals, but it is important to recognize that individualism is conducive to a higher crime rate.

Community Ties

Crime rates are low in neighborhoods that are socially integrated, because attachments of individuals to one another reduce crime by strengthening everyone's stake in conformity. In socially integrated neighborhoods, greater surveillance of behavior can reduce crime by increasing the fear of being observed, reported, and arrested. Attachment to community is strong in Japan, China, and Switzerland, three nations with relatively low crime rates.

Programs that strengthen community ties might reduce crime rates, but it would be difficult to employ such measures in a nation such as the United States, where individualism is a strongly held value and geographic mobility is common. Crime might be curbed by implementing a program tried in Puerto Rico that created a sense of community by allowing slum residents to take charge of their own lives and by requiring offenders to work to improve their community (Silberman, 1978). Another approach is for the residents of well-to-do communities to develop "sister-neighborhood" or mentoring relationships with inner-city areas that have high crime rates. Those who control more resources can help the disadvantaged develop literacy, work, and social skills and find jobs for them. Broker organizations can recruit outside volunteers to help revitalize crime-ridden neighborhoods, but the volunteers need to feel safe in those communities and must avoid patronizing attitudes that alienate local residents. The ultimate goals of such a strategy are to develop the human capital of people living in high-crime communities and to integrate those communities into the larger society (Buerger, 1994).

The Family

The family is usually a strong institution in nations that have low crime rates. Chinese and Japanese families have traditionally had close attachments between children and their parents, whose "psychological presence" minimizes the children's tendency toward delinquency. The Chinese family is organized on a hierarchical basis, emphasizing respect for elders while providing parental affection for children. As a result, the Chinese usually have low crime rates, whether they live in China or elsewhere (Count-van Manen, 1971). The Japanese family has similar characteristics, with children being taught to be concerned about the good opinion of their family and to avoid bringing shame on it. This creates an investment in conformity and keeps children from delinquency. Swiss children also learn to be concerned about the good opinion of others and to avoid law-violating behavior that would bring public censure on themselves and their families.

In the United States, people who violate the law typically come from families that differ from Chinese, Japanese, and Swiss families. Policies might be implemented to strengthen the ability of American families to prevent delinquency and crime. The closeness of adolescents and their elders in Switzerland suggests the possibility of creating programs that integrate young people and adults in common activities (Clinard, 1978).

Early-intervention programs can reduce delinquency by providing educational daycare for preschool children and by using home visits to teach parents how to raise their children and how to use community resources to get financial assistance, pediatric care, and legal advice (Lally, Mangione, and Honig, 1998). Successful programs teach parents techniques of consistent but nonphysical discipline, train family members in communication and conflict-resolution skills, and treat entire families when one member gets into trouble with the law. One study estimates that a $1 million investment in parent-training programs would prevent 157 crimes per year, compared to only 60 that would be prevented by a similar investment in the construction and operation of prisons to house more career criminals for longer terms (Greenwood et al., 1996). Not only is early intervention cost-effective, it is also favored over the construction of more prisons by Americans of all political orientations (Cullen, Wright, and Chamlin, 1999).

Welfare reform and income tax reform might also change the family. Crime and delinquency might be reduced if the welfare system encouraged families to stay together, rather than taking a neutral stance toward family breakups, or even encouraging family dissolution in order to create eligibility for certain kinds of public assistance. The income tax system might also be redesigned to encourage family stability; for example, tax incentives to discourage divorce and to encourage employers to offer flexible work hours might lead to better supervision of children and thus reduce delinquency.

The School

In China, the family's influence is reinforced by schools and government-run play centers, which tie children to adults who have authority. Schools and play centers also reduce the time that children have available to engage in delinquency and minimize the boredom that is sometimes mentioned as a cause of delinquency in the United States. In Japan, the tremendous academic pressure on students to succeed has been cited as a cause of delinquency, although Japanese schools are quite effective in controlling students' behavior.

Delinquency can be curbed by improving academic performance through the preparation of disadvantaged children for school, the development of more structured classroom environments, and the adoption of student-centered teaching strategies. According to one study, money spent on a program that offers students incentives to graduate from high school will prevent four times as much crime as the same amount spent on more prison space for serious offenders (Greenwood et al., 1996). Reforms that tie students more closely to the school and its teachers can create a "psychological presence" that keeps young people from violating the law. Curricula should provide students with the skills to achieve legitimate success but should also be designed to fit the needs and values of the community.

Nonacademic programs might also help reduce crime. Experiences such as wilderness survival training and discussion groups with elderly people in the community might develop students' self-confidence and broaden their perspectives. Programs that strengthen a sense of personal responsibility and create empathy with others might reduce crime by undermining the ability to use techniques of neutralization to justify violations of the law. Courses and tutoring can provide students with the social and emotional skills to control their anger and jealousy, negotiate with others, avoid confrontations, and develop relationships with peers and teachers.

Discrimination

Elimination of the discrimination that denies minority groups equal access to valued opportunities would help solve the crime problem, because minorities are disproportionately involved in crime. Discrimination weakens attachment to the conventional social order, increasing the chance that the group that is discriminated against will have a high crime rate. Obstacles to voting or organizing politically deny power to minority groups and thus weaken their ties to the political system. Schools that are segregated or poorly funded provide an inadequate education and leave minorities unprepared for well-paying jobs to which they can form strong attachments. Job discrimination in which minority-group members are "the last hired and the first fired" can keep them from developing loyalty to an employer. Housing discrimination that relegates minorities to the most run-down areas of the city weakens their ties to the community.

Discrimination in education, work, and housing contributes to high poverty rates among minority groups. When poverty is combined with a cultural emphasis on material success, as it is in the United States, there is a strong motivation to commit property crime. Eliminating discrimination would increase legitimate opportunities and create bonds to the conventional order among groups with traditionally high crime rates, thus helping to reduce the overall crime rate.

Conclusion

Crime can be reduced by developing policies that enhance the social support available from families, schools, friends, employers, communities, and the government. Individuals use supportive relationships instrumentally to complete an education or get a job, and expressively to meet their needs for affection and sharing (Cullen, 1994; Colvin, Cullen, and vander Ven, 2002). Policies that foster attachments to conventional people and institutions create a stake in conformity that makes the rewards of a law-abiding way of life and the risks of criminal behavior great enough to reduce violations of the law. Harsh or certain punishment is less likely to reduce crime than policies that make it more rewarding to abide by the law.

Summary

Three approaches to solving the crime problem differ in their ideas about crime causation and their recommendations for reducing crime. The conservative approach focuses on conventional crime, which is attributed to the poor and to people who have been improperly socialized. Conservatives would solve the crime problem by using the criminal justice system to deter and incapacitate criminals. The liberal approach also focuses on conventional crime, but it proposes that it can be reduced by alleviating poverty and providing legitimate opportunities for everyone. The radical approach looks at both conventional crime and white-collar crime, which are attributed to the structure of a capitalist system. According to this perspective, only a fundamental restructuring of the social order can solve the crime problem.

In the mid-1960s, a presidential commission studied crime and recommended changes in the criminal justice system, rather than changes in social conditions, as the way to reduce crime. The LEAA was unable to reduce crime by changing the criminal justice system and was disbanded in 1981. Crime was a major issue in the 1968 and 1972 presidential campaigns, contributing to the victory of Richard Nixon in both elections. President Ronald Reagan occasionally raised the crime issue, and in 1984 he signed into law a sweeping set of reforms aimed at curbing crime. George H. W. Bush used the crime issue effectively in winning the presidency in 1988, and during his time in office he made numerous proposals to reduce crime in general and drug offenses in particular. In the 1992 and 1996 elections, neither Bill Clinton nor his opponents gained a strong advantage with their positions on the crime issue. Crime was not a decisive issue in the 2000 election, but George W. Bush did benefit from the support of the National Rifle Association.

The first of three general recommendations for reducing crime is to change the criminal justice system. One way to do this is to reduce the overreach of the criminal law, so that the limited resources can be concentrated on the most serious crimes. For years, the federal government has tried to stop the importation of drugs, but the amount of drugs entering the country does not seem to have decreased as a result.

The courts might curb crime by increasing the certainty of punishment, but it is not clear that this can be done within the constraints of existing constitutional rights. Concentrated efforts to imprison organized crime leaders have had an impact on the Mafia's criminal activities in recent years. Some have proposed that crime might be prevented if juvenile court records were more accessible to criminal court judges.

A second strategy is situational crime prevention. This involves target hardening to make buildings and property less vulnerable to theft. Self-protective measures might reduce the chance that an individual will be victimized. Strategies to increase informal social control can reduce crime, and community crime prevention has had some effect in curbing crime, especially when used in conjunction with aggressive police practices.

A third strategy is to deal with the causes of crime. Economic policies can provide offenders with work and thus attach them more strongly to the conventional social order. Crime can also be curbed by minimizing the disruptive effects of social change. Attachment to the nation can keep a country's crime rate low, as it has in China and Japan; strong ties to the local community can have the same effect. Policies that strengthen the family and teach parents how to raise law-abiding children can curb crime. Schools can reduce delinquency and crime by helping young people establish close ties to their teachers and by providing them with the skills to succeed in legitimate careers. Eliminating discrimination can cut crime by strengthening the attachment to the conventional order of minority groups that have traditionally had high crime rates. In general, providing stronger ties to conventional people and institutions is an effective strategy for solving the crime problem.

IMPORTANT TERMS

conservative approach	radical approach	target hardening
liberal approach	situational crime prevention	

REVIEW QUESTIONS

1. What are the three ideological approaches to dealing with the crime problem? How would each deal with crime?

2. What role has the crime issue played in presidential elections since the mid-1960s?

3. How can crime be reduced by reforming the criminal justice system?

4. How can situational crime prevention curb crime?

5. How can crime be reduced by dealing with economic and political factors, the process of social change, community organization, the family, the school, and racial and ethnic discrimination?

FOR FURTHER STUDY

Politics and Crime   Katherine Beckett and Theodore Sasson's *The Politics of Injustice: Crime and Punishment in America* (Thousand Oaks, CA: Pine Forge Press, 2000) explores the way that politicians have developed increasingly punitive solutions for the crime problem since the 1960s. The liberal approach to the crime problem is elo-

quently presented in Elliott Currie's *Crime and Punishment in America* (New York: Holt, 1998).

Attitudes toward Punishment   A comprehensive review of the research on Americans' attitudes toward punishment can be found in Francis T. Cullen, Bonnie S. Fisher, and Brandon K. Applegate's "Public Opinion about Punishment and Corrections" (in Michael Tonry, ed., *Crime and Justice: A Review of Research,* vol. 27. Chicago: University of Chicago Press, 2000, pp. 1–79).

Solving the Crime Problem   Solutions to the crime problem are assessed in Lawrence W. Sherman et al.'s *Pre-venting Crime: What Works, What Doesn't, What's Promising* (Washington, DC: U.S. Department of Justice, July 1998) and David P. Farrington and Brandon C. Welsh's (eds.) *What Works in Preventing Crime? Systematic Reviews of Experimental and Quasi-Experimental Research* (vol. 578 of the *Annals of the American Academy of Political and Social Science,* Thousand Oaks, CA: Sage, 2001).

GLOSSARY

Age-specific arrest rate   The number of arrests per 100,000 people in a given age category.

Aggravated assault   An unlawful attack by one person on another in which the purpose is to inflict severe bodily injury and in which a weapon typically is used.

Aggregate   People who happen to be in the same place at the same time but who do not interact much and have no sense of common identity.

Amenability issue   The possibility that certain kinds of offenders are suited to a particular type of treatment.

Anomie   Normlessness, or a disjunction between institutionalized means and culturally approved goals.

Antisocial personality disorder   A pervasive pattern of disregard for, and violation of, the rights of others that begins in childhood or early adolescence and continues into adulthood. (American Psychiatric Association definition)

Appeal to higher loyalties   A technique of neutralization that justifies a violation of the law by the demands of a group that is smaller than the whole society but requires its members to conform to standards that may be incompatible with the law.

Argot   A specialized language that creates solidarity by differentiating a group from outsiders.

Arson   The willful burning of the building, motor vehicle, aircraft, or personal property of another person.

Assault   An unlawful attack by one person on another.

Atavism   A person "born out of time" and similar to primitive people or lower animals in his or her biological makeup; the basis of Lombroso's theory of the "born criminal."

Attention-deficit hyperactivity disorder (ADHD)   A syndrome characterized by inattention (failure to listen and to complete tasks), impulsivity (acting without thinking), and hyperactivity (restlessness and excessive motor activity).

Bail system   A procedure allowing pretrial release but designed to ensure that a defendant will show up to face charges when the trial is scheduled.

Behavior modification   A treatment program that tries to change behavior, rather than personality, by rewarding desirable actions and punishing undesirable ones.

Biographical method   A research strategy in which the experiences of a single individual are examined in detail.

Boot camp   A military-style program designed to scare offenders away from crime by subjecting them to harsh discipline, rigorous exercise, and strenuous work.

Brawner rule   The legal rule that a person will be found not guilty by reason of insanity if at the time of such conduct as a result of mental disease or mental defect, he lacks substantial capacity either to appreciate the criminality of his conduct or to conform his conduct to the requirements of the law.

Broken windows theory   The theory that social and physical disorder gives rise to crime.

Bureaucracy   A formal organization that is rationally organized to pursue goals in an efficient manner.

Burglary   Unlawful entry into a building to commit a serious crime, usually the theft of property.

Business organization   A permanent structure that profits from extortion and the provision of illegal goods and services; more commonly called "organized crime."

Cartography   An approach to the study of crime that uses official data to map or chart patterns of crime.

Case attrition   A funnel or sieve effect that characterizes the criminal justice system, with cases being sorted out as they proceed through the system and with relatively few crimes ending with a perpetrator's conviction and imprisonment.

Casework   A treatment program designed to help offenders cope with specific problems they face.

Certification   The social verification by the criminal justice system or by conventional people that an offender is rehabilitated.

Chronic offender   A person who has violated the law frequently; criminologists vary in their definition of "frequently" from a minimum of three to a minimum of nine offenses.

Classical school   An approach to crime that emphasizes free will and the deterrence of criminal behavior by the fear of punishment.

Clearance rate   The proportion of cases the police solve to their satisfaction.

Cognitive-behavioral programs   Treatment programs that seek to change what and how offenders think and thereby alter their behavioral choices, especially their decision to commit crime.

Cohort   A carefully defined group of people who are in a common situation at one time.

Collective efficacy   A combination of social cohesion and willingness to intervene on behalf of the common good by supervising children and maintaining public order.

Community policing   An approach that establishes two-way communication between citizens and the police through foot patrols, decentralized operations, storefront stations, community organizations, crime newsletters, and contacts with people at home and at work.

Comparative research   A research strategy that looks at crime in societies with different cultures and social structures.

Compensation   A system in which the state repays crime victims for their financial losses or physical injuries.

Computer crime   Any violation of the law in which a computer is the target or the means.

Concentric-zone model   A model of metropolitan areas based on concentric rings with distinctive characteristics.

Concordance rate   A measure of the similarity of criminal behavior that is used in studies of twins.

Condemnation of the condemners   A technique of neutralization asserting that it is the motives and behavior of the people who are condemning the offender, rather than the motives and behavior of the offender, that should be condemned.

Conduct disorder   A repetitive and persistent pattern of behavior in which the basic rights of others or major age-appropriate social norms or rules are violated. (American Psychiatric Association definition)

Conflict perspective   An approach that sees the criminal law as closely intertwined with the distribution of political power and economic resources in a society.

Conformity   A mode of adaptation in which both cultural goals and the institutionalized means to reach those goals are accepted.

Consensus perspective   An approach that sees the criminal law as representing social consensus or agreement about what kinds of behavior should be punished by the state.

Conservative approach   An approach that seeks to preserve the status quo from criminals, who are seen as challengers to the existing social order.

Containment theory   The theory that people are insulated to various degrees against pressures to commit deviant acts by external and internal factors.

Contingency   A factor that determines movement from one criminal role to another, or from one crime to another.

Control balance theory   A theory that explains crime in terms of the ratio between the control imposed on an individual by others and the control an individual exercises over others; people who have either a control deficit or a control surplus are the most likely to engage in predatory crime.

Costs related to criminal violence   The financial losses that result from violent crimes in which victims are physically hurt.

Craft organization   A small and relatively permanent group of two or three thieves or confidence tricksters, each of whom plays a well-defined role in the specific type of crime that the group commits.

Crime   An act that violates the criminal law and is punishable by the state.

Crime index   The sum of eight offenses defined by the FBI as serious crimes.

Crime rate   The number of reported crimes divided by the number of people in an area, often expressed as a rate of crimes per 100,000 people.

Criminal career   A sequence of criminal acts carried out over time by one person.

Criminal intent   The willed or conscious desire to commit an act that violates a criminal law.

Criminal propensity theory   The theory that crime is the result of causal traits that remain relatively constant over the life course.

Criminology   A discipline that gathers and analyzes empirical data to explain violations of the criminal law and societal reactions to those violations.

Cultural criminology   The study of the way that crime and crime control are given meaning by popular culture, especially the media, both as political and social issues and as entertainment.

Dark figure   The number of crimes that actually occur but are not recorded by the police.

Defensible space   The subdivision and design of housing to allow residents to distinguish stranger from neighbor and thus elicit a sense of territoriality, which can reduce crime by informal social control.

Delinquent gang   A gang that has a tight primary group structure and is organized to carry out specific profitable crimes.

Denial of injury   The technique of neutralization that claims no one is hurt by an offender's crime, even if it technically violates the law.

Denial of responsibility   The technique of neutralization that involves the denial of personal responsibility for actions that violate the criminal law.

Denial of the victim   The technique of neutralization that claims a crime is justified as a rightful retaliation against the victim.

Determinate sentencing   A system using fixed terms of imprisonment, which can sometimes be reduced by credit for good behavior while incarcerated.

Deterrence   The inhibition of criminal activity by state-imposed penalties.

Developmental criminology   The study of changes in offending within individuals over time; it acknowledges both continuity and change over time, explaining patterns of offending in terms of the life transitions experienced by individuals and the developmental processes of activation, aggravation, and desistance.

Differential association theory   The theory that crime and delinquency are learned in face-to-face interaction and occur when there is an excess of definitions favorable to violation of the law over definitions unfavorable to violation of the law.

Differential identification theory   The theory that people engage in criminal or delinquent behavior because they identify with real or imaginary persons from whose perspective their crime or delinquency seems acceptable.

Differential opportunity theory   A theory of delinquency that focuses on the discrepancy between aspirations and access to both legitimate and illegitimate means to reach those goals.

Diffusion of responsibility   The phenomenon that manifests itself among groups of witnesses to an emergency or a crime, as a result of which people say that someone should act but that it need not be they because other potential helpers are present.

Direct loss   The result of a crime in which the stock of useful things is reduced, as in arson or vandalism.

Directed patrol   The strategic redeployment of police resources based on analysis of crime statistics.

Discretion   The use of judgment to decide what action to take.

Displacement effect   A change in the pattern of crime without a reduction in the total amount of crime, resulting from criminals' efforts to avoid punishment; displacement may be from one target to another, from one area to another, or from one kind of offense to another.

Doing gender   The idea that through their social behavior men develop and act out forms of masculinity, or masculinities, while women develop and act out forms of femininity, or femininities.

Drift   A condition of limbo between a conventional lifestyle and a criminal lifestyle, with no strong attachment to either.

EFT crime   Any violation of the law involving an electronic fund transfer system.

Enforcement costs   The financial cost of crime that results from money spent on various criminal justice agencies.

Excuse   A defense to a criminal charge that denies criminal intent.

Exiting   A successful disengagement from a previous pattern of criminal behavior.

Experiment   A controlled study in which people are treated in different ways to determine the effects of that treatment on their attitudes and behavior.

Facilitating factors   Factors that increase the chance that a situation will lead to criminal violence or theft.

Family intervention   A program designed to improve communication and the expression of feelings within the family, change patterns of behavior within the family, or alter the way that parents manage their children.

Focal concern   A value or area of interest that elicits widespread, persistent attention and emotional involvement.

Forcible rape   Carnal knowledge of a female forcibly and against her will (FBI definition); some states define forcible rape in sex-neutral terms.

Formal organization   A large, complex secondary group that is deliberately created to achieve certain goals.

Formal social control   An effort to bring about conformity to the law by agents of the criminal justice system such as the police, the courts, and correctional institutions.

Fraud   The crime of obtaining money or property by false pretenses.

Gender ratio problem   The issue of why males commit more crime than females.

Gender structure   The institutional arrangements that treat men and women, and boys and girls, differently.

General deterrence The inhibition of the desire to engage in crime among the general population through the punishment of certain offenders.

General strain theory An expanded version of anomie theory that focuses on both positive and negative sources of strain, the various dimensions of strain, strategies for coping with strain, and factors that determine whether strain will be handled in a delinquent or nondelinquent fashion.

Generalizability problem The question of whether theories of crime, most of which were developed to explain offending by men and tested on male subjects, can be applied to crime by women.

Good Samaritan problem The issue of how bystanders respond to emergencies such as crimes.

Group A set of relationships among people who interact face-to-face over time.

Group counseling A treatment program that allows several inmates to be treated at the same time and at a low cost. It involves the discussion of feelings and attitudes in an effort to create mutual acceptance and a supportive environment.

Hate crime A criminal offense committed against a person, property, or society that is motivated in whole or in part by the offender's bias against a race, religion, disability, sexual orientation, or ethnicity/national origin. (FBI definition)

Historical research A research strategy that examines the same society at different times and looks at the way crime has changed as a result of economic and social development.

Illegal expenditures The costs of crimes that divert money from the legitimate economy and represent a loss of potential revenue for people who produce and supply legal goods and services.

Incapacitation The custodial control of convicted offenders so that they cannot commit crimes that affect the general public.

Incidence The frequency with which offenders commit crime, or the average number of offenses per offender, measured by dividing the number of offenses by the number of offenders.

Indeterminate sentencing A penalty imposed under a system that establishes long maximum sentences for different crimes and allows judges to impose any penalty up to the maximum; sentences are often a range of years to be served in prison, with parole boards determining actual release dates.

Individual therapy A method of treatment commonly used in prison in which psychiatrists, psychologists, or psychiatric social workers help offenders solve psychological problems that are thought to be the cause of criminal behavior.

Informal social control The reactions of individuals and groups that bring about conformity to norms and laws; they include peer and community pressure, bystander intervention in a crime, and collective responses such as citizen patrol groups.

Innovation The mode of adaptation in which cultural goals are accepted, but means are used that society regards as unacceptable.

Intensive offender A person whose criminal activity begins at an early age and is sustained over time, consciously planned, persistent, skilled, and frequent.

Intermittent offender A person who engages in irregular and opportunistic crimes with low payoffs and great risks but does not think of himself or herself as a professional criminal.

Intimate partner violence Murder, rape, robbery, or assault by current or former spouses, cohabiting partners, or dates.

Just deserts The idea that offenders should be punished because they deserve to suffer for the harm they have caused.

Justification A defense to a criminal charge that the law allows a person to act in a particular way due to force of circumstances.

Juvenile delinquent A person below a legally specified age who has been adjudged by a juvenile court to have violated the law or committed a juvenile status offense.

Labeling perspective The perspective on deviant behavior that emphasizes the effects of a socially imposed label on a person who breaks a social rule.

Larceny The unlawful taking, carrying, leading, or riding away of property from the possession of another.

Law A norm that is written down and formalized by the political system.

Learning disabilities An impairment in sensory and motor functioning that leads to deviant classroom performance.

Left realism A conflict theory emphasizing the impact that crime by the lower and working class has on other members of the same class and proposing a variety of pragmatic crime-reduction strategies.

Lex talionis The principle of "an eye for an eye, a tooth for a tooth."

Liberal approach The perspective that crime can be reduced by attacking its underlying causes through social reforms.

Life-course perspective   An approach that examines delinquency and crime in terms of patterns of change and continuity of behavior between childhood and adulthood.

Lifestyle theory   The theory that individuals who commit violent offenses and property crimes, abuse drugs and alcohol, spend more time on the streets, and associate with deviant peers are themselves exposed to a high risk of victimization.

Machismo   The concept of maleness as overly aggressive, dominant, and strong behavior.

McNaghten rule   The legal rule stating that a person will be found not guilty by reason of insanity if at the time of the crime the person was under a defect of reason so as to be unable either to know the nature and the quality of the act or, if the person was aware of the nature of the act, to know that wrong was being done.

Mandatory minimum sentence   A legal requirement that an offender who commits a particular crime be sentenced to at least a specified amount of time in prison.

Marginal deterrent effect   The extent to which crime rates respond to incremental changes in the threat of sanctions.

Marxist or radical criminology   A conflict theory that focuses on social class, defined by the relationship of a group to the means of production, and claims that capitalists, who own and control the means of production, use the law to protect their property from those who threaten it, namely, the lower and working classes.

Master status   The situation in which other aspects of a person's behavior become submerged in a particular social identity, such as that of a deviant.

Mechanical solidarity   A unity based on shared values and norms and on the similarity of functions performed by all members of the society.

Milieu therapy   A treatment method that introduces the idea of rehabilitation into all aspects of an institution, including relations between inmates and staff members.

Mode of adaptation   A way that persons who occupy a particular social position adapt to cultural goals and the institutionalized means to reach those goals.

Mood disorder   A form of serious mental illness that includes depressive disorders (unipolar depression) and bipolar disorders (manic or mixed episodes followed by major depressive episodes).

Motor vehicle theft   The theft of an automobile, truck, bus, or other type of vehicle.

Murder and nonnegligent manslaughter   The willful killing of a human being.

Network   Ties among individual members of groups or among different groups.

Norm   A rule that makes explicit certain social expectations about what is appropriate behavior for a particular person in a specific situation.

Obscene material   Material, often pornographic in nature, that has been declared illegal because it poses a threat to the state or to organized religion, violates common morality, has no redeeming social value, or appeals to the prurient or lascivious interest.

Observation   A research strategy that involves the careful and systematic watching of behavior.

Organic solidarity   A unity based on an interdependence of functions, much as in a complex biological organism.

Organized crime   Criminal activity by an enduring structure or organization developed and devoted primarily to the pursuit of profits through illegal means (see *Business organization*).

Parole   A system in which inmates are released before they complete their full sentences and are then supervised in the community and sent back to prison if they violate the conditions of their release.

Patterns of crime   A research strategy that involves the use of data to determine where crime is committed, who commits crime, who is victimized, and what are the major dimensions of the criminal act.

Peacemaking criminology   A humanistic approach that regards crime as the product of a social structure that disadvantages some groups, sets people against one another, and generates a desire for revenge.

Picaresque organization   A relatively permanent gang under the leadership of a single person who sometimes relies on the support and advice of a few officers.

Plea bargaining   An informal but structured process of negotiation in which the prosecutor and the defense attorney agree on a guilty plea and the sentence that the prosecutor will recommend to the judge.

Pluralistic ignorance   A situation in which witnesses in a group fail to help the victim of an emergency or a crime because they interpret the failure of other witnesses to help as a sign that no help is needed.

Pornography   Material that is intended to arouse people sexually by portraying sexual matters in visual or verbal terms.

Positivism A perspective that relies on the scientific method to quantify and measure behavior and the social conditions associated with behavior.

Power-control theory The theory that the class structure of the family explains the social distribution of delinquent behavior through the social reproduction of gender relations.

Premenstrual syndrome (PMS) A set of symptoms associated with the onset of menstruation, including tension, nervousness, irritability, fatigue, headaches, cramps, and depressed moods.

Pretrial diversion A program that allows a district attorney to recommend to a judge that a criminal proceeding be suspended while a suspect participates in a treatment program.

Prevalence A measure of the proportion of a population that commits crime in a given period, arrived at by dividing the number of offenders by the size of the population.

Prevention and protection costs The financial costs of crimes that result from expenditures on alarm systems, spotlights, locks, bars, and other "target-hardening" devices, as well as the money that people spend on insurance premiums to cover their losses through theft.

Preventive detention A system in which some defendants are held without bail while awaiting trial.

Primary deviation An initial act of deviance that has not been socially labeled as deviant.

Primary group A small and relatively permanent group characterized by intimate relationships.

Proactive police work Police efforts to discover and deal with crime on their own initiative.

Probation A form of supervised release imposed by judges on convicted offenders, in which they serve no time in jail or prison.

Problem-oriented policing An approach that assumes the police should deal with the underlying conditions that generate crime and should cooperate with citizens to attack local crime problems.

Professional thief A skilled offender who is committed to crime as an occupation and thinks of himself or herself as a criminal.

Project organization A group of several criminals who come together to commit one or a series of acts of robbery, burglary, fraud, or smuggling.

Protective neighboring A combination of cooperative surveillance and willingness to intervene in a crime by the residents of a community.

Racial profiling The prediction that an individual is more likely to violate the law if he or she is a member of a particular racial or ethnic group.

Radical approach A perspective that focuses on crime by both the underprivileged and the privileged, and attributes crime by both groups to the conditions of a capitalist society.

Radical nonintervention A policy to minimize official reaction to delinquency in order to prevent the labeling of adolescents that could drive them into criminal careers.

Rape See *Forcible rape*

Rational-choice perspective A reward-risk model that emphasizes offenders' strategic thinking and the ways that they process information and evaluate opportunities and alternatives.

Reaction-formation A repudiation of goals that a person emotionally supports but cannot attain, such as a reversal of middle-class goals by lower- or working-class delinquents.

Reactive police work Police response to a citizen's report of a crime.

Rebellion A mode of adaptation in which people reject cultural goals and develop a new set of goals, rejecting institutionalized means to reach cultural goals and developing a new set of means; behavior in which a person seeks to create a new social structure that will more effectively allow people to meet what the rebel considers appropriate goals.

Recidivism rate The percentage of offenders who, during a specific period after their treatment has ended, are arrested and convicted of new offenses or have their punishment made more restrictive because they have failed to meet the conditions of a less restrictive sentence.

Rehabilitation The restoration of criminals to a law-abiding way of life through treatment; the result of any planned intervention focused on the offender that reduces criminal activity.

Reintegrative shaming A process that follows expressions of community disapproval of an offender's behavior with gestures of reacceptance by the larger law-abiding community.

Relative deprivation The discrepancy between people's expectations about certain goods and conditions of life to which they are rightfully entitled and their capabilities, or the actual goods and conditions of life they believe they can attain and maintain under the current social system.

Restitution A system that requires offenders to make monetary payments or provide services, either to the victim or to the community at large.

Restorative justice A response to crime that seeks to reintegrate offenders while also attending to the rights of victims.

Retreatism A mode of adaptation in which cultural goals are abandoned and institutionalized means are also rejected.

Retribution The idea that offenders should be punished because they deserve to suffer for the harm they have caused.

Ritualism A mode of adaptation in which cultural goals are scaled down or given up, while norms about the institutionalized means to reach cultural goals are accepted.

Robbery The theft of property from another person by force or threat of force.

Routine activities theory A perspective that sees crime as a function of people's everyday behavior and stresses motivated offenders, target suitability, and guardianship.

Sanction An effort to ensure future conformity to a norm and punish past nonconformity.

Schizophrenia A serious mental disorder that involves delusions, hallucinations, disorganized speech, grossly disorganized or catatonic behavior, and negative symptoms such as affective flattening and lack of speech or will.

Secondary deviation Deviant behavior that is the result of the labeling process.

Secondary group A group that is usually larger, more complex, and less intimate than a primary group.

Selective incapacitation A system of predictive restraint that holds only those offenders who are the most likely to commit more crime if released.

Self-report study Research that measures crime by having respondents report their own violations in confidential interviews or on anonymous self-administered questionnaires.

Sense of inequity The belief that one's social position is not as great relative to one's efforts as the social positions and efforts of other people.

Sentence disparity The difference in the criminal sanctions that are handed out to people who are convicted of similar offenses and who have similar criminal records.

Sentencing guidelines A system that defines a range of penalties for offenses of a given degree of harmfulness committed by offenders of a specific degree of blameworthiness (usually measured by prior criminal record).

Serious and violent juvenile (SVJ) offender A juvenile who has committed one or more of the following crimes: homicide, voluntary manslaughter, rape or attempted rape, robbery, aggravated assault, arson of an occupied building, or kidnapping.

Simple assault An unlawful attack by one person on another in which no weapon is used and no serious injury results.

Simultaneity A reciprocal cause-and-effect relationship between two variables; for instance, sanctions by the criminal justice system may affect the crime rate, but the crime rate may also affect the sanctions that are handed out by the criminal justice system.

Situational crime prevention Measures that involve the management, design, or manipulation of the environment in order to reduce opportunities for crime and increase the perceived risks of committing crime.

Social class Social standing based on economic resources, occupational prestige, political power, or lifestyle.

Social construction of crime The way that groups with different interests they seek to promote interpret or give meaning to crime by using their resources to gain ownership of an issue.

Social control A process that brings about conformity to society's norms and laws.

Social control theory The theory that people who engage in crime or delinquency are relatively free of intimate attachments, aspirations, and moral beliefs that bind them to a conventional and law-abiding way of life.

Social gang A gang that has a group identity, a relatively permanent structure, informal leadership based on popularity, and intimate interaction among members.

Social learning theory The theory that people learn attitudes and techniques conducive to crime in both nonsocial and social situations from positive reinforcement (rewards) and negative reinforcement (punishments) that result from their own behavior, whether that behavior is criminal or law-abiding.

Social structure Recurrent, stable patterns of interaction among people.

Social structure and social learning (SSSL) theory A theory that links social learning theory to various social-structural variables.

Somatotype A body type that results from embryonic development and is thought to be associated with a particular temperament and propensity to crime and delinquency.

Specific deterrence The effect of a penalty that causes an individual who is punished for a crime not to commit that crime again because his or her reward-risk calculations have been altered by the punishment.

Status offense An act defined as unacceptable for people below a given age and used as a basis for juvenile court proceedings; included are underage drinking, running away from home, and truancy.

Strain The frustration and sense of injustice that result from experiencing socially structured incapacities as low capabilities.

Subculture A patterned way of life both similar to, and different from, the dominant culture of a society.

Subculture-of-violence theory The theory that the norms shared by a group of people may define violence as an appropriate response to certain circumstances and lead members of the group to engage in violent crime in order to conform to others' expectations.

Subterranean value A value or ideal that is subordinate or below the surface in the dominant value system and is sought by most people only occasionally and in appropriate circumstances.

Survey A research strategy in which a sample of people who are representative of a larger population are asked a series of prepared questions.

Target hardening A policy of reducing opportunities for crime by making it more difficult for offenders to carry out crimes against particular targets.

Technique of neutralization A justification used prior to a crime by an offender to render inoperative the social controls that would otherwise check law-violating behavior.

Temporal boundary conception of the criminal career A perspective that looks at the age at which criminal activity begins, the length of time over which it occurs, the kinds of crime an individual commits, and the age at which criminal activity ceases.

Terrorism Violence against innocent civilians that is designed to produce a powerful psychological impact on an audience far broader than those directly affected, in pursuit of a political, messianic, or vengeful goal.

Transfer of property The cost of crimes in which property is transferred from one person to another, such as from the victim of a theft to the thief.

Truth-in-sentencing A system that requires offenders to serve a certain percentage of their sentence (usually 85 percent) in prison.

Tutelage Instruction or socialization in criminal motives and skills, including how to spot opportunities for, plan, and carry out thefts.

Typology A set of categories.

Vandalism The willful or malicious destruction, injury, disfigurement, or defacement of property without consent of the owner.

Vengeance A private and personal response to a wrong; it does not involve an established authority such as the state.

Victim compensation See *Compensation*

Victim impact statement A detailed written report based on an interview with a victim about the effects of a crime on him or her.

Victim precipitation The situation that exists when a person who suffers eventual harm from a crime plays a direct role in causing the crime to be perpetrated.

Victim proneness The tendency for certain people to be victimized repeatedly.

Victimization survey A systematic effort to measure the experiences of the victims of crime by interviewing a cross section of a population.

Victimless crime An offense that is consensual and lacks a complaining participant.

Violent gang A fighting gang that emerges spontaneously to defend a territory against rival gangs, often resorting to violence over trivial provocations.

White-collar crime An illegal act, punishable by a criminal sanction, that is committed in the course of a legitimate occupation or pursuit by a corporation or by an otherwise respectable individual of high social status.

BIBLIOGRAPHY

Adler, Freda. *Nations Not Obsessed with Crime.* Littleton, CO: Rothman, 1983.

———. *Sisters in Crime: The Rise of the New Female Criminal.* New York: McGraw-Hill, 1975.

———. "Socioeconomic Variables Influencing Jury Verdicts," *New York University Review of Law on Social Change* 3 (1973), 16–36.

Adler, Patricia A. *Wheeling and Dealing: An Ethnography of an Upper-Level Drug Dealing and Smuggling Community,* 2d ed. New York: Columbia University Press, 1993.

———, and Peter Adler. "Shifts and Oscillations in Deviant Careers: The Case of Upper-Level Drug Dealers and Smugglers," *Social Problems* 31 (December 1983), 195–207.

Ageton, Suzanne S., and Delbert S. Elliott. "The Effects of Legal Processing on Self-Concept." Boulder, CO: Institute of Behavioral Science, 1973.

Agnew, Robert. "Adolescent Resources and Delinquency," *Criminology* 28 (November 1990), 535–566.

———. "Building on the Foundation of General Strain Theory: Specifying the Types of Strain Most Likely to Lead to Crime and Delinquency," *Journal of Research in Crime and Delinquency* 38 (November 2001), 319–361.

———. "Foundation for a General Strain Theory of Crime and Delinquency," *Criminology* 30 (February 1992), 47–87.

———. "A Longitudinal Test of Social Control Theory and Delinquency," *Journal of Research in Crime and Delinquency* 28 (May 1991), 126–156.

———. "Social Control Theory and Delinquency: A Longitudinal Test," *Criminology* 23 (February 1985), 47–61.

———. "The Techniques of Neutralization and Violence," *Criminology* 32 (November 1994), 555–580.

———. "Why Do They Do It? An Examination of the Intervening Mechanisms between 'Social Control' Variables and Delinquency," *Journal of Research in Crime and Delinquency* 30 (August 1993), 245–266.

———, and Helene Raskin White. "An Empirical Test of General Strain Theory," *Criminology* 30 (November 1992), 475–499.

———, et al. "A New Test of Classic Strain Theory," *Justice Quarterly* 13 (December 1996), 681–704.

———, et al. "Strain, Personality Traits, and Delinquency: Extending General Strain Theory," *Criminology* 40 (February 2002), 43–71.

Akers, Ronald L. *Criminological Theories: Introduction and Evaluation,* 2d ed. Los Angeles: Roxbury, 1997.

———. *Social Learning and Social Structure: A General Theory of Crime and Deviance.* Boston: Northeastern University Press, 1998.

Albini, Joseph L. *The American Mafia: Genesis of a Legend.* New York: Appleton-Century-Crofts, 1971.

Albonetti, Celesta A. "Sentencing under the Federal Sentencing Guidelines: Effects of Defendant Characteristics, Guilty Pleas, and Departures on Sentence Outcomes for Drug Offenses, 1991–1992," *Law and Society Review* 31 (1997), 789–822.

Albrecht, Hans-Joerg. "Minorities, Crime, and Criminal Justice in the Federal Republic of Germany," in Ineke Haen Marshall, ed., *Minorities, Migrants, and Crime: Diversity and Similarity Across Europe and the United States.* Thousand Oaks, CA: Sage, 1997, pp. 86–109.

Alder, Christine. "An Exploration of Self-Reported Sexually Aggressive Behavior," *Crime and Delinquency* 31 (April 1985), 306–331.

Allen, Francis A. "Criminal Justice, Legal Values and the Rehabilitative Ideal," in Stanley E. Grupp, ed., *Theories of Punishment.* Bloomington: Indiana University Press, 1971, pp. 317–330.

Allen, Vernon L., and David B. Greenberger. "An Aesthetic Theory of Vandalism," *Crime and Delinquency* 24 (July 1978), 309–321.

American Friends Service Committee. *Struggle for Justice: A Report on Crime and Punishment in America.* New York: Hill and Wang, 1971.

American Psychiatric Association. *Diagnostic and Statistical Manual of Mental Disorders,* 4th ed. Washington, DC: American Psychiatric Association, 1994.

Amir, Menachem. *Patterns in Forcible Rape.* Chicago: University of Chicago Press, 1971.

Andelman, David A. "City Crime Wave Spreading to Suburbs," *New York Times,* January 30, 1972, p. 49.

Andenaes, Johannes. *Punishment and Deterrence.* Ann Arbor: University of Michigan Press, 1974.

Andrews, D. A., et al. "Does Correctional Treatment Work? A Clinically Relevant and Psychologically Informed Meta-Analysis," *Criminology* 28 (August 1990a), 369–404.

———, et al. "A Human Science Approach or More Punishment and Pessimism: A Rejoinder to Lab and Whitehead," *Criminology* 28 (August 1990b), 419–429.

Angel, Arthur, et al. "Preventive Detention: An Empirical Analysis," *Harvard Civil Rights Civil Liberties Law Review* 6 (March 1971), 300–396.

Angier, Natalie. "Maybe It's Not a Gene behind a Person's Thrill-Seeking Ways," *New York Times,* November 1, 1996a, p. A22.

———. "Variant Gene Tied to a Love of New Thrills," *New York Times,* January 2, 1996b, pp. A1, B11.

Anglin, M. Douglas, and George Speckart. "Narcotics Use and Crime: A Multisample, Multimethod Analysis," *Criminology* 26 (May 1988), 197–233.

Apospori, Eleni, and Geoffrey Alpert. "Research Note: The Role of Differential Experience with the Criminal Justice System in Changes in Perceptions of Severity of Legal Sanctions over Time," *Crime and Delinquency* 39 (April 1993), 184–194.

Applegate, Brandon K., et al. "Assessing Public Support for Three-Strikes-and-You're-Out Laws: Global versus Specific Attitudes," *Crime and Delinquency* 42 (October 1996), 517–534.

Arbuthnot, J., D. A. Gordon, and G. J. Jurkovic, "Personality," in H. C. Quay, ed., *Handbook of Juvenile Delinquency.* New York: Wiley, 1987, pp. 139–183.

Archer, Dane, and Rosemary Gartner. *Violence and Crime in Cross-National Perspective.* New Haven, CT: Yale University Press, 1984.

Archer, Dane, Rosemary Gartner, and Marc Beittel. "Homicide and the Death Penalty: A Cross-National Test of a Deterrence Hypothesis," *Journal of Criminal Law and Criminology* 74 (Fall 1983), 991–1013.

Archer, John, ed. *Male Violence.* London: Routledge, 1994a.

————. "Violence between Men," in John Archer, ed., *Male Violence.* London: Routledge, 1994b.

Arms, Robert L., Gordon W. Russell, and Mark L. Sandilands. "Effects of Viewing Aggressive Sports on the Hostility of Spectators," *Social Psychology Quarterly* 42 (September 1979), 275–279.

Armstrong, K. G. "The Retributivist Hits Back," in Stanley E. Grupp, ed., *Theories of Punishment.* Bloomington: Indiana University Press, 1971, pp. 19–40.

Attorney General's Commission on Pornography. *Final Report.* Washington, DC: U.S. Department of Justice, 1986.

Austin, James. "Sentencing Guidelines: A State Perspective," *National Institute of Justice Journal,* March 1998, pp. 25–26.

Austin, Roy L. "Women's Liberation and Increases in Minor, Major, and Occupational Offenses," *Criminology* 20 (November 1982), 407–430.

————, and Mark D. Allen. "Racial Disparity in Arrest Rates as an Explanation of Racial Disparity in Commitment to Pennsylvania's Prisons," *Journal of Research in Crime and Delinquency* 37 (May 2000), 200–220.

Bacon, Margaret K., Irvin L. Child, and Herbert Barry 3d. "A Cross-Cultural Study of Correlates of Crime," *Journal of Abnormal and Social Psychology* 66 (April 1963), 291–300.

Baier, Colin J., and Bradley R. E. Wright. "'If You Love Me, Keep My Commandments': A Meta-Analysis of the Effect of Religion on Crime," *Journal of Research in Crime and Delinquency* 38 (February 2001), 3–21.

Bailey, Walter C. "An Evaluation of 100 Studies of Correctional Outcome," *Journal of Criminal Law, Criminology and Police Science* 57 (June 1966), 153–160.

Bailey, William C. "Murder, Capital Punishment, and Television: Execution Publicity and Homicide Rates," *American Sociological Review* 55 (October 1990), 628–633.

————, and Ruth D. Peterson. "Murder and Capital Punishment: A Monthly Time-Series Analysis of Execution Publicity," *American Sociological Review* 54 (October 1989), 722–743.

Baker, Wayne E., and Robert R. Faulkner. "The Social Organization of Conspiracy: Illegal Networks in the Heavy Electrical Equipment Industry," *American Sociological Review* 58 (December 1993), 837–860.

Barkley, Russell A. *Attention Deficit Hyperactivity Disorder: A Handbook for Diagnosis and Treatment.* New York: Guilford Press, 1990.

————. "Attention-Deficit/Hyperactivity Disorder," in Eric J. Mash and Russell A. Barkley, eds., *Child Psychopathology.* New York: Guilford Press, 1996, pp. 63–112.

Barlow, Melissa Hickman, David E. Barlow, and Theodore Chiricos. "Economic Conditions and Ideologies of Crime in the Media: A Content Analysis of Crime News," *Crime and Delinquency* 41 (January 1995), 3–19.

Barnett, Randy E. "Restitution: A New Paradigm of Criminal Justice," in Randy E. Barnett and John Hagel 3d, eds., *Assessing the Criminal: Restitution, Retribution, and the Legal Process.* Cambridge, MA: Ballinger, 1977, pp. 349–383.

Baron, Stephen W., Leslie W. Kennedy, and David R. Forde. "Male Street Youths' Conflict: The Role of Background, Subcultural, and Situational Factors," *Justice Quarterly* 18 (December 2001), 759–789.

Barr, Robert, and Ken Pease. "Crime Placement, Displacement and Deflection," in Michael Tonry and Norval Morris, eds., *Crime and Justice: A Review of Research,* vol. 12. Chicago: University of Chicago Press, 1990, pp. 277–318.

Barry, Dan. "Separating Fakes from 9/11 Victims," *New York Times,* December 31, 2002, pp. A1, A18.

Barry, Ellen. "Study Links Past Abuse, Gene to Violent Acts," *Boston Globe,* August 2, 2002, p. A2.

Barstow, David. "Hoping to Escape Life Term, Officer Admits Man's Torture," *New York Times,* May 26, 1999, pp. A1, C25.

Bartusch, Dawn R. Jeglum, et al. "Is Age Important? Testing a General versus a Developmental Theory of Antisocial Behavior," *Criminology* 35 (February 1997), 13–48.

Baskin, Deborah R., and Ira B. Sommers. *Casualties of Community Disorder: Women's Careers in Violent Crime.* Boulder, CO: Westview, 1998.

Bass, Alison. "How Jocks View Women: Old Issue Gets New Scrutiny," *Boston Globe,* December 5, 1994, pp. 39, 52.

————. "Mental State No Sure Bet for Insanity Defense," *Boston Globe,* January 9, 1995, p. 4.

Bastian, Lisa D. *Criminal Victimization 1993.* Washington, DC: U.S. Department of Justice, May 1995.

Baumrind, Diana. "Parental Disciplinary Patterns and Social Competence in Children," *Youth and Society* 9 (1978), 239–276.

Bayley, David H. "Police: History," in Sanford H. Kadish, ed., *Encyclopedia of Crime and Justice,* vol. 3. New York: Free Press, 1983, pp. 1120–1125.

Beccaria, Cesare. *On Crimes and Punishments.* Indianapolis: Bobbs-Merrill, 1764/1963.

Beck, Allen J., Jennifer C. Karberg, and Paige M. Harrison. *Prison and Jail Inmates at Midyear 2001.* Washington, DC: U.S. Department of Justice, April 2002.

Beck, Allen, et al. *Survey of State Prison Inmates, 1991.* Washington, DC: U.S. Department of Justice, March 1993.

Becker, Howard S. *Outsiders: Studies in the Sociology of Deviance.* New York: Free Press, 1973.

Bedau, Hugo Adam. "Concessions to Retribution in Punishment," in J. B. Cederblom and William L. Blizek, eds., *Justice and Punishment.* Cambridge, MA: Ballinger, 1977, pp. 51–73.

———. "Review of Walter Berns, *For Capital Punishment: Crime and the Morality of the Death Penalty,*" *Ethics* 90 (April 1980), 457–466.

Behn, Noel. *Big Stick-Up at Brinks!* New York: G. P. Putnam's Sons, 1977.

Bell, Daniel. "Crime as an American Way of Life: A Queer Ladder of Social Mobility," in *The End of Ideology: On the Exhaustion of Political Ideas in the Fifties,* rev. ed. New York: Free Press, 1962, pp. 127–150.

Bellair, Paul E. "Social Interaction and Community Crime: Examining the Importance of Neighbor Networks," *Criminology* 35 (November 1997), 677–703.

Belson, William A. *Juvenile Theft: The Causal Factors.* London: Harper and Row, 1975.

Benedict, Jeff. *Public Heroes, Private Felons: Athletes and Crimes against Women.* Boston: Northeastern University Press, 1997.

———, and Don Yaeger. *Pros and Cons: The Criminals Who Play in the NFL.* New York: Warner Books, 1998.

Bennett, Richard R., and R. Bruce Wiegand. "Observations on Crime Reporting in a Developing Nation," *Criminology* 32 (February 1994), 135–148.

Bennetts, Leslie. "Do the Arts Inspire Violence in Real Life?" *New York Times,* April 26, 1981, pp. H1, H25.

Benson, Michael L., Francis T. Cullen, and William J. Maakestad. "Local Prosecutors and Corporate Crime," *Crime and Delinquency* 36 (July 1990), 356–372.

Beristain, Antonio. "Capital Punishment and Catholicism," *International Journal of Criminology and Penology* 5 (November 1977), 321–335.

Berk, Richard A., and Phyllis J. Newton. "Does Arrest Really Deter Wife Battery? An Effort to Replicate the Findings of the Minneapolis Spouse Abuse Experiment," *American Sociological Review* 50 (April 1985), 253–262.

Berkowitz, Leonard, and Jacqueline Macaulay. "The Contagion of Criminal Violence," *Sociometry* 34 (June 1971), 238–260.

Bernard, Thomas J. "Angry Aggression among the 'Truly Disadvantaged,'" *Criminology* 28 (February 1990), 73–96.

———, and R. Richard Ritti. "The Philadelphia Birth Cohort and Selective Incapacitation," *Journal of Research in Crime and Delinquency* 28 (February 1991), 33–54.

Berns, Walter C. *For Capital Punishment: Crime and the Morality of the Death Penalty.* New York: Basic Books, 1979.

Bernstein, Jared, and Ellen Houston. *Crime and Work: What We Can Learn from the Low-Wage Labor Market.* Washington, DC: Economic Policy Institute, July 2000.

Best, Joel. *Threatened Children: Rhetoric and Concern about Child-Victims.* Chicago: University of Chicago Press, 1990.

———, and David F. Luckenbill. *Organizing Deviance,* 2d ed. Englewood Cliffs, NJ: Prentice Hall, 1994.

Binder, Arnold, and Gilbert Geis. "*Ad Populum* Argumentation in Criminology: Juvenile Diversion as Rhetoric," *Crime and Delinquency* 30 (October 1984), 624–647.

Binder, Arnold, and James W. Meeker. "Implications of the Failure to Replicate the Minneapolis Experimental Findings," *American Sociological Review* 58 (December 1993), 886–888.

Bishop, Donna M. "Juvenile Offenders in the Adult Criminal Justice System," in Michael Tonry, ed., *Crime and Justice: A Review of Research,* vol. 27. Chicago: University of Chicago Press, 2000, pp. 81–167.

———. "Legal and Extralegal Barriers to Delinquency: A Panel Analysis," *Criminology* 22 (August 1984), 403–419.

———, and Charles E. Frazier. "Gender Bias in Juvenile Justice Processing: Implications of the JJDP Act," *Journal of Criminal Law and Criminology* 82 (Winter 1992), 1162–1186.

———, and Charles E. Frazier. "The Influence of Race in Juvenile Justice Processing," *Journal of Research in Crime and Delinquency* 25 (August 1988), 242–263.

———, et al. "The Transfer of Juveniles to Criminal Court: Does It Make a Difference?" *Crime and Delinquency* 42 (April 1996), 171–191.

Black, Dan, and Daniel Nagin. "Do 'Right to Carry' Laws Reduce Violent Crime?" *Journal of Legal Studies* 27 (1998), 209–219.

Black, Donald J. *The Behavior of Law.* New York: Academic Press, 1976.

———. "Crime as Social Control," *American Sociological Review* 48 (February 1983), 34–35.

———. *The Manners and Customs of the Police.* New York: Academic Press, 1980.

———. "Production of Crime Rates," *American Sociological Review* 35 (August 1970), 733–748.

———, and Albert J. Reiss, Jr. "Police Control of Juveniles," *American Sociological Review* 35 (February 1970), 63–78.

Block, Alan A., and Frank R. Scarpitti. *Poisoning for Profit: The Mafia and Toxic Waste in America.* New York: Morrow, 1985.

Block, Carolyn Rebecca. *Homicide in Chicago.* Chicago: Center for Urban Policy, Loyola University of Chicago, 1987.

———. *Is Crime Seasonal?* Chicago: Illinois Criminal Justice Information Authority, 1984.

Block, Michael Kent, Frederick Carl Nold, and Joseph Gregory Sidak. "The Deterrent Effect of Antitrust

Enforcement," *Journal of Political Economy* 89 (June 1981), 429–445.

Block, Richard. "Victim-Offender Dynamics in Violent Crime," *Journal of Criminal Law and Criminology* 72 (Summer 1981), 743–761.

———. *Violent Crime: Environment, Interaction, and Death.* Lexington, MA: D. C. Heath, 1977.

———, and Carolyn R. Block. "Decisions and Data: The Transformation of Robbery Incidents into Official Robbery Statistics," *Journal of Criminal Law and Criminology* 71 (Winter 1980), 622–636.

Blum-West, Stephen Robert, and Larry A. Hembroff. "The Effects of Intent, Motive, Fair Play, and Real Harm upon Judgments of Offense Seriousness." Paper presented at the Annual Meeting of the Southwestern Sociological Association, San Antonio, TX, March 1982.

Blumberg, Abraham S. *Criminal Justice: Issues & Ironies,* 2d ed. New York: Viewpoints, 1979.

Blumenthal, Monica, et al. *Justifying Violence: Attitudes of American Men.* Ann Arbor, MI: Institute for Social Research, 1972.

Blumstein, Alfred. "On the Racial Disproportionality of United States' Prison Populations," *Journal of Criminal Law and Criminology* 73 (Fall 1982), 1259–1281.

———. "Racial Disproportionality of U.S. Prison Populations Revisited," *Colorado Law Review* 64 (1993), 743–760.

———. "Violence by Young People: Why the Deadly Nexus?," *National Institute of Justice Journal,* August 1995, pp. 2–9.

———, Jacqueline Cohen, and David P. Farrington. "Criminal Career Research: Its Value for Criminology," *Criminology* 26 (February 1988), 1–35.

———, Jacqueline Cohen, and Daniel Nagin. *Deterrence and Incapacitation: Estimating the Effects of Criminal Sanctions on Crime Rates.* Washington, DC: National Academy of Sciences, 1978.

———, David P. Farrington, and Soumyo Moitra. "Delinquency Careers: Innocents, Desisters, and Persisters," in Michael Tonry and Norval Morris, eds., *Crime and Justice: An Annual Review of Research,* vol. 6. Chicago: University of Chicago Press, 1985, pp. 187–219.

———, et al. *Criminal Careers and "Career Criminals",* vols. 1 and 2. Washington, DC: National Academy Press, 1986.

Blundell, William E. "Equity Funding: 'I Did It for the Jollies,' " in Donald Moffitt, ed., *Swindled! Classic Business Frauds of the Seventies.* Princeton, NJ: Dow Jones Books, 1976, pp. 42–89.

Boggs, Sarah L. "Formal and Informal Crime Control: An Exploratory Study of Urban, Suburban, and Rural Orientations," *Sociological Quarterly* 12 (Summer 1971), 319–327.

Boisjoly, Russell, Ellen Foster Curtis, and Eugene Mellican. "Roger Boisjoly and the *Challenger* Disaster: The Ethical Dimensions," *Journal of Business Ethics* 8 (1989), 217–230.

Booth, Alan. "The Built Environment as a Crime Deterrent: A Reexamination of Defensible Space," *Criminology* 18 (February 1981), 557–570.

———, and D. Wayne Osgood. "The Influence of Testosterone on Deviance in Adulthood: Assessing and Explaining the Relationship," *Criminology* 31 (February 1993), 93–117.

Bortner, M. A. "Traditional Rhetoric, Organizational Realities: Remand of Juveniles to Adult Court," *Crime and Delinquency* 32 (January 1986), 53–73.

Boston Globe. "Ask the Globe," May 7, 1980, p. 86.

———. "Panel Says Criminals Launder up to $150b," December 30, 1986, p. 10.

Bowers, William J., and J. H. Hirsch. "The Impact of Foot Patrol Staffing on Crime and Disorder in Boston: An Unmet Promise," *American Journal of Police* 6 (1987), 17–44.

Bowling, Michael, et al. *Background Checks for Firearm Transfers, 2001.* Washington, DC: U.S. Department of Justice, September 2002.

Boydstun, John E. *San Diego Field Interrogation: Final Report.* Washington, DC: Police Foundation, 1975.

Brady, James P. "Arson, Fiscal Crisis, and Community Action: Dialectics of an Urban Crime and Popular Response," *Crime and Delinquency* 28 (April 1982), 247–270.

Braga, Anthony A., et al. "Problem-Oriented Policing in Violent Crime Places: A Randomized Controlled Experiment," *Criminology* 37 (August 1999), 541–580.

Braithwaite, John. *Crime, Shame, and Reintegration.* Cambridge, England: Cambridge University Press, 1989.

———. *Inequality, Crime, and Public Policy.* London: Routledge and Kegan Paul, 1979.

———. "The Myth of Social Class and Criminality Reconsidered," *American Sociological Review* 46 (February 1981), 36–57.

———. "Reintegrative Shaming, Republicanism, and Policy," in Hugh D. Barlow, ed., *Crime and Public Policy: Putting Theory to Work.* Boulder, CO: Westview, 1995, pp. 191–205.

———. "White-Collar Crime, Competition, and Capitalism: Comment on Coleman," *American Journal of Sociology* 94 (November 1988), 627–632.

———, and Gilbert Geis. "On Theory and Action for Corporate Crime Control," *Crime and Delinquency* 28 (April 1982), 292–314.

Brantingham, Paul, and Patricia Brantingham. *Patterns in Crime.* New York: Macmillan, 1984.

Bratton, William J., and George L. Kelling. "Putting Police Officers Back on the Beat," *Boston Sunday Globe,* February 14, 1993, p. A2.

Brezina, Timothy. "Delinquency, Control Maintenance, and the Negation of Fatalism," *Justice Quarterly* 17 (December 2000), 779–807.

Bridges, George S., and Sara Steen. "Racial Disparities in Official Assessments of Juvenile Offenders: Attributional Stereotypes as Mediating Mechanisms," *American Sociological Review* 63 (August 1998), 554–570.

Bridges, James H., John T. Gandy, and James D. Jorgensen. "The Case for Creative Restitution in Corrections," *Federal Probation* 43 (September 1979), 28–35.

Brier, N. "The Relationship between Learning Disability and Delinquency: A Review and Reappraisal," *Journal of Learning Disabilities* 22 (1989), 546–553.

Britt, Chester L. "Versatility," in Travis Hirschi and Michael R. Gottfredson, eds., *The Generality of Deviance.* New Brunswick, NJ: Transaction Books, 1994, pp. 173–192.

Broidy, Lisa M. "A Test of General Strain Theory," *Criminology* (February 2001), 9–35.

———, and Robert Agnew. "Gender and Crime: A General Strain Theory Perspective," *Journal of Research in Crime and Delinquency* 34 (August 1997), 275–306.

Bronner, Ethan. "As College Costs Increase, Scholarship Fraud Follows," *New York Times,* November 15, 1998, pp. 1, 22.

Brown, Julia S. "A Comparative Study of Deviations from Sexual Mores," *American Sociological Review* 17 (April 1952), 135–146.

Brown, Richard Maxwell. "The American Vigilante Tradition," in Hugh Davis Graham and Ted Robert Gurr, eds., *Violence in America: Historical and Comparative Perspectives.* Staff Report to the National Commission on the Causes and Prevention of Violence, vol. 1. Washington, DC: U.S. Government Printing Office, 1969, pp. 121–169.

Buder, Leonard. "Sharp Drop in Bank Robberies Cited by New York City Police," *New York Times,* January 30, 1983, p. 22.

Buerger, Michael E. "A Tale of Two Targets: Limitations of Community Anticrime Actions," *Crime and Delinquency* 40 (July 1994), 411–436.

Bureau of Justice Statistics. *Corrections Statistics.* Retrieved January 20, 2003, from U.S. Department of Justice website: www.ojp.usdoj.gov/bjs/correct.htm.

———. *Prisoners and Alcohol.* Washington, DC: U.S. Department of Justice, January 1983.

———. *Probation and Parole Statistics.* Retrieved June 3, 2002, from U.S. Department of Justice website: www.ojp.usdoj.gov/bjs/pandp.htm.

———. *Reporting Crimes to the Police.* Washington, DC: U.S. Department of Justice, December 1985.

———. *The Seasonality of Crime Victimization.* Washington, DC: U.S. Department of Justice, May 1988.

Burgess, Ann Wolbert, and Lynda Lytle Holmstrom. "Rape: Its Effect on Task Performance at Varying Stages in the Life Cycle," in Marcia J. Walker and Stanley L. Brodsky, eds., *Sexual Assault.* Lexington, MA: D. C. Heath, 1976, pp. 23–33.

Burgess, Robert L., and Ronald L. Akers. "A Differential Association-Reinforcement Theory of Criminal Behavior," *Social Problems* 14 (Fall 1966), 128–147.

Burnham, Bonnie. *The Art Crisis.* New York: St. Martin's Press, 1975.

Bursik, Robert J., Jr., and Harold G. Grasmick. "Economic Deprivation and Neighborhood Crime Rates, 1960–1980," *Law and Society Review* 27 (1993), 263–283.

Bursik, Robert J., Jr., and Jim Webb. "Community Change and Patterns of Delinquency," *American Journal of Sociology* 88 (July 1982), 24–42.

Burton, Velmer S., Jr., et al. "Gender, Self-Control, and Crime," *Journal of Research in Crime and Delinquency* 35 (May 1998), 123–147.

Bushway, Shawn D. "The Impact of an Arrest on the Job Stability of Young White American Men," *Journal of Research in Crime and Delinquency* 35 (November 1998), 454–479.

Butterfield, Fox. "Are American Jails Becoming Shelters from the Storm?" *New York Times,* July 19, 1992, p. E4.

———. "How the Chinese Police Themselves," *New York Times Magazine,* April 18, 1982, pp. 32, 36–40, 50–56.

———. "Treatment Can Be Illusion for Violent Mentally Ill," *New York Times,* July 28, 1998, pp. A1, A12.

Bynum, Tim S., Gary W. Cordner, and Jack R. Greene. "Victim and Offense Characteristics: Impact on Police Investigative Decision-Making," *Criminology* 20 (November 1982), 301–318.

Calavita, Kitty, Henry N. Pontell, and Robert H. Tillman. *Big Money Crime: Fraud and Politics in the Savings and Loan Crisis.* Berkeley: University of California Press, 1997.

Cameron, Mary Owen. *The Booster and the Snitch: Department Store Shoplifting.* New York: Free Press, 1964.

Cameron, Samuel. "The Economics of Crime Deterrence: A Survey of Theory and Evidence," *Kyklos* 41 (1988), 301–323.

Campbell, Anne. *Men, Women, and Aggression.* New York: Basic Books, 1993.

———, and Steven Muncer. "Men and the Meaning of Violence," in John Archer, ed., *Male Violence.* London: Routledge, 1994, pp. 332–346.

Canter, Rachelle. "Family Correlates of Male and Female Delinquency," *Criminology* 20 (August 1982), 149–167.

Cao, Liqun, Anthony Adams, and Vickie J. Jensen. "A Test of the Black Subculture of Violence Thesis: A Research Note," *Criminology* 35 (May 1997), 367–379.

Cao, Liqun, Francis T. Cullen, and Bruce G. Link. "The Social Determinants of Gun Ownership: Self-Protection in an Urban Environment," *Criminology* 35 (November 1997), 629–657.

Caplan, Lincoln. "Annals of Law: The Insanity Defense," *New Yorker,* July 2, 1984, pp. 45–78.

Capote, Truman. *In Cold Blood: A True Account of a Multiple Murder and Its Consequences.* New York: Random House, 1965.

Cappell, Charles L., and Gresham Sykes. "Prison Commitments, Crime, and Unemployment: A Theoretical and Empirical Specification for the United States, 1933–1985," *Journal of Quantitative Criminology* 7 (1991), 155–199.

Carter, Daniel L., Robert A. Prentky, and Ann W. Burgess. "Victims: Lessons Learned for Responses to Sexual Violence," in Robert K. Ressler, Ann W. Burgess, and John E. Douglas, *Sexual Homicide: Patterns and Motives.* New York: Lexington Books, 1988, pp. 199–211.

Carter, Timothy, and Donald Clelland. "A Neo-Marxian Critique, Formulation, and Test of Juvenile Dispositions as a Function of Social Class," *Social Problems* 27 (October 1979), 96–108.

Caspi, Avshalom, et al. "Are Some People Crime-Prone? Replications of the Personality-Crime Relationship across Countries, Genders, Races, and Methods," *Criminology* 32 (May 1994), 163–195.

Cavender, Gray, and Lisa Bond-Maupin. "Fear and Loathing on Reality Television: An Analysis of 'America's Most Wanted' and 'Unsolved Mysteries,' " *Sociological Inquiry* 63 (August 1993), 305–317.

Center for Media and Public Affairs. *Media Monitor: Network News in the Nineties: The Top Topics and Trends of the Decade.* Washington, DC: Center for Media and Public Affairs, July/August 1997.

Cernkovich, Stephen A. "Conceptual and Empirical Ambiguity in Class-Oriented Theories of Crime and Delinquency," *International Journal of Criminology and Penology* 6 (May 1978a), 105–210.

———. "Evaluating Two Models of Delinquency Causation: Structural Theory and Control Theory," *Criminology* 16 (November 1978b), 335–352.

———. "Value Orientations and Delinquency Involvement," *Criminology* 15 (February 1978c), 443–458.

———, and Peggy C. Giordano. "School Bonding, Race, and Delinquency," *Criminology* 30 (May 1992), 261–291.

———, Peggy C. Giordano, and Meredith D. Pugh. "Chronic Offenders: The Missing Cases in Self-Report Delinquency Research," *Journal of Criminal Law and Criminology* 76 (Fall 1985), 705–732.

Chaiken, Jan M., and Marcia R. Chaiken. "Drugs and Predatory Crime," in Michael Tonry and James Q. Wilson, eds., *Drugs and Crime,* vol. 13 of *Crime and Justice: A Review of Research.* Chicago: University of Chicago Press, 1990, pp. 203–239.

Chaiken, Marcia R., and Jan M. Chaiken. "Offender Types and Public Policy," *Crime and Delinquency* 30 (April 1984), 195–226.

Chaiken, Marcia R., and Jan M. Chaiken. *Priority Prosecution of High-Rate Dangerous Offenders.* Washington, DC: U.S. Department of Justice, March 1991.

Chambliss, William J., ed. *Crime and the Legal Process.* New York: McGraw-Hill, 1969, pp. 360–378.

———. *On the Take: From Petty Crooks to Presidents.* Bloomington: Indiana University Press, 1978.

———. *Power, Politics, and Crime.* Boulder, CO: Westview, 1999.

Cheatwood, Derral. "Capital Punishment and the Deterrence of Violent Crime in Comparable Counties," *Criminal Justice Review* 18 (1993), 165–179.

———. "Interactional Patterns in Multiple-Offender Homicides," *Justice Quarterly* 13 (March 1996), 107–128.

———. "Is There a Season for Homicide?" *Criminology* 26 (May 1988), 287–306.

Chermak, Steven M. *Victims in the News: Crime and the American News Media.* Boulder, CO: Westview, 1995.

Chesney-Lind, Meda. *The Female Offender: Girls, Women, and Crime.* Thousand Oaks, CA: Sage, 1997.

———. "Judicial Enforcement of the Female Sex Role: The Family Court and the Female Delinquent," *Issues in Criminology* 8 (Fall 1973), 51–69.

Chevalier, Louis. *Laboring Classes and Dangerous Classes in Paris during the First Half of the Nineteenth Century.* New York: Howard Fertig, 1973.

Chin, Ko-Lin. *Chinatown Gangs: Extortion, Enterprise, and Ethnicity.* New York: Oxford University Press, 1996.

Chiricos, Ted, Sarah Eschholz, and Marc Gertz. "Crime, News and Fear of Crime: Toward an Identification of Audience Effects," in Gary W. Potter and Victor E. Kappeler, eds., *Constructing Crime: Perspectives on Making News and Social Problems.* Prospect Heights, IL: Waveland, 1998, pp. 295–315.

Chiricos, Theodore G. "Rates of Crime and Unemployment: An Analysis of Aggregate Research Evidence," *Social Problems* 34 (1987), 187–212.

———, and Gordon P. Waldo. "Socioeconomic Status and Criminal Sentencing: An Empirical Assessment of a Conflict Proposition," *American Sociological Review* 40 (December 1975), 753–772.

Christiansen, Karl O. "A Preliminary Study of Criminality among Twins," in Sarnoff A. Mednick and Karl O. Christiansen, eds., *Biosocial Bases of Criminal Behavior.* New York: Gardner Press, 1977, pp. 80–108.

———. "Seriousness of Criminality and Concordance among Danish Twins," in Roger Hood, ed., *Crime, Criminology, and Public Policy: Essays in Honour of Sir Leon Radzinowicz.* New York: Free Press, 1974, pp. 63–77.

Clark, John P., and Larry L. Tifft. "Polygraph and Interview Validation of Self-Reported Deviant Behavior," *American Sociological Review* 31 (August 1966), 516–523.

Clarke, Ronald V., ed. *Situational Crime Prevention: Successful Case Studies.* Albany, NY: Harrow and Heston, 1992.

———, and Patricia M. Harris. "Auto Theft and Its Prevention," in Michael Tonry, ed., *Crime and Justice: A Review of Research,* vol. 16. Chicago: University of Chicago Press, 1992, pp. 1–54.

Cleaver, Eldridge. *Soul On Ice.* New York: Dell, 1968.

Clelland, Donald, and Timothy J. Carter. "The New Myth of Class and Crime," *Criminology* 18 (November 1980), 319–336.

Clifford, William. *Crime Control in Japan.* Lexington, MA: D. C. Heath, 1976.

———. "Culture and Crime—In Global Perspective," *International Journal of Criminology and Penology* 6 (February 1978), 61–80.

Clinard, Marshall B. *Cities with Little Crime: The Case of Switzerland.* Cambridge, England: Cambridge University Press, 1978.

———. *Corporate Ethics and Crime: The Role of Middle Management.* Beverly Hills, CA: Sage, 1983.

———, and Daniel J. Abbott. *Crime in Developing Countries: A Comparative Perspective.* New York: Wiley, 1973.

Cloward, Richard A., and Lloyd E. Ohlin. *Delinquency and Opportunity: A Theory of Delinquent Gangs.* New York: Free Press, 1960.

Cochran, John K., Peter B. Wood, and Bruce J. Arneklev. "Is the Religiosity-Delinquency Relationship Spurious? A Test of Arousal and Social Control Theories," *Journal of Research in Crime and Delinquency* 31 (February 1994), 92–123.

Cocozza, Joseph J., and Henry J. Steadman. "Prediction in Psychiatry: An Example of Misplaced Confidence in Experts," *Social Problems* 25 (February 1978), 265–276.

Cohen, Albert K. *Delinquent Boys: The Culture of the Gang.* New York: Free Press, 1955.

Cohen, Jacqueline. "Incapacitation as a Strategy for Crime Control: Possibilities and Pitfalls," in Michael Tonry and Norval Morris, eds., *Crime and Justice: An Annual Review of Research,* vol. 5. Chicago: University of Chicago Press, 1983, pp. 1–84.

Cohen, Lawrence E., and David Cantor. "Residential Burglary in the United States: Life-Style and Demographic Factors Associated with the Probability of Victimization," *Journal of Research in Crime and Delinquency* 18 (January 1981), 113–127.

———, and Marcus Felson. "Social Change and Crime Rate Trends: A Routine Activity Approach," *American Sociological Review* 44 (August 1979), 588–608.

———, and Kenneth C. Land. "Age Structure and Crime: Symmetry versus Asymmetry and the Projection of Crime Rates through the 1990s," *American Sociological Review* 52 (April 1987), 170–183.

Cohen, Mark A. "Some New Evidence on the Seriousness of Crime," *Criminology* 26 (May 1988), 343–353.

———, Ted R. Miller, and Brian Wiersema. *Victim Costs and Consequences: A New Look.* Washington, DC: U.S. Department of Justice, 1996.

Coleman, James S., Thomas Hoffer, and Sally Kilgore. *High School Achievement: Public, Catholic, and Private Schools Compared.* New York: Basic Books, 1982.

Coleman, James William. *The Criminal Elite: Understanding White-Collar Crime,* 4th ed. New York: St. Martin's Press, 1998.

Collins, James J., Jr. *Alcohol Use and Criminal Behavior: An Executive Summary.* Washington, DC: U.S. Department of Justice, National Institute of Justice, 1981a.

———, ed. *Drinking and Crime: Perspectives on the Relationships between Alcohol Consumption and Criminal Behavior.* New York: Guilford Press, 1981b.

Colton, Kent W., et al. *Computer Crime: Electronic Fund Transfer Systems and Crime.* Washington, DC: U.S. Government Printing Office, 1982.

Colvin, Mark, Francis T. Cullen, and Thomas vander Ven. "Coercion, Social Support, and Crime: An Emerging Theoretical Consensus," *Criminology* 40 (February 2002), 19–42.

Conklin, John E. *Art Crime.* Westport, CT: Praeger, 1994.

———. *"Illegal but Not Criminal": Business Crime in America.* Englewood Cliffs, NJ: Prentice Hall, 1977.

———. *Robbery and the Criminal Justice System.* Philadelphia: Lippincott, 1972.

———. *Why Crime Rates Fell.* Boston: Allyn & Bacon, 2003.

Connell, R. W. "Foreword," in James W. Messerschmidt, *Masculinities and Crime: Critique and Reconceptualization of Theory.* Lanham, MD: Rowman and Littlefield, 1993, pp. vii–xv.

Cook, Philip J. "The Correctional Carrot: Better Jobs for Parolees," *Policy Analysis* 1 (1975), 11–54.

———. "The Influence of Gun Availability on Violent Crime Patterns," in Michael Tonry and Norval Morris, eds., *Crime and Justice: An Annual Review of Research,* vol. 4. Chicago: University of Chicago Press, 1983, pp. 49–89.

———. "Robbery Violence," *Journal of Criminal Law and Criminology* 78 (Summer 1987), 357–376.

———. "The Technology of Personal Violence," in Michael Tonry, ed., *Crime and Justice: A Review of Research,* vol. 14. Chicago: University of Chicago Press, 1991, pp. 1–71.

Copes, Heith, et al. "Reporting Behavior of Fraud Victims and Black's Theory of Law: An Empirical Assessment," *Justice Quarterly* 18 (June 2001), 343–363.

Cordilia, Ann. *The Making of an Inmate: Prison as a Way of Life.* Cambridge, MA: Schenkman, 1983.

Corman, Hope, and H. Naci Mocan. "A Time-Series Analysis of Crime, Deterrence and Drug Abuse in New York City," *American Economic Review* 90 (June 2000), 584–604.

Count-van Manen, Gloria. "A Deviant Case of Deviance: Singapore," *Law and Society Review* 5 (February 1971), 389–406.

Crawford, Charles, Ted Chiricos, and Gary Kleck. "Race, Racial Threat, and Sentencing of Habitual Offenders," *Criminology* 36 (August 1998), 481–511.

Cressey, Donald R. *Criminal Organization.* New York: Harper and Row, 1972.

———. *Other People's Money: A Study in the Social Psychology of Embezzlement.* Belmont, CA: Wadsworth, 1971.

Criminal Division, U.S. Department of Justice. Cited in *Congressional Record—Senate* 114 (July 18, 1968), 21986.

Cromwell, Paul F., James N. Olson, and D'Aunn Wester Avary. *Breaking and Entering: An Ethnographic Analysis of Burglary.* Newbury Park, CA: Sage, 1991.

Cronin, Roberta C., et al. *Evaluation of the Habitual Serious and Violent Juvenile Offender Program.* Washington, DC: Office of Juvenile Justice and Delinquency Prevention, U.S. Department of Justice, January 1988.

Cronin, Thomas E., Tania Z. Cronin, and Michael E. Milakovich. *U.S. v. Crime in the Streets.* Bloomington: Indiana University Press, 1981.

Crutchfield, Robert, George Bridges, and Susan Pritchford. "Analytical and Aggregation Biases in Analyses of Imprisonment: Reconciling Discrepancies in Studies of Racial Disparity," *Journal of Research in Crime and Delinquency* 31 (May 1994), 166–182.

Cullen, Francis T. "Rehabilitation and Treatment Programs," in James Q. Wilson and Joan Petersilia, eds., *Crime: Public Policies for Crime Control.* Oakland, CA: ICS Press, 2002, pp. 253–289.

———. "Social Support as an Organizing Concept for Criminology: Presidential Address to the Academy of Criminal Justice Sciences," *Justice Quarterly* 11 (December 1994), 527–559.

———, Bonnie S. Fisher, and Brandon K. Applegate "Public Opinion about Punishment and Corrections," in

Michael Tonry, ed., *Crime and Justice: A Review of Research,* vol. 27. Chicago: University of Chicago Press, 2000, pp. 1–79.

——, and Karen E. Gilbert. *Reaffirming Rehabilitation.* Cincinnati, OH: Anderson, 1982.

——, William J. Maakestad, and Gray Cavender. *Corporate Crime under Attack: The Ford Pinto Case and Beyond.* Cincinnati, OH: Anderson, 1987.

——, John Paul Wright, and Mitchell B. Chamlin. "Social Support and Social Reform: A Progressive Crime Control Agenda," *Crime and Delinquency* 45 (April 1999), 188–207.

——, et al. "Crime and the Bell Curve: Lessons from Intelligent Criminology," *Crime and Delinquency* 43 (October 1997), 387–411.

Curran, Debra A. "Judicial Discretion and Defendant's Sex," *Criminology* 21 (February 1983), 41–58.

Curtis, Lynn A. *Criminal Violence: National Patterns and Behavior.* Lexington, MA: D. C. Heath, 1974.

Cushman, Paul, Jr. "Relationship between Narcotic Addiction and Crime," *Federal Probation* 38 (September 1974), 38–43.

Dabbs, J. M., and R. Morris. "Testosterone, Social Class, and Antisocial Behavior in a Sample of 4,462 Men," *Psychological Science* 1 (1990), 209–211.

Dalgaard, Odd Steffen, and Einar Kringlen. "A Norwegian Twin Study of Criminality," *British Journal of Criminology* 16 (June 1976), 213–232.

Daly, Kathleen. "Gender and Varieties of White-Collar Crime," *Criminology* 27 (November 1989), 769–794.

——. *Gender, Crime, and Punishment.* New Haven, CT: Yale University Press, 1994.

——, and Rebecca Bordt. "Sex Effects and Sentencing: A Review of the Statistical Literature," *Justice Quarterly* 12 (March 1995), 143–177.

——, and Meda Chesney-Lind. "Feminism and Criminology," *Justice Quarterly* 5 (December 1988), 497–538.

Daly, Martin, and Margo Wilson. "Crime and Conflict: Homicide in Evolutionary Psychological Perspective," in Michael Tonry, ed., *Crime and Justice: A Review of Research,* vol. 22. Chicago: University of Chicago Press, 1997, pp. 51–100.

Darley, John M., and C. Daniel Batson. " 'From Jerusalem to Jericho': A Study of Situational and Dispositional Variables in Helping Behavior," *Journal of Personality and Social Psychology* 27 (July 1973), 100–108.

Datesman, Susan K., and Mikel Aickin. "Offense Specialization and Escalation among Status Offenders," *Journal of Criminal Law and Criminology* 75 (Winter 1984), 1246–1275.

Davis, John A. "Justification for No Obligation: Views of Black Males toward Crime and the Criminal Law," *Issues in Criminology* 9 (Fall 1974), 69–87.

Davis, Robert C., and Arthur J. Lurigio. *Fighting Back: Neighborhood Antidrug Strategies.* Thousand Oaks, CA: Sage, 1996.

Dawson, John M., and Patrick A. Langan. *Murder in Families.* Washington, DC: U.S. Department of Justice, July 1994.

Decker, Scott H., Tim Bynum, and Deborah Weisel. "A Tale of Two Cities: Gangs as Organized Crime Groups," *Justice Quarterly* 15 (September 1998), 395–425.

——, and Barbara Salert. "Predicting the Career Criminal: An Empirical Test of the Greenwood Scale," *Journal of Criminal Law and Criminology* 77 (Spring 1986), 215–236.

——, and Barrik van Winkle. *Life in the Gang: Family, Friends, and Violence.* Cambridge, England: Cambridge University Press, 1996.

——, Richard Wright, and Robert Logie. "Perceptual Deterrence among Active Residential Burglars: A Research Note," *Criminology* 31 (February 1993), 135–147.

DeFleur, Lois B. "Biasing Influences on Drug Arrest Records: Implications for Deviance Research," *American Sociological Review* 40 (February 1975), 88–103.

——. *Delinquency in Argentina: A Study of Córdoba's Youth.* Pullman: Washington State University Press, 1970.

DeFranco, Edward J. *Anatomy of a Scam: A Case Study of a Planned Bankruptcy by Organized Crime.* Washington, DC: U.S. Government Printing Office, 1973.

De Li, Spencer. "Legal Sanctions and Youths' Status Achievement: A Longitudinal Study," *Justice Quarterly* 16 (June 1999), 377–401.

Deming, Romine R. "Correctional Restitution: A Strategy for Correctional Conflict Management," *Federal Probation* 40 (September 1976), 27–32.

Denno, Deborah W. *Biology and Violence: From Birth to Adulthood.* Cambridge, England: Cambridge University Press, 1990.

——. "Gender, Crime, and the Criminal Law Defenses," *Journal of Criminal Law and Criminology* 85 (Summer 1994), 80–180.

Dershowitz, Alan M. *The Abuse Excuse and Other Cop-outs, Sob Stories, and Evasions of Responsibility.* Boston: Little, Brown, 1994.

Desroches, Frederick J. *Force and Fear: Robbery in Canada.* Toronto: Nelson Canada, 1995.

Dietz, Mary Lorenz. *Killing for Profit: The Social Organization of Felony Homicide.* Chicago: Nelson-Hall, 1983.

Ditton, Paula M., and Doris James Wilson. *Truth in Sentencing in State Prisons.* Washington, DC: U.S. Department of Justice, January 1999.

Dixon, Jo, and Alan J. Lizotte. "Gun Ownership and the 'Southern Subculture of Violence,' " *American Journal of Sociology* 93 (September 1987), 383–405.

Dobinson, Ian. "Pinning a Tail on the Dragon: The Chinese and the International Heroin Trade," *Crime and Delinquency* 39 (July 1993), 373–384.

Dobrin, Adam. "The Risk of Offending on Homicide Victimization: A Case Control Study," *Journal of Research in Crime and Delinquency* 38 (May 2001), 154–173.

Dombrink, John. "Organized Crime: Gangsters and Godfathers," in Joseph E. Scott and Travis Hirschi, eds., *Controversial Issues in Crime and Justice.* Newbury Park, CA: Sage, 1988, pp. 54–75.

Donnelly, Patrick G., and Charles E. Kimble. "Community Organizing, Environmental Change, and Neighborhood Crime," *Crime and Delinquency* 43 (October 1997), 493–511.

Donnerstein, Edward, Daniel Linz, and Steven Penrod. *The Question of Pornography: Research Findings and Policy Implications.* New York: Free Press, 1987.

Donnerstein, Edward, Ronald G. Slaby, and Leonard D. Eron. "The Mass Media and Youth Aggression," in Leonard D. Eron, Jacquelyn H. Gentry, and Peggy Schlegel, eds., *Reason to Hope: A Psychosocial Perspective on Violence and Youth.* Washington, DC: American Psychological Association, 1994, pp. 219–250.

Donziger, Steven R., ed. *The Real War on Crime: The Report of the National Criminal Justice Commission.* New York: Harper Perennial, 1996.

Duhart, Detis T. *Urban, Suburban, and Rural Victimization, 1993–98.* Washington, DC: U.S. Department of Justice, October 2000.

———. *Violence in the Workplace, 1993–99.* Washington, DC: U.S. Department of Justice, December 2001.

Dunford, Franklyn W., David Huizinga, and Delbert S. Elliott. "The Role of Arrest in Domestic Assault: The Omaha Police Experiment," *Criminology* 28 (May 1990), 183–206.

Durham, Alexis M., H. Preston Elrod, and Patrick T. Kinkade. "Public Support for the Death Penalty: Beyond Gallup," *Justice Quarterly* 13 (December 1996), 705–736.

Durkheim, Emile. *The Division of Labor in Society,* trans. by George Simpson. Glencoe, IL: Free Press, 1895/1933.

———. *The Rules of the Sociological Method,* trans. by Sarah A. Solovay and John H. Mueller; ed. by George E. G. Catlin. New York: Free Press, 1895/1938.

Eck, John. "Solving Crimes," *NIJ Reports,* March 1984, pp. 4–8.

———, and Edward R. Maguire. "Have Changes in Policing Reduced Violent Crime? An Assessment of the Evidence," in Alfred Blumstein and Joel Wallman, eds., *The Crime Drop in America.* Cambridge, England: Cambridge University Press, 2000, pp. 207–265.

Egan, John W. "The Internal Revenue Service and Corporate Slush Funds: Some Fifth Amendment Problems," *Journal of Criminal Law and Criminology* 69 (Spring 1978), 59–74.

Ehrlich, Isaac. "The Deterrent Effect of Capital Punishment: A Question of Life and Death," *American Economic Review* (June 1975), 397–417.

Eichenwald, Kurt. "Former Fed Chief Picked to Oversee Auditor of Enron: Talk of Crime Gets Big Push," *New York Times,* February 4, 2002, pp. A1, A19.

Elias, Robert. "Alienating the Victim: Compensation and Victim Attitudes," *Journal of Social Issues* 40 (1984), 103–116.

———. *Victims of the System: Crime Victims and Compensation in American Politics and Criminal Justice.* New Brunswick, NJ: Transaction Books, 1983.

Elifson, Kirk W., David M. Petersen, and C. Kirk Hadaway. "Religiosity and Delinquency: A Contextual Analysis," *Criminology* 21 (November 1983), 505–527.

Elliott, Delbert S. "Serious Violent Offenders: Onset, Developmental Course, and Termination—The American Society of Criminology 1993 Presidential Address," *Criminology* 32 (February 1994), 1–21.

———, and Suzanne S. Ageton. "Reconciling Race and Class Differences in Self-Reported and Official Estimates of Delinquency," *American Sociological Review* 45 (February 1980), 95–110.

———, and David Huizinga. "Social Class and Delinquent Behavior in a National Youth Panel: 1976–1980," *Criminology* 21 (May 1983), 149–177.

———, David Huizinga, and Suzanne S. Ageton. *Explaining Delinquency and Drug Use.* Beverly Hills, CA: Sage, 1985.

———, and Harwin L. Voss. *Delinquency and Dropout.* Lexington, MA: D. C. Heath, 1974.

Ellis, Lee. "Genetics and Criminal Behavior: Evidence through the End of the 1970s," *Criminology* 20 (May 1982), 43–66.

———. "Monoamine Oxidase and Criminality: Identifying an Apparent Biological Marker for Antisocial Behavior," *Journal of Research in Crime and Delinquency* 28 (May 1991), 227–251.

———. "Religiosity and Criminality: Evidence and Explanations of Complex Relationships," *Sociological Perspectives* 28 (October 1985), 501–520.

———, and Anthony Walsh. "Gene-Based Evolutionary Theories in Criminology," *Criminology* 35 (May 1997), 229–276.

Ellison, Christopher G., and Patricia L. McCall. "Region and Violent Attitudes Reconsidered: Comment on Dixon and Lizotte," *American Journal of Sociology* 95 (July 1989), 174–178.

Ellsworth, Phoebe C., and Lee Ross. "Public Opinion and Capital Punishment: A Close Examination of the Views of Abolitionists and Retentionists," *Crime and Delinquency* 29 (January 1983), 116–169.

Elmhorn, Kerstin. "Study in Self-Reported Delinquency among Schoolchildren in Stockholm," in Karl O. Christiansen, ed., *Scandinavian Studies in Criminology,* vol. 1. London: Tavistock, 1965, pp. 117–146.

Empey, Lamar T., and Steven G. Lubeck, with Ronald L. LaPorte. *Explaining Delinquency: Construction, Test, and Reformulation of a Sociological Theory.* Lexington, MA: D. C. Heath, 1971.

Engel, Robin Shepard, James J. Sobol, and Robert E. Worden. "Further Exploration of the Demeanor Hypothesis: The Interaction Effects of Suspects' Characteristics and Demeanor on Police Behavior," *Justice Quarterly* 17 (June 2000), 235–258.

Ennis, Philip H. *Criminal Victimization in the United States: A Report of a National Survey.* Field Surveys II of the President's Commission on Law Enforcement and Administration of Justice. Washington, DC: U.S. Government Printing Office, 1967.

Erez, Edna, and Pamela Tontodonato. "The Effect of Victim Participation in Sentencing on Sentence Outcome," *Criminology* 28 (August 1990), 451–474.

Erickson, Maynard L., and Jack P. Gibbs. "On the Perceived Severity of Legal Penalties," *Journal of Criminal Law and Criminology* 70 (Spring 1979), 102–116.

Erickson, Patricia G., and Michael S. Goodstadt. "Legal Stigma for Marijuana Possession," *Criminology* 17 (August 1979), 208–216.

Ericson, Richard, Patricia Baranek, and Janet Chan. *Representing Order: Crime, Law and Justice in the News Media*. Toronto: University of Toronto Press, 1991.

Ericsson, Kjersti. "Gender, Delinquency and Child Welfare," *Theoretical Criminology* 2 (November 1998), 445–459.

Eronen, Markku. "Mental Disorders and Homicidal Behavior in Female Subjects," *American Journal of Psychiatry* 152 (August 1995), 1216–1218.

———, Panu Hakola, and Jari Tiihonen. "Mental Disorders and Homicidal Behavior in Finland," *Archives of General Psychiatry* 53 (June 1996), 497–501.

Erwin, Michael. "Top Theft Areas." Retrieved April 30, 2002, from National Insurance Crime Bureau website: www.nicb.org/services/hotspotsrelease.html.

Esbensen, Finn-Aage. "Foot Patrols: Of What Value?" *American Journal of Police* 6 (1987), 45–65.

Evans, Sandra S., and Joseph E. Scott. "The Seriousness of Crime Cross-Culturally: The Impact of Religiosity," *Criminology* 22 (February 1984), 39–59.

Evans, T. David, et al. "Religion and Crime Reexamined: The Impact of Religion, Secular Controls, and Social Ecology on Adult Criminality," *Criminology* 33 (May 1995), 195–224.

———, et al. "The Social Consequences of Self-Control: Testing the General Theory of Crime," *Criminology* 35 (August 1997), 475–504.

Fagan, Jeffrey, and Richard B. Freeman. "Crime and Work," in Michael Tonry, ed., *Crime and Justice: A Review of Research*, vol. 25. Chicago: University of Chicago Press, 1999, pp. 225–290.

Fagan, Jeffrey, and Martin Guggenheim. "Preventive Detention and the Judicial Prediction of Dangerousness for Juveniles: A Natural Experiment," *Journal of Criminal Law and Criminology* 86 (Winter 1996), 415–448.

Fagan, Jeffrey, and Sandra Wexler. "Family Origins of Violent Delinquents," *Criminology* 25 (August 1987), 643–669.

Fagan, Jeffrey, and Deanna L. Wilkinson. "Guns, Youth Violence, and Social Identity in Inner Cities," in Michael Tonry and Mark H. Moore, eds., *Youth Violence, Crime and Justice: A Review of Research*, vol. 24. Chicago: University of Chicago Press, 1998, pp. 105–188.

Farr, Kathryn Ann. "Revitalizing the Drug Decriminalization Debate," *Crime and Delinquency* 36 (April 1990), 223–237.

Farrell, Ronald A., and James F. Nelson. "A Sequential Analysis of Delinquency," *International Journal of Criminology and Penology* 6 (August 1978), 255–268.

Farrell, Ronald A., and Victoria Lynn Swigert. "Prior Offense Record as a Self-Fulfilling Prophecy," *Law and Society Review* 12 (Spring 1978), 437–453.

Farrington, David P. "Longitudinal Research on Crime and Delinquency," in Norval Morris and Michael Tonry, eds., *Crime and Justice: An Annual Review of Research*, vol. 1. Chicago: University of Chicago Press, 1979, pp. 289–348.

———. "The Relationship between Low Resting Heart Rate and Violence," in Adrian Raine, P. A. Brennan, David P. Farrington, and Sarnoff A. Mednick, eds., *Biosocial Bases of Violence*. New York: Plenum, 1997, pp. 158–183.

———. "Self-Reports of Deviant Behavior: Predictive and Stable?" *Journal of Criminal Law and Criminology* 64 (March 1973), 99–110.

———, Rolf Loeber, and Welmoet B. van Kammen. "Long-Term Criminal Outcomes of Hyperactivity-Impulsivity-Attention Deficit and Conduct Problems in Childhood," in Lee N. Robins and Michael Rutter, eds., *Straight and Devious Pathways from Childhood to Adulthood*. Cambridge, England: Cambridge University Press, 1990, pp. 62–81.

———, Lloyd E. Ohlin, and James Q. Wilson. *Understanding and Controlling Crime: Toward a New Research Strategy*. New York: Springer-Verlag, 1986.

———, Howard N. Snyder, and Terrence A. Finnegan. "Specialization in Juvenile Court Careers," *Criminology* 26 (August 1988), 461–485.

Federal Bureau Of Investigation. *Crime in the United States, 2001: Uniform Crime Reports*. Washington, DC: U.S. Government Printing Office, 2002.

Feeney, Floyd, and Adrianne Weir, eds. *The Prevention and Control of Robbery*. Davis: Center on Administration of Criminal Justice, University of California at Davis, 1973.

Feld, Barry C. "Criminalizing the American Juvenile Court," in Michael Tonry, ed., *Crime and Justice: A Review of Research*, vol. 17. Chicago: University of Chicago Press, 1993, pp. 197–280.

Felson, Marcus. *Crime and Everyday Life,* 2d ed. Thousand Oaks, CA: Pine Forge, 1998.

Felson, Richard B., Eric P. Baumer, and Steven F. Messner. "Acquaintance Robbery," *Journal of Research in Crime and Delinquency* 37 (August 2000), 284–305.

Felson, Richard B., and Henry J. Steadman. "Situational Factors in Disputes Leading to Criminal Violence," *Criminology* 21 (February 1983), 59–74.

Ferracuti, Franco, Simon Dinitz, and Esperanza Acosta de Brenes. *Delinquents and Nondelinquents in the Puerto Rican Slum Culture*. Columbus: Ohio State University Press, 1975.

Ferraro, Kenneth F. *Fear of Crime: Interpreting Victimization Risk*. Albany: State University of New York Press, 1995.

Ferrell, Jeff, and Neil Websdale, eds., *Making Trouble: Cultural Constructions of Crime, Deviance, and Control*. Hawthorne, NY: Aldine de Gruyter, 1999.

Fessenden, Ford. "They Threaten, Seethe, and Unhinge, Then Kill in Quantity," *New York Times,* April 9, 2000, pp. 1, 20.

Figueira-McDonough, Josefina. "Discrimination or Sex Differences? Criteria for Evaluating the Juvenile Justice System's Handling of Minor Offenses," *Crime and Delinquency* 33 (July 1987), 403–424.

———. "Feminism and Delinquency," *British Journal of Criminology* 24 (1984), 325–342.

———, and Elaine Selo. "A Reformulation of the 'Equal Opportunity' Explanation of Female Delinquency," *Crime and Delinquency* 26 (July 1980), 333–343.

Finckenauer, James O. *Scared Straight! and the Panacea Phenomenon.* Englewood Cliffs, NJ: Prentice Hall, 1982.

Fishbein, Diana H. "Biological Perspectives in Criminology," *Criminology* 28 (February 1990), 27–72.

———. "The Biology of Antisocial Behavior," in John E. Conklin, ed., *New Perspectives in Criminology.* Boston: Allyn & Bacon, 1996, pp. 26–38.

———, and Robert W. Thatcher. "New Diagnostic Methods in Criminology: Assessing Organic Sources of Behavioral Disorders," *Journal of Research in Crime and Delinquency* 23 (August 1986), 240–267.

Fisher, Bonnie S., Francis T. Cullen, and Michael G. Turner. *The Sexual Victimization of College Women.* Washington, DC: U.S. Department of Justice, December 2000.

Fisher, Bonnie, and Jack L. Nasar. "Fear of Crime in Relation to Three Exterior Site Features: Prospect, Refuge, and Escape," *Environment and Behavior* 24 (1992), 35–65.

Fishman, Sima, Kathleen Rodenrys, and George Schink. "The Income of Organized Crime," in President's Commission on Organized Crime, *The Impact: Organized Crime Today.* Washington, DC: U.S. Government Printing Office, April 1986, pp. 413–494.

Fisse, Brent, and John Braithwaite. *The Impact of Publicity on Corporate Offenders.* Albany: State University of New York Press, 1983.

Flanagan, Timothy J., and Dennis R. Longmire. *Americans View Crime and Justice: A National Public Opinion Survey.* Thousand Oaks, CA: Sage, 1996.

Forde, David R., and Leslie W. Kennedy. "Risky Lifestyles, Routine Activities, and the General Theory of Crime," *Justice Quarterly* 14 (June 1997), 265–294.

Foreman, Judy. "How to Tell If You Are 'Muggable,' " *Boston Globe,* January 20, 1981, pp. 20, 21.

Forst, Brian E., and Jolene C. Hernon. *The Criminal Justice Response to Victim Harm.* Washington, DC: U.S. Department of Justice, June 1985.

Foster, Jack D., Simon Dinitz, and Walter C. Reckless. "Perceptions of Stigma Following Public Intervention for Delinquent Behavior," *Social Problems* 20 (Fall 1972), 202–209.

Foucault, Michel. *Discipline and Punish,* trans. by Alan Sheridan. New York: Pantheon, 1978.

Fowler, Floyd J., Jr., and Thomas W. Mangione. *Neighborhood Crime, Fear and Social Control: A Second Look at the Hartford Program.* Washington, DC: National Institute of Justice, U.S. Department of Justice, 1982.

Fowler, Glenn. "More 'Career Criminals' Convicted in State Effort," *New York Times,* January 8, 1981, p. B7.

Fowles, Richard, and Mary Merva. "Wage Inequality and Criminal Activity: An Extreme Bounds Analysis for the United States, 1975–1990," *Criminology* 34 (May 1996), 163–182.

Fox, James Alan. "A Disturbing Trend in Youth Crime," *Boston Globe,* June 1, 1995, p. 19.

———, ed. *Methods in Quantitative Criminology.* New York: Academic Press, 1981a.

———. *Models in Quantitative Criminology.* New York: Academic Press, 1981b.

———. " 'They Seek to Kill the Company,' " *Boston Globe,* December 31, 2000, pp. D1, D3.

———, and Michael L. Radelet. "Persistent Flaws in Econometric Studies of the Deterrent Effect of the Death Penalty," *Loyola of Los Angeles Law Review* 23 (November 1989), 29–44.

———, and Marianne W. Zawitz, *Homicide Trends in the United States.* Washington, DC: U.S. Department of Justice, January 1999.

Franklin, Alice. "Criminality in the Work Place: A Comparison of Male and Female Offenders," in Freda Adler and Rita James Simon, eds., *The Criminology of Deviant Women.* Boston: Houghton Mifflin, 1979, pp. 167–170.

Franklin, James L. "The Churches and the Death Penalty," *Boston Globe,* March 14, 1982, p. 30.

Freedman, Lawrence Zelic. "No Response to the Cry for Help," in James M. Ratcliffe, ed., *The Good Samaritan and the Law.* Garden City, NY: Doubleday, 1966, pp. 171–182.

Freeman, Richard B. "Crime and Unemployment," in James Q. Wilson, ed., *Crime and Public Policy.* San Francisco: ICS Press, 1983, pp. 89–106.

French, Howard W. "Japan's Troubling Trend: Rising Teen-Age Crime," *New York Times,* October 12, 1999, p. A6.

Fyfe, James J. "Observations on Police Deadly Force," *Crime and Delinquency* 27 (July 1981), 376–389.

Gagnon, John H. "Sexual Conduct and Crime," in Daniel Glaser, ed., *Handbook of Criminology.* Chicago: Rand McNally, 1974, pp. 233–272.

Gallup, George. "Safety Fears Swelled Nixon Vote," *Boston Globe,* November 11, 1972, p. 7.

Gardiner, Muriel. *The Deadly Innocents: Portraits of Children Who Kill.* New Haven, CT: Yale University Press, 1985.

Garfinkel, Harold. "Conditions of Successful Degradation Ceremonies," *American Journal of Sociology* 61 (March 1956), 420–424.

Garner, Joel H., and Christy A. Visher. "Policy Experiments Come of Age," *NIJ Reports,* September/October 1988, pp. 2–8.

Garofalo, James. "Reassessing the Lifestyle Model of Criminal Victimization," in Michael Gottfredson and Travis Hirschi, eds., *Positive Criminology.* Newbury Park, CA: Sage, 1987, pp. 23–42.

———, and Maureen McLeod. "The Structure and Operations of Neighborhood Watch Programs in the United States," *Crime and Delinquency* 35 (July 1989), 326–344.

Gebhard, Paul H., et al. *Sex Offenders.* New York: Harper and Row, 1965.

Geis, Gilbert. "Avocational Crime," in Daniel Glaser, ed., *Handbook of Criminology.* Chicago: Rand McNally, 1974, pp. 273–298.

———. "The Crime Intervenor: Samaritan or Superman?" Lecture presented at University of California, Irvine, February 5, 1981.

———. "White Collar Crime: The Heavy Electrical Equipment Antitrust Cases of 1961," in Marshall B. Clinard and Richard Quinney, eds., *Criminal Behavior Systems:*

A Typology. New York: Holt, Rinehart and Winston, 1967, pp. 139–151.

Geller, William, and Kevin J. Karales. "Shootings of and by Chicago Police: Uncommon Crises. Part I: Shootings by Chicago Police," *Journal of Criminal Law and Criminology* 72 (Winter 1981), 1813–1866.

Gelles, Richard, and Murray A. Straus. *Intimate Violence.* New York: Simon and Schuster, 1988.

Georges-Abeyie, Daniel E., and Keith D. Harries, eds. *Crime: A Spatial Perspective.* New York: Columbia University Press, 1980.

Gerbner, George, and Larry Gross. "Living with Television: The Violence Profile," *Journal of Communication* 26 (Spring 1976), 173–199.

Gibbons, Don C. *Society, Crime, and Criminal Behavior,* 6th ed. Englewood Cliffs, NJ: Prentice Hall, 1992.

Gibbs, John J., and Peggy L. Shelly. "Life in the Fast Lane: A Retrospective View by Commercial Thieves," *Journal of Research in Crime and Delinquency* 19 (July 1982), 299–330.

Gifford, Sidra Lea. *Justice Expenditure and Employment in the United States, 1999.* Washington, DC: U.S. Department of Justice, February 2002.

Gillis, A. R., and John Hagan. "Density, Delinquency, and Design: Formal and Informal Control and the Built Environment," *Criminology* 19 (February 1982), 514–529.

Ginsburg, B. E., and B. F. Carter. *Premenstrual Syndrome: Ethical and Legal Implications in a Biomedical Perspective.* New York: Bantam, 1987.

Giordano, Peggy C. "Girls, Guys and Gangs: The Changing Social Context of Female Delinquency," *Journal of Criminal Law and Criminology* 69 (Spring 1978), 126–132.

——, Stephen A. Cernkovich, and M. D. Pugh. "Friendships and Delinquency," *American Journal of Sociology* 91 (March 1986), 1170–1202.

Glaberson, William. "Killer Blames His Therapist, and Jury Agrees," *New York Times,* October 10, 1998, pp. A1, A10.

——. "Lawyers' Math in Sept. 11 Deaths Shows Varying Values for Life," *New York Times,* November 11, 2001a, pp. B1, B10.

——. "Racial Profiling May Get Wider Approval by Courts," *New York Times,* September 21, 2001b, p. A16.

Glaser, Daniel. "The Classification of Offenses and Offenders," in Daniel Glaser, ed., *Handbook of Criminology.* Chicago: Rand McNally, 1974, pp. 45–83.

——. "Criminal Theories and Behavioral Images," *American Journal of Sociology* 61 (March 1956), 433–444.

——. "A Review of Crime-Causation Theory and Its Application," in Norval Morris and Michael Tonry, eds., *Crime and Justice: An Annual Review of Research,* vol. 1. Chicago: University of Chicago Press, 1979, pp. 203–237.

Glueck, Sheldon, and Eleanor Glueck. *Physique and Delinquency.* New York: Harper and Brothers, 1956.

Glueck, Sheldon, and Eleanor Glueck. *Unraveling Juvenile Delinquency.* Cambridge, MA: Harvard University Press, 1950.

Goldberg, Jeffrey. "The Color of Suspicion," *New York Times Magazine,* June 20, 1999, pp. 50–57, 64, 85–87.

Golden, Daniel. "It's a Crime," *Boston Globe,* September 11, 1995, pp. 39, 52.

Goldstein, Jeffrey H. *Aggression and Crimes of Violence,* 2d ed. New York: Oxford University Press, 1986.

——, ed. *Sports Violence.* New York: Springer-Verlag, 1983.

Goldstein, Michael J., and Harold S. Kant. *Pornography and Sexual Deviance.* Berkeley: University of California Press, 1973.

Goldstein, Paul J. "The Drugs/Violence Nexus: A Tripartite Conceptual Framework," *Journal of Drug Issues* 14 (1985), 493–506.

Goleman, Daniel. "Brutal Sports and Brutal Fans," *New York Times,* August 13, 1985, pp. C1, C3.

——. "When the Rapist Is Not a Stranger: Studies Seek New Understanding," *New York Times,* August 29, 1989, pp. C1, C6.

Gonnerman, Jennifer. "Life without Parole?" *New York Times Magazine,* May 19, 2002, pp. 40–44.

Gonzalez, David. "Sliwa Admits Faking Crimes for Publicity," *New York Times,* November 25, 1992, pp. B1, B2.

Gordon, Alan R., and Norval Morris. "Presidential Commissions and the Law Enforcement Assistance Administration," in Lynn A. Curtis, ed., *American Violence and Public Policy: An Update of the National Commission on the Causes and Prevention of Violence.* New Haven, CT: Yale University Press, 1985, pp. 117–132.

Gordon, David M. "Capitalism, Class, and Crime in America," *Crime and Delinquency* 19 (April 1973), 163–186.

Gordon, Margaret T., and Stephanie Riger. *The Female Fear.* New York: Free Press, 1989.

Goring, Charles. *The English Convict: A Statistical Study.* London: His Majesty's Stationery Office, 1913.

Gottfredson, Michael R. "Treatment Destruction Techniques," *Journal of Research in Crime and Delinquency* 16 (January 1979), 39–54.

——, and Travis Hirschi. *A General Theory of Crime.* Stanford, CA: Stanford University Press, 1990.

Gove, Walter R., Michael Hughes, and Michael Geerken. "Are Uniform Crime Reports a Valid Indicator of the Index Crimes? An Affirmative Answer with Minor Qualifications," *Criminology* 23 (August 1985), 451–501.

Grabosky, P. N., and Russell G. Smith. *Crime in the Digital Age: Controlling Telecommunications and Cyberspace Illegalities.* New Brunswick, NJ: Transaction Publishers/The Federation Press, 1998.

Graham, Mary G. "Controlling Drug Abuse and Crime: A Research Update," *NIJ Reports,* March/April 1987, pp. 2–7.

Grasmick, Harold G., and Donald E. Green. "Legal Punishment, Social Disapproval and Internalization as Inhibitors of Illegal Behavior," *Journal of Criminal Law and Criminology* 71 (Fall 1980), 325–335.

Grasmick, Harold G., et al. "Testing the Core Empirical Implications of Gottfredson and Hirschi's General Theory of Crime," *Journal of Research in Crime and Delinquency* 30 (February 1993), 5–29.

Green, Donald E. "Measures of Illegal Behavior in Individual-Level Deterrence Research," *Journal of Research in Crime and Delinquency* 26 (August 1989a), 253–275.

———. "Past Behavior as a Measure of Actual Future Behavior: An Unresolved Issue in Perceptual Deterrence Research," *Journal of Criminal Law and Criminology* 80 (Fall 1989b), 781–804.

Green, Gary S. "Citizen Gun Ownership and Criminal Deterrence: Theory, Research, and Policy," *Criminology* 25 (February 1987), 63–81.

Green, Penny A., and H. David Allen. "Severity of Societal Response to Crime: A Synthesis of Models," *Law and Society Review* 16 (1981–82), 181–205.

Greenberg, David F. "The Correctional Effects of Corrections: A Survey of Evaluations," in David F. Greenberg, ed., *Corrections and Punishment.* Beverly Hills, CA: Sage, 1977, pp. 111–148.

———. "Methodological Issues in Survey Research on the Inhibition of Crime," *Journal of Criminal Law and Criminology* 72 (Fall 1981), 1094–1101.

———. "The Weak Strength of Social Control Theory," *Crime and Delinquency* 45 (January 1999), 66–81.

———, and Ronald C. Kessler. "The Effects of Arrests on Crime: A Multivariate Panel Analysis," *Social Problems* 60 (March 1982), 771–790.

———, Ronald C. Kessler, and Colin Loftin. "The Effects of Police Employment on Crime," *Criminology* 21 (August 1983), 375–394.

———, Ronald C. Kessler, and Colin Loftin. "Social Inequality and Crime Control," *Journal of Criminal Law and Criminology* 76 (Fall 1985), 684–704.

Greenberg, Stephanie W. "Alcohol and Crime: A Methodological Critique of the Literature," in James J. Collins, Jr., ed., *Drinking and Crime: Perspectives on the Relationships between Alcohol Consumption and Criminal Behavior.* New York: Guilford Press, 1981, pp. 71–109.

———, and Freda Adler. "Crime and Addiction: An Empirical Analysis of the Literature, 1920–1973," *Contemporary Drug Problems* 3 (Summer 1974), 221–269.

Greenfeld, Lawrence A. *Alcohol and Crime: An Analysis of National Data on the Prevalence of Alcohol Involvement in Crime.* Washington, DC: U.S. Department of Justice, April 1998.

———. *Sex Offenses and Offenders: An Analysis of Data on Rape and Sexual Assault.* Washington, DC: U.S. Department of Justice, February 1997.

———, and Steven Smith. *American Indians and Crime.* Washington, DC: U.S. Department of Justice, February 1999.

Greenhouse, Steven. "Poles Find Crime Replacing Police State," *New York Times,* March 4, 1990, p. 20.

Greenwood, Peter W. "Differences in Criminal Behavior and Court Responses among Juvenile and Young Adult Defendants," in Michael Tonry and Norval Morris, eds., *Crime and Justice: An Annual Review of Research,* vol. 7. Chicago: University of Chicago Press, 1986, pp. 151–187.

———. "Selective Incapacitation: A Method of Using Our Prisons More Effectively," *NIJ Reports,* January 1984, pp. 4–7.

———, et al. *Diverting Children from a Life of Crime: Measuring Costs and Benefits.* Santa Monica, CA: Rand, 1996.

———, et al. *Three Strikes and You're Out: Estimated Benefits and Costs of California's New Mandatory-Sentencing Law.* Santa Monica, CA: Rand, 1994.

———, with Allan Abrahamse. *Selective Incapacitation.* Santa Monica, CA: Rand, 1982.

Greer, William R. "Most Burglars Look for Easy Ways to Slip Unseen into Empty Homes and Head Straight for the Bedroom," *New York Times,* July 10, 1986, pp. C1, C6.

Grinnell, Richard M., Jr., and Cheryl A. Chambers. "Broken Homes and Middle-Class Delinquency: A Comparison," *Criminology* 17 (November 1979), 395–400.

Grogger, Jeff. "An Economic Model of Recent Trends in Violence," in Alfred Blumstein and Joel Wallman, eds., *The Crime Drop in America.* Cambridge, England: Cambridge University Press, 2000, pp. 266–287.

Groth, A. Nicholas, Robert E. Longo, and J. Bradley McFadin. "Undetected Recidivism among Rapists and Child Molesters," *Crime and Delinquency* 28 (July 1982), 450–458.

Hackney, Sheldon. "Southern Violence," in Hugh Davis Graham and Ted Robert Gurr, eds., *Violence in America: Historical and Comparative Perspectives.* Staff Report to the National Commission on the Causes and Prevention of Violence, vol. 2. Washington, D.C.: U.S. Government Printing Office, 1969, pp. 387–404.

Hafner, Katie, and John Markoff. *Cyberpunk: Outlaws and Hackers on the Computer Frontier.* New York: Simon and Schuster, 1991.

Hagan, John. "The Social Embeddedness of Crime and Unemployment," *Criminology* 31 (November 1993), pp. 465–491.

———. *Structural Criminology.* New Brunswick, NJ: Rutgers University Press, 1989.

———, and Holly Foster. "Youth Violence and the End of Adolescence," *American Sociological Review* 66 (December 2001), 874–899.

Hagedorn, John M. "Homeboys, Dope Fiends, Legits, and New Jacks," *Criminology* 32 (May 1994), 197–219.

Hakim, Simon, and George F. Rengert, eds. *Crime Spillover.* Beverly Hills, CA: Sage, 1981.

Hamilton, V. Lee, and Laurence Rotkin. "Interpreting the Eighth Amendment: Perceived Seriousness of Crime and Severity of Punishment," in Hugo Adam Bedau and Chester M. Pierce, eds., *Capital Punishment in the United States.* New York: AMS Press, 1976, pp. 502–524.

Hamilton, V. Lee, and Steve Rytina. "Social Consensus on Norms of Justice: Should the Punishment Fit the Crime?" *American Journal of Sociology* 85 (March 1980), 1117–1144.

Hamilton, V. Lee, and Joseph Sanders. *Everyday Justice: Responsibility and the Individual in Japan and the United States.* New Haven, CT: Yale University Press, 1992.

Hamilton, V. Lee, and Joseph Sanders, et al. "Punishment and the Individual in the United States and Japan," *Law and Society Review* 22 (1988), 301–328.

Hamlin, John E. "The Misplaced Role of Rational Choice in Neutralization Theory," *Criminology* 26 (August 1988), 425–438.

Hamparian, Donna Martin, et al. *The Young Criminal Years of the Violent Few.* Washington, DC: U.S. Department of Justice, June 1985.

Hanson, Bill, et al. *Life with Heroin: Voices from the Inner City.* Lexington, MA: D. C. Heath, 1985.

Harcourt, Bernard E. *Illusion of Order: The False Promise of Broken Window Policing.* Cambridge, MA: Harvard University Press, 2001.

Hare, R. D., S. D. Hart, and T. J. Harpur. "Psychopathy and the DSM-IV Criteria for Antisocial Personality Disorder," *Journal of Abnormal Psychology* 100 (1991), 391–398.

Harlow, Caroline Wolf. *Injuries from Crime.* Washington, DC: U.S. Department of Justice, May 1989.

Harring, Sidney L. *Policing a Class Society: The Experience of American Cities, 1865–1915.* New Brunswick, NJ: Rutgers University Press, 1983.

Harrison, Lana, and Joseph Gfroerer. "The Intersection of Drug Use and Criminal Behavior: Results from the National Household Survey on Drug Abuse," *Crime and Delinquency* 38 (October 1992), 422–443.

Hartjen, Clayton A., and Don C. Gibbons. "An Empirical Investigation of a Criminal Typology," *Sociology and Social Research* 54 (October 1969), 56–62.

Hartjen, Clayton A., and S. Priyadarsini. *Delinquency in India: A Comparative Analysis.* New Brunswick, NJ: Rutgers University Press, 1984.

Harvard Magazine. "Understanding Terrorism: A *Harvard Magazine* Roundtable," *Harvard Magazine,* January–February 2002, pp. 36–49, 99–103.

Hawkins, Darnell, and Kenneth A. Hardy. "Black-White Imprisonment Rates: A State-by-State Analysis," *Social Justice* 16 (1989), 75–95.

Hawkins, Gordon. "God and the Mafia," *The Public Interest* no. 14 (Winter 1969), 24–51.

Hay, Carter. "Parenting, Self-Control, and Delinquency: A Test of Self-Control Theory," *Criminology* 39 (August 2001), 707–736.

Heinz, Anne M., and Wayne A. Kerstetter. "Pretrial Settlement Conference: Evaluation of a Reform in Plea Bargaining," in Burt Galaway and Joe Hudson, eds., *Perspectives on Crime Victims.* St. Louis: C. V. Mosby, 1981, pp. 266–276.

Hembroff, Larry A. "The Seriousness of Acts and Social Contexts: A Test of Black's Theory of the Behavior of Law," *American Journal of Sociology* 93 (September 1987), 322–347.

Hennessy, Michael, Pamela J. Richards, and Richard A. Berk. "Broken Homes and Middle Class Delinquency," *Criminology* 15 (February 1978), 505–528.

Hepburn, John R. "The Impact of Police Intervention upon Juvenile Delinquents," *Criminology* 15 (August 1977), 225–262.

Herrnstein, Richard J., and Charles Murray. *The Bell Curve: Intelligence and Class Structure in American Life.* New York: Free Press, 1994.

Hickey, Eric W. *Serial Murderers and Their Victims,* 3d ed. Belmont, CA: Wadsworth, 2002.

Hindelang, Michael J. "Causes of Delinquency: A Partial Replication and Extension," *Social Problems* 20 (Spring 1973), 471–487.

———. "Class and Crime," in Sanford H. Kadish, ed., *Encyclopedia of Crime and Justice,* vol. 1. New York: Free Press, 1983, pp. 175–181.

———. *Criminal Victimization in Eight American Cities: A Descriptive Analysis of Common Theft and Assault.* Cambridge, MA: Ballinger, 1976.

———. "Race and Involvement in Common Law Personal Crimes," *American Sociological Review* 43 (February 1978), 93–109.

Hirschel, J. David, and Ira W. Hutchison, 3d. "Female Spouse Abuse and the Police Response: The Charlotte, North Carolina Experiment," *Journal of Criminal Law and Criminology* 83 (Spring 1992), 73–119.

Hirschi, Travis. *Causes of Delinquency.* Berkeley: University of California Press, 1969.

———. "Crime and the Family," in James Q. Wilson, ed., *Crime and Public Policy.* San Francisco: ICS Press, 1983, pp. 53–68.

———, and Michael J. Hindelang. "Intelligence and Delinquency: A Revisionist Review," *American Sociological Review* 42 (August 1977), 571–587.

Hochstetler, Andy. "Opportunities and Decisions: Interactional Dynamics in Robbery and Burglary Groups," *Criminology* 39 (August 2001), 737–763.

Hodgins, S. "Mental Disorder, Intellectual Deficiency, and Crime: A Birth Cohort," *Archives of General Psychiatry* 49 (1992), 476–483.

———, et al. "Mental Disorder and Crime: Evidence from a Danish Birth Cohort," *Archives of General Psychiatry* 53 (1996), 489–496.

Hoffman-Bustamante, Dale. "The Nature of Female Criminality," *Issues in Criminology* 8 (Fall 1973), 117–136.

Hohler, Bob. "N. H. Neighbors React to a Rape and Witnesses Who Did Not Act," *Boston Globe,* August 16, 1987, p. 44.

Hollinger, Richard C., and John P. Clark. *Theft by Employees.* Lexington, MA: D. C. Heath, 1983.

Holzman, Harold R. "Learning Disabilities and Juvenile Delinquency: Biological and Sociological Theories," in C. R. Jeffery, ed., *Biology and Crime.* Beverly Hills, CA: Sage, 1979, pp. 77–86.

Hooton, Earnest A. *The American Criminal: An Anthropological Study.* Cambridge, MA: Harvard University Press, 1939.

Horney, Julie D., Wayne Osgood, and Ineke Haen Marshall. "Criminal Careers in the Short-Term: Intra-Individual Variability in Crime and Its Relation to Local Life Circumstances," *American Sociological Review* 60 (October 1995), 655–673.

Horning, Donald N. M. "Blue-Collar Theft: Conceptions of Property, Attitudes toward Pilfering, and Work Group Norms in a Modern Industrial Plant," in Erwin O. Smigel and H. Laurence Ross, eds., *Crimes against Bureaucracy.* New York: Van Nostrand Reinhold, 1970, pp. 46–64.

Horowitz, Ruth. *Honor and the American Dream: Culture and Social Identity in a Chicano Community.* New Brunswick, NJ: Rutgers University Press, 1983.

———, and Gary Schwartz. "Honor, Normative Ambiguity and Gang Violence," *American Sociological Review* 39 (April 1974), 238–251.

Hoyt, Dan R., Kimberly D. Ryan, and Ana Mari Cauce. "Personal Victimization in a High-Risk Environment: Homeless and Runaway Adolescents," *Journal of Research in Crime and Delinquency* 36 (November 1999), 371–392.

Ianni, Francis A. J., with Elizabeth Reuss-Ianni. *A Family Business: Kinship and Social Control in Organized Crime.* New York: Russell Sage Foundation, 1972.

Ignatieff, Michael. *A Just Measure of Pain: The Penitentiary in the Industrial Revolution, 1750–1850.* New York: Pantheon, 1978.

Inciardi, James A. *Careers in Crime.* Chicago: Rand McNally, 1975.

———. "Heroin Use and Street Crime," *Crime and Delinquency* 25 (July 1979), 335–346.

———, Ruth Horowitz, and Anne E. Pottieger. *Street Kids, Street Drugs, Street Crime: An Examination of Drug Use and Serious Delinquency in Miami.* Belmont, CA: Wadsworth, 1993.

Ireland, Timothy, and Cathy Spatz Widom. "Childhood Victimization and Risk for Alcohol and Drug Arrests," *International Journal of the Addictions* 29 (1994), 235–274.

Irwin, John. "Adaptation to Being Corrected: Corrections from the Convict's Perspective," in Daniel Glaser, ed., *Handbook of Criminology.* Chicago: Rand McNally, 1974, pp. 971–993.

———. *The Felon.* Englewood Cliffs, NJ: Prentice Hall, 1970.

Jackson, Bruce. *A Thief's Primer.* New York: Macmillan, 1969.

Jackson, Pamela Irving, and Leo Carroll. "Race and the War on Crime: The Sociopolitical Determinants of Municipal Police Expenditures in 90 Non-Southern U.S. Cities," *American Sociological Review* 46 (June 1981), 290–305.

Jacobs, Bruce A. *Robbing Drug Dealers: Violence beyond the Law.* Hawthorne, NY: Aldine de Gruyter, 2000.

Jacobs, David, and Robert M. O'Brien. "The Determinants of Deadly Force: A Structural Analysis of Police Violence," *American Journal of Sociology* 103 (January 1998), 837–862.

Jacobs, James B., and Kimberly Potter. *Hate Crimes: Criminal Law and Identity Politics.* New York: Oxford University Press, 1998.

Jacobs, Jane. *The Death and Life of Great American Cities.* New York: Vintage, 1961.

James, Jennifer, and William Thornton. "Women's Liberation and the Female Delinquent," *Journal of Research in Crime and Delinquency* 17 (July 1980), 230–244.

Jang, Sung Joon, and Terence P. Thornberry. "Self-Esteem, Delinquent Peers, and Delinquency: A Test of the Self-Enhancement Thesis," *American Sociological Review* 63 (August 1998), 586–598.

Jankowski, Martín Sanchéz. *Islands in the Street: Gangs and American Urban Society.* Berkeley: University of California Press, 1991.

Jeffery, C. Ray. "Biology and Crime: The New Neo-Lombrosians," in C. R. Jeffery, ed., *Biology and Crime.* Beverly Hills, CA: Sage, 1979, pp. 7–18.

Jenkins, Patricia H. "School Delinquency and the School Social Bond," *Journal of Research in Crime and Delinquency* 34 (August 1997), 337–367.

Jenkins, Philip. "Fighting Terrorism as if Women Mattered: Anti-Abortion Violence as Unconstructed Terrorism," in Jeff Ferrell and Neil Websdale, eds., *Making Trouble: Cultural Constructions of Crime, Deviance, and Control.* Hawthorne, NY: Aldine de Gruyter, 1999, pp. 319–346.

———. *Using Murder: The Social Construction of Serial Homicide.* New York: Aldine de Gruyter, 1994.

Jensen, Gary F. "Inner Containment and Delinquency," *Journal of Criminal Law and Criminology* 64 (December 1973), 464–470.

———. "Power-Control vs. Social-Control Theories of Common Delinquency: A Comparative Analysis," in Freda Adler and William S. Laufer, eds., *New Directions in Criminological Theory: Advances in Criminological Theory,* vol. 4. New Brunswick, NJ: Transaction, 1993, pp. 363–380.

———, and David Brownfield. "Gender, Lifestyles and Victimization: Beyond Routine Activities," *Violence and Victims* 1 (1986), 85–99.

———, and Kevin Thompson. "What's Class Got to Do with It? Further Examination of Power-Control Theory," *American Journal of Sociology* 95 (January 1990), 1009–1023.

Jensen, Michael C. "Business Students Disagree on Bribes," *New York Times,* March 27, 1976, p. 37.

Jesilow, Paul, Henry N. Pontell, and Gilbert Geis. *Prescription for Profit: How Doctors Defraud Medicaid.* Berkeley: University of California Press, 1993.

Joe, Delbert, and Norman Robinson. "Chinatown's Immigrant Gangs: The New Young Warrior Class," *Criminology* 18 (November 1980), 337–345.

Johnson, Bruce D., Andrew Golub, and Jeffrey Fagan. "Careers in Crack, Drug Use, Drug Distribution, and Nondrug Criminality," *Crime and Delinquency* 41 (July 1995), 275–295.

Johnson, Byron R., et al. "A Systematic Review of the Religiosity and Delinquency Literature," *Journal of Contemporary Criminal Justice* 16 (February 2000), 32–52.

Johnson, David R., and Laurie K. Scheuble. "Gender Bias in the Disposition of Juvenile Court Referrals: The Effects of Time and Location," *Criminology* 29 (November 1991), 677–699.

Johnson, Elmer H., and Israel L. Barak-Glantz. "Introduction," in Israel L. Barak-Glantz and Elmer H. Johnson, eds., *Comparative Criminology.* Beverly Hills, CA: Sage, 1983, pp. 7–17.

Johnson, Jeffrey G., et al. "Television Viewing and Aggressive Behavior during Adolescence and Adulthood," *Science* 295 (March 29, 2002), 2468–2471.

Johnson, Richard E. "Social Class and Delinquent Behavior: A New Test," *Criminology* 18 (May 1980), 86–93.

Johnston, David Cay. "Affluent Avoid Scrutiny on Taxes Even as I.R.S. Warns of Cheating," *New York Times,* April 7, 2002, pp. 1, 23.

Joint Committee on New York Drug Law Evaluation. *The Nation's Toughest Drug Law: Evaluating the New York Experience.* Washington, DC: U.S. Government Printing Office, 1978.

Jordan, B. K., et al. "Prevalence of Psychiatric Disorders among Incarcerated Women: Convicted Felons Entering Prison," *Archives of General Psychiatry* 53 (1996), 513–519.

Joyce, Fay S. "Some Victims' Families Find Relief in Executions," *New York Times,* January 19, 1984, p. A18.

Judson, Horace Freeland. *Heroin Addiction in Britain: What Americans Can Learn from the English Experience.* New York: Harcourt Brace Jovanovich, 1974.

Junger, Marianne, and Ineke Haen Marshall. "The Interethnic Generalizability of Social Control Theory: An Empirical Test," *Journal of Research in Crime and Delinquency* 34 (February 1997), 79–112.

Junger-Tas, Josine, and Ineke Haen Marshall. "The Self-Report Methodology in Crime Research," in Michael Tonry, ed., *Crime and Justice: A Review of Research.* Chicago: University of Chicago Press, 1999, pp. 291–367.

Kalven, Harry, Jr., and Hans Zeisel. *The American Jury.* Boston: Little, Brown, 1966.

Kaplan, Howard B., Steven S. Martin, and Robert J. Johnson. "Self-Rejection and the Explanation of Deviance: Specification of the Structure among Latent Constructs," *American Journal of Sociology* (September 1986), 384–411.

Kappeler, Victor E., Mark Blumberg, and Gary W. Potter. *The Mythology of Crime and Criminal Justice,* 2d ed. Prospect Heights, IL: Waveland Press, 1996.

Karmen, Andrew. *New York Murder Mystery: The True Story behind the Crime Crash of the 1990s.* New York: New York University Press, 2000.

Karp, David R. "Harm and Repair: Observing Restorative Justice in Vermont," *Justice Quarterly* 18 (December 2001), 727–757.

Kassebaum, Gene, David A. Ward, and Daniel M. Wilner. *Prison Treatment and Parole Survival: An Empirical Assessment.* New York: Wiley, 1971.

Katz, Jack. *Seductions of Crime: Moral and Sensual Attractions in Doing Evil.* New York: Basic Books, 1988.

Kellermann, Arthur L., et al. "Gun Ownership as a Risk Factor for Homicide in the Home," *New England Journal of Medicine* 329 (October 7, 1993), 1084–1091.

Kelley, Barbara Tatem, Terence P. Thornberry, and Carolyn A. Smith. *In the Wake of Childhood Maltreatment.* Washington, DC: U.S. Department of Justice, August 1997.

Kelley, Clarence M. *Crime in the United States, 1975: Uniform Crime Reports.* Washington, DC: U.S. Government Printing Office, 1976.

Kelley, Thomas M. "Status Offenders Can Be Different: A Comparative Study of Delinquent Careers," *Crime and Delinquency* 29 (July 1983), 365–380.

Kelling, George L., et al. *The Kansas City Preventive Patrol Experiment.* Washington, DC: Police Foundation, 1974.

Kelling, George., et al. *The Newark Foot Patrol Experiment.* Washington, DC: Police Foundation, 1981.

Kempf, Kimberly L. "Specialization and the Criminal Career," *Criminology* 25 (May 1987), 399–420.

Kempf-Leonard, Kimberly, Paul E. Tracy, and James C. Howell. "Serious, Violent, and Chronic Juvenile Offenders: The Relationship of Delinquency Career Types to Adult Criminality," *Justice Quarterly* 18 (September 2001), 449–478.

Kennedy, Leslie W., and David R. Forde. "Routine Activities and Crime: An Analysis of Victimization in Canada," *Criminology* 28 (February 1990), 137–152.

Kenney, Dennis Jay. *Crime, Fear, and the New York City Subways: The Role of Citizen Action.* New York: Praeger, 1987.

Kessler, R. C., et al. "Lifetime and 12-Month Prevalence of DSM-III-R Psychiatric Disorders in the United States," *Archives of General Psychiatry* 51 (1994), 8–19.

Kifner, John. "New Immigrant Wave from Asia Gives the Underworld New Faces," *New York Times,* January 6, 1991, pp. 1, 20.

Kilpatrick, Dean G., David Beatty, and Susan Smith Howley. *The Rights of Crime Victims—Does Legal Protection Make a Difference?* Washington, DC: U.S. Department of Justice, December 1998.

King, Harry, and William J. Chambliss. *Harry King: A Professional Thief's Journey.* New York: Wiley, 1984.

Kirkpatrick, John T., and John A. Humphrey. "Stress in the Lives of Female Criminal Homicide Offenders in North Carolina," in James H. Humphrey, ed., *Human Stress: Current Selected Research,* vol. 3. New York: AMS Press, 1989, pp. 109–120.

Kirkpatrick, Sidney D. *Lords of Sipán: A True Story of Pre-Inca Tombs, Archaeology, and Crime.* New York: Morrow, 1992.

Klaus, Patsy. *Carjackings in the United States, 1992–96.* Washington, DC: U.S. Department of Justice, March 1999.

———. *Crimes against Persons Age 65 or Older, 1992–97.* Washington, DC: U.S. Department of Justice, January 2000.

Kleck, Gary. "Life Support for Ailing Hypotheses. Modes of Summarizing the Evidence for Racial Discrimination in Sentencing," *Law and Human Behavior* 9 (1985), 271–285.

———. "Racial Discrimination in Criminal Sentencing: A Critical Evaluation of the Evidence with Additional Evidence on the Death Penalty," *American Sociological Review* 46 (December 1981), 783–805.

———. *Targeting Guns: Firearms and Their Control.* New York: Aldine de Gruyter, 1997.

———, and Marc Gertz. "Armed Resistance to Crime: The Prevalence and Nature of Self-Defense with a Gun," *Journal of Criminal Law and Criminology* 86 (Fall 1995), 150–187.

Klein, Stephen P., Susan Turner, and Joan Petersilia. *Racial Equity in Sentencing.* Santa Monica, CA: Rand, 1988.

Klemke, Lloyd W. "Does Apprehension for Shoplifting Amplify or Terminate Shoplifting Activity?" *Law and Society Review* 12 (Spring 1978), 391–403.

Klinger, David A. "Demeanor or Crime? Why 'Hostile' Citizens Are More Likely to Be Arrested," *Criminology* 32 (August 1994), 475–493.

———. "More on Demeanor and Arrest in Dade County," *Criminology* 34 (February 1996), 61–82.

Klockars, Carl B. *The Professional Fence.* New York: Free Press, 1974.

Kohlmeier, Louis M. "The Bribe Busters," *New York Times Magazine,* September 26, 1976, pp. 47–60.

Kolata, Gina. "Racial Bias Seen on Pregnant Addicts," *New York Times,* July 20, 1990, p. 13.

Kolbert, Elizabeth. "Television Gets Closer Look as a Factor in Real Violence," *New York Times,* December 14, 1994, pp. A1, D20.

Kovandzic, Tomislav V., Lynne M. Vieraitis, and Mark R. Yeisley. "The Structural Covariates of Urban Homicide: Reassessing the Impact of Income Inequality and Poverty in the Post-Reagan Era," *Criminology* 36 (August 1998), 569–599.

Kramer, John H., and Jeffrey T. Ulmer. "Sentencing Disparity and Departures from Guidelines," *Justice Quarterly* 13 (March 1996), 81–106.

Kramer, Ronald C. "Corporate Crime: An Organizational Perspective," in Peter Wickman and Timothy Dailey, eds., *White-Collar and Economic Crime.* Lexington, MA: D. C. Heath, 1982, pp. 75–94.

Krohn, Marvin D., James P. Curry, and Shirley Nelson-Kilger. "Is Chivalry Dead? An Analysis of Changes in Police Dispositions of Males and Females," *Criminology* 21 (August 1983), 417–437.

Krohn, Marvin D., et al. "Social Status and Deviance: Class Context of School, Social Status, and Delinquent Behavior," *Criminology* 18 (November 1980), 303–318.

Krost, Jack. "He Tries to Determine What Makes Criminals Tick," *Boston Globe,* October 24, 1982, p. 8.

Kruttschnitt, Candace. "Women, Crime, and Dependency: An Application of the Theory of Law," *Criminology* 19 (February 1982), 495–513.

———, Christopher Uggen, and Kelly Shelton. "Predictors of Desistance among Sex Offenders: The Interaction of Formal and Informal Social Controls," *Justice Quarterly* 17 (March 2000), 61–87.

Kutchinsky, Berl. "Pornography and Sexual Violence: The Criminological Evidence from Aggregate Data in Several Countries." Paper presented at the Fourteenth International Congress on Law And Mental Health, Montreal, 1988.

Kvålseth, Tarald O. "Seriousness of Offenses: An Experimental Study Based on a Psychological Scaling Technique," *Criminology* 18 (August 1980), 237–244.

Lab, Steven P. "Patterns in Juvenile Misbehavior," *Crime and Delinquency* 30 (April 1984), 293–308.

———, and John T. Whitehead. "An Analysis of Juvenile Correctional Treatment," *Crime and Delinquency* 34 (January 1988), 60–83.

———, and John T. Whitehead. "From 'Nothing Works' to 'The Appropriate Works': The Latest Stop on the Search for the Secular Grail," *Criminology* 28 (August 1990), 405–417.

Labaton, Stephen. "Milken's Sentence," *New York Times,* April 26, 1990, pp. D1, D11.

LaFree, Gary D. "Adversarial and Nonadversarial Justice: Comparison of Guilty Pleas and Trials," *Criminology* 23 (May 1985), 289–312.

———. "The Effect of Sexual Stratification by Race on Official Reactions to Rape," *American Sociological Review* 45 (October 1980), 842–854.

———. *Losing Legitimacy: Street Crime and the Decline of Social Institutions in America.* Boulder, CO: Westview, 1998.

———. *Rape and Criminal Justice: The Social Construction of Sexual Assault.* Belmont, CA: Wadsworth, 1989.

———, and Kriss A. Drass. "The Effect of Changes in Intraracial Income Inequality and Educational Attainment on Changes in Arrest Rates for African Americans and Whites, 1957 to 1990," *American Sociological Review* 61 (August 1996), 614–634.

LaGrange, Randy L., and Helene Raskin White. "Age Differences in Delinquency: A Test of Theory," *Criminology* 23 (February 1985), 19–45.

LaGrange, Teresa C., and Robert A. Silverman. "Low Self-Control and Opportunity: Testing the General Theory of Crime as an Explanation for Gender Differences in Delinquency," *Criminology* 37 (February 1999), 41–72.

Lakshmanan, Indira A. R. "58 Chinese Paid with Their Lives; Smuggling Thrives Despite Cost, Risks," *Boston Sunday Globe,* June 25, 2000, pp. A1, A26.

Lally, J. Ronald, Peter L. Mangione, and Alice S. Honig. "The Syracuse University Family Development Research Program: Long-Range Impact on an Early Intervention with Low-Income Children and Their Families," in Douglas R. Powell, ed., *Annual Advances in Applied Developmental Psychology: Parent Education as Early Childhood Intervention: Emerging Directions in Theory, Research and Practice,* vol. 3. Norwood, NJ: Ablex, 1998, pp. 79–104.

Land, Kenneth C., David Cantor, and Stephen T. Russell. "Unemployment and Crime Rate Fluctuations in the Post–World War II United States: Statistical Time-Series Properties and Alternative Models," in John Hagan and Ruth D. Peterson, eds., *Crime and Inequality.* Stanford, CA: Stanford University Press, 1995, pp. 55–79.

Langan, Patrick A. "Racism on Trial: New Evidence to Explain the Racial Composition of Prisons in the United States," *Journal of Criminal Law and Criminology* 76 (Fall 1985), 666–683.

———, and John M. Dawson. *Spouse Murder Defendants in Large Urban Counties.* Washington, DC: U.S. Department of Justice, September 1995.

———, and David P. Farrington. *Crime and Justice in the United States and in England and Wales, 1981–1996.* Washington, DC: U.S. Department of Justice, October 1998.

———, and David J. Levin. *Recidivism of Prisoners Released in 1994.* Washington, DC: U.S. Department of Justice, June 2002.

Lanza-Kaduce, Lonn, Donna M. Bishop, and Lawrence Winner. "Risk/Benefit Calculations, Moral Evaluations, and Alcohol Use: Exploring the Alcohol-Crime

Connection," *Crime and Delinquency* 43 (April 1997), 222–239.

Larzelere, Robert E., and Gerald R. Patterson. "Parental Management: Mediator of the Effect of Socioeconomic Status on Early Delinquency," *Criminology* 28 (May 1990), 301–323.

Latané, Bibb, and John M. Darley. *The Unresponsive Bystander: Why Doesn't He Help?* New York: Appleton-Century-Crofts, 1970.

Laub, John H., Daniel S. Nagin, and Robert J. Sampson. "Trajectories of Change in Criminal Offending: Good Marriages and the Desistance Process," *American Sociological Review* 63 (April 1998), 225–238.

Laub, John H., and Robert J. Sampson. "Understanding Desistance from Crime," in Michael Tonry, ed., *Crime and Justice: A Review of Research,* vol. 28. Chicago: University of Chicago Press, 2001, pp. 1–69.

Laudon, Kenneth C. *Dossier Society: Value Choices in the Design of National Information Systems.* New York: Columbia University Press, 1986.

Lauritsen, Janet L., Robert J. Sampson, and John H. Laub. "The Link between Offending and Victimization among Adolescents," *Criminology* 29 (May 1991), 265–291.

Lavrakas, Paul J. "Fear of Crime and Behavioral Restrictions in Urban and Suburban Neighborhoods," *Population and Environment* 5 (1982), 242–264.

———, and Elicia J. Herz. "Citizen Participation in Neighborhood Crime Prevention," *Criminology* 20 (November 1982), 479–498.

Layson, Stephen K. "Homicide and Deterrence: A Reexamination of the United States Time-Series Evidence," *Southern Economic Journal* 52 (July 1985), 68–89.

LeBlanc, Marc, and Rolf Loeber, "Developmental Criminology Updated," in Michael Tonry, ed., *Crime and Justice: A Review of Research,* vol. 23. Chicago: University of Chicago Press, 1998, pp. 115–198.

Lefkowitz, Monroe M., et al. *Growing Up to Be Violent: A Longitudinal Study of the Development of Aggression.* New York: Pergamon, 1977.

Lejeune, Robert. "The Management of a Mugging," *Urban Life* 6 (July 1977), 123–148.

Lemert, Edwin M. "Isolation and Closure Theory of Naive Check Forgery," *Journal of Criminal Law, Criminology and Police Science* 44 (September–October 1953), 293–307.

———. *Social Pathology.* New York: McGraw-Hill, 1951.

Leonard, Eileen B. *Women, Crime, and Society: A Critique of Criminology Theory.* New York: Longman, 1982.

Leonard, William N., and Marvin Glenn Weber. "Automakers and Dealers: A Study of Criminogenic Market Forces," *Law and Society Review* 4 (February 1970), 407–424.

Lesieur, Henry R. "Compulsive Gambling," *Society* 29 (May/June 1992), 43–50.

———. "Gambling, Pathological Gambling and Crime," in Thomas Galski, ed., *The Handbook of Pathological Gambling.* Springfield, IL: Charles C Thomas, 1987, pp. 89–110.

Letkemann, Peter. *Crime as Work.* Englewood Cliffs, NJ: Prentice Hall, 1973.

Levin, Jack, and Jack McDevitt. "Yes, We Need Hate Crime Laws," *Boston Globe,* July 28, 1998, p. A15.

Levine, Dennis B. *Inside Out: An Insider's Account of Wall Street.* New York: Putnam, 1991.

Levine, James P. "Jury Toughness: The Impact of Conservatism on Criminal Court Verdicts," *Crime and Delinquency* 29 (January 1983), 71–87.

Levitt, Steven D. "Using Electoral Cycles in Police Hiring to Estimate the Effect of Police on Crime," *American Economic Review* 87 (June 1997), 270–290.

Lewis, Dan A., Jane A. Grant, and Dennis P. Rosenbaum. *Social Construction of Reform: Crime Prevention and Community Organizations.* New Brunswick, NJ: Transaction Books, 1988.

Lewis, Dan A., and Greta Salem. "Community Crime Prevention: An Analysis of a Developing Strategy," *Crime and Delinquency* 27 (July 1981), 405–421.

Lewis, Dan A., and Greta Salem. *Fear of Crime: Incivility and the Production of a Social Problem.* New Brunswick, NJ: Transaction Books, 1986.

Lewis, Dorothy Otnow, et al. "Homicidally Aggressive Young Children: Neuropsychiatric and Experiential Correlates," *American Journal of Psychiatry* 140 (February 1983), 148–153.

Lewis, Dorothy Otnow, et al. "Violent Juvenile Delinquents: Psychiatric, Neurological, Psychological and Abuse Factors," *Journal of the American Academy of Child Psychiatry* 18 (1979), 307–319.

Lewis, Neil A. "Justice Department Opposes Lower Jail Terms for Crack," *New York Times,* March 20, 2002, p. A20.

Lichter, Linda S., and S. Robert Lichter. *Prime Time Crime: Criminals and Law Enforcers in TV Entertainment.* Washington, DC: Media Institute, 1983.

Lichter, S. Robert, Linda S. Lichter, and Stanley Rothman. *Prime Time: How TV Portrays American Culture.* Washington, DC: Regnery, 1994.

Liddick, Don. "The Enterprise 'Model' of Organized Crime: Assessing Theoretical Propositions," *Justice Quarterly* 19 (June 1999), 403–430.

Liebman, James S., Valerie West, and Jeffrey Fagan. "A Broken System: Error Rates in Capital Cases 1973–1995." Retrieved June 12, 2002, from www.law.columbia.edu/news/PressReleases/liebman.html.

Lilienfeld, S. O., and I. D. Waldman. "The Relation between Childhood Attention-Deficit Hyperactivity Disorder and Adult Antisocial Behavior Re-examined: The Problem of Heterogeneity," *Clinical Psychology Review* 10 (1990), 699–725.

Link, Bruce G., Howard Andrews, and Francis T. Cullen. "The Violent and Illegal Behavior of Mental Patients Reconsidered," *American Sociological Review* 57 (June 1992), 275–292.

———, and Ann Stueve. "New Evidence on the Violence Risk Posed by People with Mental Illness," *Archives of General Psychiatry* 55 (May 1998), 403–404.

Lipsey, Mark W. *Juvenile Delinquency Treatment: A Meta-Analytic Inquiry into the Viability of Effects.* New York: Russell Sage, 1991.

Lipton, Douglas, Robert Martinson, and Judith Wilks. *The Effectiveness of Correctional Treatment: A Survey of Treatment Evaluation Studies*. New York: Praeger, 1975.

Liska, Allen E., and Mark D. Reed. "Ties to Conventional Institutions and Delinquency: Estimating Reciprocal Effects," *American Sociological Review* 50 (August 1985), 547–560.

Liska, Allen E., and Barbara D. Warner. "Functions of Crime: A Paradoxical Process," *American Journal of Sociology* 96 (May 1991), 1441–1463.

Little, Craig B., and Christopher P. Sheffield. "Frontiers and Criminal Justice: English Private Prosecution Societies and American Vigilantism in the Eighteenth and Nineteenth Centuries," *American Sociological Review* 48 (December 1983), 796–808.

Lizotte, Alan J. "Extra-Legal Factors in Chicago's Criminal Courts: Testing the Conflict Model of Criminal Justice," *Social Problems* 25 (June 1978), 564–580.

Loeber, Rolf, and David P. Farrington, eds. *Serious and Violent Juvenile Offenders: Risk Factors and Successful Interventions*. Thousand Oaks, CA: Sage, 1998.

Loeber, Rolf, David P. Farrington, and Daniel A. Waschbusch. "Serious and Violent Juvenile Offenders," in Rolf Loeber and David P. Farrington, eds., *Serious and Violent Juvenile Offenders: Risk Factors and Successful Interventions*. Thousand Oaks, CA: Sage, 1998, pp. 13–29.

Loeber, Rolf, Larry Kalb, and David Huizinga. *Juvenile Delinquency and Serious Injury Victimization*. Washington, DC: U.S. Department of Justice, August 2001.

Loeber, Rolf, et al. "Initiation, Escalation, and Desistance in Juvenile Offending and Their Correlates," *Journal of Criminal Law and Criminology* 82 (Spring 1991), 36–82.

Loftin, Colin, Milton Heumann, and David McDowall. "Mandatory Sentencing and Firearms Violence: Evaluating an Alternative to Gun Control," *Law and Society Review* 17 (1983), 287–318.

Loftin, Colin, and Robert H. Hill. "Regional Subculture and Homicide: An Examination of the Gastil-Hackney Thesis," *American Sociological Review* 39 (October 1974), 714–724.

Loftin, Colin, and David McDowall. " 'One with a Gun Gets You Two': Mandatory Sentencing and Firearms Violence in Detroit," *Annals of the American Academy of Political and Social Science* 455 (May 1981), 150–167.

Loftin, Colin, and David McDowall. "The Police, Crime and Economic Theory: An Assessment," *American Sociological Review* 47 (June 1982), 393–401.

Logan, Charles H. "Arrest Rates and Deterrence," *Social Science Quarterly* 56 (December 1975), 376–389.

———, and Gerald G. Gaes. "Meta-Analysis and the Rehabilitation of Punishment," *Justice Quarterly* 10 (June 1993), 245–263.

Lombroso, Cesare. "Introduction," to Gina Lombroso Ferrara, *Criminal Man According to the Classification of Cesare Lombroso*. New York: Putnam, 1911.

Lott, John, and David B. Mustard. "Crime, Deterrence, and Right-to-Carry Concealed Handguns," *Journal of Legal Studies* 26 (1997), 1–68.

Lowman, John, and Brian D. MacLean, eds. *Realist Criminology: Crime Control and Policing in the 1990s*. Toronto: University of Toronto Press, 1992.

Luckenbill, David F. "Criminal Homicide as a Situated Transaction," *Social Problems* 25 (December 1977), 176–186.

———, and Joel Best. "Careers in Deviance and Respectability: The Analogy's Limitations," *Social Problems* 29 (December 1981), 197–206.

———, and Daniel P. Doyle. "Structural Position and Violence: Developing a Cultural Explanation," *Criminology* 27 (August 1989), 419–436.

Ludwig, Jens. "Concealed-Gun-Carrying Laws and Violent Crime: Evidence from State Panel Data," *International Review of Law and Economics* 18 (1998), 239–254.

———. "Gun Self-Defense and Deterrence," in Michael Tonry, ed., *Crime and Justice: A Review of Research*, vol. 27. Chicago: University of Chicago Press, 2000, pp. 363–417.

Lundquist, John H., and Janice M. Duke. "The Elderly Victim at Risk: Explaining the Fear-Victimization Paradox," *Criminology* 29 (May 1982), 115–126.

Lupsha, Peter A. "Individual Choice, Material Culture, and Organized Crime," *Criminology* 19 (May 1981), 3–24.

Lynch, James. "Crime in International Perspective," in James Q. Wilson and Joan Petersilia, eds., *Crime: Public Policies for Crime Control*. Oakland, CA: ICS Press, 2002, pp. 5–41.

MacAndrew, Craig, and Robert B. Edgerton. *Drunken Comportment: A Social Explanation*. Chicago: Aldine, 1969.

McAuliffe, William E., and Robert A. Gordon. "A Test of Lindesmith's Theory of Addiction: The Frequency of Euphoria among Long-Term Addicts," *American Journal of Sociology* 79 (January 1974), 795–840.

McCaghy, Charles H. "Child Molesters: A Study of Their Careers as Deviants," in Marshall B. Clinard and Richard Quinney, eds., *Criminal Behavior Systems: A Typology*. New York: Holt, Rinehart and Winston, 1967, pp. 75–88.

———. "Drinking and Deviance Disavowal: The Case of Child Molesters," *Social Problems* 16 (Summer 1968), 43–49.

McCain, Nina. "James Q. Wilson Talks about Crime and Punishment in the U.S.," *Boston Globe*, August 11, 1984, p. 2.

McCarthy, Bill. "Not Just 'For the Thrill of It': An Instrumentalist Elaboration of Katz's Explanation of Sneaky Thrill Property Crimes," *Criminology* 33 (November 1995), 519–538.

McCarthy, John D., and Dean R. Hoge. "The Dynamics of Self-Esteem and Delinquency," *American Journal of Sociology* 90 (September 1984), 396–410.

McClam, Erin. "Whites Live Six Years Longer than Blacks, Says CDC Report," *Boston Globe*, September 14, 2001, p. A6.

McCleary, Richard, Barbara C. Nienstedt, and James M. Erven. "Uniform Crime Reports as Organizational Outcomes: Three Time-Series Experiments," *Social Problems* 29 (April 1982), 361–372.

Maccoby, Eleanor E., and Carol Nagy Jacklin. "Sex Differences in Aggression: A Rejoinder and a Reprise," *Child Development* 51 (December 1980), 964–980.

McCord, Joan. "Family Relationships, Juvenile Delinquency, and Adult Criminality," *Criminology* 29 (August 1991), 397–417.

———. "A Longitudinal Perspective on Patterns of Crime," *Criminology* 19 (August 1981), 211–218.

———. "Some Child-Rearing Antecedents of Criminal Behavior in Adult Men," *Journal of Personality and Social Psychology* 37 (1979), 1477–1486.

———. "A Thirty-Year Follow-up of Treatment Effects," *American Psychologist* 33 (March 1978), 284–289.

McCord, William, and Joan McCord. *Origins of Crime: A New Evaluation of the Cambridge-Somerville Youth Study.* New York: Columbia University Press, 1959.

McCorkle, Richard C. "Research Note: Punish and Rehabilitate? Public Attitudes toward Six Common Crimes," *Crime and Delinquency* 39 (April 1993), 240–252.

MacDonald, John M. "The Effectiveness of Community Policing in Reducing Urban Violence," *Crime and Delinquency* 48 (October 2002), 592–618.

———, and Meda Chesney-Lind. "Gender Bias and Juvenile Justice Revisited: A Multiyear Analysis," *Crime and Delinquency* 47 (April 2001), 173–195.

McDowall, David, Alan J. Lizotte, and Brian Wiersema. "General Deterrence through Civilian Gun Ownership: An Evaluation of the Quasi-Experimental Evidence," *Criminology* 29 (November 1991), 541–559.

McFarland, Sam G. "Is Capital Punishment a Short-Term Deterrent to Homicide? A Study of the Effects of Four Recent American Executions," *Journal of Criminal Law and Criminology* 74 (Winter 1983), 1014–1032.

McGahey, Richard M. "Economic Conditions, Neighborhood Organization, and Urban Crime," in Albert J. Reiss, Jr., and Michael Tonry, eds., *Communities and Crime.* Chicago: University of Chicago Press, 1986, pp. 231–270.

McGarrell, Edmund, Steven Chermak, and Alexander Weiss. *Reducing Firearms Violence through Directed Police Patrol: Final Report on the Evaluation of the Indianapolis Police Department's Direct Patrol Project.* Indianapolis, IN: Crime Control Policy Center, 1999.

McGarrell, Edmund, et al. "Reducing Firearms Violence through Directed Police Patrol," *Criminology and Public Policy* 1 (November 2001), 119–148.

McGlothin, William H., M. Douglas Anglin, and Bruce D. Wilson. "Narcotic Addiction and Crime," *Criminology* 16 (November 1978), 293–315.

McGuire, William J., and Richard G. Sheehan. "Relationships between Crime Rates and Incarceration Rates: Further Analysis," *Journal of Research in Crime and Delinquency* 20 (1983), 73–85.

McIntosh, Mary. *The Organisation of Crime.* London: Macmillan Press, Ltd., 1975.

MacKenzie, Doris Layton. "Boot Camp Prisons in 1993," *National Institute of Justice Journal,* November 1993, pp. 21–28.

McKinley, James C., Jr. "It Isn't Just a Game: Clues to Avid Rooting," *New York Times,* August 11, 2000, pp. A1, C24.

McLarin, Kimberly J. "Welfare Fingerprinting Finds Most People Are Telling Truth," *New York Times,* September 29, 1995, pp. B1, B4.

McMillan, Jon. "The All-American Fire Trap," *New York Times,* April 17, 1995, p. A17.

McNamara, Joseph D. "Preface," in George L. Kelling et al., *The Kansas City Preventive Patrol Experiment.* Washington, DC: Police Foundation, 1974, pp. iii–iv.

Maguin, Eugene, and Rolf Loeber. "Academic Performance and Delinquency," in Michael Tonry, ed., *Crime and Justice: A Review of Research,* vol. 20. Chicago: University of Chicago Press, 1996, pp. 145–264.

Maguire, Kathleen, and Ann L. Pastore, eds. *Sourcebook of Criminal Justice Statistics 1994.* Washington, DC: Bureau of Justice Statisics, 1995.

———, and Ann L. Pastore, eds. *Sourcebook of Criminal Justice Statistics 1998.* Washington, DC: Bureau of Justice Statisics, 1999.

———, and Ann L. Pastore, eds. *Sourcebook of Criminal Justice Statistics 2000.* Washington, DC: Bureau of Justice Statisics, 2001. Retrieved from www.albany.edu/sourcebook.

———, and Ann L. Pastore, eds. *Sourcebook of Criminal Justice Statistics 2001.* Washington, DC: Bureau of Justice Statisics, 2002. Retrieved from www.albany.edu/sourcebook.

Maguire, Mike. "The Needs and Rights of Victims of Crime," in Michael Tonry, ed., *Crime and Justice: A Review of Research,* vol. 14. Chicago: University of Chicago Press, 1991, pp. 363–433.

Mann, Coramae Richey. *When Women Kill.* Albany: State University of New York Press, 1996.

Mannuzza, S., et al. "Adult Outcome of Hyperactive Boys: Educational Achievement, Occupational Rank, and Psychiatric Status," *Archives of General Psychiatry* 50 (1993), 565–576.

Margolick, David. "Chorus of Judicial Critics Assail Sentencing Guides," *New York Times,* April 12, 1992, pp. 1–40.

Markowitz, Fred E., and Richard B. Felson. "Social-Demographic Attitudes and Violence," *Criminology* 36 (February 1998), 117–138.

Mars, Gerald. "Dock Pilferage: A Case Study in Occupational Theft," in Paul Rock and Mary McIntosh, eds., *Deviance and Social Control.* London: Tavistock, 1974, pp. 209–228.

Marshall, Ineke Haen. "Minorities and Crime in Europe and the United States: More Similar than Different!" in Ineke Haen Marshall, ed., *Minorities, Migrants, and Crime: Diversity and Similarity across Europe and the United States.* Thousand Oaks, CA: Sage, 1997a, pp. 224–241.

———. "Minorities, Crime, and Criminal Justice in the United States," in Ineke Haen Marshall, ed., *Minorities, Migrants, and Crime: Diversity and Similarity across Europe and the United States.* Thousand Oaks, CA: Sage, 1997b, pp. 1–35.

Martin, Douglas. "Kitty Genovese: Would New York Still Turn Away?" *New York Times,* March 11, 1989, p. 29.

Martin, John Bartlow. *My Life in Crime.* New York: Harper, 1952.

Martin, Michael J., Thomas K. Hunt, and Stephen B. Hulley. "The Cost of Hospitalization for Firearm Injuries," *Journal of the American Medical Association* 260 (November 25, 1988), 3048–3050.

Martin, Susan E. " 'A Cross-Burning Is Not Just an Arson': Police Social Construction of Hate Crimes in Baltimore County," *Criminology* 33 (August 1995), 303–326.

———. "Policing Career Criminals: An Examination of an Innovative Crime Control Program," *Journal of Criminal Law and Criminology* 77 (Winter 1986), 1159–1182.

———, and Lawrence W. Sherman. "Selective Apprehension: A Police Strategy for Repeat Offenders," *Criminology* 24 (February 1986), 155–173.

Martinson, Robert. "New Findings, New Views: A Note of Caution Regarding Sentencing Reform," *Hofstra Law Review* 7 (Winter 1979), 243–258.

———. "What Works?—Questions and Answers about Prison Reform," *The Public Interest* no. 35 (Spring 1974), 22–54.

Marvell, Thomas B., and Carlisle E. Moody, Jr. "The Impact of Prison Growth on Homicide," *Homicide Studies* 1 (August 1997), 205–233.

Marvell, Thomas B., and Carlisle E. Moody, Jr. "Prison Population Growth and Crime Reduction," *Journal of Quantitative Criminology* 10 (1994), 109–140.

Marvell, Thomas B., and Carlisle E. Moody, Jr. "Specification Problems, Police Levels, and Crime Rates," *Criminology* 34 (November 1996), 609–646.

Marx, Gary T., and Dane Archer. "Citizen Involvement in the Law Enforcement Process: The Case of Community Police Patrols," *American Behavioral Scientist* 15 (September–October 1971), 52–72.

Marx, Gary T., and Dane Archer. "Picking Up the Gun: Some Organizational and Survey Data on Community Police Patrols." Paper presented at the Symposium on Studies of Public Experience, Knowledge and Opinion of Crime and Justice. Washington, DC: Bureau of Social Science Research, Inc., March 1972.

Massey, James L., Marvin D. Krohn, and Lisa M. Bonati. "Property Crime and the Routine Activities of Individuals," *Journal of Research in Crime and Delinquency* 26 (November 1989), 378–400.

Masters, Brooke A. "Women's Shelters Save Mostly Men," *Boston Globe,* March 15, 1999, p. A3.

Matsueda, Ross L. "Reflected Appraisals, Parental Labeling, and Delinquency: Specifying a Symbolic Interactionist Theory," *American Journal of Sociology* 97 (May 1992), 1577–1611.

———, and Kathleen Anderson. "The Dynamics of Delinquent Peers and Delinquent Behavior," *Criminology* 36 (May 1998), 269–308.

———, and Karen Heimer. "Race, Family Structure, and Delinquency: A Test of Differential Association and Social Control Theories," *American Sociological Review* 52 (December 1987), 826–840.

Matthews, Roger, and Jock Young, eds. *Issues in Realist Criminology.* London: Sage, 1992.

Matza, David. *Delinquency and Drift.* New York: Wiley, 1964.

———, and Gresham M. Sykes. "Juvenile Delinquency and Subterranean Values," *American Sociological Review* 26 (October 1961), 712–719.

Mauer, Marc. *Americans behind Bars: U.S. and International Uses of Incarceration, 1995.* Washington, DC: The Sentencing Project, 1997.

Maurer, David W. *The American Confidence Man.* Springfield, IL: Charles C Thomas, 1974.

———. *Whiz Mob: A Correlation of the Technical Argot of Pickpockets with Their Behavior Pattern.* New Haven, CT: College and University Press, 1964.

Maynard, Douglas W. "The Structure of Discourse in Misdemeanor Plea Bargaining," *Law and Society Review* 18 (1984), 75–104.

Mazerolle, Lorraine Green, Colleen Kadleck, and Jan Roehl. "Controlling Drug and Disorder Problems: The Role of Place Managers," *Criminology* 36 (May 1998), 371–403.

Meadow, Arnold, et al. "Self-Concept, Negative Family Affect, and Delinquency: A Comparison across Mexican Social Classes," *Criminology* 19 (November 1981), 434–448.

Medinnus, Gene R. "Delinquents' Perceptions of Their Parents," *Journal of Consulting Psychology* 29 (December 1965), 592–593.

Mednick, Sarnoff A., William F. Gabrielli, Jr., and Barry Hutchings. "Genetic Factors in the Etiology of Criminal Behavior," in Sarnoff A. Mednick, Terrie E. Moffitt, and Susan A. Stack, eds., *The Causes of Crime: New Biological Approaches.* Cambridge, England: Cambridge University Press, 1987, pp. 74–91.

Mednick, Sarnoff A., and Jan Volavka. "Biology and Crime," in Norval Morris and Michael Tonry, eds., *Crime and Justice: An Annual Review of Research,* vol. 2. Chicago: University of Chicago Press, 1980, pp. 85–158.

Mednick, Sarnoff A., et al. "Biology and Violence," in Marvin E. Wolfgang and Neil Alan Weiner, eds., *Criminal Violence.* Beverly Hills, CA: Sage, 1982, pp. 21–80.

Mednick, Sarnoff A., et al. "EEG as a Predictor of Antisocial Behavior," *Criminology* 19 (August 1981), 219–229.

Megargee, Edwin I. "Psychological Determinants and Correlates of Criminal Violence," in Marvin E. Wolfgang and Neil Alan Weiner, eds., *Criminal Violence.* Beverly Hills, CA: Sage, 1982, pp. 81–170.

———, and Martin J. Bohn. *Classifying Criminal Offenders: A New System Based on the MMPI.* Beverly Hills, CA: Sage, 1979.

Meier, Robert F., and Gilbert Geis. *Victimless Crime? Prostitution, Drugs, Homosexuality, Abortion.* Los Angeles: Roxbury Publishing Company, 1997.

Meisenhelder, Thomas. "An Exploratory Study of Exiting from Criminal Careers," *Criminology* 15 (November 1977), 319–334.

Menard, Scott. "The 'Normality' of Repeat Victimization from Adolescence through Early Adulthood," *Justice Quarterly* 17 (September 2000), 543–574.

———, Sharon Mihalic, and David Huizinga. "Drugs and Crime Revisited," *Justice Quarterly* 18 (June 2001), 269–299.

———, and Barbara J. Morse. "A Structuralist Critique of the IQ-Delinquency Hypothesis: Theory and Evidence," *American Journal of Sociology* 89 (May 1984), 1347–1378.

Merton, Robert K. "Social Structure and Anomie," in *Social Theory and Social Structure,* 1968 enlarged ed. New York: Free Press, 1968, pp. 185–214.

Messerschmidt, James W. *Crime as Structured Action: Gender, Race, Class, and Crime in the Making.* Thousand Oaks, CA: Sage, 1997.

———. *Masculinities and Crime: Critique and Reconceptualization of Theory.* Lanham, MD: Rowman and Littlefield, 1993.

Messner, Steven F. "Economic Discrimination and Societal Homicide Rates: Further Evidence on the Cost of Inequality," *American Sociological Review* 54 (August 1989), 597–611.

———. "Regional and Racial Effects on the Urban Homicide Rate: The Subculture of Violence Revisited," *American Journal of Sociology* 88 (March 1983), 997–1007.

———, and Kenneth Tardiff. "The Social Ecology of Urban Homicide: An Application of the 'Routine Activities' Approach," *Criminology* 23 (May 1985), 241–267.

Miethe, Terance D. "Citizen-Based Crime Control Activity and Victimization Risks: An Examination of Displacement and Free-Rider Effects," *Criminology* 29 (August 1991), 419–439.

———, and Robert F. Meier. *Crime and Its Social Context: Toward an Integrated Theory of Offenders, Victims, and Situations.* Albany: State University of New York Press, 1994.

———, Mark C. Stafford, and J. Scott Long. "Social Differentiation in Criminal Victimization: A Test of Routine Activities/Lifestyle Theories," *American Sociological Review* 52 (April 1987), 184–194.

Milgram, Stanley. "The Experience of Living in Cities: A Psychological Analysis," *Science* 167 (March 13, 1970), 1461–1468.

———, and Paul Hollander. "The Murder They Heard," in Renatus Hartogs and Eric Artzt, eds., *Violence: Causes and Solutions.* New York: Dell, 1970, pp. 206–212.

Miller, J. L., Peter H. Rossi, and Jon E. Simpson. "Perceptions of Justice: Race and Gender Differences in Judgments of Appropriate Prison Sentences," *Law and Society Review* 20 (1986), 313–334.

Miller, Jody. "Up It Up: Gender and the Accomplishment of Street Robbery," *Criminology* 36 (February 1998), 37–66.

Miller, Joshua D., and Donald Lynam. "Structural Models of Personality and Their Relation to Antisocial Behavior: A Meta-Analytic Review," *Criminology* 39 (November 2001), 765–798.

Miller, Stuart J., Simon Dinitz, and John P. Conrad. *Careers of the Violent: The Dangerous Offender and Criminal Justice.* Lexington, MA: D. C. Heath, 1982.

Miller, Ted R., and Mark A. Cohen. "Costs of Penetrating Injury," in Rao Ivatury and C. Gene Cayten, eds., *Textbook of Penetrating Trauma.* Philadelphia: Lee and Civiga, 1995.

Miller, Walter B. "American Youth Gangs: Past and Present," in Abraham S. Blumberg, ed., *Current Perspectives on Criminal Behavior: Original Essays in Criminology.* New York: Knopf, 1974, pp. 210–239.

———. "Lower Class Culture as a Generating Milieu of Gang Delinquency," *Journal of Social Issues* 14 (no. 3, 1958), 5–19.

Milligan, Susan. "Many Turns on the Trail: NRA Power in Elections Grows as Ranks Swell," *Boston Globe,* August 7, 2000, pp. A1, A9.

Minor, W. William. "Techniques of Neutralization: A Reconceptualization and Empirical Examination," *Journal of Research in Crime and Delinquency* 18 (July 1981), 295–318.

Mintz, John. "NRA Official Boasts of 'Unbelievably Friendly Relations' with Bush," *Boston Globe,* May 4, 2000, p. A9.

Miranne, Alfred C., and Michael R. Geerken. "The New Orleans Inmate Survey: A Test of Greenwood's Predictive Scale," *Criminology* 29 (August 1991), 497–518.

Mitford, Jessica. *Kind and Usual Punishment: The Prison Business.* New York: Knopf, 1973.

Moffitt, Terrie E. "Adolescent-Limited and Life-Course Persistent Antisocial Behavior: A Developmental Taxonomy," *Psychological Review* 100 (1993), 674–701.

———. "Juvenile Delinquency and Attention Deficit Disorder: Boys' Developmental Trajectories from Age 3 to Age 5," *Child Development* 61 (1990), 893–910.

———, and Avshalom Caspi. *Findings about Partner Violence from the Dunedin Multidisciplinary Health and Development Study.* Washington, DC: U.S. Department of Justice, July 1999.

———, Donald R. Lynam, and Phil A. Silva. "Neuropsychological Tests Predicting Persistent Male Delinquency," *Criminology* 32 (May 1994), 277–300.

———, Richard W. Robins, and Avshalom Caspi. "A Couples Analysis of Partner Abuse with Implications for Abuse-Prevention Policy," *Criminology and Public Policy* 1 (November 2001), 5–36.

Monachesi, Elio D., and Starke R. Hathaway. "The Personality of Delinquents," in J. N. Butcher, ed., *MMPI: Research Developments and Clinical Applications.* New York: McGraw-Hill, 1969, pp. 207–219.

Monahan, John. *Mental Illness and Violent Crime.* Washington, DC: U.S. Department of Justice, October 1996.

Moon, Melissa M., et al. "Is Child Saving Dead? Public Support for Juvenile Rehabilitation," *Crime and Delinquency* 46 (January 2000a), 38–60.

Moon, Melissa M., et al. "Putting Kids to Death: Specifying Public Support for Juvenile Capital Punishment," *Justice Quarterly* 17 (December 2000b), 663–684.

Moore, Charles A. "Taming the Giant Corporation? Some Cautionary Remarks on the Deterrability of Corporate Crime," *Crime and Delinquency* 33 (July 1987), 379–402.

Moore, Elizabeth, and Michael Mills. "The Neglected Victims and Unexamined Costs of White-Collar Crime," *Crime and Delinquency* 36 (July 1990), 408–418.

Moran, Richard. "The Insanity Defense: Five Years after Hinckley," in Robert J. Kelly and Donal E. J. MacNamara, eds., *Perspectives on Deviance: Dominance, Degradation and Denigration.* Cincinnati, OH: Anderson, 1991, p. 77–87.

Morash, Merry, Timothy S. Bynum, and Barbara A. Koons. *Women Offenders: Programming Needs and Promising Approaches.* Washington, DC: U.S. Department of Justice, August 1998.

———, and Meda Chesney-Lind. "A Re-Formulation and Partial Test of the Power-Control Theory of Delinquency," *Justice Quarterly* 8 (1991), 347–377.

———, Robin N. Haarr, and Lila Rucker. "A Comparison of Programming for Women and Men in U.S. Prisons in the 1980s," *Crime and Delinquency* 40 (April 1994), 197–221.

———, and Lila Rucker. "A Critical Look at the Idea of Boot Camp as a Correctional Reform," *Crime and Delinquency* 36 (April 1990), 204–222.

Moriarity, Thomas. "Crime, Commitment, and the Responsive Bystander: Two Field Experiments," *Journal of Personality and Social Psychology* 31 (February 1975), 370–376.

Morris, Norval. "Punishment, Desert, and Rehabilitation," in Hyman Gross and Andrew von Hirsch, eds., *Sentencing.* New York: Oxford University Press, 1981, pp. 257–271.

———, and Gordon Hawkins. *The Honest Politician's Guide to Crime Control.* Chicago: University of Chicago Press, 1970.

Morsch, James. "The Problem of Motive in Hate Crimes: The Argument against Presumptions of Racial Motivation," *Journal of Criminal Law and Criminology* 82 (Fall 1991), 659–689.

Moshavi, Sharon. "Wave of Violence by Teenagers Leads to Japan Hand-Wringing," *Boston Sunday Globe,* May 21, 2000, p. A20.

Mosher, Donald L., and Ronald D. Anderson. "Macho Personality, Sexual Aggression, and Reactions to Guided Imagery of Realistic Rape," *Journal of Research in Personality* 20 (March 1986), 77–94.

Mosher, Donald L., and Mark Sirkin. "Measuring a Macho Personality Constellation," *Journal of Research in Personality* 18 (June 1984), 150–163.

Murray, Charles A., and Louis A. Cox, Jr. *Beyond Probation: Juvenile Corrections and the Chronic Delinquent.* Beverly Hills, CA: Sage, 1979.

Mydans, Seth. "Sexual Violence as Tool of War: Pattern Emerging in East Timor," *New York Times,* March 1, 2001, pp. A1, A10.

———. "Videotape of Beating by Officers Puts Full Glare on Brutality Issue," *New York Times,* March 18, 1991, pp. A1, B7.

Myers, Steven Lee. "Captain and Crew Charged in Voyage of Chinese to U.S.," *New York Times,* June 8, 1993, pp. A1, B2.

Nagel, Ilene H., and John Hagan. "Gender and Crime: Offense Patterns and Criminal Court Sanctions," in Michael Tonry and Norval Morris, eds., *Crime and Justice: An Annual Review of Research,* vol. 4. Chicago: University of Chicago Press, 1983, pp. 91–144.

Nagin, Daniel, and David P. Farrington. "The Onset and Persistence of Offending," *Criminology* 30 (November 1992a), 501–523.

———, and David P. Farrington. "The Stability of Criminal Potential from Childhood to Adulthood," *Criminology* 30 (May 1992b), 235–260.

———, and Raymond Paternoster. "Enduring Individual Differences and Rational Choice Theories of Crime," *Law and Society Review* 27 (1993), 467–496.

———, and Raymond Paternoster. "On the Relationship of Past to Future Participation in Delinquency," *Criminology* 29 (May 1991), 163–189.

———, and Greg Pogarsky. "Integrating Celerity, Impulsivity, and Extralegal Sanction Threats into a Model of General Deterrence: Theory and Evidence," *Criminology* 39 (November 2001), 865–891.

Nasar, Sylvia, and Kirsten B. Mitchell. "Booming Job Market Draws Young Black Men into Fold," *New York Times,* May 23, 1999, pp. 1, 21.

National Fire Protection Association. "Arson in Structures Drops 5% in 1999, NFPA Reports," March 30, 2001. Retrieved from www.nfpa.org/PressRoom/newsreleases/arsondrops/arsondrops.asp.

National Institute of Justice. *1998 Annual Report on Drug Abuse among Adult and Juvenile Arrestees.* Washington, DC: U.S. Department of Justice, April 1999.

———. "Restorative Justice: An Interview with Visiting Fellow Thomas Quinn," *National Institute of Justice Journal,* March 1998, pp. 10–16.

National Research Council. *Understanding and Preventing Violence.* Washington, DC: National Academy Press, 1999.

Navarro, Mireya. "After Carjacking Surge, Puerto Rico Is Wary Behind the Wheel," *New York Times,* July 31, 1994, p. 28.

Neapolitan, Jerome L. "Cross-National Variation in Homicides: Is Race a Factor?" *Criminology* 36 (February 1998), 139–156.

Neubauer, David W. *Criminal Justice in Middle America.* Morristown, NJ: General Learning Press, 1974.

New York Times. "As Audits Decline, Fewer Taxpayers Balk at a Bit of Cheating," January 19, 2002, p. A9.

———. "A Law Distinguishing Crack from Other Cocaine Is Upset," December 29, 1990, p. 13.

———. "Street Crime Hits Prague Daily Life," December 18, 1991, p. A21.

Newburn, Tim, and Elizabeth A. Stanko, eds. *Just Boys Doing Business? Men, Masculinities and Crime.* London: Routledge, 1994.

Newman, Graeme. *Comparative Deviance: Perception and Law in Six Cultures.* New York: Elsevier, 1976.

Newman, Oscar. *Architectural Design for Crime Prevention.* Washington, DC: U.S. Government Printing Office, 1973.

———. *Creating Defensible Space.* Washington, DC: U.S. Department of Housing and Urban Development, Office of Policy Development and Research, April 1996.

———, and K. A. Franck. "The Effects of Building Size on Personal Crime and Fear of Crime," *Probation and Environment* 5 (1982), 203–220.

Nisbett, Richard E., and Dov Cohen. *Culture of Honor: The Psychology of Violence in the South*. Boulder, CO: Westview, 1996.

Normandeau, André. *Trends and Patterns in Crimes of Robbery*. Ph.D. dissertation. Philadelphia: University of Pennsylvania, 1968.

O'Brien, Robert M. "The Interracial Nature of Violent Crimes: A Reexamination," *American Journal of Sociology* 92 (January 1987), 817–835.

O'Brien, Timothy L. "Officials Worried over a Sharp Rise in Identity Theft," *New York Times*, April 3, 2000, pp. A1, A19.

Office of Justice Programs, National Institute of Justice. *The Extent and Costs of Crime Vicimization: A New Look*. Washington, DC: U.S. Department of Justice, January 1996.

Office of Juvenile Justice and Delinquency Prevention. *1998 National Youth Gang Survey*. Washington, DC: U.S. Department of Justice, November 2000.

———. *Promising Strategies to Reduce Gun Violence*. Washington, DC: U.S. Department of Justice, February 1999.

———. "Targeting Serious Juvenile Offenders for Prosecution Can Make a Difference," *NIJ Reports*, September/October 1988, pp. 9–12.

Oliver, Mary Beth, and G. Blake Armstrong. "The Color of Crime: Perceptions of Caucasians' and African-Americans' Involvement in Crime," in Mark Fishman and Gray Cavender, eds., *Entertaining Crime: Television Reality Programs*. New York: Aldine de Gruyter, 1998, pp. 19–35.

Orcutt, James D. "Differential Association and Marijuana Use: A Closer Look at Sutherland (with a Little Help from Becker)," *Criminology* 25 (May 1987), 341–358.

Osbun, Lee Ann, and Peter A. Rode. "Prosecuting Juveniles as Adults: The Quest for 'Objective' Decisions," *Criminology* 22 (May 1984), 187–202.

Osgood, D. Wayne, et al. "Routine Activities and Individual Deviant Behavior," *American Sociological Review* 61 (August 1996), 635–655.

Ousey, Graham C., and Matthew R. Lee. "Examining the Conditional Nature of the Illicit Drug Market–Homicide Relationship: A Partial Test of the Theory of Contingent Causation," *Criminology* 40 (February 2002), 73–102.

Outlaw, Maureen C., and R. Barry Ruback. "Predictors and Outcomes of Victim Restitution Orders," *Justice Quarterly* 16 (December 1999), 847–869.

Padilla, Felix M. *The Gang as an American Enterprise*. New Brunswick, NJ: Rutgers University Press, 1992.

Paik, Haejung, and George Comstock. "The Effects of Television Violence on Antisocial Behavior: A Meta-Analysis," *Communication Research* 21 (August 1994), 516–546.

Palmer, Ted. "Martinson Revisited," *Journal of Research in Crime and Delinquency* 12 (July 1975), 133–152.

———. *A Profile of Correctional Effectiveness and New Directions for Research*. Albany: State University of New York Press, 1994.

Parker, Donn B. *Crime by Computer*. New York: Scribner's, 1976.

Paschall, Mallie J., Robert L. Flewelling, and Susan T. Ennett. "Racial Differences in Violent Behavior among Young Adults: Moderating and Confounding Effects," *Journal of Research in Crime and Delinquency* 35 (May 1998), 148–165.

Paternoster, Raymond. "Examining Three-Wave Deterrence Models: A Question of Temporal Order and Specification," *Journal of Criminal Law and Criminology* 79 (Spring 1988), 135–179.

———, and Paul Mazerolle. "General Strain Theory and Delinquency: A Replication and Extension," *Journal of Research in Crime and Delinquency* 31 (August 1994), 235–263.

———, and Sally Simpson. "Sanction Threats and Appeals to Morality: Testing a Rational Choice Model of Corporate Crime," *Law and Society Review* 30 (1996), 549–583.

Patterson, Gerald R., and Thomas J. Dishion. "Contributions of Families and Peers to Delinquency," *Criminology* 23 (February 1985), 63–79.

Pease, Ken, and Gloria Laycock. *Revictimization: Reducing the Heat on Hot Victims*. Washington, DC: U.S. Department of Justice, November 1996.

Pennell, Susan, et al. "Guardian Angels: A Unique Approach to Crime Prevention," *Crime and Delinquency* 35 (July 1989), 378–400.

Pepinsky, Harold, and Richard Quinney, eds. *Criminology as Peacemaking*. Bloomington: Indiana University Press, 1991.

Perkins, Craig A. *Age Patterns of Victims of Serious Violent Crime*. Washington, DC: U.S. Department of Justice, September 1997.

———, and Patsy Klaus. *Criminal Victimization 1994*. Washington, DC: U.S. Department of Justice, April 1996.

Peters, Michael, et al. *Boot Camps for Juvenile Offenders*. Washington, DC: U.S. Department of Justice, September 1997.

Petersilia, Joan. "Criminal Career Research: A Review of Recent Evidence," in Norval Morris and Michael Tonry, eds., *Crime and Justice: An Annual Review of Research*, vol. 2. Chicago: University of Chicago Press, 1980, pp. 321–379.

———, Peter W. Greenwood, and Marvin Lavin. *Criminal Careers of Habitual Felons*. Santa Monica, CA: Rand, 1977.

Peterson, Mark A., and Harriet Braiker, with Suzanne M. Polich. *Who Commits Crimes: A Survey of Prison Inmates*. Boston: Oelgeschlager, Gunn and Hain, 1981.

Peterson, Ruth D., and William C. Bailey. "Felony Murder and Capital Punishment: An Examination of the Deterrence Question," *Criminology* 29 (August 1991), 367–395.

Peterson, Ruth D., and William C. Bailey. "Murder and Capital Punishment in the Evolving Context of the Post-*Furman* Era," *Social Forces* 66 (March 1988), 774–807.

Petrosino, Anthony, Carolyn Turpin-Petrosino, and James O. Finckenauer. "Well-Meaning Programs Can Have

Harmful Effects! Lessons from Experiments of Programs Such as Scared Straight," *Crime and Delinquency* 46 (July 2000), 354–379.

Pfuhl, Erdwin H., Jr. "Police Strikes and Conventional Crime: A Look at the Data," *Criminology* 21 (November 1983), 489–503.

Phillips, David P. "The Deterrent Effect of Capital Punishment: New Evidence on an Old Controversy," *American Journal of Sociology* 86 (July 1980), 139–148.

———. "The Impact of Mass Media Violence on U.S. Homicides," *American Sociological Review* 48 (August 1983), 560–568.

———, and John E. Hensley. "When Violence Is Rewarded or Punished: The Impact of Mass Media Stories on Homicide," *Journal of Communication* 34 (Summer 1984), 101–116.

Phillips, Llad, and Harold L. Votey, Jr. *The Economics of Crime Control.* Beverly Hills, CA: Sage, 1981.

Phillips, Phillip D. "Characteristics and Typology of the Journey to Crime," in Daniel E. Georges-Abeyie and Keith D. Harries, eds., *Crime: A Spatial Perspective.* New York: Columbia University Press, 1980, pp. 167–180.

Pierce, Glenn, and William J. Bowers. "The Bartley-Fox Gun Law's Short-Term Impact on Crime in Boston," *Annals of the American Academy of Political and Social Science* 455 (May 1981), 120–137.

Piliavin, Irving, and Scott Briar. "Police Encounters with Juveniles," *American Journal of Sociology* 70 (September 1964), 206–214.

Piquero, Alex, and George F. Rengert. "Studying Deterrence with Active Residential Burglars," *Justice Quarterly* 16 (June 1999) 451–471.

Piquero, Alex, and Stephen Tibbetts. "Specifying the Direct and Indirect Effects of Low Self-Control and Situational Factors in Offenders' Decision Making: Toward a More Complete Model of Rational Offending," *Justice Quarterly* 13 (September 1996), 481–510.

Platt, Anthony M. "Prospects for a Radical Criminology in the USA," in Ian Taylor, Paul Walton, and Jock Young, eds., *Critical Criminology.* London: Routledge and Kegan Paul, 1975, pp. 95–112.

Ploeger, Matthew. "Youth Employment and Delinquency: Reconsidering a Problematic Relationship," *Criminology* 35 (November 1997), 659–675.

Podolefsky, Aaron, and Fredrick DuBow. *Strategies for Community Crime Prevention: Collective Responses to Crime in Urban America.* Springfield, IL: Charles C Thomas Publisher, 1981.

Polk, Kenneth. "Delinquency and Adult Criminal Careers," in Delos H. Kelly, ed., *Criminal Behavior: Readings in Criminology.* New York: St. Martin's Press, 1980, pp. 143–150.

———. *When Men Kill: Scenarios of Masculine Violence.* Cambridge, England: Cambridge University Press, 1994.

Pollard, Paul. "Sexual Violence against Women: Characteristics of Typical Perpetrators," in John Archer, ed., *Male Violence.* London: Routledge, 1994, pp. 170–194.

Polling the Nations. Gallup Poll, 2002. Retrieved from http://lib3.tufts.edu:2362/poll/lpext.dll?f=templates& fn=main-h.htm.

Pollock, Vicki, Sarnoff A. Mednick, and William F. Gabrielli, Jr. "Crime Causation: Biological Theories," in Sanford H. Kadish, ed., *Encyclopedia of Crime and Justice,* vol. 1. New York: Free Press, 1983, pp. 308–315.

Poole, Eric D., and Robert M. Regoli. "Parental Support, Delinquent Friends, and Delinquency: A Test of Interaction Effects," *Journal of Criminal Law and Criminology* 70 (Summer 1979), 188–193.

Porterfield, Austin L. *Youth in Trouble: Studies in Delinquency and Despair, with Plans for Prevention.* Fort Worth, TX: Leo Potishman Foundation, 1946.

Povey, David, et al. *Recorded Crime, England and Wales, 12 Months to March 2001,* July 19, 2001. Retrieved from www.homeoffice.gov.uk/rds/pdfs/hosb1201.pdf.

Powers, Edwin, and Helen L. Witmer. *An Experiment in the Prevention of Delinquency: The Cambridge-Somerville Youth Study.* New York: Columbia University Press, 1951.

Prentky, Robert Alan, Murray L. Cohen, and Theoharis K. Seghorn. "Development of a Rational Taxonomy for the Classification of Rapists: The Massachusetts Treatment Center System," *Bulletin of the American Academy of Psychiatry and the Law* 13 (1985), 39–70.

President's Commission on Law Enforcement and Administration of Justice. *The Challenge of Crime in a Free Society.* Washington, DC: U.S. Government Printing Office, 1967.

President's Commission on Obscenity and Pornography. *Report.* Washington, DC: U.S. Government Printing Office, 1970.

Proband, Stan C. "Canadian Parliamentary Report Rejects U.S. Crime Control Approach," *Overcrowded Times: Solving the Prison Problem* 4 (April 1993), 2.

Prugh, Jeff. "In Atlanta, a Pall of Fear," *Boston Globe,* February 14, 1981, p. 3.

Pruitt, Charles R., and James Q. Wilson. "A Longitudinal Study of the Effect of Race on Sentencing," *Law and Society Review* 17 (1983), 613–635.

Puzzanchera, Charles M. *Delinquency Cases Waived to Criminal Court, 1988–1997,* OJJDP Fact Sheet. Washington, DC: U.S. Department of Justice, February 2000.

Quinney, Richard. *The Social Reality of Crime.* Boston: Little, Brown, 1970.

Raab, Selwyn. "Mob's 'Commission' Believed Defunct," *New York Times,* April 27, 1998, pp. A1, A16.

———. "Officials Say Mob Is Shifting Crimes to New Industries," *New York Times,* February 10, 1997, pp. A1, B4.

Radelet, Michael L., and Ronald L. Akers. "Deterrence and the Death Penalty: The Views of the Experts," *Journal of Criminal Law and Criminology* 87 (Fall 1996), 1–16.

———, Hugo Adam Bedau, and Constance E. Putnam. *In Spite of Innocence: Erroneous Convictions in Capital Cases.* Boston: Northeastern University Press, 1994.

Radzinowicz, Sir Leon, and Joan King. *The Growth of Crime: The International Experience.* New York: Basic Books, 1977.

Raine, Adrian, Peter H. Venables, and Sarnoff A. Mednick. "Low Resting Heart Rate at Age 3 Years Predisposes to

Aggression at Age 11 Years: Evidence from the Mauritius Child Health Project," *Journal of the American Academy of Child and Adolescent Psychiatry* 36 (1997), 1457–1464.

Raine, Adrian, et al. "Reduced Prefrontal Gray Matter Volume and Reduced Autonomic Activity in Antisocial Personality Disorder," *Archives of General Psychiatry* 57 (2000), 119–227.

Rankin, Joseph H., and Roger Kern. "Parental Attachments and Delinquency," *Criminology* 32 (November 1994), 495–515.

Rantala, Ramona R., with technical support from Thomas J. Edwards. *Effects of NIBRS on Crime Statistics.* Washington, DC: U.S. Department of Justice, July 2000.

Rapaport, Elizabeth. "The Death Penalty and Gender Discrimination," *Law and Society Review* 25 (1991), 367–382.

Ratcliffe, James M., ed. *The Good Samaritan and the Law.* Garden City, NY: Doubleday, 1966.

Rausch, Sharla. "Court Processing versus Diversion of Status Offenders: A Test of Deterrence and Labeling Theories," *Journal of Research in Crime and Delinquency* 20 (January 1983), 39–54.

Rawls, Wendell, Jr. "Fear Linked to Killings Rises among Atlanta Youths," *New York Times,* March 22, 1981, p. 24.

Rebellon, Cesar J. "Reconsidering the Broken Homes/Delinquency Relationship and Exploring Its Mediating Mechanism(s)," *Criminology* 40 (February 2002), 103–135.

Reckless, Walter C. "Containment Theory," in Barry Krisberg and James Austin, eds., *The Children of Ishmael: Critical Perspectives on Juvenile Justice.* Palo Alto, CA: Mayfield, 1978, pp. 187–193.

———. *The Crime Problem,* 5th ed. New York: Appleton-Century-Crofts, 1973.

Reed, Gary E., and Peter Cleary Yeager. "Organizational Offending and Neoclassical Criminology: Challenging the Reach of a General Theory of Crime," *Criminology* 34 (August 1996), 357–382.

Reichman, Nancy. "Insider Trading," in Michael Tonry and Albert J. Reiss, Jr., eds. *Beyond the Law: Crime in Complex Organizations,* vol. 18 of *Crime and Justice: A Review of Research.* Chicago: University of Chicago Press, 1993, pp. 55–86.

Reiman, Jeffrey H.. *The Rich Get Richer and the Poor Get Prison: Ideology, Class, and Criminal Justice,* 6th ed. Boston: Allyn & Bacon, 2001.

Reiss, Albert J., Jr. *The Police and the Public.* New Haven, CT: Yale University Press, 1971.

———, and Albert Lewis Rhodes. "The Distribution of Juvenile Delinquency in the Social Class Structure," *American Sociological Review* 26 (October 1961), 720–732.

Rennison, Callie Marie. *Criminal Victimization 2001: Changes 2000–01 with Trends 1993–2001.* Washington, DC: U.S. Department of Justice, September 2002.

———. *Intimate Partner Violence.* Washington, DC: U.S. Department of Justice, May 2000.

———. *Violent Victimization and Race, 1993–98.* Washington, DC: U.S. Department of Justice, March 2001.

Reppetto, Thomas A. *Residential Crime.* Cambridge, MA: Ballinger, 1974.

Ressler, Robert K., Ann W. Burgess, and John E. Douglas. *Sexual Homicide: Patterns and Motives.* New York: Lexington Books, 1988.

Rettig, Richard P., Manual J. Torres, and Gerald R. Garrett. *Manny: A Criminal-Addict's Story.* Boston: Houghton Mifflin, 1977.

Reuter, Peter. "The Cartage Industry in New York," in Michael Tonry and Albert J. Reiss, Jr., eds., *Beyond the Law: Crime in Complex Organizations,* vol. 18 of *Crime and Justice: A Review of Research.* Chicago: University of Chicago Press, 1993, pp. 149–201.

———. *Disorganized Crime: The Economics of the Visible Hand.* Cambridge, MA: MIT Press, 1983.

Rezendes, Michael. "Jackson's New Target: Black-on-Black Crime," *Boston Globe,* November 6, 1993, pp. 1, 4.

Rhodes, William C. *Behavioral Threat and Community Response.* New York: Behavioral Publications, 1972.

Richards, Pamela, Richard A. Berk, and Brenda Foster. *Crime as Play: Delinquency in a Middle Class Suburb.* Cambridge, MA: Ballinger, 1979.

Roberts, Julian V. "The Role of Criminal Record in the Sentencing Process," in Michael Tonry, ed., *Crime and Justice: A Review of Research,* vol. 22. Chicago: University of Chicago Press, 1997, pp. 303–362.

Roberts, Sam. "Mafia Infiltration of Business Costing Consumers Millions," *New York Times,* December 19, 1985, p. B13.

Robins, L. N. "Epidemiology of Antisocial Personality," in G. L. Klerman et al., eds., *Psychiatry: Social, Epidemiologic, and Legal Psychiatry.* New York: Basic Books, 1986, pp. 231–244.

———, et al. "Lifetime Prevalence of Specific Psychiatric Disorders in Three Cities," *Archives of General Psychiatry* 41 (1984), 949–958.

Robison, James, and Gerald Smith. "The Effectiveness of Correctional Programs," *Crime and Delinquency* 17 (January 1971), 67–80.

Rodman, Hyman. "The Lower-Class Value Stretch," *Social Forces* 42 (December 1963), 205–215.

Rogers, Joseph W. *Why Are You Not a Criminal?* Englewood Cliffs, NJ: Prentice Hall, 1977.

Roiphe, Katie. *The Morning After: Sex, Fear, and Feminism on Campus.* Boston: Little, Brown, 1993.

Rojek, Dean G., and Maynard L. Erickson. "Delinquent Careers: A Test of the Career Escalation Model," *Criminology* 20 (May 1982), 5–28.

Rojek, Dean G., and Maynard L. Erickson. "Reforming the Juvenile Justice System: The Diversion of Status Offenders," *Law and Society Review* 16 (1981–82), 241–264.

Roncek, Dennis W., and Pamela A. Maier. "Bars, Blocks, and Crimes Revisited: Linking the Theory of Routine Activities to the Empiricism of 'Hot Spots,' " *Criminology* 29 (November 1991), 725–753.

Rosenbaum, Dennis P. "Community Crime Prevention: A Review and Synthesis of the Literature," *Justice Quarterly* 5 (September 1988), 323–395.

———. "The Theory and Research behind Neighborhood Watch: Is It a Sound Fear and Crime Reduction Strategy?" *Crime and Delinquency* 33 (January 1987), 103–134.

———, and Linda Heath. "The 'Psycho-Logic' of Fear-Reduction and Crime-Prevention Programs," in John Edwards et al., eds., *Social Influence Processes and Prevention.* New York: Plenum, 1990, pp. 221–247.

Rosenfeld, Richard. "Patterns in Adult Homicide: 1980–1995," in Alfred Blumstein and Joel Wallman, eds., *The Crime Drop in America.* Cambridge, England: Cambridge University Press, 2000, pp. 130–163.

———, and Scott H. Decker. "Are Arrest Statistics a Valid Measure of Illicit Drug Use? The Relationship between Criminal Justice and Public Health Indicators of Cocaine, Heroin, and Marijuana Use," *Justice Quarterly* 16 (September 1999), 685–699.

Rosenquist, Carl M., and Edwin I. Megargee. *Delinquency in Three Cultures.* Austin: University of Texas Press, 1969.

Rosenthal, Elizabeth. "Health Insurers Say Rising Fraud Is Costing Them Tens of Billions," *New York Times,* July 5, 1990, pp. A1, B7.

Rosett, Arthur, and Donald R. Cressey. *Justice by Consent: Plea Bargains in the American Courthouse.* Philadelphia: Lippincott, 1976.

Ross, R. R., and H. B. McKay. "Behavioral Approaches to Treatment in Corrections: Requiem for a Panacea," *Canadian Journal of Criminology* 20 (1978), 279–298.

Rossi, Peter H., and Richard A. Berk. *Just Punishments: Federal Guidelines and Public Views Compared.* New York: Aldine de Gruyter, 1997.

Rossi, Peter H., Richard A. Berk, and Kenneth J. Lenihan. *Money, Work, and Crime: Experimental Evidence.* New York: Academic Press, 1980.

Roth, Jeffrey A. "Prosecutor Perceptions of Crime Seriousness," *Journal of Criminal Law and Criminology* 69 (Summer 1978), 232–242.

Rothman, David J. *The Discovery of the Asylum: Social Order and Disorder in the New Republic,* 2d ed. Hawthorne, NY: Aldine de Gruyter, 2002.

Rowe, David C. *Biology and Crime.* Los Angeles: Roxbury, 2002.

———. "Biometrical Genetic Models of Self-Reported Delinquent Behavior: A Twin Study," *Behavior Genetics* 13 (1983), 473–489.

———, and D. Wayne Osgood. "Heredity and Sociological Theories of Delinquency: A Reconsideration," *American Sociological Review* 49 (August 1984), 526–540.

Rubin, Robert T. "The Neuroendocrinology and Neurochemistry of Antisocial Behavior," in Sarnoff A. Mednick, Terrie E. Moffitt, and Susan A. Stack, eds., *The Causes of Crime: New Biological Approaches.* Cambridge, England: Cambridge University Press, 1987, pp. 239–262.

Rushton, J. Philippe. *Race, Evolution, and Behavior: A Life-History Perspective.* New Brunswick, NJ: Transaction Publishers, 1995.

Russell, Diana E. H. *The Politics of Rape: The Victim's Perspective.* New York: Stein and Day, 1975.

———. *Rape in Marriage,* rev. ed. Bloomington: Indiana University Press, 1990.

Russell, Gordon W. "Psychological Issues in Sports Aggression," in Jeffrey H. Goldstein, ed., *Sports Violence.* New York: Springer-Verlag, 1983, pp. 157–181.

Rutenberg, Jim. "Survey Shows Few Parents Use TV V-Chip to Limit Children's Viewing," *New York Times,* July 25, 2001, pp. B1, B7.

Rutter, Michael, et al. *Fifteen Thousand Hours: Secondary Schools and Their Effects on Children.* Cambridge, MA: Harvard University Press, 1979.

Rydell, C. Peter, and Susan S. Everingham. *Controlling Cocaine: Supply Versus Demand Programs.* Santa Monica, CA: Rand, 1994.

Saad, Lydia. "Fear of Conventional Crime at Record Lows," *Gallup Poll Monthly,* October 2001, pp. 2–10.

Sack, Kevin. "Hate Groups in U.S. Are Growing, Report Says," *New York Times,* March 3, 1998, p. A11.

Samenow, Stanton E. *Inside the Criminal Mind.* New York: Times Books, 1984.

Sampson, Robert J. "Crime in Cities: The Effects of Formal and Informal Social Control," in Albert J. Reiss, Jr., and Michael Tonry, eds., *Communities and Crime.* Chicago: University of Chicago Press, 1986, pp. 271–311.

———. "Structural Sources of Variation in Race-Age-Specific Rates of Offending across Major U.S. Cities," *Criminology* 23 (November 1985), 647–673.

———, and Jacqueline Cohen. "Deterrent Effects of the Police on Crime: A Replication and Theoretical Extension," *Law and Society Review* 22 (1988), 163–189.

———, and W. Byron Groves. "Community Structure and Crime: Testing Social-Disorganization Theory," *American Journal of Sociology* (January 1989), 774–802.

———, and John H. Laub. *Crime in the Making: Pathways and Turning Points through Life.* Cambridge, MA: Harvard University Press, 1993.

———, and Janet L. Lauritsen. "Deviant Lifestyles, Proximity to Crime, and the Offender-Victim Link in Personal Violence," *Journal of Research in Crime and Delinquency* 27 (May 1990), 110–139.

———, and Janet L. Lauritsen. "Racial and Ethnic Disparities in Crime and Criminal Justice in the United States," in Michael Tonry, ed., *Ethnicity, Crime, and Immigration: Comparative and Cross-National Perspectives, Crime and Justice: A Review of Research,* vol. 21. Chicago: University of Chicago Press, 1997, pp. 311–374.

———, and Stephen W. Raudenbush. *Disorder in Urban Neighborhoods—Does It Lead to Crime?* Washington, DC: U.S. Department of Justice, February 2001.

———, Stephen W. Raudenbush, and Felton Earls. "Neighborhoods and Violent Crime: A Multilevel Study of Collective Efficacy," *Science* 277 (August 15, 1997), 918–924.

———, and William Julius Wilson. "Toward a Theory of Race, Crime, and Urban Inequality," in John Hagan and Ruth D. Peterson, eds., *Crime and Inequality.* Stanford, CA: Stanford University Press, 1995, pp. 37–54.

Samuel, William, and Elizabeth Moulds. "The Effect of Crime Severity on Perceptions of Fair Punishment: A California Case Study," *Journal of Criminal Law and Criminology* 77 (Fall 1986), 931–948.

Sanday, Peggy Reeves. *Fraternity Gang Rape: Sex, Brotherhood, and Privilege on Campus.* New York: New York University Press, 1990.

Sanders, William B. *Gangbangs and Drive-Bys: Grounded Culture and Juvenile Gang Violence.* New York: Aldine de Gruyter, 1994.

Scales, Ann. "Polls Say Blacks Tend to Favor Check," *Boston Sunday Globe,* September 30, 2001, p. A16.

Schafer, John, Raul Caetano, and Catherine L. Clark. "Rates of Intimate Partner Violence in the United States," *American Journal of Public Health* 88 (November 1998), 1702–1704.

Schafer, Stephen. *The Political Criminal: The Problem of Morality and Crime.* New York: Free Press, 1974.

———. *The Victim and His Criminal: A Study in Functional Responsibility.* Englewood Cliffs, NJ: Prentice Hall, 1968.

Schiraldi, Vincent, and Mark Soler. "The Will of the People? The Public's Opinion of the Violent and Repeat Juvenile Offender Act of 1997," *Crime and Delinquency* 44 (October 1998), 590–601.

Schneider, Anne L., and Peter R. Schneider. *Private and Public Minded Citizen Responses to a Neighborhood-Based Crime Prevention Strategy.* Eugene, OR: Institute of Policy Analysis, 1978.

Schur, Edwin M. *Crimes without Victims: Deviant Behavior and Public Policy.* Englewood Cliffs, NJ: Prentice Hall, 1965.

———. *Narcotic Addiction in Britain and America.* London: Tavistock, 1962.

———. *Our Criminal Society: The Social and Legal Sources of Crime in America.* Englewood Cliffs, NJ: Prentice Hall, 1969.

———. *Radical Nonintervention: Rethinking the Delinquency Problem.* Englewood Cliffs, NJ: Prentice Hall, 1973.

Schwartz, Martin D., and Walter S. DeKeseredy. *Sexual Assault on the College Campus: The Role of Male Peer Support.* Thousand Oaks, CA: Sage, 1997.

Schwartz, Richard D., and Jerome H. Skolnick. "Two Studies of Legal Stigma," *Social Problems* 10 (Fall 1962), 133–142.

Schwendinger, Herman, and Julia Schwendinger. "Defenders of Order or Guardians of Human Rights?" in Ian Taylor, Paul Walton, and Jock Young, eds., *Critical Criminology.* London: Routledge and Kegan Paul, 1975, pp. 113–146.

Schwendinger, Julia R., and Herman Schwendinger. *Rape and Inequality.* Beverly Hills, CA: Sage, 1983.

Scimecca, Joseph A. "Labeling Theory and Personal Construct Theory: Toward the Measurement of Individual Variation," *Journal of Criminal Law and Criminology* 68 (December 1977), 652–659.

Scott, Joseph E., and Fahad Al-Thakeb. "The Public's Perceptions of Crime: Scandinavia, Western Europe, the Middle East, and the United States," in C. Ronald Huff, ed., *Contemporary Corrections: Social Control and Conflict.* Beverly Hills, CA: Sage, 1977, pp. 77–88.

Scully, Diana, and Joseph Marolla. "Convicted Rapists' Vocabulary of Motive: Excuses and Justifications," *Social Problems* 31 (1984), 530–544.

Sechrest, Lee, Susan O. White, and Elizabeth D. Brown, eds. *The Rehabilitation of Criminal Offenders: Problems and Prospects.* Washington, DC: National Academy of Sciences, 1979.

Sellin, Thorsten. "The Basis of a Crime Index," *Journal of Criminal Law and Criminology* 22 (September 1931), 335–356.

———. *Culture Conflict and Crime.* New York: Social Science Research Council, 1938.

———, and Marvin E. Wolfgang. *The Measurement of Delinquency.* New York: Wiley, 1964.

Serrill, Michael S. "A Cold New Look at the Criminal Mind," *Psychology Today* 11 (February 1978), 86–92, 106.

Shah, Saleem A., and Loren H. Roth. "Biological and Psychophysiological Factors in Criminality," in Daniel Glaser, ed., *Handbook of Criminology.* Chicago: Rand McNally, 1974, pp. 101–173.

Shannon, Lyle W., with Judith L. McKim, et al. *Criminal Career Continuity: Its Social Context.* New York: Human Sciences Press, 1988.

Shapiro, Susan P. "Collaring the Crime, Not the Criminal: Reconsidering the Concept of White-Collar Crime," *American Sociological Review* 55 (June 1990), 346–365.

Shaw, Clifford R., and Henry D. McKay. *Juvenile Delinquency and Urban Areas,* rev. ed. Chicago: University of Chicago Press, 1969.

Shelden, Randall G., John A. Horvath, and Sharon Tracy. "Do Status Offenders Get Worse? Some Clarifications on the Question of Escalation," *Crime and Delinquency* 35 (April 1989), 202–216.

Sheley, Joseph F., and James D. Wright. *In the Line of Fire: Youth, Guns, and Violence in Urban America.* New York: Aldine de Gruyter, 1995.

Shelley, Louise I. *Crime and Modernization: The Impact of Industrialization and Urbanization on Crime.* Carbondale: Southern Illinois University Press, 1981a.

———. "Urbanization and Crime: The Soviet Case in Cross-Cultural Perspective," in Louise I. Shelley, ed., *Readings in Comparative Criminology.* Carbondale: Southern Illinois University Press, 1981b, pp. 141–152.

Shenon, Philip. "The Mobsters Who Lurk behind the Corporate Veil," *New York Times,* December 8, 1985, p. E4.

Sherman, Lawrence W. "Attacking Crime: Police and Crime Control," in Michael Tonry and Norval Morris, eds., *Modern Policing,* vol. 15 of *Crime and Justice: A Review of Research.* Chicago: University of Chicago Press, 1992a, 159–230.

———. "The Influence of Criminology on Criminal Law: Evaluating Arrests for Misdemeanor Domestic Violence," *Journal of Criminal Law and Criminology* 83 (Spring 1992b), 1–45.

———. "Police Crackdowns: Initial and Residual Deterrence," in Michael Tonry and Norval Morris, eds., *Crime and Justice: A Review of Research,* vol. 12. Chicago: University of Chicago Press, 1990, pp. 1–48.

———. *Policing Domestic Violence: Experiments and Dilemmas.* New York: Free Press, 1992c.

————, and Richard A. Berk. "The Specific Deterrent Effects of Arrest for Domestic Assault," *American Sociological Review* 49 (April 1984), 261–272.

————, Patrick R. Gartin, and Michael E. Buerger. "Hot Spots of Predatory Crime: Routine Activities and the Criminology of Place," *Criminology* 27 (February 1989), 27–55.

————, and Barry D. Glick. *The Quality of Police Arrest Statistics,* Police Foundation Reports 2. Washington, DC: Police Foundation, August 1984.

————, and Dennis P. Rogan. "Effects of Gun Seizure on Gun Violence: 'Hot Spots' Patrol in Kansas City," *Justice Quarterly* 12 (December 1995), pp. 673–693.

————, James W. Shaw, and Dennis P. Rogan. *The Kansas City Gun Experiment.* Washington, DC: U.S. Department of Justice, January 1995.

————, and David Weisburd. "General Deterrent Effects of Police Patrol in Crime 'Hot Spots': A Randomized, Controlled Trial," *Justice Quarterly* 12 (1995), 625–648.

————, et al. "From Initial Deterrence to Long-Term Escalation: Short-Custody Arrest for Poverty Ghetto Domestic Violence," *Criminology* 29 (November 1991), 821–850.

Short, James F., Jr. "Introduction to the Revised Edition," in Clifford R. Shaw and Henry D. McKay, *Juvenile Delinquency and Urban Areas,* rev. ed. Chicago: University of Chicago Press, 1969, pp. xxv–liv.

————, and F. Ivan Nye. "Reported Behavior as a Criterion of Deviant Behavior," *Social Problems* 5 (Winter 1957), 207–213.

Shotland, R. Lance, and Margret K. Straw. "Bystander Response to an Assault: When a Man Attacks a Woman," *Journal of Personality and Social Psychology* 34 (November 1976), 990–999.

Shover, Neal. *Aging Criminals.* Beverly Hills, CA: Sage, 1985.

————. *Great Pretenders: Pursuits and Careers of Persistent Thieves.* Boulder, CO: Westview, 1996.

————. "The Later Stages of Ordinary Property Offender Careers," *Social Problems* 31 (December 1983), 208–210.

————. "The Social Organization of Burglary," *Social Problems* 20 (Spring 1973), 499–514.

————, Glenn S. Coffey, and Dick Hobbs. "Crime on the Line: Telemarketing and the Changing Nature of Professional Crime," *British Journal of Criminology* (2003), forthcoming.

————, Greer Litton Fox, and Michael Mills. "Long-Term Consequences of Victimization by White-Collar Crime," *Justice Quarterly* 11 (March 1994), 301–324.

————, and Carol Y. Thompson. "Age, Differential Expectations, and Crime Desistance," *Criminology* 30 (February 1992), 89–104.

Silberman, Charles E. *Criminal Violence, Criminal Justice.* New York: Random House, 1978.

Simon, Rita J., and David E. Aaronson. *The Insanity Defense: A Critical Assessment of Law and Policy in the Post-Hinckley Era.* New York: Praeger, 1988.

Simons, Ronald L., et al. "A Test of Latent Trait versus Life-Course Perspectives on the Stability of Adolescent Antisocial Behavior," *Criminology* 36 (May 1998), 217–243.

Simpson, Sally S., and Christopher S. Koper. "Deterring Corporate Crime," *Criminology* 30 (August 1992), 347–375.

Singer, Simon I., and Murray Levine. "Power-Control Theory, Gender, and Delinquency: A Partial Replication with Additional Evidence on the Role of Peers," *Criminology* 26 (November 1988), 627–647.

Skogan, Wesley G. "Citizen Reporting of Crime: Some National Panel Data," *Criminology* 13 (February 1976a), 535–549.

————. "Crime and Crime Rates," in Wesley G. Skogan, ed., *Sample Surveys of the Victims of Crime.* Cambridge, MA: Ballinger, 1976b, pp. 105–119.

————. *Disorder and Decline: Crime and the Spiral of Decay in American Neighborhoods.* Berkeley: University of California Press, 1990.

————. "Fear of Crime and Neighborhood Change," in Albert J. Reiss, Jr., and Michael Tonry, eds., *Communities and Crime.* Chicago: University of Chicago Press, 1986, pp. 203–229.

————. "Reporting Crimes to the Police: The Status of World Research," *Journal of Research in Crime and Delinquency* 21 (May 1984), 113–137.

————, and Susan M. Hartnett. *Community Policing, Chicago Style.* New York: Oxford University Press, 1997.

————, and Arthur J. Lurigio. "The Correlates of Community Antidrug Activism," *Crime and Delinquency* 38 (October 1992), 510–521.

Skolnick, Jerome H. *Justice without Trial: Law Enforcement in Democratic Society,* 3d ed. New York: Wiley, 1994.

————, and James J. Fyfe. *Above the Law: Police and the Excessive Use of Force.* New York: Free Press, 1993.

Skorneck, Carolyn. "683,000 Women Raped in 1990, New Government Study Finds," *Boston Globe,* April 24, 1992, pp. 1, 32.

Sloan, John Henry, et al. "Handgun Regulation, Crime, Assaults, and Homicide: A Tale of Two Cities," *New England Journal of Medicine* 319 (November 10, 1988), 1256–1262.

Smigel, Erwin O., and H. Laurence Ross. "Introduction," in *Crimes against Bureaucracy.* New York: Van Nostrand Reinhold, 1970, pp. 1–14.

Smith, Brent L., and Kelly R. Damphousse. "Punishing Political Offenders: The Effect of Political Motive on Federal Sentencing Decisions," *Criminology* 34 (August 1996), 289–321.

Smith, David E., and George R. Gay, eds. *"It's So Good, Don't Even Try It Once": Heroin in Perspective.* Englewood Cliffs, NJ: Prentice Hall, 1972.

Smith, Douglas A. "The Plea Bargaining Controversy," *Journal of Criminal Law and Criminology* 77 (Fall 1986), 949–967.

————, and Robert Brame. "On the Initiation and Continuation of Delinquency," *Criminology* 32 (November 1994), 607–629.

————, and Patrick A. Gartin. "Specifying Specific Deterrence: The Influence of Arrest on Future Criminal

Activity," *American Sociological Review* 54 (February 1989), 94–106.

Smith, Dwight C., Jr. "Organized Crime and Entrepreneurship," *International Journal of Criminology and Penology* 6 (May 1978), 161–177.

Smith, Tom W. "A Call for a Truce in the DGU War," *Journal of Criminal Law and Criminology* 87 (Summer 1997), 1462–1469.

Snell, Tracy L., and Laura M. Maruschak. *Capital Punishment 2001*. Washington, DC: Bureau of Justice Statistics, December 2002.

Snyder, Howard N., Melissa Sickmund, and Eileen Poe-Yamagata, *Juvenile Offenders and Victims: 1996 Update on Violence*. Pittsburgh, PA: National Center for Juvenile Justice, February 1996.

Snyder, Howard N., Melissa Sickmund, and Eileen Poe-Yamagata. *Juvenile Transfers to Criminal Court in the 1990's: Lessons Learned from Four Studies: Summary*. Washington, DC: U.S. Department of Justice, August 2000.

Sorensen, Jon, et al. "Capital Punishment and Deterrence: Examining the Effect of Executions on Murder in Texas," *Crime and Delinquency* 45 (October 1999), 481–493.

Sparks, Richard F. "Multiple Victimization: Evidence, Theory, and Future Research," *Journal of Criminal Law and Criminology* 72 (Summer 1981), 762–778.

———. *Research on Victims of Crime: Accomplishments, Issues, and New Directions*. Washington, DC: U.S. Government Printing Office, 1982.

Sparrow, Malcolm K. *Fraud Control in the Health Care Industry: Assessing the State of the Art*. Washington, DC: U.S. Department of Justice, December 1998.

Spears, Jeffrey W., and Cassia C. Spohn. "The Effect of Evidence Factors and Victim Characteristics on Prosecutors' Charging Decisions in Sexual Assault Cases," *Justice Quarterly* 14 (September 1997), 501–524.

Spelman, William. "What Recent Studies Do (and Don't) Tell Us about Imprisonment and Crime," in Michael Tonry, ed., *Crime and Justice: A Review of Research*, vol. 27. Chicago: University of Chicago Press, 2000, pp. 419–494.

———, and John E. Eck. *Problem-Oriented Policing*. Washington, DC: U.S. Department of Justice, January 1987.

Spitzer, Steven. "The Political Economy of Policing," in David F. Greenberg, ed., *Crime and Capitalism*. Palo Alto, CA: Mayfield, 1981, pp. 314–340.

Spohn, Cassia, and Jeffrey Spears. "The Effect of Offender and Victim Characteristics on Sexual Assault Case Processing Decisions," *Justice Quarterly* 13 (December 1996), 649–679.

Stack, Steven. "Publicized Executions and Homicide, 1950–1980," *American Sociological Review* 52 (August 1987), 532–540.

———. "Social Structure and Swedish Crime Rates: A Time-Series Analysis, 1950–1979," *Criminology* 20 (November 1982), 499–513.

Stafford, Mark C., and Omer R. Galle. "Victimization Rates, Exposure to Risk, and Fear of Crime," *Criminology* 22 (May 1984), 173–185.

Stark, Rodney. "Deviant Places: A Theory of the Ecology of Crime," *Criminology* 25 (November 1987), 893–909.

Stattin, Håkan, and David Magnusson. "The Role of Early Aggressive Behavior in the Frequency, Seriousness, and Types of Later Crime," *Journal of Consulting and Clinical Psychology* 57 (December 1989), 710–718.

Steadman, Henry J. "Empirical Research on the Insanity Defense," *Annals of the American Academy of Political and Social Sciences* 477 (January 1985), 58–71.

———, et al. "Violence by People Discharged from Acute Psychiatric Inpatient Facilities and by Others in the Same Neighborhoods," *Archives of General Psychiatry* 55 (May 1998), 393–401.

Steffensmeier, Darrell J. "Assessing the Impact of the Women's Movement on Sex-Based Differences in the Handling of Adult Criminal Defendants," *Crime and Delinquency* 26 (July 1980), 344–357.

———. *The Fence: In the Shadow of Two Worlds*. Totowa, NJ: Rowman and Littlefield, 1986.

———. "Organization Properties and Sex-Segregation in the Underworld: Building a Sociological Theory of Sex Differences in Crime," *Social Forces* 61 (June 1983), 1010–1032.

———, and Michael J. Cobb. "Sex Differences in Urban Arrest Patterns," *Social Problems* 29 (October 1981), 37–50.

———, and Stephen Demuth. "Ethnicity and Judges' Sentencing Decisions: Hispanic-Black-White Comparisons," *Criminology* 39 (February 2001), 145–178.

———, and Stephen Demuth. "Ethnicity and Sentencing Outcomes in U.S. Federal Courts: Who Is Punished More Harshly?" *American Sociological Review* 65 (October 2000), 705–729.

———, and Miles D. Harer. "Is the Crime Rate Really Falling? An Aging U.S. Population and Its Impact on the Nation's Crime Rate, 1980–1984," *Journal of Research in Crime and Delinquency* 24 (February 1987), 23–48.

———, John Kramer, and Cathy Streifel. "Gender and Imprisonment Decisions," *Criminology* 31 (August 1993), 411–446.

———, Jeffery Ulmer, and John Kramer. "The Interaction of Race, Gender, and Age in Criminal Sentencing: The Punishment Cost of Being Young, Black, and Male," *Criminology* 36 (November 1998), 763–797.

Steinhart, David. "California Opinion Poll: Public Attitudes on Youth Crime," *NCCD Focus*, December 1988, pp. 1–7.

Stenross, Barbara. "Police Response to Residential Burglaries: Dusting for Prints as a Negative Rite," *Criminology* 22 (August 1984), 389–402.

Stephens, Richard C., and Rosalind D. Ellis. "Narcotic Addicts and Crime: Analysis of Recent Trends," *Criminology* 12 (February 1975), 474–488.

Sterngold, James. "Firms Act in Wake of 2 Scandals," *New York Times*, June 7, 1986, pp. 33, 36.

Stiles, Beverly L., Xiaoru Liu, and Howard B. Kaplan. "Relative Deprivation and Deviant Adaptations: The Mediating Effects of Negative Self-Feelings," *Journal of Research in Crime and Delinquency* 37 (February 2000), 64–90.

Stoddart, Kenneth. "The Enforcement of Narcotics Violations in a Canadian City: Heroin Users' Perspectives on the Production of Official Statistics," *Canadian Journal of Criminology* 23 (October 1982), 425–438.

Stolzenberg, Lisa, and Stewart J. D'Alessio. "Sentencing and Unwarranted Disparity: An Empirical Assessment of the Long-Term Impact of Sentencing Guidelines in Minnesota," *Criminology* 32 (May 1994), 301–310.

———, and Stewart J. D'Alessio. " 'Three Strikes and You're Out': The Impact of California's New Mandatory Sentencing Law on Serious Crime Rates," *Crime and Delinquency* 43 (October 1997), 457–469.

Stookey, John Alan. "A Cost Theory of Victim Justice," in Burt Galaway and Joe Hudson, eds., *Perspectives on Crime Victims*. St. Louis: C. V. Mosby, 1981, pp. 80–89.

Straus, Murray A. "Trends in Cultural Norms and Rates of Partner Violence: An Update to 1992," in Murray A. Straus and Sandra M. Stith, eds., *Understanding Partner Violence: Prevalence, Causes, Consequences, and Solutions*. Minneapolis: National Council on Family Relations, 1995, pp. 30–33.

Stuart, Reginald. "Atlanta Deaths: Fear Felt by Young," *New York Times,* January 26, 1981, pp. A1, A12.

Surette, Ray. "Media Echoes: Systemic Effects of News Coverage," *Justice Quarterly* 16 (September 1999), 601–631.

Sutherland, Edwin H. *The Professional Thief*. Chicago: University of Chicago Press, 1937.

———. *White Collar Crime: The Uncut Version*. New Haven, CT: Yale University Press, 1949, 1983.

———, and Donald R. Cressey. *Criminology,* 10th ed. Philadelphia: Lippincott, 1978.

———, Donald R. Cressey, and David F. Luckenbill. *Principles of Criminology,* 11th ed. Dix Hills, NY: General Hall, 1992.

Suttles, Gerald D. *The Social Order of the Slum: Ethnicity and Territory in the Inner City*. Chicago: University of Chicago Press, 1968.

Swigert, Victoria Lynn, and Ronald A. Farrell. *Murder, Inequality, and the Law*. Lexington, MA: D. C. Heath, 1976.

Swigert, Victoria Lynn, and Ronald A. Farrell. "Normal Homicides and the Law," *American Sociological Review* 42 (February 1977), 16–32.

Sykes, Charles J. *A Nation of Victims: The Decay of the American Character*. New York: St. Martin's, 1992.

Sykes, Gresham M., and David Matza. "Techniques of Neutralization: A Theory of Delinquency," *American Sociological Review* 22 (December 1957), 664–670.

Szasz, Andrew. "Corporations, Organized Crime, and the Disposal of Hazardous Waste: An Examination of the Making of a Criminogenic Regulatory Structure," *Criminology* 24 (February 1986), 1–27.

Taylor, Bruce, and Trevor Bennett. *Comparing Drug Use Rates of Detained Arrestees in the United States and England*. Washington, DC: U.S. Department of Justice, April 1999.

Taylor, H. Gerry. "Learning Disabilities," in Eric J. Mash and Russell A. Barkley, eds., *Treatment of Childhood Disorders*. New York: Guilford Press, 1989, pp. 347–380.

Taylor, Ian, Paul Walton, and Jock Young. "Critical Criminology in Britain: Review and Prospects," in Ian Taylor, Paul Walton, and Jock Young, eds., *Critical Criminology*. London: Routledge and Kegan Paul, 1975, pp. 6–62.

Taylor, Ian, Paul Walton, and Jock Young. *The New Criminology: For a Social Theory of Deviance*. London: Routledge and Kegan Paul, 1973.

Taylor, Ralph B. *Breaking Away from Broken Windows: Baltimore Neighborhoods and the Nationwide Fight against Crime, Grime, Fear, and Decline*. Boulder, CO: Westview, 2001.

———, and Steven Gottfredson. "Environmental Design, Crime, and Prevention: An Examination of Community Dynamics," in Albert J. Reiss, Jr., and Michael Tonry, eds. *Communities and Crime*. Chicago: University of Chicago Press, 1986, pp. 387–416.

———, Stephen D. Gottfredson, and Sidney Brower. "The Defensibility of Defensible Space: A Critical Review and a Synthetic Framework for Future Research," in Travis Hirschi and Michael Gottfredson, eds., *Understanding Crime: Current Theory and Research*. Beverly Hills, CA: Sage, 1980, pp. 53–71.

———, and Adele V. Harrell. *Physical Environment and Crime*. Washington, DC: U.S. Department of Justice, May 1996.

Taylor, Robert W., Eric J. Fritsch, and Tory J. Caeti. "Core Challenges Facing Community Policing: The Emperor *Still* Has No Clothes," *ACJS Today,* May/June 1998, pp. 1, 3–5.

Tennenbaum, Abraham N. "The Influence of the *Garner* Decision on Police Use of Deadly Force," *Journal of Criminal Law and Criminology* 85 (Summer 1994), 241–260.

Tennenbaum, D. "Personality and Criminality: A Summary and Implications of the Literature," *Journal of Criminal Justice* 5 (1977), 225–235.

Teplin, L. A., K. M. Abram, and G. M. McClelland. "Prevalence of Psychiatric Disorders among Incarcerated Women: Pretrial Jail Detainees," *Archives of General Psychiatry* 53 (1996), 505–512.

Terrill, William, and Stephen D. Mastrofski. "Situational and Officer-Based Determinants of Police Coercion," *Justice Quarterly* 19 (June 2002), 215–248.

Thomson, Douglas R., and Anthony J. Ragona. "Popular Moderation versus Governmental Authoritarianism: An Interactionist View of Public Sentiments toward Criminal Sanctions," *Crime and Delinquency* 33 (July 1987), 337–357.

Thornberry, Terence P., and R. L. Christenson. "Unemployment and Criminal Involvement: An Investigation of Reciprocal Causal Structures," *American Sociological Review* 49 (June 1984), 398–411.

———, et al. "Delinquent Peers, Beliefs, and Delinquent Behavior: A Longitudinal Test of Interactional Theory," *Criminology* 32 (February 1994), 47–81.

———, et al. "Testing Interactional Theory: An Examination of Reciprocal Causal Relationships among Family, School, and Delinquency," *Journal of Criminal Law and Criminology* 82 (Spring 1991), 3–35.

Thorsell, Bernard A., and Lloyd W. Klemke. "The Labeling Process: Reinforcement and Deterrent?" *Law and Society Review* 6 (February 1972), 393–403.

Thrasher, Frederic M. *The Gang: A Study of l,313 Gangs in Chicago,* abridged ed. Chicago: University of Chicago Press, 1963.

Tien, James M., Thomas F. Rich, and Michael F. Cahn. *Electronic Fund Transfer Systems Fraud: Computer Crime.* Washington, DC: U.S. Department of Justice, April 1986.

Tillman, Robert. *Global Pirates: Fraud in the Offshore Insurance Industry.* Boston: Northeastern University Press, 2002.

———. "The Size of the 'Criminal Population': The Prevalence and Incidence of Adult Arrest," *Criminology* 25 (August 1987), 561–579.

Timnick, Lois. "Psychic Trauma Follows Chowchilla Kidnapping," *Boston Globe,* January 24, 1981, p. 3.

Timrots, Anita D., and Michael R. Rand. *Violent Crime by Strangers and Nonstrangers.* Washington, DC: U.S. Department of Justice, January 1987.

Tittle, Charles R. *Control Balance: Toward a General Theory of Deviance.* Boulder, CO: Westview, 1995.

———. "Social Class and Criminal Behavior: A Critique of the Theoretical Foundation," *Social Forces* 62 (December 1983), 334–358.

———, and Robert F. Meier. "Specifying the SES/Delinquency Relationship," *Criminology* 28 (May 1990), 271–299.

———, and Raymond Paternoster. "Geographic Mobility and Criminal Behavior," *Journal of Research in Crime and Delinquency* 25 (August 1988), 301–343.

———, and Alan R. Rowe. "Certainty of Arrest and Crime Rates: A Further Test of the Deterrence Hypothesis," *Social Forces* 52 (June 1974), 455–462.

———, Wayne J. Villemez, and Douglas A. Smith. "The Myth of Social Class and Criminality: An Empirical Assessment of the Empirical Evidence," *American Sociological Review* 43 (October 1978), 643–656.

Titus, Richard M., Fred Heinzelmann, and John M. Boyle. "Victimization of Persons by Fraud," *Crime and Delinquency* 41 (January 1995), 54–72.

Tjaden, Patricia, and Nancy Thoennes. *Extent, Nature, and Consequences of Intimate Partner Violence: Findings from the National Violence against Women Survey.* Washington, DC: US Department of Justice, July 2000.

Tjaden, Patricia, and Nancy Thoennes. *Prevalence, Incidence, and Consequences of Violence against Women: Findings from the National Violence against Women Survey.* Washington, DC: U.S. Department of Justice, November 1998.

Tjaden, Patricia, and Nancy Thoennes. *Stalking in America: Findings from the National Violence against Women Survey.* Washington, DC: U.S. Department of Justice, April 1998.

Tobias, J. J. *Crime and Industrial Society in the 19th Century.* New York: Schocken, 1967.

Toby, Jackson. "The Socialization and Control of Deviant Motivation," in Daniel Glaser, ed., *Hand-book of Criminology.* Chicago: Rand McNally, 1974, pp. 85–100.

Tonry, Michael. "Ethnicity, Crime, and Immigration," in Michael Tonry, ed., *Ethnicity, Crime, and Immigration: Comparative and Cross-National Perspectives, Crime and Justice: A Review of Research,* vol. 21. Chicago: University of Chicago Press, 1997, pp. 1–29.

———. "The Failure of the U.S. Sentencing Commission's Guidelines," *Crime and Delinquency* 39 (April 1993), 131–149.

———. *Malign Neglect: Race, Crime, and Punishment in America.* New York: Oxford University Press, 1995.

———. *Sentencing Matters.* New York: Oxford University Press, 1996.

Tracy, Paul E., Jr. "Race and Class Differences in Official and Self-Reported Delinquency," in Marvin E. Wolfgang, Terence P. Thornberry, and Robert M. Figlio, *From Boy to Man, from Delinquency to Crime.* Chicago: University of Chicago Press, 1987, pp. 87–121.

———, and Kimberly Kempf-Leonard. *Continuity and Discontinuity in Criminal Careers.* New York: Plenum, 1996.

———, Marvin E. Wolfgang, and Robert M. Figlio. *Delinquency Careers in Two Birth Cohorts.* New York: Plenum, 1990.

Traub, Stuart H. "Battling Employee Crime: A Review of Corporate Strategies and Programs," *Crime and Delinquency* 42 (April 1996), 244–256.

Treaster, Joseph B. "Behind Immigrants' Voyage, Long Reach of Chinese Gang," *New York Times,* June 9, 1993, pp. A1, B2.

———. "Empty Graves and Full Wallets; Fake Deaths Abroad Are a Growing Problem for Insurers," *New York Times,* July 1, 1997, pp. D1, D4.

Trojanowicz, R. *An Evaluation of the Neighborhood Foot Patrol Program in Flint, Michigan.* East Lansing, MI: Michigan State University, 1983.

Tunnell, Kenneth D. *Choosing Crime: The Criminal Calculus of Property Offenders.* Chicago: Nelson-Hall, 1992.

Turk, Austin. "Back on Track: Asking and Answering the Right Questions," *Law and Society Review* 27 (1993), 355–359.

———. *Criminality and Legal Order.* Chicago: Rand McNally, 1969.

Uggen, Christopher. "Work as a Turning Point in the Life Course of Criminals: A Duration Model of Age, Employment, and Recidivism," *American Sociological Review* 67 (August 2000), 529–546.

———, and Candace Kruttschnitt. "Crime in the Breaking: Gender Differences in Desistance," *Law and Society Review* 32 (1998), 339–366.

Uhlman, Thomas M., and N. Darlene Walker. " 'He Takes Some of My Time; I Take Some of His': An Analysis of Sentencing Patterns in Jury Cases," *Law and Society Review* 14 (Winter 1980), 323–341.

U.S. Department of Justice. "National Correctional Population Reaches New High; Grows by 126,400 during 2000 to Total 6.5 Million Adults," press release. Washington, DC: U.S. Department of Justice, August 26, 2001.

U.S. Department of Justice, Attorney General's Task Force on Violent Crime. *Final Report*. Washington, DC: U.S. Government Printing Office, 1981.

U.S. General Accounting Office. "Death Penalty Sentencing: Research Indicates Pattern of Racial Disparities," in Hugo Adam Bedau, ed., *The Death Penalty in America: Current Controversies*. New York: Oxford University Press, 1997, pp. 268–274.

Unnever, James D. "Direct and Organizational Discrimination in the Sentencing of Drug Offenders," *Social Problems* 30 (December 1982), 212–225.

van den Haag, Ernest. *Punishing Criminals: Concerning a Very Old and Painful Question*. New York: Basic Books, 1975.

van Ness, Daniel, and Karen Heetderks Strong. *Restoring Justice*. Cincinnati, OH: Anderson, 1997.

van Voorhis, Patricia, et al. "The Impact of Family Structure and Quality on Delinquency: A Comparative Assessment of Structural and Functional Factors," *Criminology* 26 (May 1988), 235–261.

Vélez, Maria B. "The Role of Public Social Control in Urban Neighborhoods: A Multi-Level Analysis of Victimization Risk," *Criminology* 39 (November 2001), 837–864.

Visher, Christy A. "The Rand Inmate Survey: A Reanalysis," in Alfred Blumstein et al., eds., *Criminal Careers and "Career Criminals"*, vol. 2. Washington, DC: National Academy Press, 1986, pp. 161–211.

von Hirsch, Andrew. *Doing Justice: The Choice of Punishments*. New York: Hill and Wang, 1976.

———. *Past or Future Crimes: Deservedness and Dangerousness in the Sentencing of Criminals*. New Brunswick, NJ: Rutgers University Press, 1985.

———. "Proportionality in the Philosophy of Punishment," in Michael Tonry, ed., *Crime and Justice: A Review of Research*, vol. 16. Chicago: University of Chicago Press, 1992, pp. 55–98.

——— "Selective Incapacitation: A Critique," *NIJ Reports*, January 1984, pp. 5–8.

———. "Utilitarian Sentencing Resuscitated: The American Bar Association's Second Report on Criminal Sentencing," *Rutgers Law Review* 33 (Spring 1981), 772–789.

Voss, Harwin L., and John R. Hepburn. "Patterns in Criminal Homicide in Chicago," *Journal of Criminal Law, Criminology and Police Science* 59 (December 1968), 499–508.

Waegel, William B. "The Use of Lethal Force by Police: The Effect of Statutory Change," *Crime and Delinquency* 30 (January 1984), 121–140.

Waldo, Gordon P., and Simon Dinitz. "Personality Attributes of the Criminal: An Analysis of Research Studies, 1950–1965," *Journal of Research in Crime and Delinquency* 4 (July 1967), 185–201.

Wallerstein, James S., and Clement J. Wyle. "Our Law-Abiding Law-Breakers," *Probation* 35 (April 1947), 107–112.

Walsh, Anthony. "Placebo Justice: Victim Recommendations and Offender Sentences in Sexual Assault Cases," *Journal of Criminal Law and Criminology* 77 (Winter 1986), 1126–1141.

Walters, Glenn D.. "A Meta-Analysis of the Gene-Crime Relationship," *Criminology* 30 (November 1992), 595–613.

Warr, Mark. "Age, Peers, and Delinquency," *Criminology* 31 (February 1993), 17–40.

———. "Life-Course Transitions and Desistance from Crime," *Criminology* 36 (May 1998), 183–216.

———, and Christopher G. Ellison. "Rethinking Social Reactions to Crime: Personal and Altruistic Fear in Family Households," *American Journal of Sociology* 3 (November 2000), 551–578.

———, and Mark Stafford. "The Influence of Delinquent Peers: What They Think or What They Do?" *Criminology* 29 (November 1991), 851–866.

Warshaw, Robin. *I Never Called It Rape: The Ms. Report on Recognizing, Fighting and Surviving Date and Acquaintance Rape*. New York: Harper and Row, 1988.

Weatherburn, Don, Bronwyn Lind, and Simon Ku. "'Hotbeds of Crime?' Crime and Public Housing in Urban Sydney," *Crime and Delinquency* 45 (April 1999), 256–271.

Weber, Max. *Economy and Society: An Outline of Interpretive Sociology*. Berkeley, CA: University of California Press, 1979.

Weisburd, David, and Rosann Greenspan, et al. *Police Attitudes toward Abuse of Authority: Findings from a National Study*. Washington, DC: U.S. Department of Justice, May 2000.

Weisburd, David, Elin Waring, and Ellen Chayet. "Specific Deterrence in a Sample of Offenders Convicted of White-Collar Crimes," *Criminology* 33 (November 1995), 587–607.

Weisburd, David, Elin Waring, and Ellen F. Chayet. *White-Collar Crime and Criminal Careers*. Cambridge, England: Cambridge University Press, 2001.

Weisburd, David, et al. *Crimes of the Middle Classes: White-Collar Offenders in the Federal Courts*. New Haven, CT: Yale University Press, 1991.

Welch, Michael, Melissa Fenwick, and Meredith Roberts. "Primary Definitions of Crime and Moral Panic: A Content Analysis of Experts' Quotes in Feature Newspaper Articles on Crime," *Journal of Research in Crime and Delinquency* 34 (November 1997), 474–494.

Welch, Michael, Melissa Fenwick, and Meredith Roberts. "State Managers, Intellectuals, and the Media: A Content Analysis of Ideology in Experts' Quotes in Feature Newspaper Articles on Crime," *Justice Quarterly* 15 (June 1998), 219–241.

Wellford, Charles, and James Cronin. "Clearing Up Homicide Clearance Rates," *National Institute of Justice Journal*, April 2000, 2–7.

Wells, L. Edward. "Self-Enhancement through Delinquency: A Conditional Test of Self-Derogation Theory," *Journal of Research in Crime and Delinquency* 26 (August 1989), 226–252.

———, and Joseph H. Rankin. "The Broken Home Model of Delinquency: Analytic Issues," *Journal of Research in Crime and Delinquency* 23 (February 1986), 68–93.

———, and Joseph H. Rankin. "Direct Parental Controls and Delinquency," *Criminology* 26 (May 1988), 263–285.

———, and Joseph H. Rankin. "Families and Delinquency: A Meta-Analysis of the Impact of Broken Homes," *Social Problems* 38 (1991), 71–93.

Wells, William. "The Nature and Circumstances of Defensive Gun Use: A Content Analysis of Interpersonal Conflict Situations Involving Criminal Offenders," *Justice Quarterly* 19 (March 2002), 127–157.

West, D. J. *Delinquency: Its Roots, Careers and Prospects.* Cambridge, MA: Harvard University Press, 1982.

———. *Present Conduct and Future Delinquency.* London: Heinemann, 1969.

———, and D. P. Farrington. *The Delinquent Way of Life.* London: Heinemann, 1977.

———, and D. P. Farrington. *Who Becomes Delinquent?* London: Heinemann, 1973.

Whitaker, Catherine J. *Black Victims.* Washington, DC: U.S. Department of Justice, April 1990.

Wiatrowski, Michael D., David B. Griswold, and Mary K. Roberts. "Social Control Theory and Delinquency," *American Sociological Review* 46 (October 1981), 525–541.

Wicks-Nelson, R., and A. C. Israel. *Behavior Disorders of Childhood,* 2d ed. Englewood Cliffs, NJ: Prentice Hall, 1991.

Widom, Cathy S., and Michael G. Maxfield. *An Update on the "Cycle of Violence."* Washington, DC: U.S. Department of Justice, February 2001.

Wiehofen, Henry. "Punishment and Treatment: Rehabilitation," in Stanley E. Grupp, ed., *Theories of Punishment.* Bloomington: Indiana University Press, 1971, pp. 255–263.

Wiley, Norbert. "The Ethnic Mobility Trap and Stratification Theory," *Social Problems* 15 (Fall 1967), 147–159.

Wilkerson, Isabel. " 'Crack House' Fire: Justice or Vigilantism?" *New York Times,* October 22, 1988, pp. 1, 6.

Williams, Franklin P., 3d. "Conflict Theory and Differential Processing: An Analysis of the Research Literature," in James A. Inciardi, ed., *Radical Criminology: The Coming Crisis.* Beverly Hills, CA: Sage, 1980, pp. 213–232.

Williams, Terry. *The Cocaine Kids: The Inside Story of a Teenage Drug Ring.* Reading, MA: Addison-Wesley, 1989.

———. *Crack House: Notes from the End of the Line.* Reading, MA: Addison-Wesley, 1992.

Willott, Sara, Christine Griffin, and Mark Torrance. "Snakes and Ladders: Upper-Middle Class Male Offenders Talk about Economic Crime," *Criminology* 39 (May 2001), 441–466.

Wilson, James Q. *Thinking about Crime,* rev. ed. New York: Basic Books, 1983.

———. *Varieties of Police Behavior: The Management of Law and Order in Eight Communities.* Cambridge, MA: Harvard University Press, 1968.

———, and Barbara Boland. "Crime," in William Gorham and Nathan Glazer, eds., *The Urban Predicament.* Washington, DC: Urban Institute, 1976, pp. 179–230.

———, and Barbara Boland. "The Effect of the Police on Crime," *Law and Society Review* 12 (1978), 367–390.

———, and Richard J. Herrnstein. *Crime and Human Nature.* New York: Simon and Schuster, 1985.

———, and George L. Kelling. "Broken Windows: The Police and Neighborhood Safety," *Atlantic Monthly* 249 (March 1982), 29–38.

Wilson, Margo, and Martin Daly. "Sexual Rivalry and Sexual Conflict: Recurring Themes in Fatal Conflicts," *Theoretical Criminology* 2 (August 1998), 291–310.

Wilson, William Julius. *The Truly Disadvantaged.* Chicago: University of Chicago Press, 1987.

Winner, Lawrence, et al. "The Transfer of Juveniles to Criminal Court: Reexamining Recidivism over the Long Term," *Crime and Delinquency* 43 (October 1997), 548–563.

Wittebrood, Karin, and Paul Nieuwbeerta. "Criminal Victimization during One's Life Course: The Effects of Previous Victimization and Patterns of Routine Activities," *Journal of Research in Crime and Delinquency* 37 (February 2000), 91–122.

Wolfgang, Marvin E. *Patterns in Criminal Homicide.* Philadelphia: University of Pennsylvania Press, 1958.

———, and Franco Ferracuti. *The Subculture of Violence: Towards an Integrated Theory in Criminology.* Beverly Hills, CA: Sage, 1982.

———, Robert M. Figlio, and Thorsten Sellin. *Delinquency in a Birth Cohort.* Chicago: University of Chicago Press, 1972.

———, Terence P. Thornberry, and Robert M. Figlio. *From Boy to Man, from Delinquency to Crime.* Chicago: University of Chicago Press, 1987.

———, et al. *The National Survey of Crime Severity.* Washington, DC: U.S. Department of Justice, June 1985.

Wolverton, Troy. "Online Auction Fraud Rate Dips," *CNET News.com,* April 16, 2001. Retrieved from http://news.com.com/2100-1017-255905.html.

Wood, Peter B., and Harold G. Grasmick. "Toward the Development of Punishment Equivalencies: Male and Female Inmates Rate the Severity of Alternative Sanctions Compared to Prison," *Justice Quarterly* 16 (March 1999), 19–50.

Wood, Peter B., et al. "Nonsocial Reinforcement and Habitual Criminal Conduct: An Extension of Learning Theory," *Criminology* 35 (May 1997), 335–366.

Worden, Robert E., and Robin L. Shepard. "Demeanor, Crime, and Police Behavior: A Reexamination of the Police Services Study Data," *Criminology* 34 (February 1996), 83–105.

Wordes, Madeline, Timothy S. Bynum, and Charles J. Corley. "Locking Up Youth: The Impact of Race on Detention Decisions," *Journal of Research in Crime and Delinquency* 31 (May 1994), 149–165.

World Health Organization. *World Report on Violence and Health.* Brussels: United Nations, 2002.

Wright, Bradley R. Entner, et al. "The Effects of Social Ties on Crime Vary by Criminal Propensity: A Life-Course Model of Interdependence," *Criminology* 39 (May 2001), 321–351.

Wright, James D., and Peter H. Rossi. *Armed and Considered Dangerous: A Survey of Felons and Their Firearms.* New York: Aldine de Gruyter, 1986.

Wright, James D., Peter H. Rossi, and Kathleen Daly. *Under the Gun: Weapons, Crime, and Violence in America.* New York: Aldine, 1983.

Wright, John P., Francis T. Cullen, and Michael B. Blankenship. "The Social Construction of Corporate Violence: Media Coverage of the Imperial Food Products Fire," *Crime and Delinquency* 41 (January 1995), 20–36.

Wright, John Paul, and Francis T. Cullen. "Parental Efficacy and Delinquent Behavior: Do Control and Support Matter?" *Criminology* 39 (August 2001), 677–705.

Wright, John Paul, Francis T. Cullen, and Nicolas Williams. "Working While in School and Delinquent Involvement: Implications for Social Policy," *Crime and Delinquency* 43 (April 1997), 203–221.

Wright, Richard T., and Scott H. Decker. *Burglars on the Job: Streetlife and Residential Break-ins.* Boston: Northeastern University Press, 1994.

Yablonsky, Lewis. *The Violent Gang.* New York: Macmillan, 1966.

Yochelson, Samuel, and Stanton E. Samenow. *The Criminal Personality,* vol. 1: *A Profile for Change.* New York: Jason Aronson, 1976.

Yochelson, Samuel, and Stanton E. Samenow. *The Criminal Personality,* vol. 2: *The Change Process.* New York: Jason Aronson, 1977.

Yoder, Stephen A. "Criminal Sanctions for Corporate Illegality," *Journal of Criminal Law and Criminology* 69 (Spring 1978), 40–58.

Young, Robert L., David McDowall, and Colin Loftin. "Collective Security and the Ownership of Firearms for Protection," *Criminology* 25 (February 1987), 47–62.

Young, Warren, and Mark Brown. "Cross-National Comparisons of Imprisonment," in Michael Tonry, ed. *Crime and Justice: A Review of Research,* vol. 17.

Chicago: University of Chicago Press, 1993, pp. 1–49.

Yu, Jiang, and Allen E. Liska. "The Certainty of Punishment: A Reference Group Effect and Its Functional Form," *Criminology* 31 (August 1993), 447–464.

Zarr, Gerald H. "Liberia," in Alan Milner, ed., *African Penal Systems.* London: Routledge and Kegan Paul, 1969.

Zeisel, Hans. "A Comment on 'The Deterrent Effect of Capital Punishment' by Phillips," *American Journal of Sociology* 88 (July 1982), 167–169.

Zeitz, Dorothy. *Women Who Embezzle or Defraud: A Study of Convicted Felons.* New York: Praeger, 1981.

Zenoff, Elyce H., and Alan B. Zients. "Juvenile Murderers: Should the Punishment Fit the Crime?" *International Journal of Law and Psychiatry* 2 (1979), 533–553.

Zhang, Lening, and Steven F. Messner. "Family Deviance and Delinquency in China," *Criminology* 33 (August 1995), 359–387.

Zhang, Lening, et al. "Crime Prevention in a Communitarian Society: *Bang-Jiao* and *Tiao-jie* in the People's Republic of China," *Justice Quarterly* 13 (June 1996), 199–222.

Zhang, Sheldon, and Ko-Lin Chin. "Enter the Dragon: Inside Chinese Human Smuggling Organizations," *Criminology* 40 (November 2002), 737–767.

Zillmann, Dolf, and Jennings Bryant. "Effects of Massive Exposure to Pornography," in Neil M. Malamuth and Edward Donnerstein, eds., *Pornography and Sexual Aggression.* New York: Academic Press, 1984, pp. 115–138.

Zimring, Franklin E., and Gordon Hawkins. *Crime Is Not the Problem: Lethal Violence in America.* New York: Oxford University Press, 1997.

Zingraff, Matthew T., et al. "Child Maltreatment and Youthful Problem Behavior," *Criminology* 31 (May 1993), 173–202.

———, et al. "The Mediating Effect of Good School Performance on the Maltreatment-Delinquency Relationship," *Journal of Research in Crime and Delinquency* 31 (February 1994), 62–91.

Zorea, Aharon W. *In the Image of God: A Christian Response to Capital Punishment.* Lanham, MD: University Press of America, 2000.

NAME INDEX

Aaronson, David E., 127, 131
Abadinsky, Harold, 73, 169
Abbott, Daniel J., 30, 33, 78, 144, 195, 239, 249, 321
Abram, K. M., 125
Acosta de Brenes, Esperanza, 78
Adams, Anthony, 158
Adler, Freda, 160, 195, 234, 356
Adler, Patricia, 19, 281, 299–301
Adler, Peter, 281, 300
Ageton, Suzanne S., 94, 98, 183–184, 193, 224
Agnew, Robert, 151–152, 153, 161, 178, 197, 198
Aickin, Mikel, 272
Akers, Ronald L., 198, 215–216, 237, 380
Albini, Joseph L., 305
Albonetti, Celesta, 394
Albrecht, Hans-Joerg, 81
Alder, Christine, 218, 301
Allen, Francis A., 398
Allen, H. David, 320
Allen, Mark D., 352
Allen, Vernon L., 231
Alpert, Geoffrey, 372
Al-Thakeb, Fahad, 388
Altheide, David L., 336
Amir, Menachem, 14, 50, 95, 249, 251
Andelman, David A., 317
Andcnaes, Johannes, 369, 370, 375
Anderson, Kathleen, 193
Anderson, Ronald D., 121
Andrews, D. A., 131, 404, 405
Andrews, Howard, 125
Angel, Arthur, 349
Angier, Natalie, 109
Anglin, M. Douglas, 234
Apospori, Eleni, 372
Appelbaum, Kenneth, 128
Applebome, Peter, 188
Applegate, Brandon K., 384, 414, 434
Arbuthnot, J., 116
Archer, Dane, 203, 331, 380
Archer, John, 121, 160, 164
Arms, Robert L., 209
Armstrong, G. Blake, 314
Armstrong, K. G., 385, 386
Arneklev, Bruce J., 194
Ashcroft, John, 259, 419
Atta, Mohamed, 289
Augustus, John, 351
Austin, James, 392
Austin, Roy L., 190, 352
Avary, D'aunn Wester, 232

Bacon, Margaret K., 186
Baier, Colin J., 194

Bailey, Walter C., 404
Bailey, William C., 380
Baker, Wayne E., 310
Barak-Glantz, Israel L., 11
Baranek, Patricia, 1
Barkley, Russell A., 111
Barlow, David E., 2
Barlow, Melissa Hickman, 2
Barnett, Randy E., 364
Baron, Stephen W., 157
Barr, Robert, 377
Barry, Don, 62
Barry, Ellen, 190
Barry, Herbert, 3d, 186
Barstow, David, 344
Bartusch, Dawn R. Jeglum, 265
Baskin, Deborah R., 147, 230, 280
Bass, Alison, 110, 128, 208
Batson, C. Daniel, 328
Baumer, Eric P., 52
Baumrind, Diana, 188
Bausell, Carole R., 250, 251
Bayley, David H., 338, 340
Beatty, David, 365
Beccaria, Cesare, 22–23, 369, 373
Beck, Allen J., 147, 357
Becker, Howard S., 263, 265
Beckett, Katherine, 433
Bedau, Hugo Adam, 387, 397
Behn, Noel, 203, 244, 296
Beittel, Marc, 380
Belknap, Joanne, 169
Bell, Daniel, 150
Bellair, Paul E., 321
Belson, William A., 216
Benedict, Jeff, 208, 209
Bennett, Richard R., 34
Bennett, Trevor, 252
Bennett, William, 417
Bennetts, Leslie, 206
Benson, Michael L., 201, 391
Bentham, Jeremy, 369
Beristain, Antonio, 395
Berk, Richard A., 19, 147, 189, 230, 374, 394
Berkowitz, Leonard, 207
Bernard, Thomas J., 45, 158, 383
Berns, Walter, 396
Bernstein, Jared, 146, 169
Bernstein, Nina, 385
Best, Joel, 10, 263, 290
Bibi, Zafran, 363
Binder, Arnold, 374, 399
bin Laden, Osama, 58, 288
Bishop, Donna M., 6, 252, 253, 356, 370, 395
Black, Dan, 256
Black, Donald J., 32, 267, 313, 341, 342

Blakey, G. Robert, 306
Blankenship, Michael B., 2
Block, Alan A., 141
Block, Carolyn R., 32, 49, 81
Block, Michael Kent, 372
Block, Richard, 32, 255
Blumberg, Abraham S., 349
Blumberg, Mark, 10
Blumenthal, Monica, 326
Blumstein, Alfred, 88, 255, 264, 271, 352, 369, 374, 378, 380, 410
Blum-West, Stephen Robert, 388
Blundell, William E., 219
Boesky, Ivan, 133
Boggs, Sarah L., 321
Bohn, Martin J., 122
Boisjoly, Russell, 137
Boland, Barbara, 376, 377
Bonaparte, Napoleon, 298
Bonati, Lisa M., 240
Bond-Maupin, Lisa, 2
Bonta, James, 131
Booth, Alan, 109, 323
Bordt, Rebecca, 357
Bortner, M. A., 394
Bowers, William J., 258, 377
Bowling, Michael, 259
Boydstun, John E., 377
Boyle, John M., 62
Boyle, Mary, 213
Brady, James P., 62, 132
Braga, Anthony A., 378
Braiker, Harriet, 275, 276, 277
Braithwaite, John, 97, 98, 135, 198, 226, 371, 406, 424
Brame, Robert, 267
Brantingham, Patricia, 79
Brantingham, Paul, 79
Brashear, Donald, 209
Bratton, William, 378
Brezina, Timothy, 171
Briar, Scott, 19, 267, 341
Bridges, George S., 352, 353
Bridges, James H., 364
Brier, N., 111
Britt, Chester L., 275
Broidy, Lisa M., 152, 161
Bronner, Ethan, 61
Brooke, James, 204, 330
Brower, Sidney, 323
Brown, Elizabeth D., 397, 403, 404
Brown, Julia S., 9
Brown, Mark, 359, 360
Brown, Richard Maxwell, 329
Brownfield, David, 241
Bruguière, Jean-Louis, 288
Bryant, Jennings, 211
Buder, Leonard, 426

Buerger, Michael E., 239 , 430
Burgess, Ann Wolbert, 121, 317, 423
Burgess, Ernest W., 78
Burgess, Robert L., 215
Burnham, Bonnie, 298
Bursik, Robert J., Jr., 79
Burton, Velmer S., Jr., 126
Bush, George H. W., 354, 417, 432
Bush, George W., 134, 418–419, 432
Bushway, Shawn D., 267
Butterfield, Fox, 125, 196, 371
Bynum, Tim S., 292–293, 347, 353, 357

Cabey, Darrell, 324
Caetano, Raul, 53
Caeti, Tori J., 378
Cahn, Michael F., 139
Calavita, Kitty, 134, 136, 310
Cameron, Mary Owen, 19, 59, 150,
    216, 220, 223, 242, 243
Cameron, Samuel, 375
Campbell, Anne, 162
Canter, Rachelle, 86, 189
Cantor, David, 144, 238
Cao, Liqun, 158, 257
Caplan, Lincoln, 128
Capone, Al, 64
Capote, Truman, 319
Cappell, Charles L., 378
Carlesimo, P. J., 208
Carmody, Dianne Cyr, 163
Carneal, Michael, 92, 93
Carroll, Leo, 340
Carter, B. F., 109
Carter, Bill, 205
Carter, Daniel L., 121
Carter, Timothy J., 98, 356
Cashin, Jeffrey R., 251
Caspi, Avshalom, 54, 119
Cauce, Ana Mari, 241, 246
Cauvin, Henri E., 75
Cavender, Gray, 2, 68, 137, 233, 237
Cernkovich, Stephen A., 42, 98, 156,
    192, 193, 221
Chaiken, Jan M., 234, 253, 269, 270,
    383
Chaiken, Marcia R., 234, 253, 269,
    270, 383
Chambers, Cheryl A., 189
Chambliss, William J., 7, 13, 28, 174,
    297, 303, 371
Chamlin, Mitchell B., 431
Chan, Janet, 1
Chayet, Ellen, 277–278, 286, 372
Cheatwood, Derral, 81, 248, 380
Cheney, Dick, 419
Chermak, Steven M., 1, 35, 66, 237,
    259
Chesney-Lind, Meda, 86, 159–160,
    165, 356
Chevalier, Louis, 411
Child, Irvin L., 186
Chin, Ko-Lin, 303, 309
Chiricos, Theodore G., 2, 144, 314,
    353, 356
Christenson, R. L., 99
Christiansen, Karl O., 105
Clark, Catherine L., 53

Clark, John P., 42, 137
Clarke, Ronald V., 30, 60, 237, 425
Cleaver, Eldridge, 173
Clelland, Donald, 98, 356
Clifford, William, 9, 196
Clinard, Marshall B., 30, 33, 78, 133,
    144, 191–192, 195, 239, 249, 256,
    321, 372, 430
Clinton, Bill, 417–418, 432
Cloward, Richard A., 152–153, 154,
    168, 171, 267, 268
Clymer, Adam, 55
Cobb, Michael J., 161, 346
Cochran, John K., 194
Cocozza, Joseph J., 128
Coffey, Glenn S., 173, 175, 278
Cohen, Albert K., 154–155, 168, 171
Cohen, Dov, 158, 169
Cohen, Jacqueline, 264, 369, 374,
    377, 378, 380, 383
Cohen, Lawrence E., 91, 238
Cohen, Mark A., 53, 64, 388
Cohen, Murray L., 121
Coleman, James S., 193
Coleman, James William, 73, 168, 177
Coles, Catherine M., 336
Collins, James J., Jr., 252
Colton, Kent W., 139
Colvin, Mark, 432
Comstock, George, 207
Conklin, John E., 52, 91, 101, 146,
    199, 203, 243, 247, 255, 297, 299,
    312, 343, 371, 375
Conly, Catherine H., 139
Connell, R. W., 159
Conrad, John P., 271, 272, 275
"Conwell, Chic," 13, 297
Cook, Philip J., 52, 254, 257, 428
Copes, Heith, 34
Cordilia, Ann, 212, 283
Cordner, Gary W., 347
Corley, Charles J., 353
Corman, Hope, 375
Cornish, Derek B., 237
Count-van Manen, Gloria, 430
Cox, Louis A., Jr., 372
Crank, John P., 367
Crawford, Charles, 353
Cressey, Donald R., 3, 19, 177, 203,
    212, 303, 351
Cromwell, Paul F., 232
Cronin, James, 347
Cronin, Roberta C., 383
Cronin, Tania Z., 415
Cronin, Thomas E., 415
Crutchfield, Robert D., 352
Cullen, Francis T., 2, 16–17, 43, 68,
    115, 125, 137, 147, 188, 233, 257,
    391, 398, 401, 404, 405, 407, 410,
    414, 431, 432, 433
Cullen, Kevin, 302
Curran, Debra A., 357
Currie, Elliott, 433
Curry, James P., 345
Curtis, Ellen Foster, 137
Curtis, Lynn A., 14, 50, 52, 53, 96,
    247, 249
Cushman, Paul, Jr., 234

Dabbs, J. M., 109
D'Alessio, Stewart J., 384, 392
Daley, Suzanne, 55
Dalgaard, Odd Steffen, 105
Daly, Kathleen, 159–160, 178, 254,
    256, 357
Daly, Martin, 107–108, 131
Damphousse, Kelly R., 151
Danner, Mona J. E., 163
Darley, John M., 19, 326–327, 328
Datesman, Susan K., 272
Davis, John A., 178
Davis, Robert C., 333
Dawson, John M., 54, 250
DeAngelis, Tony, 136
Decker, Scott H., 26, 58, 232, 244,
    292–293, 373, 383
DeFleur, Lois B., 26, 154
DeFranco, Edward J., 141
DeKeseredy, Walter S., 218, 219
De Li, Spencer, 225
Deming, Romine R., 364
Demuth, Stephen, 354
Denno, Deborah W., 112, 113
Dershowitz, Alan M., 172
Desroches, Frederick J., 255
de Waard, Jaap, 76, 360
Diallo, Amadou, 344
Dietz, Mary Lorenz, 178
Dinitz, Simon, 78, 116, 225, 271,
    272, 275
Diniz, Angela, 204
Dishion, Thomas J., 198
Ditton, Paula M., 392
Dixon, Jo, 157, 158
Dobinson, Ian, 309
Dobrin, Adam, 241
Doherty, William F., 306
Dole, Bob, 418
Dombrink, John, 141
Donnelly, Patrick G., 323
Donnerstein, Edward, 206, 207, 210,
    211, 248
Donziger, Steven R., 67
Douglas, John E., 121, 423
Dowdy, Zachary R., 93
Doyle, Daniel P., 158
Drass, Kriss A., 147
Drew, Fred, 299
DuBow, Fredrick, 318
Duhart, Detis T., 77, 145, 146, 169
Dukakis, Michael, 417
Duke, Janice M., 91
Dunford, Franklyn W., 374
Durham, Alexis M., 380
Durkheim, Emile, 4, 8, 23–24, 313,
    314, 320

Earls, Felton, 321
Eck, John, 347, 375, 378, 410
Eckholm, Erik, 381
Edgerton, Robert B., 252
Egan, John W., 41, 92
Egan, Timothy, 93, 188
Ehrlich, Isaac, 19, 380
Eichenwald, Kurt, 134
Elias, Robert, 363
Elifson, Kirk W., 194

Elliott, Delbert S., 94, 98, 183–184, 193, 224, 272, 374
Ellis, Lee, 106, 109, 113, 194
Ellis, Rosalind D., 234
Ellison, Christopher G., 158, 315
Ellsworth, Phoebe C., 380
Elmhorn, Kerstin, 41
Elrod, H. Preston, 380
Empey, LaMar T., 192, 193, 198
Engel, Robin Shepard, 341
Ennett, Susan T., 95
Ennis, Philip H., 36
Erez, Edna, 365
Erickson, Maynard L., 274, 275, 389, 399
Erickson, Patricia G., 225
Ericson, Richard, 1
Ericsson, Kjersti, 86
Erlanger, Steven, 288, 289
Eron, Leonard, 206, 207, 211
Eronen, Markku, 125
Erven, James M., 34
Erwin, Michael, 60
Esbensen, Finn-Aage, 377
Eschholz, Sarah, 314
Evans, Sandra S., 388
Evans, T. David, 199, 194
Everingham, Susan S., 421

Fagan, Jeffrey, 144, 169, 198, 230, 253, 255, 349, 397
Fainaru, Steve, 93
Farhi, Paul, 205
Farr, Kathryn Ann, 420
Farrell, Ronald A., 221, 223, 389
Farrington, David P., 15, 42, 111, 124, 254, 264, 270, 271, 272, 273, 434
Faulkner, Robert R., 310
Feeney, Floyd, 52
Feld, Barry C., 5
Felson, Marcus, 238, 261
Felson, Richard B., 52, 159, 248
Fenwick, Melissa, 9
Ferracuti, Franco, 77, 78, 156–157
Ferraro, Kenneth F., 315
Ferrell, Jeff, 9, 21
Ferri, Enrico, 24–25
Fessenden, Ford, 122
Figlio, Robert M., 15–16, 93, 95, 114, 160, 192, 269–271, 272, 273, 274
Figueira-McDonough, Josefina, 87, 161, 192
Finckenauer, James O., 308, 312, 379
Finnegan, Terrence A., 272
Fishbein, Diane H., 104, 106, 109, 110, 111, 112, 113, 131
Fisher, Bonnie S., 16–17, 43, 241, 323, 414, 433
Fishman, Mark, 237
Fishman, Sima, 69
Fisse, Brent, 424
Flanagan, Timothy J., 314
Flewelling, Robert L., 95
Forde, David R., 119, 157, 240
Foreman, Judy, 245
Forst, Brian E., 364
Foster, Brenda, 189, 230
Foster, Holly, 54

Foster, Jack D., 225
Foster, Jodie, 127
Foucault, Michel, 359
Fowler, Floyd J., Jr., 427
Fowler, Glenn, 383
Fowles, Richard, 147
Fox, Greer Litton, 68
Fox, James Alan, 19, 88, 146, 255, 380
Franck, K. A., 323
Franco, Francisco, 144
Franklin, Alice, 87
Franklin, James L., 395
Frantz, Douglas, 289
Frazier, Charles E., 353, 356
Fream, Anne M., 220
Freedman, Lawrence Zelic, 326
Freeman, Richard B., 144, 146, 169, 230
French, Howard W., 197
Fritsch, Eric J., 378
Fyfe, James J., 343, 344, 367

Gabrielli, William F., Jr., 105, 106, 107, 109, 111
Gaes, Gerald G., 407
Gagnon, John H., 210
Galle, Omer R., 91
Gallup, George, 416
Gandy, John T., 364
Garfinkel, Harold, 222
Garner, Joel H., 19
Garofalo, James, 240, 332, 333, 334
Garofalo, Raffaele, 24–25
Garrett, Gerald R., 13, 21, 203, 267, 286
Gartin, Patrick A., 239, 372
Gartner, Rosemary, 203, 380
Gay, George R., 233
Gebhard, Paul H., 251
Geerken, Michael R., 34, 40, 383
Geis, Gilbert, 3, 65, 69, 173, 175, 176, 224, 328, 371, 399
Geller, William, 343
Gelles, Richard J., 190
Genovese, Kitty, 325, 326, 327, 328
Georges-Abeyie, Daniel E., 79
Gerbner, George, 2
Gertz, Marc, 257, 314
Gfroerer, Joseph, 253
Gibbons, Don C., 269
Gibbs, Jack P., 389
Gibbs, John J., 275
Gifford, Sidra Lea, 338
Gilbert, Karen E., 398, 404, 407
Gilliam, Franklin, 93
Gillis, A. R., 323
Ginsburg, B. E., 109
Giordano, Peggy C., 42, 161, 192, 193
Glaberson, William, 58, 172, 188, 345
Glaser, Daniel, 214, 267, 284
Glick, Barry D., 35
Glueck, Eleanor, 104, 185
Glueck, Sheldon, 104, 185
Goering, Hermann, 298
Goetz, Bernhard, 324
Goldberg, Jeffrey, 345
Golden, Andrew, 92, 93
Golden, Daniel, 208
Goldstein, Jeffrey H., 209, 210

Goldstein, Michael J., 210, 211
Goldstein, Paul J., 253
Goleman, Daniel, 16, 208, 210
Golub, Andrew, 253
Gonnerman, Jennifer, 362
Gonzalez, David, 331
"Goodman, Sam," 13
Goodroe, C., 423
Goodstadt, Michael S., 225
Gordon, Alan R., 415
Gordon, D. A., 116
Gordon, David M., 7
Gordon, Margaret T., 317
Gordon, Robert A., 233, 267
Gore, Al, 418–419
Goring, Charles, 104
Gottfredson, Michael, 2, 3, 65–66, 107, 118–119, 187, 264, 287, 291, 303, 309, 405
Gottfredson, Stephen D., 323
Gove, Walter C., 34, 40
Grabosky, P. N., 138
Graham, Mary G., 253
Grant, Jane A., 334
Grasmick, Harold J., 79, 119, 370, 389
Grattet, Ryken, 73
Grayson, Betty, 245
Green, Donald E., 370, 371
Green, Gary S., 256
Green, Penny A., 320
Greenberg, David F., 181, 198, 340, 370, 375, 376, 404
Greenberg, Stephanie W., 234, 251, 252
Greenberger, David B., 231
Greene, Jack R., 347
Greenfeld, Lawrence A., 51, 95, 250, 252
Greenhouse, Steven, 368
Greenspan, Rosann, 341, 342
Greenwood, Peter W., 147, 252, 263, 274, 276, 277, 280, 382–383, 384, 395, 424, 431
Greer, William R., 58
Griffin, Christine, 176, 224
Grinnell, Richard M., 189
Griswold, David B., 191, 193
Grogger, Jeff, 19, 253
Gross, Larry, 2
Groth, A. Nicholas, 403
Groves, W. Byron, 321
Guerry, A. M., 23, 44
Guggenheim, Martin, 349

Haar, Robin N., 404
Hackney, Sheldon, 157
Hadaway, C. Kirk, 194
Hafner, Katie, 230
Hagan, John, 54, 145, 164–165, 323, 357
Hagedorn, John M., 145
Hakim, Simon, 377
Hakola, Panu, 125
Hamilton, V. Lee, 75, 388, 390, 406
Hamlin, John E., 180
Hamparian, Donna Martin, 272, 274
Hanson, Bill, 233
Harcourt, Bernard E., 315, 336

Hardy, Kenneth A., 352
Hare, Robert D., 123
Harer, Miles D., 91
Harlow, Caroline Wolf, 50, 51, 53
Harpur, Timothy J., 123
Harrell, Adele V., 323, 324
Harries, Keith D., 79
Harring, Sidney L., 340
Harris, Eric, 92, 93, 163
Harris, Patricia M., 30, 60
Harris, Thomas, 423
Harrison, Lana, 253
Harrison, Paige M., 357
Hart, S. D., 123
Hartjen, Clayton A., 195, 269
Hartnett, Susan M., 377, 378
Hathaway, Starke R., 122
Hawkins, Darnell, 93, 352
Hawkins, Gordon, 254, 303
Hay, Carter, 188
Healy, Patrick, 385
Heath, Linda, 314
Hedges, Chris, 288, 289
Heimer, Karen, 217
Heinzelmann, Fred, 62
Hembroff, Larry A., 388
Hennessy, Michael, 189
Hensley, John E., 207
Hepburn, John R., 224, 247
Hernon, Jolene C., 364
Herrnstein, Richard J., 115, 122–123,
    131, 148, 188, 227
Herz, Elicia J., 334
Heumann, Milton, 258
Hickey, Eric W., 10, 245
Hill, Robert H., 157
Hinckley, John W., Jr., 127–128, 130,
    131
Hindelang, Michael J., 32, 52, 59, 97,
    98, 114, 179–180, 191, 192, 193, 343
Hirsch, J. H., 377
Hirschel, J. David, 374
Hirschi, Travis, 2, 3, 65–66, 98, 107,
    114, 118–119, 160, 178–180,
    181–183, 186, 187, 190, 191, 192,
    193, 198, 264, 287, 291, 303, 309
Hitler, Adolf, 298
Hobbs, Dick, 173, 175, 278
Hochstetler, Andy, 228
Hodgins, S., 125
Hoffer, Thomas, 193
Hoffman-Bustamante, Dale, 265
Hoge, Dean R., 223
Hohler, Bob, 328
Hollander, Paul, 326
Hollinger, Richard C., 137
Holmstrom, Lynda Lytle, 317
Holzman, Harold R., 111
Honig, Alice S., 430
Hooton, Earnest, 104
Hoover, J. Edgar, 34
Horney, Julie, 266
Horning, Donald N. M., 173
Horowitz, Ruth, 19, 187, 192, 231,
    233, 291
Horton, Willie, 417
Horvath, John A., 272, 274
Houston, Ellen, 146, 169

Howell, James C., 273
Howley, Susan Smith, 365
Hoyt, Dan R., 241, 246
Hughes, Michael, 34, 40
Huizinga, David, 98, 183–184, 193,
    241, 253, 374
Hulley, Stephen B., 53
Humphrey, Hubert H., 416
Humphrey, John A., 164
Hunt, Thomas K., 53
Hutchings, Barry, 106, 107
Hutchison, Ira W., 374

Ianni, Francis A. J., 19, 303, 304–305
Ignatieff, Michael, 359
Inciardi, James A., 187, 192, 223,
    233, 234, 268, 280, 291
Ireland, Timothy, 190
Irvin, Michael, 209
Irwin, John, 280, 283, 284, 400, 407
Israel, A. C., 111

Jacklin, Carol Nagy, 108
Jackson, Bruce, 232, 243
Jackson, Jesse, 95
Jackson, Pamela Irving, 340
Jacobs, Bruce A., 52
Jacobs, David, 340
Jacobs, James B., 56
Jacobs, Jane, 317, 321
James, Jennifer, 161
Jang, Sung Joon, 223
Jankowski, Martín Sánchez, 293–294,
    295, 312
Jeffery, C. Ray, 113
Jenkins, Patricia H., 192
Jenkins, Philip, 9, 10, 58, 160, 423
Jenness, Valerie, 73
Jensen, Gary F., 165, 223, 241
Jensen, Michael C., 218
Jensen, Vickie J., 158
Jesilow, Paul, 173, 176
Jhally, Sut, 163
Joe, Delbert, 194
John Paul II, Pope, 395
Johnson, Bruce D., 253
Johnson, Byron R., 194, 201
Johnson, David R., 356
Johnson, Elmer H., 11
Johnson, Jeffrey G., 207
Johnson, Lyndon B., 414
Johnson, Mitchell, 92, 93
Johnson, Richard E., 98
Johnson, Robert J., 223
Johnston, David, 289
Johnston, David Cay, 61
Jordan, B. K., 125
Jorgenson, James D., 364
Joyce, Fay S., 397
Judson, Horace Freeland, 235
Junger, Marianne, 195
Junger-Tas, Josine, 42
Jurkovic, G. J., 116

Kadleck, Colleen, 328
Kalb, Larry, 241
Kalven, Harry, Jr., 350
Kant, Harold S., 210, 211

Kaplan, Howard B., 148, 223
Kappeler, Victor E., 10
Karales, Kevin J., 343
Karberg, Jennifer C., 357
Karmen, Andrew, 70, 375
Karp, David R., 406
Kassebaum, Gene, 19, 361
Katz, Jack, 109, 228–229, 237, 280
Katz, Jackson, 163
Keating, Charles H., Jr., 134
Kellermann, Arthur L., 257
Kelley, Barbara Tatem, 190
Kelley, Clarence M., 421
Kelley, Thomas M., 274
Kelling, George L., 314, 336, 376,
    377, 378
Kelly, Michael, 299
Kempf, Kimberly L., 275
Kempf-Leonard, Kimberly, 273
Kennedy, John F., 207
Kennedy, Leslie W., 119, 157, 240,
    261
Kenney, Dennis Jay, 308, 312, 331
Kern, Roger, 181, 189
Kessler, Ronald C., 123, 340, 375,
    376
Kifner, John, 308
Kilgore, Sally, 193
Kilpatrick, Dean G., 365
Kimble, Charles E., 323
King, Alex, 6
King, Derek, 6
King, Harry, 13, 174, 297
King, Joan, 119, 147, 211, 427
King, Rodney, 343–344
Kinkade, Patrick, T., 380
Kinkel, Kipland, 92, 93
Kirkpatrick, John T., 164
Kirkpatrick, Sidney D., 299, 312
Klaus, Patsy, 60, 91
Klebold, Dylan, 92, 93, 163
Kleck, Gary, 255, 256, 257, 260, 262,
    352, 353, 355, 356
Klein, Stephen P., 353
Kleinknecht, William, 312
Klemke, Lloyd W., 222, 230
Klinger, David A., 341
Klockars, Carl B., 13, 19, 174, 175,
    177, 223, 268
Kobner, Otto, 263
Koch, Edward, 328
Kohlmeier, Louis M., 219
Kolata, Gina, 355
Kolbert, Elizabeth, 206
Koons, Barbara A., 357
Koper, Christopher S., 373
Kovandzic, Tomislav V., 147
Kramer, John H., 354, 357, 392
Kramer, Ronald C., 135
Kray, Reggie, 105
Kray, Ronnie, 105
Kringlen, Einar, 105
Krohn, Marvin D., 98, 240, 345
Krost, Jack, 117
Kruttschnitt, Candace, 265, 283, 357
Ku, Simon, 323
Kutchinsky, Berl, 210
Kvålseth, Tarald O., 388

Lab, Steven P., 272, 399, 404, 405
Labaton, Stephen, 177
LaFree, Gary D., 10, 147, 199, 248, 351, 355
LaGrange, Randy L., 198
LaGrange, Teresa C., 126
Lakshmanan, Indira A. R., 308
Lally, J. Ronald, 430
Land, Kenneth C., 91, 144
Langan, Patrick A., 54, 250, 254, 352, 402
Lanza-Kaduce, Lonn, 252
Larzelere, Robert E., 187
Latané, Bibb, 19, 326–327
Laub, John H., 185–186, 190, 201, 241, 264, 267, 274, 280, 283, 286
Laudon, Kenneth C., 35
Lauritsen, Janet L., 240, 241, 352
Lavin, Marvin, 147, 252, 263, 274, 276, 277, 280
Lavrakas, Paul J., 314, 325, 334
Lay, Kenneth, 134
Laycock, Gloria, 246
Layson, Stephen K., 19, 380
LeBlanc, Marc, 264
Lee, Matthew R., 253
Lefkowitz, Monroe M., 206
Lejeune, Robert, 232, 371
Lemert, Edwin M., 220, 221
Lenihan, Kenneth J., 19, 147
Leonard, Eileen B., 160
Leonard, William N., 135
Lesieur, Henry R., 71
Letkemann, Peter, 58, 217
Levin, David J., 402
Levin, Jack, 55
Levine, Dennis B., 231
Levine, James P., 350
Levine, Murray, 165
Levitt, Steven D., 375
Lewin, Tamar, 93
Lewis, Dan A., 314, 334
Lewis, Dorothy Otnow, 110, 111, 120, 125, 131
Lewis, Neil A., 355
Lichter, Linda S., 2
Lichter, S. Robert, 2
Liddick, Don, 306
Liebman, James S., 397
Lilienfeld, S. O., 111
Lind, Bronwyn, 323
Lindsay, Paul, 422
Link, Bruce G., 124, 125, 257
Linz, Daniel, 210, 211, 248
Lipsey, Mark W., 405
Liptak, Adam, 110
Lipton, Douglas, 403–404
Liptzen, Dr., 172
Liska, Allen E., 197, 198, 322, 376
Little, Craig B., 329, 331
Liu, Xiaoru, 148
Lizotte, Alan J., 158, 256, 354, 356
Loeber, Rolf, 111, 192, 241, 264, 270, 271, 281
Loftin, Colin, 90, 157, 257, 258, 340, 375
Logan, Charles H., 376, 407

Logie, Robert, 373
Lombroso, Cesare, 24–25, 44, 102, 103–104, 129
Loncar, Mladen, 302
Long, J. Scott, 240
Longmire, Dennis R., 314
Longo, Robert E., 403
Lott, John, 256
Louima, Abner, 344, 345
Lowman, John, 7
Lubeck, Steven G., 192, 193, 198
Luckenbill, David F., 158, 159, 212, 231, 248, 263, 290
Ludwig, Jens, 256, 257
Lundquist, John H., 91
Lupsha, Peter A., 150
Lurigio, Arthur J., 325, 333, 334
Lynam, Donald R., 114–115, 116
Lynch, James, 101, 361

Maakestad, William J., 68, 137, 233, 391
MacAndrew, Craig, 252
Macaulay, Jacqueline, 207
McAuliffe, William E., 233, 267
McCaghy, Charles H., 251
McCain, Nina, 427
McCall, Patricia L., 158
Macallair, Dan, 90
McCarthy, Bill, 229
McCarthy, John D., 223
McClam, Erin, 95
McCleary, Richard, 34
McClelland, G. M., 125
Maccoby, Eleanor E., 108
McCord, Joan, 15, 187, 191
McCord, William, 15
McCorkle, Richard C., 407
McDermott, Michael, 146
McDevitt, Jack, 55
MacDonald, John M., 356, 378
McDowall, David, 90, 256, 257, 258, 375
McEwen, J. Thomas, 139
McFadin, J. Bradley, 403
McFarland, Sam G., 380
McGahey, Richard M., 147
McGarrell, Edmund, 259
McGlothin, William H., 234
McGovern, George, 416
McGuire, William J., 378
McIntosh, Mary, 295–296, 301–302
McKay, H. B., 402
McKay, Henry D., 78–79, 99
MacKenzie, Doris Layton, 379
McKinley, James C., Jr., 210
McLarin, Kimberly J., 61
MacLean, Brian, 7
McLeod, Maureen, 332, 333, 334
McMillan, Jon, 63, 132
McNamara, Joseph D., 376
McNeil, Donald G., Jr., 55
McQueen, Anjetta, 61
McSorley, Marty, 208, 209
Magnusson, David, 119
Maguin, Eugene, 192
Maguire, Edward R., 375, 378, 410

Maguire, Kathleen, 37, 41, 45, 82, 83, 101, 250, 252, 316, 360, 384, 413, 427
Maguire, Mike, 362
Maier, Pamela A., 239
Malamuth, Neil, 16
Males, Mike A., 90
Maloy, Charles E., 250, 251
Malvo, Lee Boyd, 422, 423
Mangione, Peter L., 430
Mangione, Thomas W., 427
Mann, Coramae Richey, 164
Mannuzza, S., 111
Margolick, David, 394
Markoff, John, 230
Markowitz, Fred E., 159
Marolla, Joseph, 175
Mars, Gerald, 177
Marshall, Ineke Haen, 42, 80, 81, 101, 195, 266
Marshall, Thurgood, 358
Martin, Douglas, 328
Martin, John Bartlow, 242
Martin, Michael J., 53
Martin, Steven S., 223
Martin, Susan E., 56, 421
Martinson, Robert, 403–404
Maruschak, Laura M., 358, 382
Marvell, Thomas B., 375, 378
Marx, Gary T., 331
Massey, James L., 240
Masters, Brooke A., 54
Mastrofski, Stephen D., 342
Matsueda, Ross, 193, 217, 223, 267
Matthews, Roger, 7
Matza, David, 170–172, 177, 178, 180, 181, 243
Mauer, Marc, 359, 367
Maurer, David W., 175, 217, 243, 297
Maxfield, Michael G., 190
Maynard, Douglas W., 351
Mazerolle, Lorraine Green, 328
Mazerolle, Paul, 152, 201
Meadow, Arnold, 191
Medinnus, Gene R., 186
Mednick, Sarnoff A., 105, 106, 107, 108, 109, 111, 113, 124
Meeker, James W., 374
Megargee, Edwin I., 119, 122, 191
Meier, Robert F., 69, 98, 240, 261
Meilman, Philip W., 251
Meisenheider, Thomas, 282, 283
Mellican, Eugene, 137
Menard, Scott, 116, 246, 253
Merton, Robert K., 148–151, 152, 153, 154, 160, 168
Merva, Mary, 147
Messerschmidt, James W., 160, 162–163
Messner, Steven F., 52, 147, 157, 158, 196, 238
Miethe, Terance D., 240, 261, 426
Mihalic, Sharon, 253
Milakovich, Michael E., 415
Milgram, Stanley, 320, 326
Milken, Michael, 133, 177
Miller, J. L., 390

Miller, Jody, 162
Miller, Joshua, 116
Miller, Judith, 289
Miller, Stuart J., 271, 272, 275
Miller, Ted R., 53, 64
Miller, Walter B., 154, 155, 168, 171, 173
Milligan, Susan, 259
Mills, Michael, 68
Minor, W. William, 172, 177, 180
Mintz, John, 419
Miranne, Alfred C., 383
Mitchell, Kirsten B., 146
Mitford, Jessica, 398, 400
Mocan, H. Naci, 375
Moffitt, Terrie E., 54, 104, 107, 111, 114–115
Moitra, Soumyo, 271
Monachesi, Elio D., 122
Monahan, John, 125
Moody, Carlisle E., 375, 378
Moon, Melissa M., 5, 379
Moore, Charles A., 371
Moore, Elizabeth, 68
Moran, Richard, 128
Morash, Merry, 165, 357, 379, 404
Moriarity, Thomas, 327
Morris, Norval, 254, 386, 415
Morris, R., 109
Morris, Robert, 230
Morsch, James, 55
Morse, Barbara J., 116
Moshavi, Sharon, 197
Mosher, Donald L., 121
Moulds, Elizabeth, 390
Muhammad, John Allen, 422, 423
Muncer, Steven, 162
Muro, Mark, 306
Murray, Charles A., 115, 372
Mustaine, Elizabeth Ehrhardt, 241
Mustard, David B., 256
Mydans, Seth, 301, 344, 363
Myers, Steven Lee, 309

Nagel, Ilene H., 357
Nagin, Daniel S., 119, 229, 256, 272, 283, 369, 373, 374, 378, 380
Nasar, Jack L., 323
Nasar, Sylvia, 146
Neapolitan, Jerome L., 92
Nelson, James F., 223
Nelson-Kilger, Shirley, 345
Neubauer, David W., 349, 350
Newburn, Tim, 160
Newman, Graeme, 388
Newman, Oscar, 322–323
Newton, Phyllis J., 374
Nienstedt, Barbara C., 34
Nieuwbeerta, Paul, 246
Nisbett, Richard E., 158, 169
Nixon, Richard M., 34, 173, 176, 415, 416, 432
Nold, Frederick Carl, 372
Normandeau, André, 14
Nye, F. Ivan, 40

O'Brien, Robert M., 96, 340
O'Brien, Timothy L., 62

Ohlin, Lloyd E., 15, 152–153, 154, 168, 171, 267, 268
Oliver, Mary Beth, 314
Olson, James N., 232
Orcutt, James D., 215
Osbun, Lee Ann, 394
Osgood, D. Wayne, 109, 112, 239, 266
Ousey, Graham C., 253
Outlaw, Maureen C., 364

Padilla, Felix M., 19, 175, 217, 266, 294–295, 312
Paik, Haejung, 207
Palmer, Ted, 404, 405
Parker, Donn B., 230
Parks, Bernard, 345
Paschall, Mallie J., 95
Pastore, Ann L., 37, 41, 45, 82, 83, 101, 250, 252, 316, 360, 384, 413, 427
Paternoster, Raymond, 119, 152, 187, 195, 229, 272, 371
Patterson, Gerald R., 198
Pearce, Frank, 168
Pease, Ken, 246, 377
Peel, Sir Robert, 338
Pennell, Susan, 331
Penrod, Steven, 210, 211, 248
Pepinsky, Harold, 7
Perkins, Craig, 91
Perry, James E., 213
Pertman, Adam, 90
Peters, Michael, 379
Petersen, David M., 194
Petersilia, Joan, 101, 147, 252, 263, 269, 274, 275, 276, 277, 280, 283, 353, 410
Peterson, Mark A., 275, 276, 277
Peterson, Ruth D., 380
Petrosino, Anthony, 379
Pfuhl, Erdwin H., Jr., 375
Phillips, David P., 207, 380
Phillips, Llad, 19, 147
Phillips, Phillip D., 79
Pierce, Glenn, 258
Piliavin, Irving, 19, 267, 341
Pincus, Steven, 110
Piquero, Alex, 119, 201, 232
Pires, Osvaldo Otavio, 330
Platt, Anthony M., 4, 21
Ploeger, Matthew, 147
Podolefsky, Aaron, 318
Poe-Yamagata, Eileen, 6, 255
Pogarsky, Greg, 373
Polk, Kenneth, 164, 192, 224
Pollard, Paul, 121
Pollock, Vicki, 105, 106, 109, 111
Pontell, Henry N., 134, 136, 168, 173, 176, 310
Poole, Eric D., 191, 193
Porterfield, Austin L., 40
Posse, Hans, 298
Potter, Gary W., 10
Potter, Kimberly, 56
Pottieger, Anne E., 187, 192, 233, 291
Povey, David, 76
Powers, Edwin, 15

Prentky, Robert Alan, 121
Presley, Cheryl A., 251
Pritchford, Susan, 352
Priyadarsini, S., 195
Proband, Stan C., 424
Prugh, Jeff, 318
Pruitt, Charles R., 343, 391
Pugh, Meredith D., 42, 193
Putnam, Constance E., 397
Puzzanchera, Charles M., 5

Quetelet, A., 23, 44, 147
Quinney, Richard, 7, 9

Raab, Selwyn, 141, 303
Radelet, Michael L., 380, 397
Radzinowicz, Sir Leon, 119, 147, 211, 427
Ragona, Anthony J., 390
Raine, Adrian, 124, 131
Ramsey, Evan, 92
Rand, Michael R., 50, 52, 53
Rankin, Joseph H., 181, 187, 189
Rantala, Ramona R., 36
Rapaport, Elizabeth, 358
Rapoza, Kenneth, 330
Ratcliffe, James M., 324
Raudenbush, Stephen W., 315, 321
Rausch, Sharla, 399
Rawls, Wendell, Jr., 318
Reagan, Ronald, 127, 354, 416–417, 432
Rebellon, Cesar J., 189
Reckless, Walter C., 222, 223, 225
Reed, Gary E., 309
Reed, Mark D., 197, 198
Regoli, Robert M., 191, 193
Rehnquist, William H., 419
Reichman, Nancy, 310
Reiman, Jeffrey H., 8, 28, 367
Reiss, Albert J., Jr., 19, 32, 114, 342, 343
Rengert, George F., 232, 377
Rennison, Callie Marie, 38, 51, 53, 60, 84, 88, 91, 96, 99, 101
Reppetto, Thomas A., 58, 232, 242, 244, 245, 377
Ressler, Robert K., 121, 423
Rettig, Richard P., 13, 21, 203, 267, 286
Reuter, Peter, 2, 71, 140, 141, 142, 306
Rezendes, Michael, 95
Rhodes, Albert Lewis, 114
Rhodes, William C., 317
Rich, Thomas F., 139
Richards, Pamela, 189, 230
Riding, Alan, 330
Riger, Stephanie, 317
Ritti, R. Richard, 383
Roberts, Julian V., 389
Roberts, Mary K., 191, 193
Roberts, Meredith, 9
Roberts, Sam, 141
Robin Hood, 174
Robins, L. N., 123
Robinson, Norman, 194
Robison, James, 404
Rode, Peter A., 394
Rodenrys, Kathleen, 69

Rodman, Hyman, 156
Roehl, Jan, 328
Rogan, Dennis P., 258, 377
Rogers, Joseph W., 172, 173, 175, 176, 181, 186, 192, 203, 223
Roiphe, Katie, 165
Rojek, Dean G., 274, 275, 399
Roncek, Dennis W., 239
Rose, Pete, 209
Rosenbaum, Dennis P., 314, 325, 332, 333, 334
Rosenfeld, Richard, 26, 378
Rosenquist, Carl M., 191
Rosenthal, Elizabeth, 62
Rosett, Arthur, 19, 351
Rosoff, Stephen M., 168
Ross, H. Laurence, 174
Ross, Lee, 380
Ross, R. R., 402
Rossi, Peter H., 19, 147, 254, 256, 257, 260, 390, 394
Roth, Jeffrey A., 109, 391
Rothman, David J., 359
Rothman, Stanley, 2
Rothstein, Edward, 289
Rotkin, Laurence, 390
Rowe, Alan R., 376
Rowe, David C., 104, 105, 109, 112, 113, 124, 131
Ruback, R. Barry, 364
Rubin, Robert T., 108
Rucker, Lila, 379, 404
Rushton, J. Philippe, 92
Russell, Diane E. H., 50, 205
Russell, Gordon W., 208, 209
Russell, Stephen T., 144
Rutenberg, Jim, 207
Rutter, Michael, 193
Ryan, George, 397
Ryan, Kimberly D., 241, 246
Rydell, C. Peter, 421
Rytina, Steve, 390

Saad, Lydia, 317
Sacco, Vincent F., 261
Sack, Kevin, 55
Salem, Greta, 314, 334
Salert, Barbara, 383
Samenow, Stanton E., 116–117, 230
Sampson, Robert J., 147, 185–186, 190, 201, 240, 241, 264, 267, 274, 280, 283, 286, 315, 321, 352, 377
Samuel, William, 390
Sanday, Peggy Reeves, 301
Sanders, Joseph, 75, 388, 406
Sanders, William B., 155, 291, 312
Sandilands, Mark L., 209
Sasson, Theodore, 433
Scales, Ann, 344
Scarpitti, Frank R., 141
Schafer, John, 53
Schafer, Stephen, 151, 175, 363
Schemo, Diana Jean, 43
Scheuble, Laurie K., 356
Schink, George, 69
Schiraldi, Vincent, 5
Schneider, Anne L., 324
Schneider, Peter, 324

Schur, Edwin M., 69, 221, 235, 274
Schwartz, Gary, 231
Schwartz, Martin D., 218, 219, 250, 251
Schwartz, Richard D., 225
Schwendinger, Herman, 3, 8, 204
Schwendinger, Julia R., 3, 8, 204
Scimecca, Joseph A., 223
Scott, Joseph E., 388
Scully, Diana, 175
Sechrest, Lee, 397, 403, 404
Seghorn, Theoharis K., 121
Sellin, Thorsten, 15–16, 26, 80, 93, 95, 114, 160, 192, 269–271, 272, 274, 387–388
Selo, Elaine, 87
Serrill, Michael S., 230
Shah, Saleem A., 109
Shannon, Lyle W., 15, 271
Shapiro, Susan P., 391
Shaver, Katherine, 213
Shaw, Clifford R., 78–79, 99
Shaw, James W., 258
Sheehan, Richard G., 378
Sheffield, Christopher P., 329, 331
Shelden, Randall G., 272, 274
Sheldon, William, 104, 129
Sheley, Joseph F., 255, 256
Shelley, Louise I., 30, 78, 144
Shelly, Peggy L., 275
Shelton, Kelly, 283
Shenon, Philip, 142
Shepard, Matthew, 56
Shepard, Robin L., 341
Sherman, Lawrence W., 25, 239, 258, 374, 375, 377, 419, 421, 434
Sherrill, Jan Mitchell, 250, 251
Shipman, Harold, 268
Short, James F., Jr., 40, 78
Shotland, R. Lance, 326
Shover, Neal, 68, 173, 175, 228, 253, 269, 278–280, 282, 283, 286, 371
Sickmund, Melissa, 6, 255
Sidak, Joseph Gregory, 372
Silberman, Charles E., 90, 391, 430
Silva, Phil A., 114–115
Silverman, Robert A., 126, 247
Simon, Rita J., 127, 131
Simons, Marlise, 302
Simons, Ronald L., 265
Simpson, Jon E., 390
Simpson, O. J., 2
Simpson, Sally S., 371, 373
Sims, Calvin, 143
Singer, Simon I., 165
Sirkin, Mark, 121
Skakel, Michael, 5
Skinner, William K., 220
Skogan, Wesley G., 32, 34, 39, 314–315, 319, 334, 336, 377, 378
Skolnick, Jerome H., 19, 225, 340, 344, 367
Skorneck, Carolyn, 33, 50
Slaby, Ronald G., 206, 207, 211
Sliwa, Curtis, 331
Sloan, John Henry, 254
Sloan, John J., 43
Smigel, Erwin O., 174

Smith, Brent L., 151
Smith, Carolyn, 190
Smith, Craig S., 381
Smith, David E., 233
Smith, Douglas A., 98, 267, 350, 351, 372
Smith, Dwight C., Jr., 305
Smith, Gerald, 404
Smith, M. Dwayne, 73
Smith, Russell G., 138
Smith, Steven, 95
Smith, Tom W., 257
Snell, Tracy L., 358, 382
Snider, Laureen, 168–169
Snipes, Jeffrey B., 45
Snyder, Howard N., 6, 255, 272
Sobol, James J., 341
Soler, Mark, 5
Sommers, Ira B., 147, 230, 280
Sorenson, Jon, 380
Sparks, Richard F., 246
Sparrow, Malcolm K., 62
Spears, Jeffrey W., 353
Speck, Richard, 207
Speckart, George, 234
Spelman, William, 378, 410
Spitzer, Steven, 340
Spohn, Cassia, 353
Sporkin, Stanley, 219
Sprewell, Latrell, 208
Stack, Steven, 239, 380
Stack, Susan A., 107
Stafford, Mark C., 91, 216, 240
Stalin, Josef, 74, 144
Stanko, Elizabeth Anne, 160
Stark, Rodney, 79
Stattin, Håkan, 119
Steadman, Henry J., 125, 128, 129, 248
Steen, Sara, 353
Steffensmeier, Darrell J., 13, 91, 153, 161, 265, 346, 354, 357
Steinhart, David, 5
Stenross, Barbara, 347
Stephens, Richard C., 234
Sterngold, James, 134, 143
Stiles, Beverly L., 148
Stoddart, Kenneth, 26
Stolzenberg, Lisa, 384, 392
Stookey, John Alan, 363
Straus, Murray A., 53, 190
Straw, Margret K., 326
Street, Raul, 204
Streifel, Cathy, 357
Strong, Karen Heetderks, 406
Stuart, Reginald, 318
Stueve, Ann, 124
Surette, Ray, 1
Sutherland, Edwin H., 3, 8, 13, 64, 65, 66, 152, 212, 214, 215, 217, 224, 232, 268, 280, 282, 297, 407
Suttles, Gerald D., 322
Swarns, Rachel L., 75
Swetnam, David, 299
Swigert, Victoria Lynn, 221, 389
Sykes, Charles J., 172
Sykes, Gresham M., 170–172, 177, 178, 180, 378

Szasz, Andrew, 141
Szymkowiak, Kenneth, 169

Tarde, Gabriel, 427
Tardiff, Kenneth, 238
Taylor, Bruce, 252
Taylor, H. Gerry, 111
Taylor, Ian, 7, 8, 23, 24, 149, 214
Taylor, Ralph B., 314, 315, 323, 324
Taylor, Robert W., 378
Tennenbaum, Abraham N., 342
Tennenbaum, D., 116
Teplin, L. A., 125
Terrill, William, 342
Tewksbury, Richard, 241
Thatcher, Robert W., 109, 110, 111
Thoennes, Nancy, 53, 54, 87
Thompson, Carol Y., 279
Thompson, Kevin, 165
Thomson, Douglas R., 390
Thornberry, Terence P., 15, 99, 190, 193, 197, 223, 272, 273
Thornton, William, 161
Thorsell, Bernard A., 222
Thrasher, Frederic M., 155, 292
Tibbetts, Stephen, 119
Tien, James M., 139
Tifft, Larry L., 42
Tiihonen, Jari, 125
Tillman, Robert H., 134, 136, 168, 271, 310
Timnick, Lois, 318
Timrots, Anita D., 50, 52, 53
Tittle, Charles R., 98, 99, 195, 198, 376
Titus, Richard M., 62
Tjaden, Patricia, 53, 54, 87
Tobias, J. J., 11–12
Toby, Jackson, 186
Tonry, Michael, 80, 92, 101, 169, 286, 354, 394, 410, 417, 434
Tontodonato, Pamela, 365
Torrance, Mark, 176, 224
Torres, Manual J., 13, 21, 203, 267, 286
Torrey, E. Fuller, 125
Toussaint, Alvin, 95
Tracy, Paul E., 16, 93, 94, 269, 271, 273
Tracy, Sharon, 272, 274
Traub, Stuart H., 67
Treaster, Joseph B., 62, 309
Trojanowicz, R., 377
Tunnell, Kenneth D., 231, 252, 371
Turk, Austin, 8, 79
Turner, Michael G., 16–17
Turner, Susan, 353
Turpin, Richard, 12
Turpin-Petrosino, Carolyn, 379
Tyson, Mike, 209

Uggen, Christopher, 146, 265, 283
Uhlman, Thomas M., 351
Ulmer, Jeffrey T., 354, 392
Unnever, James D., 354

van den Haag, Ernest, 385, 396
vander Ven, Thomas, 432
van Dijk, Frans, 76, 360

van Kammen, Welmoet B., 111
van Natta, Don, Jr., 289
van Ness, Daniel, 406
van Voorhis, Patricia, 189
van Winkle, Barrick, 292
Vélez, Maria B., 334
Venables, Peter H., 124
Vieraitis, Lynne M., 147
Villemez, Wayne J., 98
Visher, Christy A., 19, 383
Volavka, Jan, 111, 113
Vold, George B., 45
Volpe, Justin, 344
von Hirsch, Andrew, 211, 383, 386, 388, 390, 410
Voss, Harwin L., 193, 247
Votey, Harold L., Jr., 19, 147

Waegel, William B., 343
Waldman, I. D., 111
Waldo, Gordon P., 116, 356
Walker, N. Darlene, 351
Walklate, Sandra, 169
Wallace, George C., 416
Wallerstein, James S., 40
Wallman, Joel, 410
Walsh, Anthony, 109, 364
Walters, Glenn D., 107, 112
Walton, Paul, 7, 8, 23, 24, 149, 214
Ward, David A., 19, 361
Waring, Elin, 277–278, 286, 372
Warner, Barbara D., 322
Warr, Mark, 201, 216, 283, 315
Warshaw, Robin, 16
Waschbusch, Daniel A., 270
Weatherburn, Don, 323
Webb, Jim, 79
Weber, Marvin Glenn, 135
Weber, Max, 290
Websdale, Neil, 9, 21
Wechsler, Henry, 251
Weimann, Gabriel, 57
Weir, Andrianne, 52
Weisburd, David, 66–67, 87, 277–278, 286, 310, 341, 342, 372, 377
Weisel, Deborah, 292–293
Weiss, Alexander, 259
Welch, Michael, 9
Wellford, Charles, 347
Wells, L. Edward, 187, 189, 223
Wells, William, 257
Welsh, Brandon C., 434
West, D. J., 15, 114, 187, 188
West, Valerie, 397
Wexler, Sandra, 198
Whitaker, Catherine J., 96
White, Helen Raskin, 152, 198
White, Jonathan, R., 73
White, Susan O., 397, 403, 404
Whitehead, John T., 399, 404, 405
Whitman, Charles, 207
Wiatrowski, Michael D., 191, 193
Wicks-Nelson, R., 111
Widom, Cathy Spatz, 190
Wiegand, R. Bruce, 34
Wiehofen, Henry, 398
Wiersema, Brian, 64, 90, 256

Wiley, Norbert, 266
Wilkerson, Isabel, 333
Wilkinson, Deanna L., 255
Wilks, Judith, 403–404
Williams, Franklin P., 356
Williams, Nicolas, 147
Williams, Terry, 19, 21
Williams, Wayne B., 318
Williamson, Wendell, 172
Willott, Sara, 176, 224
Wilner, Daniel M., 19, 361
Wilson, Bruce D., 234
Wilson, Doris James, 392
Wilson, James Q., 15, 34, 101, 122–123, 129, 131, 148, 188, 227, 314, 343, 373, 376, 377, 382, 386, 391, 410, 427
Wilson, Margo, 107–108, 131
Wilson, William Julius, 147, 158
Winn, Conrad, 57
Winner, Lawrence, 252, 395
Witmer, Helen L., 15
Wittebrood,, Karin, 246
Wolcott, G. D., 252
Wolfgang, Marvin E., 14–16, 77, 93, 95, 114, 156, 160, 192, 247, 251, 269–271, 272, 273, 274, 387–388
Wolverton, Troy, 62
Wood, Peter B., 194, 230, 389
Woodham, Luke, 92, 93
Worden, Robert E., 341
Wordes, Madeline, 353
Wright, Bradley R. Entner, 194, 198, 220
Wright, James D., 254, 255, 256, 257, 260
Wright, John Paul, 2, 147, 188, 431
Wright, Milton, 93
Wright, Richard T., 58, 232, 244, 373
Wurst, Andrew, 92, 93
Wyle, Clement J., 40

Yablonsky, Lewis, 291, 292
Yaeger, Don, 208
Yeager, Peter Cleary, 309
Yeisley, Mark R., 147
Yochelson, Samuel, 116–117
Yoder, Stephen A., 373
Young, Jock, 7, 8, 23, 24, 149, 214
Young, Robert L., 257
Young, Warren, 359, 360
Yu, Jiang, 376

Zahn, Margaret A., 73
Zane, J. Peder, 213
Zarr, Gerald H., 321
Zawitz, Marianne W., 255
Zeisel, Hans, 350, 380
Zeitz, Dorothy, 178
Zenoff, Elyce H., 120
Zernike, Kate, 289
Zhang, Lening, 196, 406
Zhang, Sheldon, 309
Zients, Alan B., 120
Zillmann, Dolf, 211
Zimring, Franklin E., 254
Zingraff, Matthew T., 190, 191
Zorea, Aharon W., 395

SUBJECT INDEX

Abductions of juveniles, 10, 318
Abortion, 58, 69
Abuse, child, 190–191
Abuse, spouse (*see* Intimate partner violence)
Accounting fraud, 134
Acquaintance rape, 17–18, 50–51
Activation, 264
Adaptation, modes of, 149–151
Adelphia Communications, 134
Adolescent-limited delinquency, 104–105
Adolescents, social class of, 98 (*see also* Juvenile delinquency)
Adoption studies, 106–107, 123
Adult activities, 182–183
Adultery and rape, in Pakistan, 363
Age
    capital punishment and, 110
    crime rates and, 88–91
    exiting from a criminal career and, 278–280
    victimization and, 91
Age of onset, 264
Age of termination, 264
Age-specific arrest rate, 88–89
Aggravated assault
    arrest rates by race, 94
    costs of, 52–53
    definition of, 27, 52
    firearms and, 53, 254
    victim–offender relationships in, 53
Aggravation, 265
Aggregate, 288–289
Aggression (aggressiveness)
    angry, 158–159
    media violence and, 205–208
    as a personality characteristic, 108–109, 119–122
    sex differences in, 108–109, 162
    sexual, differential association theory and, 218
    sports and, 208–210
AIDS, 4, 71, 75
Alcohol
    campus crime and, 18, 219, 250–251, 252
    crime and, 239
    delinquency and, 183
    drunk driving, 229
    as facilitating factor, 250–252
    mental illness, crime and, 125
    murder and, 14, 251
    sex offenses and, 250–251
Al Qaeda, 58, 288–289
Altruistic fear of crime, 315–316
Amenability issue, 403

American Indians, victimization and, 95, 96
American Law Institute, 127
American Sociological Society, 64
America's Most Wanted (television program), 2
Andersen, Arthur, 134
Angry aggression, 158–159
Annual trends in crime rates, 2, 82–83
Anomie theory, 148–152, 170
    critique of, 151, 160
    general strain theory, 151–152
    leaving a life of crime and, 282
Anti-Drug Abuse Act (1986), 417
Antisocial personality disorder, 123–124
Antitrust cases, 9, 64–65, 133, 136, 224, 372–373 (*see also* Price fixing; White-collar crime)
Apartheid, 75
Aphasia, 111
Appeal to higher loyalties, 176, 180
Architecture, informal social control and, 322–324
Argentina, 154, 329
Argersinger v. *Hamlin* (1972), 350
Argot, 297
Arousal level, 124
Arraignment, 347–348
Arrest, 421
    as career contingency, 265, 267
    demeanor and, 267, 341
    drug, 26, 233–234
    deterrence and risk of, 231, 375–376
    rates, 35
        age-specific, 88–89
        race and, 93–95
        sex differences in, 85–87
    statistics, 26, 35
Arrestee Drug Abuse Monitoring (ADAM) program, 253
Arson
    arrest rates by race, 94
    costs of, 62–63
    crack houses and, 333
    definition of, 27, 62
    fraud and, 62, 132
    in Japan, 63
    motives for, 62
    rewards and risks of, 232–233
    social, cultural, and economic sources of, 132
    in Switzerland, 132
    targets, 63
Art theft, 297–299
Assault, 27, 52–53, 87 (*see also* Aggravated assault; Simple assault)

Atavism, Lombroso's theory of, 103–104
Atlanta Georgia, murders of young blacks in, 317–318
Attention-deficit hyperactivity disorder (ADHD), 109–111, 112
Attorney General's Commission on Pornography, 210
Attorney General's Task Force on Violent Crime, 416
Attorneys
    defense, 349–350
    district, 349, 364, 383, 391, 399
Australia, 37, 323
Austria, 298, 359, 360
Authoritarian discipline, 188
Authoritative discipline, 188
Auto theft (*see* Motor vehicle theft)

Bail bonding agent, 348
Bail system, 348
Bang-jiao (China), 406
Bank of Commerce and Credit International (BCCI), 142
Bankruptcy fraud, 141
Bartley-Fox law, 258
Behavioral Science Unit (FBI), 121, 422
Behavior modification, 401–402
Belgium, 209
Bell Curve: Intelligence and Class Structure in American Life, The (Herrnstein and Murray), 115
Binge drinking, 250–251
Biographical method, 12–13, 18, 263
Biological explanations of crime
    history of, 102–104
    modern research on, 104–113
        adoption studies, 106–107, 123
        attention-deficit hyperactivity disorder, 109–111, 112
        biochemical factors and temperament, 109
        brain dysfunctions, 109–111, 112, 124
        learning disabilities, 109–111, 112
        and modern criminology, 111–113
        sex differences, 83, 107–109, 112
        twin studies, 105–106, 123
    variations in crime rates and, 91–92, 112
Biosocial Study, 113
Blacks (*see also* Race)
    crime rates of, 91–96
    discrimination against, 94–95, 147, 340, 352–356, 431–432

hate crimes, 54–57, 301
   justifications for crimes by, 178
   police and, 94–95, 342–345
   sentencing of, 352–356
   subculture of violence among,
      156–158
   victimization rates of, 95–96
   victim–offender relationships and,
      96
Blameworthiness of offenders, 386,
      388–389, 392
Block watches, 332–333, 426
Body types, 104
Bonding agent, bail, 348
Boot camp, 379
Bosnia, rape in, 301, 302
Brady Handgun Violence Prevention
      Act (1994), 259
Brain dysfunctions, 109–111, 112,
      124
Brawner rule, 127
Brazil
   lynchings in, 330
   murder and machismo in, 204
Bribery
   costs of, 65, 67
   of foreign officials, 41, 135
   market structure and, 135
   police and, 65
   political, 65, 69
British Crime Survey, 246
Broken homes, delinquency and,
      189, 216–217
Broken windows theory, 314–315
Bureaucracy, 136–137, 290
Bureau of Justice Statistics (BJS), 36
Burglary, 13 (see also Conventional
      crime; Professional theft)
   arrest rates by race, 94
   certainty of punishment for, 373
   costs of, 58
   cross-national comparisons, 75–76
   definition of, 27, 58
   differential association theory and,
      217
   fear of, 317
   firearms and, 254
   murder and, 49
   planning, 58, 244, 245
   police investigation of, 346–347
   preventing, 333, 426, 427
   rates, 30, 75–76, 77
   rewards and risks of, 232
   target hardening and, 426
   targets of, 58, 242–243, 244, 245
   victim–offender relationships in,
      58
Business crime (see White-collar
      crime)
Business organization, 296, 301–303
      (see also Organized crime)
Bystander response to crime, 19,
      324–328

California Psychological Inventory
      (CPI), 123
Cambodia, 329
Cambridge-Somerville Youth Study, 15

Campus crime (see Crime on campus)
Canada, 388, 424
   imprisonment in, 359, 360
   juvenile gangs in, 194
   professional thieves in, 217
   victimization surveys in, 37, 240
Capital punishment
   age and, 110
   in China, 381
   deterrence and, 379–382
   errors in executions, 397
   in Great Britain, 128–129, 372, 396
   insanity defense and, 128–129
   neurological problems of juveniles
      and, 109–111
   public attitudes toward, 379–380,
      396–397
   race and, 355–358
   religion and, 395
   retribution and, 395–397
   scholars' attitudes toward, 380,
      396–397
   sex and, 358
   Strike Hard campaigns, 381
Career criminal programs, 383
Careers (see Criminal careers)
Carjackings, 60
Car theft (see Motor vehicle theft)
Cartography, 23–24
Case attrition, 319, 338, 339, 358
Casework, 400–401
Causes of crime
   community ties, 430
   dealing with, 427–432
   discrimination, 431–432
   economic factors, 428–429
   family, 430–431
   political factors, 429
   public attitudes toward, 413–414,
      427
   school, 431
   social change, 429
Causes of Delinquency (Hirschi), 181
Cellular telephones, 130
Center to Prevent Handgun
      Violence, 259
Certainty of punishment, 373,
      381–382, 423
Certification, 282
Challenge, as reward from crime,
      227, 230
Challenger explosion, 136–137
Chicago Area Project, 78
Child abuse, 190–191, 251
Child molestation, 116, 251,
      402–403, 421
Children (see also Family; Juvenile
      delinquency; Juveniles)
   aggressiveness in, 108, 120,
      205–208
   fear of crime among, 317–318
   as murderers, 120
   social construction of abduction
      of, 10
China
   capital punishment in, 381
   collective response to crime in, 329
   community ties in, 196, 430

economic factors and crime in,
      428–429
   the family in, 196, 430
   migration in, 429
   organized crime and, 81, 303, 307,
      308–309
   political ideology of, 429
   schools in, 196, 431
   social bonds in, 196
   social change in, 429
Chinese-Canadians, adolescent gangs
      among, 194
Choice, crime and, 227–228
Chowchilla California kidnapping,
      318
Chronic offenders, 270–271
Cities (metropolitan areas)
   distribution of crime within,
      78–80, 239
   informal social control in, 319–322
   patrol groups in, 330–332
Class (see Social class)
Classical school of criminology, 22–23
Clearance rate, 35, 88, 346–347,
      375–376, 421
Cocaine, 233
   sentencing and, 354–355
   smuggling and dealing, 281,
      299–301, 421
Code of Hammurabi, 385–386
Cognitive-behavioral programs,
      400–401
Cohesiveness of the family,
      delinquency and, 191–192
Cohort studies, 15–16, 18, 114, 160,
      192, 269–274
Coker v. Georgia (1977), 355, 396
Collective efficacy, 321
Collective responses to crime,
      328–334
Colleges (see Crime on campus)
Colombia, 6, 209, 299, 329
   drugs and, 142, 307
   la violencia in, 157
Columbia University, 385
Columbine High School (Littleton,
      Colorado), 92–93, 163, 188
Commission on Pornography,
      Attorney General's, 210
Commitment to crime as a way of
      life, 371
Committee for the Study of
      Incarceration, 390
Community
   crime prevention and, 333–334,
      427, 430
   crime rates and, 77–78
   learning to commit crime and,
      78–79, 202–203
   reactions to crime
      collective response to crime,
         328–334
      fear of crime, 2, 314–319
      individual response to crime,
         324–328
      informal social control, 319–323
      reintegrating the offender into,
         406–407

Community policing, 333, 377–378, 421
Community Reparative Board (Vermont), 406
Comparative research, 11–12, 18
Compensation of victims, 39, 362–363
Competition, free-enterprise ideology and, 133, 135
Comprehensive Crime Control Act (1984), 416
Computer crime, 137–139, 230, 242
  differential association theory and, 220
Concealed-carry laws and firearms, 256–257
Concentric-zone model, 78–79
Concordance rate, 106–107
Condemnation of the condemners, 175–176, 180
Conduct disorder, 123
Conflict perspective, 7–9, 356
Conformity, as mode of adaptation, 149, 150
Consensus perspective, 8–9
Conservative approach, 411–414
Consumer fraud, 34, 61, 67
Containment theory, self-concepts and, 222–223
Contingency, 265–266
Control balance theory, 198
Control theory of delinquency (see Social control theory)
Conventional crime, 46–64 (see also Property crimes; Violent crime)
  deterrence and, 371
  fear of, 314–319
  organization of, 295–301
  rewards and risks of, 231–233
  self-concepts and, 223
  social, cultural, and economic sources of, 142–159
  white-collar crime and, 65–67
Conventional lines of action, 182–183
Conviction rate, 349
Corporations, 136–137, 173
  in Japan, 143
Correctional institutions (see also Prisons)
  learning to commit crime and, 211–212
  leaving a life of crime and, 283–284
Corruption, government, 28, 65, 69, 135, 303 (see also Bribery)
Cosa Nostra, La (see Mafia)
Costs of crime, 39, 46–73
  arson, 62–63
  burglary, 58
  conventional crime, 46–64
  costs related to criminal violence, 47
  direct loss, 47
  drug use, 70
  enforcement costs, 47, 338
  fraud, 60–62
  gambling, 69, 70–71

hate crimes, 54–57
illegal expenditures, 47
intimate partner violence, 53–54
larceny, 58–59
maintaining the criminal justice system, 47
motor vehicle theft, 59–60
murder, 48–50, 53–54
organized crime, 68–69
prevention and protection costs, 47–48, 316–317, 330
property crimes, 48, 58–64
prostitution, 69, 71
terrorism, 57–58
transfer of property, 47
vandalism, 63
victimless crimes, 69–71
violent crime, 46–58
white-collar crime, 64–68
Costs related to criminal violence, 47
Counseling, group, 19, 401
Counterfeit merchandise, sale of, 67, 135, 296
Courts, 347–358
  deterrence and, 378
  juveniles, 5, 225, 353, 356, 394–395, 424
  reform of, 421–424
  rehabilitation and, 399
  retribution and, 23, 391–395
Crack, 19, 333
Craft organization, 296
Credit, trust and, 136
Credit card fraud, 62
Cribs (MTV television program), 149
Crime (see also specific crimes)
  alcohol and, 14, 18, 125, 183, 229, 239, 250–252
  attitudes toward the causes of, 413–414, 427
  characteristics of, 4–5
  costs of, 46–73
  dealing with causes of, 427–432
  definitions of, 2–5, 313–314
  dimensions of, 74–101
  drug use and, 70, 183–185, 233–234, 252–253, 354–355
  excuses and, 4
  firearms and, 51, 53, 254–260, 421
  harmfulness of, 386–388, 392
  interdisciplinary research on causes of, 113
  IQ and, 113–116
  justifications and, 4–5, 178
  measuring, 22–45
  media and, 1–2, 9, 35, 66, 149, 205–208, 314, 325
  patterns of, 13–14
  politics of, 414–419
  reactions to, 313–336
  reporting and recording of, 32–34
  seriousness of, 31, 386–390
  social construction of, 9–10
  social, cultural, and economic sources of, 142–159
  specialization in, 272, 273, 275
  unemployment and, 144–147, 428

Crime and Human Nature (Wilson and Herrnstein), 227
Crime and Industrial Society in the 19th Century (Tobias), 11–12
Crime-generating cycle, 322
Crime index, 26–31
Crime in the United States: Uniform Crime Reports (FBI), 26
Crime news, 1–2, 9, 35, 66, 207
Crime on campus
  computer crime, 220
  just deserts for student offenders, 385
  measuring the problem, 43
  role of alcohol and drugs in, 18, 250–251, 252
  routine activities and, 241
  sexual assault, 16–18, 218, 219, 229
  student loans, 60–61
  surveys of rape, 16–18
  telephone fraud, 61, 138
  victimization surveys of, 16–18, 43
Crime prevention
  community strategies for, 333–334, 427, 430
  effective means of, 418, 419
  situational, 425–427
Crime rates
  age variations in, 88–91
  class variations in, 97–99
  community and, 77–78, 430
  cross-national variations in, 74–76, 92
  fear of crime and, 315, 316
  gun-control laws and, 257–259, 421
  incarceration and, 424
  index crimes, 26–31
  learning theories and variations in, 234–235
  within metropolitan areas, 78–80, 239, 321–322
  migration and, 11, 80–81, 194–195
  in nineteenth-century England, 11–12
  property crimes, 30, 77, 143–144
  psychology and variations in, 125–126
  racial variations in, 91–96
  regional variations within the United States, 76–77
  sex differences in, 83, 85–87
  social control theory and variations in, 199–200
  social, cultural, and economic factors and variations in, 165–167
  techniques of neutralization and variations in, 199–200
  temporal variations in, 81–83, 424
  victimization surveys as basis for, 16–18, 36–40
  violent crimes, 29–30, 76–77
Crime-reducing cycle, 322
Crimes against Children Research Center, 138
Crime statistics (see also Crime rates; Federal Bureau of Investigation; Victimization surveys)
  cartographic approach and, 23–24

gathering, 31–35
history, 26
official, 25–36
patterns-of-crime approach and, 13–14
political use of, 34
from self-report studies, 40–44, 85–86, 97–99
from victimization surveys, 16–18, 36–40
Crime Stoppers, 325
Crime switching, 264
Criminal careers, 263–286
adult, 217, 272–274
analyzing, 265–269
Chaiken and Chaiken's typology of, 269, 270
chronic offenders, 270–271
contingencies and, 265–266
criminal role careers, 269
definition of, 263
exiting, 278–284
incapacitation and, 382–384
juvenile delinquency and, 16, 217, 269–274
labeling perspective, 265, 266–267
leaving
anomie theory, 282
correctional system and, 283–284
differential association theory, 282
differential opportunity theory, 282
drug dealers and smugglers, 281
labeling perspective, 282
professional thieves, 279, 280
Shover's model of, 278–280
social control theory, 282–283
violent criminals, 280–281
legitimate careers compared with, 263
patterns of delinquent, 271–272
preventive detention, 349, 416
recruitment into, 268–269, 288
of robbers
career patterns, 275
intensive and intermittent careers of, 276
planning, 275–276
use of stolen money, 276
theoretical perspectives on, 264–265
typologies of, 269, 270
of white-collar offenders, 277–278
zigzag path between legitimate pursuits and, 267
Criminal courts (see Courts)
Criminal intent, 4
Criminal justice system, 337–367 (see also Courts; Police; Prisons)
costs of maintaining, 47, 338
deterrence and, 374–382
capital punishment, 379–382
courts, 378
police, 374–378
prisons, 378–379
as funnel or sieve, 319, 338, 339, 358

incapacitation and, 382–384
reforms of
courts, 421–424
overreach of the criminal law, 420
police, 420–421
prisons, 425
rehabilitation and
courts, 399
police, 398–399
prisons, 399–400, 424
retribution and
capital punishment, 395–397
courts, 23, 391–395
judges, 391–394
juvenile justice system, 5–6, 394–395
police, 390–391
prisons, 395, 424
prosecutors, 391
victims in, 362–365
Criminal law
definition of, 3
overreach of, 420
psychology and, 126–129
social construction of crime, 9–10
social origins of, 6–10
theoretical perspectives on, 3, 6–10
Criminal mind, 116–117
Criminal organizations (see Organization of criminal behavior)
Criminal personality, 116–117
Criminal Personality, The (Yochelson and Samenow), 117
Criminal propensity theory, 265
Criminal responsibility, 4, 23, 126–129 (see also Insanity defense)
Criminal role careers (see Criminal careers)
Criminal thinking, 116–117
Criminals, typologies of, 269, 270 (see also specific types of crimes)
Criminology, 10–11
biological explanations of crime and, 24, 102–113
cartographic approach to, 23–24
classical, 22–23
FBI data for research in, 36
modern, emergence of, 22–25
positivist approach to, 24–25, 104, 172
research strategies in, 18
biographical, 12–13
cohort studies, 15–16
combining strategies of, 18, 19–20
comparative and historical, 11–12
econometric techniques, 18, 19
experiments, 18, 19
mathematical models, 18, 19
observation, 18, 19
patterns-of-crime approach, 13–14
records, official and unofficial, 18–19
surveys, 16–18

Cross-national variations in crime rates, 74–76, 92
Cultural criminology, 9
Culture (cultural factors) (see also Social, cultural, and economic sources of crime)
delinquency and lower-class, 155
goals as defined by, 148–149, 154, 160
learning to commit crime and, 203–205
Culture Conflict and Crime (Sellin), 80
Curfews, juvenile crime and, 90
Czechoslovakia, crime in former, 368

Danwei (China), 196
Dark figure, 37–39, 41
Death penalty (see Capital punishment)
Decriminalization of drugs, 420
Defense attorneys, 349–350
Defense of necessity, 4–5, 176
Defense of the ledger, 176, 177
Defensible space, 322–324, 427
Delinquency (see Juvenile delinquency)
Delinquency in a Birth Cohort (Wolfgang, Figlio, and Sellin), 15–16
Delinquent Boys (Cohen), 154
Delinquent careers, 269–274 (see also Criminal careers)
Delinquent gang, 291 (see also Gangs, juvenile)
Demeanor, arrest and, 267, 341
Demonstration effect, 148, 428–429
Denial of injury, 173–175, 176, 179
Denial of responsibility, 172–173, 176, 179
Denial of the victim, 175, 176, 179–180
Denmark, 36, 37, 105, 106, 107, 210, 388
Deregulation, 134, 135–136
Desistance, 264 (see also Exiting)
Detectives, solving crime by, 346–347
Determinate sentencing, 392–394
Deterrence, 220, 337
assumptions about behavior and, 369–370
conventional crime and, 371
criminal justice system and, 374–382
capital punishment, 379–382
courts, 378, 421–424
police, 374–378, 420–421
prisons, 378–379, 424
general, 369
marginal deterrent effect, 369
other effects of penalties and, 370–371
police crackdowns and, 375
rehabilitation, 398
retribution and, 369, 386

Deterrence (*continued*)
  sanctioning process and
    certainty of punishment, 373,
      381–382, 423
    promptness of punishment,
      373, 381
    severity of punishment, 372–373
    types of punishment, 373–374,
      389–390
  specific, 369
  white-collar crime and, 371–372,
    423–424
Developmental criminology,
  264–265
Deviation, primary and secondary,
  221, 226
*Diagnostic and Statistical Manual of
  Mental Disorders (DSM-IV)*
  (American Psychiatric
  Association), 123
Diamonds (juvenile gang), 217,
  294–295
Differential association theory,
  212–221, 226
  critique of, 214–215
  delinquency and, 216–217
  evidence on, 216–221
  labeling theory and, 225, 226
  leaving a life of crime and, 282
  principles of, 212–214
  professional theft and, 217
  sexual aggression and, 218, 219
  white-collar crime and, 218–220
Differential identification theory, 214
Differential opportunity theory,
  152–153, 170
  leaving a life of crime and, 282
Diffusion of responsibility, 327
Dimensions of crime, 74–101
Direct discrimination, 354
Directed police patrol, 377
Direct loss of property, 47
Discipline, delinquency and,
  187–189
Discretion, police officer's, 340–341
Discrimination, 94–95, 147, 431–432
  (*see also* Race)
Disorganized serial murderers, 422
Displacement effect, 244, 377
Disposal of toxic wastes, 69, 141
Disputatiousness, 158–159
District attorneys, 349, 364, 383,
  391, 399
Divorce (*see* Broken homes,
  delinquency and)
Doctors, fraud by, 61, 173, 175–176
Doing gender, 162–164
Domestic violence (*see* Intimate
  partner violence)
Drexel Burnham Lambert Inc., 133
Drift, 170–171, 178, 181
Drop a Dime, 333
Drug house abatement laws, 333
Drugs, illegal
  arrests, 26, 233–234, 354–355
  campus crime and, 250–251
  community response to, 333
  costs of, 70

crime and, 70, 125, 183–185,
    252–253
  dealing, 19, 70, 142, 299–301
  decriminalization of, 420
  economic-compulsive need and,
    253
  as facilitating factor, 252–253
  firearms and, 255
  juvenile gangs and, 294–295
  law enforcement, 421
  leaving a career in selling or
    smuggling, 281
  mental illness, crime, and, 125
  organization of smuggling and
    dealing of, 281, 299–301
  organized crime and, 69, 141,
    307–308
  psychopharmacological effects of,
    253
  rewards and risks of using, 233–234
  sentencing and, 354–355, 373
  systemic factors and, 253
  use of, 70, 233–234, 239, 252–253
  as victimless crime, 69, 70, 420
Drug testing, crime and, 252
Drunk driving, 229, 373
Duration of criminal career, 264
Duress justification, 4
Dyscalculia, 111
Dyslexia, 111
Dysphasia, 111

eBay, fraud and, 62
Echo effects, 1
Ecology of crime, 79, 239
Econometric techniques, 18, 19
Economic-compulsive need and
  drugs, 253
Economic development, 75,
  143–144, 428–429
Economic factors (*see* Social, cultural,
  and economic sources of
  crime)
Economic system
  opportunity and the, 144
  organized crime and, 142
Ectomorphs, 104
Education programs, 401
EFT crime, 139, 142
Eighteenth Amendment, 140
Eighth Amendment, 348, 396
Elderly, crime and the, 91, 315
Electrical equipment price-fixing
  case, 2–3, 64–65, 136, 175,
  176, 224
Electroencephalogram readings
  (EEGs), 111
Electronic fund transfers (EFT) crime,
  139, 142
Embezzlement, 65, 67, 87, 116, 137,
  144, 150, 161, 384
  definition of, 27
  techniques of neutralization and,
    177–178, 203
Emergencies, reactions to, 326–328
Employee theft, 67–68, 173–174
  by women, 87, 161
Endomorphs, 104

Enforcement costs, 47, 338
England (*see* Great Britain)
Enron, 134
Entrapment, 4, 346
Epilepsy, 109
Episcopal Church, 384
Equity Funding Corporation of
  America, 219
Ethnicity, crime and, 92–93, 150–151
  (*see also* Race)
Evolutionary psychologists, 107–108
Excitement
  as focal concern of lower-class
    culture, 155
  as reward from crime, 227, 230–231
Excuse, 4
Exiting, 278–284
Expectations, relative deprivation
  and, 147–148
Expenditures
  on criminal justice system, 47, 338
  illegal, 47
Experiments, 18, 19, 211, 326–328,
  376–377, 403
Expressive crime, 371
Extortion, 141–142

Facilitating factors
  alcohol, 14, 18, 250–252
  drugs, 252–253
  firearms, 254–260
Family
  delinquency and, 181–194
    broken homes, 189, 216–217
    child abuse and, 190–191
    cohesiveness of the family,
      191–192
    discipline, 187–189
    holding parents responsible for
      their children's actions, 188
    peer groups and, 193–194
    power-control theory, 164–165
    separation of children from
      their parents, 189–190
    social control theory, 181–182,
      192, 193–194
    socialization, 186–187
  murder in, 14, 49–50, 53–54, 164
  power-control theory, 164–165
  reduction of crime and, 430–431
Family group conferencing (FGC), 406
Family intervention, 401, 430–431
Fear of crime
  in Brazil, 330
  children and, 317–318
  community ties and, 314–319
  consequences of, 316–319
  elderly and, 91, 315
  media and, 2, 314
  perceived risk and, 314, 315–316
  as a social problem, 314
  trust and, 317–318
Federal Bureau of Investigation (FBI),
  419, 422–423
  crime data of, 9–10, 26–36
    annual trends in, 82–83
    clearance and arrest statistics,
      35, 88, 375–376

crime index, 26–28, 30–31
  for criminological research, 36
  criticisms of, 26, 28
  National Crime Victimization
    Surveys (NCVS) compared
    with, 37
  report on hate crimes, 54, 56–57
  social construction of serial
    murder by, 10
Federal law enforcement, 421
  sentencing guidelines, 392–394, 416
Federal Trade Commission, 62
Felony murder, capital punishment
  and, 358, 381
Female offenders, violent, 280–281
Feminist criminology, 159–165
  doing gender, 162–164
  gender ratio problem, 159,
    160–162
  gender socialization, 162
  generalizability problem, 159, 160
  power-control theory, 164–165
  social construction of serial
    murder and, 10
  women as victims, women as
    resisters, 165
Feminist movement
  in Brazil, 204
  crime by women and, 161
Fence, The (Steffensmeier), 13
Fences, 13, 19, 175, 242–243, 297
Finland, 388
Firearms, 419
  in assaults, 53, 254
  concealed-carry laws and, 256–257
  cost of injuries due to, 53
  crime and, 254–260
  as facilitating factor, 254–260
  gun control, 257–260, 421
  juveniles and, 255–256
  in the media, 205
  murder, 254
  police patrol and, 258–259
  robbery, 51–52, 162–163, 254, 255
  on television, 205
  use in self-defense, 257
Focal concerns of lower-class culture,
  155
Forcible rape (see Rape)
Ford Motor Company, 137, 233
Foreign Corrupt Practices Act (1977),
  135
Formal organization, 290
Formal social control, 313, 319,
  320–321
France
  art theft by Napoleon Bonaparte,
    298
  criminal code of, 23
  "dangerous classes" in nineteenth-
    century, 411
  hate crimes in, 55
  imprisonment in, 359, 360
Frankenstein (movie), 102
Fraud, 60–62
  accounting, 134
  arson and, 62, 132
  bankruptcy, 141

business credit, 136
college scholarship, 60–61
consumer, 61, 67
definition of, 27, 60
insurance, 61–62
Internet and, 62
by physicians, 61, 173, 175–176
reporting of, 34
stock, 67, 141, 177
student loans and, 60–61
tax, 61
telemarketing, 278
telephone, 61, 138
true identity, 62
victims of, 34, 62
welfare, 61
Free enterprise, ideology of, 133–135
Free will, 22–24, 170, 369–370
Furman v. Georgia (1972), 355, 396

Gallup Poll, 379, 427
Gambling, 27, 140
  financial costs of, 70–71
  organized crime and, 69, 140, 306
  pathological or compulsive, 71
  state lotteries, 70, 148
  as a victimless crime, 69, 70–71,
    420
Gang, The (Thrasher), 292
Gangs, juvenile, 19, 173, 175, 231,
  290–295
  appeal to higher loyalties and, 176
  as business enterprises, 294–295
  in Canada, 194
  delinquent gangs, 291
  differential opportunity theory of,
    152–153
  drug dealing and, 294–295
  leadership in, 291–295
  learning to commit crime and, 203
  lower-class culture theory and, 155
  mobility trap and, 265
  organization of, 290–295
  organized, 292–295
  recruitment into, 293
  social gangs, 291
  theories of, 152–156
  unorganized, 291–292
  violent gang, 291
Gangster Disciples (juvenile gang),
  292–293
Gangsters (see Organized crime)
Gardner Museum, Isabella Stewart,
  297
Gault, in re, 5
Gender (see also Sex differences)
  doing, 162–164
  prison treatment programs and,
    357
  and the student-murder, 163
  theories of crime and, 160
Gender ratio problem, 159, 160–162
Gender socialization, 162
Gender structure, 159, 161–162
General Accounting Office, 61
General deterrence, 369
General Electric, 136, 224
General strain theory, 151–152

Generalizability problem, 159, 160
General Theory of Crime, A
  (Gottfredson and Hirschi), 2,
  118
Genetic explanations of crime (see
  Biological explanations of
  crime)
Geography of crime, 79–80
Germany, 210
  art theft and, 298, 299
  biological approach to crime in
    Nazi, 111
  collective response to crime in,
    329
  migration in, 81
  Nazis and genocide in, 111, 301
  victimization surveys in, 37
Gideon v. Wainwright (1963), 350
Globalization, 136
Goals, culturally defined, 148–149,
  154, 160
Good Samaritan problem, 324–328
Government officials, corruption
  and, 28, 65, 69, 135
Great Britain, 388
  art theft and, 299
  British Crime Survey, 246
  capital punishment in, 128–129,
    372, 396
  community organization in, 321
  crime rates in, 75–76
  criminal law in, 3
  defensible space in, 323
  delinquency in, 216, 273
  drug use in, 235, 252
  firearms in, 254
  imprisonment in, 359, 360
  McNaghten rule in, 126
  murder rates in, 75–76
  police in, 338
  schools in, 192–193
  terrorism and, 288
  Tobias's study of crime in
    nineteenth-century, 11–12
  urban patrols in, 330–331
  victimization surveys in, 37
  vigilantism in, 329
Groups, 288–290
Group counseling, 401
Guardian Angels, 331
Guardianship, 238–239
Gun control, 257–260, 421
Guns (see Firearms)

Habitual Serious and Violent Juvenile
  Offender Program, 383
Haiti, 329
Halloween trick-or-treating, 318
Hamas, 58
Handguns (see Firearms)
Harmfulness of crime, 386–388, 392
Harvard University, 385
Hate crimes, 54–57
  in France, 55
Hate Crime Statistics Act (1990), 56
Hate groups, organized, 55, 301
Heart rate, 124
Heroin addiction, 13, 233–234

Hezbollah, 58
Hispanics, victimization of, 96
Historical research, 11–12, 18
HIV virus, 4, 233
Homeless men, subculture of
    violence and, 157
Homicide (*see* Murder)
Homosexuals, 69
    hate crimes against, 56, 57
    violence in couples of, 54
Hong Kong, 308
Horizontal/commission type
    leadership, 293–294
Hormones, 108–109
Hot spots of crime, 239, 258, 376–377
Housing, informal social control and
    design of, 322–323, 426
How-to-commit crime manuals, 213
Hyperactivity, 109–111, 112
Hypermasculinity Inventory (HMI),
    121
Hypomania scale, 122

Ideological approaches to solving the
    crime problem, 411–414
Illegal expenditures, 47
Immigrants
    crime rates of, 80–81
    and organized crime, 150–151
    smuggling of illegal, 308–309
Imprisonment (*see* Prisons)
Incapacitation, 337, 424
    career criminal programs, 383
    selective incapacitation, 382–383
    three strikes and you're out policy,
        384, 424
Incest, 251
Incidence, 29
In Cold Blood (Capote), 319
Indeterminate sentencing, 391–392,
    399–400
Index crimes, rates of, 26–31 (*see also*
    Crime index)
India, 195, 388
Indiana State Prison, 399–400
Indians, American, and
    victimization, 95, 96
Individual responses to crime,
    324–328
Individual therapy, 400–401
Indonesia, 388
Industrialization, 11–12, 143–144
Inequality and crime, 147–148
Inequity, sense of, 148
Influential leadership, 294
Informal social control, 313–314,
    319, 426–427
    defensible space and, 322–324, 427
    differences among urban
        communities, 321–322
    mechanical and organic solidarity,
        320
    in small towns and large cities,
        320–321
Innovation, as mode of adaptation,
    149–151
Insanity defense, 126–129, 287,
    416–417

Insanity Defense Reform Act (1984),
    127
Insider trading, 133–134, 230–231, 310
Instrumental crime, 371
Insurance fraud, 61–62
Intelligence and crime (*see* IQ)
Intensive offenders, 276–277
Intent, criminal, 4
Interdisciplinary approach to
    criminology, 113
Intermittent offenders, 276–277
Internal Revenue Service (IRS),
    40–41, 61
International Association of Chiefs
    of Police (IACP), 26, 416
Internet, crime and the, 62, 138, 288
Intimate partner violence, 53–54,
    341, 374
IQ (intelligence quotient), 113–116
Iran, 388
Iraq, 396
Isabella Stewart Gardner Museum, 297
Italy, 30, 305, 388
"It's So Good, Don't Even Try It Once"
    (Smith and Gay), 233

Jamaican posses, 308
Japan
    community ties in, 77–78, 144,
        196–197, 430
    corporations in, 143
    crime rates in, 7, 75, 144
    economic factors and crime in, 75,
        144, 428
    family in, 196–197, 430
    firearms, 256
    informal social control, 196–197,
        319
    organized crime in, 81, 142, 143,
        307
    political factors in, 429
    schools in, 197, 431
    social bonds in, 196–197
    social change in, 75, 429
Jews, hate crimes against French, 55
Judges, 350, 351, 352–358 (*see also*
    Courts; Sentencing)
    probation and, 351–352
    retribution and, 391–394
    victim impact statements and,
        364–365
Juries, 350
Jury awards, as measure of costs of
    crime, 64, 388
Just deserts (*see* Retribution)
Justifications, 4–5, 178
Juvenile Awareness Project, 378–379
Juvenile courts (*see* Juvenile justice
    system)
Juvenile delinquency
    adolescent-limited, 105
    adult criminal careers and, 217,
        272–274
    in Argentina, 154
    attitudes toward, 5
    brain disorders and, 109–111, 112,
        124
    careers in, 269–274

chronic offenders, 270–271
class and, 16, 97–99, 152–156
cohort study of, 15–16, 114, 160,
    192, 269–274
curfews and, 90
definition, 5–6
differential association theory and,
    216–217
differential opportunity theory of,
    152–153, 170
distribution of, in urban areas,
    78–79
drift into, 170–171, 178, 181
drug use and, 183–185, 233–234,
    252–253
family and
    broken homes, 189, 216–217
    child abuse, 190–191
    cohesiveness of, 191–192
    discipline, 187–189
    holding parents responsible for
        their children, 188
    peer groups and, 193–194
    power-control theory, 164–165
    separation of children from
        their parents, 189–190
    socialization, 186–187
gangs, 152–156, 173, 290–295
in India, 195
IQ and, 113–116
labeling perspective on, 221–226,
    266–267, 399
learning disabilities and, 109–111,
    112
life-course-persistent, 104
lower-class culture and, 155, 170
neurological problems and,
    109–111
patterns of careers in, 16, 271–272
reaction-formation theory and,
    154, 170
retribution and, 5–6, 394–395
schools and, 163, 181, 183–186,
    192–193, 431
self-report studies of, 40, 42,
    85–86, 97–99, 183–185
sex differences in, 85–86
social control theory (*see* Social
    control theory)
social, cultural, and economic
    sources of, 142–159
    class differences in values,
        154–156, 171
specialization in, 272, 273, 275
subterranean values and, 171
techniques of neutralization and,
    172–177, 178–180
unemployment as cause of,
    144–147
Juvenile justice system, 5, 225
    pretrial diversion and, 399
    public attitudes toward, 5
    reform of, 6, 424
    retribution and, 5–6, 394–395
    sentencing and, 353, 356
    sex and, 85–86
    use of juvenile records, 394–395,
        424

Juveniles
capital punishment and, 110
in court, 5–6, 394–395, 424
economic development and, 144
firearms and, 255–256
murder by, 120, 255–256

Kaiser Family Foundation, 207
Kansas City (Missouri) police patrol
experiment, 376–377
Kidnapping (*see* Abductions of
juveniles)
Kuwait, 388

Labeling perspective, 221–226, 337,
399
criminal careers and, 265, 266–267
critique of, 226
differential association theory and,
225, 226
leaving a life of crime and, 282
opportunities and, 224–225
self-concepts and, 222–224
subcultures and, 225–226
Larceny, 173–174
arrest rates by race, 94
costs of, 58–59
definition of, 27, 58–59
rates of, 30, 77
types of, 59
victim–offender relationships in,
59
by women, 87, 161
Latinos (*see* Hispanics)
Laundering of money, 142
Laura Spelman Rockefeller Memorial
Foundation, 26
Law, 3 (*see also* Criminal law;
Neutralization of the law)
Law Enforcement Assistance
Administration (LEAA), 415
Lawyers (*see* Attorneys)
Learning disabilities, 109–111, 112
Learning structures, 153
Learning to commit crime, 186–189,
202–237
differential association theory,
212–221, 225, 226
labeling perspective, 221–226
reward-risk models, 226–234
sources of, 202–212
the community, 202–203
correctional institutions,
211–212
general culture, 203–205
media, 149, 205–208
peer groups, 203, 220
pornography, 210–211
sports, 208–210
variations in crime rates and
theories of, 234–235
Left realism, 7
Legalistic definition of crime, 3–4
Lex talionis, 385–386
Liberal approach, 112, 412–414
Liberia, 321
Life course, delinquency and crime
over the, 185–186

Life-course-persistent delinquency,
104
Life-course perspective, 185–186
Lifestyles of the Rich and Famous
(television program), 149
Lifestyle theory, 241
Linking penalties to crime, 390
Loan sharking, 140–141, 306
Los Angeles riot, 344
Lotteries, state, 148
Lower-class culture theory, 155, 170
Lynchings in Brazil, 330

McCleskey v. *Kemp* (1987), 355
Machismo, 204
McNaghten rule, 126–127, 128
Mafia (La Cosa Nostra), 2, 19, 46, 68,
144, 301 (*see also* Organized
crime)
as business enterprise, 305–306
as formal organization, 303
as kinship structure, 304–305
as patron–client relationships, 305
Male peer-support model, 218, 219
Mandatory minimum sentences,
258, 392, 394
Manslaughter, nonnegligent, 48–50
(*see also* Murder)
Marginal deterrent effect, 369
Marijuana, 233, 299–301
Market structure, white-collar crime
and, 135–136, 310
Marriage
crime and, 274
murder and, 49–50, 53–54, 164
rape and, 50
Marxist criminology, 7, 23, 340
Master status, 221
Mathematical models, 18, 19
Means, institutionalized, 148–149
Mechanical solidarity, 320
Media
crime and the, 1–2, 9, 66, 314, 325
learning to commit crime and,
149, 205–208
police and, 35, 325
reporting crime and the, 1–2
terrorism and, 57
Medicaid fraud, 173, 175–176
Mens rea, 4
Mental illness (*see* Psychological
explanations of crime;
Insanity defense)
Mesomorphs, 104
Methods of criminological research
(*See* Research, criminological)
Metropolitan areas (*see* Cities)
Mexico, 191, 299
Migration, crime and, 11, 80–81,
194–195, 308–309, 429 (*see
also* Immigrants)
Milieu therapy, 402
Minneapolis Domestic Violence
Experiment, 374
Minnesota Multiphasic Personality
Inventory (MMPI), 122–123
Minority groups (*see* Race [Racial
discrimination])

MMPI (Minnesota Multiphasic
Personality Inventory),
122–123
Mobility trap, 265
Model Penal Code, 127
Modernization, 143–144
Modes of adaptation, 149–151
Money laundering, 142
Monoamine oxidase (MAOA), 109,
190
Mood disorder, 124–125
Morton Thiokol, 136
Motivated offenders, 238
Motor vehicle theft
arrest rates by race, 94
carjackings, 60
costs of, 59–60
cross-national comparisons, 75–76
definition of, 27, 59
rates of, 30
rewards and risks of, 232
Murder, 175, 384
alcohol and, 14, 250, 251
arrest rates by race, 94
capital punishment as deterrent
to, 379–382
by children, 120
circumstances of, 14, 48–50, 164
costs of, 48–50
cross-national comparisons, 75–76,
92
definition of, 27, 48
disputatiousness and, 158–159
doing gender and, 162–164
fear of, 317–319
firearms and, 254, 255
inequality and, 147
justifying, 178
juveniles and, 5–6, 120, 255–256
machismo in Brazil and, 204
marriage and, 49–50, 53–54, 164
media and, 1–2, 207
neurological problems of juveniles
and, 109–111
patterns-of-crime approach to
study of, 13–14
personality traits of sexual
murderers, 120–121
police investigation of, 347
race and, 14, 49, 92, 94–96
rampage killers, 121–122
rape and, 49, 178
rates, 9–10, 29–31
regional variations in, 76–77
robbery and, 52, 178
serial, 10, 162, 245, 422–423
sex and, 49, 86–87, 107–108, 164
sexual, 120–121
in South Africa, 75
subculture of violence in
the U.S. South and, 77,
157–158
targets, 247–248
victim–offender relationships
in, 14, 48–50, 53–54, 96
victim-precipitated, 247–248
women and, 49, 87, 164, 204
Murder Incorporated, 301

Murrah Federal Building (Oklahoma
 City), 9
Muslims, 55, 56–57, 302, 344

National Aeronautics and Space
 Administration, 136
National Basketball Association, 208
National College Women Sexual
 Victimization (NCWSV)
 survey, 16–18
National Collegiate Athletic
 Association (NCAA), 208
National Crime Information Center
 (NCIC) 2000, 35, 421
National Crime Victimization
 Surveys (NCVS), 36–40 (*see
 also* Victimization surveys)
National Criminal Justice
 Commission, 67
National Drug Control Policy, 417
National Fire Protection Association
 (NFPA), 63
National Football League, 208
National Household Survey on Drug
 Abuse, 252
National Incident-Based Reporting
 System (NIBRS), 36, 90
National Institute of Justice, 19, 252,
 374
National Institute of Law
 Enforcement and Criminal
 Justice, 314
National Institute on Alcohol Abuse
 and Alcoholism's Task Force
 on College Drinking, 250
National Insurance Crime Bureau, 60
National Longitudinal Study of
 Adolescent Health survey, 54
National Opinion Research Center,
 36
National Research Council, 15
National Rifle Association (NRA),
 259, 418
National Survey of Crime Severity,
 388
National Violence against Women
 (NVAW) survey, 53–54
National Youth Survey (NYS), 40,
 178, 189, 272
Native Americans and victimization,
 95, 96
Neighborhoods (*see* Community)
Neighborhood Watches, 332–333
Netherlands, the, 37, 195, 359, 360,
 388
Networks, 289, 300–301, 310
 al Qaeda, 288–289
Neurological problems, crime and,
 109–111
Neurotransmitters, 109
Neutralization of the law, 203, 238
 critique of theory of, 180–181
 drift and, 170–171, 178
 evidence on techniques of, 177–180
  crimes by blacks, 178
  delinquency and, 178–180
  embezzlement and, 177–178, 203
  justifying violence, 178

techniques of, 172–180
 appeal to higher loyalties, 176,
  180
 condemnation of the
  condemners, 175–176, 180
 denial of injury, 173–175, 176,
  179
 denial of responsibility,
  172–173, 176, 179
 denial of the victim, 175, 176,
  179–180
 other, 176–177
 variations in crime rates and,
  199–200
Newspapers, crime and, 1, 9, 35, 66,
 207
New Zealand, 54, 114, 198
Nigeria, 329
Nonnegligent manslaughter, 48–50
Norm, 3
Norway, 6, 388
Novelty-seeking, 109

Obscene material, 210 (*see also*
 Pornography)
Observation, 18, 19
Office of Justice Programs, 48
Oklahoma City bombing, 9
Omnibus Crime Control and Safe
 Streets Act (1968), 415
Opportunities to commit crime
 economy and, 143–144
 labeling and, 224–225, 266–267
 routine activities approach to,
  238–241
 women and, 87, 161
Oregon Social Learning Center, 187
Organic solidarity, 320
Organizational discrimination, 354
Organization of criminal behavior,
 68–69, 287–312
Organized crime, 301–309 (*see also*
 Mafia)
 China and, 81, 303, 307, 308–309
 costs of, 68–69
 definition of, 68–69, 301–303
 drugs and, 69, 141, 307–308
 economic system and, 142
 extortion, 141–142
 fraud, bankruptcy and stock, 141
 gambling and, 69, 140, 306
 immigration and, 81, 150–151,
  308–309
 in Japan, 81, 142
 laundering of money and, 142
 loan sharking, 140–141, 306
 national confederation, 303
 new forms of, 68, 142, 307–309
 organization of,
  as business enterprise, 305–306
  as formal organization, 303
  as kinship structure, 304–305
  as patron–client relationships,
   305
 Prohibition and, 139, 140, 150
 prosecution of, 306, 422–423
 RICO law and, 306, 422
 in Russia, 81, 142, 308

social, cultural, and economic
  sources of, 139–142
 sources of illegal profits, 68–69,
  140–142, 305–306
 toxic wastes, disposal of, 141
Organized gang, 292–295
Organized serial murderers, 422
Overreach of criminal law, 420

Pakistan, 363
Paranoid schizophrenia, 124
Parents (*see also* Family)
 holding parents responsible for
  children's actions, 188
 separation of children from,
  delinquency and, 189–190
Parole, 361–362, 400, 416, 418
Patriarchy, 164–165
Patrol, directed police, 377
Patrol groups, urban, 330–332
Patron–client relationships, Mafia
 and, 305
Patterns of crime, 13–14, 18
Patterns of Criminal Homicide
 (Wolfgang), 14
Peacemaking criminology, 7
Peer groups
 families and, 193–194
 learning to commit crime and,
  203, 220
 social control theory and, 182,
  193–194
Penalties (*see* Punishment)
Performance structures, 153
Permissive discipline, 188
Persistence, 264
Personality (personality
 characteristics)
 aggressiveness, 108–109, 119–122,
  162
 antisocial, 123–124
 of children who kill, 120
 criminal, 116–117
 inventories, 122–123
 novelty-seeking, 109
 of rapists, 120–121
 self-control, 118–119, 186, 229
 of sexual murderers, 120–121
 and strain, 152
Peru, art theft and, 299
"Phone phreaking," 138
Phrenologists, 103
Physicians, fraud by, 61, 173,
 175–176
Physiognomists, 103
Picaresque organization, 296
Pickpockets, 217, 243, 296
Planning, criminal careers and,
 275–276
Plea bargaining, 350–351, 399
Pluralistic ignorance, 327
Poland, crime in, 368
Police, 19
 abuses of authority, 340–346
 attitudes toward, 33–34, 320–321
 brutality, 65, 175, 341–345
 clearance rate of, 35, 346–347,
  375–376

community policing, 320–321, 333, 377–378, 421
corruption, 65, 175, 303
crackdowns, 375
crime statistics, 25–36
demeanor and arrest by, 267, 341
deterrence and
    patrol tactics, 376–378
    risk of arrest, 231, 375–376
    size of police force, 375, 420
directed patrol, 377
discretion exercised by, 340–341
drugs and, 421
firearms and, 258–259, 421
history of, 338, 340
and intimate partner violence, 341, 374
juveniles and, 16
media and, 9, 35, 325
patrols, car and foot, 376–377
proactive work of, 32
problem-oriented policing, 378
racial discrimination by, 94, 340, 342–345
reactive work of, 32
recording practices of, 34
reform of, 420–421
rehabilitation and, 398–399
reporting of crime and, 32–34
retribution and, 390–391
robbery arrests by, 342–343
sex discrimination by, 345–346
shootings by, 341–342, 343–344
in South Africa, 75
use of force by, 341–342
Police Foundation, 35, 374, 421
Police patrols, 258–259, 376–378
Political corruption, 28, 69, 173, 175, 176, 303
Political issue, crime as, 34, 414–419
Political rebellion, 151
Population, crime rates and age distribution of, 89–91
Pornography, 138, 210–211
Positivism, 24–25, 104, 172
Post-Lombrosian researchers, 104
Power-control theory, 164–165
Premenstrual syndrome (PMS), 109
Presidential elections, 416–419
President's Commission on Law Enforcement and Administration of Justice, the, 414–415
President's Commission on Organized Crime, 69
Pretrial diversion, 399
Prevalence, 29
Prevention and protection costs, 47–48, 316–317, 330
Prevention of crime
    community strategies for, 333–334, 427, 430
    effective means of, 418, 419
    situational, 425–427
Preventive detention, 348–349, 416
Price fixing, 2–3, 28, 64–65, 133, 136, 175, 176, 224, 310, 372
    (see also Antitrust cases)

Primary deviation, 221, 226
Primary group, 289–290
Prisons, 358–362 (see also Correctional institutions)
    cross-national comparisons of inmates in, 359–361
    deterrence and, 378–379
    history of, 359
    learning to commit crime and, 211–212
    leaving a life of crime and, 283–284
    parole and, 361–362, 400
    population of, 359–361
    rehabilitation and, 19, 399–400, 424
    retribution and, 395
    War on Drugs and use of, 354–355, 417
    women in, 354–355, 357
Proactive police work, 32
Probation, 351–352
Problem-oriented policing, 378
Professional Fence, The (Klockars), 13
Professional theft, 174, 217, 228, 244, 276–277, 279, 295–299, 371
Profiling serial killers, 422–423
Profits, free enterprise ideology and, 133–135
Prohibition, 140, 150
Prohibition Bureau, 140
Project organization, 13, 296–299
Promptness of punishment, 373, 381
Property crimes, 46, 48, 58–64 (see also specific crimes)
    costs of, 58–64
    economic development and, 143–144
    geography of, 79
    rates of, 30, 77, 143–144
    rational-choice theory of, 227–228
    regional variations in, 77
    targets, 143–144, 241–243
    victim-precipitated, 249
Prosecutors, 349, 364, 383, 391, 399
Prostitution, 27, 69, 71, 175, 309, 420
Protective neighboring, 324
Protestant clergy, 395
Psychological explanations of crime
    criminal law and, 126–129
    evolutionary psychologists, 107–108
    intelligence, 113–116
    personality traits, 116–124
        aggressiveness, 108–109, 119–122, 162
        antisocial personality disorder, 123–124
        of children who kill, 120
        criminal mind, 116–117
        personality inventories, 122–123
        rampage killers, 121–122
        rapists, 120–121
        self-control, 118–119, 186, 229
        sexual murderers, 120–121
        and strain, 152

schizophrenia and mood disorders, 124–125
    variations in crime rates and, 125–126
Psychopath (see Antisocial personality disorder)
Psychopathic deviate scale, 122
Psychopathic personality (see Antisocial personality disorder)
Psychopharmacological effects of drugs, 253
Psychotherapy, individual, 400–401
Puerto Rico, community and delinquency in, 430
Punishment (see also Deterrence; Incapacitation; Rehabilitation; Retribution)
    classical criminology, 22–23
    justifications for, 337
    types of, 373–374, 389–390
    unpleasantness of, 386, 389–390

Qaeda, al, 288–289
Quakers, 359, 397
Quality Assurance Review (FBI), 31

Race (racial discrimination) (see also Blacks)
    biological explanations, 91–92, 112
    capital punishment and, 355–356
    crime rates and, 91–96
    delinquency and, 16, 78–79
    hate crimes and, 54–57, 301
    murder and, 14, 49, 92, 94–96
    police and, 94–95, 340, 342–345
    prisons and, 352–356
    reducing crime and discrimination by, 431–432
    sentencing and, 352–356
    and the student-murder, 92–93
    and subculture of violence, 156–158
    and unemployment, 147
    victimization and, 95–96
    victim–offender relationships and, 14, 49, 96
    War on Drugs and, 354–355, 417
Racial profiling, 344–345
Racism, 75
Racketeer Influenced and Corrupt Organizations (RICO) law (1970), 306, 422
Radical approach, 412
Radical criminology, 7
Radical nonintervention policy, delinquency and, 274
Rahway State Prison (New Jersey), 378
Rampage killers, 121–122
Rape, 14
    and adultery, in Pakistan, 363
    alcohol and, 18, 250–251
    arrest rates by race, 94
    in Bosnia, 301, 302
    on campus, 16–18, 218, 219, 229
    capital punishment and, 355

Rape (*continued*)
  costs of, 50–51
  culture and, 204–205
  definition, 17, 27, 50
  denial of responsibility and, 173
  denial of the victim and, 175
  fear of, 315, 317
  firearms and, 254
  gang, 301
  marriage and, 50, 53
  murder and, 49, 178
  organization of, 301, 302
  personality traits and, 120–121
  pornography and, 210–211
  prosecution of, 421–422
  rates of, 29–30
  reporting, 16–18, 33
  seasonal variations in rates of,
    81–82
  sex and, 50, 86
  social construction of, 10
  in South Africa, 75
  statutory, 4
  targets, 248–249
  victimization survey measurement
    of, 16–18, 50–51, 87
  victim–offender relationships in,
    49–50, 53, 96
  victim-precipitated, 248–249
Rapists
  personalities of, 120–121
  pornography and, 210–211
  recidivism of, 402–403
Rates of crime (*see* Crime rates)
Rational-choice perspective, 227–228
Rational decision making of
  corporations, 136, 137
Reaction-formation theory, 154, 170
Reactive police work, 32
Rebellion, as mode of adaptation,
  150, 151
Recidivism rates, 402–403
Records, official and unofficial,
  18–19
Recruitment into criminal careers,
  217, 268–269, 288
Regional variations in crime rates,
  76–77
Rehabilitation, 19, 287, 337
  assumptions underlying, 398
  behavior modification, 401–402
  casework, 400–401
  cognitive-behavioral programs,
    400–401
  courts and, 399
  deterrence, 398
  education programs, 401
  effectiveness of, 402–405
    amenability issue, 403
    experimental design and, 403
    measures of, 403
    recidivism rates, 402–403
  family intervention, 401, 430–431
  future of, 407
  group counseling, 401
  historical background, 23,
    397–398
  individual therapy, 400–401

  leaving a life of crime and, 283–284
  milieu therapy, 402
  police and, 398–399
  prisons and, 399–400, 424
  reaffirming, 404–405
  reintegrating the offender into
    society, 406–407
  retribution and, 398, 407, 424
  sentencing and, 399
  work programs, 401
Reintegration of offenders into
  society, 406–407
Reintegrative shaming, 198, 406
Relative deprivation, 147–148,
  428–429
Religion
  capital punishment and, 395
  delinquency and, 194
  retribution and, 395
  and serial murder, 10
  social construction of serial
    murder and, 10
Repeat victimization, 245–246
Reporting of crime, 17–18, 32–34,
  37–39, 41, 324, 325 (*see also*
    Victimization surveys)
Research, criminological, 18, 36
  biographical, 12–13
  cohort studies, 15–16
  combining strategies of, 18, 19–20
  comparative and historical, 11–12
  econometric techniques, 18, 19
  experiments, 18, 19
  mathematical models, 18, 19
  observation, 18, 19
  patterns-of-crime approach, 13–14
  records, official and unofficial,
    18–19
  strategies of, 10–20
  surveys, 16–18
Resistance by women, 165
Restitution, 363–364
Restorative justice, 406–407
Retreatism, as mode of adaptation,
  150, 151
Retribution, 23
  capital punishment, 395–397
  the courts and, 23, 391–395
  deterrence and, 369, 386
  judges and, 391–394
  juvenile justice system, 5–6,
    394–395
  linking penalties to crime and,
    386, 390
  police and, 390–391
  prisons, 395
  prosecutors and, 391
  rehabilitation and, 398, 407, 424
  sentencing guidelines, 392–394,
    416
  seriousness of crimes and
    blameworthiness of offenders,
    386, 388–389, 392
    harmfulness of crime, 386–388,
    392
    public ranking of severity of
    crimes, 388
  student offenders and, 385

  unpleasantness of penalties and,
    386, 389–390
  vengeance distinguished from, 385
  white-collar crime and, 391
Reward-risk models, 226–234
  arson, 232–233
  burglary, 232
  car theft, 232
  critique of, 234
  drug use, 233–234
  professional theft, 228, 232
  robbery, 232
  white-collar crime, 233
RICO (Racketeer Influenced and
  Corrupt Organizations) law,
  306, 422
Ritualism, as mode of adaptation,
  150, 151
Robbery, 14, 175, 387–388 (*see also*
  Conventional crime;
  Professional theft)
  age-specific arrest rates for, 88–89
  alcohol and, 252
  arrest rates by race, 94
  career patterns, 275
    intensive and intermittent,
    276–277
    planning crimes, 52, 243–245,
    275–276
    use of stolen money, 276
  carjackings, 60
  costs of, 46–47, 51–52
  definition of, 27, 51
  differential association theory and,
    217
  fear of, 317, 322
  firearms and, 51, 254, 255
  murder and, 52, 178
  police arrest practices in, 342–343,
    346–347
  rates, 29, 30
  reporting of, 32
  rewards and risks of, 232
  sex and, 86, 162–163
  in South Africa, 75
  target hardening and, 426
  targets of, 242–243, 244–245
  victim–offender relationships in,
    52, 53, 96
Roe v. *Wade* (1973), 70
Roman Catholic Church, 306, 334,
  395
Rome, ancient, 329
Routine activities approach, 80,
  238–241
  campus crime victimization and,
    16–18, 43, 250–251
  critique of, 240–241
Russia
  murder rate in, 7
  organized crime in, 81, 142, 308
  prisoners in, 359

Sanctions, 3 (*see also* Punishment)
Savings and loan industry, fraud in,
  68, 134, 310
Scared Straight program, 379
Schizophrenia, 124–125

Schizophrenia scale, 122
Schools, 163
    in China, 196, 431
    delinquency and organization of,
        192–193
    in Japan, 197, 431
    reduction of crime and, 431
    social control theory and, 182,
        183–186, 192–193
Seasonal variations in crime, 81–82
Second Amendment, 259, 419
Secondary deviation, 221, 226
Secondary group, 290
Securities and Exchange
        Commission, 134, 219
Securities fraud and theft, 67,
        133–134, 177
Seductions of crime, 228–229
*Seductions of Crime: Moral and Sensual
        Attractions in Doing Evil* (Katz),
        228
Selective incapacitation, 382–383
Self-concepts, 222–224
Self-control, crime and, 118–119,
        186, 229
Self-defense justification, 4
Self-protective measures, 316–317,
        330, 426
Self-report studies
    class–crime association and, 97–99
    dark figure, 41
    of delinquency and drug use,
        183–185
    of high school seniors, 41
    history of, 40–41
    methodological problems with,
        42–44, 97–99
    on race and crime, 94
    sex differences, 85–86
Senate Permanent Investigating
        Subcommittee, 142
Sense of inequity, 148
Sentencing (sentences)
    determinate, 392–394
    disparities, 352–358, 416
        by race, 352–356
        by sex, 356–358
        by social class, 356
    guidelines, 392–394, 416
    indeterminate, 391–392, 399–400
    plea bargaining and, 350–351, 399
    public attitudes toward, 379–380,
        390, 394, 396–397
    rehabilitation and, 399
September 11, 2001, terrorist attacks,
        55, 57–58, 62, 288, 419
    FBI interpretation of, 9–10
Serial killers, profiling, 422–423
Serial murder, 10, 162, 245, 422–423
Serious and violent juvenile (SVJ)
        offenders, 271
Seriousness of crimes, 31, 386–390
Severity of punishment, 372–373
Sex differences
    in aggressiveness, 108–109, 162
        (*see also* Aggression)
    in antisocial personality disorder,
        123

biological explanations of, 83,
        107–109, 112
    in capital punishment, 358
    in career contingencies, 265
    in crime rates, 161–162
        adult crime, 86–87
        cross-national variations in, 83
        juvenile delinquency, 85–86
        trends, 86–87, 160–161
        white-collar crime, 87
    feminist criminology and, 10,
        159–165
    in justifying embezzlement, 178
    in murder, 49, 107–108, 164
    police and discrimination by,
        345–346
    and sentencing, 354–355, 356–358
    in victimization, 87
Sex hormones, aggressiveness and,
        83, 108–109
Sex offenses, 16–18, 250–251 (*see also*
        Rape)
"Shaving," 138
Shock sentences, 378–379
Shoplifting, 18–19, 59, 228–229, 242,
        296
Signs of crime, 314
Silence of the Lambs, The, (movie and
        novel), 423
Simple assault, 52
Simultaneity, deterrence and
        problem of, 374, 378
*Sisters in Crime: The Rise of the New
        Female Criminal* (Adler), 160
Situational crime prevention,
        425–427
Smuggling
    of illegal drugs, 141, 281, 299–301,
        421
    of illegal immigrants, 308–309
    of stolen art, 299
Social change, 429
Social class
    adult crime and, 97
    bail and, 348
    definition of, 97
    delinquency and, 16, 98–99,
        152–156
    methodological problems in
        studying relationship of crime
        and, 98–99
    sentencing and, 356
    victimization, 99
Social construction of crime, 9–10
Social control, 313–314
    formal, 313
    informal (*see* Informal social
        control)
Social control theory, 160, 216–217
    adult activities and, 182–183
    conventional lines of action and,
        182–183
    critique of, 197–199
    evidence on, 183–197
        the family, 186–192, 193–194
        over the life course, 185–186
        migration and the disruption of
            social bonds, 194–195

National Youth Surveys of
        delinquency and drug use,
        183–185
    peer groups, 193–194
    religion, 194
    schools and, 192–193, 196, 197
    social bonds in other societies,
        195–197
    the family and, 181–194
    leaving a life of crime and,
        282–283
    peer groups and, 182, 193–194
    school and, 182, 183–186,
        192–193, 196, 197
    variations in crime rates and,
        199–200
Social, cultural, and economic
        sources of crime
    conventional crime
        anomie and strain, 148–152,
            160, 170
        class differences in values,
            154–156
        differential opportunity theory,
            152–153, 170
        modernization, 143–144
        opportunity and the economy,
            144
        relative deprivation, 147–148
        social class, values, and
            delinquency, 154–156
        subculture of violence, 77,
            156–159
        unemployment, 144–147
    dealing with, 427–432
    gender and feminist criminology,
        159–165
    organized crime, 28
        and the economic system, 142
        after Prohibition, 140–142, 150
        Prohibition and, 140, 150
        variations in crime rates and,
            165–167
    white-collar crime
        corporations, 136–137
        development of new
            technology, 137–139
        free enterprise ideology,
            133–135
        market structure, 135–136
        trust and credit, 136
Social gang, 291
Socialization, delinquency and,
        186–187
Social learning theory, 215–216
Social norming, 251
Social Science Research Council, 26
Social structure, 288–290
Social structure and social learning
        (SSSL) theory, 215–216
Sokaiya, Japanese corporations and,
        144
Solidarity, mechanical and organic,
        320
Somatotypes, Sheldon's theory of,
        104
South, subculture of violence and
        homicide in U.S., 77, 157–158

South Africa, crime in, 75, 329
Soviet Union (*see also* Russia)
    collective response to crime in, 329
    crime in, 7, 144
    crime statistics in, 74–75
    definition of theft in, 6
Space shuttle explosion, 136–137
Spain, crime in, 30–31, 144
Specialization in crime, 272, 273, 275
Specific deterrence, 369
Sports, learning to commit crime and, 208–210
Stalking, 54
Statistics (*see* Crime statistics)
Status offenses, 5, 85
Stock fraud, 67, 141, 177
Stolen money, robbers' use of, 276
Strain, 149, 151–152, 170
Strategies of criminological research, 10–20
Stretching values, 156
Strike Hard campaigns, 381
Student-murderers
    gender and, 163
    race and, 92–93
Student Right-to-Know and Campus Security Act (1990), 43
Subculture-of-violence theory, 77, 156–159
Subcultures, 77, 156–159, 220, 225–226
Subterranean values, 171
Suicide rate, murder rate compared with, 48
Surveys, 16–18 (*see also* Self-report studies; Victimization surveys)
Sweden, 388
    crime rates in, 210, 239
    imprisonment in, 359, 360
Switzerland
    arson in, 132
    community ties in, 78, 430
    crime in, 7
    delinquency in, 191–192
    family in, 191–192, 430
    firearms in, 256
    social change in, 429
    victimizations surveys in, 37
Systemic factors and drugs, 253

Target hardening, 426
Targets of crime, 143–144, 171, 241–249, 426
    form of, 242–243
    routine activities approach and, 80, 238–241
    value of, 243
    victim precipitation, 247–249
    victim proneness, 245–246
    vulnerability of victims and, 243–246
Target suitability, 238–239, 241–249
Tax fraud, 61
Techniques of neutralization (*see* Neutralization of the law)

Technology, development of new, 137–139
Telemarketing fraud, 175, 278
Telephone fraud, 61, 138
Television (*see also* Media)
    crime and, 1–2, 9, 149, 205–208, 314, 325
    ratings system, 207
    white-collar crime and, 66
Temperament, 104, 109
Temporal boundary conception of criminal career, 264
Temporal variations in crime rates, 81–83, 424
Tennessee v. *Garner* (1985), 341–342
Ten-Point Coalition (Boston), 334
Terrorism, 57–58, 288
    reporting, 57
    social construction of, 9–10, 58
Testosterone, aggressiveness and, 108–109
Theft (thieves) (*see also* Larceny)
    on campus, 229
    cross-cultural variations in definition of, 6
    differential association and, 217
    employee, 67–68, 173–174
    leaving a career in, 280
    organization of, 295–299
    professional, 174, 217, 228, 244, 276–277, 279, 295–299, 371
    recruitment of career criminals, 217, 268–269
    regional variations in, 77
    rewards and risks of, 232
    targets of, 143–144, 241–243
    victimization, 241
    victim-precipitated, 249
    by women, 87, 161
Therapy, behavior, 401–402
Therapy, individual, 400–401
Therapy, milieu, 402
Thinking, criminal, 116–117
Three strikes and you're out policy, 384
Tongs, Chinese, 308, 309
Toxic wastes, disposal of, 69, 141
Traffic accident deaths, murders compared with, 48
Transfer of property, 47
Treatment destruction techniques, 405
Triads, Chinese, 309
True identity fraud, 62
Trust and credit, 136
Trust and fear of crime, 317–318
Truth-in-sentencing, 392
Turkey, 299
Tutelage, 217
Twin studies, 105–106, 123
Typologies of criminal careers, 269, 270

Uganda, 195, 249, 321
Umwelt, 300–301
Unemployment, crime and, 144–147, 428
Uniform Crime Reporting Handbook (FBI), 31

Uniform Crime Reports (*see also* Federal Bureau of Investigation)
United Arab Emirates, 142
U.S. Department of Education, 61
U.S. Department of Justice, 415, 418
U.S. Immigration and Naturalization Service, 308
U.S. Senate's Violent and Repeat Juvenile Offender Act (1997), 5
U.S. Supreme Court
    abortion and, 70
    capital punishment and, 110, 355, 358, 396
    cocaine and, 355
    defense attorneys and, 350
    hate crimes and, 55
    insanity defense and, 128
    police use of deadly force and, 341–342
    prevention detention, 348
    RICO law and, 306
United States v. *Armstrong* (1996), 355
Universities (*see* Crime on campus)
Unorganized gang, 291–292
Unpleasantness of penalties, 386, 389–390
Unsolved Mysteries (television program), 2
Urbanization, crime and, 77–80, 320–322, 429

Values (*see also* Culture)
    delinquency and class differences in, 154–156
    delinquent, 171
    dominant, 171
    stretching, 156
    subterranean, 171
Vandalism, 27, 63, 154, 228, 231
V-chip (violence-chip), 207
Venezuela, 329
Vengeance, retribution distinguished from, 385
Vertical/hierarchical leadership, 293
Vicarious victimization, 314
Victim impact statement, 364–365
Victimization
    age and, 91
    on campus, 16–18, 43, 218, 219, 250–251
    fear and community solidarity, 314–319
    of high school seniors, 37
    lifestyle theory and, 241
    multiple (victim proneness), 245–246
    race and, 95–96
    repeat, 245–246
    serial murder and, 245
    sex differences in, 87
    social class and, 99
Victimization surveys
    annual trends in crime rates and, 82–83
    on campus, 16–18, 43
    community size and crime rates, 77

dark figure uncovered by, 37–39
FBI data compared with results of, 37
of high school seniors, 37
history of, 36–37
methodological problems with, 39–40
on temporal variations in crime rates, 81–83
Victimless crimes, 420
costs of, 69–71
defined, 69–70
drug use, 69, 70, 151, 183–185, 233–234, 252–253, 420
gambling, 69, 70–71, 140, 306, 420
prostitution, 69, 71, 309, 420
Victim–offender panels (VOPs), 406
Victim–offender reconciliation programs (VORPs), 406
Victim precipitation, 247–249
Victim proneness, 245–246
Victims (see also Victimization)
appearance at parole board hearings, 365
capital punishment and race of, 355
changing role of, 364–365
compensation of, 39, 362–363
in the criminal justice system, 362–365
nonreporting of crime by, 32–34
offenders' relationships with,
assault, 53
burglary, 58, 249
larceny, 59, 249
murder, 14, 48–50, 53–54, 96, 164, 247–248
rape, 17–18, 49–50, 53, 96, 120–121, 248–249
robbery, 52, 53, 96, 161–162
restitution to, 363–364
victim impact statements, 364–365
victim precipitation, 247–249
victim proneness, 245–246
victims' rights movement, 362–365
vulnerability of, 243–246
women as, 87, 165
Victims' rights movement, 362–365
Vietnamese gangs, 307
Vietnam War, 16
Vigilante groups, 329, 330, 332
Violence
in same-sex and heterosexual couples, 54
subculture of, 77, 156–159

on television, 1–2, 205–208, 314
workplace, 145–146
Violence Policy Center, 259
Violencia, la, 157
Violent crime
careers of females in, 280–281
costs of, 46, 46–58
geography of, 79
organization of, 301
rates of, 29–30, 82–83
Violent Crime Control and Law Enforcement Act (1994), 418
Violent gangs, 291
Violent predatory offenders, 269, 270
Vulnerabilities, 104
Vulnerability of victims, 243–246

War and crime, 203
War on Drugs, 354–355, 417, 421
Watergate scandal, 173, 176, 416
Welfare fraud, 61
West Side Story (play and movie), 152
Wharton Econometric Forecasting Associates, 69
White-collar crime, 28, 46, 419
appeal to higher loyalties, 176
certainty of punishment, 373
conflict perspective on, 7–8
conventional crime and, 65–67
costs of, 64–68
criminal careers of, 277–278
definition of, 64
denial of injury and, 174–175
denial of responsibility and, 173
deterrence and, 371–372
differential association theory and, 218–220
geography of, 80
labeling perspective on, 223–224
media and, 2, 66
networks and, 310
organization of, 309–310
planning, 64–65
prosecution of, 64, 391, 423–424
rewards and risks of, 233
RICO law and, 306
sex and, 87
social, cultural, and economic sources
corporations, 136–137, 173
development of new technology, 137–139
free enterprise ideology, 133–135
market structure, 135–136
trust and credit, 136

types of, 64, 65
women and, 87, 161
White-collar criminals,
characteristics of, 66–67, 87, 277–278
Witnesses, responses to crime by, 324–328
Women (see also Feminist criminology; Feminist movement; Sex differences)
biological factors affecting crime rates of, 107–109, 112
capital punishment and, 358
crime rates of, 83, 85–87, 161–162
economic development and, 143–144
employment and crime by, 87, 161
exiting from violent criminal careers, 280–281
fear of crime among, 314, 315–316, 317
illegitimate opportunity structures and crime by, 153, 161–162, 265
larceny by, 87, 161
murder and, 49, 164
police and discrimination against, 345–346
in prison, 354–355, 357
resistance by, 165
robbery by, 162–163
sentencing of, 354–355, 356–358
serial murderers, 10
as victims, 87, 165
white-collar crime and, 87, 161
Work, 186, 190, 274, 428 (see also Unemployment)
crime by women and, 87, 161
Working conditions in corporations, 136, 137
Workplace violence, 145–146
Work programs, 401
WorldCom, 134
World Health Organization (United Nations), 48
World Trade Center terrorist attacks, 9–10, 55, 57–58, 288

Yakuza, Japanese corporations and, 144, 307
Yugoslavia, 388

Zigzag path between legitimate pursuits and crime, 267
Zina (adultery), in Pakistan, 363

Photo Credits